# The Letters of SARA HUTCHINSON

SARA HUTCHINSON has never been much more than a name, though a name connected with some of the greatest in English literature. The sister of Mrs. Wordsworth, and a member of the Wordsworth household for thirty years, Coleridge's beloved Asra to whom many of his poems were written, Southey's friend and Lamb's, and a guest of the Arnolds at Rugby, she was a member of an interesting circle. For her intimate relations to Wordsworth and Coleridge it has long been apparent that we should like to know her better. Now her letters to members of her family and to friends demonstrate how worthwhile it is to know her for herself as well. The letters come from the family and from the Wordsworth collection at Dove Cottage and are here printed (almost in full) for the first time.

They show a lively and amusing woman, kind, forthright to the extent of bluntness, especially when she takes up the cudgels in the cause of what she considers truth or justice or human kindness. Coleridge describes her in one apt and characteristic sentence:

'If Sense, Sensibility, Sweetness of Temper, perfect simplicity and unpretending Nature, joined to shrewdness and entertainingness make a valuable Woman, Sara Hutchinson is so.'

Such qualities certainly make a delightful letter-writer.

*Edited by Kathleen Coburn*

THE PHILOSOPHICAL LECTURES OF SAMUEL TAYLOR COLERIDGE 1818–1819
THE INQUIRING SPIRIT

# The Letters of
# SARA HUTCHINSON
## from 1800 to 1835

Edited by
KATHLEEN COBURN

UNIVERSITY OF TORONTO PRESS
TORONTO, 1954

*Reprinted in paperback 2015*
*ISBN* 978-1-4426-3927-0 (*paper*)

TO

MISS JOANNA HUTCHINSON

# Contents

# Illustrations

# Preface

This volume presents for the first time the letters of Sara Hutchinson. They were written to members of her family from 1800 to 1835, that is, from her early days in Yorkshire to within a few weeks of her death in 1835 at Rydal Mount.

One hundred and twenty of them were handed down by Sara's devoted nieces and nephews. They were preserved through the London bombings by Miss Joanna Hutchinson, who kept some of her treasured manuscripts in the country and some of them in a suitcase under her bed as the first thing to be seized in an emergency, a procedure which strikes me as being exactly what Sara herself would have done in similar circumstances. It was Miss Hutchinson who at my importuning first showed them to me. Then through the kindness of Miss Helen Darbishire, some fifty more, written chiefly to Edward Quillinan, later Wordsworth's son-in-law, were made available from the Wordsworth collection in Dove Cottage, and are here printed with the permission of the Trustees of Dove Cottage. Miss Helen Read of Grasmere supplied one important letter and Professor E. L. Griggs another, two others are in the British Museum, and two more, to Mrs. Coleridge, are in the library of Victoria College, Toronto.

A few unimportant letters have been omitted altogether. From others some deletions, always indicated, have had to be made; they all have to do with trivial details of no personal, literary, or social consequence.

In order to avoid profuse and repetitious annotation in footnotes, I have compiled a list of names of persons and places alluded to, with some information about them, much of it very well known, but brought together to refresh the reader's memory about dates, relationships, and other small details. I have not listed everyone mentioned, the neighbours in Grasmere for instance, unless there was something to be added. Annotation of all the Grasmere names would have provided a chapter in the local history of Grasmere and as such would doubtless be full of charm. But Mrs. Rawnsley has already written such a chapter, and besides, these letters have a wider interest.

The aim has been to offer a trustworthy text. The transcribing was done by Anne Cliff Renier who did wonders, as was evident on checking her copy with the originals, with difficult manuscripts in various conditions of preservation. Often cross-written, often with Sara's everlasting postscripts closely written on fraying margins, with holes where seals were torn off and with cracks at the folds, the letters were not easy to follow or to decipher. Sara Hutchinson could and did write a beautiful hand, or rather a hand that makes the page look beautiful, as became the amanuensis of three poets. But her writing and spelling are all obviously affected by her feelings, her haste, and doubtless by disturbances around her. I have not put *sic* after all her vagaries from conventions of speech or spelling; they seem to me more enjoyable when they come naturally and unexpectedly before the eye. In the manuscript they sometimes seem to suggest a flush of feeling, a bit of controlled temper or 'plain-speaking', a degree of some sort of warmth that ought not to be damped with the cold water of pedantry. I have preferred to take her as she is. Many of her strange words and spellings are her mimicry of oddities of diction in her correspondent, or family words adopted from servants and children. These she usually underlines, and they are shown in the text in italics.

Her own Christian name she writes with and without the 'h'; Coleridge's preference is adopted here, the basis of his anagram 'Asra' and a ready way of distinguishing between her and Sarah Fricker, Mrs. Coleridge.

Her punctuation consists chiefly, almost solely, of the dash. Many of her dashes have been preserved, to convey the ease, the spontaneous and flowing quality of the letters which must often be close to her conversation. Capital letters she uses and omits with a fine unconcern. Where she relied for clarity on the end of a line, or the recipient's familiarity with her style, some additional punctuation has been introduced in accommodation to print and the eyes of strangers.

When no date is given and in the absence of a postmark, the dating of the letters is based on internal evidence. There are on some letters pencilled or ink dates in various hands; my conclusions have often agreed with these, but not always. Fortunately the dating has been fairly easily corroborated by known facts. In two cases I have accepted the pencil or ink note for lack of any other discernible evidence. I have also put the date and place of writing at the head of the letter, though Sara's practice was not consistent. Except for the deletions and slight modifications referred to, the letters are as Sara wrote them.

It is a pleasure to express my thanks to Miss Helen Darbishire to whom everyone working in the period is in debt. She took pains to make the Dove Cottage letters accessible to me and has been helpful in numerous ways. Miss Helen Read was generous with her assistance in the early stages at Dove Cottage. Both Miss Darbishire and Mrs. Rawnsley have allowed me to tap their very special knowledge of the whole Wordsworth circle. If there are gaps in the annotations that should be filled it is because I have not drawn on these sources enough. I have Fernand and Anne Cliff Renier to thank for much more than the transcribing, itself no small contribution. Professor J. R. MacGillivray has made many helpful suggestions and corrections. George and Elizabeth Whalley made the index and read the proofs with the care that has distinguished Mr. Whalley's contributions to Coleridge studies. Their generous assistance came at a time when pressure of other work made their help invaluable to me. And finally, the greatest obligation of all is expressed in the dedication of this volume. I have to thank Miss Joanna Hutchinson not only for manuscripts, helpful information, and a hospitality that seemed to suggest the ancestral atmosphere, but also for her wonderful enjoyment of these letters, all of which made working together a delightful experience. It is an honour to be permitted to present this volume to the person to whom it rightly belongs.

*August 1953*
*Victoria College, Toronto*

# Note

The italic figures at the inner end of each headline throughout the text give the date of the letter printed below and the age of Sara Hutchinson when she wrote it.

# List of Letters

The letters, unless their location is otherwise indicated (D.C.: Dove Cottage; V.C.: Victoria College; B.M.: British Museum) are in the possession of Miss Joanna Hutchinson.

| No. | Date | | Place or Postmark | Correspondent |
|---|---|---|---|---|
| 1. | 12 July | 1800 | Gallow Hill | John Monkhouse, London |
| 2. | 8 Aug. | 1800 | ,, ,, | ,, ,, ,, |
| 3. | 23 Aug. | [1800] | ,, ,, | ,, ,, ,, |
| 4. D.C. | [26 Mar. | 1805] | Grasmere | Mrs. Cookson [Kendal] |
| 5. | [Oct.] | 1808 | [Allan Bank] | Mary Monkhouse, London |
| 6. | [30] Nov. | 1808 | Grasmere | ,, ,, ,, |
| 7. | 27 Mar. | 1809 | ,, | ,, ,, ,, |
| 8. | 19 Apr. | [1809] | ,, | ,, ,, Hindwell |
| 9. | 3 Jan. | 1810 | [ ,, ] | ,, ,, London |
| 10. | [autumn | 1810] | [Hindwell] | ,, ,, ,, |
| 11. | [27 Oct. | 1811] | [Grasmere] | ,, ,, Hindwell |
| 12. | 3 Dec. | [1811] | [ ,, ] | ,, ,, ,, |
| 13. | 28 Mar. | [1812] | [ ,, ] | John Monkhouse, Hindwell |
| 14. | 19 [Nov. | 1812] | [ ,, ] | Mary Monkhouse, now Mrs. T. Hutchinson. |
| 15. | 9 Mar. | 1813 | ,, | Thomas Monkhouse, London |
| 16. | [16] May | 1813 | [Rydal Mount] | ,, ,, ,, |
| 17. | 23 June | 1813 | ,, ,, | ,, ,, ,, |
| 18. | [1 Aug. | 1813] | ,, ,, | Mary Hutchinson, Hindwell |
| 19. | 27 Aug. | [1813] | [ ,, ,, ] | John Monkhouse, ,, |
| 20. | 29 Sept. | 1813 | Stockton | Mary Hutchinson, ,, |
| 21. | 3 Aug. | 1814 | Callendar | ,, ,, ,, |
| 22. | 2 Sept. | [1814] | Kelso | Sisters, Swansea |
| 23. | 29 Ju[ne] | 1815 | Clarkson's | Mary Hutchinson, Hindwell |
| 24. | [15 Oct. | 1815] | [Rydal Mount] | Thomas Monkhouse, Penrith |
| 25. | 24 Nov. | 1815 | Kendal | Sisters, Joanna Hutchinson, Radnor |
| 26. | 24 Nov. | [?1815] | ,, | Thomas Monkhouse, London |

| No. | Date | Place or Postmark | Correspondent |
|---|---|---|---|
| 27. | 14 July 1816 | [Rydal Mount] | Thomas Monkhouse, London |
| 28. | 1 Nov. 1816 | [ ,, ,, ] | ,, ,, ,, |
| 29. | 5 Jan. 1817 | Keswick | ,, ,, ,, |
| 30. | 7 Feb. 1817 | ,, | John Monkhouse, Stow. S.W. |
| 31. | 17 Feb. 1817 | Rydal Mount | Thomas Monkhouse, London |
| 32. | 21 Feb. 1817 | ,, ,, | ,, ,, ,, |
| 33. | 15 May 1817 | ,, ,, | ,, ,, ,, |
| 34. | 28 Aug. 1817 | [ ,, ,, ] | ,, ,, ,, |
| 35. | 10 Dec. 1817 | Sundridge Rectory | ,, ,, ,, |
| 36. D.C. | 4 Jan. 1818 | London | Dora Wordsworth, Rydal Mount |
| 37. | 17 Jan. 1818 | Playford Hall, Ipswich | Thomas Monkhouse, London |
| 38. | 25 Jan. 1818 | ,, ,, ,, | ,, ,, ,, |
| 39. | 30 Jan. [1818] | ,, ,, ,, | ,, ,, ,, |
| 40. | 6 Feb. 1818 | ,, ,, ,, | ,, ,, ,, |
| 41. | 22 Feb. 1818 | ,, ,, ,, | ,, ,, ,, |
| 42. | 28 Feb. 1818 | ,, ,, ,, | ,, ,, ,, |
| 43. | 22 Mar. 1818 | ,, ,, ,, | ,, ,, ,, |
| 44. | 13 Apr. 1818 | ,, ,, ,, | ,, ,, ,, |
| 45. | 1 May 1818 | ,, ,, ,, | ,, ,, ,, |
| 46. | 8 May 1818 | ,, ,, ,, | ,, ,, ,, |
| 47. | 21 May 1818 | ,, ,, ,, | ,, ,, ,, |
| 48. | [3] Ju[ne] 1818 | Stow | ,, ,, ,, |
| 49. | [9] Ju[ne] 1818 | [Hindwell] Radnor | ,, ,, ,, |
| 50. | [Oct. 1818] | Hindwells Radnor | ,, ,, ,, |
| 51. | 16 Jan. [1819] | ,, ,, | ,, ,, ,, |
| 52. | 3 May [1819] | Rydal Mount | ,, ,, ,, |
| 53. | 7 May [1819] | [ ,, ,, ] | John Monkhouse, Stow |
| 54. | 25 July 1819 | ,, ,, | Thomas Monkhouse, London |
| 55. | 4 Aug. [1819] | ,, ,, | ,, ,, ,, |
| 56. | 26 Oct. [1819] | [ ,, ,, ] | ,, ,, Preston |
| 57. | [28 Oct.] 1819 | ,, ,, | ,, ,, London |
| 58. | [Nov.–Dec. 1819] | [ ,, ,, ] | John Monkhouse, ,, |
| 59. | 23 Dec. [1819] | [ ,, ,, ] | Thomas Monkhouse, ,, |
| 60. | 13 Jan. [1820] | ,, ,, | ,, ,, ,, |
| 61. | 27 Feb. 1820 | ,, ,, | Mary Hutchinson, Hindwell |

| No. | Date | Place or Postmark | Correspondent |
|---|---|---|---|
| 62. | 10 Apr. 1820 | [Rydal Mount] | Thomas Monkhouse, London |
| 63. | 30 Apr. [1820] | [ ,, ,, ] | ,, ,, ,, |
| 64. | [June 1820] | [ ,, ,, ] | ,, ,, ,, |
| 65. | [June 1820] | [ ,, ,, ] | ,, ,, ,, |
| 66. D.C. | 16 Aug. 1820 | ,, ,, | Mrs. Wordsworth, Geneva |
| 67. | 7 Sept. 1820 | [ ,, ,, ] | John Monkhouse, Stow |
| 68. D.C. | 11 Sept. 1820 | ,, ,, | Mrs. Wordsworth, Paris |
| 69. D.C. | 19 Sept. 1820 | ,, ,, | ,, ,, ,, |
| 70. | 15 Oct. [1820] | ,, ,, | John Monkhouse, Stow |
| 71. | 7 Nov. [1820] | [ ,, ,, ] | Thomas Monkhouse, London |
| 72. | 12 Feb. [1821] | Stockton | ,, ,, ,, |
| 73. | 27 May 1821 | Rydal Mount | ,, ,, ,, |
| 74. | 27 Sept. [1821] | ,, ,, | Mary Hutchinson, Hindwell |
| 75. | 23 Nov. [1821] | [ ,, ,, ] | Thomas Monkhouse, London |
| 76. | [26 Nov. 1821] | [ ,, ,, ] | ,, ,, ,, |
| 77. | 11 Jan. [1822] | [ ,, ,, ] | ,, ,, ,, |
| 78. | 5 Feb. 1822 | ,, ,, | ,, ,, ,, |
| 79. | 22 Feb. 1822 | ,, ,, | John Monkhouse, Stow |
| 80. | 24 Feb. 1822 | [ ,, ,, ] | Thomas Monkhouse, London |
| 81. D.C. | 28 June 1822 | ,, ,, | Edward Quillinan, Lee Priory |
| 82. | 21 Sept. [1822] | Stockton | John Monkhouse, Stow |
| 83. | 19 Oct. 1822 | ,, | Thomas Monkhouse, London |
| 84. | 9 Nov. 1822 | ,, | ,, ,, ,, |
| 85. D.C. | [8 or 15] Mar. 1823 | London | Edward Quillinan, Lee Priory |
| 86. | 28 June 1823 | Boulogne | Thomas Monkhouse, London |
| 87. D.C. | 12 July 1823 | ,, | Dora Wordsworth, Hindwell |
| 88. | 22 July 1823 | ,, | Thomas Monkhouse, Ramsgate |
| 89. | [Sept.–Oct. 1823] | [Ramsgate] | ,, ,, ,, |
| 90. D.C. | [Oct. 1823] | ,, | Edward Quillinan, Lee Priory |
| 91. D.C. | [13 Oct. 1823] | ,, | ,, ,, ,, ,, |
| 92. | 14 Oct. [1823] | ,, | Thomas Monkhouse |
| 93. | 18 Oct. 1823 | ,, | ,, ,, Penrith |
| 94. D.C. | [30 Oct.] 1823 | Gloucester Place, London | Edward Quillinan, Lee Priory |
| 95. | 23 Feb. [1824] | Hindwell | Mrs. Thomas Monkhouse, London |
| 96. | 4 Mar. [1824] | Stow | Thomas Monkhouse, London |

| No. | Date | | Place or Postmark | Correspondent |
|---|---|---|---|---|
| 97. D.C. | 15 Apr. | 1824 | Hindwell | Edward Quillinan, Lee Priory |
| 98. | 29 Apr. | [1824] | ,, | Thomas Monkhouse, London |
| 99. | 12 June | [1824] | Stow | ,, ,, ,, |
| 100. | [June–July | 1824] | ,, | ,, ,, ,, |
| 101. | [ ,, ,, | 1824] | ,, | ,, ,, ,, |
| 102. D.C. | [10 Sept. | 1824] | ,, | Edward Quillinan, Lee Priory |
| 103. D.C. | 3 Nov. | 1824 | Torquay | ,, ,, ,, ,, |
| 104. D.C. | [8 Dec. | 1824] | ,, | ,, ,, ,, ,, |
| 105. | [2 Feb. | 1825] | Newton Abbott | Thomas Monkhouse, Exeter |
| 106. | 7 Feb. | 1825 | Taunton | John Monkhouse, Stow |
| 107. | 15 Feb. | [1825] | Clifton | ,, ,, ,, |
| 108. D.C. | 28 Feb. | 1825 | ,, | Edward Quillinan, Lee Priory |
| 109. D.C. | 29 Mar. | 1825 | Hindwell | ,, ,, ,, ,, |
| 110. D.C. | 2 June | 1825 | Brinsop Court | ,, ,, London |
| 111. D.C. | 5 Oct. | 1825 | Rydal Mount | ,, ,, Lee Priory |
| 112. D.C. | 24 Oct. | 1825 | Coleorton | ,, ,, Westminster |
| 113. D.C. | 21 Nov. | 1825 | Rydal Mount | ,, ,, Lee Priory |
| 114. D.C. | 25 Jan. | 1826 | ,, ,, | ,, ,, ,, ,, |
| 115. D.C. | 28 Jan. | 1826 | ,, ,, | John Monkhouse, Stow |
| 116. D.C. | 22 May | 1826 | ,, ,, | Edward Quillinan, Lee Priory |
| 117. D.C. | 23 Aug. | 1826 | ,, ,, | ,, ,, ,, ,, |
| 118. | 19 Sept. | 1826 | ,, ,, | John Monkhouse, Stow |
| 119. D.C. | 28 Sept. | 1826 | ,, ,, | Edward Quillinan, Lee Priory |
| 120. D.C. | 5 Oct. | [1826] | ,, ,, | ,, ,, ,, ,, |
| 121. D.C. | 11 Nov. | 1826 | ,, ,, | ,, ,, ,, ,, |
| 122. | 6 Feb. | [1827] | ,, ,, | John Monkhouse, Stow |
| 123. | 11 Feb. | [1827] | ,, ,, | Mary Hutchinson, Brinsop Court |
| 124. | 18 Mar. | [1827] | Keswick | John Monkhouse, Stow |
| 125. D.C. | 10 Apr. | 1827 | Rydal Mount | Edward Quillinan, London |
| 126. | [8 Apr. | 1827] | [ ,, ,, ] | John Monkhouse, Stow |
| 127. D.C. | 21 Apr. | 1827 | ,, ,, | Edward Quillinan, London |
| 128. D.C. | 15 July | 1827 | Grassy Nook | ,, ,, ,, |
| 129. D.C. | 12 Sept. | 1827 | Rydal Mount | ,, ,, ,, |
| 130. | 13 Dec. | [1827] | ,, ,, | Mary Hutchinson, Brinsop Court |
| 131. D.C. | 27 Jan. | 1828 | ,, ,, | Edward Quillinan, London |
| 132. D.C. | 4 Mar. | 1828 | ,, ,, | ,, ,, ,, |
| 133. | 28 Apr. | [1828] | [Rydal Mount] | John Monkhouse, Stow |

| No. | Date | | Place or Postmark | Correspondent |
|---|---|---|---|---|
| 134. D.C. | 20 Apr. | [1829] | Brinsop Court | Edward Quillinan, London |
| 135. D.C. | 30 Jan. | [1830] | Rydal Mount | ,, ,, ,, |
| 136. | 26 Mar. | [1830] | ,, ,, | Miss Mary Hutchinson, Jr. Brinsop Court |
| 137. D.C. | 31 July | [1830] | ,, ,, | Edward Quillinan, London |
| 138. D.C. | 13 Sept. | 1830 | ,, ,, | ,, ,, ,, |
| 139. | 14 Nov. | 1830 | ,, ,, | ,, ,, ,, |
| 140. | 6 Jan. | [1831] | ,, ,, | Mary Hutchinson, Brinsop Court |
| 141. D.C. | [29 Apr.] | 1831 | ,, ,, | Edward Quillinan, London |
| 142. D.C. | 10 May | 1831 | ,, ,, | ,, ,, ,, |
| 143. D.C. | 16 May | 1831 | ,, ,, | ,, ,, ,, |
| 144. | 11 Oct. | [1831] | ,, ,, | Elizabeth Hutchinson, Brinsop Court |
| 145. D.C. | 6 Jan. | 1832 | ,, ,, | Edward Quillinan, St. Germaine-en-Saye |
| 146. D.C. | 10 July | [1832] | ,, ,, | Edward Quillinan, Malvern |
| 147. D.C. | 7 Aug. | 1832 | ,, ,, | ,, ,, London |
| 148. V.C. | 9 Feb. | 1833 | ,, ,, | Mrs. S. T. Coleridge, Hampstead |
| 149. | 27 May | 1833 | ,, ,, | Edward Quillinan, London |
| 150. | 27 June | 1833 | ,, ,, | ,, ,, Boulogne |
| 151. | 24 Aug. | 1833 | ,, ,, | ,, ,, ,, |
| 152. | 4 Mar. | 1834 | Rugby | Mary Hutchinson, Brinsop Court |
| 153. | 17 Mar. | 1834 | Playford Hall, Ipswich | Edward Quillinan, Boulogne |
| 154. D.C. | 1 Apr. | 1834 | ,, ,, ,, | Mary Hutchinson, Brinsop Court |
| 155. | [Apr.–May] | 1834 | Hendon | Sarah Hutchinson, Jr., Brinsop Court |
| 156. D.C. | 9 May | 1834 | ,, | Edward Quillinan, London |
| 157. | 27 May | 1834 | ,, | Mary Hutchinson, Brinsop Court |
| 158. B.M. Add. MS. 41186. | 28 June | [1834] | Rydal Mount | Mrs. Clarkson, Ipswich |
| 159. | 8 [July | 1834] | Rydal Mount | Mary Hutchinson, Brinsop Court |

| No. | Date | Place or Postmark | Correspondent |
|---|---|---|---|
| 160. D.C. | 20 July [1834] | ,, ,, | Edward Quillinan, London |
| 161. | [?3–?10 Aug. 1834] | ,, ,, | Mary Hutchinson, Brinsop Court |
| 162. V.C. | [28 Sept.] 1834 | Keswick | Mrs. S. T. Coleridge, Hampstead |
| 163. | 15 Oct. [1834] | ,, | Thomas Hutchinson, Jr., St. John's, Cambridge |
| 164. | 3 Nov. [1834] | ,, | ,, ,, ,, ,, |
| 165. D.C. | 8 Jan. 1835 | Rydal Mount | Edward Quillinan, Oporto |
| 166. | 10 Jan. 1835 | ,, ,, | J. H. Green |
| 167. | 16 Feb. 1835 | ,, ,, | Thomas Hutchinson, Jr., St. John's, Cambridge |
| 168. | [Apr.–May 1835] | ,, ,, | Mary Hutchinson, Brinsop Court |
| 169. | [?30–31 May 1835] | ,, ,, | ,, ,, ,, ,, |

# Introduction

> Stockton is just the same as ever – bright and clean and dull! but we, the Hutchinsons, are all so agreeable ourselves, and to ourselves . . . that we are quite independent of all other society.

So Sara wrote in 1821 to her cousin Tom, then enjoying the social whirl of London from a house in Portman Square. She was writing from her brother John's, at Stockton-on-Tees.

Seven years earlier she had been worried about John at Stockton;

> kind and attentive to me as he can be . . . he is so involved in his own affairs that he does not seem ever to think of anything else, and what grieves me is that though he is quite well, he never appears to enjoy anything. I never saw him laugh heartily as he used to do (except yesterday when I told him . . .).

John's eldest daughter bothered her too.

> She seems as if nothing interested her. She creeps to bed at nine o'clock and goes frequently to the Methodist Chapel for mere lack of something to do. I never saw a young person with so little life about her in my life. . . . She gets upon horseback and never stirs out of a walk – 'It is so *foolish* to see people riding hard' – and then it gives her a stitch in her side – Well, but that you must expect when you begin to ride: and if you never go out of a walk it will always be the case. 'Oh but I never shall wish to go out of a walk.' Well, thought I, but I held my tongue, it will be lucky for you if everybody that ride with you are as accommodating as your papa and I – and so we spent the whole day from nine in the morning till eight at night upon the road . . .

and the impatient Aunt goes on to 'grank' happily to her cousin Mary that she had had only one hour's gossip with her sister Betsy, not the three she had counted on, and 'John being blind as a beetle at night', she was 'obliged to be pilot', and one eye had suffered ever since from strain.

Cleanliness and dullness, work, and Methodist Chapel-going just to fill in the time, were clearly not enough for Sara, and clearly could not compensate in any way for never being eager to take your horse out of a walk. She was not one to regard as '*foolish*' persons who rode hard. It was essential to be interested, lively, companionable. The best thing was to live in the midst of a set of good enjoyers; and to be amused, to laugh, was second in importance only to being honest.

'So agreeable ourselves, and to ourselves' – that is how we see them on a certain night in October 1799. The early death of their parents having left them orphans and scattered them about among relatives and friends, they seem later in life to have especially enjoyed being together as a family, as some of them were now, at Tom's farm at Sockburn in Yorkshire. John was the eldest, then Mary, later Mrs. Wordsworth, Henry, the sailor brother, Thomas, Sara's favourite brother perhaps, Sara herself, George, and Joanna. Dorothy Wordsworth, Mary's friend of school days, and William, had been guests for some weeks. Suddenly they had two more visitors: Coleridge, about whom they had all heard a good deal from William and Dorothy, and the Bristol publisher of the *Lyrical Ballads*, Joseph Cottle. It was the 26th of October, a night indelible in Coleridge's memory, and though he and Wordsworth and Cottle left the next day to explore the Lake Country, he was back before a month was out, back to 'Conundrums & Puns & Stories & Laughter – with Jack Hutchinson, . . . round the Fire', and to holding hands with Sara, and feeling that for the first time love had really taken possession of him, 'venenato, eheu! & insanabili'. It was a lively, charming, intelligent fireside circle into which the two young poets had found their way, and one cannot escape the conclusion, especially after reading Sara's letters, that it was quite as important for the poets as the poets were stimulating for it. In the circle, Mary and Sara were probably the most forceful characters. Mary is a little better known than Sara, though not as well known as her real rôle, and her manuscript remains, ought to have made her. She has been overshadowed by Dorothy; Sara, though described by de Selincourt as 'for years . . . the family sheet anchor' in the Wordsworth household, has been overshadowed by both.

So far as she has been described at all, Sara Hutchinson has been known only by casual references to her in subordinate contexts. The people nearest to her either could not say much or did not. Coleridge, whose love for her was for ten years the focus of his emotional life but who unfortunately met her five years after he had married another Sara, wrote many poems to or about her as 'Asra'. The Wordsworths did not say much about her, not because they did not value her, but because their relation to her was of that practical day to day domestic kind, expressing itself in little acts and looks and casually spoken words and not in fine speech of any sort. Wordsworth's letter* to Southey describing her death is, however, a most moving one. The fullest description we have had of her person is given in Professor de Selincourt's *Dorothy Wordsworth.*

Sara Hutchinson was not imposing in appearance. Like Dorothy only a little over five feet in height, rather plain-featured, and with a plump, dumpy figure devoid of grace and dignity, she was only redeemed from the commonplace by a delicately fair skin and a profusion of light brown hair. But those who looked closer noted in her face a peculiarly sweet expression, and she had a real distinction of mind and character. More matter of fact than Dorothy, less excitable, and without her sensitive alertness of mind, she had a keener sense of quiet fun, and was, moreover, a woman of considerable intellectual gifts, fully worthy to be the intimate friend of two great poets. 'The combination', wrote Coleridge, 'of natural shrewdness and a disposition to innocent humour joined with perfect simplicity and tenderness is what distinguishes her from her sister (Mary), whose character is of a more solemn cast.'

He also gives from a notebook of Edward Quillinan, Wordsworth's son-in-law, the story of a revealing episode in which she played a part we can now see to have been characteristic of her. Quillinan, out of shyness, made three attempts, in three fifty-mile rides over Kirkstone and back, before he mustered courage to present his introduction to Wordsworth. Wordsworth took the delay for neglect and was huffed.

He seemed quite angry, twirled a chair about, and made short and stiff remarks. I was getting indignant and thought him disagreeable.

Then Dora Wordsworth entered, and Wordsworth's face and voice changed to the fatherly.

It was a most timely interruption. I have loved that sweet girl ever since.

Soon, however, the fine patriarchal expression vanished, the poet resumed his frigidity and his twirl of the chair. I was about to retire, much disappointed, when in came Miss Hutchinson, who saw at once that there was some awkwardness between us: she relieved me in a moment with that fine talk and benign politeness thoroughly understood only by women. She civilly accosted me, rallied the poet for twirling the chair, took it from him and appropriated it to her own use, made herself mistress of the cause of our restraint, laughed him into a good humour, and sent him out to show me the garden and the terrace.

* *Wordsworth Letters, The Later Years*, II, 747.

Hartley and Sara Coleridge are less enthusiastic. Their comments suggest a certain ill-concealed asperity in her, or at least a no-nonsense attitude not very congenial to them. We must remember, however, that Hartley is writing to his mother when he mentions her, and perhaps felt that criticism of Asra was not *wholly* unacceptable.

> Miss Hutchinson, he writes to his mother in February [1832], looks ten years older than her sister. I have seen younger looking women of eighty. As far as my observation goes, Mothers, if they enjoy tolerable health and ease of mind, bear age much better than old Maids.*

(He does not appear to have noticed that she had lost all her teeth.) He catches some of her quality, however, if not the unbiased truth about her, in a letter to his brother-in-law.

> Poor dear Miss Hutchinson, without a spark of malice in her heart, had, from the perfect faultlessness of her own life, a good deal of intolerance in her head, and yet, she could forgive in persons whom she liked, much greater derelictions than she censured in those to whom she was indifferent! Of all my friends, of whom God has given me so many more and better than I have deserved, she has been the only one in whose manner I observed a marked difference, indeed though she never surceased her good wishes for my father's son, I am afraid she did not latterly regard me with any degree of pleasurable affection. I believe politics had something to do with this coldness. Not that she was so illiberal as to dislike people for differing from her own opinions (she certainly and naturally liked them better when they agreed) but hers was preeminently a one-sided mind. Had I been an out-and-outer, she could have understood it, but my mixture of old cavalier toryism and German liberalism (for I never was and never talked like a Frenchified Jacobin or Yankee republican) puzzled her, and she was rather shocked at my almost total disbelief in the existence of political integrity in any sect or party, to which, nevertheless, the time gives too much proof. But she is gone where these things trouble not, where, I hope, no rumour of earth reaches and no memory of earth remains.†

Young Sara Coleridge described her as very short and with only one attractive feature, her light brown hair. But we see from Sara Hutchinson's letters that she considered her as not so likeable a girl as Edith Southey in the same house. If the Coleridge children were ready to pronounce Sara Hutchinson 'dumpy' and 'plain' and old-looking, she thought 'the Celestial Blue' rather self-conscious of her looks and learning, spoilt, and self-indulgent. Probably such feelings were on both sides impossible to conceal.

* *Letters of Hartley Coleridge*, ed. E. L. Griggs, 1936, p. 136.

† *Ibid.*, p. 188.

Dorothy Wordsworth's *Journal* is rather laconic in expressions of personal feeling, except where William is concerned, but even here we become aware of a quiet trust amounting to dependence. It was Sara Hutchinson who prepared the wedding breakfast for William and Mary while Dorothy lay prostrate on the bed upstairs, and Sara who warned her when it was time to pull herself together and welcome them. When the three of them went off on the tripartite honeymoon, it was to Sara they wrote their first letter, and having to stop over a few hours in Kendal they went to see the house where 'dear Sara' had lived as a child.

But what manner of woman she was, who figured so importantly, yet so unobtrusively in all their lives, her letters themselves show us for the first time. They give us as well one of the most intimate pictures we have of that great circle—the Wordsworths, Coleridges, Southeys, Lambs, de Quincey, and many lesser luminaries.

Sara was born in 1775, the second daughter of John Hutchinson of Penrith, and Mary Monkhouse. Her mother died when she was eight years old, leaving a family of five boys and five girls. When their father died two years later the family was necessarily broken up. Mary stayed with her grandmother and uncle and aunt Monkhouse in Penrith where she and Dorothy Wordsworth, also an orphan, became friends. Sara was sent to Kendal, to an aunt on her mother's side, Mrs. Patrick. David Patrick was an unusual and cultivated man. As described by Sara in later life to Wordsworth, he provided the outlines of the character of the intellectual Pedlar in *The Excursion*; it is a reasonable guess that in being in his household Sara had access to a better library and better talk than perhaps any of her brothers and sisters. Aside from this, her early life seems to have been the unremarkable one of a young girl of a respectable family and modest means in a small but busy provincial town. So uneventful were her days, in outward circumstance, or, so far as we have been told, in inward crisis, that it is impossible at first to be clear even about the changes of scene and occupation.

She keeps house for Tom and George and visits John at Stockton, and she visits her cousins the Monkhouses, and they visit her. Two poets drop in of an October evening, and they all talk round the fire. She is in love. Poems begin to come – beautiful, and terrible, ardent but hopeless. What did it feel like to receive *Dejection: an Ode*, one wonders? Her sister marries and goes off to Grasmere. Tom and George find a new farm, closer to Grasmere, and walks and visits become more frequent. Thomas and Catherine Clarkson, fiery, articulate souls, are neighbours. A new nephew at Grasmere, and she is needed there. Coleridge goes off to Malta in search of health, and to try to control his love for her, but of her feelings about his departure we have no record. Appalling word comes to her in Kendal – the loss of the *Abergavenny* with its crew and captain, John Wordsworth. She walks over to Grasmere to break the news to them. Family tradition has it, supported by an entry in one of Coleridge's notebooks, that John Wordsworth wished, or the family wished him, to marry Sara. If it was so, her reserve here too is absolute. She goes on transcribing William's poems, making shirts for her brothers, taking walks with William and Dorothy in the countryside she loved best, acting as the family letter-writer for all of them, always available when a baby was about to be born, or a household to be moved, or when illness struck anywhere in the Wordsworth, Monkhouse, Hutchinson, Southey orbit. There was the crisis over *The Friend*, when she tried to help Coleridge to pull himself back into creative work, and finally had to admit failure by going off to Wales. The conflicting intensities of these days wore her out – Coleridge's pressures, practical and unconscious, and the Wordsworths' growing criticism and hopelessness about him. Then came the black cloud of misunderstanding that darkened affection; Coleridge, with Hartley white-faced in the carriage beside him and Derwent in tears, drove through Grasmere without stopping.

Life was not easy. The Allen Bank chimneys smoked beyond enduring, and the Rectory was damp. The children were ill, little Catharine lame, probably from poliomyelitis, and Thomas, the family darling, wrung their hearts with his sweetness and patience in his illness, likewise undiagnosed. Again Sara has to be the bearer of bad news, for Catharine and Thomas died within six months of each other. Another marriage – her brother Tom and Mary Monkhouse – very dear to her – in Grasmere Church. Then her cousin Tom Monkhouse – to an unknown Jane Horrocks – she is not so sure about that. And so there are more babies, and more households for the indispensable visitor to visit. More poems are coming out; she assists at the birth there too. There is a trip to London and a visit to Somerset House, and to Coleridge, and perhaps an unappreciated glimpse of Keats. A trip to Boulogne, not a great success, from a want of enterprise and imagination in her hostess. A short stay in Ramsgate, too fashionable and the household uninteresting. But Coleridge called and came to dinner and impressed them all with his talk and enlivened a dull time.

Losses and sorrows begin to increase. Dear Cousin Tom Monkhouse, so kind to everyone, has married a selfish wife who has hounded him with anxieties. In his last months it is Sara who takes care of him and his affairs until he dies in 1825. Dora Wordsworth is delicate and often ailing; Dorothy Wordsworth becomes seriously ill and William and

Mary are distracted; Mrs. Southey has to be removed, by force, to a retreat at York. The older generation is full of ailments – and death is a frequent companion. It is the younger generation she is chiefly concerned about now – Dora's health, young Tom Hutchinson's education, Willy Wordsworth in Germany learning to be a business man, little Mary Monkhouse now an orphan, dear Ebba her god-daughter, and Sarah her namesake, the 'h' on whose name she laments. Reading the letters straight through one gets the sense of the inevitable cycle of the years and 'the unimaginable touch of time'. Coleridge is dead, and Lamb. The links with life are fewer. Dorothy Wordsworth is alarmingly low and Sara sends for William and Mary. But Dorothy lived on, a death-in-life figure for more than twenty years. It was Sara who went. Always decisive, she was no procrastinator.

> William would vouch for the perfection of my character on this point. He always says that when Sara fixes to come you may be *sure of* her.

As in the novels of her contemporary Jane Austen, the plot is secondary, the characters everything. Her letters provide private yet disinterested pictures of a large and lively group of characters. Disinterested is I think the word, even in full view of her vigorous prejudices. It is not that there is very much in the letters that is actually new. The largest addition is the two letters 21 and 22, describing for the first time the Scottish Tour taken by William and Mary and Sara in 1814. And there is quoted by Sara part of an unpublished letter by Wordsworth, interesting for its insight (161). We have known about his eyes, his constant revisions of his poems, his interest in the progressive schools of his day, the constant flow of visitors to Rydal Mount. There have been many witnesses. But there are sometimes suspicions that the testimony of other writers cannot be taken at face value; and for other reasons the words of wives and sisters have to be taken with a grain of salt also. But a sympathetic sister-in-law seems to provide a nice combination of close knowledge and detachment. Especially a sister-in-law who lived in the household for over thirty years and whose nature it was to be honest at all costs.

There are some scraps of fresh information too. The letters to Quillinan, for instance, perhaps reveal some new reasons why Wordsworth was worried about him as a husband for Dora. They all love 'Q', obviously. They knit and sew for 'the Trots' after his first wife's death and long to see them ('how the wind will blow their little bonnets to-day'); they pack up all his belongings – Dorothy may have to repack in Kendal if the box doesn't hold together; Sara makes arrangements for his garden and his hayloft, keeps accounts for him and conducts his complicated transactions with his landlord. He consults her about his children's education, and he writes her about public affairs. But he is careless about writing and leaving addresses, 'a flibbertigibbet' she says, and he tries their affectionate patience so that she becomes a trifle urgent with her advice. But it is worth noting that Quillinan kept those letters, and that he continued to flout her advice, knowing perfectly well that the friendly letters, the socks, the scoldings and teasings, the devotion to the Trots would continue. He sends her a Valentine, which she ungratefully returns, with a letter on the back. He asks her and Dora jointly to become the guardians of his children should he meet with any accident abroad, and Sara and Wordsworth decline such a responsibility both for Dora and for herself. In September 1826 he writes light-heartedly that 'It would be a very pleasant adventure to fall in love', and it is fairly clear that though Dora's affection for him and for the children was unconcealed, he does not appear to have thought, for some years after his wife's death, of marrying her. Wordsworth, we may suspect, had his doubts about something more than his finances, or his difference – Quillinan was Roman Catholic – in faith.

About various contemporaries there are small details that one stumbles on with pleasure – about the Lambs, or Lockhart, or Wilson and *Blackwood's Magazine*, and the *Quarterly*, and her remarks on minor works and figures are often acute. Some of her shrewd nips are delightful – her blunt uncharitableness towards Mrs. Hemans, for instance, whom she considered false, affected, self-important, and silly. Compared with her, Miss Douglas of New York is harmless, she thinks, 'not an *unworthy* tho' a disagreeable body'. She takes a more restrained but more penetrating jab at Maria Jane Jewsbury, who 'is determined to write and therefore fancies she *must*'.

The Wordsworth moments in the letters will be for some readers the most important of all, and they are numerous.

Wordsworth is a poet about whom in some respects we already know far too much, and yet, since he frequently suffers from not sharing Shakespeare's personal inscrutability, it is useful to know more. Sara Hutchinson's angle of incidence is a good one. She quotes him often, usually but not always with approval. He is 'fidgetty' about postage (an ungenerous, nay parsimonious thing to a zealous letter-writer), and he is fretful but unwise, she thinks, about his eyes. When it comes to public matters, politics, and poetry, his word is received with some awe, or with unconscious acceptance, and Wordsworth's masculine domination of what Quillinan called his Ladies, and S. T. C.

less respectfully his 'petticoats', is plain as a pikestaff. 'W$^{m}$ refuses to allow *Blackwoods* in to the house' – but she smuggled it in for she was determined to read it. We see the Bard's spluttering annoyance, sometimes loftily expressed, as the reviews and parodies came to Rydal Mount. But in contrast we see him also 'the life of the parties when there is any real need for it', as for instance when Thomas Monkhouse was fatally ill. We see him the over-anxious parent, burdening his boys with his disapproval when they are not interested in books, so that Sara says of Johnny at the age of eighteen that he has become 'less afraid of his father'. We see his heart-sickening fears for their health, and his attempts to be fatherly, when by temperament and by occupation he needed solitude and quiet.

> M$^{rs}$ Lloyd & her little Girls have been here all night – Mary & she have been preparing to set out for Brathay – *Doro* & the Girls hurrying the father with his shaving to accompany *them* upon the Lake to scate – He partly attending to John & Derwent who are at work with Greek – Dorothy & I with our desks before us *attempting* to write in a hurry for the post – & I about to set off for M$^{rs}$ Crumps for a few days – all this though going on in *two* rooms might as well be only in one: for – the constant opening & shutting of doors – messages & arrangements, *to, from,* & *by* all the parties – that a more *agreeable* scene of confusion you could not imagine.

Then there are the times when he is 'more busy than agreeable', or 'only agreeable by fits', and she will consider the text of his poems final only when they are 'tightly bound up *in boards*'. She is clearly all for the poet in him, and against the statesman *manqué*. She hates to see him on the hustings. 'Poetry and all great and good things will be lost in Electioneering,' she moans.

Miss Helen Darbishire has very kindly sent me her transcript of an unpublished letter of William Wordsworth to Sara Hutchinson which makes very clear the strength of the affectionate bonds between them.

> Rydale Mount. October 4th 1813.
>
> My dearest Sarah,
>
> Dorothy you know is at Kendale: but Mary and I received your letter last night which was forwarded to her by today's Post – We long for your return which I shall be most happy to facilitate. [Then he suggests plans for meeting her half-way – She is at Stockton – both on horseback.] Write immediately and tell me which plan you prefer: or if H. cannot procure a Horse exact a promise from Jack to go to Penrith, or if that promise cannot be gained and depended upon tell me,

and I will come as far even as Stockton to conduct you home again – But what I myself should like best would be to meet you at Hawes – and what I should like infinitely the worst would be that you should prolong your stay, and deprive us of your presence & company for I love you most tenderly. This is the anniversary of my wedding day and every year whether fraught with joy or sorrow has brought with it additional cause why I should thank God for my connection with your family – Mary joins with me in blessing you as we have blessed each other.

[Mary writes a postscript in the course of which she says, 'I want you my most dear Sister painfully –']

As Miss Darbishire says, 'Sara's intelligence and wit must have been much cherished by Wordsworth – and he certainly allowed her to criticize his poems and made use of her criticism.' It is a great pity that her letters to him are not extant, especially the one that led him to write the long explanation and defence of *The Leech-gatherer* in answer to her complaints about it. As Miss Darbishire has said, he found Sara's remarks 'at first unpalatable' but later 'sound and even stimulating' and they led him to put in place of a stanza she disliked a new one, 'surely the imaginative core of the poem. . . . "As a huge stone is sometimes seen to lie/Couch'd on the bald top of an eminence. . . ." ' *

What the letters reveal of the Coleridge chapter in her life is in some respects new. Heretofore I think there has not been a syllable directly from her about him. Here we see him tempting her with snuff – one would know that his snuffbox would be generously passed about; we see him 'making racket enough for twenty' with little Dora Wordsworth, then aged four, teasing her because 'she cannot be too naughty for his taste'; we see again the troubles with the *Friend*, and how she shared the Wordsworths' unsanguine views; but it comes with something of a shock, even to a shock-proof Coleridgian, to find him quoted on the subject of the stall-feeding of cattle! Of the reported success of the 1811 lectures, after the quarrel with Wordsworth, she writes as a friend still concerned about his welfare; still more defensively, in the same letter in which she regrets his having passed through Grasmere without stopping, she protests against rumours that the *Friend* had ruined the printer. By 1817, after the worrying reports of that worst period of Coleridge's life between the departure from the Lakes and his haven in Highgate in 1816, her comments are remote and negative, and when she saw him in 1818 she clearly tried to avoid him. But she inquires about his lectures and is far from detached. Then

* See *Wordsworth, Poems in Two Volumes, 1807*, edited by Helen Darbishire, Oxford, 1952, Appendix III.

comes a searing comment on the *Letters* in *Blackwood's** which 'we do not think' are S. T. C.'s – 'too stupid to induce us to read, except a sentence here and there'. They are certainly not in his best vein, but they are indubitably his and no one else's, and it is a commentary full of pathos for him, that she, of all persons, could not recognize him when she saw him. Yet when she does see him clearly, she describes without flinching, but without moralizing. Miss Barker, in Boulogne, she says, 'lives in a complete dream – planning and scheming and never executing! Yet believing as firmly as Mr. Coleridge that she never fails!'

The letters make it clear that she saw Coleridge at least five times after they parted in 1810. It has usually been suggested that the Wordsworth quarrel put an end to their relationship. We know now that she saw him in 1818 in London on her way to the Clarksons; twice or more when he called on her in Ramsgate in 1823; and in 1834 she called on him in Highgate, and realizing that the end was near, went back two or three times before she left for the North. The Ramsgate visits are interesting. She was staying with Mrs. Tom Monkhouse, not greatly believing in Mrs. Monkhouse's ill health or need for a spa, and, one gathers, bored. Coleridge arrived on Saturday night, and called on Monday, rather over-kissing the baby – and she quotes his horrifying but revealing remark that kissing a baby is as refreshing as a bathe in the sea. She considers Coleridge an inducement to Quillinan and when she finally gathered together a dinner party, Quillinan was 'astonished' and 'a little uncomfortable' because he 'could not presume to talk to him'. The picture of Coleridge as '*obliged* to have all the talk to himself' is kinder than some other interpretations of that performance. And the visit is interesting, too, for the references to Elia's letter to Southey, and the indication that much as she is devoted to Southey, she agrees with Coleridge in resenting the narrow rigidity of his views on some important questions, and particularly his insensitive bludgeoning of Charles Lamb. All in all, the Ramsgate visits seem to have been harmonious and healing, so much so that she is 'a little sorry to leave Ramsgate before the time', and she knows Coleridge will be 'in despair at our sudden determination'. I cannot help thinking that Coleridge's 'The Pang More Sharp Than All' might be dated 1823.†

* See p. 227 and n.

† *Complete Poetical Works*, 1912, I, 457–8. E. H. Coleridge gives the date as (?)1825–6, possibly linking it to the Gillman relationship. But the 'babe, that tempts and shuns the menaced kiss', and the description of Kindness in the third stanza, as well as other small details, suggest links with Sara Hutchinson, and possibly the Ramsgate meetings of 1823.

Then there are her visits to him at Highgate, and a slight flaring up of her old impatience with Mrs. Coleridge who is now not any more than of old alive to his true state. After his death she is more outspoken still about his family, who 'had more pride in him than love for him'. She makes a comment any biographer of Coleridge might covet for his final sentence: 'Poor dear Coleridge is gone! He died a most calm and happy death – tho he had suffered great pain for some time previous. He was opened – the disease was at his heart.' '*The* disease' – the phrase marks her complete recognition and acceptance of it – and there had been many doubters – 'the disease was at his heart.' This he himself knew and had known for many long years. And the Chapman's *Homer* and the mourning ring are her tokens of the positive and negative sides of such an illness. So she sends for the one and thanks for the other – Mr. Green will understand 'how precious they are' to her. One wonders if Mr. Green would be equal to anything of the kind.

The references to Coleridge may seem to be rather cool, but then she could scarcely be expected to refer to him otherwise than guardedly and dispassionately. The ambivalence in her attitude to him is clear. Indeed her perception of the two sides of most human coins is one of the best discoveries to be made in the letters. And this very perception, meeting a like sensitivity in Coleridge, must have provided both of them, in the good years, with that happy amenity of the human condition, an eye to catch. It is pleasant to see how in old age the whole story ends in the strains of pure affection that were its truest note. She was the fitting recipient of *Dejection: an Ode*, and like it, serene at the close.

There are two letters to Mrs. Coleridge, written late in life when the difficulties of earlier years are forgotten in the sadnesses she has to report; one of the letters has to do with poor Hartley's accounts, kept originally by Dorothy Wordsworth, and when her health failed, by Sara Hutchinson, Hartley being quite incapable of taking care of himself. The other letter tells Mrs. Coleridge the grim story of how Southey had had to take her sister, Mrs. Southey, to the asylum at York. Both unhappy matters Sara handles with delicacy and genuine kindness and feeling, though the letters have just that shade of extra politeness that separates them from the family letters, or those to Quillinan. A certain distance is discernible which all the goodwill in the world does not bridge, in spite of the fact that enough water has now gone under the mill for her to send her love 'to dear STC'. But the old Sara shines through in her barely concealed admonition to young Sara to 'rouze' herself, to pay no attention to advice [her mother's!] to seek 'quiet'. What she needs is 'change of scene and occupation'. In this triangle of Saras, the youngest may have been the brainiest and was certainly the most beautiful, but it is beyond doubt her admonisher who excelled in vigorous common sense if not in tact. The pen was certainly blunt that could insert such a message to a daughter in a letter to the mother who was not so stupid as not to feel a barb in it. The barb was meant to be sharp, too. Mrs. Southey had been taken off to York, and though it is of course not stated, it is between the lines that Sara might reach the same fate if firmer measures were not taken. Asra was being cruel to be kind, but one could scarcely wonder if the young Sara, whose lassitudinous illnesses probably had some physical or emotional basis, and Hartley with his gentle, twisted temperament, found her a fairly strong dose at times.

It is not possible to go around the whole circle – the Southeys, de Quincey, the Lloyds, the Lambs, and all their visitors, more and less glorious. But of the Wordsworth-Hutchinson-Monkhouse families one thing is clear: the strong ties of affection and likemindedness, generosity and disinterestedness among them. The fact that all three families were orphaned early may help to account for the high store they set on a warm and friendly family life. But it was no artificial or merely tribal bond that kept them visiting and writing long letters to one another. Their general ability to distinguish between the real and the unreal, their sense of public responsibility and recognition of general concerns greater than their own, their fondness for rural life, for natural pleasures, for literature, these are their characteristic qualities. They helped to root their poets in a natural, practical everyday world without being a brake-weight on the traces of the chariots of the sun.

Of the letters as period pieces much might be said. The broad questions on which Sara Hutchinson touches are familiar and have been illustrated many times. It is the 'Incidental Intelligence', as the newspapers of her day described it, that is entertaining, and sometimes startling; when she clamours for the suspension of the Habeas Corpus Act, for instance, to put down Brougham's 'Blues' in Westmoreland. Either she and Dorothy Wordsworth are the most rabid Tories at Rydal Mount or Rydal Mount's real political heat is being somewhat innocently exposed. More deeply felt and communicated in the letters is the acuteness of the agrarian distresses after the Napoleonic wars, when people as competent and hard-working as Tom and Mary Hutchinson begin to think about emigrating. Or again, another reference takes us straight into one of the liveliest scandals of the day – Mrs. Clarke and the Duke of York – 'Duke or Darling' as the boys say in the street instead of 'Heads or Tails'. Wordsworth's *Cintra* pamphlet, which she had transcribed, is delayed, not as de Quincey said, because of a drunken printer, not as the printer said, because of the repeated corrections, not as Wordsworth said, because of de Quincey's delays, but all because of Mrs. Clarke's *Memoirs* which as a prospective best-seller ousted Wordsworth's sober essay off the presses. Mrs. Clarke's *Memoirs* were not published in this edition by C. & R. Baldwin in 1809, being bought up for £10,000 and suppressed, but they helped to delay the *Cintra* pamphlet until interest had waned, so that of its five hundred copies many were sold for waste paper. Equally unlooked for is a glimpse of a new royal baby. She writes Mary Hutchinson who is 'expecting':

> . . . if it is a Boy & not named *John*, I will not have him for a nephew of mine – if it is a Girl you may call it 'Alexandrina Victoria', or any other daft name you like, in compliment to our future Queen that is to be in default of a better. Only think of an *English* queen with such a name!

One shocking aspect of the letters is the cumulative impression they build up of medical ignorance so short a time ago, in the profession itself and in the general public. She asks the Lambs to go and visit poor young Tom Clarkson—he is lonely and has the smallpox. And the hints of undiagnosed poliomyelitis, appendicitis, and tuberculosis, to say nothing of the unconscious cruelty with which anaemia or other conditions were treated, are horrifyingly frequent. On the other hand, it comes as an exciting surprise to one ignorant of medical history, to hear of two operations for cataract; she sees the success of one on Thomas Clarkson and persuades John Monkhouse to a similar course.

We should not think of looking in these letters for an inside picture of a famous public school – but it is here – in some detail. And did we all know that Dr. and Mrs. Arnold were known to the boys as 'The Tarts'? There is some pleasant sense of irony, too, in finding her ordering, just as she has left them, the clarion work of the Oxford Movement which had no more determined opponent than Thomas Arnold. She wishes to read the first of the *Tracts for the Times*. Books, politics, agriculture, she is interested in them at close range, and gives one the sense of being generally aware of the contemporary horizon. But the horizon is notoriously less interesting than the speck on it, and it is a truism of real cogency here that the most interesting thing in good letters is the writer himself. Sara Hutchinson, without being in the least egotistical, in fact partly because she is reticent, is the vibrant centre of interest in these letters. Like all good letter writers, she is, in a way, unsparing of herself, writing freely and generously, with a clear head and in good heart, and with the intention to entertain as well as communicate. She is a real correspondent: every letter actively involves us in at least two, often in a dozen, lives. She describes the life around her, and she imagines the life going on around her correspondent. Her penetration of her friends' affairs rises to more than questions, which she knows are tiresome. She gives orders, argues, scolds, commiserates. They kept her letters – it is perhaps not very usual for quite so many persons in a family circle to keep the letters of a perfectly unfamous cousin, sister-in-law, and aunt – because they could not destroy them. Her letters brought her, in her person as she was, right into a chair at their hearths; they were far too alive to put on the fire.

Her direct comments on herself are few but illuminating. Perhaps one of the happiest things about her is the entire absence of striving for perfection in herself, or in others.

I often congratulate myself on never having been a beauty – Mrs. Coleridge says she cannot bear to look at herself – 'and that it is not a bit a matter what one puts on when one is grown such a [? sight]'. Now I shall for ever feel that it is my duty to make myself as bonny as I can – one has no [right] to force people to look upon what is disagreeable.

She has no illusions, but lots of common sense, and more than that, zest.

John is bewitched also with the Kaleidoscope (I will spell it with a k in spite of the *Literary Gazette* to show you that I understand greek) but he was too rational to look through it at breakfast time, as *you* or I would have done.

She doesn't take herself too seriously. 'W[m] says "Let a wife drift towards you," ' she writes the lovelorn Tom Monkhouse.

. . . Old Maid as I am don't think that, though I firmly believe the balance of *comfort* is on our side, I am a favorer of a single life – comfort is but a meagre thing after all – but I have seen such misery in the marriage life as would *appal* you if you had seen it. Such millstones about the necks of worthy men! that I would have you be *wary* – . . . Of course you will not suppose that I think all the fault belongs to the women. . . .

She is Thomas Monkhouse's confidante in personal matters, and one deduces from the letters that she was the recipient of frequent confidences, especially from the young. To the younger Tom Hutchinson who is afraid of failing at Cambridge her advice is rather firm and monitory, but it is also encouraging, and supported by the practical help of a tutor arranged and paid for. And the spirit in which the thing was done must surely be a model for all well-intentioned aunts.

That you are well, and happy, is the best assurance I can receive that you are satisfied with yourself, and doing your duty: and tho' much gratified by your kind expressions of obligation to me I should be very disingennuous were I not to tell you that the favour *you say* I have done you – is not *so purely disinterested* as you may suppose – for my dear Boy I assure you the *pain* I felt when I saw you in such a state of despondency I should have been glad to be rid of at a much greater price than the payment of a little money – which I can well spare and which I trust, with God's blessing, will be well bestowed upon you – & I wish no better recompence.

Some of the choicest passages in the letters are to be found in descriptions, brief and unselfconscious, of her responses to various kinds of beauty, or activity or moments of peace: King's College Chapel, the Grasmere autumn, the children dancing, the after-church Grasmere churchyard full of the congregation, or Oxford, which she does not wish to know in any more detail but always to remember as in her first glimpse of it, whole, 'the Glory of our island'. She has an eye and can see out of the corner of it, or, as often, it is wide open. Whatever is going on, the verb is in the affirmative mood, the active voice, and the present tense. Drenched by a sudden storm, she calls on friends in Patterdale only to find them away from home, Henry not yet arrived, and nothing as it ought to be. What is she to do? Does she sit down and write an anxious letter describing all the accidents and mishaps that have led up to this uncomfortable crisis, as Sarah Coleridge would have done? No, because she is not uncomfortable and it is not a crisis. She stirs up the fire, sits down and dries herself off, has a cup of tea, and recites happily to herself some lines she has transcribed for William.

A steaming bowl, a blazing fire,
What greater good can man desire?
'Twere worth a wise man's while to try
The utmost anger of the sky:
To *seek* for thoughts of gloomy cast,
If such the bright amends at last.

It is inevitable, if very unfair, that her letters and Mrs. Coleridge's* should be compared. Asra was infinitely more favoured by events. And yet we cannot fail to see that 'Hutton', as the children called her, whatever their respective circumstances, would always have made a better life for herself than Mrs. S. T. C., and the contrast considerably increases the pathos of Mrs. Coleridge's position. For Sara Hutchinson was incomparably the freer spirit.

* As published in *Minnow Among Tritons*, by Stephen Potter, 1934.

'The Wordsworths are much in request,' Mrs. Coleridge wrote Poole. 'You have no notion how much respectability attaches to them.' Respectability and prudence, as Mr. Potter points out, are two of her words. 'The Hutchinsons are all so agreeable ourselves and to ourselves,' Sara Hutchinson writes, 'that we are quite independent of all other society.'

Sara Hutchinson will write impatiently, 'What stupes go to the university and how few are plucked!', while Sarah Coleridge in a moment of hard-won complacency thinks that 'verily he [Hartley] will not disgrace the name which now stands high at both Universities'. ''Tis a glorious thing to have a Bishop for an uncle if one has sons at the universities,' she says. 'I do not agree with Joanna,' Sara Hutchinson writes, 'in thinking a Curate of Grasmere more respectable than the Head Master of the National Schools.' They are discussing Mr. Johnson, and Sara Hutchinson, though she does not sweep respectability away altogether, puts it farther down in her list of considerations.

He no doubt will be preferred in the Church also – but in no other situation can he be so eminently useful as the one he holds – therefore, though a teacher of all the little *Ragamuffins* in London, Joanna need not be ashamed of him for a husband if she can get him.

The exact relation of sting to fun in such remarks is difficult at this distance to determine. On the whole the letters suggest if not more sugar than spice, more spice than acid.

The letters of the two Sara's present a contrast in style also. It is not just that Sara Hutchinson's have variety as she is affected by her correspondent: affectionate equality to the Monkhouses – informing, requesting, protesting, sharing poems and many interests – more polite to Mrs. Coleridge and a shade more elegant – simple without condescension to little Ebba – bracing to poor self-depreciating young Tom Hutchinson at Cambridge – whereas Mrs. Coleridge is writing only to Poole to whom she has always poured out her troubles. It is not only this difference. In Mrs. Coleridge's letters, whether the matter is cheerful or 'vexatious', all is in disorder. Everything tumbles out, helter-skelter, dropped and picked up again, repeated, apologized for, till we do not know whether to laugh, cry, or scream. Her words come freely but out of a state of perpetual consternation. Her stream of words is a cheerful but agitated and muddy one ('forgive all blunders'), full of rocks and holes, constantly swinging around corners very quickly and meeting the unexpected, picking up debris here and there, often doubling back on itself. Asra's letters flow evenly, steadily, making for their destination, showing a ripple here and there, occasionally a rock below the surface, sometimes making an interesting change of level, but always clear, under command, bringing us into a sweet vista now and then. With Mrs. Coleridge there is no time to attend to the banks that fly past – the waters themselves are too troubled. With Asra we pause occasionally, perhaps for a person to be described: – Lady Farquhar 'has a countenance so benign and expressive of enjoyment that it is evident in a moment that you must love her sometime or other' – for a quiet evening to be spent – a serious problem in some-one's life to be discussed – a joke, for its own sake, like a letter from Lamb – or for some general reflection on life – 'The painters who flatter are quite in the right. Truth gives no satisfaction.'

What Sara Hutchinson's letters give us then, is fresh light on an interesting group of persons; the sight of a human being who enhances the early nineteenth-century scene; and some charming writing. If the group of persons she lived among is distinguished, as Mr. Potter says, for its articulateness, then here is another member of it. Perhaps her unique contribution to them was her conspicuous sense of fact; and, one should add, of fun. Hartley Coleridge says she was 'naturally despondent', and S. T. C. that she was 'as deficient in hope' as himself. If so, she refused to show her despondence in her letters, though she certainly refused also to hope against hope. There is a resilient northern practicality about her that must have steadied them all at one time or another, over-wrought as they often were. This is the quality that gave rise to Professor de Selincourt's description of her as 'a sheet-anchor'. She had her blind spots and big ones, her prejudices too, but neither her reason nor her unreason precluded sensitivity and taste, and kind-ness which was not less kind for struggling to be wise.

Coleridge should have the last word, and it comes in one of his very few comments on her, made privately to Daniel Stuart:

> If Sense, Sensibility, Sweetness of Temper, perfect simplicity and unpretending Nature, joined to shrewdness and entertainingness make a valuable Woman, Sara Hutchinson is so.

Such qualities certainly make a delightful letter-writer.

# THE LETTERS

# I

*Mr Monkhouse, Mr Bush's, Pudding Lane, London*
*Messrs B & C to the care of M^r Saville, Upholsterer,*
*17 Aldgate High St*

*Gallow Hill, Wykeham by Malton, Yorkshire, July 12, 1800*

Dear John

I *ought* to apologize for not answering your Letter which I received so many months ago by M^r Dickson but you must naturally suppose I have been much engaged of late & consequently it is unnecessary – we are now tolerably settled in our new habitation and like it much better than we expected – the country is very pleasant – the farm good & the house very convenient much better than the generality of farm Houses – tho' nothing like Sockburne but that was not to be expected – Jack[1] has been over & was much pleased with every thing but as he is always in such a hurry he did not see half of what he ought – I have a request to make (in which all this family join earnestly) which I think you may comply with without much trouble to yourself – it is that you will go to the Navy Office & enquire where the Edgar* is & if Harry[1] is on board & in what capacity – we have some reason to believe he has left this Ship & cannot get any certain account by any other method – we have applied before when we were at a loss about him – but at this time we had rather the application was made personally than by Letter – if you go to the office you may have access to the Books – write here as soon as you have gained the necessary information but do not mention it to any one – we are very anxious about him therefore beg you may be as expeditious as possible – M^r

* Sara had reason to worry. Her sailor brother had by this time probably left the *Edgar* (because of a captain who ruled by frequent floggings), had pawned his pay sheet, and was jobless in London. He tells the story in a delightful poem, *The Retrospect of a Retired Mariner in Nine Cantos, written by Himself* (Stockton, 1836). The poem is dedicated to Joanna Hutchinson, and tells with a good deal of salt and savour, the story of his naval career. He describes taking Mary to visit the Wordsworths at Racedown, pays tribute to Capt. Sir Alexander Ball, a corroboration of Coleridge's eulogy, and tells a remarkable and horrible story of the slave trade, which Coleridge recorded from Henry's own telling of it, in one of his notebooks. Coleridge was fond of Henry and enjoyed his rhymes, of which there are some still in MS. signed 'The Ancient Mariner'. For S. H. on Henry's *Retrospect*, see Letter 168, p. 442.

Dickson did not tell us one *tale* about you notwithstanding he was much importuned as you had given us a hint that there *was* something to tell – we expect him & Mr Lodge soon – they are coming to see what they can pick up at Scarboro' this *Spa* season – it is a very gay place I assure you – the *spaers* are thronging past daily – our house is not very far from the road & we see Coaches *whirring* by for ever – we also expect Miss Charlotte in about three weeks – our friends are determined to find us out notwithstanding the distance – our *Gentlemen* are very busy with the Hay, it is fine weather – & I suppose Jack[1] will be as through as any body with his soon. Mary[2] & little Anna Weir are spending the Holidays with him – I had a letter from him this morning in which (in his old way) by way of a *Hoax* he tells me that Miss Weir is now in London & intends returning by Gallow Hill – we wish it was true as we should be delighted to see her – Mary[1] H. will be much obliged to you to purchase for her Stockdale's edition of Shakespear – it is bound in one volume & costs 1 Guinea – but as it may not perhaps be in print you must not get any other, if you can meet with it send it by the first opportunity – that is by the first private hand to Stockton as it is not likely you will have an opportunity of sending it hither – Tom[1] George[1] & Mary[1] join me in best wishes & I am Dr John yours affty S. Hutchinson

## 2

*Mr Monkhouse, Mr Bush's, 29 Pudding Lane, London*

*Gallow Hill, near Wykeham Malton, Yorkshire 8 Aug. 1800*

My dr John

We were much disappointed that you were not able to gain any information respecting Harry[1] at the Navy Office – we have desired Jack[1] to send you a letter of his which I hope he will not neglect. I am afraid some other folks have not left off *blushing* otherwise they would not have cared for giving the clerks offence as certainly they had no right to deny you – we were never before required to send either Letter or Register – You did flatter yourself you hum'd us completely by pretending that Miss Weir was not in London but before your letter arrived we were certain of her being there therefore it had not the desired [effect?]. I was also much amused with your *admonition* not to believe all that Jack says when you the moment after acknowledge you have swallowed all the wit which he had cramd Miss Weir with purposedly to amuse you – George[1] will thank you to go immediately upon the receipt of this to M[r] Idle's & purchase two Hats one is for him & the other for M[r] Dickson – they must be handsome fashionable but not round tops and sent by the coach directed as you address your letters – now you must not fail as George will be going to Sockburn in a fortnight at farthest & if it does not come [by] that time he will have some difficulty in getting [*torn*] – he is going to reap the crop there & is to stay at Stockton all winter to market it – You may either pay for the Hats or leave them for M[r] R. Dickson to pay when he comes to Town or in any other way you may advise – I suppose Miss W. has left Town before this – she behaved very shabbily not to call here – if she did not bring Mary's[1] Shakespear send it along with the Hats – we have not much opinion of your *friend the Author's* works if they display no more judgement than he has done in pronouncing Stockdale's the worst edition – it is an old one therefore better than those which have been *improved* by such wits as he. I am D[r] John yours affty S. Hutchinson.

I will thank you to purchase for me at your friend the Chip Hat house a Chip Hat or bonnet of the very *newest* fashion – I would have it col[d] *pea-green* else lilac I would prefer – a useful size that is one to shade the face but not too large as you know that would be out of proportion, but I have a small head [*torn*] you can order it to be sent to the Idles who will pack it carefully up – mind no flowers or kick-shaws about it let it be very modest – not hemmd with Ribband or any thing but simply the Hat itself don't give an extravagant [price?] – I will repay you [*torn*] for the Book when I return to S[tockton] with thanks. Don't be angry at the trouble we give you.

The Hats must be 23 inches round the outside of the crown.

## 3

*Mr Monkhouse, Mr Bush's – Pudding Lane, London*

*Gallow Hill, Aug[t] 23rd* [*1800*]

My d[r] John

I think it is almost necessary for me to pay the postage of my letters as I shall be an expensive correspondent to you if I contrive to write at this rate but as the Hats are not arrived I am afraid we shall lose them without some enquiry is made after them – they might have been half a dozen times down from London since I wrote and I apprehend they are laying at York or Malton – I will therefore trouble you once more to enquire what coach they were sent by, to what Inn at York and the Innkeeper's name. If they should not have been forwarded at all let George's & mine be sent to Stockton & M^r Dickson's and Mary's[1] Shakespear as I before desired to Gallow Hill – by the Mail – George[1] has left us – he is at present at M^r Wood's where he will continue 'till the crop at Sockburne is got in. Did Jack[1] ever send you one of Harry's[1] Letters? should he not we have ordered George to get & send you one. I wish you may at least be able to learn where Edgar* is – that we may write to him – Miss Weir is I find arrived at home at last – she made a pretty say, was I fancy so charmed with your gallantry that she could not *tear herself away*. I do not doubt but you were very polite – send us some account of her *proceedings* in Town as we can never get her to write and you have never mentioned her at all. Do not fail to write as soon as you can give us any information respecting the hats that we may make some enquiries at York. The players are come to Scarboro', Kemble's company & M^r J. Kemble is expected – when he arrives we intend to honor them with our presence. I find your papa is expected at Stockton Manse – I hope to be at home by that time to receive his honor write *immediately* God bless you! Tom[1] & Mary[1] send their best love – I am d^r John yours affty S. Hutchinson.

I hope you have been tolerably *warm* in London this summer. You never tell us whether you are likely to continue at M^r Bush's or not nor how the old boy & you agree now.

I have opened my Letter to say that should you not have got my last letter (which is rather improbable) that this will be a perfect riddle to you – I had desired you to send two Gentleman's hats fashionable & hansome but not round tops 22 inches round the outside of the crown to be bought of M^r Idle – one for M^r Dickson the other for George – a chip hat also for myself but as it is so late in the season it is of little consequence – you need not trouble yourself – the other hats you must forward immediately – one here the other to George at Stockton.

*Postmark: Malton*

## 4

*Grasmere, Tuesday Ev^o. [March 26, 1805]*

My dear Friend

I should have written to you before this, but I wished to tell you that my box was arrived, that you might not plague yourself about it – as I hoped it would come in its' *own time* – and it did find its' way hither

* See p. 3 note.

yesterday – The Combs &c I shall get from George's[1], & I thank you for sending them. I was glad to find by your note, that you were all well; & hope that dear little John continues so – we are all well here, so far as relates to bodily Health – but for ought more, I can say little – We have had delightful weather ever since I came, but not the Heart to enjoy it – we cannot stir from the house without meeting a thousand fresh remembrances of our loss.* The body has been found! and interred at Wyke by the directing of an aunt of Mr C. Wordsworth – it had been found very near the Ship – among the many accounts we have had is one saying that the firing was never once heard owing to the storm! – I have just rec^d a Letter from our friend at Malta† – it had escaped with part of the convoy I suppose. He is well, & intends to leave Malta for Eng^d in March – This will be a great comfort to my dearest Friends – best of all they could receive – For this we have reason to be most thankful! – I have also had a Letter from home requesting my early return – I know not how it will be managed – for they will not let me talk of it here – But *wedded* as I am I must think about it tho' I shall be loth to leave them at this time – When I think of all your & Mr C[ookson]'s kindness to me, I grieve indeed to think, that I should have been so unlucky as pay my visit to you at such a melancholy Time – for I would desire to remember it with cheerful feelings; as it is, it will ever be recollected with pain. But I will most assuredly visit you again – when I shall hope that neither you or I, will have ought to distress us – when these things will have passed into a melancholy but not painful recollection – God bless you, and all that you love! I shall ever remember your affection with unmingled feelings of pleasure. Remember me most affectionately to Mr C.— & the Children. I am going to make 4 Bonnets for four of my favorite girls – namely Jane, Bessy, little Dorothy[3] & your Elizabeth[3] – so you must make the old Beavers serve till its arrival which may not be very soon as I am not quite in the humour – but I tell you, that you may not be at that trouble yourself – Now I hope you will come to see us when you have nothing else better to do – but on this shall not as I have already promised you ever depend my coming to you – My kind remembrances to those who think me worth enquiring after – But most particularly to your Aunt, the whole Family of the Steeles, & our dear old Friend the Doctor – kiss the Bairns for me, & believe me most sincerely your Friend S. H.

Mary[1] & Dorothy[1] desire their kind remembrances – W^m[1] is gone to Brougham to Cap^t Wordsworth.‡

* John Wordsworth's death. † Coleridge.

‡ Sarah Hutchinson to Mrs Cookson of Kendal – Grasmere – End of March 1805. Miss Hutchinson was on a visit to Mrs Cookson at the time of the death of

## 5

*Miss Monkhouse, 21 Budge Row, London*

[*Oct. 1808*]

My dear Mary

You cannot conceive the strange perplexities of my mind, at the moment when I received your Letter, the other morning at Ann Nicholson's – a Letter written by you; directed by John[2]; and a few lines under the Seal by Mrs Clarkson – it was quite a Riddle! However when I had recovered from my surprize, & came to the explanation, I was most truly happy to find that you were, or had been, (for there was no date to your Letter, & I suspect it had lain a week at Rydale) with dear Mrs Clarkson – I know that it would do *her* good, if it were for nothing else but to talk about *us* – and for your own sake it was a delight to me that you should know, & love and feel, the goodness of such a noble Creature, as she most truly is – We have not heard from her since, at which I am rather surprized, and therefore I am in the dark with respect to your motions; and also the success of John's[2] farming Plans – most sincerely do I wish that he may succeed – and I have no doubt but that Tom[1] will be very glad to join him, notwithstanding his apparent luke-warmness – He is *determined* upon having a Farm, if possible – but he cannot be stirred without some probability – nay more, some certainty of success – he wants a little *Enterprize* most sadly – Now if John should meet with a farm in *Suffolk* I do not see the necessity of Tom's coming to look at it; because Sam Buck would be a much better judge, knowing as he does all the usages of the

Capt. John Wordsworth Jr. (5 Feb. 1805) and proceeded thence to Grasmere. On the 27th of March a letter was received there announcing the finding of the body and another from S. T. Coleridge 'our friend at Malta' bearing the date 19 Jan.

'Home' at this period was with her brother George at Park house between Pooley Bridge and Dacre.

Capt. John Wordsworth Senior, the Poet's 1st Cousin, was at this time tenant of Brougham Hall. – G. G. W[ordsworth].

Thomas Cookson of Kendal and his wife Elizabeth were not related to the Cooksons of Penrith from whom the mother of Wordsworth was sprung—the friendship probably arose through Sara Hutchinson who on being left an orphan at the age of ten was brought up by kinsfolk in Kendal – both she and Mrs. Cookson were born in 1775. Mr. Cookson died in 1833, and Mrs. Cookson in 1868 at How Foot in Grasmere, where with two of her daughters she lies buried. – G. G. W.

Country – and William says that he thinks it folly for them *both* to go to Wales together (a *hunting*) they had best take two different roads (as the Kings sons used to do when they went to seek their Fortunes) and then they will travel over twice as much ground with the same expence. Upon my word Mary! if you go into Wales, you will be a far-travelled Lady – there is nothing like giving up Business, living upon one's Fortune, & *fancying* one's self rich! Never mind Darling! It will bring in abundant harvest in the end: thou mayest sit by the fire hereafter, as Joanna says, and think of what thou hast seen, when other means of amusement are not in thy power – Joanna has also I find resolved to do the same – she and Miss Green are going to London & Bath; and they sent a message by George[1] (who was here last week) to try to enlist me into the scheme – but I have declined it – however I do not disapprove of it for her – she had much better spend her money in that way, than by boarding at Appleby where nothing would have come of it –

I wrote to you some time ago – at least I *think* I did – and yet I have some notion that in writing to Harry[1] I addressed you at the same time; and for that reason only I have since felt as if I had really written to yourself. I wonder that we have not heard again from Harry – I trust in God that he has not sailed, for the weather has been tremendous! you can have no conception of the uncomfortableness, not to say *misery*, of this House* in these storms – not a chimney will draw the smoke! and one day we could not have a fire except in the Study; & then you could not *see* each other. In the rest of the rooms the fire was actually blown out of the Grates – We have at last got the chimney Doctor who has begun his operations in the kitchen; but he works slowly, and I fear it will be an age before they are all cured. It has been a most ungenial Autumn – we have not been able to stir out; indeed it seems to be almost winter already, the Waterfalls are in all their glory if one could but travel abroad to see them – I have just been stimulating my Faculties by a pinch of Fribourg out of a great Canister which came in a Box from London last night – it is in vain to attempt to give over – while Coleridge is in the House one is never out of the way of temptation – You have no chance of seeing him in London – he talks of staying here all the winter – but should he change his mind you may be assured, if he is in any comfortable health or Spirits, that he will find you out; for you are a most mighty favorite with him – he never forgets the attention with which you used to listen to his long discourses when they used to lull poor Jane Addison to sleep! You will be glad to hear that his health & spirits are much amended. M[rs] C[oleridge]

* Allan Bank, to which they had recently moved from Dove Cottage.

was here last week – she came to settle the Boys at Ambleside School; and carry back little Sara[3], who has been with us for some time – the Boys are to spend Saturday & Sunday in every week here – and their great holidays at Keswick.

You are affronted that I never mention the Babe. Why it is just like all the rest – and will be the very same as Dorothy[2] – it thrives very well now though it has had the Thrush in its mouth. I wish its Mother throve well also – but she looks miserably, & is so pestered with a sore mouth that she can scarcely eat any thing – we all wish her to wean the Child, but she is as obstinate as heretofore, and will not consent – however if she goes on in this way it *must* be done. – Sissy has had a sore throat for some time, & has lost all her good looks – the glands (I forget the learned name) in her throat are so swoln as to completely fill it – she has been subject to it ever since she had the Croupe from relaxation of the Parts. The other Children are well – your Godson still talks of you '*my* Godmother'. – I am very sorry to find that John[2] has received no benefit from his Physician – however I trust that Dr Beddoes may do something for him; and if he goes into Wales it will be no inconvenience to him to consult Dr B. personally – Your poor Lover* is ill again – at Liverpool, I think, he is on a visit to the Astleys or some of his harum-scarum Friends – we have seen nothing of him lately – His Mother and Sister are at Edinburgh but they return to Elleray to spend the Winter – Tom[1], you would hear, has given up all thoughts of the Bp's Farm at Calgarth.

I hope, that though you tell me you have seen none of the Sights, you intend to see them all, notwithstanding your dislike of London – Except to see Mr Cooke in Sr Pertinax† I would not have you to spend your money at the Theatre – for as you have already seen Mrs Jordan, & the House, I am sure there is nothing else worth looking at – & though you may not be so much delighted with Madame Catalani's *singing* as those who understand it, or pretend to do so, yet *she* is worth going to see for her beauty's sake; & for the grace & elegance of her motions – and the contrast between her & all the rest of the '*objects*' upon the stage, at the Opera, is amusing – besides the *hatefulness* of the dancing is worth seeing, if it were but to know *what* it is the folks make such a rout about! You will have much more time upon your hands than we had, who were dragged about without any mercy or rest; & therefore if some things do not give you pleasure they will at

* John Wilson, or 'Christopher North'.

† G. F. Cooke was a successful actor, then playing at Covent Garden, and Sir Pertinax MacSycophant, the leading character in C. Macklin's play *The True-Born Scotsman*, was one of his famous parts.

least not fatigue you – I am glad that you have seen Cambridge it is a most interesting place – Write and tell me all about M^rs^ Clarkson & Bessy – I am afraid that nothing has come of your journey in the farming line – if there had I think that you would have written – You must not forget our Commission about the Cambric – if you can, get it ready to send by some private hand; for we are in great want; & any that we get here is both bad & dear. You must not for the world encourage your Tom[2] in his liking for the Country, till he has made a fortune, & then '*rural leisure*' will be a fine thing for him – but he has not like poor Harry[1] felt the want even of necessaries to make him forego superfluities, much less comforts. My kind love to him; and to dear John[2]; and blessing & prayers for dear Harry – and believe me most truly thy Friend S. H.

*Postmark: Keswick*

## 6

*Miss M Monkhouse, 21 Budge Row, London 4*

*Grasmere, Nov^r^, Wednesday* [*30 Nov. 1808*]

My dear Mary

Your letter was brought by M^r^ de Quincey & William last night at 10 o'clock – they had been dining with your Friends at Elleray – and I having had a lonely day in my bed-room was right glad to see it for my own sake and more for thine for I had long looked for a Letter from you, and wondered whether mine, which I sent to Budge Row, had been forwarded to you or not – I read it in Bed & began immediately to write to dear M^rs^ Clarkson and intended to write to you but was too much tired to finish even her's; for I have been very ill for some days past but have got rid of my complaint & only want strengthening – it was on Saturday morning that I was seized in my Bowels & the disease proved to be a Dysentery which confined me to my bed till yesterday at noon in violent pain, but with good doctoring & nursing the enemy was driven off & I slept from 3 o'clock yesterday afternoon till nearly 10 at night when I felt myself quite another creature – I am still as you may suppose very languid & weak – but I have no doubt but that I shall soon be quite well & the Doctors agree that it is likely to do my other complaints good in the end – We have had such miserable work with the smoke as you can have no conception of – poor Dorothy[1] is kept trotting the day through; for the Servants work is never done – a fine day comes & there is no smoke – then they clean up: & the next undoes all that they have done – even in my room, which is the best chimney in the house, while I lay in Bed I often could not discern the Ceiling – We have had a chimney Doctor for a month & he has done no good – we females wish to quit the Premises immediately but the Men will not hear of it – William is for trying for a Cure – and a *scientific* Dr is to come from Kendal, but if he does not remove the evil W^m will consent to go to Troutbeck where there is a good House vacant – M^r Wilson* *hopes* that they never may be cured he is in agonies for fear that they should & rejoices in every storm in the hope that W^m will be tired out – We have quite taken your lover into favor again he *is* a nice creature & would fain be better than he is. I am sure if he was near W^m he would never seek those wild companions of his any more – Mr de Quincey has been here 3 weeks & I daresay will make a long stay – he is a good tempered amiable creature & uncommonly clever & an excellent scholar – but he is very shy & so reverences Wm & C[oleridge] that he chats very little but is content to listen – he looks only like 18 but is nothing like either helpless or dissipid as Joanna said: but then he is in much better health than when she saw him – we are a nice round family you may think and when Coleridge's boys are here on a Saturday & Sunday a pretty noisy one – even now I hear C. making racket enough for twenty with Sissy below – he does tieze her in such a way for she cannot be too naughty for his taste; he calls her 'beautiful Cat of the Mountain'† & she is more like a cat with him than any thing else – the moment he appears she puts on her airs – else with every body else she is far more gentle than she used to be – she has been poorly & is much softened by it – and now looks very pretty again – But John[4] is the darling of all – no body ever makes a Comparison – your Godson is a naughty Boy though he denies it the day through – & if he does mischief (breaks a plate for instance) he comes immediately to the parlour door with his 'Thos[4] *not* a naughty boy. Thos diddent break a plate' which is the first information we receive of the disaster – now what do you think of your *virtuous* Godson? Are you not ashamed of yourself to be jaunting about in this manner and neglecting his '*religious & virtuous Education*'? The Baby continues a bonny babe – so I have discharged my duty to them – If you were here you would scarcely know the Place again – when I got up yesterday & looked out of the window it seemed as if I had lain

* Cf. Letter 5, p. 10 note.

† Coleridge was adapting a line from Wordsworth's 'Ruth'. Dorothy Wordsworth also records his skirmishes with Dora. See letter to Mrs. Clarkson, 8 Dec. 1808. *Wordsworth Letters, The Middle Years*, I, 256.

3 seasons instead of 3 days in Bed for I saw Trees standing by the House higher than the Portico – the railing finished; & the shrubs all planted – the gravelling will soon follow so that without doors we shall be delightful but then alas! what are we within! I have been down stairs to Tea & have seen Sissy take her medecines like a Heroine – she covenanted that if she might sit in the Parlour during Tea that she would take them which she has performed – and she *eats* her Pill, & sups the mixture with a Tea spoon!!

. . . I hardly dare hope any thing from the Wales scheme. Suffolk would have been much more desirable, & then your being near M^rs^ C[larkson] would have been such a delight – The scarcity of hands to manage the Land is one great reason for its cheapness & that is an inconvenience which no farmer can remedy –

You were lucky indeed to meet with your Friends at Cambridge – The sight of King's College Chapel was sure to astonish you; it has had that effect upon almost every body I have heard speak of it – but I myself was, I confess, disappointed in it – & I am grieved to be out of sympathy with so many that I love – every body wonders at me except M^rs^ Clarkson, who agrees with me that the ornaments destroy the simplicity of the form, & distract one's attention – but I saw it, unluckily, with a blazing sun in at the West window; which revealed every part, and brought forward every ornament most obtrusively; & it wanted that gloom & obscurity which is in my idea the charm of such buildings. To stand and look up one of the aisles of Westminster Abbey is far more delightful to my feeling – tho that is still more spoilt by the monuments yet the gloom does not force them so upon you and you can fancy what it would be if they were away – but in the other they are a part of the whole & unless I could see it in the twilight I am sure that I never could be so much impressed – But the walks at Cambridge! Did you not admire the old Trees & the shady walks of St. John's? I liked the old Colleges best – I hope you saw the Library which I did not –

Has your old Lover J. W. ever been to see you? I should think W^m^ would not fail to tell him of his happy meeting with you & you may expect a call – now I desire you may not break his Heart outright – and now for poor dear Henry[1]. I have never had the heart to ask whether he was gone – but, as if I should get an answer, have put it off till the last – It is a comfort however to find that he is in such good spirits. I hope it may be a good omen – If he is not sailed tell him I do not fear but that I shall be quite stout when he returns for my disease is not a mortal one – and also that Gill side will be ready for him as we hear that M^r^ Partridge is tired of his Bargain; it will not answer he finds for a Lake situation – God bless you all! I must give over for I am sadly tired & want to be in bed – and so good night & heaven bless thee my darling for ever S. H.

Every body sends their love

*Postmark: Keswick, N . . . 1808*

## 7

*Miss Monkhouse, 21 Budge Row, London*

*Grasmere, Monday Morn$^{g}$, Mar 27th* [*1809*]

My dear Mary

If you could have any notion how pleasantly I am seated at this moment, full in the warm sunshine in my room window, with the glittering lake and this beautiful vale before me, you would wish yourself here if you had no other desires to impel you towards us. I have changed my room, and now occupy that which William and Mary used to sleep in when you were here – it is much warmer than my own little cabin, and more cheerful; but yet I regret the old one; and if I am here in the summer I think I shall creep into it again for the sake of its coolness; and because I like the view from its window even better than this. We have had most delightful weather for a long time and the fields begin to look green; M$^{r}$ King's are already as green as an emerald.

I received your Letter on Saturday morning and intended to have written to you by last night's Post; but William employed me all the day till tea-time;* and then I was so fagged that I thought it better to lose even three posts, as I shall do than make you pay for a stupid Letter. Your's had been carried to Joanna, at M$^{rs}$ Barrow's, at Kendal – she had opened it and added a few lines, saying, that John[2] had left Kendal that afternoon (thursday) and that Miss Green would be there on the next; and that on Saturday Morning they were to set off for Hindwell – She had a miserable cold when she left us on Wednesday Evening but was in tolerable spirits; but, if Miss Green does not accompany her a good way on the road, I fear she will fall very flat, for she had quite a horror of travelling alone – I wished very much, at the last that I had been going with her; for, the weather being so very fine, if I could only have been secure of not being sick there seemed no other

* Transcribing his *Convention of Cintra* pamphlet.

objection to it – I was to have had a room to myself; *you yunkers* were to have done all the work; – nay John[2] was for *locking me up* in my room, for fear that I should be tempted to engage in the bustle – If we had had any notion that the weather would have been so favourable I should certainly have procured a Poney and have gone with John – but this scheme was not thought feasible till too late – However you may be assured that I shall be with you before the summer is over if I am alive, and able to travel; of which I have no fear, as I am certainly much better and stronger than I was; and have had very little or no pain in my side lately – and if the weather does not grow cold again I shall soon be fit for any thing – but cold pinches me terribly – I cannot use exercise enough to keep myself warm.

We have had a very sickly House since I came home – your Godson has had the measles – and little Catherine a cold, or complaint very like the measles, but no eruption – Mary is now very poorly with a cold, occasioned by relaxation from having been confined in the hot Nursery all the last week with the Children – Yesterday she was very ill indeed, but this morning she is something better – Thomas[4] is very much improved by his illness – during its continuance he was a very Tyrant; but now he is as meek and gentle as he used to be when you were here in the summer – but we expect that when his strength returns he will be the same little *Bully* that he was awhile ago – he is also much improved in beauty. I sometimes think him the handsomest – he has sweet eyes and a delightful expression of countenance – even when he puts on *his airs* he looked so sweet, that his countenance told you, that they were but *put on* – & one could scarcely refrain from kissing rather than correcting him. He is to go to School, along with Sally[5] & John[4], after Easter – John has gone ever since Sissy went away and is very fond of it – 'this Master', he says, 'has never beat me but once' – the old one, we find, used to beat him cruelly – but Johnny himself never told a word about it – though we often detected the marks left on his cheeks by the tears – He is not to be dealt with by severity – it would make him quite obstinate and stupid – but treat him gently and he is the gentlest of all gentle beings – He says now that he cannot come into Wales, because he is to be a *printer* with Mr de Quincey (who talks of having a Press for his amusement) and must stay to learn to be a good Scholar for that purpose – the hope of being with Mr de Q. would stimulate him to any thing – for he loves him better than anything in the world! Sissy, I find, is in great favour at Penrith – she behaves in a most *exemplary* manner – she is to remain as long as my aunt chuses to keep her – and then go to Appleby and return home with Miss W[eir] & the children at midsummer – for they wish very much to come, if their Father will consent to it, and let them go to Stockton (in stead) at Christmas.

I never saw my aunt while I was at Eusemere – she was too much engaged with my uncle at the time – and I could not walk there, and no horse to carry me, neither had she a bed for me – Poor Body! It is a melancholy employment which she has at present – but in this greater affliction her lesser ones will be swallowed up; and she will scarcely at present have leisure to reflect upon the loss she has had of you – yet I fear the time will soon come when she must feel herself a very solitary Being! . . . I do not think her scheme of going to Julia a good one; for though Julia must be more to her than any one else, yet she will be very dull in so retired a place – so far from all her old acquaintances – (for at her time of life People are not very ready to form new ones) – and she is very fond of a little gossiping Society – when they were at Sebergham it was quite different – my uncle was every thing to her, and the knowledge of the good she was doing by making him comfortable there made her happy – if they had been at Sebergham still my uncle might have been a healthy man at this day!

We are glad to hear such a good account of your brother Tom's[2] health and affairs – I hope he will take care of himself that he may be able to enjoy the country when he has made his fortune and is disposed to retire – but perhaps, if money comes in fast, he may grow enamoured of it and chuse to remain a little & a little longer till he is too old – or else he may give up before he gets enough & then repent – 't is a difficult matter to know when to stop – it is a pity that you should have seen so little of London – but though you are glad to get out of it you will soon forget all the disagreeables; and look forward with pleasure, at some future time, to a second visit – this has been the case with me. I now fancy that I should like very much to go again – and *we* will go, Mary, at the *Coronation*!* – You must not be *buried* in Wales. When I had read your letter to Dorothy she said 'God bless her, she is far too good to be buried alive'! Whatever may be *Joanna's* notion, *we* think we are here far more *in the World* than you will be – and when you recollect the gaieties of Windermere you must acknowledge also that we are near the *fashionable* World. Dorothy[1] and I are going to spend a while at Elleray next week, I believe – Your lover is gone to Wastwater with his sister and another Lady and we expect them here on their return either today or tomorrow. He is a nice creature for all his follies – he says that it is only 'a sense of his own

* Her equivalent for the Greek Calends and a reference to George III's procrastination in dying. The Coronation of George IV took place in 1820, but she and Mary did not get to it.

unworthiness' that makes him come so seldom to Grasmere and not his preference of other society – He wrote W^m^ a nice Letter on this Subject – You must have him Mary – if you can get him? He also enquires most particularly after you – & I will invite him to come into Wales to see you.

You were very good to send us a fresh list of the Subscribers'* names for we had much difficulty in mak[ing] the first out and were quite *capped* with 2 names – still there is a contradiction in the two – Tom's[2] had one address 'Mr Bowman Water Lane *Thames St*' the Clarks '*Tower St*'. We have taken *Tom's* down into the Book; but if it is wrong tell us, if right it will stand '*Thames St*' & you need not trouble yourself to mention it when you write.

Coleridge has been at Keswick Penrith & Brathay† for a month – I only just saw him when at Eusemere, & then he had not got his business settled – but if he did he hoped to be able to send out the first number on the 14th – He has had a vast of plague – more than suits one of his temper & habits – indeed few would have ventured to engage in it if they could have had an idea of the obstacles – and he least of any man I know is calculated to overcome them.

William's pamphlet‡ is all gone to the Press. We have desired M[r] de Quincey, who is in London, to send one to you for John[2] if it is printed before friday week – it may be *printed* but not published by that time; & therefore if he does not send you one you may be sure that it is not ready – but should you stay longer in Town than *that* you must apply to him (82 Great Titchfield St. Cavendish Sq.) or M[r] Stead for one – as John is very desirous of seeing it, and it would cost more than the value of the Book to have it sent by the Coach.

The Poem came safe in the Box – We admired your taste in the choice of Joanna's *Dress*. It was not *John*[2] who gave you a bad character for oeconomy at Grasmere – it was only *my own deduction* from our Tom's[1] telling me that John had given him a hint (when he left you together in a Shop at Clifton) not to let you purchase a *high priced* Cap.

I think I told you that M[r] de Quincey had taken our old Cottage for 6 years – It is to be made very smart – the rooms new papered – kitchen under-drawn – and many other comforts – it will be almost

* Subscribers to Coleridge's *The Friend*, for which she was amanuensis.

† Coleridge was in Keswick at home, in Penrith with Brown the printer, and at Brathay with the Hardens.

‡ The pamphlet on the Convention of Cintra was not published until 20 May 1809. Wordsworth blamed de Quincey for the delay, de Quincey a drunken compositor, and the printers de Quincey and Wordsworth for making many corrections. Sara Hutchinson gives still another cause. See Letter 8, p, 20 note.

filled with Books – and we have ordered his furniture all new (mahogany) at Kendal – so that when you come you will scarce know it again – and your Tom[2] would be quite in love with it – even Joanna must I think approve of it when it is so smartened up. I am vexed that I cannot give you any direction about the Wedgewoods Warehouse: if C[oleridge] had been here perhaps he might have given me some information – however there is a *Book* I know (& which they must have in Tom's[2] office) that gives all the addresses of the mercantile Houses in Town – apply to it – if you find it out there ('Wedgewood & Byerly') & learn by going to the House that there are *imperfect* Wares to be sold (which are good enough for common use) you can suit yourself – if not we can order a crate from Staffordshire to you – which will be easiest carriage – but the difference in the price will more than pay the carriage of it here as I have heard it stated, that they are sold for half price.

Kind love to Tom & I am dear Mary most affy yours S. H.

I shall hope to hear a very particular account of Hindwell from you – God bless thee, I love thee dearly!

*Postmark: Keswick, Mar 30, 1809*

## 8

*Miss Monkhouse, Hindwell, nr new Radnor*

*Grasmere, April 19th* [*1809*]

My dear Mary

In the first place I must send you a *kiss* from William for your nice Letter which was in his opinion (a thing rather uncommon) *well worth the postage* – He is quite delighted that you went to the Lord Mayor's Ball; and also with your excursion to Windsor – One thing I am to ask you which is – in what sense young Cookson is a Coxcomb? Whether merely a Fop? – a pedantic Coxcomb? or whether he gave himself airs of quality and combined the other? As is I suppose the character of almost all the Eaton Scholars – Dorothy[1], who was one of his nurses, is very anxious to hear more of him; and also what you thought of Elizabeth Cookson. We were very glad that you called and it was a pity that you had not dined with them –

We are rejoiced to find that you are all so much pleased with Hindwell; but it is a sad tale that you tell about the maid Servants – I know not what you will do – I should be tempted to send you one if I could hear of one that was *unexceptionable* – but it is such a long way that unless such were to be met with, that were willing to go, it would be folly to run any risk. I just long to know what sort of weather you have now – we had a deep snow last night – but this morning's sun has nearly melted it all in the valley – though now, at 12 o'clock, the sky looks as if we should have more – I hope that you would be able to talk Mr Lewis over about the House – This he must, if he does it at all, do for you females – the men are in the right of it only to mind their own – I expect that you will have a nice room for me against I come – my plan is to set off about a week after midsummer (if the children come with Miss Weir) and William approves of the plan – but our Mary[1] & D., when it comes to it, want to persuade me to stay till the autumn – Jack[1] is expected at Penrith on the 25th & says that he will come hither – but I begin to fear that the snow will frighten him – for I want to try if I cannot coax him to sell me Lilly for my expedition – I have no doubt at all but that I shall be able to perform the journey on horseback – in a coach I should be sick to death over such roads as you describe – Let me, while it is in my mind, tell Tom that I have had a Letter from Mr Clarkson making enquiry after his old mare 'is she gone into Wales' was the question – I am sadly grieved about it & at a loss – for he is sure to go & purchase her of the man at whatever price he may ask; & perhaps, which is worse than all, find her in a miserable condition – Can not Tom[1] make application to some one at Penrith or Stainton who will stir in the business & get her back? something must be done; for I dare not say to Mr C. that no steps have been taken for her recovery – Mr C. will be here the first week in June.

I have ordered your Pots – the crate will cost more than £4 which our's did – because as I knew you would want every thing – I desired that 6, instead of 2, Ewers & Basons, 8, instead of 2, Chambers, & some more Jugs – and some Egg cups might be added – but they are cheaper than any common pots *bought at a pot shop* – as to the Churn I can do nothing for you – the one Mr Taylor recommended was Beetham's (*patent* Churn I believe) he lives in London – & the particulars were in that Letter to Tom, which he used to have in his witing Desk. But I dare say there are by this time improvements upon it – Mr Taylor's only churn 12 lb – and a churn of that shape to churn nearly a firkin would be very awkward – I saw one advertized in the Courier yesterday; but it was a patent one also – & only made in Lancashire – J. Woods Ormskirk – 'It is worked by a lever with a weight & grit & performs more work with it than 2 women in the same time without it' – but then they give no account *how* it is worked – & what is very suspicious he offers to sell the right of making them for 5 Gs & has many on hand price £2. 12. 6. – What kind of Churns are used in the Country? I would on no account advise you to get one that does *not* work with a *Churn staff* – next to this mode a barrel churn is best that turns round altogether but then it requires the most art in churning – & some people always churn ill in them (our Betsy for instance). If the Letter is in being Tom[1] might apply to it for Beetham's address & you must get *your* Tom[2] to enquire of him whether any other persons are privileged to make them – that you may have a chance of getting one nearer than London – The nicest model of a churn I ever saw was in 'Barrow's account of the interior of Africa' now when we are upon farming I must tell John[2] that Coleridge, who has been staying a day or two at Workington Hall, writes from Keswick that he has 'become a convert to Sir F. Burdett's opinions concerning great Gentlemen turning fierce practical agriculturalists – and above all soiling Cattle or stall feeding has become my *horror*' – We used to have many a quarrel about this same soiling for which he used to be the advocate – M^r Curwen's book which he has sent us, namely his yearly report containing his own statements is a pack of lies – I was sure of it when I read it – and Luff who was here the other day, tells me that all his statements are false – he never charges to the Farm the work done by the Colliery horses – but takes care to make the Colliery pay the farm for the food they eat.

Tom[1] is quite in the right of it not to trouble himself any further about the *Friend* until he sees it – there are no want of subscribers to induce C[oleridge] to publish – it will not fail on that score – whether it will fail on any other or not I cannot speak with equal confidence – but I should think that he has gone too far to recede. It has been advertized in the *Courier* for the first saturday in May – William came in to me just now to read some of his additions to the *White Doe* with which he is at present busy – there is to be another canto added to it – I hope it will be finished before I come – The pamphlet was not to be published till today – the printers are so busy with M^rs Clark's memoirs*

* Wordsworth's pamphlet on the Convention of Cintra was written from November to April 1809. It was printed by C. & R. Baldwin, New Bridge St., London, for Longman, Hurst, Rees and Orme, of Paternoster Row, and appeared 27 May 1809. Mrs. Clarke was the notorious mistress of Frederick Augustus, Duke of York, son of George III. She revealed in her memoirs and in the parliamentary inquiry, Jan.–Mar. 1809, that led to his resignation as Commander-in-Chief of the Army, that promotions in the army had been arranged through her influence by bribes. I can find no surviving copy of her memoirs printed by C. & R. Baldwin, New Bridge St., London. I can only surmise that the edition Sara Hutchinson refers to as competing in the press with Wordsworth's work, was the one that was suppressed, for which Mrs. Clarke was said to have received

that M^r de Q. could not get them to attend to any thing else – we hear that the Boys in the streets toss up instead of heads or Tails? – 'Duke or Darling!' Dorothy & I are engaged to go to Elleray on Friday to stay a while – M^r W[ilson] is to come in the morning with his two poneys – he was here on sunday – arrived wet to skin – Boots & all – and would not change a rag but let them dry on! He is very obstinate – Mary! you can never manage him!

We had a Letter from my Aunt yesterday – poor body! she is in somewhat better spirits – and we are glad to find that Dorothy[2] is such a comfort to her – she seems quite wrapped up in her; & says that she cannot part with her till the very last moment – She (Sissy) was quite satisfied not to have her red shoes at Easter – because it was bad weather & black were the fashion – her *own* reason was the best; that 'the rain would wash off all the *paint* you know'. Your Godson is very handsome & very entertaining; & if he is not so good as he ought to be it is for this *last reason* which makes him more noticed – it is a truth, with regard to Children, that in some respects neglect is *tender mercy*. You say nothing of John's[2] health, so we hope he is in his better way – M^rs Patrick, poor old creature, has had a paralytic stroke but retains her faculties though there is no chance of her recovering the use of her side – but my aunt will tell you all the Penrith news – I should not have written now but for the sake of the Churn for I am sure that *my* Letter will not be worth a postage – I am glad that you are likely to have some neighbours – but if you do not go to church before you are ready to sit Bides I fear they will think you heathens – and I should think that you will not be ready till after you have got the house to yourselves – God bless you all together – I often dream about you – last night, when I did sleep, I was *pestered* with your concerns the whole time – Farewell! most affty yours S. H.

I rather think Miss Green has sent my Gown to Penrith, so Joanna dont ask about it. Have you ever heard from Miss Green? She told me that if she was flighty & gay she should never think of writing – neither if she were low spirited – but if in her sober senses perhaps she might – our Tom[1] will scold this writing. William says that you *must* marry, he sees nothing else for you – He wishes you, Mary, a good husband every time that your name is mentioned – we often joke him about his anxiety to get you married

*Postmark: Keswick*

£10,000 and £600 annuity to be continued to her two daughters. Three thousand copies were said to be burnt, for which the printers were paid £1500. No wonder the Cintra pamphlet could not meet such competition. Of it five hundred copies were printed, many of which were sold for waste paper.

# 9

*Miss Monkhouse, 21 Budge Row, London*

*Wednesday, Jany 3rd, 1810*

My dear Mary

The affectionate solicitude concerning us which prompted you to write was more pleasing to us than even an entertaining Letter could have been, or even one *worth* postage; therefore you may assure yourself that we were very happy to receive your's – and I wish that I could send you one in return really worth postage – But except to tell you that we are all well and happy, though not very rich, I have nothing to communicate – and except a few Xmas feasts lately, we go on in the old way – see only the same set over and over again – and have the same kind of conversations, which to you would be entertaining enough I know – The Children are all well and thriving – your Godson is just as innocent as ever and as much a baby – we call him the *everlasting* Child, for he never does seem a day older – though he gets a great many words yet he has the same simplicity – for instance if we are going any way & he petitions to accompany us his cry is 'do *do* et I go, I 'ont *tell*' – because he once overheard us bidding Sissy not give a hint that she was going out, for fear he should wish to go – and ever since he supposes that we cannot refuse him after he has given this assurance – Also – 'do, *do* et I go, because I is very poorly'. Little Catherine is very lively and looks very knowing, but she does not get well forward with her feet – neither can she say anything but 'pussy' – John[4] & D[ora][2] go to the Dancing School – Siss says that the Master is the *prettiest* Man in the world & has *such a pretty Leg*! – 'Just here it is so small' – pointing to the ancle. John was very shy about exhibiting himself – and went many days, before he durst dance, as a looker-on – if we had insisted upon his dancing at first he would never have gone at all – he is most distressingly shy – All the little Lloyds were here yesterday and there was a display of fireworks at the Town end at which all the Children and middle aged in the Village were assembled. Mr de Quincey's House was like a fair. We did not dine with him on Christmas day but went to Elleray to meet Mary[1] & the Cooksons from Kendal – and we stayed with the Beau two days, and filled his house – he, Mr Blair, & Mr de Q. were obliged to sleep [at] Bowness & leave us in possession of his Cottage. (His Mother & Sister are at Edinburgh.) We then came to dine all together at Brathay 99 and at

M[r] de Q. met again on Newyear's day – therefore you see we have been visiting about though without much variety – The Beau was here yesterday, but left us this morning and his friend M[r] B. is here – for the Beau has so many balls to attend which he does not relish that he often comes over here when M[r] W[ilson] is off – John[1] did but stay one day with us and as it was so short a time before Xmas we could not hope for his coming back to us at that time. W[m] & Mary were at Kendal when he arrived, and we were all in confusion here, having just got rid of the Workmen and were getting the house cleaned up in their absence – he helped us to put up the Books – the study is a divine Room – but it smokes as well as all the other sitting rooms when the wind is high – though they are much improved in ordinary weather – and now that we find them incurable, at such times, we are quite resigned to it – and will be contented to remain in the House till the end of the term ; or even longer if possible – for there is no other likely for us in the neighborhood, & the idea of leaving Grasmere becomes every day more painful – go where ever we will still when we return it seems the most beautiful place in the World.

I was very sorry to think that you should leave Hindwell again so soon after you had got settled – and especially as the winter is the most sociable time in a farm house, as there is less business for the men without doors; besides it would have been pleasant to you [to] have spent your first Xmas together – I have been sadly grieved about Henry[1] – and we are quite at a loss to know what is become of him. John[1] said that he had got a Berth to the West Indies – but he has never written to us since his return to London – Do not fail to tell us what you know concerning him. . . .

I am glad to hear such a pleasing account of M[rs] Addison & Mary[3] – I would not have any of you persuade H. Addison to be a Farmer for depend upon it you would be blamed – for it will be impossible to get the Family to look upon it in the same light which you do – they will think it little less than *standing in the way of his fortune*. Remember me very kindly to M[rs] A. Miss H. & Mary[3]. . . . I cannot help thinking that you can have no objection in the world to my putting an end to this Letter when I write such a miserable scrawl and, I do not know how it is but, I cannot have patience to write a Letter decently for the life of me, though I write Manuscripts for our Gentlemen most admirably, & have as much patience for it as any body. I am very well – my complaints are all gone – & though I have never yet been tried I daresay I could walk as well as ever though I do not like it – I have been so spoilt by riding – God bless you my dear Mary! Kind love to Tom[2] – and to Henry[1] (if he is not gone & you ever see or hear of him) &

desire him to write – every body send their love farewell – most truly yours S. H. A happy new year to you, all of us!

*Postmark: Jan. 12, 1810*

## 10

*Miss Monkhouse, Mrs Addison's, 38 Bernard St, Russell Square, London*

*Friday Even$^{g}$* [*autumn 1810*]

My dear Mary

I need not tell you that we were all rejoiced to find that your journey had not fatigued you much; and that the Doctor gives you such good encouragement. But we were not quite satisfied that you did not tell us what your complaint is for he must have told you else you could not have been so well satisfied with him, nor so confident, as you seem to be, that he will cure you – mind that you be more particular when you write – and if the D$^{r}$ should not have told you already don't fail to ask him *what ails* you or get Dorothy[1] to do it.

You managed very badly indeed not to seek after Dorothy[1] sooner – the more so as R$^{d}$ Addison was not in Town – for to him I have referred her for your address. But I am sure that my Letter could not have reached her before she left Bury, else she would have sought you out had she been able to stir. However I hope that if she does return to London that you will be more fortunate – but I have my doubts whether she will return or not – for should her Brother and Priscilla be at Binfield, and they wish her very much to go home with them, I think she would find some difficulty in refusing – If she does come desire her to write to me before she leaves Town if she can find a moment's time.

This has been our ironing day – We thought ourselves wondrous lucky to get the Clothes dried in this broken weather – Mansell's field was got in on Saturday without any rain – but alas! the *three acres* last cut are still out. Henry[3] & Tom[1] are gone to Hereford to the Shew and fair – They were at the Sale, on Wednesday, at Horn-Lacy and bought a Cow. . . . [*A long account of Mr D.'s efforts to find a farm in Wales.*]

Jack[1] sent the Catalogue of the first day's sale of M$^{r}$ Colling's stock. – John[2] will most likely see it in the newspaper. M$^{r}$ Rudd bought 3 highest priced Cows – one for 400 Gs another 410 Gs & the third 365 Gs – 'Wetherell & Co' (which Tom[1] supposes to be *Mason*) bought Comet for 1000 Gs. I cannot recollect the amount of the 16 Cows with the Heifers & Calves but it was an immense sum. Tom[1] carried the Paper with him today to shew it to the Breeders and others at Hereford.

We had a Party to Tea & Supper on Monday – the Walkers, who had come to dine at Mr Urwicke's, sent their compts & Mrs Urwicke intended waiting upon us in the evg. *Mr* U. also came with them and played at Cards and was as lively as possible – indeed there was no want of noise or life in any of the party – and we flattered ourselves that they enjoyed their visit – We have seen none else of our neighbours since you left us – we hear that Miss S. got cold with walking into the Garden with thin shoes & was laid up again.

I think I have told you all the stirrings (except that Dolly Lloyd is now making a terrible noise among the Hogsheads in the Cellar it being our second brewing night this week – we are going to have the Cellar filled with *October*) but I am mighty dull – being tired with my day's work – so had best leave some paper for Joanna to give you something more lively – God bless thee dear Mary, and send thee soon & safe back to us again! Kind love to John[2], & Tom[1] and beg John will not forget to enquire after Harry[1] before D[orothy] goes away – & if he sees him to beg of him to write to me. Remember me to Mrs A[ddison] Miss H. and the young ones – again God bless you. S.H.

Don't fail to write soon. Bring some *cheap* writing Paper, if you can get any. I know *your* Friends don't deal in cheap articles of that kind – but if you see D[orothy] she can ask Mr Lamb where & how it is to be come at – outsize folio would do for the Lads and common uses.

[*Joanna H. writing.*]

My dear Mary I am happy to be able to inform you that your *Turtle* bears your absence much better than I expected he would; tho' he was rather in the pathetique order for 2 days after you left us; his arm is still very weak – and he does not take much care of it, do all we can. You will be surprized to hear that I have had two jaunts single upon Johns Mare – once to the post – and to the carpenters and was not in the least afraid, tho much tired, and Sarah[1] would have it I sat as if I was sitting upon a Cockle. . . . I must not forget to tell you that D. Lloyd has fallen deeply in love with Sara[1] – she tells Peggy she is the prettiest woman she ever saw – so there is now in the press and speedily will be published 'the Loves of Dorcas and Sara' a new Novel in 3 Vols. . . .

. . . We have got a most beautiful Tea pot. It is the real Lupton. I cannot admire it, but Tom[1] and Sara[1] think it quite divine. God bless you my dear Mary. . . . J. H.

*Postmark: Radnor*

# II

*Miss Monkhouse, Hindwell, Radnor*

*Thursday, Oct*$^{r}$ [*27, 1811*]

I thank you dearest Mary! for your two Letters – the latter did not reach me till yesterday Morning: I believe it had lain at Ambleside since Monday. We are all rejoiced, more than I can express, at the good account you give of yourself and Heaven grant that you may continue to go on so well – we will sing the praises of D$^{r}$ Thomas for ever! I wish I could give you any advice or comfort respecting your teeth – but alas! I have nothing profited by my own sad experience. I believe that the tincture of Myrrh is an excellent thing – and also to clean at night. M$^{r}$ Crump as I have before told you, never fails to do this – and his teeth are admirable – Do this, and avoid sweet things (at least never eat them without washing your mouth afterwards) wrap up your head warm at night (this I *know* is good) and try to keep off the enemy this winter if possible in the hope that you may be more able to struggle with him hereafter. William always contends that it was my winter's tooth ache at Coleorton with the sleepless nights consequent upon it that '*undermined my constitution*' – therefore take care & if they will ache – out with them.

We are all very well here – but have been much confined to the house of late – since I wrote last we have but had 2 fair days throughout – on the one (the Wednesday on which M[ary] A[ddison] left you) I rode [to] Ambleside the only time I have been on horseback when I found that the Poney had a dreadful Cough so we got Luff to prescribe for it, but as it does not cough but when it is ridden I cannot tell you whether it is better or not – however Luff satisfied us that it was not the Colt Strangles as he had feared – and the Poney is in very good condition – it had a little cough when we got here which had been increased by being turned out in the rain – for W$^{m}$ has such a notion of making it 'hardy'. Our other fair day was last Sunday, a bitter biting frost which came down in a clash next day – this morning was fine & bright but is now clouding in – yesterday afternoon was very fine & we were hoping for a change. To settle your mind about the Bairns, I did buy Godson a Hat for you, & Boots for his Godfather – I bought John[4] a Hat myself – but as for the other they were too young to care about it – Tott's Boots did not fit – so were sent back *to Wales* to be changed – the second pair arrived on Monday night and proud

Creature was he when I laced them on, & promised him he should should have them on on Sunday to go to *Chich*, as he calls it. He sate upon the Carpet admiring them without saying a word & then with a sigh, tracing his finger along the heel, said 'I wish there was a pair of *spirs* on here'. I told him that his Godfather would have sent him a pair but there were none to be had little enough – so he was satisfied. I do not think Mary[1] will bring him – it would not be worth while for so short a time, there being no School she could not leave him; John[4] learns so badly that they are sadly frightened about them all – Tom[4] is very quick & witty – but he does not learn at school; he never looks at his books, but is always peeping out at the ends of his eyes to see whether the Master is angry or not – (By the Bye Mr Johnson the Schoolmaster was one of those 3 black coats that were sitting up stairs in the inn at Chester where he was attending the ordination). Tottie is very thin and sallow but he has the most *radiant* countenance I ever saw in my life; but he looks so weak and feeble that I often fancy he will not live. He is very little bigger than when I left Grasmere – I suppose he was most terribly held in the hooping Cough & worst of all the fever that succeeded it – Mr de Q. thinks Kate *beautiful* & our neighbours & Mrs Luff, who said she used to think her the plainest child ever born, say that she is now so pretty & improved so fast that they expect to see her the handsomest – I do not go thus far with them – but she is certainly a *bonny little lass* with a most sweet & clever countenance. William[2] does not improve upon acquaintance – Johnny[4] does – he looks infinitely better than when I first came. Mrs Luff is just gone by in 'My folks' Gig – Mr Crump & his friend went yesterday – the Luffs today – the de Qs go on Tuesday – Mrs King & her Ladies the Monday following – & then the Crumps will drive up the rear in Novr – and we shall be left alone. Mary & D. talk of going to Watermilloch – & Penrith – and I have half promised Mrs Luff to go to her house with my Poney for a few days if the weather takes up before the autumn is over, that she may have a companion to ride with, & to shew me the beauties of Patterdale – & for this last reason I intend to go. I have never written to H. Addison yet – indeed I wish to hear something about L[l]anthony, and besides we have had so much company that I could not ask him to come conveniently; but I shall now write to him and I hope he will come over. L[l]anthony must be (as Mr Sharp said in a Letter to Wm concerning Bolton Abbey 'what a spot for a Honeymoon') the very place for an elderly man to live at with a young wife – but he is a nice creature, I suppose, so that in any situation, if she has sense, she can have no desire to go astray – It seems more a place for Hermits than farmers who are to profit by their intercourse with the world – I wish it had been as 'handy' a place as the Land is good – in which case my scheme was, that they would take it in partnership with H[enry] A[ddison] – that H. would have resided & they visited occasionally; and so, if no better could have been done, I had intended to offer myself as Housekeeper for 3 years; in which time I should hope that some of the three would take unto themselves a wife – Poor Henry[3]! I am afraid he will be upon a low key – no prospect of a farm – and no great satisfaction in his present connection with his great cousin. . . .

Mary W. sends her kind love to my Aunt to whom she intended writing (but as I was writing to you thought double postage useless) to thank her for her handsome present – I assure you they are well off in the dress gown way – they have already each a nice poplin that D. bought, besides their old sarsenets. They admire Joanna's presents very much, & intend to wear them according to order – The Caps too are much approved; though till they saw themselves '*look bonny*' in them they did not relish the notion of a ribbon border. By this you will understand that my goods & chattels are safe arrived – the first two packages at least – the last I hope are sent off for I am in great want of shoes & my stuff gown. William who is busy teaching at the School, after D^r^ Bell's fashion, is just come in & up to me saying that he will saddle the Poney & walk by my side if I will go & give it & myself an airing – so if the rain keeps off we will go to Ambleside to hear the News – for we expect a battle – and I will finish my Letter tomorrow – This afternoon another *route* at M^r^ de Qu's – of the Kings, Crumps & ourselves – we have lost all the beaux – Quince & W^m^ alone remain – but W^m^ is always the soul of the Parties – the Ladies say they are nothing without him – but I must away Miss Eliza would say – God bless you all!

Afternoon – I am glad to tell you that this is a heavenly day and so we hope for change along with the moon. I had a pleasant ride to the Town-head. W^m^ & D. walked by my side – I was obliged to set off first – they were not ready – so we were to meet at the White Bridge & I went round by Allan Bank & over Butterlip How to make my way longer – the Poney did not like to leave the road & cross over the field to the gate by M^r^ Crump's stable, but began with its airs – however I basted him & though he was saucy at the gates yet he went on very well afterwards. When I rode him to Ambleside he went very nicely, & called at the houses, rode into Gardens, & was as tractable as possible – only once whipped round – Johnny[4] says he *will go his own way* when he takes him a little ride at watering time – but Johnny has only the Halter on, & can do nothing with him; else he is not afraid & could manage him very well – their new saddle is not come from Kendal. I know not whether my saddle is any better for its alteration because it has not been sufficiently tried – but I must tell you of the cheapness of the Saddler – He stuffed it anew – repaired the lining, indeed made it quite new behind – put a new stirrup leather from the far side (the part which goes under the belly is a great broad thing like a girth with buckles to the other) – all costing only 4/–!! I am sure that at Kington they would have charged 7/6 or maybe ½ a guinea – I have told you all about the Poneys freaks because you desired it – It's cold continues very bad.

The Montagus went to Plymouth – I would gladly have persuaded Mary[1] to go to Worcester with them & then come on to Hindwell. I am confident that it would do her good. The change of air and a little of Joanna's pampering her would do good – for she has no regular appetite – if she does not like a thing well then she will not eat – & it is variety she wants – she tires with all things – She bids me say that nothing shall prevent her coming in the spring – and that she expects you will bear in mind that you *are* to return with her – else she says she will not come. William is quite uneasy about her thinness, want of appetite, & the head ache which she frequently has – and says he will consult some London Physician – I wish it had been a better season, for change of air I am sure would do her good. She had far too much anxiety, and uncomfortableness to cope with when at the sea side to reap the benifit.

I have been dipping into Bingley's *Tour of N. Wales** which would have been a most useful book for us had we seen it before we set out – because he has seen every thing though certainly not with the same eyes that we saw – for instance in Powis Castle he says 'the Apartments have a *heavy* and *unpleasant* appearance from the great thickness of the walls; and the furniture is chiefly in the ancient stile of elegance. In some of the chambers the *old* & *faded* tapestry is yet left!!!' From this sentence could any body have had a notion of the place – though to do him justice he speaks of the Building as magnificent tho' spoilt by the chimneys & the red mortar. But he does not appear to have said 'Oh! dear!' once either *in* the Park or *in* the house. – Indeed I can scarcely believe he has been there though he mentions the *length* of the gallery & that some of the antiques are supposed to be valuable. He has quoted some pretty lines at Valle Crucis Abbey which I will transcribe you.

* Bingley, William – *North Wales: including its scenery, antiquities, customs, and some sketch of its natural history: delineated from two excursions . . . during the summer of 1798 and 1801*. (2 vols. Longman and Rees, 1804, 2nd ed., 1814.)

We do not know where they come from nor has he given the name of the author

I do love these auncient ruynes,
We never tread upon them but we set
Our foot upon some reverend historie;
And questionless here in this open Courte
(Which now lies naked to the injuries
Of stormy weather) some men lye interr'd
Who lov'd the Church so well & gave so largely to 't,
They thought it should have canopied their bones
Till domesday: but all things have their end;
Churches & cities (which have diseases like to men)
Must have like death that we have.*

That Pillar is called the Pillar of Eliseg erected 1000 years ago in memory of some Prince of Powis who was slain in the battle of Chester (in 600 & something) & was thrown down in the civil wars – then raised from the rubbish by the Mr Lloyd of *Trevor* (that ugly great house under the wood on the other side of Langollen which by the bye Bingley admires) but as the original inscription is efaced they have I suppose in gratitude to Mr *Lluids* memory put his upon it instead of Elisegs' –

Mr Lloyd of Brathay has lost a Brother lately in the Typhus – and the other day a sister who was recovering from the fever but unfortunately broke a blood vessel which carried her off instantly. Mrs Ll. is gone to Birmingham to console the Family – a shocking thing, we think, for her whose life is of more value to her family than any one of them can be to theirs – for she is both Father & mother. Dorothy[1] has got the little Class (Tom[4] & 3 others) into the Parlour to their a-b abc. But she can make nothing of them. Of all Trades keep me from being a School mistress!! William is off again – he has attended regularly 2 or 3 hours every morning and Evg since monday. Dr Bell is at Keswick – we wish he would give us a call [*torn*] how *very easy* the mode is. D. says that one of the Boys taught in this way at some of the London Schools organized the School at Coleorton – he was there 6 weeks and every thing was easy [*torn*] & went on like Clock-work. I wish we had one of them here – but there is not room in the School House for so many Classes to say at one time, as they ought, to do to save time.

I forgot to tell you in my last that the beautiful white bind-weed in the hedges is only an annual; so that you must try to get some seed if

* Sara Hutchinson's quotations are from vol. II, pp. 87 and 164; it is interesting to notice that she takes the best of Bingley's lines, omitting the last five which are more conventional and sentimental.

it be not too late. M^rs King has two varieties of it in her garden – she culti[vates] the major convolvulus – one lilac & one blue & white – but neither is so beautiful as the [*torn*]. [If] you can get any seed send us one or two from time to time in a Letter. M^rs K. has [a de]sire for some. M^rs K. sows it & lets it run up sticks as scarlet beans which is not near so gr[ace]ful as when it hangs its wreaths upon other plants & shrubs – so that I would always sow them in hedges or at the foot of shrubs – I hope you have got some planting done and your garden in order – mind and tell me every particular. It was a sad job your being thrown from the Mare in her fall – poor creature it is all owing to her blindness so she can never be safe. I hope they will get a Poney for you – I was sadly grieved at what you told me concerning Overton Bridge. Bingley says that the yews in Overton Church yd are accounted among the wonders of Wales – but I think those in Grey* (what-do-you-call-it) Church yd far finer – so here he is wrong again! I have been interrupted fifty times I believe by Mary, who is making a gown & D. coming to tell me of the progress of her Pupils so that I am weary as you may be with reading such an unconnected *Piece* – however I will fill up my paper with something or other before I send it that the *appearance* of it at least may please you when you open it at Radnor. Tell me if you continue to go. The weather here I ought to say has been warm enough in all conscience, quite mug – but we could not do without fires – in the absence of the sun it would have been cheerless indeed – Sunday. I was prevented from sending off my Letter on Saturday by such a bustle! A chaise drove up to the door containing M^r and M^rs Southey, M^rs Coleridge, Sara[3], Edith & Herbert S[outhey], & on Horseback D^r Bell & his Servant – they had been at Patterdale & just gave us a call – W^m rushed D^r B off instantly to the School to hear the Bairns their Lessons & to give the Masters instructions – D^r B. fell in love with Joanna's lover† & said he should like to steal him from us – then when this party went off came M^rs King's Man with a load of shrubs. D. & I were deep in a *Novel* when the party drove up, & we had gone back to it when the shrubs arrived – so though we kept at it we got many a *blessing* from below for not going to help, it being nearly 5 oclock & the de Qu's coming to tea – Then yesterday D. & I went to Ewedale with the D. Qu's & M^r Johnson they going on to Coniston & joining us again in Ewedale where we drank Tea & did not get home till nearly 9 o'clock last night – Dear Mary[2], I wished that you had been with us! at the head of Ewdale there is the most divine situation for a house or rather Cottage I ever saw; & the prettiest little Estate, which belongs to an old Man and Woman whose daughter was

* Greyhurst. † Mr. Johnston, *q.v.*

a servant of M[r] Patrick's & with whom I spent a fortnight there when I was 10 years old. I recollected every particular of that place as distinctly as if I had but been there yesterday & had often described it to Dorothy – but as the old People had left the House they used to live in she used to persuade me that I was mistaken that it was a neighbour's place I meant – However I found it out & every thing remained just as it used to be except the house which was not in the same neat order – the Son's wife not being so tidy as the old woman. We then went to see the old woman who with her husband had retired to a cottage hard by, leaving the Farm & family *Mansion* to their son so after our call upon her we went further down the vale to Fanny's sisters where we were to meet the de Qs again & drink Tea. The Day was delightful – but poor M[rs] de Qu was very bad in a cold & hoarseness & I turned sick with riding in the dark among the hills – the Poney behaved admirably when I was on but it would not go with Johnny[4] who was of the Party. Your Godson was in an agony to go with us – Johnny & the Poney both going & he not of the Party was more than his slender stock of patience could endure – When his Mother & I both denied him he went to his father who was talking to Luff about the Spaniards in the parlour, & he, not knowing what the child asked, answered Yes – this drove him ranting so his mother promised that he should go to a nice place with her – & she & W[m] carried him with them to call [at] Rydal Hall, at Miss Prichards & Lloyds – 3 calls that had been long owing – & he was dressed in his *Boots* – but alas! he told Sarah[3] that at Rydal the Ladies neither said he was a fine Boy or a *pretty* Boy. I have now found out that Catherine is like your Tom[2]. She has exactly his looks – his nose – & the whole shape of her face reminds me of him – Since I have found this out I can see her likeness to Harry[1] – and now I am sure that it was only because she so very strongly reminded me of *somebody* that I fixed it upon him – I know my Aunt, & perhaps more of you, may be affronted at this because they have such a high notion of the beauty of the one & the plainness of the other. We had a Letter from Henry[1] yesterday. He says that after the races he means to pay us a visit if convenient – that Jack[1] sets off for Penrith this week & talks at times of bringing M[rs] H.* *along*: if they come it will be in a chaise but that they have not offered him a seat though they know he is coming & intending to walk – This is the whole of his Letter except that he will tell us of M[rs] H's elegant behaviour to him when he comes & sends love to all hands – he never *asks our pardon* for not answering our Letters. Southey was surprized that T[om] should think L[l]anthony a very narrow Valley & was sorry it did not suit. He &

* The second Mrs. John Hutchinson.

Mrs S. was at L[l]anthony this summer – They were also at L[l]angollen as Mrs de Q. tells me visiting Lady Elinor B[utler] & Miss P[onsonby] but we had no time for talk: but I shall enquire all about them when we meet again – Mrs C[oleridge] & S[outhey] pressed me much to go to Keswick – but Southey's kind & affectionate greeting of me, & his earnest and unfeigned wishes that I should go had much more effect – and I shall certainly go – So D[orothy] with whom the Ladies pretend to be affronted for her never going near them & I am to be off in a short time to K[eswick]. You see I am still to be the real jaunter – Peggy Ashburner says that surely Miss Joanna wod like Grasmere now when there is so much visiting – 'I never expected to see Grasmere come to sic a pass.'

Farewell dear dear Friends! Tell me every thing I hope John[2] will some time or other write me a novel as to Tom[1] I do not ask him though I should be most proud of a letter farewell again God bless thee dear Mary

I wish you saw the number of scarlet Cloaks & silk Pelisses assembled in the Church yard – the Norths – the Tillmans – de Qus – Crumps – Kings – & Miss W. all as fine as [?] & now come the Peddins of Dove Nest in their Landeau – and behind follows the Ladies Fleming & Mrs Howard of Levens and another Carriage. Mrs Treemay past a while ago – So what think you of live Grasmere? Hartley & Derwent are here – D[orothy] and I tell you that H[artley] is quite a man – Sara C. is very pretty but she looked ill. Edith is pretty & genteel. Herbert is a *beauty* he will be like his father – but at present wants *nose* which makes prettier as a child – H[erbert] can read *Robinson Crusoe* or any Book – Godson is a very little younger & does not know his ab abs.

Tell me if my long Letter tries you – so that I may not err in this way again – if I know what sort of a Letter you all like I would try to write it – but as they used to tell me that my Letters were *good-for-nothing* I am afraid I cannot please do what I will.

*Postmark: Kendal*

## 12

*Miss Monkhouse, Hindwell, Radnor*

*Thursday Evening, Decr 3rd* [*1811*]

My dear Mary

I have written five Letters today – and yet I have the courage to take this long sheet, at which you will wonder the more when I tell you that Dorothy seeing that I am *in for it*, has asked me to write a sixth – namely one to M^rs^ Clarkson – But as I have a snug fire up in my own room I suppose she is resolved that I shall *earn* it – The Masons have had another bout at the Dining-room fire place without effect, it still smokes – and we are all crammed into William's little Parlour which is a most inconvenient thing – and particularly so to him at present, for he is very busy working. However since we find my chimney will carry smoke we shall not in future be quite so ill off; and the Chimney in the Dining-room is to be re-built as soon as M^r^ Jackson gets his corn out of the Barn – then if it is not better they will leave the House in the spring if another can be got. If I could have foreseen this I would most certainly have spent my winter with M^rs^ Clarkson – for even one less in that little room would have made it more comfortable.

I thank you dear Mary for your long Letter – before it arrived I was half-vexed at you, thinking that you made one serve for my two – however Joanna has given me one also and we are nearly straight. As Joanna does not mention your health, and says that you are gone to Penfannon, I trust that you are quite well – and my Aunt is again in her *better fashion* for I begin to fear that she will not be able to throw off her complaint entirely – I hope you will neither of you suffer by this very cold weather. M^rs^ Clarkson, whom I look upon as an excellent Doctoress, says that *chills* are the worst things in the world for you – so mind & keep yourself warm. I am perished for want of my stuff Gown – and long for it also that I may wear my brown stockings *along* – for I pity to wear them without, lest they should not last till the end. I wish that the Gown may have been sent by John Hall; for the Carriers will be an age in bringing the Box – Tell me what *oddments*, as Joanna calls them, are left out – because I know not what came & what was left – my Toothpick Case I miss & some other trifles which I fancied ought to have been in the Trunk already arrived. I thank you for the Hereford Papers which came last week – they are above a month old – however quite new to me. I wonder among the number of advertiz^ts^ that there should be no Farms to suit H[enry] A[ddison]. . . .

Henry[1] is still here – He and I have been a week at Appleby where we found Miss Weir in good health and spirits, but so much ashamed of her '*conduct*' with respect to Joanna that she now dare not write – Her Teapot, worsteds, &c all arrived safe, and she will make her own acknowledgements when she can muster courage. She has 9 Boarders at present all of whom will return after the Vacation; and two more promised – a Miss Shepherd of Shaw End near Kendal, & Parson

Stephenson's Daughter from Glencoe. The day-school she fears will fall off as there are no Children in the Town to succeed. Henry & I set off on our journey to Appleby by way of Kendal on Saturday week. He walked by my side & we spent Sunday with M^r^ and M^rs^ Cookson[2] – and proceeded to A. on Monday. The weather was heavenly, more like April than Nov^r^ and so it continued all the week. The Ball we expected to be on Wednesday Miss Weir had sent *that* word to hasten us with Dorothy's[2] frock, little expecting our Company, when we got there we found it not till friday & Miss Weir *happy* to have *cheated* us into a longer stay – The Children as well as herself were, as you may suppose delighted to see us. Siss could not keep her eyes off me the whole Evening. I thought her the most beautiful Creature I ever saw in my life, notwithstanding all that Henry[1] had said, *bewitchingly* so – for your life it seemed impossible not to admire her – there is such a life and variety in her countenance as I never saw – then she was so modest & pretty-behaved that it gave her face a milder & sweeter expression than I thought it capable of – The next day I did not think her so *perfect*, because you found out that her complection was not so good as at night it appeared to be, for though healthy and blooming she is not *fair* & her neck is a *bad* colour. The Ball was like one of M^r^ Yewdale's Balls – abundant in *bad* dancing – There was not one Child except a little Heelis that turned out her toes *well* – even Jane who is a good, & very graceful, Dancer – & Eliza very promising – neither of them excell in this respect. Watts attends Miss Conis's [?] Scholars – but Miss Weir dare not have him because Yewdale is such a favourite at Appleby they say 'he is the only Master that can make every one dance'. There were many enquiries made after you all. Every body had heard that Joanna was going to be married. M^rs^ Hickson gave this intelligence to Jack[1], & he has taken care to make the most of it. They were all happy to hear that my Aunt is so well pleased with Wales. . . . We could not get away from Miss Weir's till Monday and then the weather was broken. However we feared a storm and that we should be weather-bound we set off home by way of Pooley & Patterdale and a dreadful journey we had – the morning look[ed] blustring but did not rain but before we got to Pooley we had rain, hail, snow & sleet in perfection so that I believed the skin of my face had been cut & we were once forced to shelter in a Cottage on Cliburn moor – at P. we dried ourselves by an excellent fire among some entertaining Company (Abbot of Gowtray one) & had a nice dinner, & proceeded to Patterdale I having the Courage to go alone & let Henry[1] follow at his own pace for I was starved with going so slow. It was fair when we set off but the *seasons returned* before we had gone far, & after

Harry[1] being completely drenched he arrived about an hour after me at Luffs where I was sitting Mistress of the House over a blazing stick fire in their nice little parlour with the Tea things before me in complete comfort having thought of Ben & the Sailor at the Cherry Tree & repeated the lines many times.* Here we were detained all day on Tuesday; and on Wednesday morning it snowed & blew & rained, *as usual*, and he expected if it continued that Kirkstone would be impassable. At length it cleared about 12 and we had a bitter blast but got fair home to the great astonishment of all here, who never dreamed of our setting out in such weather, notwithstanding we had so much exceeded our time. The Luffs were at Ambleside – when we went away they were coming here – but begged we would go to the House if we came that way so we did & the maid made us right comfortable. It is a nice spot yet after all they are going to leave it. It will most likely be sold. Askew is in want of money – but this is only surmise. They had refused the place in the Isle of Bourbon but have now written again to accept – but we hope it will have been disposed of in the mean time. The estate in Silverthwaite he can dispose of. He has 1000£ more offered than he gave but then he has laid out some hundreds 4 or 5. Mrs Luff is as happy as possible in the idea of all her preparations for her voyage &c &c as if she were 15 and never had had a disappointment in Life. Luff poor Fellow! is very low-spirited & hopeless – but he feels himself constrained to go by dire necessity. It is a sad grief to him to leave his Cottage and all that he has done about it – and truly he may for it is a little Paradise. What do you say to de Q's having polled the Ash Tree & cut down the hedge all round the orchard† – every Holly, Heckberry, Hazel, & every twig that skreened it – & all for the sake of the Apple trees that he may have a few more Apples – Mrs Jones now stands quite alone, that nice high hedge behind her and all above, & where the Moss hut stood, levelled to the ground. D. is so hurt and angry that she can never speak to him more: & truly it was a most unfeeling thing when he knew how much store they set

* 'A steaming bowl, a blazing fire
What greater good can man desire?
'Twere worth a wise man's while to try
The utmost anger of the sky:
To seek for thoughts of gloomy cast,
If such the bright amends at last.'

Wordsworth's *The Waggoner*. Sara Hutchinson had herself transcribed the poem, which was not yet published. That she can refer to it in this way, as well known to her cousin, indicates how much William's poems were read aloud, or passed about in transcription, in the family circle.

† The orchard at Dove Cottage which he took in 1811.

by that orchard – the Apple trees also are so pruned that instead of its being a little wood, as it used to be, there is neither shade or shelter. My hand is so stiff that I cannot write any more so must finish to-morrow.

Thursday. Dorothy[1] and I have been chatting over my nice little fire and she bids me tell you Joanna that she is delighted to find that you do not despair about the Champion as I told her, when Mary said that she was resolved to come to the wedding. She was to be the Bride's Maid & pay the first visit into Kent – Yet I am somewhat at a Loss how to reconcile this with what I heard from Miss Weir – namely – that the Lincolnshire Champion fully expects you to be his Housekeeper – he told Miss Weir that his House was in great forwardness & that he should enter in the Spring. When I asked him something about his House &c he did not seem very communicative so I did not proceed on the subject – If this be the case, and you are not setting us upon a wrong scent, there will be a war between the Champions which is to have the Prize. D. bids me tell you that she is very fond of her Gown – it is made up but [she] does not mean to wear it till we pay our visit to Keswick after Xmas. You will perhaps hear from Tom[2] that Coleridge's Lectures* have gone on to the 4th – more than this we have not had an opportunity to learn – and that they give great satisfaction and are very well attended – though I am afraid they will not prove very profitable. You ask, Joanna, what I think of Mr Johnson – who is a canny† like Person – but not the least like one that I should suspect either of you to be *in love* with. He is not likely to stay here long for Mr Jackson's son is to come as soon as ready for his title so in the mean time Mr J is looking out for himself. Mrs de Q. has offered 2 situations to him and Dr Bell has promised, at William's request, to do something for him on the first opportunity. Peter has called upon me so I must go down for D. will not go in to him & Mary[1] is going to walk. Quincey reads the newspapers standing, or rather stooping with Catherine on his back – he is very fond of her but yet does not like to be plagued with her when he feels any thing like a duty which as he has engaged to teach her to read &c, towards her – but he will contrive some how or other to shake this off for he lives only for himself and his Books. He used to talk of escorting

* Coleridge's Lectures on Milton and Shakespeare, Nov. 1811 – Jan. 1812, Mondays and Thursdays at the London Philosophical Society. Fifteen lectures were announced, seventeen given.

† Probably not in the Scottish sense of 'shrewd' but in the Lancashire–Yorkshire sense of 'agreeable to the eyes, . . . seemly, comely, good, worthy, "nice", very satisfactory'. – *N.E.D.*

Mary[1] into Wales but I do not believe that she will have his company – Ma[r]y continues very full of her jaunt but I believe it will be a hard thing to get her off after all. I am sure it would do her good if she does not think too much about Home & the Bairns. Godson is a sweet little Fellow – but such a *worrits* he certainly worries all the flesh off his bones for he is thin as a lath & does not grow a bit though he has an excellent appetite and never ails any thing except that he has a husky cough at times which makes one fear that his lungs are not strong. I wish she would bring him and leave him for a year or two – I think you might contrive to make him a scholar for he is very quick though he gets on badly at school he – learns his Lessons by heart & in reality knows nothing of them – John[4] is terribly slow & Catherine will not attend to her Letters so I fear there will be no great Scholarship amongst them. Sissy is far the best but she is giddy & inattentive and has not improved so much (tho a good deal) as she might have done owing to this nasty dancing school which has been in their heads for 11 weeks – She is very tall though I do not think she will be a tall woman – she is stiff made & her neck is shortish – she is fat also. Joanna's Godson has been very bad in his Teeth & is much reduced by it & plainer than ever. Catherine is as fat and firm as a little Porker – her lameness does not improve – but in the cold weather it cannot be expected. I think we shall have a deep snow very soon it has every appearance of it at present – so I shall get no more rides for some time. My Poney continues in high favour and is as tractable as any poney in the world & as sensible as needs be – he will try all in his power to open a gate when he finds I have any difficulty by putting his nose or teeth to the latch – & will come up for me to get on again if I am obliged to get off – He is in excellent heart & condition, but he wants polling sadly – he is very ragged about his head – Henry trimmed his mane nicely but he durst not touch the head & ears. Luff promised to do this but he has not had opportunity. I can make him go wherever I like – come home & turn back again & go any where. I am completely his master notwithstanding Tom's[1] auguries. Oats cost me 12/6 per Bushell (I believe 3 winchesters)* Wheat is expected to be very dear & wool is rising. M^r^ Cookson and his Partner have been riding all over the Country to buy it up in the hope of an accommodation with America. Are not you delighted, John[2], with General Hill's affair? William says that General Blake's Battle & defeat has been the most creditable to the Spaniards of any action that they have ever been engaged in; for by Suchet's own account the victory was very doubtful at one time. I thank John for his [*two words illegible – crack in paper*] & I beg that

* The Winchester bushel abolished in 1835.

when he makes us [*hole in paper – seal*] takes stock at Christmas that he will communicate the result. Surely as Corn sells so well there will be a better account than the last. You said not a word about John Harrison. He is a nice Lad. I could have found in my heart to have spoken a word to him on the subject the other day at Patterdale but as I knew if he did wish to come he would want great wages, & having no authority, I did not – but he would be an invaluable Servant. Mrs Luff has the very best Poney in the world – able to carry any weight – a good size – quite a cart horse for strength & size to mine & very handsome & gay-looking; he would suit you nicely for he is fit for any work – He cost 20£. I wish you had had it – I do not like to hear of your any of you riding Duchess [*torn – seal*] will never be quiet till you get a broken Limb – But I forgot to tell you that my Poney has fa[llen o]n his knees several times with me – once coming down a steep hill when H[enry] A[ddison] & I were [*torn*] I was nearly off – but he has never broken his knees. Luff said it must [be his] shoes & I h[ave n]o doubt it is for he never made a false step till he lost his Kington [shoe] which the Grasmere Blacksmith set on I had taken off at Ambleside & I do not think [it is] much better. They put far too much iron on – the very sound of his feet is different he [sounds] like a Cart Horse – but sometimes I think it is mainly carelessness for when [*crack and torn*] though he was clogged by the snow & it was very slippery, he never stumbled – because he [*torn*] & more careful. Luff has not seen these shoes but I must consult him, he is my head Far[rier]. Tom[1] is quite in the wrong respecting the Virginian Creeper, it has feelers & will hold against any wall – at Downton Castle the wall is smooth free stone. The Ayrshire rose is an evergreen & looks very pretty against Luffs Cottage but that wants nailing – They have 3 different Clematis – a variety of the White besides the Virgin's Bower, and a beautiful purple one. When you have got such abundance of Shrubs I guess Tom will have his Darling plantation nicely tricked out.

Henry[1] talks of leaving us about the 20th. He intends to walk to Bdcastle where he will meet Miss Weir with the Children and proceed with them. He talks with great pleasure of his new house & I hope he will be more comfortable at the Farm than he is at Stockton for though I have no doubt but Jack[1] is kind to him yet Mrs H[utchinson] when he is not there pays H. no attention & the Servants never – He wants me sadly to go and see him at his house in the summer he says that he will come and walk by my side. Miss Weir says she will be of the party – but I want her to come to Wales she says that must be when she is richer. If H. A. does not want me (for I must stick to my promise) or my services are not required in any more urgent way I shall certainly go for it would give him so much pleasure poor Fellow & I shall have an opportunity of seeing Betsy. I was most sadly grieved when I came home that there was no Letter from Jack respecting his settlement. Jack ought to have made up his mind before H[enry][1] came & he should not have been an hour in Stockton without having been set at rest as to his future circumstances. I am quite ashamed when any one speaks to me upon the subject & hopes that this has been done & I can only give an evasive answer – Poor Fellow he never breathes murmur and is in far better spirits than I should be in his case – but it is evident that it presses upon his spirits at times though he says nothing – and the conduct of our *rich* relations to him is more mean than you could have imagined when they invite the rest of the Family to their houses they never ask him. Geo.[1] did say, you never come over to see us (they are at Whiten). Why they never came to see him & when they sent a note to invite Jack's[1] family to dine he was not named! This was before Geo. had said the above. Jack was angry and was not for going – but when I am there I will not go to their houses if he is not invited & will tell them so should they do it – if he declines the invitation that will be a different thing. . . . I am glad to tell you, Joanna, that Jack expects to get 40£ a year more for your Estate – it is worth far *more now* than before mine was bought, and mine now is worth *any money* – and in his esteem the nicest spot in the world. It is now called Grassy Nook – Either this year or the last the hay that grew upon it was worth 300£ – so after all I hope I have not taken him in – I ought to have told my Aunt about her Goddaughter's dress which was not fine but neat and she was very well contented. My Aunts frock was preferred by Miss Weir before a thin Lens* one given by M^rs^ Cookson – Mary[1] bids me say that you Joanna have been the real Pincey (which she never expected of *you*) with the Gowns for unless we can get it matched it will not make up and we contrived the best we could by cutting them together. It only wants cuffs for we were forced to cut the sleeves short – so if it is not matched we must make Ribbon or velvet Cuffs. I intend to send it up with Algernon Montagu to Mary Addison who will I dare say take the trouble to go to the place where it was bought if she recollects it. Did you enquire of Tom[2] respecting the Rum which was consigned to him? Harry[1] suspects that it is lying at the Wharf – of course it is of some consequence to him and he expects it to be worth near 80£. This Letter is a bit to every one I think you must make them subscribe towards the postage. I hope you will think that there is enough at least for the money. I will send you a little Poem

* Lens: from *lense*, an obsolete verb 'to make lean' or 'to become lean' ? i.e. north country for 'skimpy'?

or two by way of encreasing it's value. Farewell and may God bless you all & keep you healthy and happy during the winter & for ever – Make my kind love to the Donaldsons, and I hope to hear that they are in somewhat more comfort – My compts to Mrs Urwick & the rest of your neighbours. I am glad the Blackslands are so agreeable – Again God bless you all! S.H.

Inscription for an Urn, placed by Sir G.B. at the end of a double row of Limes, to the Memory of Sir Joshua Reynolds in the Grounds at Coleorton.*

Ye Lime Trees, ranged before this hallowed Urn
Shoot forth with lively power at Spring's return;
And be not slow a stately growth to rear
Of Pillars branching off from year to year;
'Till ye at length have framed a darksome aisle,
Like a Recess within that awful Pile
Where Reynolds, mid our Country's noblest Dead,
In the last sanctity of Fame is laid.

There though by right the excelling Painter sleep,
Where Death and Glory a joint Sabbath keep;
Yet not the less his Spirit would hold dear
Self-hidden praise & Friendship's private tear;
Hence an obscure memorial without blame
On these domestic grounds may bear his name;
Unblamed this votive Urn may oft renew,
Some mild sensations to his Genius due;
From One a zealous Follower of the Art
That he professed – attached to him in heart,
Admiring, loving, and with grief and pride
Feeling what England lost when Reynolds died.

Inscription on a stone nr a Cedar of Lebanon.†

The embowering Rose the Accacia and the Pine
Will not unwillingly their place resign
If but the Cedar thrive that near them stands
Planted by Beaumont's & by Wordsworth's hands

* De Selincourt says, *Wordsworth's Poetical Works*, IV, 196–7, 'Composed November 1811. Published 1815.' He gives some MS. variants. Sara Hutchinson's version here is closer to the variants than to the final version, but is not identical with any of them.

† *Wordsworth's Poetical Works*, IV, 195, 'Composed 1811 – Published 1815.' Lines 13–14, not given in the final version, are cited by De Selincourt as extant in a MS. of 1815–20. They appear to have been in the poem from 1811.

One wooed the silent Art with studious pains
These groves have heard the Others pensive strains
Devoted thus their Spirits did unite
By interchange of knowledge & delight.
May Nature's kindliest powers sustain the Tree
And Love protect it from all injury –
And when its' potent branches, wide outthrown
Darken the brow of this memorial stone
And to a favourite resting-place invite,
For coolness grateful and a sober light,
There may some Painter sit in future Days
Some future Poet meditate his Lays –
Not mindless of that distant age renown'd
When Inspiration hovered oer this ground –
The haunt of Him who sang how spear & shield
In civil conflict met on Bosworth Field:
And of that other famous Youth removed
From earth by mighty Shakespeare's self approved,
Fletcher's Associate, Jonson's Friend beloved.

I know not that I have transcribed the latter part of the Reynolds Inscrip. right. W^m is out & I cannot correct it if it is not right as I suspect, GodSon says to Henry[1], seeing him sewing, Uncle you'll be a Tailor when you'se a Man – 'Why what am I now?' says H., a Gentleman replied Tom[4] – Upon further enquiry we find he thinks all Gentlemen grow into men because when old they are not so smart-looking I suppose. Just now when he was putting on my glove, he expressed his surprize that he had as many fingers as his Aunt Sara[1]!!

## 13

*M^r Monkhouse, Hindwell, Radnor*

*Sat. 28 Mar:* [*1812*]

My dear John

If it had not been for Joanna's Letter which Dorothy[1] received today I should perhaps have delayed my promised Letter a little longer, for I am at present busily employed in transcribing for William; but as she says that you daily expect it it would be the height of *ingratitude* to defer it any longer, though I feel that I shall be obliged to *make it up* having very little to say except to return you thanks for your nice long and entertaining Epistle. I was kind enough to send it to H[enry] A[ddison] but I know not what has got into him for it has neither produced any acknowledgement to myself nor answer, I find, to you concerning the farm. I cannot but wonder what he is about; and am truly sorry to find him so undecisive. When I saw him at Patterdale he seemed resolved to have nothing to do with the Fell – but yet he was not *in fact* so much averse to farming in *that country* as his *words* would have made me believe; for he had thoughts of buying M^r^ Elwoods Estate – at least he had given it a consideration. I strongly suspect there is a *Loadstone*, in or about Penrith; and you know I have great faith in the influence of the *tender passion*.

I was very sorry to find by your Letter that farming prospects were no brighter this year than the last – but I fully expected to have had 'chapter and verse' from you after you had taken stock, which I doubt not you have done by this time. I have thought of your poor Ewes and Lambs with much concern during the late stormy weather; which has been quite as bad here as it could possibly be with you. To-day is the 'first mild day of March'*. I rode to Ambleside in the morning, and returned slowly in the rain, which fell so sweetly that there *seemed a blessing in* it; and the change in the face of the Country was like magic – every thing had been for some weeks past quite frost bound – the leaves on the oaks so shrivelled up that one considered them as almost leafless – but today the woods at Rydale were of the richest colour, and the various colours of the rocks and mountains seen through the soft air were quite enchanting – Did I ever tell any of you that the Goth (M^r^ Younghusband) has ploughed Grasmere's green Island? He has scarcely left one green sod in any of the fields of Dale End – William says his Motto must be

'Ye Sons of Britain venerate the Plough!!'

We are very glad indeed that you will have a Gig for Mary[1] – otherwise she would have seen nothing. I have never once been able to prevail upon her to mount 'black Radnor' – and though she pretended she durst ride with some one by her side (on horseback also) we had no hope of it – and consequently she must have been a prisoner, for no one at Hindwell, yourself excepted, and I know you prefer a *tivvy*, would have been disposed to take long walks with her. I wish she was off; and I hope you will be able to keep her a decent time; so that she may get some flesh upon her bones; for at present she is a miserable object. I too shall be obliged to come back to fatten if we do not get

* Wordsworth's 'To my sister', published in the *Lyrical Ballads*, 1798.

a healthier house – for I verily believe that this* is in a deadly situation, and you would all say the same if you knew the *bog* which it stands in – add to this the comforts of the smoke within, and it is without doubt a hateful house – and yet William clings to the notion of staying in it if it can be in the least improved. I cannot but wish that a good Schoolmaster may be procured for the sake of the Vale, – but I wish he may not be quite good enough for Johnny – and that perhaps may drive him to Ambleside when there is a house at liberty there.

I do not agree with Joanna in thinking a Curate of Grasmere more respectable than the head Master of the National Schools.† It is one of the most; nay it is hoped it will prove *the most* useful institution in the Country – and as W^m^ says this new method of teaching and the establishment of these Schools is, with the exception of the abolition of the Slave trade, the most happy event of our times. We have had a Letter from M^r^ J[ohnston]. He is delighted with his situation; with London; and with every body in the Concern. D^r^ Bell also writes that M^r^ J. bids fair to fulfil all that has been said of him, and do great credit to W^m^'s recommendation. He is in the eye of all the Bishops and men of power – and no doubt he will be preferred in the Church also – but in no other situation can he be so eminently useful as the one he holds – therefore, though a teacher of all the little *Raggamuffins* in London, Joanna need not be ashamed of him for a husband, if she can get him.

Harry[1] writes us that a report prevails in that neighbourhood that our George[1] is married but they cannot find out how it has come. I greatly fear that there is something not quite right going on, else he would write – if this should be true it is no good match depend upon it – for though perhaps no match would be *wise at present* yet he would not have kept it had it been a good one. Joanna's Champions are I fear both faithless to her. I shall perhaps see M^rs^ Hugesson in the Summer; as Harry continues to expect me notwithstanding Jack's[1] prohibition – but if this prohibition was anything more than a joke, which Miss Weir might *bouge* into something serious, I shall not go, sorry as I should be to disappoint him – Sissy is to *go along* if I *do* go. Harry says that Jack has never opened his lips to him since his return concerning the provision promised him.

I am most deeply grieved to hear that dear Mary's[2] pain has returned though I had anticipated it; for it is evident that the weather has great effect upon her and that a warm climate would I have no doubt soon restore her. It is very unlucky that Hindwell should be such a cold situation. I fear indeed that it will never agree with her – We must be

* The Rectory, Grasmere.

† Mr. Johnston had just left his curacy at Grasmere for such a headmastership.

forced to spend the next winter *together in Devonshire* – but alas! her old Lover John Ashworth has taken to himself a Wife. I talk of spending the next winter with M^rs^ Clarkson if I can raise the wind – for she wants me to go – and if I can do it, it is best to go in my *youth*, and here they will be less unwilling to part with me when they have such an uncomfortable house than is we could have complete enjoyment together. It really is deplorable to think how much of William's time has been stolen from him by these petty inconveniences – Sometimes within the last Month we have had no room to sit in but Dorothys[1] bedroom – not another Chimney would carry the smoke – then the Sun never shines upon the house except when we are in bed; so that we need more fires than any body else – the other day when the sun shone so hot that you were almost oppressed by it out of doors – when we came in the house felt like a well & made us shiver

Sunday Morning

We have just now at breakfast settled that the Travellers are to set off on this day fortnight – they will stay one day at Kendal – and 2 at Liverpool therefore if there is a Coach from Liverpool to *Chester* on *friday* the 17th of April they will be there on that day. Mind John[2] that you direct Tom[1] to go up that road to see Greyhurst (I think that is the name) Church & Yew Trees. M^r^ Crump tells me that one of the most beautiful views upon the Dee is behind or rather about one hundred yards to the *right* of the Church (*coming* from Liverpool) where there is a *Cottage ornée*, belonging to a Gentleman most delightfully situated.

Totts is in great glee about his journey he has been teizing me with questions as to what I am saying to you &c – and I told him that he shook my table so much that you would not be able to read what I said & then there would be no Uncle Thos[1] with his Carriage to meet him – this Gig delighted him exceedingly. He will *prim* no little when he gets into it; though if it is not rather smart he will be mortified, as his notion of Carriages is pitched high from seeing so many gay ones at the Church every Sunday. His Aunt has been making him two p^r^ of new Trowsers this week & he could scarcely be prevailed upon to leave her side; and they never were out of his thoughts – and yet after all we believe that we could persuade him to stay at home – if he did not lose his *Clothes* he would not be much distressed.

We heard from M^rs^ Coleridge last night that C[oleridge] is gone back to London – he came thro' Grasmere without calling but went back by Penrith – He is offended with William, or fancies himself so – and expected W^m^ to make some advances to him which as he did not he was miserable the whole time he was in Keswick, & M^rs^ C. was right glad to get him off again, for she had no satisfaction in him – and would have given the world, I dare say, to have had him well again with W$^{m}$. We are all very sorry that his visit has ended so; being persuaded that he never would have come down at all but in the hope of a reconciliation.* He is going to Lecture again in London.† Did I tell you that Brown the Printer‡ is gone off & left his affairs to be settled by his Creditors? Anthony Harrison agrees with me that it is impossible the *Friend* should have done him harm for he is sure that B. rec$^{d}$ as many subscriptions as paid him – besides he has the Types which C[oleridge] paid 37£ for himself; so that C. is rather a Creditor than debtor – No claim has been made upon C. & the Types were not known to be his. C. intended to enquire into the matter at Penrith which I hope he would do as some people are pleased to say that the *Friend* has ruined Brown.§

The Luffs are gone down to Portsmouth but do not yet know when they are to sail. They have been greatly wronged and ill-used by Askew who would have persuaded the World that he had half maintained them – whereas nothing could be further from the truth – and all obligation was on the other side – No money could have repayed the services which Luff had rendered W[illiam] A[skew] – King offered them the Cottage again immediately if they would have returned to it – indeed I believe there is not a Friend they had who would not have made great sacrifices to have kept them in the Country. L[uff] will be greatly missed in Patterdale. Joanna enquires after the Clarksons – We have not heard from M$^{rs}$ C. since I wrote to J. but M$^{rs}$ Luff has seen her and she is quite well (in her way) and in excellent spirits – Poor Mary Lamb is under confinement again –

I have been transcribing the *Peter Bell*|| which is now completely finished and improved – and I intend to make another copy for myself when William has done with my Pen – A few weeks ago I transcribed the Preface¶ to Wilkinsons Sketches for Luff with which I think I was almost more delighted than with anything else Willam ever wrote and intend to make another Copy as a *present* for you – but I shall not have time to do it before Mary comes. William has been busy with

* With Wordsworth, after the quarrel in Oct. 1810 precipitated by Montagu's reporting some alleged remarks, derogatory to Coleridge, by Wordsworth.

† The lectures of 1812, a course of six, May–June, at Willis's Rooms.

‡ The printer of Coleridge's *The Friend*, 1809–10.

§ The facts as Sara Hutchinson states them can be gleaned from various sources, but biographers have not always done so. This is valuable corroboration from one so close to the whole enterprise.

|| Not published until 1819.

¶ The first version of Wordsworth's *Guide to the Lakes*.

the *Recluse* but the smoke put him off and he will not now begin again before his journey. We are all very well – Bairns and all – I trust that this mild weather will restore dear Mary[2]. I hope that 'black Radnor' & I shall be at home again before she comes as I must resign him to her while she is here. If I am able to get M^rs^ Luff's Poney from the Maggs I will not sell M^rs^ King mine till after Mary[2] has been here and then we could travel all over the Country together – and I am determined to have it if I can. God bless you all! You must write immediately to *confirm* the propriety of the plan proposed for the meeting. Every body sends their love – We are glad that my Aunt & Joanna are better. . . . Yours truly S. H.

*Postmark: Kendal, Penny Post*

## 14

*M^rs^ Hutchinson, Hindwell, Radnor*

*Thursday 19th* [*November 1812*]

My dear Mary now by Law and custom my dear *Sister* though neither law or custom have the power to alter my feelings toward you, for you have always been and ever will to me as dear as the dearest Sister. God bless you all! and send you health – this being granted I feel confident of your happiness. We thank you most heartily for your Letter. I hoped for it on that evening; but if it had not come should not have been *angry*; because I know it requires a little time to settle oneself before writing can be anything but a task. You have indeed been the luckiest people in the world; yet we flatter ourselves that the weather has been finer with us than even with you. The day, at least, on which you reached home was far better here than with you; but you have not done fairly not to send us particulars. John[2] will compare mine with his journal & give us the balance in whose favour so ever it may turn out.

I scarcely know where I left off & what I have to tell you – but a few lines I must scribble to be ready for the Lloyds to take to the post when they return – they are coming hither to tea. In the first place I must tell you that we are all well at present – tho' Willy[2] has had a sickness which we were in hopes portended the measles but I think it is now gone off and I have never been out of the house except once since the day on which I carried my last to Ambleside – I caught cold by going there to see that fond man's daub of a picture (Dawe's) and have had a swoln face & gums & all the uncomfortables belonging to a severe cold – now I am quite well again. Willm & Mary did not return from Keswick till Tuesday last – They had had a very pleasant visit – parties for ever visiting all the gentry round – so Marys dress clothes would come into play. And William had a very agreeable visit at Lowther – My Lord mighty kind & disposed to do all in his power to serve him – he has written to Secretary Long and Mary is now *afraid* that something will be offered that he cannot undertake – The Ladies sent him to Penrith in the Carriage & then he escorted them back as far as T. Wilkinson's and went to Sockbridge – He called upon Miss Green but she was ill in bed; & she has never been well since she went to her new lodgings. Dorothy[1] went off yesterday over the Halse to Watermilloch – Wm set her over the hill – I suppose she will not stay more than 10 days, as the Marshalls go home before Xmas. Here is a letter just come for her from the dear Andrew.* I will transcribe what relates to you or what may amuse you. 'My dr Antelope. Wish to be with you sometime & scold you? No! I wish to be with you always that you may scold me; which I can find no body to do, as you do, such a scold you are! – I beg you will waft my gratulations (for I suppose she has left you) to Mary[2] Monkhouse, my Madras Mistress: no longer I suppose M. M.: but Mrs Mary Hutchinson – Happy Man Mr H. to have such a sweet creature for his wife. If he be such a man as his sister is a woman – such a Husband as she is a wife, I could wish nothing better for the sweet Lady or the sweetest Lady of them all! Now she is gone, there will be full scope for the talents of Sara Hutchinson in the Mad[ras] School. What a favourite will she then be next summer having no M. M. to rival her. It will behove you then to take care that she does not supplant even you.' He then speaks of his only intending to stay at Coleorton a day or two but his 'kind Host & hostess cast 4 chains over my inclinations by talking for ever of Mr. & Mrs. H. Miss W. S. H. who begins to regain her lost ascendancy, now the Madras girl is no more, and of our Keswick Friends & Coleridge.' He then sends his respects &c to Parson J[ackson] & the school master who he says he wishes nothing better to him than that 'he may have any share of the real & indefatigable exertions of Sr G[eorge] & Lady B[eaumont]. Day by day, & hour by hour they attend the school, & do all that ought to be done, & as it ought to be done. Let me hear that he is not outstript by all the grave & good.' He says that in Brunswick Sq. Mad[ras] Schools are opened for their own & neighbours Childn by the good Ladies their Parents finding it in vain to wait for

* Dr. Andrew Bell.

School mas$^{ts}$ & M$^{ss}$'. He is going to Ludlow Birmingham & Oxford in his way, I suppose to London. We intend sending his Letter to D. so if she writes to him she will give him an inviti [*sic*] to come & see his sweet M. M. & then you may try to get him to set the school a-going. If he should come this might be done if you were to introduce him to the Landlord. If I had read his Letter in Japan I could have known whose it was it is so characteristic. I am not very proud of his flattering of me – indeed I think we are all very good natured! He is a queer creature – god knows!

I have just put on my wedding cap* & dressed myself ready for our party & come up stairs to finish my Letter. Willy[2] is following His Mother up & down full of chat – he very often talks of you – is sure the carriage will come back. 'Godfather will bring Godmother back to William.' Totts talked much about you till he heard you were at home – every morning in bed the first thing he used to say was either 'Now Aunt Sarah let us talk about Wales' or 'How far aunt S. do you think they have got, Welsh Pool?' or some other place he would name & always had a pretty good guess taking the road they went. You cannot conceive what a quiet house we had during Dorothy's[2] absence – Totts never whined, & Willy very seldom cried – Now that she is come back she tiezes Totts & he can neither bear it or keep from her. He improves daily at school & is as anxious as ever – he is seldom without a book in his hand when in the house, & I hear him getting his spelling all the time after he is up till he goes to school of a morning. He slept with me when D. was absent & many a piece of nice chat we had about you all before he got up.

We were pleased to find that you were so much satisfied with your House & parlour – you tell me not a word of the Garden – but all in due time. I suppose you got no shrubs – our lasses have been doing up our Court – but our shrubs are not come though they have been ordered some time. Did I tell you that Miss Penny does not go to live at Rydall Mount – she is going near Silverthw[aite] but as My Ladies we understand do not intend to let the house for longer than a year at a time W$^{m}$ would not have it – most likely it will stand empty. Some say they wish to have a single Lady in it. It might do for Miss Green but nobody would like such an uncertain tenure. The Norths are not yet gone – they exhibit themselves & their beautiful Girls at Church constantly now since M$^{r}$ Jackson has ceased coming to do duty. I have never been at the School, but I understand that they come on very well – M$^{r}$ Powley is very much interested in the School &

* The wedding of Thomas Hutchinson and Mary Monkhouse had been at Grasmere, 2 Nov. 1812.

expressed himself (at P. Ashburners's where he drank tea last Sunday) as being very anxious for it's welfare and delighted with the Boys whom he said were the finest set of Lads he ever saw. There is going to be a Mad. School established at Keswick; and it was proposed that D[orothy] should go & set them forward – this was W^m^'s wise proposal but M[ary] prevented it; knowing that it would be mighty disagreeable for her to have to *fight* (without Dr. B[ell]'s weapons cough & mint drops) among such a number – many of them bigger than herself – & what is worse against 18 trustees & not more than 2 or 3 of them *for* the system. Therefore Mary recommended it to Southey that the Master should be sent to Carlisle for instruction. – As a piece of gossip I must tell you that M^rs^ Calvert says that the dear Doctor actually offered himself to M^rs^ Kennedy – she being an heiress – Mary had forgot the Lady's name but it must have been Miss D. from the time, her being an heiress, having a mother, and being a ward of old Mitchinson of Carlisle. I do not believe him such a fool or so interested for they thought it was for her money *alone* – besides he did not think very highly of her – I should like well to have a dish of (scandal shall I call it) with 'Mistiss Obinson.'

I have had a letter today from dear M^rs^ Clarkson. She is very well and in better spirits than when she last wrote having ridded her house of a set of bad [*word left out*?] that had made her very uncomfortable. She is going to spend the Christmas Holidays with Tom[5] at Perndon (W^m^ Smiths) and will visit her sister in Town before she returns to Bury – Her Father is as gay as a Lark and expects to shame them all by his clever housekeeping. She does not mention more than the name of the d^r^ Till[brook] – in connection with Bloomfield who she says are both grieved that Hartley & Derwent are not at a better school where something might be made of their great Talents. The Crumps are all gone except M^rs^ C. Miss (who is returned from Scotland) & Louisa – and they go next week, so then the vale will be left to its *ancient* & quiet inhabitants.

I begin to think that the Friends, with old Dame Pemberton & her 'nice new toppin', are not coming. Cha^s^ keeps quite well – somewhat fidgetty but that must be expected. I think I have told you all the *news* and I am too stupid to *make up* the Letter so I will bid you all good bye, begging that you will write soon and often. Tell us if you have heard again from Geo.[1] – No news of Johnsy!! God bless you all for ever! & your affectionate & faithful

Sister
S. H.

Mary[1] does not look any better for her journey – though she seems to have enjoyed herself while out – but as she returned thro' the Church she went to throw herself upon the poor Child's grave* – so that we had no cheerful meeting. You did not say particularly (or else we could not read it) in what state that poor sufferer is at the Stone House. – Tell us as we are very anxious to hear how you find him if you go to see him – I hope Joanna has written to Miss Weir. De Q. is still at Ilfracombe but he was going to London to keep his Term at the Temple & *says* he will be here in about a fortnight.

D.

| | |
|---|---|
| Monday. | There was a shower while we were in Ambleside ab^t noon. The afternoon & Ev^g mild & beautiful. no frost at night. |
| 10. Tues. | a most delicious day! mild & sunny & warm. |
| 11. Wed: | Here it was a dullish day but no rain; Mary spoke of it's being remarkably fine at Keswick. |
| 12. Thurs: | |
| | Rain & mug. (at K. fair & pleasant). |
| 13. Frid: | |
| 14. Sat. | Fine day – heavy shower after dark. |
| 15. Sun: | Beautiful day. |
| 16. Mon: | Fine till Even^g then a heavy shower & high wind. a little snow on the hills. |
| 17. Tues: | Cold wind fair all day except a shower afternoon. frosty night. |
| 18. Wed: | Bright frosty day a light shower of hail about noon. clear moonlight night. |
| 19. Thurs: | A glittering day. the frost not hard & the sun hot. |

Remember me to your Neighbours – Poor James! If he is as bonny as he can be is he as happy?

*Postmark: Keswick, 298*

## 15

*Thos Monkhouse Esq^re*

*March 9th 1813*

My dear Tom

I had a small parcel to send to Joanna and to make it worth the Carriage have enclosed in the Box a Pot of Char which I hope will be

* Catharine's. Two weeks later, Catharine's brother Thomas died, 1 Dec. 1812.

acceptable to you – If the News papers are not arrived do not lose any opportunity of forwarding the Books to Luff but send them without the Papers – we have sent a Letter to be enclosed in the Parcels.

Perhaps you, or whoever Joanna has commissioned to purchase the Carpet, may find no difficulty in procuring 2 – both of a good size – and quality – Wilton, Brussels or Turkey whatever may be *good* & cheap.

I should not wonder if you were to find Joanna quite as reluctant to leave Town as she was to return to it last time – The magnet will now be at the Central School instead of Kent. I am afraid she is somewhat fickle –

Be so good as write to tell me the name of the Ship &c when you have sent off the Parcel – and I will write to apprize my Friends of it – I have the means of writing to them through Lord C. Somerset.

If you or Joanna could take the trouble of writing a note to a Friend of mine 'Miss Dowling, at the R$^{t}$ H$^{ble}$. the Earl of Galloway's Charles S$^{t}$ S$^{t}$ James'' saying that you have a parcel to send to M$^{r}$ L. in which you can enclose her a Letter it would be a great favor to us both – But perhaps there may not be time for all this – I will only apologize for all the trouble I give you by saying that I hope you would with no more scruple employ me.

God bless you! – Remember me to your Friends in St Mary Axe. All here are well, and join in kind remembrances – Very affy your's
S. Hutchinson

The Pots were not so large as I supposed therefore I send two. I should be glad to hear of their *safe* arrival.

## 16

*Thomas Monkhouse Esq$^{re}$, Budge Row, London*

*Sunday Even$^{g}$ [16 May, 1813]*

My dear Cousin

I received your Letter on Friday Evening – but our Distribut*er** (this is the *official* mode of spelling the word, therefore you must not question my orthography) being from home we could not decide upon the important part of its contents. He is now returned and it is determined

* Wordsworth was made Distributor of Stamps for Westmoreland in Apr. 1813.

that a Turkey carpet must be had for the dining-room – the dimensions of which are $\overset{\text{F}}{19}.\overset{\text{I}}{4}$ by 13.4 – The proper measurement for the Study Carpet, which room is to serve also for drawing room, you will find on the other side. This *you say* must be Brussels – we should be very well contented with the old-fashioned Wilton, if it is to be had at a cheaper rate – only we must confine you to colour and pattern – the pattern to be as *small as possible* without regarding the fashion; and the colour to be of drabs, and a light yellow; which last is the colour of the window hangings. I have also a commission for Mary Addison in connection with this last part of my direction to you in which she will be greatly assisted by your procuring her a patch of the carpet for the study. We are quite ashamed to give you such troublesome jobs – but we hope you will sometime have the satisfaction of seeing how smart you have made us – But nature has done more for us than we can all do – for surely this is the most beautiful and gay place you ever beheld. I wish you could at this moment behold the splendor of Winandermere which lies before my eyes illuminated by the setting sun with the lovely green veil of Ambleside between us and it. – But I have forgotten part of my commission which was that you would be so good as buy for William 2 pair of Pantaloons, of the knit kind, – such as you got him before when he was in Town – one grey & the other drab. The money for all these things including Mary Addison's you must get at Staple Inn to be placed to account.

William sets off tomorrow to Appleby to take upon him his new office – The income of it we expect will be about 500£ per an: – and the duty very easy. He will keep a Clerk therefore we hope it will not very much interfere with his other pursuits – He will be most happy to see Mr Wheelwright if he is lucky enough to be at home when he passes this way – and I think that he will not be more than a week from home upon this business at present. His late absence was caused by the melancholy fate of the *Peacock Frigate* – the brave Captain of which was the husband of his Cousin Mary[4] Wordsworth who had been here spending a few days, about three weeks ago, full of hope and joyful anticipation of her husband's being made Post Captain and returning to spend two or three years on shore before he got a ship – What a dreadful change – What a blight to her in the very threshold almost of life! Her Brother also was in the ship – but there is hope that he may be saved among the Prisoners – he was a young Lad of great promise – the only hope of his parents, for Joseph, who was appointed to the Lowther Castle Indiaman, is utterly helpless from disease.

Mrs Peake is now at her Father's house near Cockermouth whither

William has been and where he left her and all the family in the deepest affliction – M^rs^ P. is a most amiable woman – doated on her Husband by whom she was equally beloved – indeed every body who knows her loves her she is of such a sweet, and gentle, and loving nature. I know not whether M^rs^ Addison's family are any of them acquainted with [her] but poor Isabella & she were very intimate.

I am rejoiced as well as you by every account which we have from our dear Friends in Wales – and may heaven continue to them the blessings that they enjoy – that they deserve them it is a comfort now to contemplate – and should they be deprived of them hereafter it will be no less their consolation to feel that they have not abused them – Two more innocent contented and gentle dispositions never were united.

I have been so much interrupted by company that I have not time for more – it is 9 o'clock, & I have yet to send my Letter to Ambleside; for we cannot wait another post we are in such a hurry for our Carpets – The gay time is coming on and we want our house in order that we may have time to enjoy ourselves. I am going to Keswick for a fortnight next Wednesday to pay a long-promised visit to a Miss Barker a friend of Southey's – I hope the Carpets will be here at my return for I know that in Town you do all things in an instant. – God bless you! and believe me very affty yours S. H.

You must make my excuses to M[ary] A[ddison] for this shabby note.

My dear Mary[2]

I leave it to T[om][2] M. to make my apologies for troubling you with a commission – which is to procure me 5 shades of drab rug worsted from the darkest drab nearly black to white included – 2 pounds of each shade; and 6 pounds of a *lightest* bright yellow. T. M. has to get a Carpet with these colours in & he will perhaps be able to shew you the colour. Also 16 yards of Canvas not coarse rug canvas neither the finest kind used for Tent Stitch but proper for cross stitch rather open.

Our best remembrances to your Mother Aunt and all your brothers. God bless you very truly. Your's S. H.

If you think proper to send the parcel by sea direct to M^r^ Cookson Kendal to the care of J[ohn] H. Stockton whom you must advise of its shipping. If by Land to M^r^ C. Kendal – without any other name – except W. W. at a corner.

*Postmark: Kendal Penny Post, My 19, 1813*

## 17

*Thos Monkhouse Esq$^{re}$, Budge Row, London*

*Rydal Mount, 23rd June* [*1813*]

My dear Coz

I did not intend to have written to you till the arrival of the Carpets; but Joanna in a Letter which I had from her the other day, says, that she is '*happy* to find that we like them' – Having had, we suppose, some Kentish Swains in her head she has mis-read what I had told her; which was merely that your account of the prices had not frightened us, and that we were glad that we had taken your advice &c &c – Now if *she* has also expressed her *happiness* to you – you must think *us* very *ungrateful* not to have communicated our's to you – but the truth is – that the Carpets are not yet arrived – but we have not the least doubt that we shall approve your choice – and the prices were below our expectations – The Nankeen, worsteds, & Canvas, *Dog Cheap* compared with any thing we could have got here. I hate to dwell upon grievances and should not have noticed the delay but for your information. If ever you have any thing to send North again, in a hurry, never trust it to any Canal – the Kendal People say that the Carriage has been irregular ever since they were opened – and that no mode of conveyance is to be depended upon, from London but the *Leeds* Waggon – from Stockton to Penrith, or Kendal, the Carriers also are very punctual; but the fault was entirely mine in not telling you to *avoid* the Canals.

We are all very well and comfortable in our new residence notwithstanding the noise which little Willy makes with his strong shoes upon the carpetless floor – and we have so much pleasure from the beauty which is around us without doors that we care little for the want of ornament within. I do wish you could have come to see us this summer – I fancy that much as I enjoy this place that I should love it far better if all my friends had seen and enjoyed it with me – It is the admiration of every body – the *crack* spot, and the envy, of the whole neighbourhood. – We looked out after the Coach, which passes very near to us for many evenings in expectation of M$^{r}$ Wheelright but he never arrived – neither have your matrimonial Friends given us a call – they, I suppose, were too much occupied with each other to care for anything else; and M$^{r}$ W. too busy to lose a day among the Lakes. We have had abundance of other visitors; I think we have scarcely been one day unengaged for the last month – You who are fond of visiting and parties should always come into this neighbourhood in June, or July, or August – and then you would think that we live *in* the world; especially if you came at the Regatta season when there are most genteel Balls. I wish I could persuade you to come this year for I believe we are to have a party here whom William is engaged to attend to them – and Miss Green expects her nephew and M[r] Hutchinson to come – and the boat races among the beautiful scenery of Winandermere surely a far more taking thing than Horse Races – tho' upon Penrith Fell – beautiful as is the ground it cannot be compared with our *liquid course*.

I have not heard from Wales for an age. Joanna tells me that they have been very gay at the Stow – therefore I suppose Mary[2] has been too much engaged to write – God bless her! I am glad to find that her health enables her to enjoy herself so much. Joanna I guess will not be able to leave her Kentish Friends for some time yet – it is most likely that she will not be ready to return to Hindwell till you go which will make it pleasant for you both. We should have been glad if she had made us a call here while she was on the wing, for I fear it will be long before she can raise Cash for another Expedition.

I suppose you are all in doleful mood about this Armistice. – We can scarcely contain our indignation – and that Profligate the *Courier* tells the tale without one word of either indignation or sorrow. If the Ministers do not put forth their whole power now in aid of Lord Wellington, Buonparte's days of exultation will come again – and we shall be left alone in the Combat if no worse – However *we here* like the present ministers rather than their opponents who would, if they were in, do nothing for the good Cause – and Peace with the Tyrant I trust no friends of the Nation can wish for.

William was at Penrith about a fortnight ago where he saw Henry Addison who continues in a bustle among his Farming concerns. Miss Green says that he is also a constant attendant at the Tea parties and that his partiality for Miss Parker is still one of subjects of conversation.

We hope that you have according to order made your demand at Staple Inn for the sum which William is indebted to you for the Carpets &c. They will [take your] word without any previous advice from home. I [do] sadly grieve whenever I think of the failure of my [friend to] get the Kendal papers &c sent out to Mauritius [especially] since I have learnt that another Friend of Luff [failed] also in a like purpose. If one Vol. only of the Regis[ter] if you should have any opportunity of sending it with the last or two last Nos of the *Quarterly Rev*: it would oblige me greatly if you could forward them or any Book or Papers relating to public affairs that you think, would be interesting – I have heard from them once since they arrived at the end of their Voyage – Poor Souls! they are very little satisfied with their situation and pine after what they have left behind.

Remember me kindly to Miss R. and the rest of your Friends at Hampstead if they are not gone into Wales – and to all M^rs^ Addison's Family – Everyone here joins me in kind love to you – and I am dear Tom most truly. Your's S. H.

John[1] Hutchinson writes us that he is much pleased with his daughter's improvement while in Town – You will have occasion to complain, as William sometimes does when (to use his own phrase) a Shilling is 'whipt out his pocket' for a worthless Letter – God bless you!

*Postmark: Kendal, Penny Post, 28 Ju, 1813*

# 18

## *Mrs Hutchinson, Hindwell, Radnor*

*Sunday Morn^g^ [Aug 1, 1813]*

My dearest Sister

I was not one bit angry at your silence – I was only disappointed when the post days were passed by without bringing me a Letter. I guessed that you were so much engaged with visitors that you had not time to write how much soever you might wish it; and had not I been occupied in the same way I should have written to you notwithstanding you were the debtor. I got your's, & one from Joanna, last night upon my return from the Station whither I had *been with Miss* Green, M^rs^ Ellwood, and Willy Whelpdale and was not at home the evening before when they arrived having gone to Brathay to see poor Lloyd and there I was detained all night by a thunder storm. Lloyd has been very bad ever since I last wrote – It has been a sad stroke to his poor wife who had been in such good hope concerning him – We have some of us made a point of going to see her every day at his request; as we are the only people to whom she can entirely open her mind – and this task, added to our numberless visitors, has employed us all fully. Were I to give you a list of the folks we have had & our consequent engagements it would make a list as long as that of Crossthwaite's Museum – at present Dorothy & I except the Children including the Coleridges are alone; W$^{m}$ & Mary went to Whitehaven yesterday – W$^{m}$ to pay his respects at the Castle & both of them to visit M$^{r}$ Blakeney. I hope it will do her good, she went off I believe very cheerfully – though it was a struggle to bring her to consent. She is very well except the rheumatism & a pain – in her back – Her spirits have I think been better – at least in company – and except when in bed she has never been out of it for many weeks – We have had the Stoddarts, that is the D$^{r}$ and his Lady and a Poetess along – the Crackanthorpes – M$^{r}$ Cookson, M$^{r}$ Kinneson [?] & his son & M$^{rs}$ Marshalls 2 eldest sons—all staying in the house at different times – except the Miss C's who did not last time they were in this neighbourhood – they slept at Ambleside but we had them in the day time – and after they went to Rayrigg, where they now are. M$^{rs}$ C. stayed with us & we expect them all again tomorrow – Then we had M$^{r}$ Thorpe constantly at our parties which he enlivened most agreeably – and callers and daily visitors among our neighbours without end – It has been weary work I assure you! & I see no end of it. – Tomorrow, or next day comes M$^{rs}$ Coleridge, Sara[3] & Miss Eliz. Fricker – M$^{rs}$ Clarkson too was to have been here this week but she must not come till W$^{m}$ & M. return – and we are also to have the Marshalls – the Calverts & Miss Barker & the new Governess we expect daily – This new Governess perhaps you have never heard of – she is a friend of Miss B[arker] and is going to set up at Ambleside to teach the Lloyds – Jane Harding – Whites Miss Scambler – Miss Newton & our D[orothy][2] – She comes a year upon tryal for if no more than these scholars turn up & no more are in the place it cannot answer to her – but we have engaged to remunerate her for one year's tryal; & as there are a good many children in the neighbourhood she may get Boarders in the way M$^{r}$ Dawes has them – and she is competent to teach German, french & Italian – to M$^{r}$ Dawes' Boys if she can but manage them – which she will give two evenings a week to – She is also an excellent musician & will teach grown people the Harp &c &c. – Her name is Fletcher – they are a musical family at Birmingham & she has played the organ there – also been private governess to Baroness Howe's daughter & in other families where she has given great satisfaction but is tired of that kind of situation – though she has a *passion* for teaching as Miss Fricker says. – So Miss B. has persuaded her to set up for a 'romantic Governess' among the Lakes – I hope it may answer to her & the advantages to us will be incalculable – For Dorothy is the most unteachable creature alive: though as quick as thought – but there is no nailing her to her books – and indeed she cannot but be sadly neglected at such a season as this, when one is obliged to attend so much to Strangers. There is I am sure a no way of teaching children at home without a governess if you do not live in complete solitude or give yourself up entirely to it for some hours in the day as M[rs] Chippendale used to do – but then it is better worth while when there are ½ a day than only one – Sara[3] Coleridge is the only exception I have yet seen – but then she has so much pleasure in her book, & learns without teaching, that she is no example. Hartley tells me that John[4] is much improved since he was at M[r] Dawes' school before – he has only returned since the Holidays – we were quite satisfied with M[r] Powley and indeed had rather that he had continued under his care, if the Boys at Grasmere school had been as fit companions for him. Willy[2] will be very quick I have no doubt; but he is too much of a Duke to look at his book – *because he is desired* – and the first business of teaching them will be a terrible job for he is such a rebel as you never knew – but he knows *every thing* and is a witty creature – we think he grows every day more like dear Tom[4] in the face – i:e: in feature – for he can never have the same expression of countenance; their tempers & characters being so different.

I ought to tell you that we like all our 'Cousin Cracken crokes', as Willy calls them, *very* well – The Girls are being unaffected & well behaved – very affectionate and were as agreeable & happy as possible. William is affected in his manners – and *has been* much more so; but I believe it is now mere habit. I was as much prejudiced against them all as any body could be before they came – but it is entirely removed – indeed I like M[r] C. exceedingly and he has as good and affectionate a heart as can be; & it is a great pity that his manners should be so much against him – Miss Green & M[rs] Ellwood had all sorts of disagreeable stories against him – but he removed all disagreeable impressions by his kindness & politeness to them. We D. & I & Miss G's party went with him to the Ragatta – and Miss Green M[rs] Ellwood & Willy went to the Ball – where they enjoyed themselves very much. They were introduced by M[rs] Harden. The Miss C's went with M[rs] Fleming [*torn*] for we could not go to the Ball. I had sad work to get [*torn*]; & indeed I wish I could have brought myself to go on M[rs] Ellwood's account – for Miss G. was so *primmy* at the Station, on the Regatta day, that I was afraid she would have had a disagreeable ball with her. Not *primmy* with us, but did not chat with the folks when she had an opportunity of chatting with – and it was good fun to us to see so many people & no small share of oddities among them who were quite new to D. & me.

I must give over all this news & nonsense & tell you that 4 or 5 pair (I forget which) of Gentlemen's Stockings, the Castors, Jug Rugs (I hope M[rs] C[ookson] did not forget to put in) and Irish Tabissten Gowns for you and Joanna were all forwarded in a parcel from M[r] Cookson, above a month ago, to M[r] James Symonds Draper Hereford – Therefore John[2], who I should suppose will attend that Market, must enquire after them – I hope the Tabissten will not be singed like poor Joanna's goods – I could not get a grey one for my Aunt else I should have been sorry to have made her a *Bispill* – What will you say when I tell you that 3 breadths of our Brussells Carpet has been burnt with vitriol in the Carriage along with 11 yds of my canvas – Oh it has been a vexatious case! & we are yet uncertain whether we can get any redress – but as Joanna says I am sick of the subject & will reserve particulars till we meet – only I must tell you that, to use W[m]'s words, the Carpets are as 'beautiful articles as ever came into a house' – & cheap – the nankeen too is dog cheap – if ever you want another Camp bed have nothing else – our study is beautiful – I wish you could see it – and the dining room looks so comfortable, warm, & *genteel* you would be delighted with it – I do so wish you could see this place – you can have no idea of it – for even we who have lived so long near it, never had till we came to reside at it. Our neighbours the Ladies are very fond of us – and we hope that W[m1] will quite cut out Miss Penny – indeed if it were not a point of honour we are sure they had rather have us than any body else – & we do not believe that Miss P. will ever claim the promise – We have unrestrained right to walk in the Grounds as if they were our own – & Lady Di pops in and takes a friendly cup with great pleasure – poor Lady F[leming] is in bad health & they are gone to Brighton – it would be a sad thing if she were to die for then Sir D[aniel] would be at the Hill for his life. However we console ourselves with the hope in that case that Lady Di would sell the place to W[m] – We rue sadly that we did not buy it as we find it would have been quite as agreeable to them & more convenient – for they only wanted to be rid of the Norths. I have little room to say any thing about the Marshalls. It is a hopeless case – we will try what we can do. I wish I had known before Sharp went for I have no doubt but he would have given me 10 Gs for them. In the meantime D. & I will contribute 2£ which you will place to our account – & if we can raise any more among our friends will – it will help them on their journey. I do not wonder at Toms[2] being weary – he smiles [?] very justly; & ought not to do any more as he knows doubtless many more deserving objects.

I have no patience when I think of that Lad's being taken from the Sea. I hope Tom H. will send him back – he is fittest there & it is no duty of Tom's to keep him – Therefore I wish his humanity may not tempt him to do so foolish a thing. You must save this & *read* it to Joanna for I cannot write all this over again.

You must tell me Mary[2] if you do not like your Gowns & I will try to get others – but depend upon it they will be becoming – My Aunt Gamage used to say *yallow* was becoming to every body & it set off linen the best of any colour.

God bless you all together. I will write to John M.[2] to whom I am greatly obliged for his Letter when I am more at leisure to write *legibly* for this is scandalous but I have two other Letters to write this morning – and the Party from 'Rotha Side' are coming to dine with us – I have not given up the hope of seeing you before Xmas – but I must go to Stockton if I can get – and I hope we shall go to Bolton Abbey when Lloyd is better.* We intend to make a party. But I have sad news of my poney – They say it is broken winded – tho' opinions are various – Mr Scambler says it is – but Wilcox & his Hostler [*sic*] say that it has better wind than Mr S. It has been bled & is somewhat better – so I have hopes – but it is such an unlucky creature that I cannot turn it out and at present we have no grass to cut for it – I give it mashes twice a day – It *had* a dreadful cough but it does not puff and blow as Lily used to do. Again God bless you all. Remember me to your visitors – and ask Geo.[1] when he intends to visit this part of the Country.

We have no doubt of the report concerning L. L. D.

I wish I had known of the want of fish Hooks before they had gone to Whitehaven in time to have got a Cargo for them to have got franked at the Castle – but I will have some ready for the first opportunity of that kind which offers. We have two nice new boats upon Rydale at command & it is a sweet Lake to fish upon – there are plenty of Perch & Pike, & we take our Tea bathing & load with fuel at [the island]. I stand and dr[ink] Tea on the opposite shore for the Islands are so full of wood that there is no safety in making a fire upon them – and from the opposite shore in an evening we have the most beautiful scene among the Lakes. I know not whether ever you were there at sun-set. It is beautiful beyond all description. I forgot to tell you that we had a call from Mr & Mrs Chippendale their two eldest Girls & their little Boys who were making a Tour of the Lakes which the Girls chose in preference to going to a watering place. Mrs C. is as handsome as ever though somewhat fatter [&] does not look a day older – her *Teeth* are most beautiful. Her Girls are almost as tall as

* Lloyd's illness affected them all, for Dorothy Wordsworth was staying a good deal with Mrs. Lloyd, being one of the very few persons Lloyd could tolerate in the house.

herself. And she is as fond of talking about her school days as ever. She gave me and all of us a most pressing invite to go & see them. Mr C. & the Wordsworths are related.

We have heard nothing of poor Miss Peake lately. Her father said the last time he wrote that she was somewhat better – & as soon as she could would come hither. This *is* the last *bit*!!!!!

*Postmark: Kendal, Penny Post*

## 19

*Mr Monkhouse, Hindwell, Radnor*

*Friday, Augt 27th [1813]*

My dear John

I ought to have thanked you for your Letter long before this; but I hoped every day to be able to say something decisive respecting Anne Hatton; and till this morning I have heard nothing from her. I should have gone over on purpose to try my eloquence upon her but we have been so much engaged with company, and I have every day been expecting to set off for Stockton, that I really have not had a *moment to call my own.* I therefore commissioned Mrs Ellwood, who passed thro' Keswick on her way home, last Monday to speak to Ann, & the message which I have had is that she will let me know when she has heard from 'our Folk' – but 'our folk' will be '*very mad*' if she goes so far from home. The truth is however, I am inclined to believe, that she is herself very desirous to come – she told Miss Green she should like much to live with you; and if it were not for the formidable journey she would *jump* at the place. I would have you write to her & tell her all the particulars; what services will be required of her; and what wages you will give her. She does not understand a dairy – and *I* am not certain that you have not more Cows than are necessary for the Family – therefore I could not satisfy her on this point. I am very anxious that you should have her; because I am certain she would be a real treasure to you; and I know of no other likely to suit. I shall make all possible search for you in the County of Durham if Ann does not consent.

Henry[2] came hither this day week; and on Tuesday last we were to have set off together for *Grassy Nook* but alas! when our Man went into the stable in the morning his Poney (Lilly) was found in no condition for travelling – it had been fastened in the Halter all night in some terrible manner, by having thrown itself down, and in the struggling to get free had so maimed and bruised itself that we were obliged to send for the farrier – and it is now suffering greatly from the bruise above its eye – and whether it will recover or not we are in doubt – if it is not better we must set off without it in a day or two. Henry is very well and seems perfectly happy & contented in his situation – though he says sometimes he wishes he had not come hither, for, after having seen this beautiful place, he does not think he shall like his own so well.

I am very glad to find you in such good heart about your farm notwithstanding all your provocations connected with the building – This fine season must make you all rich however it may tend to lower the prices – Crops of every kind are here abundant; and I believe that there will be very little corn uncut in this neighbourhood at the end of this week. The weather seems so firmly settled that it will serve for your longer harvests I hope – I never remember so fine a summer as we have had – and though the weather has been sufficiently dry to house the crops yet we have had rain enough to keep the pastures green and freshen the woods – so that the country, except for the corn-fields, retains all the verdure of spring. The Lakers* have had a glorious time of it – and for the last month I suppose there has been more travellers than ever were known to be in the same space of time. It has been truly *ridiculous* to see the numbers of Carriages driving along – and Ambleside has been as full of Lodgers as it could hold – even to overflowing. We have had Stuart† and his Bride – they came ten days ago when we were full of company & spent one day with us & then went to Keswick intending to return & take up their abode with us for a week; but upon their coming back they found Letters hurrying him to Town so we only had them for two Evenings. We are all delighted with the bride who is only *18* – tall, well grown – a fine figure with a fine complection & an agreeable face – very lively & perfectly unaffected – They have not yet settled where they will reside – sometimes they talk of Ambleside – and if they do fix upon the Lakes it will be in this neighbourhood which will be very agreeable to us as we like them so much – Cælebs‡ looked mighty brisk and somewhat younger than when I last saw him – but certainly the pair were more like Father & Daughter than Husband & Wife.

Southey set out for London on Wednesday. I hope you will see him – I sent your Message to him by M[rs] C[oleridge?] but I know not

* A comic opera, *The Lakers*, 1798, by [? James Plumptre].

† Daniel Stuart, *q.v.*

‡ Hannah More's *Cœlebs in Search of a Wife*, 1808.

that it would be delivered – but I am sure he will be at Hindwell if he has time.

We are all pretty well – Mary[1] is at times in tolerable spirits i.e. when she is obliged to exert herself – but when she is alone she seems to have gained nothing towards subduing her affliction*; and she is as thin and looks as miserably as ever. William is over head & ears in his verses so what with them, & company, & stamps, he is more busy than agreeable – but we all enjoy our house & the situation – and are as happy as it is permitted to most people to be – And we are all greatly rejoiced to hear such good accounts from you all; and above all that Mary's[2] health is so much improved – I think of you much & often and only grieve that the distance betwixt us is so great – not so much this for my own sake, for the journey to me would be pleasure, but Death has made such a coward of my poor sister that she cannot hear [bear?] the notion of any one of us leaving her for any length of time.†

I know you will be sadly provoked at this scribble – Mary tells me that nobody but she tolerates my penmanship – I did intend writing coperplate when I began but I find that time will not permit – for we have company to tea & there is nobody ready to receive them tho' the time draws on fast. I shall write to Mary[2] as soon as I get to the end of my journey or perhaps before if we are detained longer than I expect – for I have a deal to say to her – Tell Tom[1] that M[r] Cookson will do his best to send him some flies – M[rs] C. said they would put a few, to be doing with, into the Newspaper – and would send more by W. Cookson from whom I suppose, by this, you are to be *favoured* with a visit – So *don't go to bed.* I hope you have got my parcel from M[r] Symonds by this time – I shall send the Sheep Skins to London as soon as Mary's Gloves are made –

Tell them to write to me at Stockton, if they are not too busy, without waiting for my Letter – I am desirous to hear from Joanna that she is got safe home – and it will be a great comfort to me to have frequent Letters from you all when I am there for it is such an age since I was there before that I still feel quite like a Stranger in the Land.

Saturday – The Poney is in the same state – all our Doctoring, for we have had Physician Apothecary & Nurse, has not brought the wound to digest & when we shall get off I know not – My Clothes have been gone a week and it is a most uncomfortable state to remain

* The loss of Catharine and Thomas within six months of each other.

† Mary had been away visiting in Wales when Catharine died; Dorothy was away when Thomas died.

in such uncertainty one cannot enjoy anything. If you have any commissions for me in the Land of Farmers you must write. I can buy horses, hire servants, or aught else you may require . . . I must be forced to direct my Letter to Hindwell for I know not your address – and worthless as the Letter is I had rather it reached you than not – Our best love to all – God bless you! Most truly yours. S. H.

## 20

*Mrs Hutchinson, Hindwell, Radnor*

*The Farm, 29th Sep*[r] *[1813]*

Your letter which I received at Stockton yesterday morning dearest Mary *pricked* my conscience sadly and I provided myself instantly with pens and paper intending to write to you against this days post, but in my hurry I left them behind me and now when they are arrived, I shall be too late. However I hope you have already received my last and are satisfied that I am well and that my silence proceeded from nothing but a state of *indifferentism* which I have caught since I came into this part of the world. I fancy that all people here are affected with it and that it is contagious – but perhaps the cause exists in myself; for living as I do with those who think and feel exactly as I do upon most subjects and are interested by the same things no wonder when I get among another set that I should fancy that they are interested about *nothing* when I find them actually dead to all that concerns me – and therefore all that happens to me here seems of so little worth that I have never had any inclination to write about it. However Joanna as you wish for a novel I must give you the best I can and as an exception to the above remarks, I must say that my visit to Eryholme tho' short was very interesting to me for there – added to a most kind reception, I found every body just the same as I had ever known them and as anxious after the welfare of those I love as ever they were – they talked to me of you all, and heard me talk as if they had forgotten their own concerns in the pleasure of seeing me. Do not suppose that I am really uncomfortable – quite the contrary – for I have great satisfaction in knowing that it is a pleasure to Henry[1] to have me here and our John[1] is as kind and attentive to me as he can be – but he is so involved in his own affairs that he does not seem ever to think of any thing else and what grieves me is that though he is quite well he never appears to enjoy any thing – I never saw him laugh heartily as he used to do except yesterday morning when I told him that Joanna had named your Molly Slingsbys Allemand – and his daughter Bessy is exactly his fellow – She seems as if nothing interested her – She creeps to bed at 9 o'clock and goes frequently to the Methodist Chapel for mere lack of something to do. I never saw a young person with so little life about her in my life. I often compare her with you, Mary[2], at her age and with Mary Addison when she was at Hindwell. Dorothy[2] has the life of 50 such in her. She gets upon horseback & never stirs out of a walk – "It is so *foolish* to see people riding hard – & then it gives her a stitch in her side' – Well but that you must expect when you begin to ride; and if you never go out of a walk it will always be the case – 'Oh but I never shall wish to go out for a walk' – Well thought I, but I held my tongue, it will be lucky for you if everybody that you ride with are as accommodating as your papa and I – and so we spent the whole day from 9 in the morning till 8 at night upon the road betwixt Stockton & Hartlepool except 2 hours which we stayed at the latter place and one at Greatham with Betsy where I had expected to stay at least 3 and after all came home for the best part in the dark and John being blind as a beetle at night I was obliged to be pilot – the consequence of which was that I strained my eyes so with looking that my bad one has been bloodshot & weak ever since – M[rs] J. H. is certainly the life of the House – we are very kind. She always wishes me to stay & presses my return – She conducts herself admirably with respect to the children – and it is to me marvellous that they are so obedient to Bessy – in *all things* they are to obey her – whatever she prohibits cannot be obtained. M[rs] H. never interferes neither with one thing or other respecting them – and I wish I could say that I think Bessy impartial – Anne[1] is the favorite – & poor Mary[8] can never do right – except at her Book & then she is the superior of them all. She is uncommonly clever and if she were in judicious hands might perhaps be cured of her disagreeable ways which are, I suppose, so many that she has no credit given for any other. Charley is a sweet fellow very quick at his book and so full of life & enjoyment that it is delightful to see him – Henry[2] is graver & slow at his book – dislikes school and is fond of the farm and working – he wishes he were Wilson that he might go with the cart – and since the Triton came in he has never been seen in the house except at meal times being busy carrying in hemp. He maunders & talks for ever and comes out with very droll sayings – Little William[3] is exactly like Charles – He is very well but has not got the use of his legs – for both are now affected. Lucy is a Hutchinson – her hair brown & her under Chap comes forward – she has as well as Anne quite the *tach*[*e*]. They are to come from

Hartlepool on Saturday and I have advised John[1] to consult D^r Addie – for it appears to me to be no sprain – the child feels no pain – and if it were weakness it could not have come on so suddenly. I fear it is something of a Paralysiss. I shall go with M^rs H. on Saturday as far as Greatham & stay a few days with Betsy – she came to Stockton last Wednesday and stayed all night. The morning was wet & Henry[1] would not let me go to meet her being certain that she would not come – however I could not be easy so got an early dinner & went off when I found her & got a fine scold – or rather Henry got it for me – She had come on purpose to make purchases upon which she wished for my advice & had wept for mortification at my non-arrival – However we got all completed to her satisfaction; except that M^rs Elstob & I would *only* let her have *5* yds of Flannel for *2* pr of Drawers instead of *8* which she had set down in her list, & insisted upon it that it was the proper quantity. Every time I see M^rs Elstob I am more pleased with her and confident in the propriety of her conduct towards Betsy – She governs her without seeming to do so and Betsy feels as if she were her own Mistress entirely and M^rs Elstob is as respectful towards her as if she were a servant at one time & without losing any of her own importance. She is a very superior woman and [would] do herself credit in any situation. The husband is a worthy creature any body may see the first moment they are in his company.

Miss M[aynard] is an evergreen & jockies about as usual alone on Jenny. M^rs Lambert I am sorry to say looks aged but she did not appear less active than heretofore. David was there; & with him I was quite charmed. He is a nice intelligent unaffected young man in perfect health & spirits; & so like to Henry Addison that though I knew who he was the first moment I saw him and addressed him as David Maynard, yet I had a feeling as if I ought to ask him if he were not Henry A. His features are not the same entirely; but his eyes, mouth, teeth & complexion very like but above all the expression of his Countenance is so like that at times it alters his features till you could fancy they were the very same – and this especially at the corners of his eyes when he smiles it is Henry's very self & M^rs Addison. . . . This puts me in mind of poor Tilbroke who had been at Rydal upon *crutches*. He was thrown out of a Gig in Scotland & though no bones are broke he is lame in his hip – Mary[1] says he is not a bit cast down by his accident but is just the same honest creature whom they like better & better though he continues to comb his hair & dress his nails in company. Blomfield is gone into Russia – He was one of the Candidates along with D. M. for some of the honours. He beat David last year but D. was conqueror this – so we may conclude that D. is an excellent Scholar for Blomfield is an acknowledged one. You must indeed write to the dear Doctor* (Mary[2] *Monkhouse* will find out the connection of my ideas though to others the parts of my Letter may seem to have none) just to thank him for the notice he took of our request, any answer to all his love and affection you are not called upon to give. I hope they have written to you from Rydal for I really have not room to tell you of all their goings on – only I must say that they have been as full of company as ever – Poor Mary[1] says she wishes I were at home again & that they were closed up by snow for till that time they will never be at rest. M[rs] Peake her Mother & two Sisters have been with them & John W. who is returned from Prison. He & his two elder sisters are going to Chester. Dorothy[3] is to spend the winter at Rydal.

I have had a short Letter from the Luffs they are going to be removed from the Isle of France to its neighbour Bourbon, as soon as Luff is able; but he had been confined by the Gout for 6 weeks. 'The Commander in chief (S[r] Al[x] Campbell) has appointed me Head of the paymasters Gen[l] Staff, & also *Chaplain* to his *M[ys] Forces* on that station, & I shall enter on my *clerical* duties early the next month (May). It would not be delicate in me to make any comments on this arrangement; I leave the discussion in excellent hands & I know that you will make the most of it –' This is the only part of the Letter of any general interest – the rest is mere longings to be back again & some hopes that he will be able to accomplish the end for which he left, as he calls it, his blessed little Cottage – He has sent over to Woodriffe [?] 1600 Spanish dollars to pay off some of his old scores; & in a short time he hopes to send enough to pay the whole as his income is now increased by this new arrangement & amounts to 1300£ pr an: so that except for this nasty gout the news is very comfortable. He rejoices in the news from Europe concerning the discomfiture of the Arch-fiend – it has been as the bread of life to him. He sends his love to all of you – and he has 26 sheets of his '*Letters from the Mauritius*' written which I am to have by the next conveyance – I am going to write to them today; for it is shamefully long since I have written – and of the many Letters it does not appear that they have rec[d] more than one of mine. It was said in the newspaper that Lord C. Somerset was going to the Cape – as Governor I suppose – If so I should hope he will find some post for Luff there, which would be a fine thing as it is the most delightful of all our foreign Stations – when I send my Letter I shall perhaps hear from his Ldship if this be true; because it will be necessary to prevent my letters from being forwarded to him in future – and he is exceedingly polite & attentive to their concerns – This reminds me

* Dr. Andrew Bell.

of Horse racing – & I must tell you Tom[1] that yesterday it was said at Stockton that Williami has been a great winner by the success of his Horse or mare that won the St. Leger Stakes*. He had been heard to say that if *it* won he should never want money again as long as he lived. I grieve for the accident which has happened to your Horse. Radnor has the most horrible cough you can imagine – all Horses here have coughs and all the way we came along the complaint was prevailing. Tell *your* Tom[2] (this is now no distinction) T. M. I mean, when you write to him, that when he has opportunity, to get one yd of the Carpet border for that it is now found out is damaged & keep it by him till some convenient opportunity offers of sending it. What a plague he has had – & what a vexation they with those nasty Carriers! – This is Market day. Our Maid is gone to Stockton. Henry[1] has been gathering & shelling Pease & I must go & help him to make the dinner ready. I know not how long I shall stay in this neighbourhood. William & Mary talk of meeting me at Bolton Abbey but I know not how to get thither without taking Henry on purpose – and I dread the notion of going by way of Appleby & Penrith with Jack[1]; for Bessy is to accompany him & we must go in a walk the whole way. Jack wants William to come hither to take a look at Lyric Lodge. I am glad you like your Gowns – they will not be so gay *made up* – do wear them – & they will dye what colour you like when dirty – Joanna! I did not get one single article of dress clothes to come here – & since I came have bought nothing but three cambric muslin Gowns which I wanted sadly. I hope to avoid all visiting (as I profess to be always at the Farm) except just *particulars*. I was at G[eorge][1] H's on Sunday. M^rs^ H. down stairs for the first time. She is very well was glad to see me & entreated me to go often – G. & Henry[1] are very kind and affectionate but they are all very dull because they are all so [*S. H's. blank*]. I am going to Aunt Polly's on Friday – poor Body she is very paralytic. Gordon Tidy is dead – he blessed Aunt P. in his last moments saying she had always been his kindest Friend. T. H. I have never spoken to – his wife & sister called but I shall waive a visit there if possible. M^rs^ Scurfield & her daughter also called – and these are all the visits I hope that I shall be called upon to pay. I went to see M^rs^ Stephenson & drank Tea with her for the sake of Sockburn. She looks younger than either of her elder daughters who are complete old maids in appearance. Rebecca is forgetful [still] but she is in much better health than she used [to be]. Franky Dickson is to be at Stockton on Sunday unluckily [I] shall be at Greatham and as our John[1] says he he is such 'a [*torn*]-minded man' I suppose he will not think it worth

* She wrote 'States'.

while to ride 8 miles to see me. I am vexed about Anne Hutton because I beli[ev]e that she herself is inclined to come & I do not see what need she has to ca[re a]bout 'our folk'.

Dorothy[1] said I was to get her money from Tom[1] for her as she wanted a little private Cash – say what it is & I can get it of John[1] – Mary[2] you must tell me the size of your Table. Miss B[arker] & M[rs] Southey get very handsome Draper Clothes of a man that comes over from Ireland. I could perhaps meet with one or two for you because you know I mean to spin you a fine one which is to be your very best as soon as I get my wheel set up but perhaps this may not be this winter – I cannot expect to buy a damask one here *cheap* – but it will be this good & handsome *answer*. Farewell & may God bless you all and may you dance & enjoy yourselves to your life's end. Your most afft Sister S. H.

We came from Eryholm by way of Sockburne it did not look as it used to do – not absolutely in decay but going fast that way – the trees do not help cover the house many branches must be dead & those left though not absolutely in disorder were not in order. The Greens were knee-deep in rough Grass – There was a stubble in the Gilystone [?] field quite black – all about the farm house looked ruinous – no corn stacks in his stack yard those I suppose are all at the [?] White's House & the wall in decay – Beverley Wood alone and the River was the same – even the fields & hedges looked diserdly [?] I did not long to live there. I thank you dearest Mary[2] for your long Letter. I daresay I have not noticed all that I ought to have done in it – and I know many of you will hold this scrawl; this *is* the last bit.

Perhaps G. may come hither – but no – I guess he will go direct to Brough-hill – else I could have returned with him, rather than with the *reading* Flies.*

* The reference is to a story old in the Hutchinson family, a pun on reading and Reading. Coleridge tells the anecdote in his *Statesman's Manual*, 1816, pp. 46–7; he had jotted down a note of it on his first visit to the Hutchinsons in Oct. 1799.

'But the phrase which occasioned this note [the Reading Public], brings to my mind the mistake of a lethargic Dutch traveller, who returning highly gratified from a showman's caravan, which he had been tempted to enter by the words, The Learned Pig, gilt on the pannels, met another caravan of a similar shape, with The Reading Fly on it, in letters of the same size and splendour. "Why, dis is voonders above voonders!" exclaims the Dutchman, taking his seat as first comer, and soon fatigued by waiting, and by the very hush and intensity of his expectation, gives way to his constitutional somnulence [*sic*], from which he is roused by the supposed showman at Hounslow, with a "In what name, Sir!

As you never gave me any answer about the Castors I suppose they were right. I hope John[2] does not think of sleeping in the new house this winter. He will get his death. Remember me to poor Mrs Urwick, I am very sorry for her. If M^rs L. or Sir H. G. should buy the farm I hope it may be got for George[1].

*Postmark: 'Stockton', 1 Oc, 1813*

*MS note* by Miss Elizabeth Hutchinson: 'John' is *my* GdFather elder Brother (and S.H.'s) 'Bessy' his eldest daughter by 1st wife. 'Mrs. J. H.' is the 2nd wife – the other children are hers.

## 21

*Mrs. Hutchinson, Hindwell, Radnor, South Wales*

*Callendar* Wednesday* [*3 Aug. 1814*]

My dear Mary

I promised to write to you as soon as our departure was fixed, or immediately upon our setting out – and lo! we have travelled 290 miles before my promise is performed. This is however the very first moment of leisure – a wet day is likely to detain us here and if it were not that we fear the weather is completely broken, I should not be sorry for it; as a rest is grateful; & we can come by it in no other way. Till yesterday we have been most lucky – the rain mostly fell at nights or when we were housed – we never were wet but once – & never out in the rain but twice till yesterday, when it came down by wholesale all the way from the Trossachs hither – & a pretty pickle we were in! – Notwithstanding our journey has been delightful – & as fortunate as possible – but I must tell you where we have been &c – after I have enquired after you all; & most especially concerning dearest Joanna, whose uncomfortable situation has often crossed me in the midst of my enjoyment – I cannot tell you where to write to us except to Edinburgh, & there we do not expect to be till three weeks – if the weather permits us to do all we intend – for sometimes we have changed our route & by that means Letters may miss us – but we are *sure* to be at Edin^gh on our way home – so direct to W. W. post office – & don't delay lest the weather should force us homeward.

was your place taken? Are you booked all the way for Reading?" – Now a Reading Public is (to my mind) more marvellous still, and in the third tier of "Voonders above voonders".'

* This letter and the following one, give the only detailed account we have of this Scotch Tour.

It is a fortnight gone Monday since we left home for Keswick (where we stayed all night). Johnny[4] *along* upon black Radnor – & Miss Alms (a Lady from Carlisle who has been staying at Lloyds) with us in the Car*; upon which account we had another horse tandem – The little Lads at Dalston nʳ Carlisle asked Johnny if we were the Mountebanks; and even plain matter-of-fact Johnny said 'yes', enjoying the Joke – Wᵐ we set down as the Dʳ, the postillion as the Merryman, Johnny a little tumbler with his poney for horsemanship feats, and we Ladies for Tamborine players &c – I tell you these particulars because I know they will amuse Tom; but if I were to continue to recount all the *admiration* we have met with I should never have done – my Letter must be mere hints which you may keep to rub up my memory when I come; & then I will give you the whole – But we have been much admired – although our machine, as they call all carriages, is not new to their eyes [?] [*ink faded*] – every one seems to know that it is a jaunting Car – & we saw two at Glasgow – some call it a 'consated Machine' & many other epithets equally droll – I am delighted with the People they are the most polite folk I ever met with – All the Inns have been very comfortable so far; and the *Highlanders* (the farmers I mean for we have not been into any of the cottars habitations) into whose Huts we have occasionally gone, or met with & joined them in our way are quite *Gentlefolk* – Men living in such hovels as you would not think good enough for Cattle you will find far more intelligent & expressing themselves much better than any person you can meet with in England who has not had, as I may say, an *university* Education or one as liberal – and the women living in the same Huts in manners much superior to any farmers wives I ever saw in any rank – though their dress is in many instances a kind of dirty *Ladylike* – in others worse than you can conceive – the common people sail (women I mean) about in a long red cloak with the hood up no bonnet on the hottest days – in Glasgow streets even we met them thus dressed at every step; & that day was a complete West India heat. But to my Itinerary. From Keswick we went to Carlisle by Sebergham where we dined & walked up to Werned Hall – slept at Carlisle where we met first with Mʳ James Losh, & afterwards with A. Harrison; the first drank tea with us & the latter supped at Mʳˢ Pearsons Miss Alms sisters house & where we had dropped her. Next morning we breakfasted at Brampton & while the horses were resting took a post chaise & went to Haworth & Lanacost Priory – at the first place we drank a glass of wine & had *bride* cake with Mʳ Ramstars & his youthful bride

* The same jaunting car Wordsworth and Dorothy Wordsworth and Coleridge had used for their Scotch Tour in Aug. 1803.

D. Maunsly – he being a Distributor of Stamps was very polite to us but we did not claim any acquaintance with the Bride – Returned to Brampton & dined at Longtown – Pressed on 4 miles beyond Langholm to Burnfoot Miss Malcolms where we were to leave our sweet Johnny – our ride from Longtown was beautiful beyond expression – I wished you had farmed there – the Land very rich fine large farms & princely houses – the oats, wheat, barley, beans all of *giant stature*, & not a weed to be seen in any of them – the potatoes & turnips excellent crops & so beautifully clean!! The Esk is a beautiful river – we crossed it five times over stone bridges all handsome, some elegant & one magnificent, the country richly wooded and Langholme lying sweetly at the head of the broad vale – after this the river is closed in by green hills – smooth & high winding away before us without a house or tree to be seen, and then opening into a little level plot with a house which is the farm of Miss Malcolm with the Esk running close by – I should have told you that the Esk constantly reminded me of the Dee – It was 9 o'clock when we arrived – we found a houseful of company from *Enbro'** & I know not where; but we had a truly highland reception – the Miss Malcolms were fit to devour us – there are 4 sisters – so scotch so merry & so noisy!! But I should never be done if I were to go on in this way – Well when introduced to the visitors one proved to be Miss Milward of Porton whom I have seen at Miss Ritson's & two of the others were friends of M^rs^ Spencer & Lady Maxwell, whom Tom knows, & one of these had stayed with Fanny at Stockton & was well acquainted with all our family and friends – these meetings made us think of M^r^ Sharp & repeat his observation 'How we touch!' Next morning we assembled a strong party at breakfast – some to tea some pobs, some *brose* some to boiled milk eggs, ham & all snacks – the forenoon was spent in Miss Mina (Wilhelmina) Malcolm's Museum which is a many chambered cottage in the woods, a beautiful thatched building containing curiosities, most valuable tastefully arranged, from every part of the globe brought by her Brothers & Friends – they have many brothers all of whom have raised & distinguished themselves. Sr. John Malcolm (one of them) in India – Col. Malcolm now likely in America – another an admiral – and one is an eminent scholar & clergyman a friend of Christopher. They were 14 children I believe – all educated at this Burnfoot in the true highland fashion – and the nephews are sent to their Aunts house to be educated in the same fashion; there are 4 at present besides a lad of the parish which they make a companion for the first that come –

* Her italics suggest a possible reference to Coleridge's *Epitaph* of 1803. See *Coleridge's Poetical Works*, II, 970.

the tutor is a clever young man & they teach the Latin most admirably. We hope John may get some good – but all this should have been left hereafter or I shall never leave Burnfoot. This was a wet day but we met one of the sisters going off to Western Hill as she said to fetch Lady Johnson to dinner 'for they always made a point of inviting each other when they had company in this lonely place & Lady J. did not mind the rain' – though it was two miles off Lady J. came & instead of a weatherbeaten highland Dame as I expected she was a beautiful & elegant young woman – courtly in her manners – for her time has been at Court – but with just a delightful portion of scot[t]ish frankness, tempered by English reserve – We had a big dinner – scotch soup – sheeps head singed – besides many other good things spoilt by the cooking – often I was reminded of Pintlaith tho' it was very different the noise was intolerable everybody talked at once, at least all the scotch; & we also were forced to seem to be heard – there was a nice honest sea captain there with his old aunt who we are to go and see at Edinburgh – Well, to proceed at night came the dancing master & all stood up to dance young and old with the Bairns – Lady J as happy as if she were dancing at Carleton house – all but W^m^ & I & the old lady who looked on – Next morning we left Burnfoot promising to stay on our return – & went to Moffat to sleep – this was a dullish ride nothing but moor after we had left the Esk – Next day (Saturday) to Elvanfoot & Douglas Mile – & to Lanark next morning to breakfast – we then went to the 'Established Kirk' & heard a screaming scotch parson you never heard anything like it – The falls of the Clyde are the grand object here; but these could not be seen on a Sunday – it was roasting hot. I slept all the afternoon; W^m^ & Mary were delighted with the sight of all the mill [desporting?] in their gay clothes by the side of the river – the Mills are magnificent buildings & there is no appearance of wretchedness as in other manufacturing places – we saw the falls of the Clyde before breakfast next morning; which, though there was comparatively little water in the river, far exceeded our expectations – set off for Hamilton & saw those little hanging Gardens of Baron Cleugh which D[orothy] describes by the way* – at Hamilton House saw the grand collection of pictures which they were denied in their Tour – then set out for Glasgow seeing Bothwell Castle by the way which D. has described so well that my idea of it was perfect – & we did wish to linger out the evening there – I never was so loath to leave any place – Got to Glasgow in the dusk – walked in the streets in the morning shopping & to see the Cathedral which is the only perfect building of gothic architecture

* *Cf. Dorothy Wordsworth's Journals*, I, 230–1 (2nd ed., 1952).

remaining in Scotland; & a noble specimen it is – stayed 3 nights one at the inn & two at Mr Grahames about a mile from Glasgow. M^r G. is eldest brother of the Poet who is dead – M^rs G. & her daughters were at Bath – but we had a pleasant visit notwithstanding for he is an angel of a Man. I wish you could see him; you could not but love him; his countenance is *really* angelic – & his manners so mild & affectionate – he is quite a perfective person – their carriage being away we hired a *Landeau* & acted the Duchess of Oldenburg through the streets, & to all the *curiosities* – which *are* most curious & of which henceforth. – Thursday went to Dumbarton – and Ardencaple a sweet ride down the Clyde & Firth of Clyde – and the sea Loch Gair, upon which Ardencaple Inn stands – Friday morning crossed the Loch to RoseNeath Castle, the Duke of Argyles, which is a grand building, but not finished; the situation divine on a peninsula – returned to Ardencaple & set out after having breakfasted traveled further up [the] Loch, going to the head, when rain came on & we housed at the toll Bar where *M^rs* Turner received us kindly; and astonished me by the *comforts* of the house – proceeded & were obliged to shelter again at a farm house of stone where we were again well received by a Lady & her daughters, who had come from Dumbarton for a few weeks, her husband the provost – their kindness was extreme – they dried & made us comfortable & whatever the house afforded they would have pressed upon us – we gave them our name & find they had some of them been at Rydal – the Lady and her eldest daughter who was a [*torn*] creature – they were a large family Boys and Girls – this was by the side of Loch Long, which is a most interesting sea loch, & which we did not see to perfection owing to the rain tho' it was greatly accompanied by sailing mists – dined at [?Arraganda] at [? and] proceeded to Luss upon Loch Lomond to sleep – Here we rested all next day visiting the Islands which are enchanting – & upon the deer Island met with a canty highland woman – who would have delighted Joanna – she was all heart – and lived in happy laziness as all the highlanders do – her husband is deer keeper & they have no children, yet they keep a maid who was sitting upon a kind of straw long settle by the fire (I in my simplicity asked her if she was ill 'troth no' was the reply) – & except once I never saw a woman with a bit of work in her hand – & they *can* have nothing else to do for they never clean their houses – From Luss on Sunday morning we went to breakfast at Drymen & attended the kirk where there was an excellent preacher – this was a sweet drive by the side of Loch Lomond and then across an excessive, rich, & well cultivated strata just like English Parks well wooded – and surrounded by all the magnificent hills of scotland – the duke of Montrose's property – from Drymen to Aberfoyle where we spent the night & the next forenoon in viewing Loch Earn & Loch Con above Aberfoyle and then we met with a friendly Highlander who went with us; he lived in an abject house but was a *Gentleman* & his wife a Lady – we passed also another highland farm where the genteel appearance of the Inhabitants surprized us; for you can have no idea of the deep solitude of these places – but they go many miles to kirk – & during the interval of morning & afternoon service those who have not friends near almost all the congregation indeed sit in the church yard – From Aberfoyle we passed a sweet Lake in a vale which hilly scene is called Menteith with 2 islands, upon which are five ruins – & here we saw Stirling Castle at a great distance – the walls brightened by the setting sun – slept at Callendar & went to the Trossachs where we were drenched – and this morning rain abating as I was writing the first pages I left my pen & am now scribbling at Lochearnhead in an inn literally as clean as an private English house need to be – the scotch dont need cleanliness – & this house just seemed as marvellous to me as that Inn at Frodsham after we had been among welch dirt – We had a sweet ride this morning Callendar and the neighbourhood are enchanting; our road was through the Ness of Long high mountains on each side a sweet stream first & then the winding Lake Lubenaig – then strata & sea & now we are at the head of Lochearn. W^m^ & M. are gone to walk to see a waterfall & Castle but it is too far for me – I should have said that in our way from Callendar to the Trossachs we passed Loch Venechar & Loch Achray – the Trossachs were magnificent with mists & flying clouds & even more beautiful than if the day had been finer; it was showery all the time we were at the lake but is come pell-mell when we got to the Highlanders house where our Car was left – We sate by the fire & had some whisky, the first Mary ever tasted; we wished we had eaten our cold chickens & ham by the Lake side – & we were very sorry that we had not remained there all night as there were two clean beds in the *spence* – but the house was *lovely* & the smoke delightful!! the man sate making a rake (for the Hay is not begun) & conversed sensibly upon all subjects – he had an excellent Library in the *spence* – many new books such as Mrs Grant on the Highlands, Scotts poems – and many country histories – besides some old Books of value – a large party of young Gentlemen had stayed there the winter before who had left their carriages & servants at Tarbet & crossed over the mountains from Loch Lomond, to Loch Katrine, as W^m^ & D. did – but we go by the roads in a less ambitious way. After all you will be most happy to hear that we are all well – no accident has befallen either Horse or man (our horse performs admirably) & dearest Mary is much improved by her journey; she truly enjoys herself; & William is happy that the journey has accomplished this his chief aim – If all goes on well we hope to be at Edinburgh as I have said in 3 weeks at most – 10 days more will bring us home. If it is too late for the Welsh Tour I shall be grieved, more for your sake than my own – it shall not however prevent my coming and I will contrive to give as little trouble as possible – but of this hereafter – perhaps I had best try the Coach & leave my poney behind – if we should go to France this will be best – To France D[orothy] is resolved to go – if it be practicable – but this I will tell you about when we meet. Only advise me. I wish that H[enry] A[ddison] would come – because I do not like to make Wm come with me after this long absence from home. Besides they are so unwilling for me to co[me that] obstacles will be thrown in their way. Our Joanna, in every [letter says she does not expect me this winter; so then there [is the good] reason for my staying that 'you see they do not expect you' – However [in spite of] the chapter of possibilities I will come, unless [you] think as they do heer that it is *wiser* to wait till spring.

I finish my Letter at Killin which place we reached last night and a most enchanting place it is upon two beautiful rivers the Dockhart & Lochy both of which are full the former rushing over such a broad bed of rock as I never before beheld & we crossed it at this place last night in the dusk & while upon the bridge it seemed as if the whole world of waters had been let loose for the water gushes were on every side & you might fancy yourself among some of the mighty waters of north America. There is an ancient residence in ruin of the earls of Bredalbane & a burial place with finer & older wood than any I have seen in Scotland & not often surpassed in England. Indeed I must say that Scotland has in this respect far exceeded my expectations – there is less barrenness & more beauty & fertility than I expected and unquestionably the Lakes Mountains & Rivers are upon a much grander scale than [ours]. Farewell I must finish we are to set off & I know not where else we shall get the Letter posted – tomorrow night we hope to be at Cairndon & the next day at Inverary. Heaven bless you all, do not fail to write your true sister & friend S. H.

Heaven bless you all. If Joanna were here she would be vexed to see Land so wasted, farmland unenclosed with only pocket handkerchief pieces cultivated & full grown women herding a cow or two all day long.

*Postmark: Aug 7, 1814, 1/3½*

## 22

*Mrs Hutchinson, Somerset House, Swansea*

*Kelso, 2nd of Sept., Friday* [*1814*]

My dear Sisters

for I suppose you are both together at Aberystweth I must write to express the disappointment which I felt at Edinburgh in not finding a Letter there for me from Mary[2] – if one from Dorothy[1] had not told us that Joanna was better & how you were going on I should have been very uncomfortable at your silence – and I am not so much satisfied with her account as not to be very anxious to hear immediately from one of you – therefore I hope you will not fail to forward a Letter to meet me upon my return to Rydal – I am very glad that the Doctor disordered all poulticing and outward applications – If Joanna's lump had ever been as big as one which Mary Jameson had she would have been miserable it is always as big as a bird's egg ugly and sore upon any cold – yet there is no doubt of it's being a simple glandular swelling which if touched or trifled with would inevitably *come* to *some*thing – this is the opinion of all people concerning these swellings, or enlargements, rather, & I have scarcely conversed with any one upon the subject that has not one – for myself during this tour with turning my neck so much mine has never been at ease & I could have fancied it often much larger than usual – but a days rest has made me forget it again.

We arrived at this place, from Selkirk, this evening or rather to a late dinner – we breakfasted by the way with Mrs Scott then the Poet being from home and went with her to Melrose & lunched with Ld Buchan at Dryburgh Abbey & have had a most delicious ride down the capital Tweed – I know not whether Tom[1] went on so far or not but it is a glorious farming country – Joanna would also have been bewitched with the sight [of] young Farmers who rode from this town today it being market day – this is a truly beautiful country, rather [*word omitted*?] than most part of England – and the situation of the town is very fine – I wish you could see Melrose Abbey – the ornamental part of it is quite wonderful, it really seems a fine & distinct as lace work – & there are numberless windows the tracery of which is quite perfect – though the outside is much more beautifull, the inside does not give you the solemn feeling of Taste but the workmanship is in every part a thousandfold more elegant. You will scold this pen &

I am vexed with it myself – but I have no knife at hand – and I have little time or patience to write at present – We came to Edinburgh on Thursday week, & left it on Tuesday last – our Time was spent very pleasantly there – chiefly at M^rs^ Wilsons – twice we dined with other friends & met all the *wits* who were in town – but unfortunately the Season had driven them all into the country – The weather of late has been most delightful – it is now only that we have summer – many a good drenching, as D. would tell you, we had in the Highlands – but I trust that this fit will last till we reach home which we hope will be on Saturday week – tomorrow we go to Hawick – the next day to Burnfoot where we shall stay a couple of days & take up dear Johnny again. I ought to have told you that yesterday we visited Yarrow & we shall soon have a poem *Yarrow Visited* – but for the rest of our travels I must leave them till we meet or till I have more leisure – we are going to tea & then to Bed – for when travelling *we are* off, or *ready* at least (for the Ostlers are not always so) at 6 o'clock so most gladly do we go to bed by 10 at the very latest. I wrote you, Mary, a very long Letter from Killin in Argyleshire, & in it I begged to hear from you at Edinburgh – I recollected having said direct to W. W. & it came into my head that you might think I meant the initials only to be written & He went to enquire again for a Letter for *W. W.* to his great annoyance however he was very anxious to hear from you himself – & would not let the Letter be lost on that account – If you told D. that her letter was to serve as all she was inexcusable in not telling us as it would have saved us a thousand conjectures. If this weather is general you will be far advanced with the harvest – but I do not expect, Mary, that you will be disposed for a Welsh tour this autumn after having been a month at Aberystwith – Have you heard of Williams poem* yet? doubtless it would be delivered long ago in Budge Row for you. I must conclude this Epistle though it is a wretched piece to send so far – we shall not return by Penrith therefore I cannot see Henry Addison – Did D. tell you she had seen him and Mary[3] with M[rs] Buchanan & the bold Capt & a party at the Lakes. I am glad to find that Joanna has seen George[1] – I began to think he had cut us all – farewell! best very best love to all – you have not told me lately how John[2] is getting on [? among] his Maidens [?Minders] – again I must say God bless you! S. H.

I think it is best after consideration to direct this to Hindwell if you should have left the sea my Letter may be lost (little matter you will say) & if not it will only detain it one day as I hope Thomas will either

* *The Excursion*, published July 1814.

forward it or repeat my earnest request by the next post – kind love to my aunt –

## 23

*Mrs Hutchinson, Hindwell, Radnor*

[*29 June 1815*]

My dear Mary

I was greatly relieved by the arrival of your Letter; I had, in vain, tried to persuade myself that no news was good news. My aunt's attack which was the worst part of your communication I trust will not prove serious and here is weather able almost to revive the dead. In this Town I see fifty '*Dickey*' carts (as M^r^ C[larkson] calls them) in a day, driving about the streets with Gentlemen or Ladies in them – elderly ladies often driving from one door to another – & I always wish my aunt had one – how nicely we could air her out – even Joanna might be her own charioteer! for when you are in them you feel as secure as if you were sitting on a chair, & the creatures are so much broken that they are no trouble in the world – we have two to carry us to M^r^ C's farm one morning – & Mary[1] was so much in love with her ride, that she persuaded W^m^ to consent to purchase an *ass curricle* & drive home in it, & yesterday they actually were upon the point of giving 25£ for a curricle & *pair* – but something *came out* that made it not prudent to venture upon these asses for so long a journey – but yet if we can meet with a *complete apparatus* we are to buy it & send it to Cambridge. W^m^ was induced to consent to it on the score of its being such a comfort to her in going to church & there was no chance of getting an *accomplished* pair in the North – & everybody said that *time only* was necessary to enable them to perform the journey. Well but enough of asses &c. We came hither on the day last specified viz. Monday week, had a pleasant journey *on the Coach* though I was sick, & in despair. We found M^r^ C. and the Men at the door ready to herd us off – & found dear M^rs^ C. well and much stronger & in every way better than when I was last here – though she had had a very severe attack about 6 weeks ago. We have been quiet, & happy, & comfortable as you may guess. Mary is just the same. Mr Buck & his daughter Thisby who is here, looking as if no time had elapsed since I last saw her. I have seen none of the brothers except Wm, & that by chance since I came – they are odd creatures & live so much *to* themselves that they have such a high opinion *of* themselves as to think nobody else worthy of regard. Mary & W^m are this morning set off to Bocking where they will remain till Saturday – thence to Cambridge & home by Coleorton. I have fixed in my own mind to be with you on the twentieth. If you wish me to come before write I entreat you for *my sake* if not for your own – I shall have no comfort in staying if I cannot depend upon this – I shall have no satisfaction in being useful by halves; & any fear of being too late will spoil all my enjoyment.* M^rs Clarkson will not urge me to stay beyond my time she only says she wishes Mary[2] Monkhouse had managed her matters better; she wished I could have come in the autumn, rather than at this time, & stayed the whole winter. They have taken a house & land near Ipswich 25 miles from this place. We shall go over to see it while I stay. I propose leaving this place on any day between the twelfth & fifteenth on which I can hear of a companion. If it should be the *first* day I shall be with you before the twentieth; as a couple of days will do for Hampstead; the day I am in town I shall spend with Miss Lamb and sleep at M^rs Addisons – hoping they will be ready to set off though I have heard nothing further of their intentions; only I am sure that they wanted no inclination, if M^rs A. felt herself equal to the journey, & assured that it was convenient to John[2] to receive them. I grieve to hear of the distress in Kington – and what is worse there is no hope of an end to it for some years. Rents must however be reduced – the Legilsation will do nothing – *can* do nothing at present and individuals must submit to the oppression; for no one can but rejoice at the general effects of it – the ability with which we have resisted the domination of Bonaparte. No Landholder whatever I am sure can resist the entreaties of his tenant – those who cannot pay must give up their farms – and I hope no landlord will be so [*torn*] as wish to be fined but from the produce of his Land – therefore I trust Tom[1] will speak out as well as John[2] – M^r L[ewis] will *expect it* depend upon it – it is but justice to himself & the concern to try at least. Stocks are up again & I shall lose no opportunity of having the money sold out if it is wanted – but John[1] told me that the Deed would not be ready for a year perhaps. W^m's money we suspect – indeed R^d Addison said as much – is already invested in R^d W's Land. But no answer is to be had from him – nor money scarcely – & W^m is as you may guess *when it comes into his head* sadly vexed about it as you may guess. Tom[2] would tell you that W^m came to Town to refuse the Collectorship – Instead of My Lord's keeping it a secret it was known all over the

* She was going to take charge of the household for Mary Hutchinson who was expecting a child.

Town before Wms arrival & he was also informed by those he met in the street of his refusal as soon as given – The papers however were not so ready to proclaim his disinterestedness as they were to publish what they conceived the contrary in his acceptance of the Stamp Office.

What does George[1] say to the news? Does he now believe that Bonaparte is the choice of the people – nobody but the *English* Jacobins believe this – not one in France save the Marshalls & not half of the army ever ventured to say it but there is evidently a strong party *against* the Bourbons – though *by all* the old King is respected though not thought fit to govern. What they will do now God knows! So far W$^{m}$ has been a true prophet & in London his words will now be remembered though not many believed him at the time. If the Marshalls & army, (what is left of it) with the Republicans have the upper hand, it is in vain that Boney is put down – the spirit still remains which has disturbed the peace of Europe – but it is in vain to speculate – let us rejoice that He *is* put down; & that the Army has been beaten & forced to confess it – and above all that the Belgians & Italians have proved to the world that they did not prefer the yoke of the Tyrant to their present Rulers. For him, surely no voice can be raised. Cappel Lofft is so distressed by his downfall [no one] durst even mention the subject yesterday when we dined there – Now I must give up this, & give Joanna an answer to her postscript. The fashion for the hair is to be *stroaked up* very high behind & fastened in plaits & bows at the crown of the head, & these bows attached by flowers – the front dressed full in *careless curls* – or cross parted all the way from the crown curled at the sides & down into the neck – Gowns made *plain* but rather loose – drawings are *out* at the fashionable dress makers though still worn by those who have them – *deep* flounces or none, by the genteelest folk; & the *furbelows* are only seen in the streets; blond is the most fashionable trimming – col$^{d}$ waists are worn – & white ones to col$^{d}$ gowns – & plain muslin waists with sprigged ones; *disebled** gowns may come in places – & silk spencers both in the house & out of doors universal – but in the genteel circles made very plain, only not in the old fashioned way of plainness but *slack* at the back, wide sleeves & if sarsenets, faced with satin or capes – those gymp trimmings are only for the *street folk* – white muslin spencers very much worn. Straw Hats unusual – a plume of feathers standing high or *bobs for ever* – but *this* you will see at Kington – for the Hats are to be seen in all shop windows & those cannot be missed – but I suppose Kington milliners go to the cheapest Houses. Miss Bibb is a far better mantua stitch than Miss F. Green is the prevailing colour – the colour

* A family word, for 'dishabille'?

of the Watch Ribbons – & shoes of all colours, boots legs of one col. & feet of another the *flashyer* seems the better – & in spencers & Gowns the gayest most prevailing – Your yellow is only such as may be seen any day in the streets as a common morning gown – Now I think I have given you enough only I must add that I shall bring my Aunt a real French Cap made from one Mrs C[larkson] bought in Paris – and which kind she has adopted. You shall have one too for a bandling [? farthing]. You do not mention John's[2] Scratch so I trust he is well again. I congratulate you upon your change of Servant; it is no use to lament the plague, now that it is over which you have had. There is no print of Mr Clarkson – but sometime I trust there will – there once was one but a very bad one – Dr B[ell] & he would make an excellent pair – we had the same wish with Thomas.[2] Thom[5] C. is quite a Man. He is at home on account of the fever at Cambridge & does not return till October. Mrs C. says she intends to come & see you some time. . . . Farewell & God bless you all for ever.

I must go to Edward Street & enquire after the spoon & fork – It is very provoking for I congratulated myself with having got *everything*; they got the same quantity of Tapes &c but thread she did not & would like some of yours if you have too much. I would not part with it to her. The tapes &c cost almost nothing. Needles were most extravagant.

For your comfort I must add that Wm does not now advise Tom[1] to continue in Basings any longer than his taste since he has heard from me a part of Toms plan which he was associated with & which he approves mightily – of this when we meet. Only it has nothing to do with his return into Cumbd or any *particular* spot. So don't take the alarm. I will tell you when we meet. The Guineas are condemned and *more* at *Joel Emenuels* – but we have credit there. I have enough to carry me to town (you must send Julia the five £ if necessary, I cannot) & by the time I get there my dividend will be due & I must contrive to get it from Downs else I shall be aground. Joel told us Guineas were high but we *durst* not *sell*. I suppose my aunt has not liked her Toppin. Mine was the same colour & is now far too light I must have a new one. I shall expect another Letter from some of you whilst I am here – but as I have little to say & cannot get franks here dont expect one from me; but conclude that I hold my intentions & as soon as I arrive in Town & have our journey settled I shall write. adieu!

*Postmark: 29 Ju 1815*

## 24

*Thos Monkhouse Esq^re^, A. Harrison's Esq^re^, Penrith*

*Sunday Afternoon* [*15 Oct. 1815*]

My dear Coz.

I was vexed at myself after our parting that I had not begged of you to write to us to tell us how you fared after your journey, and the fatigues of Carlisle, as I feared you might not think this necessary while you had any expectation of seeing our Friends at Watermilloch. I am sorry to tell you that all chance of your meeting them is over – M^r^ Marshall is gone to Buxton with M^r^ Jones – so the visit is deferred till Nov^r^ as they had no relish for encountering the *circle* when it would be composed entirely of the Stuff Damasks – On your account they regret it extremely; but we are not quite without a hope that you will give us a call *in your way* to Stockton – and though a good many miles about, if the weather should prove favorable, you would be amply repaid by travelling through a much pleasanter country – for, except the road from Greta Bridge to Darlington, the direct road is a very dreary one. We have had some delicious days since you left us – it is provoking to think how very unlucky you were with regard to the weather! I did not return from Keswick till Thursday Evening – I found it quite impossible to make Miss B[arker] consent to my going on Tuesday; so I consented to stay till Wednesday; and on that day she contrived that I should miss the Coach. If I had known that the visit to M^r^ M's had been put off I should perhaps have stayed another day for the purpose of going to Penrith with Miss B. – which was a thing she had in her head – and I, having some business there which must be done in a short time, should have been glad to accompany her – and if I had had any chance of seeing you there I believe I should have proposed the journey seriously. I found all well at my return except little D[orothy][2] who has caught cold by attending the conjurer on Monday Evening – but she has thrown it off and is quite well again – If you can continue to come this way you might have a touch of the music meeting & to finish off in style. Miss B. goes with [the] Hardens – and if Dorothy[1] does not go you would be sure of being, through her, introduced to a pleasant party – for she knows all the folk in these parts. *My Lady** and her *respectable* Friend do not go – She & her Brother have

* Lady Fleming.

both been let into the *secret* – the young one took it in high dudgeon that she should have been so duped, and was for breaking off all intercourse immediately – The Old Lady reckoned little of a faux pas *before* marriage which, according to her creed, sets all to rights; and therefore appearances were to be kept up & the Friend dismissed quietly – only they would not appear in public with her – However it is now known in the neighbourhood that she is an exceptionable personage – fifty odd things have come out against her – with the Wiltons she had exposed herself while on their Tour – & drank 17 glasses of wine with the Capt after the other Ladies had retired & then finished with 3/– of Brandy. However My Lady Di finds that she is, or has been, recd among the great; and if all other sins, except *low extraction*, were proved against her it would make, comparatively, little impression with My Lady Di. – Now here is a nice budget of scandal for you – of course it is entre nous – for though we had enough of it by our own fire side we would not spread it farther. The *Rector* is very indignant – we females also – Wm promised he would go in to help Lady F[leming] through – who certainly was in the humour to send her off instantly – but how they will get rid of her we cannot divine, as the straight forward road has not been adopted. If you have any curiosity remaining I shall send you the sequel hereafter.

I had a letter from dear Mary[2] on Friday – they were all well. Maybush [?] very much delighted with the Porth [Pants ?] – and Joanna has captivated the Parson, who was going to escort them to the top of Wimble. She said nothing of Mary's journey so I hope she had performed well, neither did she mention her health therefore I augur well. William[1] talks for ever about your Horse and his horsemanship – I wish you could have stayed longer it seemed as if you were only beginning to be settled amongst us when you went away; and I do believe that the weather will become more settled – I hope it will favour you at the Races. If we do not see you again Mary[1] begs you will tell my Brother John[1] that she received his Letter & the money – & I will thank you also to say that I have recd my Midsummer's Divid from Thos[1] – at a venture 35£ 16/ which was the sum specified by him at Xmas – so I guessed that it was the now same.

Now do let us hear from you – and pray take care of yourself. If it was not too much to require of human virtue I should say do not dance – for I think it must be very bad for your side.

Remember us kindly to the Harrisons – especially to Mrs B. Tell me how you found Julia – God bless you my dear Tom – and may health & every good attend you! Yours very affty S. H.

W^m^ was very sorry that the Letter to Haydon had been forgotten, but we will send it by the first opportunity.

*Postmark: Kendal, Penny Post*

## 25

*Miss J. Hutchinson, Radnor*

*Kendal, Nov^r^ 24th 1815*

My dearest Sisters

If you do not always bear in mind that no news is good news you will have been both anxious about us and angry with me – Your anxiety, if you have had any, is without foundation – but I certainly deserve your anger, if ever laziness did deserve it. I have had two Letters from you since I wrote, I believe there was nothing in either that required an answer, except about the little Darlings *flannels* which the goodwives here say must not be cast *at night* till spring or warm weather – a little Honey, I long to see him!* and we think, Mary[2], that you *ought* to come to shew him off in the Spring. As Joanna intends staying over the Races I should guess she will not leave home till the middle of Summer; therefore there will be warm weather enough, before that time, for Totsy's [Tom[3]] travels. I know the want of cash will be (excuse, I will not say) but the real cause – and truly I fear it is unanswerable. We are all very much concerned when we think of you in connection with your farming concerns – and wish that the Farmers would be a little clamorous for redress – but the Legislature will be very short-sighted if they do not take their interests into consideration; for the consequence will be that all Capitalists will decline the Trade which will fall into the hands of the poor – improvements in agriculture will decline also, & we shall be again obliged to send our money to other countries for corn – this the Manufacturer rejoices in, because then his goods will go in exchange but I believe that other countries will soon manufacture for themselves. It is therefore your *Duty* all of you to besiege your Landlords with complaints, that something may be done next session towards relieving the farmers from Taxes. This is a terrible season for them! and the frost seems set in for a continuance – a thin covering of snow fell last Thursday but one & since that the frost has been intense – it is very pleasant for walking about & now that one is used to the cold it is endurable – but it came so very

* She had superintended his arrival. See Letter 23, p. 81 note.

suddenly that we were all sadly pinched. I came hither last friday – the Watermilloch expedition was deferred till another season, so I immediately resolved upon paying my long-owed visit to Mrs Cookson – I shall probably stay a fortnight longer & then go to Penrith to send off your goods & return home by way of Keswick – If Miss Fletcher is not with Miss B[arker] I shall make some stay with her but if she is I will get off as she will have no want of me & we should not enjoy ourselves with Miss F. *along* who is so deaf that Music is the only way in which you can hold communion with her – so Miss B. & she strum on the harpsichord & sing Duets all day long.

I left them all well at Rydale – Willy in his best fashion & therefore his Father in good Spirit for it would distress you to see how a pale look of that childs has the power to disturb his father – He is far more anxious about him than Mary[1] – he will scarcely suffer the wind of heaven to come near him & he watches him the day through. Johny[4] is greatly improved by his residence with Mr Dawes – grown much sharper & Mr Dawes with whom he is a great favourite says *he will do* in his learning if he is encouraged – I do think he has one of the sweetest dispositions that a human being can have & he will at least be sufficiently beloved if he should excite no other feeling – but I trust he will after all be a respectable scholar. Siss is very much improved also – and is a bonny creature – at night when you do not see the defect of her complection & she is sitting quietly & looking pleased she is quite bewitching. She & John[4] are going to the dancing School at Mrs Lloyds during the holidays. John would not have gone to a public School without being forced against his will – but luckily he has no objection to the Lloyds seeing his clumsy performance as they are only like his own family being so much with them. I think I have not written to you since Mrs Ll[oyd]'s return. She has left her Husband under the care of Doctors & his friends & will I hope stay some few months of the winter at Brathay where she may recover a little from her fatigue & exhaustion. She was in tolerable spirits when I left home – but since that time the accounts of Charles have been very bad & I fear she will sink again. I am very sorry to hear such bad accounts of Mrs Joseph Stephens – remember me kindly to her. I hope dearest Mary[2] that you will take care of yourself & not suckle too long for notwithstanding the fine tales you tell me of your strength it is evident by the falling-off of your hair, & weakness in your eyes it takes great hold of you – this latter being often the effect of it disagreeing with the constitution. I shall send you a pattn Night Cap when I send off the Bed &c & if you want aught else from this country you need but mention it & it shall be done – You often disbelieved me about the cheapness of articles here – for instance we can get handsome cut glass wine glasses at 15/ per doz the common 12/. Tumblers common at 8$^{d}$ & 1/ a piece the best 16$^{d}$ & 19$^{d}$ cut &c – & Scotch carpetting handsome at [*torn*] & mahogany furniture is dog cheap by comparison [*torn*] at Younghusbands till I longed to buy a side board which was sold for 3£ made by Gillow of the very kind which would have suited you but the Carriage is so promiscuous that I feared it might be spoilt or broken. Dont say anything about my going to Penrith if you write thither. I intend to go in the Mail which gets in at 8 in the Morning & shall claim the bed which they offered me at the Capt's but if it be engaged I shall go to M$^{rs}$ Whelpdales. If they are very glad to see me I shall stay a few days because I would not have them suppose that I merely made a convenience when in fact I shall have great pleasure in seeng them – but if the contrary I shall write to Miss Barker to come & fetch me next day which we settled she was to do when she was at Rydale. I have a long list of commissions from Betsy about silk Gowns & Silver spoons – which last articles I believe are at Hindwell or Radnor. I am glad that Mary has spent such a pleasant time among you. She is I am sure as kind natured a creature as ever lived. I hope M$^{r}$ Lewis will reduce George's[1] Rent for it would be a pity to break up the House now when it is so comfortable & you like the situation so much. If you like it I will send you a frame for D$^{r}$ B[ell]'s picture – a Glass you may have at the Glaziers & Humphry can frame it – I am getting ours done along with a print of S$^{r}$ G[eorge Beaumont] & another of my Lady all excellent likenesses which are to grace our dining room the frames are plain gilt & will cost 13/ a piece – if you wish a handsomer you may say so ours will be 1¾ inches broad concave – The old Boy has been in Scotland but he did not return our way at least we guess so though he had intended it. Banford who is his *secretary* was at Ambleside. Quince has gone off to Edinburgh at last with M$^{r}$ Wilson who was in the neighbourhood about a fortnight – we saw him pretty often & W$^{m}$ & M. were all night at Elleray with him – he was tolerably steady though Quince was often tipsey & in one of his fits has lost his gold Watch val: 60 Gs which was given to him (being his Uncles) as being according to his own [words] '*the very properest person*' to take care o[f i]t. We believe that he will marry Peggy S[impson] after all – He doses himself with Opium & drinks like a f[ish] – and tries in all other things to be as great a [*torn*] legs as M$^{r}$ Wilson. M$^{rs}$ C[ookson] begs her love.

Do not follow my example but write soon. I hope my Aunt bears this severe weather well. Remember me to the Bairns – but tell Nanny I fear I shall not have a *place* for her. Farewell ever yours S. H.

Henry[1] is very well – He talks of buying a Cottage & garden which is to be sold near Hawkshead. But he has no idea of having Betsy – [*torn*] he will not buy this cottage it has no land & he would have nothing to do – he ought to have a cow & pig – if he does set up for himself – but [*torn*] had much better if he is determined upon it be nearer to us – & I want him to have Quinceys if Q. leaves it which I think he must do if he marries – He has been enquiring after Tail End which is to let.

Tomorrow is Joannas Birth Day. Heaven send her many returns of it & happy ones.

## 26

*Thos Monkhouse Esqre, Budge Row, London*

*Kendal, Novr 24* [*1815*]

My dear Tom

I know not whether you expected me to acknowledge the receipt of your last but I have felt as if I ought to have done it before now, though I have little to say that can be worth postage – for I trust it is needless for me to assure you that we remember your visit to Rydall with as much pleasure as you can do; and hope that when it is repeated you will be at liberty to make the next longer, and that you will be more favoured by the weather – We rejoiced in the fine week after you left us for your sake – and William was much gratified by the attention which *my Lord* had shewn you, as a favor done to himself, and an evidence of my Lord's *discernment* of *your merits* – for you know you are quite a child of his own – he is determined that nothing shall be wanting, on his part, to persuade people that you really are all that he predicted you would be – We often laugh at him when he is *puffing you* off, as we call it, telling him to beware & not, like Lady B[eaumont] with his poems, cram you down everybodys throat – and overshoot his mark as she does.

I left Rydall on this day last week – the visit to Watermilloch was put off till another season, so I, finding myself at liberty, resolved to pay off an old score here which has been due for some years. I shall return by Penrith and Keswick, having at the former place some business to transact for my Aunt among her goods and chattles there – therefore if you have commissions which I can execute for you there I shall be glad to be useful, and a Letter will find me here during the next fortnight.

. . . I am glad to tell you that our Johnny[4] is greatly improved by his residence with M[r] Dawes with whom he is a great favourite. He says that he will do well, if he is encouraged, but his shyness & the very humble opinion which he has of himself are his greatest enemies – one thing is certain that, let him go where he will, he will be beloved; for never human being had a sweeter nature and more honorable feelings than he. The other children are both well – & D[ora] much improved in *beauty* at least. Dear Mary[2] tells me that the young squire at Hindwell *disimproves* in this respect; but he waxes in health & strength. I want sadly to persuade her to bring him to see us in the Spring; but, as Joanna has a scheme of spending the summer amongst us I fear it cannot be accomplished. We are very anxious concerning their farming affairs – which will become very serious if Parliament does not lessen the burthens upon occupiers of land – and very short-sighted it will be if this is not done – for Capitalists will retire from the Trade – improvements decline – & we shall be again obliged to send out money for corn – the manufactories rejoice in this prospect – goods they say will be sent out in exchange – but, depend upon it, other countries will manufacture as well as we; if there is peace what else can they do? and we know that they can do it much cheaper.

M[r] Blakeney wants to sell his place sadly; but nobody bids him more than £1500. I wish you could have it for that – but I could not in my conscience wish you to purchase in our country if I thought it would prevent your settling near John[2] & Mary[2] knowing that to them it would be such a comfort – therefore I hope you will be rich enough to have *wings* which may enable you to give them a good share of your society, & yet not exclude yourself from all other. Miss Barker came to stay with us after the music meeting – besides we had much other occasional company; so that for the last 6 weeks we have been almost as gay as if it had been summer. The Old Lady from the Hill* was dispatched at last; but would not move without being plainly told that her company was not desired, and a sum of money given to pay her expences home – this last was but justice – & a proper penalty for My Lady who had given her such a pressing invitation which she had accepted under the idea of being provided for, for the winter at least. . . Tell M[rs] R[awson] that I do not forget my promise – and I hope also to have another campaign in Town before I am too old to enjoy it. Southey is returned from the Continent greatly delighted with his tour – they are at present in, or about, London but are expected at home in a fortnight. I hope I shall be at Keswick in time to hear of their adventures in their first freshness. We are to have another Waterloo

* A guest of Lady Fleming.

Poem* – I hope it will be better than Scott's, which I hear is despicable but for my part I cannot see much poetry in a battle field. You would be grieved to hear of the death of Priscilla Wordsworth whom you saw apparently flourishing in health & spirits in Ed. Street. Her Husband bears up under his loss like a true Christian as he is. God bless you my dear Coz. I have said nothing concerning your own health – but you must not fail to say how you are going on. Farewell – my fingers are so cold that I scarcely hold my pen. I have been writing to Mary H. & am tired – so good bye & God bless you. Truly yours. S. H.

*Postmark: Kendal*

## 27

*Thos Monkhouse Esq$^{re}$, Budge Row, London*

*Sunday, 14th July, very rainy* [*1816*]

My dear Tom

A wet Sunday is an excellent day with me for paying off my old scores to my correspondents – but a wet Sunday is also an affliction to us now-a-days; for since we have had such a good Parson we are led to Church as well by pleasure as duty – when we are left again, as I fear we shall be to his Father's care, perhaps we may sometimes be so graceless as to rejoice in the rain which shall absolve us of our duty. Our Rector's Son is Curate at present, and is a most admirable preacher – he has been educated at Oxford, and is not likely to be contented to remain here – at least if he is wise, and follows his own inclinations, he will not.

I received your Letter duly by M$^{r}$ Cookson; and you will hardly believe me when I tell you that I wished *nothing so much* as to be able to join you in your tour – and I turn it over and over in my mind in the hopes of finding out some possible method of accomplishing it – but all in vain! I had had a Letter from Mary[2] H. a few days before, in which she begged I would write & try to *persuade* you from it – She says that you made such a short visit to them last year, that you ought not to cheat them so again – Now I do wish that you would gratify *her* this year, and *me* the next; for if 'I live, and flourish, & keep *unmarried*,' as the saying goes (part of which I hope, & the rest am sure of) *I will* accompany you – meet you on the borders of Wales – and

* *Occasioned by the Battle of Waterloo*, Poems Dedicated to National Independence and Liberty, XLI, XLIII, Feb. 1816. *Wordsworth's Poetical Works*, III, 149, 150.

be dropped at Hindwell according to your own plan – for *entre nous* it is not likely that M. can be your companion next summer, any more than this. However if you have already met with one, this proposal is useless – but if that is not the case, and you are disinclined to go alone, you may gratify us both without much self-denial. Your Friend William says 'He is quite in the right of it; one may see enough of one's friends in a day or two'. But Mary says that there is plenty of beautiful Country, in their neighbourhood, also which you have not seen; & till that is done why go into North Wales? Now, in spite of your own declaration, that you will not if possible abandon your own plan, I hope you will adopt mine, and satisfy all the Parties concerned.

William[1] and Mary[1] are at present at Stockton – She went a month ago with my Brother John[1] who came hither with one of his Boys, whom he left, and M. returned on the Poney which brought him. William set off on Horseback accompanied by little Henry[2] upon Radnor last Monday & he and M. are to return by Studley, Hackfal, Bolton Priory, the Caves &c in Yorkshire. Mary performed her journey so well, that we hope this little tour will be of service to her health – and indeed to William too – in as much as it will divert his mind, which has been lately much harrassed by his Brother's affairs; unused as he is to business of any kind a trust which will be executed with so much difficulty was most unfit for him – and I greatly fear it will be long before the Ex^rs will see their way clearly through it. We saw in yesterdays Kendal *Chronicle* a notice of a death which alarmed us very much 'M^rs Addison wife of M^r A. Solicitor in London on the 8 inst.' If it had been in any but the Kendal paper we should not have noticed it – but *there*, if it had not been interesting to the neighbourhood, it was not likely to have found it's way so speedily, if at all. I hope before this reaches you we shall hear that it is not Richard's Wife.

Death has made great havoc in this neighbourhood lately. – The head of one of our great Houses was carried to his grave yesterday – The B^p of Landaff who was buried at Bowness – and the same evening brought the remains of poor Lady Diana to the Hall, where she lies till tomorrow, when she will be placed in the same grave with her Husband; a situation which in her life time, I guess, she would have shuddered to think of; and if she had chosen would rather have been lain by her father to whom she was most tenderly attached – However as she made no choice – for she never talked of death – it was most natural for her daughter to bring her home – & She poor woman, has followed the Herse for the long fortnight which it has been upon the road. Willy[2] and Dorothy[2] went down the hill to a neighbour's house to see the *show* – for such we expected it would be to them – and poor things! they came home almost broken-hearted – we could not pacify them – the doleful procession, & the recollection of the old Lady, who was always kind to them, quite overcame them. Willy's great distress was that she had bid him come to see her before she went away, '& I *never* did!' Poor Lady F[leming] has lost her *only* Friend – the Poor a most benevolent one – and we, and the country round, an excellent neighbour – You say very truly that she is the greater loss. Rydal Hall will be a stupid place now – and the Bps. family will not remain at Calgarth – so we shall have little left but *Irish*, and broken-down Tradesfolk. Of the former we have swarms at present, but we keep aloof from them – indeed the neighbourhood is so crammed with new settlers and summer lodgers, that we scarcely meet a '*kent* face'. Among the rest we have *14* Cantabs, who are to be scattered about Ambleside and Bowness for three months – Some have been introduced, & I suppose most of them will find means to get a sight of the Poet before the summer is past. Our friend Tillbroke will add to the number of the Cantabs in a day or two – but his lodgings are at the foot of the hill, under the same roof as Miss Green's house – he is going to *edify* the Ivy Cottage, and next summer, when you come, I hope we shall have the pleasure of introducing you to a seat with him upon his stone bench at the door; where he hopes to enjoy himself in chatting to all wayfarers, as is his custom. We expect to have a treasure of a neighbour in him; for he is an honest, worthy, preacher and free from all affectation, and overflowing with the milk of human kindness.

William and I spent three days, the week before last, with M^r^ Marshall at Scale Hill, Lowess Water, Buttermere, & Crum[m]ock, viewing his estates and manor there, and planning his proposed plantations and Improvements. He is going to plant very largely by the side of the two last lakes – and, as he will only plant native wood, and in no wise sacrifice beauty to convenience, we expect that his labours will not only be profitable but ornamental. If you have any longing for a Lodge, or Retreat, in this Country there is no doubt but you may be gratified at little cost; for many old proprietors have dropped off, and no new ones are *rich* enough to purchase – But we are happily situated here in the main; for we see nothing of the distresses so prevalent in the Island; except in the encreased number of travelling beggars, there is nothing like *poverty* among us – and very little or no complaining – only just as much as serves to keep our faculties awake – now when we have not Bonaparte and the War to talk about. Would to heaven it were the case all over the Island! In Wales they have ceased to write about the badness of the times, and in spite of them seem to enjoy themselves. For my part I should be glad to hear that all the Farms were given up, for it seems impossible that they should ever be able to pay their rents, much less to redeem the capital which has been expended in improvements. Poor Mary[2], what a joy it will be to her to see Joe! When do you expect him? I hope we shall see him, as I understand John[2] calculates upon a journey into the North with him. I wish we were sure that his affairs were more prosperous than those of his European Friends. Mary W. tells us that they were thrown into a bit of *quandary*, at the Tees Bank by the stoppage of the New-castle, Sunderland, & Huddersfield Banks; but they had no fears for themselves – only that there is an entire want of confidence in the country notes there – Here we go on blindly – take Scotch notes of all sizes, shapes, & figures – and all that comes – but though we swal-low a camel, strain at a gnat, for the Country folk are as afraid of a *plain* shilling as if it would ruin them! I hope, and trust, that you will suffer no serious injury till the end of your term – and then that you may attain, and enjoy, that leisure & exemption from anxiety, which you have so long sighed for.

God bless you! Dorothy sends her kind remembrances – I have almost got to the end of my paper *in a legible* hand!! and you may thank my pen for this, which is made from the quill of one of the Hindwell swans, and which is so stiff and awkward to hold that I am perforce constrained to a slow pace – I had hoped that some of these swans gracefulness might be in the quill – and that it would impart it either to my hand or style – to the first it has completely failed for my wrist aches past endurance; of the other I leave you to judge – Again God bless you. Tea is ready, & a good fire. Adieu! very truly your's S. H.

I finished my Letter à la *our Betsy* went in to tea & found that our Post Man was gone without enquiring for Letters as I had given him one to carry in the morning – not giving myself credit for sufficient virtue to enable me to perform in this way *twice* a day – but my Letter will keep till Wednesday – that *it is written* is a comfort – I have in-*tend*ed to write John[2] ever since last Sep$^{r}$ and have not yet done it!! I used to have no objection to Letter writing; but now I cannot endure it – though my pleasure in receiving Letters is as great as ever – so mind write soon.

*Postmark: Kendal Penny Post, 17 Jy 1816*

# 28

*Mr Monkhouse, Budge Row, London*

*Nov^r 1st [1816]*

My dear Tom

We have often thought of you and the fair Widow & have wondered that neither of you should have written to tell us how you had sped upon your journey; for to her it was a serious undertaking – I should have written to scold her long ago, for *she* can have little else to do but write, but I did not think that a scold was worth paying for. If you should see her soon tell her this, & that I will not excuse her from writing to me. We are all very well. Miss W. is still at Halifax, but William is returned from his Whitehaven visit – at which place he saw Blakeney who is well disposed to be rid of his Cottage & land here – & said, *voluntarily*, that he would take 1600£ for it – therefore I think one may fairly conclude that it may be had for a reasonable price – and I hope you will *turn the matter* over in your mind in spite of William's *lukewarmness*.

I have been looking for Joe all this week – the Races are over I presume – and if he is to sail about the 10th inst: he ought to be making his appearance here on his way to Liverpool; more especially if he gives them a pop at Hindwell as he hoped to be enabled to do. It is an age since I have heard from Hindwell, for they are almost as idle correspondents as I am! – but their last gave me some hope of seeing John if he came to meet Joe at Liverpool. I have not yet given up all thoughts of travelling Southward – but it will entirely depend upon my meeting with an agreeable companion, as I am not disposed to trust my precious self alone upon such a journey.

I know not that we have any news in *this* part that can amuse you – the Country is thinned, almost deserted, by the Strangers – and we are settling into our old quiet winter habits – The Beaumonts left us on Monday for Coleorton. Lady B. has been laid up by a sprained ancle. Sir G. was as nice and lively as ever – and said that this *was* the nicest place in the World – As you also said, after all the glories of North Wales – *therefore* if you do not snatch the opportunity, which is offered, of having a hold in this neighbourhood I shall say that when you are absent you have no love for it. You know how well Mary & I have promised to manage matters for you; & there is no doubt that the house will let *better than ever*, since the rage for continental residencies is so much abated, & retirement is become so necessary from the embarrassed state of every bodys affairs. This brings me again to our Hindwell friends for whom I am indeed seriously alarmed – I hear of no reduction in *their* rent, although Mr L[ewis] has reduced George's[1] considerably – & the late rise in the price of grain is the most undesirable thing possible, in the present distressed state of the labouring poor, which makes them too readily listen to the advice which is so industriously disseminated among them by the dissatisfied & discontented – We are happy & quiet here thank God! And I trust they will continue the same at Hindwell, where the population is like our's, purely agricultural – which though not less aggrieved is yet in general more peaceably disposed than the manufacturing.

Give my love to Mrs R. and tell her that wherever they may fix their abode to take care to be out of the reach of manufactures – though there may be less wealth, there is more quiet & security among the simple tillers of the earth. Don't forget to remember me to the whole family at Hampstead.

William had a letter from Longman the other day in answer to his enquiries respecting the Goldfinch Books* which were charged in his account wherein he says, as you did, that upon enquiring of the Publisher the books were sent to you at Hampstead – but that they were not recd at his Shop – Now we think that it is very unlikely that Longmans People would pay the money except upon delivery of the Books, & Wm has told them so – suggesting that the parcel may be still lying at their shop – However if you can, without much trouble, enquire at the Publishers & inform Longmans of the result W. will thank you – but I think it is very unlikely that they will remember anything of the transaction if (as we suppose) you said that you retd them by the bearer but if sent by a Porter of your own the matter will easily be rectified.

Wm & M. both send their love and best wishes to you ... God bless you! & believe me very affty your's S. H.

*Postmark: Kendal, Penny Post, 4 No. 1816*

* A series of little books of words for popular songs was published under the title of *The Goldfinch* in many editions from 1748–1806.

## 29

*Mr Monkhouse, Budge Row, London*

*Keswick, 5th Jan$^{y}$. 1817*

My dear Coz.

In the first place let me say that I hope *you* have had a merry Christmas, and that *I* wish you a happy new Year – then I must thank you for your last Letter, which I should have done long ago but I had nothing to say that was worth writing – the weather is so intolerable that it puts out of tune – and talking or writing one can do little else but complain. Southey says that the last winter only ended when this began – and in truth it has been so, at Keswick at least; for they say it has been little better (than what I have been favored with here for the last three weeks) for many months – which has been a succession of rain, wind & snow – I could not live at this place for worlds – notwithstanding it is one of the pleasantest *in doors* residences in the Island; for we have good apartments, good fires, plenty of nice books, music, painting, and excellent company with now & then a pool at Quadrille – Yet one '*would*' die for want of exercise – it is impossible to stir to the door without danger of being blown away – except one day in which I took a walk with M$^{r}$ S. there has not been two hours sunshine in succession – and on Xmas day as we came from Church I expected my Cloathes to be torn off by the wind. I trust you fare better – M$^{rs}$ Clarkson says 'I hope we shall have a mild winter' – Now this augurs well for you Southerns, if she has not gone to sleep in the autumn and awoke during some chance gleam of sunshine.

I have been here, as *aforesaid*, three weeks; and shall probably remain a fortnight longer – therefore before my departure, I hope to hear that you are, *comfortably*, at least, lodged in your new habitation – so *happily*, as you have hitherto been, cannot be expected until you have a home of your own, and some loving countenance, or countenances, of your own about you; for as to your talk of remaining a batchelor 'tis all nonsense – though a *batchelor's* state is best in London; but when you retire into the country upon your fortune we must have you tossed up into a more social Being. Give my kindest love to M$^{rs}$ R. and my best wishes that she may meet with a retirement to her heart's content – and tell her that I bear in mind my promise of visiting her which I shall most surely perform if life and health be granted me, in whatever part of the Island she take up her abode – my love also to all the rest of the Family. Mary Wordsworth is sadly afraid that her Cousin James has forgotten the Indian Matts. Perhaps if they go to reside in Devonshire you and I, the next time we meet in Wales, may beat up their quarters together; for Sister Ma[ry][2] will now be tied to home, and there is no chance of any fema[le] equestrian companion but me.

They were all well at Rydal on friday – on which day the last Bulletin was issued – but poor William[1] was forced to set off with his 'chancellor', as Southey calls him, to Kirkby Stephen to lay violent hands upon the effects of one of his *Subs* – a task which will be very disagreeable to him – and Mary[1] says she is half afraid to be left in such a weak house – however, in spite of the bad times, I believe we have nought but honest people about us and I trust she is in no danger. Miss Wordsworth is still at Halifax – and will not be home for a fortnight to come. I came hither intending to stay till her return, which was then expected in ten days – but if she prolongs her stay till midsummer my Hostess vows I shall do the same – and indeed no force has hitherto kept me; for it is impossible not to spend ones time agreeably here, for Miss B., if one had no other, is excellent company – then we have variety enough from the next house – and those sweet little Girls whom I do not love much less than I do our own, for their own sakes, are a constant amusement and delight to us. M[r] Southey is well & in tolerable spirit – but poor M[rs] S. is much more melancholy than she was in the summer, when the society of indifferent Persons forced her to exertion – whereas the sight of me only brings to her recollection the last days of her poor lost Darling.*

No Parcel which Southey has lately rec[d] has contained the 'wanderings of a Goldfinch' from Longman's – however as it is not lost we shall get it some time – William will I believe be in Town in the Spring – Southey goes in March – so they will probably travel together. S. is writing a political work at present.† William is doing nothing – except when he is obliged to bother himself with the affairs of his Trust which are twice as much *work* for him as any one else. He wishes Mary very much to accompany him to London – and I should suppose either she or Dorothy will; as he does not like to stir without one of Females.

Miss Barker is very busy painting (in oils) and some sweet Pictures she has made – the artists are quite astonished with them for she has not practised for 5 years – Southey has had a M[r] Nash staying with him all the summer – the same who sketched the engravings in his 'Pilgrimage'‡ – He is a miniature painter, and has made some beautiful

* Herbert Southey died, at the age of nine, 17 Apr. 1816. Sara Hutchinson stayed to relieve Mrs. Southey during his five weeks' illness.

† *A Letter to William Smith, Esq., M.P.*, 1817.

‡ *The Poet's Pilgrimage to Waterloo*, 1816.

pictures of the five little Girls which are here – and one also of Sara & Edith which I have not seen, but which will appear in the next Exhibition – of water colours – I suppose as they are done in that material.

Your Friend Willy[2] is become quite a man – dressed in man's attire he goes to M[r] Dawe's school every day upon an Ass – and a very great personage he is I assure you. I have no other Rydal news – and of the Hindwell you are better informed than I – then from the Addisons or M[rs] Ellwood you may *have* all the secrets, and scandal too perhaps, of Penrith. . . .

I have often thought of poor Joe during our storms. Heaven grant that he may have a more prosperous voyage than the last – He managed ill to leave his heart behind him – however I trust he will have no need of it upon the Sea. God bless you, my dear Friend, and may he send you all good Things! – Most affty your's S. H. . . .

*Postmark: Keswick, 8 Ja 1817*

## 30

*Mr Monkhouse, Stow, n[r] Hay, Brecon*

*Keswick, 7th Feb[y] 1817*

My dear John

I rejoice with, and congratulate, you upon the safety of our dear Sister & the birth of our little niece – May God almighty bless them both & continue to them his goodness and protection! I have not written to Hindwell, as in these hard times I bear in mind William's[1] reprobation of 'an accumulation of useless letters', & therefore *restrain my transports* knowing that there will be no doubt concerning this subject, tho' I may not express them. I wish that Tom may put his plan in execution of coming to show off his '*nonpareils*' in the North – We are all disposed to give them their due. When I rec[d] the Letter I sent Edith to tell her Aunt Coleridge the news that M[rs] T. H. had got a daughter 'a *great beauty*, very like *me*'. She halted with the door in her hand as I gave *this part* of the message – & Miss B[arker] added 'you may go, it is quite true' – & off she went & returned with this *compliment* which I must repeat 'that they hoped it would always continue like me in every thing'.

I am very obliged to you for your nice long Letter which I should have acknowledged long ago had I not been very busy – a more industrious creature than I have been, since I came hither, you cannot imagine – writing all the morning – reading in the evening & sometimes playing *a pool at quadrille* – in short, not a moment to call my own, for there are 50 books here which I want to read, and quires to be written – which I would gladly do, if the time would serve. Southey is going to write a History of the War*; & he has got all Lord Wellesley's papers respecting Spanish & Portuguese affairs and I have been assisting to transcribe them, which has been a most delightful employment; as nothing could be more interesting than the whole, & many very entertaining also – especially the Letters of the Officers, and the Memorandum Books & journals of the secretaries – We have had the secret history of all these affairs. L$^{d}$ Wellingtons private opinions upon the Ministers, his officers, the Spanish and portuguese Gov$^{ts}$ & policy, &c &c and it has given us not only a greater general but even a personal interest in the war. I have become every day more & more attached to my occupation, & this has made me prolong my stay here with great pleasure in addition to that which I felt in complying with Miss Barker's entreaties – for Southey has so much work and is so industrious that it is a good work to assist him. I hope you have seen his last article in the Quarterly.† I forget the Title of the Books *meant to be reviewed*, which are however never noticed but in the Title – but is something about 'the working classes' – the State of the Country & review of the War is the subject of his Article (the Review of Ali Pasha is also his) – there is to be another article in the next on the same subject – and then the whole to be incorporated into a Book on the State of the Times. We have a rumour today of sad doings in London upon the opening of Parliament – but the Newspaper failed and we are in the dark.

I am glad to find that you are in better heart with your farming concerns – and tho' M$^{r}$ Lewis has not been very generous to Tom[1] yet it is better than nothing. If you were not absolutely losing money I should be contented, for this is even more than is I suppose done in any trade at present. Poor William has had a disagreeable job at Kirkby

* Southey's *History of the Peninsular War* (1822, 1827, 1832, 3 vols.). Sara's letter contradicts the statement that Southey did not see Wellington's private papers (*cf.* Jack Simmons, *Southey*, 1945, p. 175).

† The article may be Article XI, a review of various books and articles on social questions under the heading 'Parliamentary Reform', *Quarterly Review*, Oct. 1816, vol. XVI, 225–78, the article to follow being 'The Rise of Popular Disaffections', in the January number, 1817 (XVI, 511–52). '*The Review of Ali Pasha*' is I think an error; there is no such review in vol. XVI. There is in vol. XV, for July 1816, a review of *Travels of Ali Bey*, etc., which might be Southey's (pp. 299–345).

Lonsdale – Nothing less than to sell up one of his *Subs*, and the business has worried him even more than altering & mending his verses.

I hope you are not set off to London – this fine weather will detain you at home I think or make you very fidgetty if you are there as it promises to be an admirable *skidness* – we have had most delicious weather lately and if winter does not return upon us in the spring no reason to complain of what is past. Mrs Clarkson is the only person however who seems to hold any constant hope respecting agricultural matters – but I suppose that their farm is so very cheap that it is impossible to do ill upon it – and she seems to extend her hopes to her Sisters farm also who with her husband have lately been settled upon one in the neighbourhood of Bury greatly to their satisfaction. By the bye tell Mary[2] that Mrs Corsbie is at last in the family way to the great joy of her friends.

If this fine weather continues we shall be daily expecting Bessy Hutchinson, as she is to return to Stockton in March with George[2] who was to leave Grasmere in that month his Tutor intending to go at that time to Oxford – however the poor Man has had another violent attack of his old complaint, in the chest, and if he gets better will be unfit for much labour of any kind – this has been a great sorrow to us, for he is a most exemplary young man and one to whom we are all most affectionately attached. If it should please God to restore him so as to enable him to take upon himself his duties at Oxford you will find him very kindly disposed to shew you all any civility he can whenever you go thro' Oxford – this I tell you having felt myself so much disappointment when I passed through at having nobody there (it being Vacation) who could shew me the Lions – Hartley Coleridge you will at any rate find at Merton Col: who will be better than nothing but if William Jackson should be there let Hartley introduce you to him & by making yourself known to him he will do all you require. He is of Queen's – but I fear he will not be able to return. When you go to town or rather return from, it will be a *shame* if you do not stay a day to see the place. I must not forget now when I am travelling to tell Joanna for her comfort that the coach between Liverpool and Kendal is only 7/– the fare – so if they do not get to the right coach they must seek it out.

I do not know whether your Friend Dorothy[2] is returned or not – she was to be at Kendal on Tuesday last, but as she purposed staying a few days with Mrs Cookson I suppose she is scarcely yet arrived at Rydal. I know not whether I told them at Hindwell that Mrs Cookson had got another son – having now half a score of bairns. We expect Mr Owen of Lanark here every day – He wants sadly to engage Southey

& Wm enter into his feelings & schemes – but William has very little sympathy with him on this score & S. not much more I dare say. He has I have no doubt done wonders at Lanark but if his scheme was acted upon it would tend to the subversion of all religion & existing Governments – which they are not convinced that the perfection of the 'human character' could dispense with. He is a good Man & a great enthusiast but must be a little *cracky*. Miss B. has a brother with him at Lanark – who superintends his land & agricultural labourers. He was originally an Iron Master but failed during the great depression of that Trade. He is delighted with every thing at Lanark and enchanted with Mr Owen's philanthropy.

I am provoked to find that your little Landlord turns out so stingy – however he is not so bad as Tom's[1] – though one is vexed because one expected that more might be made of him. I am glad that you keep upon Terms, for it is a sad annoyance to have a hostile Landlord near one and not to have had the pleasure of a little chat with his pretty wife now and then would be a sad privation to a plain batchelor who had been used to it. My next Letter must be to your Tom who complains bitterly of his lonely state – it is no charity to write to Hindwell where they have so much for hope '& forwardlooking thoughts', it is only we who live in singleness that require such aids to give zest to life. But I am become a wretched correspondent – every body complains of me – if I have nothing in the shape of duty or business to stir me I am too idle to write. Miss Barker has set on to build in Borrowdale and thus given herself cares enow – more I fear than she looked for; for like all builders she finds the expence greatly exceeds the estimate, and like many her means not commensurate to her ends. The situation of her house is very delightful but her plan is too large for the situation; & I should not have liked to have been the first to break into the sacred retirement of that vale – however time will, as in other places, repair the injury she has done & I hope time also will bring her satisfaction in her work & relieve her from the difficulties in which it has involved her. I hope when you come into this country that we shall spend a pleasant day or two there for she is hospitality itself – and in her house I can make quite as free as if it were my own – She is as good and noble minded a woman as ever breathed. Tell Joanna that she is very happy to hear of her intended journey – and hopes that it will not fail. I was sorry for your disappointment in not seeing the *Poetess* & her beautiful sister – but Mrs King I should suppose will return to Lion's hall* and then you may go to pay your respects. I have no *news* for you. I know nothing about the Penrith Folk – and

* At Kington, Herefordshire.

I fear you will find tis a dull letter which I must close, as I am under promise to the two Girls, Edith & Sara[3], to go with them upon Castlet to gather moss to make baskets – they persuade me out of my senses sometimes, they are so pretty, so good, & so agreeable that they can make what they will of me. Farewell & may God bless you! Most affty your's S. Hutchinson.

*Postmark: Keswick*

## 31

*Mr Monkhouse, Budge Row, London*

*Rydal Mount, Feb^y 17th 1817*

My dear Tom

I am afraid you will think me very unkind not to have written to you sooner after having received such a *feeling petition* to myself in particular, and so many agreeable compliments to my sex in general; all of which I was however truly sensible of, and not a little gratified with. But during the latter part of my stay at Keswick I was so much employed with writing, and so much interested in my employment, that all letter writing was given up. M^r Southey has received a Box of papers from Lord Wellesley,* respecting the war in the Peninsula, many of which were necessary as documents for his History of that war, which he is about to write; and therefore I thought myself well employed in assisting to transcribe them. It was, as I have said, a most agreeable employment; for many of the papers were Letters of Officers engaged in the contest – private despatches – opinions of L^d Wellington respecting the officers civil and military; and the conduct & intrigues of both Spanish, Portuguese, South American, & English, Ministers & Governments – besides interesting descriptions of the Battles, Countries, &c &c. So that with this, many more books to read and the society of my agreeable Friends I spent my time very pleasantly, and not unusefully, and I did not return to Rydal Mount till last monday. I found all friends at home well, except little Dorothy[2] who has scarcely ever been free from a bad cold all the winter, & which has reduced her so much that she is not like the same child. However, God be thanked! she is now free from any disease, and if the weather were but a little more favorable I trust she will pick up her crumbs

* See p. 100 *.

again. *Aunt* Dorothy[1] only returned home on Saturday last; she is very well and glad to [be] herself at Rydal Mount again – but we are all out of humor with the weather – it is scarcely ever settled for two days alike; and I am afraid its very *nature* is changed, or that it is resolved to be in unison with other things; for all seems to be *out-of-joint* at present. Southey says *this* winter began when the *last* ended; and war at home I think is to be begun now when there is an end to it abroad – yet I hope the discontents & disturbances appear worse to us, in the Newspapers, than they are in reality, for here we are as quiet as ever – though there exists, even here, great cause of complaining – however we think patience is the only remedy – and heaven give us a sufficient portion!

. . . I am glad to hear that you intend returning to Hampstead in the summer. Miss Barker, to whom I delivered your message, hopes to visit H. in September, on her way to the continent, on a visit to an uncle who is residing with his family at Boulogne – we used to talk of coming to H. together; & if I should resolve to spend the next winter in Suffolk, who knows but I may come and see how you manage your housekeeping, if you have no objection to receive a *young* Lady into your abode, but if you are more afraid of your *carracter* than I am of mine we must try to persuade Mary[2] H. to come also to *take care of us*, she being a married Lady will smooth down all indecorums. We hope that William will not be obliged to go to Town this spring; but he is very much obliged to you for your kind attention, though he would have deemed it proper to stay at Lambeth while he was there . . .

I ought to have congratulated you before this on the Birth of our little niece, and the well-doing of our dear Sister & I have requested that the Baby may be called Mary *Monkhouse* – I like the mother's name to be carried down to posterity,* and for *that name* in particular I have a great liking – so much so that I never call Mary H. by any other – we have often regretted that one of the children here were not called Hutchinson, especially poor little Thos[4]; and while he was alive we used some times to discuss the practicability of altering the Register.

You will have heard of the death of M[rs] J. Hutchinson's uncle, & the honey fall which has descended upon the Tees Bank – George[2] will have between 6 & 7000£ per ann. 10,000 among the younger children 100 per An to his mother & father – besides an estate & the annuity which I suppose will be worth 500 per An more will eventually be George's. It is a *wicked will* inasmuch as he has passed over M[r] Sleigh as his heir & only left him the estate above ment[d] for his life, & 5000£. However M[r] S., who is the most noble-minded man breathing, is

* In this she shared Coleridge's view. See *Inquiring Spirit*, 1951, p. 307.

perfectly satisfied; except what he must feel at being slighted & unjustly dealt by for in reality the money would have been no encrease to his comforts he having such an abundant fortune. My brother John[1], to his honor be it told, expresses himself with great indignation at this injustice done to Mr S. and rejoices that Mr S. is made George's sole guardian with power to transfer the property to his Brother should he prove unworthy. George is a sweet-tempered innocent Boy – very quick, but of a frivolous turn; and tho I have no doubt of his being an amiable man, he is too unsteady to be a good scholar. We expect Mr Sleigh and his father and Mother soon to settle George's future plans – At present it is in agitation to send him to Oxford with his present Tutor, our young Parson, who is returning to Oxford next month to take some college duties upon himself; and, if this is resolved upon, he will live with Geo. in the Town as his private Tutor, till Geo is of age to be entered a Gent Commoner at some of the Colleges in that University, Mr J[ackson] continuing to be his private Tutor. G. and Mr J. are very much attached to each other, and the former is very desirous of continuing with Mr J. who is in all respects, except that his health is very precarious, most suitable for the task. I believe Geo is to take his uncle's name (Sutton) so this great wealth will not add any lustre to that of *Hutchinson.*

Have you seen Mr Coleridges 'Lay Sermons'?* The first they say addressed to the higher classes is of all obscures the most obscure – we have not seen either and hear very little that is satisfactory of his goings-on† – and especially that his health is much impaired. He is still your neighbour, at Highgate – But I forget that you are now an inhabitant of the west end of the great city. I know the street very well – Dr Southey lives in it – I hope you are settled in and find your lodgings comfortable.

I have just heard by a Letter from Joanna that you have had a bad fall from your Horse – but thank God! that you are recovering from its effects. Do write soon & tell me how you are, and that your *beauty* will not be injured by the cut upon your lip – Your Brother John's[2] was a most frightful looking wound before it was dressed and we feared his beauty was gone for ever – but it is now very little of a

* She is echoing Wordsworth's opinion apparently, but not Southey's, if the article 'The Rise and Progress of Popular Disaffections' was Southey's; it contains a complimentary reference to Coleridge's *Lay Sermons*, 1816, 1817. See p. 100 †.

† Sara's information was probably out of date. Coleridge by this time had made real progress in controlling the opium addiction, and was entering on a period of productivity that amounted almost to a rejuvenation. See p. 122 †.

disfigurement to him, except that it in some degree alters the expression of his mouth.

We transferred your communication respecting the Dividends to Sir G. Beaumont but they have not noticed it in return. W^m says that perhaps he might get you a ticket to the Gallery* on an assembly night by application to M^r Rogers or Sir G. – if he had come to town he has no doubt but he could have got one from somebody, but it is an *aristocratic* thing and the Tickets are so charily dispersed that the holders have membership candidates for them when they do not use them themselves – to have the Assembly *select* is the main aim. But it is too soon to see it in *high fashion* he will try for you if you cannot succeed yourself before the season is over.

I am so cold I can scarcely hold my pen – The children are all at home, it being holiday, and I crept into my own room that I might be out of their noise – for neither dining room or study are free from it. I hope you have heard from Joe, and that in Jamaica he has regained his heart. Joanna talks of coming to see us soon; if so she will doubtless spend the summer, & you must give her the meetings at the Races. Now do write soon, for I am very anxious to hear of your amendment, and I promise you to be a better correspondent in future. I have no news from this neighbourhood that will amuse you – except that M^r de Quincey is at length married to his rustic beauty. Tell M^rs Ellwood the piece of news when you see her, with my love – God bless you my dear Coz. Every one here join me in best wishes for your recovery. Mary[1] is in despair about her Indian Matts. Would not M^r Hall purchase some at your request for her? Farewell most affty your's S. Hutchinson.

*Postmark: Kendal Penny Post, 21 Fe 1817*

## 32

*Thos Monkhouse Esq^re, Budge Row, London*

*21st Feb^y, Rydal Mount* [*1817*]

My dear Coz.

You would observe that my last must have crossed your's on the way, which I was very glad of; for, bad as I had been it would have been still worse if two Letters from you had been necessary to rouze me from my laziness.

* The British Gallery. See p. 109.

William whom you know to be such a *wary* man, looking always on both sides of the shield before he gives an opinion, is decidedly against Mr Blakeneys Estate as a residence for Mr Wheelwrights family – The House doubtless might easily be enlarged – but the situation is unfit for an *all-the-year* residence of a large family and only calculated for a few months in the Summer – The road is bad for a carriage, & the meadows, in the middle of the vale, so frequently overflown in winter that the *direct* communication between the House & Ambleside is consequently cut off (I do not mean the meadows belonging to the farm) – But above all the want of sun in the winter is the great objection; & to one of Mrs W's delicate constitution insurmountable – It is a beautiful *fancy spot* – but is utterly wanting in conveniences – We know of none other at present in this neighbourhood to sell – there are some to let I believe – but Wm recommends Mr W. to have his eye upon the Whitehaven, Kendal & Carlisle Papers, where he will be sure to see every thing that *comes to market*. – Near to Ambleside is certainly the best situation, among the Lakes, because of the Schools – but I think that Mrs W., who has always been accustomed to the accommodations of a town, would not be contented with those that are afforded by that village. There is a good house near Hawkshead at present inhabited by a Mr Vernon which I believe will be vacant soon – but not for sale – however there is no doubt, if Mr Wheelwright is bent upon *this* neighbourhood, but there will be plenty of small estates coming to the hammer. Wm would like to know what Mr W's object is – whether he intends to amuse himself by agriculture, or fishing, or field sports – if the two latter he would be disappointed in this neighbourhood – as we have little or no game – and a thoroughbred fisherman disdains lake fishing – all our Gentlemen here who are Anglers take off to the Emont, Eden, or other streams out of the mountainous region, as we have little or no trout in the becks – and in the Lakes there is nothing to be got by Anglers but Perch and pike by trolling or floating lines – You know William always wishes People who retire from Business to *know what they are seeking after*, lest they should encounter a disappointment. Remember us all three very kindly to Mr & Mrs Wheelwright. You do not speak of her health so I hope she is better.

I am as much in the dark respecting the Hindwell news as yourself – but I trust it is nothing bad – on the contrary something lively by the manner in which it seemed to be mentioned to you – though I guess it is not very important else it would have furnished matter for a Letter to me.

Since I last wrote there has been some Letters from London which appeared to make William's presence there necessary – however we think they may do very well without him – D[r] W[ordsworth] must bestir himself – and I am sure he will do it far better for W. is so little fit for business that it worries him beyond all measure – These affairs of his Brother and some plaguy Stamp concerns have deranged him in a piteous manner – when he is thus employed – he is in a fever the whole time and unable to sleep – besides the expence of the journey is a serious affair – the times being so bad and he & D[orothy] having been so long kept out of a part of their income by Richard's embarrassments & demise. I should like very well to come with him – but I must be a little richer before I can venture upon another journey. Want of cash also will prevent D. & I taking our long-talked-of trip to Paris – unless we can get a lottery prize or some such honey-fall. I shall be very sorry too to think that I shall never see the continent – We are all very glad to find that you intend coming down this year. Now I beg that you may not delay your journey till the rainy season, & when you do come give us a *genteeler* portion of your time than you hitherto done – I hope by that time to be *remounted*, and able to accompany you upon your expeditions – for you have not *half* seen this country yet, and I think you ought to have a trip into Scotland before you need leave the Island to seek for varieties.

As you do [not] mention the wound on your lip which Joanna spoke of I hope it has been trifling – you must most industriously endeavour to have your arm rubbed, nothing else will restore it. I hope you have parted with your horse – I guess you must have been in a Gig by the manner of the accident.

Dorothy[1] desires particularly to be remembered to you and that she regretted much not having seen you in the Autumn. Wm is now quite of yours & M[r] W's opinion about retiring, and the folly of endangering the independence you have gained however small –

God bless you. every body sends their kind love – We have a complete winter's day, snow & storm – Farewell most affty yours S. Hutchinson.

I shall direct my Letters in future to your Lodgings because as M[r] Clarkson would say it is *genteeler* – and because I think after business is over & you return to your rooms it will be far more agreeable to receive a friend's Letter – but you have only given me the No & Street – not the whole direction necessary which is I believe Portman Sq.

*Postmark: Kendal Penny Post, 24 Fe 1817*

# 33

*T. Monkhouse Esq$^{re}$, Budge Row, London*

*Rydal Mount, 15th May 1817*

My dear Coz.

Mere lack of materials 'to make up a Letter', to use Joanna's phrase, and no want of inclination, has prevented my so long leaving your last unnoticed. I have little more at present to say than that William applied, a few days ago, to M$^{r}$ Rogers for an admittance to the British Gal[lery] which we hope will be sent to you in St Anne's St. – But should R. not be able to do this W$^{m}$ will then apply to the Beaumonts where he may be more successful – He did not think an earlier application so eligible as the Town will now be full of fashion, and the rooms the best worth seeing. I trust you have continued to enjoy yourself, and have entirely recovered the effects of your unlucky accident.

We are all well – the season is delicious – and the country in perfect beauty. Joanna & Henry[1] arrived from Wales twelve days ago. the latter left us on monday last, and is again settled at his favorite Hawkshead, and busy fishing I have no doubt every day upon Conistone. Joanna is very well & looks so – We are to set off on Monday to Penrith to sell up my Aunt's worldly goods – which is to me no small mortification – but I hope we shall not be tempted to stay many days – for it is quite a *sin* to leave this sweet spot at present. I wish that the Races were not so attractive to you – and then we should have a chance of seeing you in better weather and you might enjoy a spring sometimes amongst us which taking the weather into consideration is decidedly the most favorable time for visiting this country – and I am not sure that even the woods are as beautiful now as in the Autumn – the tints are almost as various. William has given up all thoughts of visiting Town this year – He had very nearly gone upon the Continent with Southey; another year I think he will want little persuasion for a trip – and I intend to scrape up all the money I can for the same purpose – but I do not *talk* about it – such things are best done in a hurry without consideration.

William's advice to M$^{r}$ Wheelwright concerning a residence in this neighbourhood is, that he should first *rent* a House, & try whether he likes it – and then he will have leisure to look about for a situation – for houses are often very easily had & at easy rents – for instance there is Watermilloch at present unoccupied, and likely to be so, which would hold Mr W's family very conveniently. Wm thinks it a very hazardous thing for Mr W to settle without previous trial as the kind of life he would be doomed to here must be so different from anything he has been accustomed to. There is a sweet spot upon Windermere upon sale at present, an excellent house and beautiful grounds, with eleven acres of land – but *6000£* are *asked* for it!! In these times it is not likely that so much will be given – but, being a fancy place, it will certainly be sold for far more than it's value.

Joanna will not say that this country is more beautiful than Wales – and that she likes Wales better she is free to declare – This amazes me – setting aside all feeling of its being our native country I cannot conceive such a *perversion* of taste – though I allow that their situations in Wales are as beautiful as heart need desire. Mary[2] however God bless her still retains her affection for this country and I hope she will end her days in it after all – I am sure that *prosperity* is not the cause of what will endear her to it. Joanna gives us good accounts of the children – there never were such on earth before.

We desired a friend of ours, Miss Alms, to call at Longmans and bring down the *Goldfinches* with her, as they have failed to arrive in any of Mr Southey's parcels – but she received the same wise answer 'that they were sent to Mr M. at Hampstead'. Will you then have the goodness to desire John[2] to call & set them right once again, get the books and do you keep them until some opportunity offers of sending them hither....

Joanna says she has nothing to say to you but 'love respects' in which all here join – Let us hear from you soon I pray – and I hope you will be able to give a good account of yourself. God bless you! and believe me very affty your's S. H.

My kind regards to the Robisons when you see them.

*Postmark: Kendal, Penny Post, 19 My 1817*

## 34

*Thos Monkhouse Esqre, Budge Row, London*

*28th Augt* [*1817*]

My dear Coz.

We were sadly vexed when your Letter arrived that I had not given you proper notice of our Winandermere gaities – Mr Crump, three of his Daughters, Mr Gee, our neighbour, Mr Tillbrook, & a friend of his, our young Parson, George H., Joanna, Miss Cookson, & myself spent a most pleasant Day upon the lake & dined, gipsey fashion, upon a rock – the boat races were not worth looking at – but the sail boats, barges, wherries, & the number of well dressed persons, besides happy children, and a decent band of music made the whole scene very enlivening and it was well worth the wetting which we got in the evening – William was engaged at home with Mr Carruthers, and as neither you or he could attend Joanna to her ball she did not go, though we learned from Tillbrook & his friend that there was a great lack of Ladies – Before I have done with Balls let me tell you that there is to be one on the 9th of next month at Kendal at which Joanna intends to be, and *William*[1] also. It is on the Evening of the Book Club dinner at which all the Gentlemen of the county attend, & William always goes as a compliment to Lord L[onsdale] – and also for the benefit of the Landlord of the *King's Arms* – therefore Joanna intends to *go along* – & she hopes you will be here in time to meet them at Kendal & attend upon both these important occasions – it is reckoned the *genteelest* Ball at Kendal – No *Towns people* attend!!!!!!!

Mr Carruthers has nearly finished one picture of Wm – but he is not satisfied himself neither are *we* though the picture will be thought like by all common observers – but he erred in chusing the attitude – one in which William is never seen – and the face is too fat & the expression unnatural – but this was not the artist's fault for Wm himself sate, as Joanna told him, in '*a perpetual smirk*' – and would not put on one Schedoni* glance – However C. we are almost certain will succeed in the next which he commences tomorrow – we are very anxious that he should [do] one his own account – as everybody says that it would help him on in his profession were he to take a successful likeness of a person so celebrated – and we are very much interested for him and so is every one who has seen him he is such a modest, amiable, youth. . . .

We had your 'Lickness' as Joanna says here lately – a Mr Alsasser with whom we were acquainted at Lamb's – and to him Joanna nearly lost her heart – [*3 lines crossed out*]. Depend upon it that it was only for your advantage that I disclosed your secret – but it is to no purpose for the Lady does not arrive – We should have been very glad to call upon the Waltons but we should be really overrun if we were to call upon all who arrive – as it is we have scarcely a moment to call our own during the season – The Country has been, and is very full

* Schedoni, as I am indebted to Anne Renier for pointing out, is the monk with the eyes and the frightening glance in Mrs. Radcliffe's *The Italian*. Coleridge had reviewed it in 1798 in the *Critical Review*.

at present – but I fear the gaeitty will be passed away before you arrive – we have had rather better weather lately & would fain hope for 'a Michaelmas summer'.

Joanna has made me scratch out the three lines above, as you will see, as they related to her Love Affairs which not being of a very serious nature I thought very suitable for the enlivening of my page – God bless you, Every Body send their kindest love – we are all well – Miss W[ordsworth] & Willy[2] are in Borrowdale – I am in great haste yours truly S. H.

This Letter when you come to the end you may say is of little use but Joanna wished you to have a chance for the Ball at K. –

*Postmark: Kendal, Penny Post, 1 Se 1817*

## 35

*Thomas Monkhouse Esq$^{re}$, 28 Queen Anne's St, Cavendish Sq:, London*

*Sundridge Rectory, Wednesday* [*10 Dec. 1817*]

My dear Tom

We had a very agreeable ride, and find this one of the nicest places in the world – i.e. this south country world – However the comforts and accomodations within door may vie with that of any world – It is a nice old-fashioned crincum-crankum house and so quiet that I do not wonder at its being greatly preferred to the turmoil of the Lambeth Parish.

We wish very much for William[1] and you also *along* – I am sure he would like this house greatly – The Doctor fully expects you & shewed us the room he intended to be your's – If you are so *ungracious* (which I cannot believe you to be) as not to come, you must not fail to send by W. an especial message – as we were forced to *make up* one for you before – you not having understood our invitation as especially *from* the D$^{r}$ – at least I fancied so upon recollecting your having said 'Do you think the Dr will be glad to see me' – this you may be assured will be the case – and *prospectively* it is polite in you to cultivate an acquaintance with the *Clergy*.

I hope our Baggage has reached you safely – Desire John[2] to seek out a change of linen from among that which comes from the Laundress for W^m to *bring* along with him as M[ary] has nothing for him here – I hope he will be back on Saturday so that you may spend Sunday with us – The road turns off to the right at the foot of a long hill within sight of Seven Oaks and this parish is to be seen from the Hill – The Snow has come very provokingly and prevents our going out this morning to reconoitre the premises & the country around – but we have very fine Trees to look at from the windows and a sloping field with the Church at the Top. . . . Mary's best love – God bless you! most truly yours S. H.

Dont let William stay a moment in Town but do you both come hither immediately.

What a sad business if he should have to go North!

Your Bed is made up.

*Postmark: 12 Dec 1817*

## 36

*Miss D. Wordsworth, Rydal Mount*

*Mortimer S^t, 4th Jan^y 1818*

My dear Dorothy[2]

As you are become such an excellent correspondent I must put in my claim to a Letter from you, and also express to *yourself* the very great pleasure which your Letters have given us, as well as the good accounts which your dear Aunt sends us of your steadiness and industry – Your writing is indeed very much improved; and the Translation Mr Tillbrook says is as good as it could be, and that you are quite right in being *literal*. I sent it to Lambeth last night to your Cousin John[6] – who is there at present – they all depart, with their Father, for Sundridge tomorrow and we shall see no more of them – we were to have dined at Lambeth today, but on account of some Gentlemen who were engaged to meet your Father here at dinner we could not go – Mrs Ellwood is with us again – She & George[2] are gone out together – your Father breakfasted with Mr Rogers & is going with Mr. W. J[ackson] to call upon your Uncle. Your Mother & Mr. Monkhouse are at Church – I was not very well & preferred staying at home, though the day is now beautiful – the morning having been wet we could not go to Battersea to see Mrs. Whelpdale & her Children as we had intended. Mr W^m [Jackson] & George[2] leave Town tomorrow;

I dare say Mr W$^{m}$. is tired of it, for they have had too much play-going – the plays being very stupid and farcical – only fit for Children, and *giddy* Boys, like your Coz Geo: I have very often wished for you my dear D[orothy] and then I have thought you were far better at home; for I am sure you would be half-killed with the delight of seeing so many gay sights – The Shops, and the Baazars would soon steal all your money from you – and want of rest & sleep your health. Mr William says that George was very steady at his Books before he came but he thinks he is *giddier* than ever now. Mr W. has bought you a beautiful amulet, with the Ps Charlotte upon it, which you must put to your chain & wear for her sake. Your Mother will buy you the Books you mention tomorrow if we do not go to Battersea – Mrs Ellwood, George, & I went yesterday* to call upon Mrs Bradley whom we luckily found at home, her husband was just going out in his gig (He is a Surgeon) but stepped back to receive us and was very polite, and she seemed very well & happy. Her Husband is a very nice looking man – tall, & appears to be about 45 – We saw the *Hats* of 6 Boys in the Passage, & the little Girl, who appears about 10 years old, came into the drawing room – a very pretty-behaved girl & seemed very fond of her new Mama. Mrs B. was rejoiced to see me, and your Father & Mother intend going to see her and to ask her & her Husband to come hither – Today we have Mr Nash, Mr Haydon, Mr J[ohn] Coleridge, & Mr Alsager to dine – and expect Mr, Miss Lamb, & Mr Manning in the Evening – on Tuesday we dine with Mr Rogers and I *hope* we shall go out in the evenings no more. We have still some pictures to go to see, but I suppose if we were to stay two months longer, we should be busy every day – the days are so short that little can be done – and they are often so dark that the Houses in the narrow Streets are forced to be lit up at mid-day. – When your Father Mother & Mr M[onkhouse] went to Hampstead the other day they were forced to leave the coach a mile distant from home, the fog being so

* Sara was staying with Thomas Monkhouse, in company with William and Mary Wordsworth. This letter was written on the Sunday (4 Jan. 1818), following Haydon's immortal dinner (28 Dec. 1817), at which Wordsworth, Lamb, Keats and others were present. On Saturday, 3 Jan., Keats called on Wordsworth in Mortimer St. 'and saw his Spouse and I think his Daughter' (Keats's *Letters*, ed. Buxton. Forman, 1935, p. 75). But Dora Wordsworth was with her aunt Dorothy at Rydal. Could it have been Sara, returned from her call on Mrs. Bradley? In a later letter Keats refers to 'Wordsworth's beautiful wife and enchanting sister' (Keats's *Letters, ed. cit.*, p. 118). Probably he had clarified his mind as to the relationship and formed his impression of Sara Hutchinson when he dined with them on 5 Jan. (*ibid.*, p. 78). Her only reference to him is less flattering. See Letter 44, p. 133.

thick that the coachman could not find his way – & I, as I sate in the House, could not see the Houses on the other side of the street – the fog is not only thick but of a yellow color and makes one as dirty as smoke.

Mr Carruthers was here yesterday Evening. He brought your Fathers Picture with him which is nearly finished & put into a frame – but it does not strike the London people as being such a good likeness, because here your father is not in his thoughtful way and therefore the picture is not lively enough – indeed it does not seem half so like him as it did, even to me – beside your father looks so well & rosy, that the picture appears sickly. Mr C was so good as try to make a pencil drawing of your Mother last night but it is not like her – Mr Haydon intends to make a chalk drawing of your Father for your Mother – Mr Carruthers has bought a fine stock of paper, Chalks, Pencils & a pont Crayon for John[4] so it will be a shame if he does not work hard when he is so well provided with materials.

Thursday. Your Father could not procure me a frank till yesterday, so my Letter will be very old news. We rec[d] your's yesterday, and I shall employ Mr Tillbrook to purchase the Music for you – but I am afraid t[hat] there will be some trouble attending it – as one does not know the right shops to go to – every one selling different kinds – Your Mother & I went yesterday to see some fine Casts from Statues of Phidias – and of the famous *Moses* by M. Angelo of which you may have seen Prints – if not your Aunt will tell you about them – after which we went to see some fine Deer which came from the Upper Missouri with beautiful large branching Horns and the creatures themselves half as tall again as the Red Deer – they are going to Blair, being the Property of the Duke of Athol. – there were 2 pairs – the female had no horns – I hope to go to Drury Lane Theatre this Evening to see Mr Kean in S[r] Giles Overreach* – and we are to go to the Opera on Saturday the day of its opening. – Your Father went yesterday to hear the famous Organ, (your Mother & I had heard it before with Mrs Ellwood Mr Tillbrook & Mr J.) and who should me meet there but Mrs Lloyd. – She was greatly surprized as you may suppose your father to be also. I am happy to hear that you have had such an agreeable Christmas – Give my kind love to Jennetta & to Mr Gee & Mr Crump, if he is still at Rydal –

God bless you all! my dearest Children – most truly yours S. H.

Mr Haydon has bought a set of drawing materials &c so there will be one for you –.

* In Massinger's *A New Way to Pay Old Debts.*

# 37

*T. Monkhouse Esq$^{re}$, 48 Mortimer Street,*
*or*
*28 Queen Anne Street, Cavendish Square,*
*London*

*Playford Hall, Saturday Morn$^{g}$* [*17 Jan. 1818*]

My dearest Friends

For as Mary[1] bid me I address you all; & should my Rydal Mount friends have left Town, you (Tom)[2] will be so good as either forward my Letter or tidings of my *well-being* – I had as pleasant a journey as ever I can expect to look for in a Coach; indeed I should not have been sick at all if I had had the forethought to eat something as soon as I was hungry – but in truth the Coach did not allow us much time the horses were changed so promptly – we some times travelled at the rate of 10 miles an hour – but unluckily one horse fell ill & we were obliged to travel with 3 for 6 miles on the other side of Colchester which detained us, & the coach arrived at Ipswich later by an hour than usual. I found M$^{r}$ C[larkson] had been there on Thursday Evening – He had gone in on horseback & sent his horse back by his Servant *sure* of riding home in the chaise with me – I found he had indeed a chaise to be in readiness if I came the next night which was soon brought to the door & I and my goods set off – When we came to the Turnpike Gate I could not but smile when the old woman came out saying you need not *stop* to pay M$^{r}$ Clarkson will pay me – and half a mile further on at the turning of the road hollaed out a voice (observe it was broad moonlight) 'hoa a post chaise that? Going to Playford? a Lady in it aye' – The post Boy stopped – & there was dear M$^{r}$ C. come out (though they had not the least expectation of my coming) in the chance of meeting me to prevent our going into a narrow lane which was a new cut till a Gig had passed – when this difficulty was over & he had walked on to open a gate or two he got in to the Chaise & asked me how I was and welcomed me – for all our previous conversation had been about the *road* & *why* his meeting us was necessary &c. Dear M$^{rs}$ C. is very well – and this is just such a place as I expected to find it – though I have seen little but the interior – It is surrounded by a moat brim full of clear water which washes the walls of the room in which I write – the Study – all is *tidy* within & immediately without, but in a perfectly unfinished state taking the house altogether, though some rooms are complete – My bedroom I think is as large as a whole floor in the house in Mortimer Street & the best bed room where *your* new bed (Tom's I mean) stands is still larger – indeed mine is the smallest room but one in the house – M^r^ C. is very well and as nice & droll as ever – he has made me laugh all this morning with his odd questions and observations – He is now dressing for market – whither he will take my Letter – but he has allowed me a *whole hour* to write it in!! which however I shall not avail myself of as I have nothing to say further – I hope to hear soon of the termination of W^m^ & Marys London visit, & the settlement of all their business by some of you – . . . And I am to each and all most faithfully Yours – S. H.

If M[ary] is still in Town I would say that I left my sponge & Bazaar Frill, and some other useful trifles which may be given to Johns[2] care & T. M. will bring them – Don't fail to send off my Trunk; direct it to M^r^ C. at the 'Post Chaise Inn'. M^r^ C. does not know when the Ipswich Carrier comes from in Town.

*Postmark: Ipswich, 19 Ja 1818*

## 38

*Thos Monkhouse Esq^re^, 28 Queen Anne's St, Cavendish Square, London*

*Playford Hall, 25th Jan^y^* [*1818*]

My dear Tom

Why really instead of despairing that you will not meet with a mate I shall begin to fear that you will be over head & ears in love again before you know what ails you – but joking apart I rejoice to find that there are more females than one to your taste & therefore that you will take *hope once more to your bosom.* It was D^r^ Southey whom I heard offer to introduce us to S^r^ W^m^ Knighton's, but perhaps M^r^ Nash did the same – I wish we could contrive to pay the Lady another visit when I pass through.

M^rs^ Clarkson & I have lamented daily, since we heard of your visit to Cambridge, that you had not arranged your matters in Town so as to have come hither with Tom[5] (who is to stay at home the next week) and take a shot at the Partridges & Pheasants along with him – his Father & he are to set off together on Saturday when he is to be settled in Lodgings in Mr John Clarkson's Counting House, & to study with a Mr Manning in the Temple – o that he may do well! Tillbrook talks of being here in the course of the next 10 days. Mr C. twitted him with his blunder about the blue Coach, but he sticks to his text that one does not go from Fetter Lane –

I greatly bewail your forlorn condition – and therefore I shall direct this Letter to Queen Anne St, for though of small worth it will, as they say in Scotland, be '*just*' better than nothing to meet you upon your return home in the evening – I do hope that you may come to an agreement with Mr Winter, else what will become of you? Not one of your favorite schemes can be accomplished. You must not fail to write & tell me when all is settled –

We are as quiet & comfortable as possible, and as regular as the sun – but it is not the *dull* regularity of Sundridge – Mr C[larkson] puts his watch upon the Table the moment supper is over – & from time to time consults it & reports progress till half past 10 – when Mrs C. & I retire together & she stays ten minutes with me by my fire – and by 11 we are in bed – at 8 I am called and Mr C. gives me a second hollow as he passes my room door, & I am always ready by the time the Urn arrives so that he has not a moment to wait & we suit mightily – indeed to his great dismay I have been down twice before him – we have charming weather and this is a very cheerful house, and but for the cold winds I should have been able to enjoy everything out of doors also – but my tooth ache has plagued me greatly, & made me shrink from the cold. I rode to Ipswich upon Mrs C–s Poney one day with Mr C. It is a pretty little fidgetting thing which has been educated in the menage – and by attending to *his directions* a most funny ride I had – I want my own or some other poney sadly that Mrs C. and I might ride together for we cannot ride alone without either a Gentleman or the Servant. It would not be decorous for Ladies of *our consequence*.

I have received my Trunk all safe and *well* – and I thank you both for it – and the long Letter which, by the bye, I had the greatest possible difficulty in reading – though I did not care as it prolonged the pleasure – I have heard also from both the Maries as you will have done – I cannot be quite happy without that *other* Copy of Percy's Ballads, though such expences should ruin me – therefore you will be so good as buy it if it is to be had – & also a Princes[s] Charlotte Snuff Box which you may send by Mr C. if you can meet with one (and they used to be very *rife* in the Windows) without much trouble – for Mrs C. wants a Snuff Box sadly & she wished I had brought her one – I dont mean the Books to be sent here. Do not forget Mary's[2] Books, & mention the Carpet yourself when you write to her as she has again spoken of it to me. I have told her that as I pass through London I will try to get her a new one cheap – but I would advise them to have a *Turkey*. Mrs C. has a beautiful new one 24 by 23 which cost only 32£ – a scotch one of the very cheapest kind will cost them 12£ & not last decent above 3 years on their floors whereas the other will last a life time.

Mrs Clarkson would have accompanied her Husband & Tom[5] to Purfleet next week if I had not been here – so Mrs J[ohn] Clarkson says that as I have prevented her I must come with her in the Spring – & this I shall do, as I have been under promise to pay her a visit long & I shall be glad of an opportunity of spending a few days among her nice little Lasses. Mary[2] H. tells me that Joanna intends to return with Jack[1] & Jane in the spring; & that this will prevent her visit to the North – This will be very provoking – and will disarrange every Body's plans – I do not think I shall go into Wales if they have such a lot of people – it were far better to postpone one's visit till it would tell more – & therefore I hope I shall get slipped down into the North again next summer, unless I take a trip to the Continent with someone or other – I hear nothing of our poor Borodale Friend – I grieve about her constantly – that her kindness & benevolence is to do nothing for her but produce mortification & disappointment!!

You must not let the worthlessness of my Letter prevent your answering it – you are too gallant I hope for that – you must take the will for the deed but you cannot expect much materials to be found for Letter writing here – & I never enter upon morals, literature, fine Arts, or the Belles Lettres – God bless you – If you [have] seen the Lambs give my very best love & tell them we are all well & that they will most likely see Mr C. next week – If you should see Mrs Ellwood tell her I have nothing to say worth postage else I would write – Farewell most truly yours S. H.

Do not make any apology for the length of your Letters – I had rather have a long one from a friend, if it were ever so dull, than a short one – but yours was very lively & agreeable notwithstanding the despairing mood in which it was written – Mary tells me that William was *delighted* with the beauty of his picture.* The Painters who flatter are quite in the right – Truth gives no satisfaction.

*Postmark: Ipswich 27 Ja 1818*

* The second one, by Richard Carruthers. See p. 111.

## 39

*Mr Monkhouse*

*Friday, Jan^y 30th* [*1818*]

My dr Tom

Mr C. goes to Ipswich to sleep to-night to be in time for the Coach in the morning – I have little to say only I think I may as well give you a line or two as it will not cost much more than my trouble in writing and your in reading it. . . . Tom[5] has had fine sport among the Game – yesterday he shot 3 pheasants 2 Rabbits & a brace of partridges, & he has done very well every day – he went off again this morning, in the rain, & will work like a slave after it these 2 days, which are the last of the season – then next week he intends to attack the Pike in the *mere* – till Thursday, when he is to go to Town to the study of the law – He would suit far better a Life of liberty in the wilds of America, than the confinements of civil society.

O I must not forget to tell you that should Mary[2] Hutchinson commission you to buy her a Carpet you must go to purchase it at Cross's in Aldersgate St. Mrs Clarkson says that she, & all her family, & the Hardcastles who are knowing people always purchase carpetting there – Mrs Corsbie had some, lately; excellent scotch at 3/6 per yd & that old patterns of *Wilton* or Brussels (but *Wilton* is the best for Mary if she orders any but scotch or Turkey) may be had at 5/–. I know that at Kington or Hereford no Scotch Carpet can be had for less than 5/– or 6/–.

Mr Clarkson will be at William Allens; he purposes staying 10 days or a fortnight – Do get a snuff Box if you can & send it by him – He goes to Purfleet to morrow, & will not be in Town I suppose till Monday. I am quite amazed at the fine weather. I am sure that we have more sun here in one day than we have among the mountains during a week of finest winter weather – & yet they say there has been an unusual *quantity* of rain – which to me only appears like trifling showers among the sunshine. Did I tell you that we had heard from our poor Friend Mrs Luff and that she was to leave the Isle of France in November. She is to return with Gov: Farquhar & his Lady (who are coming home on leave of absence) with whom she has lived ever since her Husband's death – When I hear of her arrival in Town, if she does not come hither immediately, I shall ask you to call upon her if it should not be disagreeable to you – but I think the contrary – as she speaks of the Farquhars as delightful people, & M$^{rs}$ F. is very desirous of an acquaintance with your *Small Cousin.** It is a very lucky thing that I shall be so near upon M$^{rs}$ L's arrival as I should have felt it my duty to come up to see her if she had not travelled North immediately upon her arrival. Now do write to me – what else have you to do in the solitude of Queen Anne's St? Have you been at Coleridge's Lectures† which I see puffed and advertized in the Morning Chronicle – We have been well pleased with L$^{d}$ Stanhope's speech in the House of Lords & think it has made an excellent exchange between him & his Predecessor – Farewell! My best wishes & kindest love be with you – S. H.

Please put the Inclosed into the twopenny post.

## 40

*Thomas Monkhouse Esq$^{re}$, 28 Queen Anne's St,*
*Cavendish Square, London*

*Playford Hall, 6th Feb$^{y}$* [*1818*]

My dear Tom

'Too ready answers' never '*plague*' me – Indeed were it not for the hope of receiving an answer in return I should not be *virtuous* enough to write any Letters at all – the pure motive of giving pleasure I fear is above my cut – and though I never wish to extort Letters from my friends, if it be absolutely disagreeable to them, yet I always hope that they may *like writing* and I be the gainer – Not that I am uneasy under the idea of being the object of their *benevolence*, therefore from whatever motive you write the Letters will always be welcome, for dear William's[1] lectures upon Postage never tell upon me – and here it is the only way in which one can spend money – there is no other temptation. We send every day to the Post, so it is a great disappointment when nothing comes but that dull 'Morning Chronicle' – By the bye M$^{r}$ C[larkson] is you know a sort of a Whig – and M$^{r}$ Brougham is one of his Coadjutors in his works of benevolence – (whether the two are *equally* sincere christian charity will not let us stop to enquire – ) and he has written to him on the matter of the

* Sara Hutchinson was very short of stature.

† The very successful course of fourteen lectures, 27 January to 13 March 1818, beginning with the Dark Ages and ending with English prose style since the reign of Anne.

ensuing contest for West[d] which he says he has been dragged into – I should not mention this, not deeming myself at liberty even to Rydal; but, in case Mr C. & you should meet, to warn you, if the subject should be named, not to say a word concerning Williams interference* which you might inadvertently do, thinking that Mr C. as his friend, might espouse the same cause – I wish Mr C. knew William's sentiments upon the matter – though I do not think that would turn him – although I do not know that he intends to assist Mr B[rougham] though most probable – and he can do much among the Quakers if he chuses to interfere. I think Mr B. is the most formidable opponent my Lord could have had – the fuss that has been made at Kendal with his Brother does not tell for much – it might be expected among the rabble – but they are not Freeholders. I hope & trust he will not be elected.

We see Coleridge both advertized & puffed in the *M.C.* I am glad to find that he intends publishing the Lectures & wish he may do it – because then he will have his own – else it is scattering his knowledge for the profit of others – it is wonderful that the first Lecture was true to the Prospectus – but indeed he has exhibited many wonders lately† – pray have you any conversation with him? & did he inquire after 'my dear' or his other Friends – I was afraid that he would have favored Mrs C. or me with a Letter because he asked me‡ the address, but I hope he has forgotten it – if he should ask you try to evade the question – for we are neither of us ambitious of the favor, especially as an answer *would be required.*

Let me tell you now while it is in my head that it *is* Milton & Cowper, but *not* Spencer that Mary[2] wants. *Thomsons* works is the other book – she did not say the whole of his works but William advised that the Plays as well as the Poems should be procured – I hear by Joanna, though she only gives Charles H. for her authority, that dear

* Wordsworth campaigned actively for Lord Lonsdale, writing on his behalf his *Two Addresses to the Freeholders of Westmoreland*, Kendal, 1818. They were published in part of the Kendal *Chronicle.*

† From 1816 onwards, Coleridge, receiving more medical care than he had every had, made a remarkable recovery from the worst aspects of his opium addiction and his publications were impressive in number and quality, especially to one who had seen him sink under *The Friend—Christabel, The Statesman's Manual*, both in 1816, and in 1817, *A Lay Sermon, Biographia Literaria, Sibylline Leaves, Zapolya.*

‡ Sara evidently saw Coleridge when she and the Wordsworths were in London staying with Thomas Monkhouse, Coleridge and Hartley. She left before his lectures began and H. Crabb Robinson dined with them at Thomas Monkhouse's on 27 Dec. 1818 (*H. Crabb Robinson on Books and their Writers*, I, 214).

Mary[2] is in the family way – so that being the case her spring journey to the North is at an end – yet I think she would not be so disingenuous as talk of it as only depending upon John[1] Hutchinsons movements, who has talked of accompanying Joanna in the Spring – We I suppose shall move in May when the Quakers come up to Town to their yearly meeting – and if I go into Wales you will accompany me, as I am under promise to stay at Oxford with the Mentor & Telemachus to see all the Lions thoroughly –

I am extremely happy to find that you have settled so comfortably in Budge Row – & I hope & pray that your Cambridge plan may produce entire satisfaction to yourself – Till. is a false friend – he has never come near us or told us the reason of his faithlessness – we have excellent weather though it is bitter cold – but the clear atmosphere is my daily & hourly wonder and delight – I am sure that a day without sun is unknown here – and the days are at least an hour longer than at Rydal – yet notwithstanding all this – and this pretty valley to boot – how tame does every thing appear compared with our country – how much more does one gleam of sunshine tell, among the mountains, than this uniform brightness of the whole twelve hours! But I have no doubt that the longer I stay the more I shall be satisfied – and as the Spring advances I shall find out numberless beauties – In Wales I used at the last to fancy that nothing *could* be more beautiful – but when I returned home my error was quickly rectified – though I do always say that at Hindwell there *is enough* to satisfy any reasonable creature. Mary[2] says, in speaking of their situation, that the worst of it is that they do not hold their due rank in society – This you & I have always felt as a great evil – & I think it will be little less than injustice to their children if they continue there this continuing to be the case – At any rate I hope they will send off their Boys into a *Christian* Country – and I know that they will do their best to give them a liberal education – Poor Things! I long to see them. Tom[1] is so wrapped up in his Bairns that my last Letter gave him no pleasure because I had not named them. I have been here 3 weeks & have not had one line from Rydal. Dorothy[1] has got William home again so she for a while will have no thoughts [to] send abroad, and Mary[1] is the worst correspondent in the world – she will write none except home to and about her Bairns –

I shall be glad to hear that Greek and Latin have filled up the dreary void made by the false Cupid – but best of all that you have met with some more congenial aid – Farewell & may God bless you – M[r] C. will be most glad to see you whenever you can come – You will perhaps call upon Tom[5] – but I hardly know for what purpose only if you saw him one might hear how he was going on if he keeps to his work he will be sufficiently engaged – but I sadly fear him. If Mary W. left a pair of shoes of mine in your care and you could send me them by M[r] C[larkson] it would be a good deed – but I know the trouble of doing these things & therefore would only have them sent if an opportunity should occur of getting them to Budge Row – My kindest love to the Lambs & also Condolences to Charles whom you may tell that if he had come with me I have no doubt but his eyes would have been both cured & strengthened. I could not make what your *fears* were respecting John Coleridge – that he was not a *Tuynning* that is just the word as written & I construed it into a *Twining* for I could make no other sense M[r] T. being a very polite Gentleman of the old School – Farewell S. H.

*Postmark: Ipswich, 7 Fe 1818*

## 41

*Thomas Monkhouse Esq[re], 28 Queen Anne's St, Cavendish Square, London*

*Playford Hall, 22nd Feb[y]* [*1818*]

My dear Tom

I should have noticed the receipt of your doleful Letter immediately (and have assured you that you [are] at liberty to write as often as you are inclined how doleful so ever the Letters may be they are most welcome) if I had had any comfort to bestow – but all the wise saws & rational consolations that I might have strung together must have already suggested themselves to your mind and have I fear had no effect – Your solitude might have been lightened if I could have been with you – and I am sure if it could have been comfortably managed I should have been most happy to have 'ministered' &c – The Spring is coming up, and not *slowly**, in the Summer I hope you will make leisure to leave Town for a while when change of scene & lively society will do much I well know – in the mean time we hope to see you here – for altho' M[r] C[larkson] did not invite you when you are here he will make far more *fuss* about you than M[rs] C. who has so often invited you. I told her what you said & her reply was yes he *may venture* – We are all well – and were right happy to have M[r] C. back

* *Christabel*: 'And the spring comes slowly up this way.'

again – he has nearly got rid of his hoarseness & cough which were terrible when he came home – and a pretty account he gave us of the state of London during his visit – He told us that you looked very ill – so I beg of you to rouse yourself up & ride out every day – else you will do a serious injury to your health.

I write rather in a hurry this morning for I expect my Letter to be called for every moment – & we are dying to see the Kendal Paper which Mary W. says she bade you forward hither – Now I suppose you have detained it because of the hint I gave you about M[r] C. – but this precaution was only necessary so long as M[r] C. was not aware of the pecularity of W[ms] situation – but he had learnt that in Town & wrote to us post haste to warn William lest he was ignorant of the predicament in which he stood & knowing that both gratitude* & conscience would induce him to take an active part. M[r] C. of course is for B. although he is very sorry that he should oppose L[d] Lonsdale for whose character he has the highest respect but he thinks Brougham is an *essential* that *they* his friends cannot do without him – and he has already so far assisted the African cause (& so actively) that whatever he may be individually they are bound to support him – however he has done as little as possible only written one or two Letters – He knows that W[m] will take up the subject in a manly way & not like a mere *electioneerer* – and what he may write I should like M[r] C. to read – though he does not read much – but M[rs] C. & I have been very anxious to see the paper ever since we first heard that W[m] was at work – You will not be able to read this – but there is not a drop of ink in the standish & as the servants are at Breakfast we must not ring for the world – Now mind send off the Paper directly, for one half of her last Letter to me is unintelligible to me & refers me to you & the newspaper. It amuses me to think that the electioneering spirit should have got into our quiet vales – (I have told M[r] C. that I must ring & ring I will.) Little D[orothy][2] sends me word that she shall not write till the Lowthers have been there – I think Willy[2] at least will be disappointed to find that Members of Parliament, about whom all this fuss is made, are only men.

I see that Coleridge proceeds regularly. Tell us what sort of a figure he cuts & in what spirits he appears to be – The *Morning Chronicle* puffs him very much – this is the only paper we see & it is quite against my party – M[rs] C. leans a little to her husbands side but she thinks if that were in they would do precisely like the others – and neither of them believe that there is any positive evil at the bottom – although the

* See p. 122. It was through Lord Lonsdale's influence that *Wordsworth* was made *Distributer* of Stamps for Westmoreland.

means they take are abominable – The fact is that Mr C. measures everybody by himself – who *did not oppose the* abolition – & thinks them incapable of acting against their consciences. I do not believe that his equal lives for uprightness in essentials; many may, but his extends to the smallest minutiae – in things of no value as well as those of importance – But he is an odd creature – & I do like him most dearly with all his oddity – which always amuse me – and he does not dislike being laughed at – indeed he often says things for the purpose of making us merry with him – though he *never* laughs himself & seldom smiles even.

. . . God bless you for ever – Write as often as ever you feel inclined & happy shall I be if unburdening yourself to me does in the least lighten your heart – May peace be with you – Most affty your's S. H.

I wanted to amuse myself by knitting you some nice soft Lambs wool Stockings & went to Ipswich to procure yarn for the purpose – but what I have got turns out so *hard* that it wont do so I am knitting it for Mrs C. whose skin is not so delicate as yours – she tells me that it may be had in Town – Mrs Ellwood will buy me some if you tell her & you can bring it – it must be as fine wool as possible – she is not to mind the price. I intended to have done it myself but am ashamed to say forgot.

My love to the Lambs.

*Postmark: 23 Fe 1818*

## 42

*Thos Monkhouse Esqre, Budge Row, London*

[*28 Feb. 1818*]

My dear Tom

I write to say that Mrs Clarkson and I shall be obliged to you to call upon the Lambs, or send them a note, *immediately* to ask them to be so kind as call upon Tom[5] at 'Clarkson's Lime Wharf Earl Street Black friars' who is now, poor Fellow, lying ill in the *Small Pox* as we know that a little company will be a great charity for he is not *formed for solitude*; and we think that Mr Clarksons Friends William Sutton &c will not be the most *lively* society for him – You also will be good enough to give him a call. He has been ill some days; but only last night did we hear that the complaint was the small pox; which however, God be thanked! the Doctors report to be of a very mild sort – He had caught the Infection at Hatchem, from his cousin Emma Hardcastle, who has had the disease after being innoculated for the Cow Pox – Tom also was *twice* innoculated by D[r] Harrison as M[rs] C. was not satisfied the first time (tho' the D[r] was) but the second did not even inflame the Arm which the first did – and then she was perfectly satisfied. You may suppose they are very anxious about him, notwithstanding the good report of him by the Doctors, & their confidence that every thing proper will be done – but M[r] C. thinks he will pine for a little lively company & therefore I have preferred his request to you – but *observe tell the Lambs* that *he believes* his complaint to be the *Chicken* Pox, as the Doctors did at first, & have not undeceived him lest he should be alarmed therefore you must be careful not to undeceive him –

My dearest Cousin I was most sorely grieved to find that you had been so shaken by the rencontre at the Lecture, and have wished every day to write & give you my advice – but I could not make up my mind what was the best to offer you – However as I find that absence has had no salutory effect, but has made, & will continue to make you more suseptible at any chance meeting, I would not avoid but seek opportunity of being in Her society – habit may enable you [to] meet her with firmness if not with indifference & (but that I would not for the world suggest a hope which might sink you even deeper in despair) as you feel that she does not dislike you (for how can she knowing how much you admire her & have not intruded upon much less persecuted her with your attentions) perseverance may secure her – at least as a friend & valuable associate – for I cannot believe that the time will *not* come when you may look upon her in this light – if not you are not constituted like others – at any rate nothing has been gained by your keeping aloof – and you certainly have had encouragement not to give up her society. Write to me as often as you like – & say all that you think, however doleful, if it relieves you in the least I shall be happy – If poor Tom Clarkson is worse – I have no doubt that his mother will not rest here – she is anxious to go to him, but we hope it will not be necessary, & if we have good accounts of him she is far better here. . . . I thank you for Marys[1] Letter & the Paper which were very welcome – M[rs] C. only was sorry that there was not a little more of Williams good sense in it – She leans to our side & dear M[r] C. is in his heart ashamed of his Friends (tho' he does not confess it) – for the Kendal Paper has not left him an excuse for them – their own party blaming their proceedings – But the *M. Chronicle* &

M[r] B. lies the riot at the door of the Lowthers – they 'hired Irishmen from the Canal at 1 Guinea a piece to draw their carriages' (the members carriages, when forsooth the[y] came in to Town on horseback!! And M[r] B. in his speech at the meeting in London (if you saw it) you would see adverted to the *Freeholder* who he said had represented the people as poor and the Country having no commerce & this he dwells upon as if to rouse their pride – whereas the *Freeholder* says 'poor in soil & poor in the materials of commerce' – but the whole of their conduct is as bad and what they assert, as false as possible – Dont forget to send us the other Papers which may reach you – The Brougham's made M[r] C. believe that they were greatly a-head of the L's – Certainly this does not appear from the Kendal Paper – at any rate all the respectable are on their side. Do not forget a Snuff Box for me for M[rs] C. who has set her heart upon one with the Princess's head – and bring it when you come – but I would not have you come in this cold weather for I have been very bad with the Tooth-ache (ever since Sunday having got cold at Church) and gum boils without number so that I cannot bear the wind to blow upon me – in consequence we should be kept prisoners – [Farewe]ll & may God bless you & send peace to your min[d –] Most truly & affty Yours S. H.

M[r] Clarkson has been watching me all the time wanting to send off the Man therefore no wonder that I have expressed myself in such a *muddly* way, as upon reading over my Letter I find I have done – excuse it. I think that you will make out my meaning which at least means to be a *good one.*

*Postmark: Ipswich, 28 Fe 1818*

# 43

*Thos Monkhouse Esq[re], 28 Queen Anne's St,*
*Cavendish Square, London*

*Playford Hall, 22nd March* [*1818*]

My dearest Coz.

I cannot but own that I was glad that you had resolved to postpone your visit until M[rs] Clarkson's return; because I wish you so much to know her more familiarly, she is so good & so entertaining. Poor woman! I do lament over her present situation, & have every day repented that I did not accompany her to Town – However, I trust, that her troubles are drawing towards a close; & after she has once removed from that nasty Earl Street, that she will soon feel herself in a situation to return home; it has been a great privation to me her long absence when I had anticipated such a long enjoyment of her society. But I have been very happy and comfortable, even alone with M^r^ C.; & it was a great satisfaction to me that I was here to receive poor M^rs^ Luff who would have been very solitary alone. We have had Tillbrook since Thursday, and I believe he intends remaining two or three days longer. He does not mean to come to Town; but he will write to you himself as he is anxious to have you settle about your rooms &c –

M^rs^ Luff's affairs are so unsettled that she can decide upon nothing; and as I feel my motions somewhat dependent upon her's I know not when I shall be able to leave this place – She is very anxious to go into the North – and yet she will find many things which will prevent her – and I rather hope that she may be detained till I have paid my visit into Wales – whither I hope to be able to turn my steps before the Oxford vacation – because I promised to stay a day with those Youths that they might shew me the Lions there – as W^m^ J[ackson] would give me up his Bed at Georges Lodgings & go himself into College so I might be very comfortable, and never again could have such an opportunity of seeing Oxford – but this only if I come through Town – which I should wish to do for the Sake of seeing you – but it would be but a passing view – for I have no place to stay at – at least no place that I should chuse to make a convenience of, which would be the case, as there is no one else I care about seeing – but if M^rs^ L. & I come together we can manage it. M^rs^ Clarksons going to Town again is out of the question so I shall not go to Purfleet.

I know not whether I told you that I had had a doleful account from Joanna of her health – We live such a quiet life here – one day is so like another that I always forget whether, & when, I have written to my Friends – She is determined upon going to Buxton; & therefore as her return into Wales is so uncertain she wishes me to go & indeed I feel as if I ought to do it, *in duty*, if my inclinations did not lead me – & yet I had far rather have gone there in the winter than have lost a Rydal summer. I think poor Mary[2] will be sadly hurt if you do not go to see her after such a long absence & the (what she considered) shabby visit you paid her last.

I have not patience with Wheelwright – Your continuance in business was much more for his pleasure & advantage than your own, and I should take care to tell him so, & would not any longer submit to his ill humours & maggots – I'll be bound that he is one of those People who would behave far better if he were steadily opposed – giving way to him, as you do, only encreases his unreasonable desires – & if you go on this they will be beyond endurance – and your residences at Cambridge will be nothing less than a torment to you – Therefore I would try to cut the matter short as soon as possible – it ought to have been put on a right footing when you were in treaty with the Young Men, & he was so anxious that the concern should not be given up.

I wish I could give you any advice, comfort, or consolation upon the matter nearest your heart – but it is quite one of Williams '*inexplicables*.' I think in such a case if *I* had been concerned, I should have taken an interest in the Man more than in a common acquaintance, but in such an unequivocal manner as should have left no room for the *tortures* of hope, by which means I think his lost heart might be restored – I could not but have spoken myself on the subject, had I been a Man suffering & feeling as I am sure it must have been apparent to her that you are – Every body tells me they are sure you are in love – and how much more clear sighted must She be? – I don't entirely like her – forgive me – but I think she must be a fantastical person – Her imagination dwells upon some phantom which will never be anything else to her – and if I knew her intimately I should soon advice her to take warning of her poor Friend Lady B. – I dont pretend to say that she ought to have constrained her affections – but she might have *tried*, & not have decided so rashly – this with a different subject to deal with might have been for his advantage – but with such a tender & constant swain as you are it has not had the desired effect – and I see no hope for you but from a *transfer* which I do not imagine to be so impossible as you may at present feel – therefore I say 'Speed it o father let thy Kingdom come' the use of which quotation I hope you do not think profane –

I am glad that you have been somewhat alive to the pleasure of your Friend Sartorius's Society – I wish William[1] could have gone upon the Continent with you this Summer – but perhaps this might have interfered with your preparatory college studies. I hope you have some one to assist you – I should suppose you might get on much better with a person at your elbow to solve difficulties, which, if you are obliged to turn over books & ponder upon alone, consume more time than adults have to spare. It is different in Children – what they learn with difficulty they retain – but explanation to them is of no use for it goes in at one ear and out at the other – How have I seen this exemplified in little D[orothy][2] – with no creature to assist her in music she made 10 times the progress that she did in any other study – because on herself only she relied – & what was acquired easily was not valued – but the contrary is the case with adults – difficulties disgust & make one despair when there is no *obligation* to encounter them, and you are at liberty to throw aside the work at pleasure.

You will probably have heard from Rydal that poor Willy[2] has had the Jaundice & to his own amusement, has been *Lowther** all over – If one may judge from the *West^d^ Advertizer* there is still hot work – & William gets many a wipe – Some body has sent M^r^ C. the Paper since the Broughams have had it all their own way – but it is too low & vulgar to read – quite disgusting – I find by private accounts that both Parties express themselves confident of success. I care less about the Lowthers indeed nothing, but my desires are very strong for the discomfiture of this factious Party – for in any other point of view it is a matter of no moment to that family. I saw a sort of a Quizz of our Friend Crack[enthorpe] even by his own party in the last paper –

. . . Again God bless you & send you peace & all good things – most affty your's S. H.

Mary[1] W. says she left my shoes to John's[2] care – so most likely he sent them to M^rs^ Ellwood.

*Postmark: Ipswich, 23 Mr 1818*

## 44

*Thos Monkhouse Esq^re^, 28 Queen Anne's St,*
*Cavendish Square, London*

*Monday, 13th Ap^l^* [*1818*]

My dearest Coz.

I hope that my not hearing from you is not the consequence of the fall from your Horse by which M^rs^ Ellwood tells me you had hurt your arm – for as she speaks of your having been at Battersea I think your accident has not been very serious – however I must give you a bit of advice – either ride those horses more frequently or sell them at once or they will some day or other be the death of you – fed up as they are & kept in idleness they must become wanton & vicious.

So you have had Mentor & Telemachus in Town – I hope the former was well – as to the latter the old proverb will take care of him. Tillbroke writes that he wonders he has neither seen nor heard a word of

* See Letter 61, p. 175 *.

you – I fear that the unhappy state of your mind makes you irresolute – so write to me and tell me how you are going on. I shall begin to be quite out of humour with that little Puss if she continues to cling so closely to you.

I have had several Letters from the North since I last wrote to you. Dorothys all full of election matters. I wish it were over for they are all possessed by it – and, as Mary says, it is pitiable that William should be thus diverted from his natural pursuits. I suppose you will soon receive a pamphlet* – the copy for me you may give to M[rs] C[larkson] who will bring it – as I hope we shall see her at home by the beginning of next week. She is now, as perhaps you may know, at M[r] Buck's 18 South St right – happy shall I be to see her here again – though nobody could be more comfortable than I have been here – but it is very mortifying that so much of the time of my stay should have been passed without her society – yet I hope she will be able to visit us in the North next summer. You said the snuff box should be sent by her but as it is for her & not for *M[r]* C. it must be a Lady's box. By the bye M[r] C. & I have a wager about the election, 2 lbs of snuff to one on my part against Brougham, yet I find his party affect at least to be as confident of success as the other. I hope you will fix some time for your visit to us before M[rs] C. leaves Town – though I am selfish enough to wish that it may be deferred till the time of my departure that I may have the pleasure of your company on my journey as far as Town – but I am as yet quite uncertain concerning my motions – I wish to hear from Mary[2] H. who has been long a Letter in my debt and I am half afraid that either she or the Children are unwell. Tell me if you have heard of them lately. Poor Joanna is still in bondage by the rheumatism – and as the last summer did not cure her I have small faith in this which is to come. However she is going to try a bath in the neighbourhood of Stockton which is famous† for the cure of this complaint; and if does not suffice she will as a last hope repair to Buxton.

M[rs] Luff begs me to enquire how you have sped among the prizes – She has not seen *her* number attached to any of the capital ones so fears it is a blank as might be expected. It is very odd that never any of ones friends get a prize! Poor Miss Barker how often has she failed! Now I am afraid she has not had even spare cash to purchase a chance – so is saved from disappointment at present.

Have you ever seen '*Zapolya* my dear' since the lectures‡ – or do you hear how he is going on? I was glad to see that Lamb's scattered

* Referred to Letter 40, p. 122 *.

† Coleridge had tried it in 1801.

‡ A mocking reference to Coleridge's *Zapolya*, but whether to Coleridge himself or one of his audience is not clear.

writings are in the way of being collected* – I hope the volumes will be out before I go into Wales – as I should be proud to carry them to Tom[1] who is a great admirer of Charles. Little Keats too I see is in the publishing line – but the Title of his Poem† has no charms for me – however beautiful it may be I am sure it cannot awaken my interest or sympathies – I wonder anybody should take such subjects now-a-days.

You will not perhaps be much interested at my telling you that a Friend of M^rs^ Luffs & mine, Miss Dowling, who has been 6 years Governess in L^d^ Galloways family, has undertaken the school at Ambleside to our great delight – as she is a most admirable woman & very accomplished in the *solid* sense of the word – Little Dorothy[2] is to be placed under her care at which *she* is greatly delighted having been much taken with Miss D. during her visit to Ambleside – So now if you have any young Ladies to settle in the North at School you must patronize her – and you may recommend her with perfect confidence. I hope we shall be able to get her some scholars from Penrith. She has *finished* two of their Ladies Stuart – and previously Miss Carlyle of Carlisle – She was 2 or 3 years with the Askews, seven years ago. I hear great accounts of little D's improvements in music, french &c from M^rs^ Gee – so I hope she will not be wanting in acquirements after all her waywardness about her books & I am sure that there will be wanting no goodness of heart to make her an interesting woman.

God bless you. I have written in a canter all the time. M^r^ C. has been to my room 3 times to see if my Letter is ready. farewell. M^rs^ Luffs kind remembrance – truly Yours S. H.

Write soon

*Postmark: Ipswich 14 Ap 1818*

# 45

*T. Monkhouse Esq^re^, 28 Queen Anne St,*
*Cavendish Square, London*

*Playford Hall 1st May* [*1818*]

My dearest Coz.

I cannot learn from your Letter whether you meant to go to Bath before your visit to Playford or not, however I trust that your journey

* Lamb's *Works* (2 vols.), with the moving dedication to Coleridge, came out in 1818.

† *Endymion*, 1818.

will not stand in the way of our seeing you very soon – The weather has been very delightful this week that we have wished very much for you, and therefore I hope you will come as soon as convenient – not later than the middle of the month because if you do not come I shall certainly not miss the opportunity of going to Town with Mr C., who will set off in about 3 weeks – & this is the longest time I have proposed to myself of delaying my journey into Wales. I wrote to Mary[2] to tell her that if she could make it convenient to go into the North I would set out at a moments warning to release her from the duties of house-keeping – but she has declined my services – because their are other more important obstacles to her journey – So I am very glad that the (to use an elegant illustration) saddle is set upon the right horse. I could not help twitting M[ary][1] Wordsworth for having expressed her sense of the hardship of Mary[2] H.'s condition in not being able to move about at will, like Joanna & myself, by telling her that neither she or the object of her com*misser*ation would be willing to exchange *their bonds* for our *liberty*, that she ought to have added – 'tis pity that they have neither Husband or Children to make their homes more interesting – so our lots are equal' –

Mary[1] tells me she has a few commissions for me as I pass through London – and I have a few for myself and should like also just to go to Somerset House to see the exhibition but as the Ludlow Mail does not go out till evening I shall have time for this, for stay all night I fancy I *must* & *where shall I get a lodging*? for I should not like to go to any place merely as a *convenience* – (and except for seeing you I have no desire to stay an hour in Town, & I shall see you here I hope) where I should be obliged to stay longer than I wished, out of courtesy, & incur an expence which I am not at present disposed to do – therefore what am I to do for one night as I fear I cannot sleep at the *Blue boar* or any of the Coach Houses. If I went to any *private* House it must be Miss Alms' because she would think it unfriendly if I did not – but then as I have said I could not go without staying a few days for her pleasure if she wished it – & I am not disposed to do this at present – and I should see little of you. Now you must try to get me out of this hobble – else I must come up in the early Coach & take the Ludlow Mail the same night – which I had rather not do – as to going to Battersea to beg a bed I might as well be where I am – at Miss Lambs I *durst* not sleep, & these are the only two places where I could make free enough to beg one as a convenience – what a provoking creature you are not to have a wife – or even a house of your own, without one, would do just the same. I suppose even if there was a spare bed at your lodgings they would not take me in.

I hope you have written to Tillbrook before this time. He seemed quite hurt that you had not. In a Letter which I had from him about 3 weeks ago he said it was absolutely necessary that you should have your name put on the Books, or something of that kind, I forget exactly the expression – however I am glad that you have been amusing yourself in society, & hope that you will be quite lively when you come down to us. I wish we had something attractive to set before you – but you must expect nothing but our *own selves* – for we have very little intercourse with the neighbourhood – indeed it is the most retired place I was ever in – if we were not very lively and *agreeable* ourselves we might die of the vapours. M[rs] Clarkson delights in the place, & it is a sweet spot; but yet it surprizes me that she who is so calculated for society, & enjoys it so much, should never feel the want of it here – when she felt it so heavily at Eusemere. I never saw her so well for many years – *never* look so healthy – Tom[5] is gaining strength very fast – & recovering his looks – all else well – & if this fine weather continues we shall feel ourselves quite young as well as in health – Great complaints are made of the lateness of the Spring – but to me it appears early – & compared with the accounts I receive from the North it is so – We have shoals of Nightingales – all round the house – and on the Heaths, at a short distance, the air is full of skylarks – birds whose songs I have been unaccustomed to in Westmoreland – we have neither among the Mountains – & no Nightingales you know (I believe) north the Trent.

What a shocking scrawl I have written! But I have so many Letters to write that I am all impatience. I know not how they have accumulated upon me but I am at present all in a *Mess*, & know not how I shall get through them – They were all well at Rydal when I last heard from them, which was on Sunday – I suppose Betsey is with them at present – Did my Brother John[1] go into Wales? He is incorrigible if he did not – & I shall say his money *is* of more importance to him than all the relations of life! God bless you for ever Your's truly S. H.

Don't say anything to M[rs] Ellwood if you should see her of my dilemma respecting lodgings for reasons obvious – I sh[d] think it wrong not to see her if she could come to London only for an hour – but to go there would defeat all my plans – If it is necessary as perhaps it may for M[rs] Luff to come to Town I shall have no *bother* at all.

M[rs] Clarkson has suggested the scheme of your coming on horse back, as you would find it convenient to have one here & then some of us Ladies could ride along always as there is only one saddle horse (besides her poney) which T. rides – but I think you would not think it worth while to spend 2 days over the journey – & there being no inn in the village & the beds here will be all full when you are here – you could not have John[2]* along – Only your Horse would be well taken care of. Perhaps if you were to send him 40 miles on the road the day before, & then ride yourself the last 30 this might be managed – But you will judge for yourself.

It is possible M[r] C. may go to Town on the 20th.

*Postmark: Ipswich 4 My 1818*

## 46

*Thos Monkhouse Esq[re], 28 Queen Anne's St,*
*Cavendish Sq[re], London*

*Playford, Friday Morn[g] [May 8, 1818]*

My dear Coz.

Your Letter & proposal, which I rec[d] last night, perplexed us a little for, – 'know we not that he, who intermits the appointed tasks & duties of the day, untunes full oft the pleasures of the day; checking the fine spirits that refuse to flow, when purposes are lightly changed?' – So it is, & would be, with me if I were to accede to your otherwise agreeable porposal; for my mind has been fully made up to remain here until the time of M[r] C[larkson]s departure, unless you had come down before, & then I should have returned with you. M[rs] C. says it is very shabby of you not to have proposed to come & *fetch* me at any rate – however you know that I should not require that – especially as I shall have an escort if I wait his time. For my own part I have not the least wish to stay an hour in Town, longer than to execute my commissions & see the pictures, independent of your company, which I had much rather enjoy here at this delightful season – & M[rs] C says that she always hoped to see you in Sep[r] also to take a little shooting with Tom[5] – and as you *must* go to Cambridge as soon as possible why cannot you come this way back & spend a few days? & then M[r] C. & we could all go to Town together – It is 50 Miles from C. to this place, so by this arrangement you would only have to travel the road betwixt this & town *once* – there is a Coach direct from Cambridge to Ipswich, through Bury St Edmunds, so that you would have no trouble about conveyance. M[r] C. has fixed his going to Town on the

* Probably his brother, but possibly a servant.

25th inst. & his resolutions, like the laws of the Medes & Persians altereth not. Therefore I hope you will reconsider the matter & set off to Cambridge with all convenient speed, & when you have paid us a short visit, if a long one cannot be, I shall be ready to attend you to Town & be your guest for a day or two – but a longer residence than that at present would not suit my already shattered finances, & *inadequate wardrobe*, therefore I must be contented with a morning view of the Pictures – even if Tickets could be procured which is not likely at this early season – they are not yet become cheap enough to be offered to small People like us – who would not presume to ask for them. Notwithstanding do not suppose that I should not very much enjoy a few weeks residence with you in Town – but yet though I am *my own Mistress* I am often forced to submit to the bondage of prudence & circumstance. At *present now*, if I had my own pleasure, & cash for the need, I should go from Town into the North with Mrs Luff to spend the summer – then go to Wales at the end of Autumn – but as this cannot be I must put on the Philosopher (a title which Tillbrook honors me with) & make the *inevitable* my choice; or, better, the good christian – My duty my pleasure.

The pamphlets were duly received – and William's[1] most assuredly fathers itself – the close comments are De Q's. I have got another copy therefore you may have one of them if you wish it – It is very well done only a little too violent at the end; & *we* are very sore here upon such subjects. Brougham seems, in his Letters to Mr C. I find, quite as confident of his election as the other party are. How can this be, in so small a county where the number of votes are so easily ascertained? I do hope from the bottom of my heart that he will lose it –

I am sorry for the fate of Carruthers' pictures but it could not be much of a disappointment to him as the disposition of the Academy is so well known. How do you like Wilkies Picture of Scott & his family, I have a great desire to see it. If Carruthers perseveres in his intention of going to Lisbon there is good reason to hope that his health will be improved by it.

I saw Miss Towgood's marriage in the papers – She did not look a bit like being upon the eve of such an important event when we saw her – pray do you know her spouse? I hope she has got a nice one for I am sure she is a deserving creature. God bless you! I am glad to find you are enjoying yourself which I conclude from your saying the Town is lively. Write & tell us if you agree to my proposal which I hope will not be *disagreeable* or inconvenient to you – . . . Your's most affty S. H.

. . . If C. Lamb's Books come out before I am in Town get a Copy for me when you purchase one for yourself to save trouble as I must have one.

*Postmark: Ipswich, 9 My 1818*

## 47

*Thos Monkhouse Esq$^{re}$, 28 Queen Anne's St, Cavendish Square, London*

*Playford, Thursday 21st [May, 1818]*

My dear Coz.

I have expected a Letter from you every day since I wrote my last. I do not know that there was anything in it that really req[d] an answer, if you had made up your mind not to visit us, but calculating upon your known *courtesy* I thought you would have written – and in consequence of your silence I have sometimes had a faint hope that you would pop in upon us some day – However all such hope is now over – and I write to say that our journey will, as I told you, be on Monday in the *blue Coach* & expect to be at the 3 Swans in B[isho]psgate Street at ½ past 5 – but it appears that there is a bother about the Coach which distresses M[r] C[larkson] greatly lest you should not know exactly where to come or send to meet me – as sometimes it stops at the *Bull* in Aldgate & at the *Spread Eagle* in Gracechurch St. But I do not see that there is any use in anybodys meeting me. I can have a coach in a moment & if I only find you at your lodgings I shall do, but I hope you will be in to receive me – and if you cannot accommodate me with a bed you will give me dinner or Tea & we can settle that some way. I wish that M[rs] Ellwood may not be gone into Wales, though I advised her to go because of my intended stay at Oxford – & other chances which may delay me & make her journey more troublesome to her – but now there is no likelihood of me being delayed & she might have followed me to Oxford the next day & I could have proceeded with her if there was room in the Coach – but as I did not know anything about the Hereford Coach & the Ludlow one in which I had travelled passes through Oxford at such an *unreasonable* time of night that I was in hopes of getting forward in some other way – I therefore did not like to propose her waiting for me if it was more convenient to her to go before, as she had intended – And now when the time draws near my horror of Coach travelling returns upon me, & I am half-inclined strong as my desire to see Oxford is, to give up that scheme.

I do not see the use of sending you this Letter at all – except that I should like you to be at home when I arrive – that the folk may not look strange at me – we are all well. Tom[5] C. comes up to town with us – He is quite well but the spots on his face & redness will I dare say continue for some months yet. I had a Letter from Mary[2] H. the other day to tell me of Mrs Ellwoods visit & propose our coming together. She bade me also tell you that my Aunt was in despair about her money & begged you to send it by the first of us that went – that she (my Aunt) would forward to you a Ham & 2 legs of Mutton by the first Carrier but she did not think you *deserved* them – by the bye I hope the Mutton will be better than the last was.

God bless you. Mrs C. is very sorry that you did not come while I was here – but I hope you will make it up in september or it would be quite a slighting of her invitations. She & Mrs L[uff] desire their kind regards with my dr Coz Yours most affty S. H.

*Postmark: Ipswich 22 My 1818*

## 48

*Thos Monkhouse Esqre, 21 Budge Row, London*

*Stowe, wednesday morning* [*3 June 1818*]

My dearest Coz.

Mercy on me, what a Pen & ink! The Pen is as bad looking as one of Mr Clarkson's, the ink is literally *moulded* over – therefore you may guess the extent of your Brother's labour in this way and of its exquisite color you have ocular demonstration. Now do you not think I am a good creature to sit down & write to you so soon? To tell you the truth I feel particularly in the humour for writing to you – & shall I confess why – in truth to scold you – This morning when I produced Lambs Book* which I had intended to give John[2], he opened it & read to my dismay your *presentation* to Mary[2]!! When I was disappointed in the other copy of the *Reliques*† I had determined to give the Copy of Lambs Book to him, which I supposed you had bought for me; & having got 2 beautiful silk Handfrs at Glocester for George[1]

* See p. 133. *

† Thomas Percy's *Reliques of Ancient English Poetry.*

*congratulated* myself in having obtained a *present* for each of the Gentlemen. Now you must get me the other copy of Percy & send it with the rest of my Baggage which I hope will arrive before next Saturday as all the Electioneering papers are there which John is desirous of seeing – John is bewitched also with the Kaleidoscope (I will spell it with a K. in spite of the literary Gazette to shew you that I understand *greek*) but he was too rational to look through it at breakfast time, as *you* or I would have done.

Well now for our journey which has ended so happily that I feel not the least fatigue but rather could fancy myself 20 years younger than when I was fagging my Body & puzzling my Brains about those plaguy Coaches in Town. I wish from my heart that you had come with us – never did I see a Country look so beautiful as it did all the way from Cheltenham – After being in Suffolk – though it is really very pretty at Playford, & very fine at Ipswich – the road from Hereford with the view of the Welsh mountains, which were made transparent by the lights of evening, seemed to me more beautiful than anything upon earth – I could scarcely believe that our own dear Country could be more so. Mrs E., from whom I expected little sympathy, was almost as much enchanted as myself. Then the woods were in their most exhilarating garb – all the freshness of spring with tints as various as autumn – the Hawthorn Trees in the parks white with blossom & some apple trees still retain their bloom – surely no country is so beautifully wooded as this! Art with her '*cunning hand*' may toil till she is weary before she can plant as nature has planted here – but it is of no use to talk I cannot communicate my transports you must *come & see* – How much better than parading & masquerading as Sartorius & you do, if you had both accompanied us! But I have dropped the matter of fact of our Journey. We arrived at Cambridge at 4 o'clock – where they told us the Coach breakfasted & stayed ½ an hour – but as we were not hungry we chose rather to walk about the cool & silent streets which we did to our much gratification – we saw a solitary student in his Cap pacing the Cloisters of Queens College & he put his head through the Boss of the window to look at us – whether it was study or *love* that had thus early drawn him from his pillow I know not; but if I had had a pencil about me I should have written a note to *Mentor* & delivered it to his care by way of turning his *vigils* to account. It was such a beautiful morning that I was provoked to think that our two youths were fast asleep probably in bed when they might have been enjoying it, & our agreeable company into the bargain. Except this I had no regrets – for I do not think I can ever bring myself to wish even to know more of Oxford than I do. I feel still as I did when

I first saw it, from the hill at the entrance, as if seeing it in *detail* would destroy the perfect recollection which I have of it as a whole – It is truly a beautiful city and the Glory of our Island!

At Glocester we learnt that no Coach went thence to Hereford till next morning, & this would be too late for the Day Coach of today; but were a little comforted to find that the Mail, after waiting 2 hours, would proceed to Monmouth through Ross for which last place we took places & then went to the Inn, & made an ample meal of tea, Tongue &c &c then went to the Cathedral & walked about the Town – At one oclock we set out with one young Lady in the Coach – & about a mile off were favoured with the Company of a drunken young man, something like a horse dealer, who smelt of liquor & slept all the way, tossing about his legs & arms to our great disgust as you may suppose which caused us to make many reflections on our *unhappy lot* in being subjected to such indignity, which would not have been the case had any Gentleman been in the Coach – for he was not a regular passenger. At Ross we went to the Church yard while the horses were putting to – as we had no alternative but taking a Chaise to Hereford – and when we got there I was resolved we would have no more coaching, & so proceeded like *ourselves* in another to this place, & arrived here just as the sun was sinking behind the welsh hills after a most delicious ride. John[2] was in the fields & the servants looked very strange at us – however this was nothing to us – we gained entrance & the boy soon mounted a horse & galloped into the meadows to fetch his master – from whom you may be sure we had a kind & cordial welcome – He had been at Hindwell on Sunday to meet me – for they, notwithstanding your opinion of my *indisision*, were in confident expectation that I should be there by that time – & William W. also would vouch for the *perfection* of my *character* on this point. He always says that when Sarah fixes to come you may be *sure of* her – & they at Hindwell went further – were sure of me though I had *not fixed* – only said that a few days I must stay in Town. So I beg of you to *recant* the opinion you have taken up – If you can read this I am sure it is more than I can do – but my wits outstrip my pen this morning, they are sharpened by the beauty & influence of all around me & I wish I could communicate to you, in your *dull* abode, some of my own delightful feelings, both as a relief to myself & for your *spiritual* benefit.

To descend from my flights – I must tell you that we had no charge made for our luggage, which was some set-off towards our subsequent extra expences. Tell our good friends at Battersea of our well-doing. Jane will write from Hindwell so shall I – when I can give you a sober & rational account of all there 'when these wild extacies shall be subdued into a sober pleasure'* & my pen shall be able to write even to satisfy Mr Clarkson. I believe we shall stay here till tomorrow night when John will escort us to Hindwell. John is very well & in good spirits about this farm. He is to have his House painted & made smart very soon. Farewell! God bless you. Remember us kindly at Battersea & my kind regards to the Captain. Yours most affy S. H.

Write soon – dont wait for my next – Do not forget to send the Parcel to Miss D[owling] in time & the Kaleidoscopes.

Be sure to put some prettier glasses into John[4] Wordsworths Kaleidoscope – this of ours is not *true* but it is quite as beautiful as yours now that I have altered the Glasses – & Johns wants nothing but some better in his, so contrive to get it open for it will disappoint him sadly if sent in its present state. I did make Willys[2] *perfect.*

I owe Miss Lamb for seeds 2/6 – pray pay it for me – *don't forget* & give my love to her.

*Postmark: 8 Ju 1818*

## 49

*Thos Monkhouse Esqre, 21 Budge Row, London*

Song – for T

Shall I, wasting in despaire,
Die because a woman's faire?
Or make pale my cheeks with care,
'Cause another's rosie are?
Be shee fairer than the Day,
Or the flowery meads in May;
    If shee be not so for me,
    What care I how faire shee be?

Shall my foolish heart be pin'd,
'Cause I see a woman kind?
Or a well-disposed nature
Joined with a lovely feature?

* Wordsworth, 'Lines Composed a few miles above Tintern Abbey'.

Be shee meeker, kinder, than
The turtle-dove or pelican;
    If shee be not so to me
    What care I how kind shee be?

Shall a woman's virtues move
Me to perish for her love?
Or her well-deservings known
Make me quite forget mine own?
Be she with that goodness blest,
Which may merit name of Best;
    If shee be not such to me
    What care I how good shee be?

'Cause her fortune is so high
Shall I play the fool & dye?
Those that beare a noble minde,
Where they want of riches find,
Thinke what with them they would doe
That without them date to woe;
    And unless that mind I see
    What care I how great shee be?

Great or good, or kinde or faire;
I will never more despaire;
If shee love me, this believe;
I will die ere shee shall grieve.
If shee slight me when I wooe
I can scorn and let her goe:
    If shee be not fit for me
    What care I for whom shee be?
George Wither.

[*9 June, 1818*]

My dear Coz.

I think that from the next leaf of the book from which I have transcribed the above I could find a song that would suit your Friend S[ertorius], viz. Cowley's '*Chronicle*' – but it would prove too long for my sheet – so, as I doubt not you have Cowley's works, I beg that you may read it to him – I am sure that he will approve of Withers' sentiment & philosophy, as applied to your case – & I could not resist the pleasure of copying for your *benefit* – and by way of giving value to my epistle.

This is Tuesday, the 9th of June – Your brother John[2] escorted us hither on thursday Evening after we had spent two very pleasant days with him at the Stow – He is in excellent Spirits – and his stock & crop look very promising in spite of the drought – but really the weather is intolerable – so hot and dusty that there is no stirring with comfort – However the house is so cool & pleasant that for ourselves, who have no need to stir, there is no cause for complaint; and I trust the rain will come in time for the good of the Crops.

We found all here well – My aunt is quite another creature compared with what she was during my last visit – She has been cured of her last *threatened* bilious attack by an acid bath for the feet, which relieved her as by a charm – Mary[2] is very well, but thin as a lath – She is just the same in every other respect and as happy in her Husband and Children as human being can be – Tom[1] is very well & looks not a day older – The Children are nice healthy *round-about*-things – very short, with round faces, & cheeks plump & rosy – They are neither of them handsome – and not the least like any body in either family except little Thomas'[3] mouth which in shape & expression reminds me of your Father – and I should guess that he will grow up like him though he does not at present promise to be so handsome – yet he is rather a pretty looking boy – but Mary[6] is very plain – yet I do not entirely despair of her either – and it seems impossible that they should continue such dwarfs having such *sizeable* Parents & *relatives* – myself included. Thos is a little bit of a pet – but *very* little – & my aunt may (entre nous) be thanked in a great measure for it – Mary is as sweet-tempered and quiet as a Lamb – though sufficiently lively. Your present of the Doll gave her great delight – The Waggon also though he does not return to it so frequently as you would suppose he being so much at home among live Horses & real waggons. The Kaleidoscope is above their comprehension; & therefore it is entirely the plaything of the Adults – but I do not think it gives quite as much delight here as at the Stow – perhaps because here are more interesting playthings – the Bairns.

I had a long letter from Rydal – but I forget it had come through your hands, & I was glad to find you had opened it – You would see how acceptable our Kaleidoscope will be there – By the bye what an Ignoramus that *Gazette* Man must be with all his elaborate prosing about the pronunciation – nobody but himself that I see or hear of spells it with a C. so how can he, who knows nothing of its derivation, be any judge of its proper pronunciation?

This place looks very beautiful – The Pool is as full of fish as possible – yet we have nobody to catch them – and the Boat looks too crazy for any one to venture out in it – so the fish are left in quiet possession. What a delight it is in these hot days to look upon cool water! How I pity you when I think of you being doomed to tread those hot stones & have your eyes scorched by the reflection of the sun from those brick walls! London *is* a delightful place & I like it well – but I never *can live* in it until I keep a Carriage and never have any *business* in it but *pleasure* – I hope you have written to me before this – and that you are comfortably settled in your new lodgings – Mary desires that you may use my Aunt's Mutton as speedily as possible; for she is sure that you must hitherto [have] keept* it too long else it could not be in the state which that leg was which you had in Mortimer St. Can you tell whether that came from Hindwell or the Stow? if from the former she says it must have been changed (*a bull observe*) upon the road, for the last she sent you was the finest mutton to be had in Kington – & if you had kept it till last Dc^r^ it must have been spoilt –

If my Trunk is not forwarded I hope it will not be later than next Saturday. M^rs^ Whelpdale has some thing to send us from Battersea which I hope will be forwarded in Time to send with it. We shall also thank you to purchase for us one of the pads which are made, I guess, for Donkies, & which you see at almost every Saddlers shop window, they are without a Tree & stuffed & cost about 30/–. It must have a crutch which it were better should *unship* as it will hereafter be useful for Thomas[3] and Mary[6] – at present we are so badly off for *hackneys* that we must ride, for one, a little wee wee poney far less than Radnor – & without a saddle to fit it would be intolerable; besides there is not a saddle about the premises fit for *a Lady* to ride upon. John Hall is already commissioned to buy a side saddle for Mary[2] & we beg that you will send us this pad off by the very first Carrier, & if you see John[1] H. ask him if he has forwarded his & hasten him – My Aunts Carriage, as we call the Gig it having been sent-for for her use, is on its way from Rydal Mount – So if we had but our Saddles we should be fit for any expeditions – I wish you were here to *tivy* with us. God bless you! Remember me to our Friends at Battersea – (Jane wrote to them yesterday) – and also to Sartorius – I expect you to write me a very entertaining Letter & tell me all what you are about – I have but written 3 Letters yet since I came into these parts & 2 of them have been to Your Grace –

I believe M^rs^ Luff will be in Town soon; She talks of going into the North with Miss Dowling – Do not forget to send the parcel in Time,

* 'Keept' appears again in Letter 51, p. 149.

if you have not already forwarded it by the coach which I trust *prudence* & frugality prevented. I desired you on the edge of my last to pay 2/6 to Miss Lamb for me which quite went out of my head – & I repeat it now lest it was not legible – I believe they are gone into *the Country* near *Shore* Ditch – Charles talked of going to Birmingham at the holidays – Again farewell & God bless you – Your afft *Kinswoman* S. H.

. . . My aunt says you have omitted paying Rich[d] Addison for the News Paper & begs you to do it – She is still in distress about her money but the merits of the case I cannot find out – I tell her I have 20£ she may draw upon me any day!! What better banker can she have? . . .
In a letter which I have had from M[rs] Clarkson she enquires very particularly after you. Mary[2] says if you could send her a piece of very strong Calico for Night Shirts it would be a great favor. None can be got here stout enough – but if you have it not at Budge Row dont trouble yourself further – Dont forget to send Tom[5] C, a special invitation – You will find him very agreeable as he is in such excellent health he has cast off all his humours.
Have you seen Miss C. since you abode near her? Tell me all about the meeting if you have one. –

*Postmark: Radnor 11 Ju 1818*

## 50

*Thos Monkhouse Esq[re], Penrith, Cumberland, care of A. Harrison Esq[re]*

*Saturday* [*Oct. 1818*]

My dear Cousin
I am most happy to announce to you the birth of a second Nephew, and the safety of our dear Sister. She & the child are both doing well at present & I trust will continue so – She has been very anxious that the business might be over in time for you to receive the intelligence at Penrith that you might not set off without knowing in what plight we were to receive you – and as I guess, though the Sports *are* over, you will not be able to tear yourselves away very soon from the other facinations of Cumberland, I hope this Letter will find you there – Mary says that the Capt & you had best pay your visit at the Stowe

first by which means she hopes to be able to enjoy your company *here*. We expect you to stay over the Christenting which has in the case of the other Children been *performed* at the end of a month – *We* have had delicious weather all the week, & wish often that yours in Cumberland might be the same – beautiful, soft, gleaming, days – a truly '*pensive*' Autumn without the least *tinge* of melancholy in it. John[2] was here on Sunday & is quite well – in excellent spirits & meditating a journey to Town during the winter. My Aunt, Jane Hutchinson, & little Thomas[3] are at Radnor – we sent them off by way of keeping the house quiet.

I hope you have all your sporting Apparatus along with you. Tom[1] can give you good Sport at *Gawyndovepark** where he has plenty of Pheasants which are excellent shooting, especially *sitting*, for City Sportsmen – If the weather do but continue fine you could not possibly have chosen a more beautiful season to shew off the beauties of our neighbourhood to the Capt. – I regret that we have nothing but the beauties of rural nature to exhibit to him – I fear he will find it a dull joke – after the Assemblage of *beauty & fashion* which I suppose he has found among the Mountains – Mary W. told us that you had met with romantic adventures at Windermere but left it to yourselves to relate them after exciting our curiosity – I also will leave all that I have to say till we meet which I trust will be very soon. God bless you! My kind regards to the Capt & all our Penrith Friends – Farewell very truly Your's S. H. . . .

*Postmark: Radnor*

## 51

*Thos Monkhouse Esq^re^, London*

*Hindwell, 16th Jan^y^ [1819]*

My dear Coz.

We thank you *kindly* for your lively Letters – i.e. My Aunt, Mary[2], & myself – the former says that she has a very handsome New years gift in *pickle* for you – 2 beautiful *hams*!! which is more than any of her other Nephews & nieces will get from her – so you who are, as you say, the most meritorious will be rewarded accordingly.

I left the Stow on New years day after having made nearly a 2 months sojourn with the Bachelor – and I am under promise to return again upon the arrival of the Curtains to superintend their hanging up.

* Gwerndyffnant: an instance of her mimicry of odd or local pronunciation.

John[2] has often groaned over the expence that was hanging over him; but the Bill was an agreeable surprize being less than he had expected – It is a *sad job tho'* that the Muslin is forgotten, as neckclothes are greatly wanted at both houses. I have no fear that the broach will not suit all parties. 'Tis the emblem of 'chaste Dian' & therefore suits the *Donee* as well as the Donor.

I send this by John Hall who purposes leaving the Stow on Monday & will also take charge of My M.S. [manuscript] & 3 pair of your stockings for you – the Stockings are so coarse that I think your *delicate* skin cannot endure them – but no better could I get here – but if they are wearable, & fit, you shall have as many more pairs of the same kind as you like only let me know soon; and when I can meet with better yarn I will knit you some nicer. The M.S. was finished at the Stow, therefore I could not attend to your orders – but even had I known your wishes before I know not how I could have made you a Selection if I had left out all which are to be found in Percy's* – it would be a difficult matter to make one of any size out of *scarce books* that would [be] worth transcribing or would answer the purpose for which my book is intended, that is a book to take up when you shall meet with nothing to dislike. William[1] thinks it such an agreeable one that he has often talked of having it printed – He is very fond of Books of Extracts, & has often had schemes about one – & he gives me great credit for my arrangement of these poems. But as you have sent a Book I will try to fill it for you according to your own *receipt* but this cannot be till I am better provided with Books and perhaps it may be many years before it is accomplished therefore in the mean time you will I hope accept my '*Keepsake*'† and get it bound – for I could not meet with a *Book* at Hereford & the paper is not very nice, though they would persuade me it was the best possible. Mary[2] also sends the Old Doctors print‡ which she will thank you to get framed – *not too smart* –

* Thomas Percy's *Reliques of Ancient English Poetry*.

† Sara Hutchinson transcribed at least five 'Keepsakes', anthologies of poems chosen by her – sometimes with advice from the prospective recipient. Two handsome quarto volumes still exist, beautifully written. The choice of poems provides an interesting sidelight on her taste which ran clearly to seventeenth- and nineteenth-century writers, and those not the most obvious ones. But Sara's 'Keepsakes' are a subject for an article, not a footnote. After the original one, she did one for Thomas Monkhouse, one for Henry, her sailor brother, one for Mrs. Cookson, her friend in Kendal, and one for little Mary Monkhouse. There may have been others. There is also her private collection of the poems of Wordsworth and Coleridge known as 'Sara's Poets'. Cf. Appendix III of Wordsworth's *Poems in Two Volumes*, 1807, edited by H. Darbishire (2nd ed. 1951).

‡ Of Dr. Andrew Bell.

I think one of those broad flat black frames would be the neatest and most suitable.

How grieved I have been about this Charter House affair I need not say – It really has been quite an affliction to me. I was sure that William [?Jackson] had marred the business before I saw the Letter – And wonder that Wm[1] & D.[1] did not try to prevent his sending such a Letter – but they are so accustomed to his strong mode of expressing himself that they forget what effect it has upon others. Russell would conclude that the Boy was an amiable Boy about half wise – & withal *a Pet* – that whatever was said in favour of him was prompted by, & had no foundation but in the imagination of a fond Parent. I hope you told Dr W[ordsworth] how William [JJ.] had libelled the dear Boy. I am sure that he is not of 'slow faculties' – He is only slow at his Book – And if the Master had but seen him he would not have been rejected – Southey always says that something *must* come out of that circumstance. It is evident that the rule, tho' general, *can* be dispensed with on particular occasions – and I have no doubt that it is only keept* with regard to the Boys upon the foundation. I wish this matter could yet be accomplished – and I think it might if anyone who knew John[4] & W[illy][2], also was acquainted with the Master – for I am sure he will be quite lost at home. His Father will I have no doubt do his very best – but it is impossible that he can be kept so regularly to it – besides the exercises in a public school are so much more fitted for ensuring their success at the University hereafter – We hear on all hands that Hartl[e]y failed only of being in the first class because he had not been properly drilled – that in some things he exceeded even the great expectations that were formed of him from being C[oleridge]'s Son – I do not ever expect anything of this kind from John but I speak comparatively. And then what is worst of all it is very unfit that his Father's time should be consumed in a task that an inferior Person could perform much better.

I am so vexed about this matter that I have no patience to write about it; & yet I have thought of nothing else – & to this you must attribute my bad penmanship, & stupid Letter, which is a poor return for your lively one – however this will cost you nothing – & I will write again when I am in a *better humour*. Mary[2] & her Bairns are all well – she says it is too soon for her to think of leaving home in May – Baby will not be weaned – And as John[2] says how can she leave her Bairns & he his Bullocks. I should like vastly to join such a party – but I am as you know a bankrupt – and long to be at home again – yet if I had had the money to spend I should have been glad enough to come

* Also used in Letter 49, p. 145.

round by London home for the sake of company – as my friend M^rs Luff would have been most glad to have mine along with her into the North. I think of leaving this place in March – but I do not talk about it – Remember us to the Capt when you write – This Letter will be quite as difficult to read as your own. Nobody here can read them *directly* but myself. – farewell and may God bless you and send you many happy Years – affty yours S. H.

Joanna desires you will forward the enclosed.

Mary thanks for the trouble you have had about the Habit. I hope M^rs Millar is somewhat stouter than heretofore for I certainly am –

## 52

*Thos Monkhouse Esq^re, Budge Row, London,*

*Sunday Morn^g, May 3rd* [*1819*]

My dear Coz

Your Letter followed me to Kendal where Mary[2], the Children & I arrived in safety on the evening of saturday sen'night, having left Hindwell on the thursday preceeding. Tom[1] accompanied us to Shrewsbury, where we staid, the first night – and our journeying was altogether more prosperous & agreeable than we had any reason to expect with such a party – We were sadly crammed in the chaise at first – but the last day we turned nurse out upon the Dickey & were much more comfortable – The weather was tolerable – but since our arrival here it has been very unfavorable – (until yesterday) cold piercing winds with hot sun – we have now had a refreshing rain such as you describe – & this day is delicious – All are gone to Church except myself – who have a *little sore throat* & worst of all no *bonnet* to put on my head! Mary H. has ridden to Church on an Ass – John[4] & Willy[2] her attendants – the former on his Poney, a new purchase & Willy on his ass. I am glad to tell you that Mary is quite well – I never saw her look so strong – She had a cold when we set out, but it left her immediately & she improved in health & looks during the whole journey & has continued to do so ever since – She says this Country always agreed best with her....

I was extremely glad to hear that you had enjoyed yourself so much at Bath & hope you will continue to do so in the same way as long as you are able & can relish it – depend upon it you will, if you live, have time enough to exercise your quiet & domestic propensities – and do not be in such a violent hurry to thrust yourself into the noose of matrimony – this playing the part of '*Coelebs*' will never do. Wm[1] says 'let a wife *drift* towards you,' and you will have a better chance of success – if you go positively in search you are sure to create the necessary qualities where they may not exist – as in the portrait you have sent of your present favorite there seems to be poking out that 'commonplace' quality, '*worth*' which you and your Friend set so lightly by to John's[2] great amusement. Mary H. says that you used to quiz her for recommending Miss Sanford to John[2] – & she does not see that your Lady has the advantage of her in any one thing, except music – Come now dont turn lazy – something better than this will *drift* towards you I have no doubt if you will be a little patient – and so long as you enjoy your present mode of life I cannot see why you need be in such a violent hurry – I should think that even a solitary fire side would be very agreeable after the bustle & gaiety of the day in town – but I would come & spend a winter or a summer with you any time, if I could enliven it, rather than you should *throw yourself away* before you have well considered what you are about. We all do most sincerely wish that you had your heart's desire – that is were suitably matched – and I should, so would Mary H., delight rather to come & pay the Brides visit than visit you as a bachelor – but in that character you say you have had a happy year & you can only be happy – and you may be – what God forbid – but what nevertheless is possible. Old Maid as I am, don't think that, though I firmly believe that the balance of *comfort* is on our side, [I] am a favorer of a single life – *comfort* is but a meagre thing after all – but I have seen such misery in the marriage life as would *appal* you if you had seen it. Such millstones about the necks of worthy men! that I would have you to be *wary* – and you have time enough upon your hands to be so. Of course you will not suppose that I think all the fault belongs to the women – but in your case, or I am mistaken, I believe if you were unhappy it would be the Lady's fault or unfitness – God bless you! & guide you aright – for most sincerely do I wish for your success & happiness in all things.

I found every body here quite well, & looking just the same as I left them. John[4] & Dorothy[2] excepted – the former is much grown – & not so well-looking – the latter in every way greatly improved & is certainly a most sweet-looking girl. John is I believe much improved in his latin – but I cannot approve of this home-tuition in any respect – either for tutor or Scholar. I do wish that Willy[2] would be got to the Charter house – he will do nothing at home – and unless he goes there

I am sure they will not part with him soon enough. They are so much afraid of his health that they dare not trust him alone. – His Aunt wants to bring him to the Central School – but that is an unfeasable scheme though I think it would answer for the Boy the best of any thing – You will be glad to hear that dear little Tom's[3] journey has had a very good effect upon him – it has made him much more sociable – He is quite at home here and as good a boy as anybody could wish – His father & Aunt Joanna are the *Spoilers*. Little M[ary][6] M[onkhouse Hutchinson] has been unwell from Teething but is now perfectly recovered and as sweet & good humoured as ever – the Baby is a little one but very healthy and lively. Mary[2] will I believe leave them here & meet Tom[1] at Stockton, pay a short visit there & return to us. Joannas trip to France is yet unarranged. I hope there will be no need for it. William[1] is very much disposed for a trip somewhere – He talks sometimes of *Norway* – but John[4] ties him to home – to Norway he would take him – but nobody here will consent, I hope, to his going thither. Tillbrook will be here in June – I am sure it is not from want of inclination that he has not found you out – but it is very inconvenient your being in the country 'tis a long way to come for a *chance* of seeing you. His Cottage is about to be made most beautiful under Mr Gee's hands though he has in some things gone far astray from Tillbrook's original intentions – and his purse will be sadly drained – the expence is enormous – but it will be an *exquisite* spot. Mary H. is greatly delighted with Rydal M. it far surpasses her expectations much as they were raised – great improvements have been made in the garden &c which you will see when you come. The Parcel had not arrived at Hindwell when we left it. We saw the print at Kendal & think it is pretty good for a Mag: print – De Quincey writes in *Blackwoods Mag*: so used Mr Wilson. If you saw some Letters from the Lakes purporting to be written by a German* either in that Mag: or the West[d] paper into which they were copied you would be disgusted – but I am glad to say that Mr de Q. did not know of them being put in till too late – those Letters were written by *Wilson*!! Mary[1] wishes to know if you have remembered Dr Bell – if not – have him framed against the next parcel you may have occasion to send. God bless you – Every bodys love truly yours ever. S. H.

*Postmark: Kendal, Penny Post, 5 MY 1819*

* The articles referred to appear to be 'Letters from the Lakes (Translated from the German of Philip Kempferhausen—written in the summer of 1818)', *Blackwoods*, January and March 1819 (IV, 396–404, 735–44) in which are given reports of conversations with Southey and Wordsworth.

# 53

*Mr Monkhouse, Stow, n^r^ Hay, Brecon*

*Saturday 7th May* [1819]

My dear John

Mary[6] tells me that I shall use my 'Tunt' very ill if I do not write him a Letter, after the very active correspondence which we kept up when I was in your neighbourhood. I doubt not but you have seen her Letters to Hindwell, or have heard of our successful journey and subsequent well-doing; and I have the pleasure to say that we all continue Well – I never saw Mary[2] look so strong in my life, and she is very strong, and in excellent spirits – so are the Children whose behaviour is not only beyond our expectation, but *above all praise* – A sweeter Creature than little Tom[3] cannot be – he never cries, but is as happy as the day is long – and though he is not familiar with strangers he never pouts or sets out his lip, but chats as usual with those in the room who are not strangers – Mary[6] is the more shy of the two; & though she is very *wordy*, at her own pleasure, she never condescends to talk to those who address her, be they *friends* or *foes* – and she amuses every body by her oddity – Dorothy[2] is sure she will be a *genius*. George[3] improves very much and is as quiet as a Lamb – the best proof we can have of his being in good health – Tom[3] has kissed my paper knowing that I was writing to you. I think he is the greatest favorite – in the parlour at least – but Kitchen and parlour alike are pleased with them – the Servants, one & all, are at any time ready to leave their work to talk *to them*, or to talk *of them* when they meet with a listener – One would think that I was writing to their Father – indeed such a long prosing is inexcusable addressed to anyone else – but it is the best way in which I could prove to you that dear Mary[2] is comfortable, for if the children had been unhappy of course she must have had little pleasure in her visit. We have now most delicious weather. A fine rain fell on the last day of April since which the air or rather wind, has been very hot (it even reminded us of a sirocco) as well as the sun – Yesterday again we had a sweet soft rain, & now the wind is gone – The Country has improved greatly in beauty since the first rain – the birches, larches & oaks, are all green – and the wild cherries in full bloom – so that the woods are in their greatest beauty. Every one but myself are going to spend the Day in Langdale – Mary[2] rides one of the *Asses*, which she likes exceedingly; John[4] accompanies her on his poney

& whips the ass on, with his long whip, so that she has no trouble – but when we get George's[1] poney we shall be very well off – John's is a very useful *stiff* creature – he bought it with his own money – his Father wishing him to have it for an amusement to take care of, and an inducement to take exercise (he having no companions) after poring over his books which he does with the most dutiful attention. I never saw any creature so anxious to get forward – so obliging and tractable as he is. He is greatly improved in his Latin – he construes admirably and I hope he will do so with the Greek when he has surmounted the difficulty of reading it, which as yet he does very slowly. Dorothy[2] goes on very well at School – and is much improved in beauty. Willy[2] also in health – but is still a sad pickle – however I hope he will be sent to the Charter-house before it is too late for reformation – He [is] delighted with his little cousins & wishes for no better companions.

You will have seen by the Newspapers that *Peter Bell* is published – as also a spurious Peter who made his appearance a week before the true one – Some People attribute the latter to H. Smith (one of the Authors of the *Rejected Addresses*) but I believe it is Hazlitt (tho W^m[1] says H. could *not* write anything so foolish) because there are some expressions & rhymes, in the extracts which we have seen, that occur *only in Peter Bell* which Hazlitt saw many years ago – besides we find that Hazlitt's new Lectures have been printing at the same time & at the same office with William's *Peter* – The false one is very stupid, but I have no doubt that it has helped the sale of the true one – which has nearly all been sold in about a week, now a new Ed: is called for – Some good-natured person – the Author no doubt – sent William a No. of the '*Literary Gazzette*' in which is a most abominably abusive critique – it can only be written from personal *malice* – for the most beautiful passages are selected for ridicule – in many cases the very ones which are pointed out for admiration in the complimentary Letters which W^m has received – however, notwithstanding, it is exactly what I expected – and I wish you could see the article – for after all they confess indirectly that he influences all the poetry in the Coun*try* – This critique made us advise him to publish the *Waggoner*, just to give them another bone to pick, which he has consented to – and it will come out as soon as possible I hope with the second Ed: of *Peter*. If you want *a* PETER *of your own* (Mary[2] has one) & can't wait send for one immediately, that you may have a good print as the second Ed: will not be so good as the first & there are no corrections except in printing. We see in the Papers that Col. Gwynne has met to fight a duel – pray who was his antagonist? Or has it only been, as we suspect, a sham duel to retrieve his character? I hope you have had the *West^d*

Letter to her cousin, John Monkhouse, 7 May, 1819

*Gaz.* regularly – it is always sent from this house the day after it is published – so you *ought* to have it both early & regularly – By the bye could you find among your papers ([the] Carlisle *Patriot* I am *sure* contained it) that account of a mans being blown to pieces in blowing out a candle – it was in two of our papers about 2 months ago – William wishes very much to see the account.

I had a Letter from T. M. while we were at Kendal – He is all alive & in the midst of enjoyment. He means to be here in August – I hope you will come also – but *times* I fear are very bad with you Farmers – I wish you had each a snug Stamp Office here in this Country – Mary[2] wishes it every day. She bids me tell you with her Love, that she has never yet *rued* of her Jaunt which she believes you expected she would do – I hope John Perrington is better & will soon be able to start with my Palfrey. Tom[1] must send me a nice Bridle along – for here are nothing but plated bits to be had at Kendal of a Poneys size.

Now I hope you will write to us and tell us all the news of the Farm. Mary[2] will I suppose see your large West^d Estate today – it would do exactly for your *old* Cottage scheme. We were very much shocked to hear of your poor Neighbours melancholy end – Tell us how his Daughters bear up under their affliction – I am sure you will feel a great loss in him. he was a nice cheerful good humoured creature apparently. Farewell & God bless you! All here desire their kindest regards along with your most afft S. H. My compliments to Harriet, who I hope does not intend to leave you.

M^r Wilson wrote those 'Letters' which appeared in the *Patriot* &c, pretending to be written by a German – they were copied into the *Gaz*: without M^r De Qs knowledge. W^m stopt their going on – I believe they came out originally in *Blackwoods Edin: Magazine* which now takes upon it to praise W^m through thick & thin – M^r W. – *we know* writes both *for* and *against* him – & all that about Southey, true as it was, with some exceptions was not written with sincerity – for W[ilson] does not admire either the P[oet] L[aureate] or his works – *quite otherwise.* Could you conceive such indelicacy not to say want of principle – M^r de Q. writes in the same Mag: which has a wide circulation – & is clever enough – but pre-eminent among the periodical publications – for Gossip personality & scurrility – you have heard of all their manuevres to enduce W^m to contribute to it – but he would not even receive it at their hands – or read it. However after all as they have taken to praise him he cannot be so unpopular as might be supposed as these people do not praise & dispraise from any motive but that of making their books sell – If it becomes a fashion to praise him the *Ed. Rev:* will [soon] be as [taking?] as the rest. Miss Barker is gone to Boulogne.

*Postmark: Kendal, Penny Post*

# 54

*Thos Monkhouse Esq^re^, Budge Row, London*

*July 25th. Rydal Mount [1819]*

My dear Cousin

I cannot conceive how you can possibly exist in London during this hot weather when we, notwithstanding all the clouds which our Mountains gather about us are almost dying with the heat. This morning I walked to Church, & with *unfeigned sincerity* declared that I would not walk back again for 500 Gns. So one of our good neighbours, in charity, gave me a seat in a Donkey cart. I have a poney of my own but it is a *blue* – a true independent – and a worshipper also of the 'mountain nymph sweet Liberty' & having once been turned a-field is resolved to remain there, pursuing its own will while I am forced to trudge on foot – but conquered & enslaved it shall be this very evening – & we will see who shall be master in future – But notwithstanding the heat the country looks beautiful – we have had plenty of rain – even today a water spout burst over Ambleside, & the torrents ran in numbers down the mountain as if it had rained for a month – I wish you could have come while dear Mary[2] was with us – Rydal is, & has been, full of *agreeable People* – At the foot of the Hill we have M^rs^ Hilton & her family consisting of S^r^ John & M^r^ Hilton, 3 Daughters, two of whom are *very pretty* & all more than very agreeable – besides a young female Friend with her Brother whose names I forget – Then M^r^ Gee has no less than *12* Females under his protection who though some of them elderly Gentlewomen are nevertheless very accomplished – being skillful in music, & draw delightfully – you would be enchanted with the music of one of them, in particular, & with the sketches of all – Our Friend Till's Cottage looks even more beautiful in their sketches than in reality – & that is needless – I am sure if it once caused him to break the 10th commandment it now makes all who looks upon it do the same. Tillbrook was here a week ago. He only stayed 10 days & is now upon a visit at Stanwix near Carlisle – He will return here again for a short time, & then intends paying a visit at Hindwell, as he is engaged to return by Shrewsbury where he spent some time in his way down. He is delighted with his cottage & does not in the least regret the money which has been spent over it, or the deviations which Mr Gee has made in the original plan – which have certainly made it a much more habitable concern, & has not injured the *picturesque*. Blakeney's Cottage has again lost its Tenants they *decamped* leaving their furniture to pay their creditors, & it is at present let for the benifit of the Creditors to a Mr Montague Burgoyne & family – It is a very pretty place – but all places must give place to the Ivy Cot.

You will perhaps have heard that dear Mary[2] & her husband & Children left us on monday – we seem quite lost without them – the house appeared as still as death for some days – The children were so happy & good that they were nothing but pure delight to us. I can assure you that Mary has not the least inclination to spoil them – whatever work is done in that way is by Father & aunts. Tom[3] who cares for no one when his father is by was not nearly so tractable after he arrived – but he has quite got rid of his shyness & never once put on a sour look, as he used to do when strangers were by – but I fear he may relapse into his old habits when he goes home & sees strangers so very rarely.

I suppose you are not gone to Paris or we should have heard from you – Pray do not go this year but come & make a long stay with us – for William[1] is sure to go upon the continent next year – he cannot possibly refrain any longer. Mary W. Mary H. Tom[1] & myself spent 3 days very agreeably at Penrith a fortnight ago – Capt B. & Henry A. came to Patterdale with us – and Henry even came over here the week after to see us & the children – indeed nothing could exceed the kindness of the Capt & he would most gladly have fetched the whole party to spend a week with him & his wife at Penrith but their civility came too late as all Tom's & Mary's plans were arranged, & their time consumed else they would most gladly have complied with their wishes. We stayed at Mrs Whelpdales who was most truly happy to see us – and we spent one day with poor Mr M. of Langwathby which visit was most *worthily bestowed*.

. . .We have not had many strangers for the last fortnight – but before that we had some *one or other dropping* in, to see the *Lions* – By the bye we females have a great curiosity to see the Reviews &c of Wms Poems &c in *Blackwood's Magazine*; but as Wm will not suffer it to come into the house with his knowledge *we must smuggle it* – So if *you take it in* bring those Nos – but do not buy it I entreat you if you have it not already for it is not worth the money – only your having spoken to me of those *puffs* made me suppose you had it. We are sorry that the false Benjamin, & the 'battered Tar' have not had the same agreeable effect upon the true Benjamin as the false *Peter* had upon the true – for there has been no call for a second Ed: We had a most droll Letter from Lamb concerning Ben: & the Dedication* – It was worth while to have written the poem for the sake of the Letters.

If your Friend the Capt is with you remember me to him & say that if he makes his appearance in these parts with a stout poney I am at Leisure to attend him as guide among the mountains – Remember me at Battersea to our Friends there – and write soon to tell us what you are about – Every Body sends their love to you – Your's very truly & affty S. H.

Tom[1] & Mary[2] expected to reach Stockton Wednesday last – where I suppose they will remain a week or 10 days – they mean to spend a day in their way home with the Hugessons at Ripon when they will have an opportunity of seeing Studley & Hackfall. Joanna's rheumatism is much better & she has been as busy as a Bee during their absence which is the best possible remedy for all her complaints –

*Postmark: Kendal, Penny Post, 30 Ju 1819*

## 55

*Thos Monkhouse Esq[re], Budge Row, London*

*Rydal Mount, 4th Aug[t]* [*1819*]

My dear Coz.

I have this moment heard a piece of news which, if true, most satisfactorily solves the mystery of your long silence – viz. that you are going to be married! 'To a Counsellors Daughter – a *dashing Dame*'. This intelligence William has picked up at Penrith – was brought there by a Gentleman of your neighbourhood, but the names of the Parties he has forgotten. Now I think you have used me – *your old confidant*, a little scurvily not to have informed her of this most important matter; but I suppose you intend to bring your Bride & surprize us – William bids me tell you to *beware* of a *dashing Dame* – & that you ought to have 20,000£ at least with a wife – especially if she is a *Dasher*, and not one who will sit down quietly at home with you tied to her ApronString, as you told me would be your taste in married

* Benjamin: *The Waggoner*, dedicated to Charles Lamb, was published in 1819.

Life. Be this as it may I hope you will speedily make your peace with me by writing me all particulars, as to birth, parentage, education &c &c with a true confession of the state in which matters stand between you & this said Lady, if such there be, and whether she is the fair one of whom you sent me the description a while ago, which certainly was not drawn by the pen of a Man very deeply in Love – But, joking apart, my dear Cousin, why have you not written to me? We hear such doleful accounts of the commercial world that I half fear you are not so agreeably employed as in making love – Most happy shall I be to hear that you are, and of every thing that promises you present gratification and permanent happiness – And though you may perhaps thank this idle report for my writing at this time – yet at all times I am anxious for your welfare and desirous of hearing from you – So do not place my enquiries to the account of mere idle curiosity for they spring from a more worthy source. –

We are all well – but oppressed by the heat – There is scarcely a possibility of stirring during the middle of the day – but the country looks beautiful and the Tourists do not seem to care for the heat – they roll on amid the dust, and in spite of the flaring Sun. William has been a week at Lowther, and we have had an almost lonely house compared to what it was when dear Mary[2] and her Darlings were with us – I suppose they will now be bending their steps homewards – but I have had no exact intelligence concerning their movements since the day after their arrival at Stockton – they had rather an unlucky journey thither, the chaise having broken down, but no accident happened to any of them except that they all had a good wetting having had a mile to walk for shelter during a heavy rain – however as good comes often out of evil Mary was by this favored with the sight of Aysgarth Fall which had given her great delight, & which she said was by far the most beautiful waterfal[l] she ever saw.

We have had fewer visitors than I ever knew at this Season – I suppose the Continent is still more in vogue than this country – We had a Letter from Lady B[eaumont] at Tarente last monday – they seem to be enjoying themselves greatly – She says She thinks Sir G[eorge] could live for ever within sight of Mont Blanc. Southey is going to make a Tour in Scotland with M^r^ Rickman – He sets out on the 10th.

We have heard from Miss Barker several times – She lives at Boulogne just as if she were in an English watering place – nothing but company & dissipation – without any intercourse with French people & therefore little opportunity of seeing any thing in men or manners that she might not have seen at home – If you do travel in France (*as perhaps you may chuse rather to take your Bride thither)* & should be at Boulogne dont fail to call upon her – you will find her at the Hotel de Prefecture with her uncle Sir J[ere] Homfray. William is sadly [disappo]inted that he cannot go abroad this summer – [though] he does not say so – but among other obstacles that of having John[4] to attend to is an insurmountable one.

Our Friend Westall arrived last night – poor Fellow in wretched spirits – a true Don Dismal – if the cause were not too lamentable to bear a joke – but he has lost a most valued friend – the wife of M^r^ Stephens of Sedbergh and mother of twelve living Children – She died in childbed suddenly while he was in the house on Monday – He is a most worthy creature full of kind feelings – and tenderness to all living things – I have not seen his engravings of the Lakes – but he has got one number out – M^r^ Gee has a beautiful painting of his of Lodore.

God bless you! Do write soon & believe me ever, Very truly, Your's S. H. . . .

## 56

*Thos Monkhouse Esq^re^, Sam^l^ Horrocks' Esq^re^, Preston*

*Rydal Mount, 26th Oct^r^* [*1819*]

My dear Coz.

You cannot conceive how anxious I have been about you ever since we parted – Your pale & jaded countenance convinced me that you had suffered more from the disappointment than you expected to do – and for my own part I am sadly grieved also; as from the little I could gather of the affair the Lady has risen many degrees in *my* estimation, therefore what must she have done in *your's*! Had I not been engaged to return immediately with the old Parson (who had waited for me) I should most certainly have seated myself between you & dear little Willy[2] in the Chaise to have heard all the particulars, both for my own satisfaction and *your's*, as I guess you would have been relieved by detailing them. I have thought of little else, & though I hope for a Letter, to tell me how you are, by next post at farthest; yet I cannot help writing – because I know you are too much given to despairing whilst I, if I understood you aright, think there is much Hope in the case; as I have far too high an opinion of the Party to believe she would have written to you and talked about 'circumstances' had she not determined to *alter* those circumstances, if *possible*; & if *not* possible why recur to the matter at all? – But I am so much in the dark, and so hurried were your communications that I may have misunderstood them & be reasoning upon false *premises* – However I will suspend my reasonings, being unwilling to foster false hopes – although I do think the Lady is worth a *pause* – So do not go and fill up the *void* she may have left hastily* – as is often the case – a sore heart sometimes applies the first *plaster* (to use an elegant application) that comes *to hand*. Well but I long to hear that you do not stand in need of one – for though I counsel you to *pause* and not *forget* in a hurry, yet I should grieve to think that you suffered a hundredth part as much as I saw you suffer on a former occasion. It was unfortunate that you were obliged to *rush* off from us so hastily but I hope you are enjoying yourself, notwithstanding, among your Preston Friends – Now do write soon & often.

William[1] came home yesterday to dinner – His eyes are much better, & he is in other respects well – Southey was at Whitehaven also – W. stayed a day at Keswick on his return –

I found Mary[1] & Dorothy[1] very doleful after parting with poor Willy[2]; but they have got up their spirits again, & I trust that his well-doing will make them rejoice in his absence – Tell him that John[4] & the Donkey came home in 2 hours – and that the pigeons are all alive, & today were put into the Cote – they pick about on the front as tame as possible – Mary forgot to bid you tell M^r^ Johnson that Willy was not to have any *Beer* given him to drink – Poor Fellow you must tell us all about his behaviour &c – else his mother will be sadly disappointed & beg M^r^ J. will make him write to her which he can do very well if he chuses – I hope you read her paper of *In*structions, which inclosed Willy's key – I pointed them out to you but have been afraid that you did not attend. The most material was concerning the *vaccination* which Willy would tell you could not be done at Kendal or Ambleside for want of *matter*. If it cannot be had at P[reston] name it immediately to M^r^ J.

A Bee hive full of honey is come in this morning for you which we shall forward as soon as possible – (also your little *Play* Books which have been left behind) – I fear it will not contain more than half the quantity you required but it is most exquisite in flavour – My fingers are so cold I can scarcely guide the pen – We have had very cold weather since Saturday – Sunday was the coldest I *ever* experienced – Take good care of yourselves, & pray do not travel in any of those

* The wisdom of Sara's caution was borne out by events. Thomas Monkhouse, who confided his many troubles of the heart to her, in the end married Jane Horrocks of Preston, who does not appear to have been his match in affection or sensitivity.

morals that they are (or to speak more charitably *would be*) distestable horrible Opposition Coaches – Apropos to 'Opposition' – the *meeting* at Kendal was very flat – the Fell-*siders* were disappointed that their Leaders disavowed the Radicals – and were heard to say that B[rougham] was as bad as the rest & would no doubt take a *place* when he could get one – not one huzza of 'B. for ever!' was uttered and the number collected not above 1200 or 1500 – mostly without *Coats* & was manifest by the holding up of hands – The dismissal of the L[d] Lieut of the West Riding proves that Ministers are strong – and we are delighted to think that the office of Clerk of the Peace goes along with the Lieutcy (Wybergh to wit) – Farewell ever your's truly, & may God bless you & Willy! – S. H.

Remember me to the Lambs & all Friends at Battersea. I must tell you a pretty trait of Willy – As we rode through Ambleside on our way to K. we spied his companion Joe Bankes of Rydal in the street. We stopped that they might shake hands & I found by his Mother on my return home that he had slipped a Shilling into Joes hand – At Kendal I had questioned him about his money as I found his purse reduced 2/– but he evaded my question & only confessed with 1/– he had spent on a knife. He had taken every rag of his old Clothes to Joey the night before –

*Postmark: Kendal, Penny Post*

## 57

*Thos Monkhouse Esq[re], Budge Row, London*

*Thursday Ev[o]* [*28 Oct. 1819*]

My dear Cousin

I delay not a moment in returning you the enclosed, as I do not wonder that you should be anxious for its safe keeping, it being so highly honorable to the parties concerned. I thank you for sending it – for thȯ' somewhat, as you say, mysterious it was impossible not to be gratified by the perusal – It is in vain to utter ones regrets, or to repeat your exclamation of, 'unlucky wight!' – but surely you *have missed* a *Treasure* – However I see nothing of *hope* in the matter, she seems *to me* not only engaged but *attached* else where, and however one may lament this one ought not to wish it otherwise – The principle of doing as one would be done by I have no fear that you will ever have a desire to *flinch* from – All the hope I ever had was from an idea that the nature of her regard to the other person might have been mistaken – and therefore it was more honorable to undeceive him than to proceed to an engagement which must ultimately be a misery to both. Most sincerely do I join with you in wishing her every possible happiness – – & with her in hoping that you will speedily regain your wonted calmness of mind – I wish I could have half an hours chat with you since now comfort for five minutes is worth volumes of idle scribble per post –

I fear when you are alone & at your quiet fireside you will pull a long face & heave many a deep sigh. God bless you! &, after all, make you as happy as I believe your deserve to be! –

We thank you for your detailed account of dear Willy[2], and are rejoiced that he has done himself so much credit trusting that he will continue so to do. Before this reaches you all his pastimes for the present will be over, & you will most probably have resigned him to the care of Mr J[ohnston]. We shall be anxious to hear how he settles to School. His Letter gave great delight – it will make his mother very happy if he takes pleasure in writing to us. Wm & Mary talked of setting out to day for Sedburgh – but it is put off till next week – for my own Part I have not much satisfaction in thinking of that School for John[4] – but M. says if they find it unpromising she will prevail upon Wm to proceed to Richmond – but will not speak upon this till she gets W. off – So do not name it –

You *must* see the *Cumbd Paquet* of Wednesday last if possible – there is a defence by S[outhey] of the address you speak of, which was certainly written by him – But this is *entre nous* – We all agree that tho' it contained nothing but the *truth*, & was approved by the Cabinet, yet the spirit of it was too harsh and unconciliatory. Mr Waller disapproved – from *pique*, it is believed, more than anything else so another is adopted which *is neither one thing or other* & most wretched composition. Wm does not know its author, but he supposes it Mr W. Wm says it is an elegant specimen of the '*lathery* style'. However he signed it – & it will be presented – the names will I suppose be transferred to it – Calvert approved & signed the first – altho' a Whig – S's Defence is signed A. B.

I delivered your Message to Mr Gee & he will order the Char to be sent as soon as possible – We have had a Vol: of Poems from C. Lloyd* some of which I am sure would give you great pleasure – but the [*torn*], though clever & well expressed, are so diseased in feeling &

* *Nugae Canorae: Poems.* [By Charles Lloyd] Third Edition With Additions. 1819.

if one did not know the state of the poor creatures mind – It is a sad pity they should have been published –

We have no News . . . M^rs^ Gee & I take a sober ride together – but the country looks cold and *unlovely* as the travelling Linen Draper observed today. We have no 'autumnal beauty' – the frost & previous rain have prevented that *gradual* change in the foliage, which is necessary to perfect beauty & harmony of colour – The Newspapers tell us that there has been deep snow in the South – we have a *sprinkling* on the mountain Tops, and very severe cold, but the sun shines & the weather is very pleasant for exercise out of doors – Farewell & may God bless you!

Every body here desire their kindest remembrances to you & to dear little Willy – Write often which I trust you will be able to do cheerfully – if not however doleful you may be your Letters will be more acceptable from the consideration that in spending a part of your dolefuls upon me you may be relieved thereby.

I have re-perused the [*torn*] is certainly very mysterious perhaps even more so [*torn*] you – however you must not *hope* there is no *sure* [*torn*] able as yourself justly feel foundations to build [*torn*]. You must not wish that she could change her mind – [*torn*] *own sake* even.

*Postmark: Kendal, Penny Post, 1 No 1819*

## 58

*John Monkhouse Esq$^{re}$, at 21 Budge Row, London*

[*Nov–Dec, 1819*]

My dear John

I mean this Letter to reach you on Sunday when you have nothing else to do but read it, so that if it proves dull no matter, as I trust it will not contain anything improper to be read on a holiday – I have often thought of you during our late storm – which has now passed away, and the fields look all the greener for the snow which has been cherishing them – but perhaps you have not had any snow and have not been confined to the house – for I find that in the South at least it fell six weeks before it visited us. I put on my habit for a ride this morning but I verily believe the rain will keep me in as the frost has done for 10 days past.

I have taken this long sheet, intending to fill it if possible, & by that means to *extract* a long Letter from you in return, for I want to hear all about the *Cattle* &c & whether you are making a *fortune*. Your farming concerns are the only ones among my friends in which I have any hope so pray do not disappoint me.

We are all well here – Our family is at present rather small, having lost little Willy[2] & M^rs^ Ellwood – She left us the day before yesterday & this is the only time we have been without visitors staying in the house since my return from Wales. We have excellent accounts of Willy as far as health & behaviour go – but no very flattering accounts of his scholarship; but he has been so much noticed & invited out that he has had far too much pleasure. So I find you are going to pay your respects to the Smithfield market after all! – Well I wish you every possible pleasure – yet I must still think that you would have met with more things to your taste, than Bullocks even, in the Spring. – William intends to publish a batch of small poems immediately – & when a new Ed: of the other poems is called for, which will be in a few months, these with *The White Doe*, Benjamin, *Peter*, & the Odes, will make a third volume – this ed: will be a small octavo in a cheaper style* – then *he says* he will never trouble himself with anything more but the *Recluse* –

By the bye have you read 'Peter's Letters to his Kinsfolk'† – as I doubt not they are in your Club for every body reads them – It is a most audacious Book – written by a M^r^ Lockhart, and *Wilson*, though Lockhart only is spoken of as the author – but there is Wilson in almost every page. L. is a young Scotsman – the translator I find of Schlegel's Book which we read together – I said when I was reading the Letters that the style reminded me of those *Lectures*‡, & was then told that L. had translated them – but the style of the translation is much better, the original has *steadied* him – here he runs wild, often into nonsense & bombast, & terribly is the book disfigured by bad English & scotticisms – but there is great power & spirit, though perhaps not so much originality as may seem to some folk who are not acquainted with the '*Hessians*', as we used to call Coleridge's German books – for Peter,

* *Poems, including the Lyrical Ballads*, by William Wordsworth (3 vols., 1820).

† *Peter's Letters to His Kinsfolk*, by Peter Morris, the Odontist (3 vols., Edinburgh, 1819). The work is attributed to John Gibson Lockhart, Scott's son-in-law, but the literary relations of the Blackwood team are probably inextricable. Sara does not refer to the high praise of Coleridge in this work.

‡ Schlegel, C. W. F. von, *Lectures on the History of Literature, ancient and modern. From the German* (2 vols., Edinburgh, 1818). Lockhart made the translation in repayment of Blackwood's financing a trip to Germany for him. The fact that Lockhart translated these lectures, adds interest to his praise of Coleridge's lectures later in the *Quarterly Review*, Feb. 1835.

(as also C. in some degree), is greatly indebted to them for most of his opinions – However you must read the book – though do not *order* it, it is not worth possessing – & it is almost a pity that it should be encouraged – for as I have said it is a most *audacious* & *unprincipled performance* – full of gossip & personality – & contradictions – They say the Authors are sent to Coventry – in Ed. & I am sure they ought to be at Glasgow – though they do try to make the amendé honourable – indeed it is praise & censure so extravagant that you see in a moment that they have no principle at all – William cuts a great figure in the book* – Southey is the *best used* because he is scarcely noticed* – but all the poor Lawyers of Ed. how ridiculous he made them!! The following is the motto which was added to the book at Rydal Mount –

Here's a bra' Scot what say you to that!
Here's another as good as that
Here's the best of all the three
And here's the Lord Provost of Auld Reekie.

Another Book which we have been reading is well worth your ordering, although it may not be quite so entertaining as the above it is more deeply interesting i.e. the 'Memoir of the life & writings of the Rev^d^ Claudius Buchannan D.D.' – Also his 'Christian Researches' without which the other is not compleat – as it contains a great part of the journal of his visit to the Syrian Churches – I always forgot to tell you that the Article in the *Quarterly* respecting the Churches in which Brougham is so properly chastised was not Southey's – It was the joint production of Professor Monk, of Cambridge, M^r^ Croker, & Gifford –

Perhaps you may have heard that it was Williams intention to send John[4] to Sedburgh School – and he went thither for that purpose – but found M^r^ Stephens the Master in such a deplorable state of body & mind that he was obliged to give it up – and not a week had elapsed before we heard of M^r^ Stephens death. A most distressing case! – his wife died about 4 months ago leaving 12 Children, the eldest 18 – 8 of them Girls – They are now completely destitute – for their father was not able to lay up any provision for them save 1000£ upon an insurance for his Life – Their Friends are doing the utmost to procure a subscription, & trying to get some into different charities – and I trust will succeed as the extremity of the case will rouse every one to exertion – The elder Girls are excellent Scholars the Father intended them to be fitted for Teachers – Sedburgh School is in the Gift of St Johns Col:

* Wordsworth at I, 122–3, 179; Southey at II, 143–4.

Camb. – the stipend is 600£ per Ann. – so we hope that a competent Person will be appointed in which case John is to go there.

We expect Doro[2] home in three weeks – She is a great *strapping* Lass now & very pretty – I suppose she is to continue at school at least 18 months longer. We have had a most agreeable Man here – a Mr Kenyon a friend of Southeys – he was at Ambleside & spent the greatest part of 4 days with us about a fortnight ago – and is again returned – He has been four years on the continent, is full of anecdotes – & tells his stories in the most agreeable way without exception I ever saw. He is a man of Fortune without profession – a scholar – He buried his wife at Naples – Tom[1] may remember his bringing Mrs Coleridge & Derwent to Park House, 15 years ago – He says he remember[s] Tom – but did not remember having seen me or any Lady there. He has been as he says ever since his residence at Keswick at that time *bit* by Wms Poems – & indeed he seems to have a better verbal knowledge of them than the Author himself.

*Humboldt, being asked how he liked Lady Morgan's treatment of him in her 'France'*, replied, 'Poor Denon is far *worse off* than me' – If you have not read the Book I must tell you that they are praised up to the skies – A Nephew of Miss Williams (Helen Maria) observed to Mr Kenyon when he was in France – that *Lockhart* was 'a man of exaggerated opinions' – which you will find when you read the Book.

Mr Carruthers has sent William a sweet little picture which he has painted at Lisbon of a view of Cintra through the arch of an aqueduct containing the House of the Marquis Marialva in which was signed the *Convention* – It arrived yesterday & we are all very proud of it for it is very beautiful – and gratifying to William to receive it from him – One of his Brothers – I believe poor 'luculent' is dead lately – Wm, who was with your Father, was here in the Summer when Tom[2] M. was with us.

The last news we had of Tom[2] was from Mrs Luff who says he looks very ill – He has had a bad cold ever since his return to town – & I fear he does not take care of himself. He looked uncommonly well when he was here – quite stout & *fresh* – not the pale face he was wont to have some years ago – Sartorius is I suppose as gay as the gayest at Paris notwithstanding he was second in a duel there lately which terminated fatally – God bless you! my kind love to all. I think this letter may

* *France*, by Lady Morgan (formerly Sydney Owenson) (4th edition in 2 vols., 1818). A gossiping book, and very silly; it was given a devastating review in the *Quarterly Review*, Apr. 1817, vol. XVII, 260–86.

serve both houses – for why should I multiply postage – Kiss the bairns all of them as you like for me & tell them that their Aunt Sarah loves them dearly – What follows I have kept to the last for a bon bouche – & also out of policy as certainly all my own scribble must have appeared dull stale and unprofitable after it – It is a reply to a letter of Dorothys[1] to Mary Lamb asking her no doubt what she thought of Willy – & is a complete Quizz throughout, *founded on facts*, on the part of Charles – Ever your affty Coz. S. H.

The dear Myers is just arrived – alas, alas! for we expect Mr Kenyon to dinner.

*25 Novr 1819*

Dear Miss Wordsworth

You will think me negligent but I wanted to see more of Willy, before I ventured to express a prediction. Till yesterday I had barely seen him – Virgilium Tantum Vidi – but yesterday he gave us his small company to a Bullock's heart – and I can now pronounce him a lad of promise. He is no pedant nor bookworm, so far I can answer. Perhaps he has hitherto paid too little attention to other men's inventions, preferring, like Lord Foppington, the 'natural sprouts of his own'. But he has obversation, & seems thoroughly awake. I am ill at remembering other people's bon mots but the following are a few. Being taken over Waterloo Bridge, he remarked that if we had no mountains, we had a fine river at least, which was a Touch of the Comparative, but then he added in a strain which augured less for his future abilities as a Political Economist, that he supposed they must take at least a pound a week Toll. Like a curious naturalist he enquired if the tide did not come up a little Salty. This being satisfactorily answered, he put another question as to the flux & reflux, which being rather cunningly evaded than artfully solved by that She-Aristotle Mary, who muttered something about its getting up an hour sooner & sooner every day, he sagely replied, 'Then it must come to the same thing at last' which was a speech worthy of an Infant Halley!

The Lion in the 'Change by no means came up to his ideal standard. So impossible it is for Nature in any of her works to come up to the standard of a Child's imagination. The Whelps (Lionets) he was sorry to find were dead, & on particular enquiry his old Friend the Ouran Outang had gone the way of all flesh also. The grand Tyger was also sick, & expected in no short time to exchange this transitory world for another – or none. – But again, there was a golden Eagle (I do not mean that of Charing) which did much arride and console him. Williams genius, I take it, leans a little to the figurative, for being at play at Tricktrack (a kind of minor Billiard table which we keep for smaller wights, & sometimes refresh our own natures fatigues with taking a hand at) not being able to hit a ball he had iterately aimed at, cried out, 'I cannot hit that Beast' – Now the balls are usually called Men, but he felicitously hit upon a middle term, a term of approximation & imaginative reconciliation, a something where the two ends, of the brute matter (ivory) & their human & rather violent personifications into Men, might meet, as I take it, illustrative of that excellent remark in a certain Preface about Imagination, explaining 'like a Sea-beast that had crawled forth to sun himself'.* Not that I accuse William Minor of hereditary plagiary or conceive the image to have come ex traduce. Rather he seemeth to keep aloof from any source of imitation, & purposedly to remain ignorant of what mighty poets have done in this kind before him. For being asked if his Father had ever been on West^r Bridge, he answered that he did not know.

It is hard to discern the oak in the acorn, or a Temple like St Paul's in the first stone that is laid, nor can I prefigure what distinction the genius of William Minor hath to take. Some few hints I have set down, to guide my future observations. He hath the power of calculation in no ordinary degree for a Chit. He combineth figures, after the first boggle, rapidly, as in the Tricktrack board, where the hits are figured, at first he did not perceive that 15 & 17 made 22, but by a little use he could combine 8 with 25 – & 33 again with 16, which approacheth something in kind (far let me be from flattering him by saying in degree) to that of the famous American Boy. I am sometimes inclined to think I perceive the future Satirist in him, for he hath a sub-sardonic smile that bursteth out upon occasion, as when he was asked if London were as big as Ambleside, & indeed no other answer was given, or proper to be given, to so ensnaring & provoking a question. In contour of Scull certainly I discern something paternal. But whether in all respects the future man shall transcend his father's fame, Time the trier of geniuses must decide. Be it pronounced peremptorily at present that Willy is a well-mannered Child, & tho' no great student, hath yet a lively eye for things that lie before him! Given in haste from my desk at Leadenhall – yours & your's most sincerely C. Lamb.

M^r de Q. has given up the Editorship of the *Gaz.* & we have given it up also. I have said nothing about your health – but do not you forget

* Lamb refers to Wordsworth's Preface to his *Poems*, 1815, and to his quotation there from his own 'Resolution and Independence'.

to notice it – & also tell me how your eyes are. Dorothy[1] desires 'her tenderest regards'. Goodbye again – John[4] & I are just going to ride – My Poney is in *high fettle* – John's is off with J[ohn] C[arter] on his journey – but he borrows M[r] Gees.

*Postmark: Kendal, Penny Post*

## 59

*Thos Monkhouse Esq[re], 28 Queen Anne St, Cavendish Square*

*Tuesday, 23rd Dec[r]* [*1819*]

My dear Coz.

As I have the opportunity of sending you a few lines free of postage I must thank you for your nice long Letter though I have nothing to say that would have justified my putting you to *any expence* – I had qualms enow I assure you about the honey – & it was not sent without *mature deliberation.* William is just this moment set off for D[r] Satterthwaites – on business which he has to transact at Penrith relative to his Trust as Ex[r] of his Brother – We have had tremendous weather but this is a fine day & I hope it will continue – Mary[2] would tell you how glad we all were to hear of your convalescence & warn you to take care of yourself in future – I was glad to find that dear John[2] is so near you – his society will enliven you & give an interest to what is going on around you – & drive away I trust painful regrets – I heartily wish that a certain persons *fate* was decided – so that all speculations upon it were at an end – for the end of all things is peace!

Tell John that I wrote him an immense Letter a short time ago which I hope he received before he set out – else it will fall very flat upon him after he returns home – Do not fail to *carry* him to C. Lamb's – especially when there is a chance of meeting the Worthies who assemble there on their public Evenings – I shall long to hear how he is amused at the Smithfield Meeting which *I would not allow* him to attend last year – at least he used to say so – Poor Willy I hope will not get another *surfeit* this Xmas, as I find he was no better for all the Beefsteak & mince pies with which you had crammed him – His Father was in a terrible alarm – so you must mind in future not to give him as much as he would eat, for he is a little inclined to gluttony & is poor Darling very bilious – He never could in his life eat a raw Apple without its having a visible effect upon his stomach – indeed, John[4] excepted, not a Child of all the five but were effected by it – What a change must have been wrought in his reading by so short a time! It is certainly a marvellous *system* & fully deserves all the old D[rs] devotion – I am glad that John[3] has been to the school for I think London does not exhibit a sight so interesting. M[r] Johnson tells us that the D[r] is very anxious to establish a preparatory School for the Classics – I wish if dear little Tom[4] lives that they may send him to it, for he promises to be so steady at, and fond of his, book that it will be a pity if they cannot give him every advantage – I am afraid my Brother John[1] will think Henry[2] has been sadly slighted in not having seen Willy – but he being the bigger Boy and such a *fendy* (if you understand a word) one might have contrived to see him of his own accord –

God bless you! This is scarcely worth even the 2[d] that it will cost you – but I am not in a writing humour & shall [? should] delay the packing of M[r] Gees Parcel if I were – Ever yours, truly with kind love from all to you & John – S. H.

If Willy is at Lambeth send him his Letter if not it will keep till he returns from Sundridge – I promised him a Crown at Xmas before he went away – and intended sending it but they say it will be stolen out of a 2[d] post Letter – so ask him if he wants it & give it him for me & I will repay you with thanks.

## 60

*T. Monkhouse Esq[re], 28 Queen Anne St,*
*Cavendish Square, London*

*Jan[y] 13th [1820],*
*Rydal Mount*

My dearest Coz.

Mary[1] desires that I will not fail to ask you in the very first part of my Letter if we are to have the Nicholson–Charity for the two children that she has named to you, as the families are both anxious for an answer; & if you have rec[d] or do receive the money soon, she wishes you to keep it to go in part of payment of two Bills – one to M[r] Prince & the other at Twinings – therefore she begs you will answer this immediately that she may send the remainder of the money necessary – Mary thanks you for your Letter & most particularly am I charged to express them for your kindness in going to Sundridge to bring Willy up – and indeed for all your kindness to him they are never weary in expressing their grateful sense of it – I did not wonder at what you said about M^r J[ohnston] there is something in his character that always *appears undecided* or not *straight forward*; but it is merely his fear of giving pain, & his endeavours to do all things by gentle means rather than by opposition – You know that W^m wished Willy to be as much out of B. Gardens as he could be, on account of his health, & also as a relief to M^r J. – but after his stomach had been deranged M^r J. said he was sorry that it was thought necessary to remove him always at the end of the week, besides other visits, as he supposed his stomach had been deranged by eating apples & mince pies – & with much visiting he must unavoidably get improper food – but I am sure that neither he, or anyone, cast the least shadow of blame upon you – he seemed hurt that W^m had thought it necessary that the child should always be removed from him except at school time – However the best way for you to do is to tell M^r J. that whenever he wants *rid* of Willy & you are not otherwise engaged you will take him – if he gives you notice – for W^m has no anxiety comparatively, about the Situation now & M^r J. will take him out for a breathing – we did not think that you would stuff him – what I said was only a *warning* to you, because he can bear less of that kind of spoiling than any child I ever knew – and from his habit of eating *quick* even the plainest viands are often hurtful to him – In the case of his parents – & you need not mind M^r J. – I am sure if you know how sensible they are of your watchfulness over him, & your provisions & affectionate treatment, you would feel that you had all the recompence which gratitude can bestow – So on this head you may be perfectly at ease – but I am very sorry that you should have let M^r Js opinion vex you – because I think it must have been misunderstood. I congratulate you on your happy state of mind with regard to Miss P. & I trust that you will in the end be rewarded for all your sufferings occasioned by the *tender passion* – The right one will come at last no doubt – when you will have nothing to do but love both *wisely & well*.

I have written thus far in such a bother that if you make any sense of it – it is more than I expect – M^rs Lloyd & her little Girls have been here all night – Mary[1] & she have been preparing to set out for Brathay – *Doro*[2] & the Girls hurrying the father with his shaving to accompany *them* upon the Lake to scate – He partly attending to John[4] & Derwent who are at work with Greek – Dorothy[1] & I with our desks before us *attempting* to write in a hurry for the post – & I about to set off for M^rs Crumps for a few days – all this though going on in *two* rooms might as well be only in one; for – the constant opening & shutting of doors – messages & arrangements, *to*, *from*, & *by* all the parties – that a more *agreeable* scene of confusion you could not imagine, if you had not been at Rydal Mount when a *moving* was *about to be* – Right gladly did I assent to Mrs Ll. when she said '*Are you not glad to get rid of us?*' – but they have scattered my faculties so that I shall not gather them together again until I have finished a solitary walk or ride to Allan bank – We are all well – Wms eyes tolerable – but he is still sadly afraid of the light so that we sit much in the darkness. We had a gay ball at Mr Gees on Tuesday – upwards of 40 – 30 of whom were children – The Hall had a famous hearth fire in it, & had a good old English look – the dancing of course was in the drawing room – We had also a ball at Mr Hardens on New years eve – & to night the Children have one at Mr Scamblers – Derwent is here – He has left his situation & is going to town to be with his father previous to his entrance at Cambridge in August next – I am going to Keswick in about a fortnight, & shall probably return via Penrith, Appleby, & Kendal – but I have not quite made up my mind to the performance of these latter which are partly *duty visits*.

. . . God bless you & send you many happy new years – write soon & believe me ever most affty Yours S. H.

Remember me to the Lambs – I am sorry that the *wits* do not shew more tact than expose their libertinism in your society – They are a sad *set* I fear – but Lambs wit makes him appear worse than he is – else he never could have written *Rosamond Grey* – that surely comes from the heart. Mrs Lloyd told us that one day Miss L. brought her a list of places of worship in the neighbourhood where she would find evening services performed adding that she knew it would be a relief to her to quit the society she would find at her husbands lodgings generally in an evening – Mrs Ll. expressed her obligation which she felt the more as it was a thing so much out of Miss Lambs way – upon which Miss L. replied, 'not so much out of my way as you may suppose but I am forced into another' –

## 61

*Mrs Hutchinson, Hindwell, Radnor*

*Rydal Mount, 27th Feby 1820*

My dearest Mary

I should not have been so long in acknowledging the rect of your last nice long letter could we have succeeded in seeing Mr Scambler sooner – but the neighbourhood has been so sickly that he could scarcely ever be found at home – poor M^rs^ Gee was thrown down by the wind the other day & hurt herself sadly, & till yesterday she was obliged to be contented to have her wound dressed by the apprentice – Yesterday when he came they sent up for Mary[1], & she laid dear little Thomas'[3] case before him. He does not think it has anything to do with teething – therefore must not be neglected – You must attend to his *diet* & he must wear a flannel belt over his '*little Bowels*' give him strong broth, & animal food; no vegetables or watery diet – and he will send you a prescription for medicine which he has promised to write tomorrow; but so much is he hurried that he begged we would not send for it until then – However I hope & trust that the sweet Darling is better before this time; & that the delay will be of little consequence. How I long to see him, a sweet fellow! and that little comical stumpy creature of a sister of his – and George[3] also I should have no objections to get a *skie* at (to use M^r^ Clarksons favorite phrase) although he is less of an *acquaintance* of mine. Yet I dare say I should take him into favor, if it were only for his beauty's sake – but he never can rival Tom in my affections – From a hint in yours, concerning the coronation, I guess there is another claimant upon one's affections about to make its appearance – but remember if it is a Boy & *not* named *John*, I will not have him for a nephew of mine – if it is a Girl you may call it 'Alexandrina Victoria', or any daft name you like, in compliment to our future Queen that is to be in default of a better – only think of an *English* queen with such a name!* Further I must add that if you have *Twins* they *must* be *John & Joanna* – if 2 Boys *John & Johannes*, or *Hans*, or the same name in some *other* language – If 2 Girls, still by the same name in two different languages – This is the only pretty way to manage these matters in case of twins, & I have it very *much at heart* that it should be adopted. M^rs^ Grant is the only Person whom I have heard of that had the same idea. She had a *Peter & Petrina* – I am not joking although I have written this to make you smile.

I need not tell you that we have been sadly grieved about the affairs at R[adnor] – & fear that Tom will suffer more than he ought to do – indeed it is not for him to suffer at all. Your own affairs are sufficiently hazardous – and I wish we could see any hope of better prospects – such as you must not think of emigrating – you must stick by old England – but I think it would be well if G[eorge][1] would turn his thoughts towards the Cape. He & his wife are young enough, & able,

* Queen Victoria (Alexandrina after the Czar of Russia, and Victoria after her German mother) was born May 1819. The much-loved Princess Charlotte had died 5 Nov. 1817.

to labour – William[1] is quite on the side of the landed labour & what he has seen of G. W. Hall's statements he thinks are accurate – but wishes he had seen the whole. He has mentioned the case of the farmers, & what you say respecting their case in your last, to Lord Lonsdale & L[d] Lowther, & will speak further on the subject. M[r] Bolton is of the same opinion, & is gone to Liverpool to assist M[r] Canning upon whom also he will urge the subject; & as he M[r] C. is member for a mercantile Town it will come with greater effect from him. M[r] B[olton] wished to have a Letter containing a statement of facts & opinions from a respectable & intelligent capital farmer – which he says would have more weight than from any body of men – therefore W. & he wish that Tom[1] or Johnny[2] who is more likely not to object to writing would write to W[m] & give their private opinion. We hope to see one or both of them at the Election; though we hope also that it may not be a matter of necessity – but it might be worth while for John to come to have some conversation with the members on the above subject; as he may be *sure* that he will be attended to. Southey is also of the same opinion but he is, he says, ignorant on the subject & therefore, unless he were enlightened, can do nothing else. I have no doubt but he would give the Farmers a helping hand. I returned from Keswick last Thursday week where I had been 3 weeks – the last of which was consumed in nursing a sore throat – and I was obliged to come home in a chaise, with a *raw neck* & very weakly, before I had finished my visit; & was obliged also to postpone my intended *tour* by Penrith, Appleby, & Kendal, home, on account of poor M[rs] Luff, who after all returns to Mauritius next month with the Farquhars, and whose luggage I had to send off with all speed. I have therefore given up my intended visit for the present – as I do not wish to encounter the bustle of the election at Appleby or Kendal. We were in hopes that the Blues* intended to be very quiet – but Mr B[rougham]'s address, which you would see in yesterdays Paper, has destroyed these hopes, & proved that it was only the restrictions which have kept the mob quiet – I fear there is no chance of their disregarding his call. How has the dreaful intentions of those miscreants in London proved a necessity of these restrictions! It is well that this has happened *before* the *dissolution* of Parlia[t]. It will surely open the eyes of the blind – William always dread any measures that may be necessary to strengthen Gov[t] – but I hope they will suspend the Habeas Corpus† – & make an example of all they can get hold of. They have been far

* At that date Blues were Whigs, Yellows Tories.

† De Selincourt says: 'No sensible woman ever lost her head more completely than Dorothy [Wordsworth] in the prejudices and passions of the Brougham

too lenient thus far. Mr B. is in great favor with us at present for his proper & temperate speech about the Queen, & Lord Castlereagh's compliment to him is an assurance that the King seems to submit himself to the Laws, & will silence all clamour & speculation on the subject until the laws shall be put in force – and her case determined. If she is guilty, which no one seems to doubt, she will surely keep away – but if she thinks they cannot *prove* her so she is audacious enough to come – and a pretty *row* she will make.* French affairs were frightful enough, but our own has put them quite in the back ground. William[1] & Dorothy[1] intend going into Switzerland this summer with your Tom[2] – they wished me to '*go along*' but if Mary W. will go I had much rather, as I can link myself on with some other party at a future time, which she can not – and as all the children will be off at school I shall not object to remaining behind, for I should not have that constant anxiety or responsibility concerning them as if they were in the house with me. John[4] goes to Sedburgh as soon as school is set up – He does not express any reluctance – He feels himself so much improved in his learning that he does not fear to encounter other Boys – indeed he must know that he is in many things superior to most of his age – Willy[2] you know is doing admirably – everybody speaks of him with delight. He is quite a *miracle* of *goodness*. His dear Mother is so happy now that nothing could bribe her to have him taken from school – and he is himself so happy! feeling the good effect of doing his duty – poor thing! he had a miserable life at home with all the indulgencies that were heaped upon him. D.[2] is doing very well at school – They also continue to like school – their Parents have all written the most flattering Letters to Miss D[owling] & one and all were so eager to return after the holidays that they could not be prevented from coming through the storm – while Julia even came in a cart the day before, because she would not wait until a chaise could be sent for – altho she had been at deaths door before the holiday – but papa must do as Julia likes – Miss Ds receipts for *this* year, with her present number, I have reckoned at £1000 odd pounds – and the school is more likely to increase than diminish after midsummer – She means to have another sister if it does increase, at Xmas – who is nearly as old as

election' (*Dorothy Wordsworth*, p. 309). Sara is a rival. Fear of revolution seems to have been real, supported as it was by the extreme poverty in the period after the Napoleonic Wars.

* Queen Caroline, separated from George IV in 1796, arrived back in England 5 June 1820. Divorce proceedings began 19 Aug., in which Brougham defended her against charges of adultery. The proceedings were not completed; on 29 July 1821 she was refused admission to the Coronation, as Sara predicted, 'a pretty row'. She died the following month.

herself – as well educated, & has been many years engaged in Tuition – she is previously to go to France to improve herself in dancing & speaking the language – D. comes on admirably with her French & they all chatter away as *flip* as may be. The children at Keswick are as sweet as ever – Edith is my delight. She is just what a girl of that age ought to be. Sara[3] is somewhat spoilt by so much learning – she has no enjoyment of any thing else & never seems interested but when she has a classical author in her hands – takes no part in any conversation but what relates to books, & *personal beauty** – and she is perfectly useless & helpless as far as regards the ordinary occupations of life – Yet it is a wonder that she is not more spoilt for her Mother & Brothers think there is not such another Being upon earth – & be she absent or present their discourse always tends to her. Derwent is so conceited there is no enduring him – but when he gets into the world this will be rubbed off I hope. Southey's Baby† is greatly improved in liveliness since you saw it – it is a sweet lovely creature – very forward – except its *feet* – & in a fair way to be spoilt, for the whole house doates upon it – The father never hears its voice that he does not come out of his study to greet it – and many an half hour is employed there to shew the pictures – 'Go to Papa in the Study' would at any time make him put out his hands to come to me, although he would not come willingly at any other time. Capt Southey with his wife's [sister?] & *six* Children live in Newlands – a seventh is expected soon! We have had a very nice Letter from Miss B. I hope she will get some of her [debts] worked off – she is very comfortable; lives at a small expense – and has already had a good deal – but it is a sad pity that she has thus banished herself. Keswick seems so odd with out her! Her nice house standing empty – But I had a very agreeable visit – The Ladies were very pleasant – and S[outhey] as kind and delightful as could be. He is as lively as a Lark – always busy, & yet always at leisure; his *Life of Wesley* is just finished printing, & will be out soon – you will find it very entertaining. . . .

[*about a third of the page torn off*]

* A brochure by Edith Coleridge, Sara's daughter (*Some Recollections of Henry Nelson Coleridge and his Family*, Torquay, 1910), provides an amusing gloss at this point. 'In a girlish essay, unpublished, entitled 'The Disadvantages of Beauty', she describes the difficulties which beset a beautiful girl on her entering into society, especially from jealousy, not the jealousy of the younger women her contemporaries, whom she ever found kind and generous, but the jealousy of their mothers and aunts, who could not bear to see their dear ones eclipsed by a rival's claims. With characteristic naïveté, Sara never perceived that no one could possibly have written such an Essay, except from the standpoint of personal experience.'

† Cuthbert.

– M^r^ [?] W^m^ & D. were at Kendal yesterday – L^d^ L. arrived just as they were setting off – I hope he will get his canvass over before the mob is let loose by the dissolution of Par^t^ – They are all at Church except myself.

My aunt will be sorry to hear that Doctor Cookson is dead – one Letter which came today brought this intelligence – He died last Wednesday – He has been ailing long – and his son says that had his life been prolonged it would have been one of suffering. His last complaint was a dysentery. He heard the bell toll for the funeral of the King, & said 'the good old king is gone, may my end be like his' – and he did die without a struggle. Mrs C. and all the family were as well as could be expected – Christopher said she set him a noble example of fortitude & resignation.

M^r^ Gee is, as you may guess, as hot as pepper after electioneering business. He means to carry up the Title deeds tied with a bunch of yellow glorying in the boast which he will make of having made himself a Freeholder for the very purpose of voting against the Blues.

I do not wish Tom[1] to interfere at all with respect to my Trunk; if my last demand is not attended to I must serve a writ in due time, upon George Young. My Poney is in most excellent condition quite a beauty – too frisky almost for me to ride now when I am not over strong – but M^r^ Gee will cool it during this election. He has had it off one excursion & is going to Lowther tomorrow. . . .

You will be angry at this small hand but I did not think I had so much to say. . . .

All the resident gentry and clergy are yellow, & do not object to what is called the domination of the House of Lowther – it is only strangers who have no natural connection with the country with the exception of Crackanthorpe & Wyburgh, that are against it. If Col Lowther had retired B[rougham]s chance would have been much better – but the Col: was loudly called for by all the yellows & there was no one else to stand. The blues fully expected young Hazel & were evidently disappointed but he is yet too young to have the confidence of the County. No contest is at present expected in Cumb^d^ notwithstanding the advantagement respecting an *independent* member. Farewell & God bless you all. I hope my Aunt and you are all well again. . . .

## 62

*Thos Monkhouse Esqre, 28 Queen Anne Street,*
*Cavendish Square, London*

*Monday, 10th Apl [1820]*

My dear Coz.

Thanks for both your Letters – The one from Preston was very *entertaining* inasmuch as you know that there is always something in the misfortunes of our best friends even that gives us pleasure – but in your case there was something more for we had our *revenge* in your disappointments – I would not for a trifle that they should know of your detention in Wales – Mary would say you were tender Brother not to have changed your purpose – But now I suppose your regrets are all passed away – the sweet society of the Misses Horrocks made amends for all – By the bye Mr Gee tells me that Miss O[aks], the lady whom you mention as staying at Hendon, is a very charming Girl – and that by your praises of her he thought that was also *your opinion* – *his is* that you would be lucky if you could succeed there –

Well, but no matter of such nonsense, I must tell you that your yesterdays Letter made Mary W. very happy – She had looked for it every day since Wednesday – and *of course* concluded by your silence that the dear, poor, helpless little Boy was wretched at the Charter House – & was half angry with me who could hope that he *could be happy* there – I am glad that the dear little Fellow will have a holiday at the end of this week, when his Aunt will be in Town, so that there will be no interruption or irregularity & she may enjoy his company without scruples of conscience – Dr W[ordsworth] said he hoped to be in Town on thursday but that was I think the very soonest – Dorothy[1] will inform you the moment of her arrival – Tell her that William expects she will lose no time in communicating with Longman – We have heard nothing from him since she went – & he is very anxious that the Vol: should be out & the reprint of the Poems commenced* – John[4] leaves us this week – the house seems already as still as it can be – but what will it be when I am left alone – nothing less than *awful*. I wish for dear Dorothy back every hour although I would not be so *cruel* as take her away from her good Brother who I am sure must have so much pleasure in having her beside him – And you also

* The 1820 edition. See Letter 58, p. 165 *.

will feel Lambeth like another home when she is there – I hope you will write to us often & not give up the pen because you know that Dorothys is always ready.

William & I went to Kendal on Thursday Ev^g & stayed till saturday morning – and he is to be off again on Wednesday to meet Lord Lonsdale at Keswick & proceed with him to Whitehaven – This work will never have an end – Poetry & all good & great things will be lost in Electioneering – Your Friends Freeholds will be attended to – M^r Crump is going to sell Scone Crag in Parcels for Freeholds by public Auction – but unless they can be got at a fair price W. will not bid up any *blue* Property above its value – else they would be pretty Freeholds –

We were greatly surprized with the news of the arrival of another Niece in Wales – I hope dear Mary[2] will take care of herself for the weather is very treacherous, and she has had a succession of bad colds during the winter which have caused her present weakness – Added to this her great anxiety concerning the state of their affairs preys upon her mind & must injure her health – Most heartily do I wish that they were more in the world for she is so naturally disposed to cheerfulness that in society she would perforce sometimes cast off her anxieties – Yonder they seem all alike the whole house constantly repeating the same strain – If George[1] were disposed of I think it would be some relief to them but till he himself proposes some scheme *heartily* of what use is it for others to scheme for him. He is not a Child that one can make do as he ought, & yet he is as helpless as any child when he has once got into difficulties –

Do not forget Henry[2] Hutchinson when you have Willy[2] with you – And Dorothy[1] must give Anne a call at Miss Babbington's in or about Sloane Street when she may chance to pass that way. I think I should have gone to Penrith this week to pay my long-intended visit if I was sure that A. Whelpdale was still there, because he sent so kind a message & offer of coming for me which I could not do when D^r W. was here & D. on the eve of such a long absence. Remember me very kindly to him & M^rs W. when you see them – We are all well except myself who am now writing with a distracting tooth and ear ache which I suppose I brought on yesterday by *walking* to Church – Farewell Kindest remembrances to Dorothy – D^r W. & Willy – Yours ever most truly S. H.

W. is just come from the post and has got the proof title page &c – So D. will have no care about that.

*Postmark: 15 Ap 1820*

# 63

*T. Monkhouse Esqre, 28 Queen Anne Street*

*Sunday, 30th Apl [1820]*

My dear Coz.

Although I suppose you do not intend to favor me with another Letter while Miss Wordsworth is in Town, as through her means you can hear all the Rydal news, yet I am resolved to remind you of your duty to a faithful correspondent, which I can do without putting you to the expence of postage. Mr Whelpdale who has been with us since friday leaves us by tomorrows coach. He seems to enjoy himself very much amongst us – we have had two pleasant rides together, & in the morning if the weather proves favorable intend going to the Station. What a pity that he did not bring his wife with him to astonish her among our mountains! William talks of setting [off] tomorrow fortnight, but it will be a week at least before they reach Town – being to spend some days in Oxfordshire – Mr Jones proposes that they shall visit Stowe, & Blenheim, from his house – which will consume two days at least. When the time draws near I cannot help wishing to be of the Party – altho I have no regrets at being left behind, as this could only have been to the exclusion of dear Mary – who certainly could have had no other opportunity of visiting the Continent. I hope you will be able to accompany them – and, as you have said nothing to the contrary, I suppose you have arranged matters with the Wheelwrights – By the bye if they come into the North, I hope they will not pass Rydal Mount without giving me a call. Mrs A. W. tells her Husband that she hears from Mrs Chatfield that you are *going to be married* with a Lady who draws exquisitely – so Mr Gee & he, laying their heads together, have made it out to be Miss Oaks – the Lady upon whom you called at Hendon – but I am afraid this is not the case after your declaration in favor of the Preston young Ladies – I hope you do not mean to exclude me from your confidence this time, as I have always been most faithful so prepare for a confession.

Miss Wordsworth will read you some of the entertaining parts of Miss Barkers Letter which I shall send her – if she were at any other place than Boulogne I think I should at some convenient time accept of her invitation as one might have some good fun together – she is so lively & finds entertainment wherever she is – but the society of B[oulogne] is not the most choice – and it is not in high repute among the English as a residence. You must go to see her – William talks of going by Rouen & returning by the Netherlands – and you, now that I recollect, are only to join them at Paris so this cannot be – well but when *I go* you shall escort me – unless you are engaged with a more interesting female companion at home – which if M[r] Chatfield is right will most probably be the case before I shall be at liberty. . . .

William has had a delightful Letter today from Haydon who seems in great spirits as to the success of his Picture*, which he says will meet all his present exigencies – I know not when any Letter has given me more pleasure – poor Fellow! what a relief it must be to him – & what an encouragement to persevere which I hope & trust he will do – I long to see a Picture, which must be almost new to me the principal figure being entirely painted since I saw it – one cannot wish it not to be sold – but I hope it will not then be wholly inaccessible after this season. I wonder how much he will realize by the exhibition of it.

M[r] W. tells me that all the Penrith folk *cry out* concerning a late marriage – & the part which the Ladies parents acted towards a certain coz. of ours – but all seem to think that he has not broken his heart after the Lady – Pray do you hear anything of the *worthy Couple* – I suppose you will meet hereafter as cooly as possible though I think she must look a little queer. I am writing to D. by the same conveyance – so you have no need to shew all this nonsense to her – I have nothing else to say else I should not have written it – for I took up the pen merely to shew you that I did not mean you should be relieved of the burthen of my correspondence. So I beg you will write soon. God bless you! & believe me most affty Yours S. H.

## 64

*Thos Monkhouse Esq[re], 28 Queen Anne St, Cavendish Square*

*Sunday Night [June 1820]*

My dear Coz.

What a precipitate young Man you are! Take care what you are about! and consider well what you are about to *lose* as well as *gain*. It will be no more '*the handsome* Mr Monkhouse' – You may grow more beautiful every day, after you are married, and old Miss Pritchard,

* Haydon's painting, 'Christ's Entry into Jerusalem', for which Wordsworth sat as one of the figures, had a public triumph in Edinburgh, London, etc., when he exhibited it in 1820.

even, will not espy out the half of your charms – Nay I should not wonder if the young Ladies were to fancy you were rather plain, & they would be sure to pronounce your Brother *more agreeable*, although heretofore he used to complain of being thrown into shade by his younger Brother – O such a change will be wrought in your situation as you are not aware of! – You may come into the country year after year, & nobody will talk about you – except M^rs Anthony Harrison & a few elderly Ladies like ourselves – Think I say of all these things *& can you endure the neglect that awaits you*? – Upon your first visit to the North, of course, you will '*come in*' for *some* share of the notice which your Lady will attract – but after that all will be over! There will be nothing left but *humdrumming it*, as William would say, over the fire side together – Well – without a joke – God bless you! for it is a most serious affair I have no doubt in which you are at present engaged, and for *that very reason* I have written *nonsensically* – Yet from the very bottom of my heart I send you my best wishes & prayers for all the blessings that this world can give – & that the first may be a wife as good as you deserve – You need not caution me as to our neighbours – I should never have mentioned your name connected with such a subject seriously except at home – but by chance M^r Gee hit upon this Miss Oaks knowing she was at Hendon at the time you called –

How will your present engagements square with the continental Trip? I begin to fear that this will end like poor Mary[2] Hutchinsons & my long-talked-of attendance at the Coronation – in disappointment – Schemes executed as soon as formed are best – those long contemplated are seldom executed – every day some new obstacle starts up – & I shall expect to hear that the Tour is relinquished, until I know that you are all fairly out of London, & on your way to the Coast. William's Eyes are in a very precarious state – and if not greatly amended I am sure he will not have the heart to set out – neither I think will D. be happy to leave her brother C[hristopher] unless his health is perfectly reestablished. How much more serious his illness has been than we supposed when W^m & M. set out – although Mary thought it would be much better that they should not go to Lambeth while he was in so weak a state, as Company is injurious to him.

Doro[2] has just left me – she came to dine and we have had a nice cozy evening together – I assure you we look forward to much enjoyment during the holidays notwithstanding our solitary condition – I think of your 'parading & masquerading' every evening – for the country is at present most enchanting, & though I should have no objection to join you – yet I cannot but wonder that *every body* does *not come here* to see how beautiful we are – I cannot but admire the good-nature of your Friends in taking Willy[2] to Sadlers Wells* – I think the whole amusement which you adults could have must have been in seeing his transports.

Good night & God bless you! I hear nothing of our dear Friends at Hindwell & Stow – but I hope better times are awaiting them – at least their case will not again be thrown aside but deliberated upon – you do not mention the Wheelwrights – are they coming North? Col: Salkeld is dead – no very mighty loss I should suppose to any one – I can give you no news of the Carlisle election that will not be *old* before this reaches you. Whenever you are inclined to write I shall be happy to hear from you – but my claims must give way for the present. Farewell most affty yours S. H.

## 65

*Thos Monkhouse Esq^re, Queen Anne St*

*[June, 1820]*

My dearest Cousin

After such a Letter as your last you had a right to expect a somewhat speedier acknowledgement – But nonsensical as my last was I looked upon it as something of an answer, for what further can I say than wish you all possible happiness – You have certainly had better opportunities of knowing the Lady – than any other that you have *aspired to* – & therefore one may reasonably hope that you are not deceived in her – The picture you have drawn is very amiable, & I do believe not flattering – all I have to wish is that you may find her as good a wife as you deserve & may God bless you together! – I shall give you my opinion when I see her – till then I shall adopt your's – and *Miss Wordsworths* which is sufficiently favourable for any reasonable Person – and I *give my consent* if that is what you wished for when you begged me to write immediately.

I am writing in a great hurry to save the post so excuse this wretched scrawl – I think it is more than probable that you will all be prevented going to the Continent – M^r Renshaw's Death will perhaps be an obstacle to Wms leaving Eng^d in time. So after all we may see you, &

* Then a playhouse for lighter plays and pantomimes. Possibly they took Willy to see the famous Grimaldi who in old age was still acting occasionally.

perhaps your Bride in the North – By the bye if *you* mean to come with your Horses, pray give me timely warning that I may cater for them with more advantage than I was able to do last year.

God bless you! & believe me ever most affty Your's S. H.

## 66

*Mrs Wordsworth, à la Poste restante, à Geneva*

*Wednesday 16th Aug*[t] [*1820*] *Doro's Birth-day & yours dearest Mary altho I was not aware of it when I began to write God preserve you both for many happy years*

My dearest Friends

Once more I am left quite alone – for the first time since dear Doro came from school – she returned 3 weeks ago – John[4] on Thursday last, & Henry[1], who came over to see John before he went, left me this morning, having been detained since sunday by the rain. Such weather we have had for the last month, constant rain for whole days together – on others thunder & showers, very heavy – & sometimes soft drizzling uncomfortable weather which was worst of all. In spite of it we are all well and happy – and thankful to hear such good accounts of the Rydal Mount party, and wish that your fellow Travellers were as comfortable. It will be a sad pity if poor Mrs M[onkhouse] is excluded – but better see no sights at all than run any risk of being laid up entirely – I am glad that dearest Dorothy is resolved to take care of herself – much as it grieved me to find how ill she had been yet I fully expected it from her eagerness, and unwillingness to believe that she is not as strong as possible – How glad dearest Mary[1] to find that you are so strong – Pray tell me whether your appetite is improved that I may know whether you *can* be strong without food or not. I was sorry to hear of William's using your Spectacles – '*Use Eyes* & have eyes' shall for ever be my maxim! I have worked more since you left me than I have done for many years – and my eyes are far better than I used to fancy they were when I had the fit of taking care of them upon me – if I work till 12 o'clock at night they do not ache in a morning as they used to do – I am sure, *Mary*, you gave up too soon – mine are now as good as ever they were – Well but enough about this – though I have said we are all well I have not heard one word of Willy[2] since you left Town – except that Mrs C[larkson?] when she forwarded the

Coblenz Letter said she *expected* him that day; & by a Letter which Doro received from Sophia Lloyd I found he had been spending the day before that at Kensington, very well and happy – Ned Lloyd, whom I did not see, told John[4] that he was a great Dandy – & talked like a *Londonner* & sported all their phrases – Sophia did not mention her Uncle at all – so I hope he is better – though I cannot say but that I felt rather hurt that no one should have written to me as if I had no interest either in him or Willy after you were out of the Kingdom – Of course I was not *uneasy* – but I should have been better pleased if you had desired some one to do this – & not leave me to hear even of Willy by mere chance (& of the D^r^ [Wordsworth] not at all – the public papers would have told me if he had been dead & in that way I should have heard of such an event) Doro wrote to Willy & I expect he will answer the Letter from Playford – Mrs C[larkson] will of course write to you at Berne or Geneva – John[4] went to school in great spirits – He was most industrious all the while he was here notwithstanding his propensity to lying in bed – and this was not *general* – latterly he used to read the larger Ed. of Goldsmiths *Hist: of Rome* in bed of a morning – *that* Book he really did devour. Mr. W. had ordered it to be read, & he found it so entertaining that he was quite possessed by it – If he had two minutes, only, to spare he was up to the office and reading; & we might call for ever if we did not go to his elbow to rouze him – He sometimes read to me, but not often, & he is very much improved – as to Latin he reads it as fluently as any body, & used to have great pleasure in reading it to Doro. He *has* great pleasure in Latin – but the difficulties which are before him in Greek prevented his taking the same pleasure in it, & therefore I fear he did not look much in his Greek books – and the Latin also I guess stole much of his time from Arithmetic. He intended spending Friday Sat: & part of Sunday, at Mr Cookson's as Mrs C had invited him so often he thought it was proper altho' I believe he had rather have remained at his books – however he took one in his pocket which he would *ply* when he was there, as he said James was always in the Warehouse which was no amusement to him – He has not written yet – but perhaps my Letter may not be sent off before next Wednesday. I saw Doro this morning – She & Miss Knott came to see if I were alive after the two last rainy days – She is very well, & quite happy as she keeps the top of the Class – Eliz Crump told me that she had heard Miss D. say that Doro had improved more than any Girl in the school the last half year – this much she never said to me, but I was perfectly satisfied with her improvement – She devours your Letters but John[4] can be quite satisfied with *just knowing* that there *is a Letter arrived*, neither would he be unhappy if no one read its contents to him – but as to reading it himself that is a matter quite out of the question! If you do not return this winter, which seems to be the prevailing opinion that you will not, we intend to take off all together to Stockton to spend the Holidays, unless I pay a visit there before which John[1] is desirous that I should do, & says that I have quite turned my back upon them. George[2] & Charles who are at present upon the moors intend to pay me a visit – & as they will travel on horseback he proposes that I should return with them – and this I would gladly do – but the warrant from the Stamp Office is not yet arrived & till John C[arter] has been to take the Stock &c of the new Towns I cannot leave home for such a distance – On any other account there is no objection – I have weighed the matter seriously & find none – I am not in the least dull even when alone – I can find employment enough – indeed I have hitherto had far too much – no time even to read the news papers – and I have not been a very good neighbour to the Gees lately – they are very bad ones to me – or rather *would be* but if I had not callers plenty – and Mr W. Jackson has been very attentive in coming to see me – The Old Gentleman is something better; he sate an hour with me yesterday – he is at the Hall – was very sorry to hear of his *Turtle's* indisposition – and enquired 'if Mr *Wads*worth was not *fearfully suspicious of being imposed* upon' & whether you found it expensive &c – –

Since I wrote to Scone[?], I had a call from Mr Fergusson & Dr Griffiths of New York – It was last Tuesday but one – they told me that Mr & Mrs Rawson had been 3 weeks at Halstead & I was not a little mortified, as you may suppose, for I should most certainly have gone over with Doro & John to see them – They were to leave H. in a day or two & by the Yorkshire road – However tho' Mrs M. had not sent any message I was resolved that John & I would go to make a *morning call at* least, though I found they were engaged to dine out the two following days – both these days were very wet – & on the 3$^{rd}$ though we rose at 6 did not get off till 10 – however we had a delightful ride – met Mr R. about a mile from H. in a *white Hat* & did not know him – yet his features were familiar – but his complexion so different that tho I said to John that Gen$^{t}$ is like Mr R. yet it seemed impossible & I was satisfied with Johns reply, '*Why that Man is not above 40*', and passed on – Mrs R. too, God bless her!, much improved – as fair as a lily, & so beautifully dressed! – if she had a *silvery toppin*, instead of a flaxen one, I should have had more pleasure in looking at her than I ever experienced from the sight of any youthful beauty – they were at Old Church, & we dined with them, having first ate Luncheon at H[alstead] – Mrs M[arshall] much improved by her two winters in

London – and Mary Anne very pleasant but for the constant pulling down of her shoulders – we left them at 6, & had three heavy showers in coming home, but were not wet, each being provided with an umbrella – John took one to please me – & he did not suffer a drop to fall without unfurling it – 'You made me bring it,' he said (when I quizzed him for taking the trouble so often) 'So I am resolved to have all the advantage I can from it' – We had a very pleasant day altogether, & I believe *they* thought it, a pretty *break in*, and me a very *agreeable* Person – for I was so glad to see the dear old People, after being afraid I should miss them, that being in good spirits it was no *fash* to make myself agreeable – Mrs M. pressed us to stay all night – and seemed to feel that she ought to have told me of the Rawsons being there – for she said – 'I should have sent to invite you to stay with us while they were here but I supposed you could not leave home' – There wanted nothing but Doro to make our visit compleat – but that could not be – John was very chatty with Mrs Marshall who thinks of Sedbergh School for Henry – & hoped if he went John would be like a Brother to him – He is the same pretty delicate-looking boy – Dr Griffiths is a thin *yanky* person – but they say like his Father he is so desirous of seeing W^m^ and Dorothy that he intends to address a Letter to you at the Post Office Paris whither he is going in a short time – so that you must find him out – Mrs R. said his Father would be sadly disappointed if he did not see you – and indeed the young man, though not very enthusiastic about any thing else, seemed very anxious on this point – Mr F[ergusson] looked as usual. John & I walked with them to Ambleside, Mr F. wished to see Doro – & John went with him to Stock Gill Waterfall & saw them off to Bowness in their way to Kendal – they left their Keswick chaise at the foot of the hill – so made a very short visit to us & the waterfalls. Mrs Rawson made fifty enquiries after you all – and wished that you, D[1], could find time to give her *one Letter* – Pray do – I will give up one of mine to her freely. They go home via Scarborough. By the bye that reminds me of Priest Wrangham who I find by *Blackwood* is promoted to the Archdeaconry of Cleveland. Wilson is elected the M[ora]l Philos: chair – & all the Letters of recommendation have been printed in several newspapers; Parties run very high at Ed: upon the matter – He is a Tory & therefore he was elected says Mrs I. Harden – Such a fulsome Letter, Walter Scott's! Mr Roscoe's not a degree less so. Southey's & Williams both Jesuitical – especially the Latter – but every body does not know that never was man *opened out* as he has been – all his drinkings – Cockfightings – Clubs for the purpose of coining new oaths &c besides his unprincipled treatment of W^m^ & other Friends all laid open – Mr Gee says he heard him say such things of Wm as made him despise the man. . . . People seem afraid there will be a *row* about the Queen – they have taken her a house nr the H. of L. which she means to occupy in the day – but cannot resist the pleasure of a parade thro' the streets to & from Brandenbergh house evening & morning – she cannot be innocent being so impudent! – Mr Gee is upon the moors with the 'Lowther Lads' – We talk of spending a few days at the *Fawleigh* as Southey calls Miss B[arker]s house – but the weather has prevented our executing any schemes out-of-doors – Poor Mrs Coleridge wants sadly to see me to talk about her unfortunate Son* – It appears that the Fellows have stretched their power to the utmost – nothing can be proved against him but indiscretions – such as would not have stood in the way of any other Probationer – but they wanted to be rid of him – Wm J[ackson] was sure of it from the very first and said if he had been guilty of any intemperance he must have heard of it being Proctor – I am truly sorry for her – for what can the poor helpless creature do for himself! She is very anxious that the best of it shd be made to the Beaumonts – and it is to be feared they will hear the very worst as John Coleridge's Letter was not *over delicate*.

. . . There have been very few Lakers – and fewer Lodgers – One Gent in veneration of Wm called to ask to see *the Study* – he had named his first-born Son after Wm – I did the *honors* & found that he was a friend of Talfourd – and acquainted, or connected in some way, with Mr Poole – & had been so *wretched* as to miss seeing Wm in Town – not arriving there till a very few days previous to Wms departure – He had been on a Pilgrimage to the Duddon – His name Irvinge – And now God bless you all – I am tired for the present having got rid of most which was upon my mind to say to you & which would not have appeared worth the writing had I been in a hurry to send off a Letter – but all of it will be readable, stupid as it is, at such a distance from home, & when Letters are become rarities – I wish I could *just* know where you all are – and if Mrs M[onkhouse] is better. Henry[1] & Mr W. J. were quite shocked that the Brid[e]groom should separate for a moment – In vain did I advocate his cause – & quote Milton & I know not what other worthies in his favor – it was a perfect scandal to go even to the top of a mountain & leave one's Bride at the bottom!!! My kindest best love & good wishes to all –

17th Mr Gee came home yesterday Evg & returns on Sunday to Lowther to go round the east wood with Ld Lowther who was so busy that he could not go out for one day shooting – so Mr Gee & the Keepers had all the sport to themselves which was *glorious* when the

* Hartley, deprived of his Oriel fellowship, for alleged intemperance.

weather allowed them to go out – he had 20 shots one day & killed 20 – another 22 or 3 & killed nineteen – this information is for the Gent: And he has not brought us one bird to Rydal! Col. L. is not down. Lady E. has been very ill – constant attacks of fever since her confinement – but I believe she is now considered safe – I find that Mr Wilsons election is considered quite a triumph over the Whigs – who had become so insolent in Ed: as to be unendurable – alas they are poorly off if such be a triumph! Better no champion at all than such as he – The Crumps say – *Mr Wilson a Tory!* No such thing!! But he is all things to all men.

18th I think I must not wait till Wednesday for John's[4] Letter – better have nothing further said about him than you be disappointed altogether of a Letter at Geneva. We have another weeping day – yesterday was fine throughout & a frosty night – the air has had an autumnal feeling in it for the last fortnight, & all the birds are as still as mice – The woods at Lowther Mr Gee says are already changed – what a short summer it has been! Indeed but for one 10 days or a fortnight we have had no summer weather – I have been obliged to add more cloathing to my bed – though I have still persisted in doing without a fire – the Gees have one constantly. The Garden has been very productive, except for Peas & these entirely failed – off 3 crops not one was gatherd – they grew not the height of my ancle and never filled – the Jays also reaped most of the 2 first; we had but 3 times at Table – Apples most abundant – Gooseberries & Raspberries also – and such a profusion of fine black Cherries as you never saw – but these are out of our reach – John used to sit up in a Tree & feast for half an hour at a time – and Doro with the young Ladies stripped the lower branches. The Patterdale farmer is this moment arrived – so I have sent John to settle with him – Mr Gee sold the bark at Peniton long ago. John thinks there must be some blunder about the Stamp Office. I have desired Mr Gee to make enquiry of Mr James if he has rec[d] his warrant . . . the weather prevents our putting the Borodale scheme* in execution – we shall defer it until Mr G returns again from Lowther – Sally who has not been lucky enough to let the house this year (although there are 25 Cantabs at Keswick) is very happy to hear of our intention – but said we must delay a little as the flood had mad sic *wark* that she must have the house &c *rightled* up a little – I hope you will continue to see Miss B[arker] if you do not go to Boulogne she will be glad to meet you at Calais or elsewhere – The Queen has written such an impudent [?intemperate] radical Letter to the King!! She will not submit to the verdict of the house of Lords if they condemn her – The whole house

* To stay in Miss Barker's house there.

is under the influence of the King &c – and she wished to be tried by a common Jury – but I have not yet seen the Letter altho it is published – S[r] F Burdett called upon her – previous to the Westminster Meeting they called for an address – to ask her some questions the answers to which were to regulate his conduct – Had she raised this Bergami from a menial condition to be her Chamberlain &c – *Yes* – Had he, as was reported, slept in the same room with her? '*Yes* – she was afraid of being poisoned' – a good joke while asleep – So S[r] F. took leave satisfied & stirred not in the affair of the meeting (This is Lowther news by Mr Gee) – indeed I do not know whether there has been one or not for as I said I have not read the papers – but I shall take to them again now that the trial is come on – and doubtless all that has passed will be raked up again so I shall have lost nothing. Brougham has carved out employment for his 2 brothers – Jimmy is counsel – & the other her secretary & gone to Italy after witnesses – The Treasury has already granted 10,000 to the Queens Law Agents – B. & Mr Denman tho' both waited upon her to dissuade her from going to the Play – & in case she did resolved to have no more to do with her. I am going with Mrs Gee to call upon Miss Taylors – so God bless you all for ever and ever! I hope you really do not intend to stay away all the winter – If you do not I shall begin to look for your return as the days shorten so fast it will be little pleasure in travelling – To be in the Towns in the dark is no fun at all – I trust I shall have a better account of Mrs M. in the next Letter – Kindest love to all ever & ever most truly yours
S. H.

*Postmark: Kendal, Penny Post, 21 AU 1820*

## 67

*John Monkhouse Esq[r], Stow, n[r] Hay, Brecon*

*7th Sep[r]* [*1820*] – *Thursday Ev[g] the day of the Eclipse which I never looked for, it was so cloudy that I supposed the sun was not visible but I find every body else looked – and Saw.*

My dear John

I have intended writing to Hindwell every day for a week past – but upon the receipt of yours it has occurred to me that by writing to you I shall kill two Birds with one Stone – thank you for your Letter

– and communicate all I have to say to Hindwell besides; which is chiefly to tell of the Travellers, from whom I had a Letter last week dated Lucerne – *all well* & in full enjoyment – M[rs] M[onkhouse] & her sister were however to be left at Lucerne & to make themselves comfortable there, and at Geneva, until the return of the rest of the party from Italy – Geneva was to be a sort of headquarters from which they would make excursions – so that the Ladies were not [to] be entirely left – Our Gentlemen here, viz. William Jackson & Henry[1], were quite scandalized at the notion of the Brides being left for an hour – nay the bridegroom *ought not* to *climb* a *hill if his wife were* to *stay at the bottom* – Such ardour can the charms of Miss Crump inspire! They do not say one word about their return – so I suppose they intend to go to Rome – & when they will be at home God knows! But as the Ladies go no further than Geneva, I should think too that Rome will be abandoned.

I have had such a disappointment that I am quite *out of sorts*! & have the tooth ache, & a bad pen into the bargain! So you must not expect a bright epistle in return for your *most deserving* one; with so many kind expressions in it to boot – My Brother John[1] & his son Charles came hither on Saturday last. I was in Borrodale with the Gees – & though I had expressly ordered John Carter to send for me over the Fells in case George Sutton & Charles (whom I partly expected) should come yet he relied upon a Letter by the Coach, which did not reach me until Monday Evening, instead of Saturday. However I set off at 4 next morning but they were gone – having no time to spare except *that one day Sunday*, which was spent in expecting me every moment. Dorothy[2] came to them & she & Charles went on Sunday morning to fetch Henry[1] – and they had spent the Evening before with John[4] at Sedburgh – so that they did not entirely lose their errand – though one part of it was to take me back with them – We are all 3 & Henry to go at Xmas, if our Travellers do not come home & say nay. My pen is so bad, & I am so uncomfortable, from my wretched Teeth which I wrenched yesterday with *pretending* to eat a pear, that I must give up writing tonight; else your eyes will suffer by attempting to make out what will not prove worth the trouble; so good night & God bless you! –

Friday Morning. If you knew how many Letters I have had to write, in which the same Tale has been told, you would not wonder at my closing last night in disgust – the rest of my time, while awake, was passed in unavailing regrets that the distance between us is so great that dearest Mary[2] could not come hither for change of air, instead of going to Aberystyth – She was so well when with us that I am sure the change would do quite as well for her – and quiet we have in abundance – and the place is so beautiful, & the Country in full beauty also, that it is little less than able to revive the dead to look upon it – I often think of poor Miss Smiths reply to her Friends, when they recommended a change of scene, 'If I cannot live here, I can live no where'. So deep a feeling has she of the beauty of the Country and its power over her – Even if the road were but more direct one might manage it – for the expence would not be so great as a maintenance at Aberistyth – Do think about it, it is not such *a very wild* scheme – and I am sure she would be more comfortable here without her Bairns than at any other place – We would have both the Poneys in, & she should ride every day – and I would nurse her so carefully – and I think Tom would be happier to have her here than at Aberistyth if he were not there also – besides we could go to the sea if that were found necessary – I warrant you I would set her up for the winter & I have no fear that we shall have a long season of fine weather. – I was glad to hear that you had found a substitute for medicine in fruit & hope it will continue to provide the effect desired. For I often *yoused* (just now look at the manner in which I was going to spell) *used* to think with pity upon your nightly visitations.

Mary Bell *does come back*, and you may quiz me as you like! It is her own doing – She feels that she likes us better than her faithless swain, who will never give pleasure to any human being as long as he lives; & whose diabolical temper prevents his having any in himself except what arises from self conceit. I have only one Damsel now so you may guess how solitary I am – and she can never be anything further to me than *my slave*; for I cannot like her in spite of many taking qualities – and I shall be glad, handsome as she is, when Martinmas comes to take her from my sight.

If your Views of the Lakes are upon the smaller paper I can furnish you with a good 2nd No & we shall also have the 3rd down [done?] immediately – Westal[l]* always sends us some of the best impressions – I have been very unlucky this year – not having sold one copy yet for him – indeed I have had but few visitors, & those staying so short a time the Poet being absent that I could not *rush* upon them – but the work has answered very well; though I am sorry to say he talks of abandoning it, for the present at least. He was married last week – only a foolish *trick for him* though she is a respectable woman – and

* Wm. Westall (1765–1836) was a popular engraver and painter. But there is so far as I know no collected edition of his views of the Lakes, and no attribution in the Southey bibliographies, of any such letter-press to him. In later life Westall impoverished himself by unwise speculation in pictures, and Sara Hutchinson is obviously trying to help him.

Southey tells me that he is going to introduce his wife to Lady Hester Stanhope i.e. he is going into that part of the world – and elsewhere, in foreign parts to lay up a stock of sketches – as the rage for foreign scenery is so great at present – The last No. is exquisite – the view of Derwent Water in twilight is above praise. That Lake is complete, & the Letter press (furnished for him by Southey) accompanies it – I hope he will change his mind as so many lovely subjects are yet to be delineated. Tell me if yours are *large paper* & I will desire him to order them to be sent for you to Hereford – if small I can send them through M^r^ Cooksons means.

I am vexed at you for enjoying *Blackwoods Mag*: It is such an unprincipled publication that I have no patience with it, in spite of its abuse of the *Ed. Rev.*, & its Toryism – because I look upon it as a disgrace to any cause it undertakes – What do you think of the same pen abusing, quizzing, & lauding to the very third heaven, William in the same No.! Nay even writing an abusive article in one No (of him or any other) merely to have an opportunity of writing on the other side next month; & thereby accommodate all parties, and sell their work!! Such is the principle & plan of that said Mag. & our *Friend* Wilson is the Editor! Did you ever read *Peters Letters*? Those are by Lockhart – who married Walter Scotts daughter & who also translated Schlegel – just such another genius as Wilson – and who has, as appears by his writings, as little principle as his Coadjutor. Clever enough they both are, and amusing; but I have always been ashamed to think that I *could* be amused by their gossip, personality, scurrility &c &c – They are both sent to Coventry at Edinburgh, & no wonder – yet W. has been elected to the Chair of *Moral* Philosophy in that university – a most worthy occupant truly! – Perhaps you might see the Testimonials which he published – a Letter of Williams among the rest – Jesuitical as it was I would not have written it, when he knew how he had been used by W. – But W^m^ said he was beneath his resentment, & he could not look upon any Man as a Gentleman who could so far act in opposition to his principles, either for the sake of gain, or to make an impression upon the public, or be the caterer to their bad passions.

Have you seen Southey's *Wesley*? – You will find it a most entertaining Book. He is gone to the Press, at last, with his *History of the War** – but it will be a ponderous work, & long before it is out. He is also writing a life of George Fox† as a companion to *Wesley*. What an

* Southey's *Life of Wesley* (2 vols., 1820). His *History of the Peninsular War* (3 vols.) came out 1823–32.

† His life of George Fox was not written.

indefatiguable creature he is! He came to see us in Borodale with Mr Nash, a young Mr Varden & all the Ladies & a very merry day we had – He is quite as lively as he used to be – the dear little boy is a second Herbert – I never can call him anything else – Edith is coming to stay with me – She said if 'our Folk' did not come home she would come & stay all winter – She is a sweet creature & a merry companion, for she has much of her fathers turn for fun. Sara[3] C. is more of the Piano – poor thing she mopes herself with her learning – altho she is far less indifferent to admiration than Edith – Our Doro[2], who naturally comes to my mind, is a nice creature as ever breathed – She is very well & happy – and improving greatly to the satisfaction of her Governess – Tell Joanna that she has had a long french letter from Miss B[arker] the contents of which I cannot communicate, for she was too eager after the Letter from Lucerne to read it to me – but she is an excellent French scholar as far as she has gone – and every body is daily more & more delighted with the school which encreases every quarter – They have now 22 Boarders – I had a visit from Miss Graves, Miss Bab Harrison, the Twins & their *St Preux* (shall I call him) Bowman, when Margaret Harrison was brought to school – They had *blash* [blast?] weather – but little Bab did enjoy the country in spite of it – altho' she was a little annoyed by the appearance she made after having been wetted so often – a thing of very little consequence in the case of elderly damsels *like me*. Yet I often congratulate myself upon never having been a beauty – for Mrs Coleridge says she cannot come to look at herself – 'and that it is not a bit a matter what one puts on when one is grown such a [*torn*]'. Now I shall for ever feel that it is my duty to make myself as bonny as I can – one has no [right] to force people to look upon what is disagreeable.

I am sorry that you see such factious newspapers. What I hear from Southey & from Lr Lowther, through Mr Gee, leads me to believe that the Que*an* has not a chance of proving her innocence – that she *is* innocent no one believes not even *the Times* newspaper itself. She takes I know not, or rather I *dare* not say, how many copies of that paper – but the weekly cost is 500£ – the like sum was paid to the mob daily at first – but I hope that will not be longer in her power – unlimited power to draw upon the Treasury for the small expences of the Suit were given to her & a quarters allowance of her income in advance – 1000£ was drawn for by her Law Agents for their expences – then 4 – then 3 – & then I think the Treasury demanded – knowing as it did to what use this was put – yet all the time the Faction talked of her poverty. Her House her furniture besides were provided – I forget whether Majocci was the first witness but if he was we thought his examination very good – he soon contradicted himself and as for his *non mi ricordi* – What were the questions put to him? nothing worthy of remembrance – one of importance has never been asked – The Queen did not expect to see him then – she believed him dead – poisoned – Another whose name I forget was poisoned – And L^rd^ Milsington – (I think his name) was stabbed by mistake for another that they wished out of the way – She is a true Messalina – and the indecencies are they say more horrible than any thing that can be conceived – far worse the Lords say than simple Adultery in its worst shape – People say it is all Ministers fault – How can that be when they resigned their places twice because they would not condemn her to banishment instead – and as to the omission of her name in the Liturgy being a sine qua non – Brougham at first said it was a mere Bagatelle – Even B. himself in his speech did not seem to think she had any chance of proving herself innocent though he was forced to say so – He will make a pretty thing of it – that is all he cares – all his Brothers are profiting also by the business – He cannot now say that he does not touch the public money. S^r^ F. Burdett called upon the Queen when a meeting was proposed to address her from West^r^ to ask her a few questions for the regulation of his conduct – viz. Had she raised Bergami from the rank of a courier to be her Chamberlain? Yes – Had he ever slept in the same room with her as was reported? 'Yes – She was afraid of her life – being poisoned' – In her sleep a good joke – So Sir F. made his Bow – & disclaimed having any hand in an address – & whether there was one and I know not for I have not read one 10th part of the stuff about her – Now and then when all her folly is condensed in one Article I read it – or the inconsistency of her advocates – & some of the precious sedition – sickening sentiment – and bombast – and nonsense which have been culled from the answers to addresses – Cobbett is they say her scribe – but Cobbett does not write such nonsense – that is put in by the 'Hoary Traitor' D^r^ Parr* – and some most likely are from the Pen of '*Absolute Wisdom*' – which nick-name the worthy Alderman† will not lose on this side the grave. – But I have given to [*sic*] much of my paper to this worthless subject. If you were but to read two violent papers of opposite parties the Evidence seems scarcely the same. Yesterday I opened a large parcel of the new volumes – there are 2 Sonnets new to me which were written at oxford in *their* way to London & I intended to have transcribed them for you – they

* Dr. Samuel Parr, 1747–1825, the notorious controversialist.

† Alderman Wood, of St. Audley St., with whom Queen Caroline took up residence on her return to England in June 1820. Sara Hutchinson's attitude was not the popular one which was much more sympathetic to the Queen.

are 4 nice pocket volumes* – far more agreeable to my mind than the last ones. – I had a letter on the day of my return from M[rs] Clarkson with a bad account of poor Willy[2] who had been very ill but was recovering – however I believe that he must have brought on his complaint by eating fruit, which he never can do with impunity, though she does not say so – He was recovering & I trust that by this time he is well though he does not recruit as fast as other Children – She & they all were delighted with him – and think him a sweet Boy & of most agreeable manners – So you see how much travel can improve. Thank you for your entertaining account of my *likeness* – I wish most heartily that I had her here – She would be quite as welcome in this Kitchen when I were tired of her as with Harriet – Pray remember me kindly to Harriet whom I am glad to find continues with you & who will not I trust be subject to the tender passion & consequently derange the oeconomics of the Stowe. I suppose you have plenty of Apples this year – we have a super abundance. If 'our Folk' do not come home I shall not know what to make of my stores. Fruit has been plentiful of all kinds – but I daily discover fresh stores among the plumb Trees &c &c. And what a load of nuts upon the Hazels – We were at Wastwater on Saturday & might have gathered bushels by the way side without ever lifting ones arm above head –

I hope M[r] Cookson will compromize with the Carriers – for it is very unreasonable to think that one is to sit down with all the loss – and if I could spare the money I would with pleasure spend a little more for sake of justice – but really I cannot (throwing bad money after bad is the saying) and therefore would be glad that the matter was settled as well as the rogues will suffer it . . . God bless you all! My kindest love to every one – Hope my Aunt is well & Joannas rheumatism not returned. Kiss all the Darlings for me. Yours most affty S. H.

Since I wrote this I have been reading Mad: Dumont evidence – which proves that she is herself just such another as the Queen that while it suited her purpose she thought the Queen a charming Person but she has confirmed the other depositions – & I don't see why Italian Chambermaids are not as good evidence as English ones which are taken in all our crim. cons.

*Postmark: Kendal, Penny Post*

* *The Miscellaneous Poems of William Wordsworth in Four Volumes*, 1820.

# 68

*Mrs Wordsworth, à la poste restante, Paris*

*Rydal Mount, 11th Sep$^{r}$, Monday Morn$^{g}$* [*1820*]

My dearest Friends

We are all well – John from whom I hear regularly seems quite happy, & likes his new Mistress very well. They have several Boys in the House – H. Marshall among the rest – '*one from the South 15 years of age who is farther on in Greek than I am*' but adds '*I do not think he is well grounded*' – I begin to observe that he has a better conceit of himself since he has had an opportunity of measuring his attainments with those of other Boys. He continues to be very *careless* (for they are now all blunders of carlessness) in spelling; but he appears to write with more freedom, though I cannot say that his penmanship looks much better. Dorothy[2] is *charmingly* – I never saw her look better. She is somewhat fatter than at Midsummer (anxiety about the prizes makes them work a little too hard perhaps before a vacation) – but it is nothing but the fatness of health & content. The young Ladies & their Governesses danced a Contra Dance nearly at the top of Langdale pikes last wednesday, & another at the Mill beck – It was their farewell excursion – for the party becomes too unwieldy to move in a body – Dear little Willy[2], I am sorry to say, has had a feverish attack at Mrs Clarkson's – but he was recovering before I was informed of it & I trust he is now quite strong again – Mrs C. was going to Bury & would take him along with her as she thought he would be less likely to exert himself too much there – of course she never thought of leaving him behind but she determined upon her visit thither in the hope of doing him good & amusing him till he was quite strong again. From the account which she gave me of his illness I have little doubt but that it has been occasioned by eating apples – as he could get as many as he liked there – change of diet also was likely to affect his weak stomach & Mr C. would cram him. – Mrs C. says he took most kindly to them all – and she is delighted with his manners & says she loves him very much – & he was as tractable as possible during his illness – I wrote instantly to beg that she would talk seriously to him – if she believed that he had eaten too much fruit – as I hope he would be impressed by what *she* said – and also (if it were true, as the Lloyds reported, that his former illness was occasioned by eating green-gooseberries) he will see how the pleasures of his holidays are curtailed by his want of forbearance. Now do not be uneasy – I am sure if he had not been quite well I should have heard again – for I wrote to Mrs. C. the moment after I had read her Letter – and I am sure she could *doctor* him better than any of us. Her Letter was *one* of the '*vexatious*' things, to use poor Mrs Coleridge's phrase, that awaited my return from Borodale – where the Gees & I had spent a fortnight very happily – another was that my Brother John[1] & Charles had been here from the Saturday night until Monday morning & altho' I had expressly ordered J[ohn] C[arter] to send a man over the fells for me in case the Boys came (whom I told you I expected but as they had not signified the time I did not think it proper to disappoint the Gees on their account) he depended upon a Letter of John's which he had forwarded by the Coach & which I did not receive until the Monday night – I set off early next morning & found them gone after their having spent Sunday here in watching for, & expecting me, every minute. Doro[2] was sent for on Saturday Night & she spent the next day & night with them; they took her to school early in the morning in their way over Kirks[t]one. Chas & she had gone on Sunday morning in the Gig to fetch Henry[1] – so that they enjoyed themselves very much I have no doubt – and she had done the honors very properly – and I dare say her Uncle was not a little pleased with her – for he allowed that Anne would have been better, or as well, at the School, & he told her he should send Lucy. He also insists that we are all 3 to spend the Xmas holidays at Stockton – and so we intend if you are not at home to say nay – John came on purpose to take me home with them – This reconciled me to the disappointment in some degree for I should have found it very difficult to refuse him – and if the Stamp Office business had been settled I should not have hesitated – George[3] Sutton has sprained his foot & could not come. They left Henry with Mr Tate – and spent one night at Sedbergh with John[4] – who was much pleased with his Coz. Charles, & with his uncle you may be sure who is always so pleasant with youngsters – besides he opened his purse & gave him a Guinea. (Of the Stamp Office I will speak when I see Mr Gee whom I commissioned to make enquiries at Penrith). The next and most sorrowful thing was poor Mr Scambler who was then upon his death-bed where he lingered in extreme torture for nearly 3 weeks – and died last Saturday Night at 10 o'clock leaving the whole neighbourhood filled with lamentations for his loss, & anxiety for his poor wife & 9 children – However I learn from Mrs North that they are not quite destitute – that, to use her words, he has done wonders in the time – Yet his last moments were disturbed by the idea of their forlorn situation which he often expressed to his wife – and seldom could he bear the sight of his

Children – He was perfectly sane in mind the whole time, & watched the progress of his disease & could at intervals when the pain abated have given as correct an opinion upon any one's case as ever he did in his life. He was perfectly aware of his situation, & talked as calmly as possible & made all the arrangements he could for the future. He even on the day of his death signed a paper relating to a Chancery suit – not of his own – knowing that it was necessary – He begged to do it saying 'Let me do what good I can while I am alive'. Miss Dowling, generous creature that she is, hearing of his anxiety about his Children told Mrs S. that she would be answerable for the Education of Eliz. – and when Mrs S. told him this at sometime when he had been expressing his solicitude on her account he replied 'She knows not what a load she has taken from my mind!' For he had always set a great value upon Miss Ds instructions – & of course he knew that they could not hereafter be procured – Col: Taylor also had engaged to send the second boy to school for a year to fit him for a Cadetship which he would give him. He also is dead and there is an end of that interest – A young Man of the name of Carr is come to the business. . . . Many candidates are talked of – Another piece of melancholy news is the death of John Wordsworth of Whitehaven on board the *Atlantic* of that port – His disease the yellow fever. The Newspaper informed me of this event. His family no doubt know of your absence else they would have written – Poor Fellow he is provided for for ever! Young Smith called here, as I believe I told you; he appears in very tolerable health altho' his complexion is very sallow – Poor Mrs Wordsworth what a life of sorrow has her's been!

I have told you these melancholy tidings that they must not all come upon you at your return and damp the pleasure which I trust you will feel when once again at your own homes where heaven grant that you may meet with no change, except what the seasons have wrought since your departure! – I should not have named Willys illness but to give you confidence that I tell you all the truth – Mary[2] Hutchinson is better but the Doctor advises her to go to Aberistyth to lay up a stock of strength for the winter – She was much improved by a residence of a fortnight at the Stow – I wish she had been near enough to come to me I am sure she would have done quite as well as at Aber$^{th}$. All else well in Wales – Miss Cookson says that *Miss Mary*[6] *Hutchinson* was the greatest beauty upon the Kington race ground – and that Mrs Frankland Lewis, being smitten with her, took her Brother to Hindwell next day to see her. J. M., from whom I had a Letter last week, says 'your *Likeness* is a most entertaining companion for a visit but is a "*real windy*" & would prove too much for a person of moderate patience who had her all to himself – her tongue is in perpetual motion. She talks to herself when she has nobody else to talk to, & we thought it rather fortunate that Harriet (Johns Maid) never thought the day too long in her society so that when *the paroxysm was at its height* & she was dispatched into the Kitchen she always met with a welcome reception – besides the gift of the gab she retains her taste for insects &c, & set Uncle to catch Butterflies till he spoilt his Hat in her Service' – He complains of bad times – that his wheat has not made so much by 500£ this year as last – but he is cheerful & happy notwithstanding – working away to feed the public without any profit this last year – his actual loss he cannot state at less than 300£ – I hear nothing of George[1] good or evil. John[1] H. takes no notice of him in his Letters.

We spent as I have said a very pleasant time in Borodale – the house in spite of the late floods was very comfortable – and Sally most happy to give us every accommodation – Upon our return we felt quite dissatisfied with our own selves – Nabscar even looks still poor & mean compared with those beautifully wooded rocky steeps – The Family at Greta Hall all well; Southey as lively as a lark and his little Boy well and the image of poor Herbert – They all spent a day with us, accompanied by Mr Nash & a young Varden, at the *Fawleigh* – and Mr Gee & I spent one with them at R[ydal] H[all] where we met with a merchant of Trieste & two Germans at Tea – & who I find upon my return home have been here & left a card – Mr Tickny, the Gent. from Trieste, had seen W^m^ in Town I suppose – Cards also from Rev^d^ Arch^d^ Allison – Rev^d^ Dr Batfield a friend of T. M's who has been at Grasmere some days with a young wife no *bigger* than myself. Lots of People come upon the Mount who say they know Mr W., & should have called if he had been at home – & some have been impudent enough to peep in at the windows when I have been sitting in the room – but this is only owing to Jane Dawson's *daftness*. Old Mary's *Quality* are much more decorous. Here is a Letter from *Archdeacon* Wrangham – who has ordered a copy of his Horaces Odes, 3^d^ Book for a specimen, 50 copies of which only are printed to W. '*in full confidence* that your accustomed & affectionate friendship would have led you to suggest whatever alteration your excellent taste & scholarship might deem necessary – If it should have reached you, know that I am impatient for your communication – If not, & you feel inclined to give me a half hour or two of your leisure, pray let me know' – If not I suppose the book will be *dis*ordered – However it is a nice affectionate Letter, & I shall write a few lines to tell him of your absence as I think William would not like the Letter to seem neglected – especially as it contains a request of service from him.

10 o'clock P.M. I am just come from Mr Gees but he has gained no information whatever respecting the *New Towns* – we have learnt from Mr Garnett that Mr James only began to distribute Stamps last week; but it is odd that the Warrant *for us* was not made out at the same time. I desired Mr Gee to learn whether Mr J. supplied Cockermouth &c – & if he did to ask Dr Satterthwaite if he knew of any subsequent arrangement – if not there must be a blunder, those Towns must be supplied somewhere & no application has been made here – of course if it is got into Mr James' hands it will stay there as J[ohn] C[arter] cannot interfere without authority – Mr Gee did not see Dr S. – This is the third time he has been at Lowther without asking the question which I desired – this last time I put them upon paper – We have heard nothing either of Col. Salkeld's Legacy duty – It will without doubt be a great loss to William having Mr J[ames] in his district – I am quite vexed when I think of his having given up his claim to the whole – or that it should ever have been thought of by the other party.

Miss Charlotte [Lockier] has had a Letter from Miss Louisa at Geneva – I hope you would meet upon their return from Italy – Miss C[harlotte] was rather poorly in Borowdale but she is better all else well – as are the rest of our neighbours who are at home excepting poor Mr Jackson who still continues, and will I fear remain an invalid all his life – He has been at Cartmel a fortnight & was somewhat better while there – but since his return he has been as heretofore and is only comfortable when made so by Laudanum. William will return to Oxford in 3 weeks or a month & then he will be left alone – He manages himself very ill no doubt – He even wanted to drink Cowslip wine at dinner on Sunday. He sent for me to dine with them – and we had venison, Hare Soup, & Stickle Tarn Trout! what think you of such sumptuous doings! The Cooksons are all well except James who has a slow fever.

And now I think I have told you all about ourselves – and our neighbours which I have done first for your gratification – for my own I should have talked about you & expressed the satisfaction that I feel in hearing that you all enjoy your *Travels* so much and that Mrs M[onkhouse] is better. I grieved at your disappointment in finding no Letters at Berne – I wrote thither and also to Geneva – quite in time for the Berne Letter to have reached you at Lucerne, it would leave London about the 30th of July. Miss Lockiers Letter came even from Geneva hither in 12 days – Her friends say it saves many days by directing the Letters by Calais – both to & from Geneva. I trust you have received both my Letters by this time & also one from Mrs Clarkson who I understood had written to you before W^ms^[2] illness. I long to hear of your turning your faces homeward – though if you can continue to enjoy yourselves & do not find it too expensive, I hope you will leave nothing undone. I am comfortable enough altho' I have not any pleasure in my present inmates – but Mary [Bill will re]turn to me at Martinmas – she has got up her heart & her looks – and is I hope reconciled [to giving?] up all chance of ever fixing her worthless swain. I have also hired another Cook – Mary Anne as smooth & polite as possible – but I do not like such smoothness – if I were to say black was white *to my face* she would agree to it – Cross-tempered maids shall always have my favor in preference. Betty is quite well but sadly vexed that you like foreign parts & that there is no hope of your speedy return. Jonathan has been lame both hand and foot & only able to 'pettle' about the Garden for some weeks – but today he is gone to the Quarry again. We have abundance of Apples – though I am sorry to say that a thief has been in the Garden last night – So I fear they will all be gone before they are ripe – Good night & God preserve us all! It is bed time, & I am rather cold for I have no fire – the weather has been unusually sultry for some days past very fine for a fortnight – but until that time we had rain incessant – and very cold – constant fires at Mr Gees & in Borodale – though I have but had a fire twice since the week after you left me, I have profited by my neighbours luxuries.

Wednesday – I must send off my Letter today lest you should begin to be anxious – I long to hear of you again & when I may begin to look for you – I often *hear* that you intend to winter abroad – and I hope there is just as much truth in the report as those which I used to hear before you set off that you had given up all idea of it – for various reasons every one had a new one – one I remember Mr Dawe's had because of the disturbances in France – Mr Sunderland of Ulverstone has sent you a commission in case *you winter in Rome* – If I have room I will give it you at the End, it came through John[4] from whom I had a Letter today. He is quite well. No News except that he has done the first proposition in Euclid to Mr W. – A Letter from L^d^ Lowther to Mr Gee – mentions that Thompson of Appleby he hears wishes to succeed Atkinson, who is about to decline the distribution, & proposes another person in preference, a *yellow* – Mr Atkinson had told J. C. that he would provide a proper person. If it is Thompson I suppose we must prefer the other – but we shall manage so as not to let the *interest* appear else we should perhaps be thwarted – J. C. says that he shall propose 800£ security as he was not satisfied with Atkinson – Lord L. is coming next week to visit his Friends in these parts. Mr Gee in his reply will ask him about the new Towns – as he has condescended to interest himself about a Sub: we may certainly ask him a civil question.

This is a *weary* long Letter – I can not read it over myself so most probably you may find many repetitions in it – what a folly & slavery it is to write such long Letters about nothing – and yet I dare say there are 50 things which you will want to know neglected – pray ask *a list* of questions at the end & they shall be answ$^{d}$ in like form. My kindest dearest love and best wishes to all & each. Doro has your last Letter (she could not find time to read it the short time she was here & put it in her pocket to read upon Lang dale pikes which I hope she accomplished) therefore if any questions are unanswered you must excuse me. The Books are come – Johns[4] & Henrys[1] sadly scratched by bad packing – D's[2] very pretty but she was unhappy that the leaves were not gilt. I disposed of 3 copies as you ordered to S. Cookson Edith & Sara[3] – and the rest are here – a good many copies – I am quite well except for my Teeth which plague me worse than ever – I *pretended* to eat a pear & wrenched the only useful one so much that it is now sore & useless & I am reduced to masticate with my tongue upon the roof of my mouth. Let me not forget to tell you that today when I sate down to work almost for the first time since we went to Borodale, above 3 weeks, my eyes were as *quivery* and queer as possible – but before I went having exercised them very much they were as strong & clearsighted as in all my life – so do not any of you give up exercising them in all things – farewell & may God preserve you all for ever! & send you safe home to us. We have delicious weather at present – unnaturally hot for Sep$^{r}$ – I have had no further news of Willy – so fear not but all is well. The Gees always desire their kindest remembrances – I say nothing of the *Quean* or her worthless supporters – such lies do the newspapers put forth on her side as would surprize you – I see them in our infamous radical papers – Mr B[rougham] after all his impudence during the examinations – did not know what to say when the examinations for the prosecution closed & he was asked when he would enter upon his defence – He hummed & *ha ed* until they were obliged to bid him *speak up* – !!! Nobody could hear him. . . .

You must not fail to provide for Doro's[2] work Box – It is all that she is anxious about – winders, bodkins, skillets, measure &c &c of ivory or mother of pearl – scissars & knife I tell her are far better in Eng$^{d}$. She has had a long French Letter from Miss B[arker]. Mrs Ellwood desires that you will if you can bring them conveniently buy 6 pr of white silk stockings for her & her Sister – 3 plain & 3 embroidered. You are to wear them first – I hope you can do it – as we give them so much trouble in the dress line. Dont forget my seeds – I put these commissions in a rememberable corner now when they are in my mind.

John Carter desires to know what is to be done if W$^{m}$ is not in Eng$^{d}$ before the 21st Oct$^{r}$ the last day on which the quarterly acc$^{t}$ can be signed. *Do not fail to give express orders in your very next.*

*Postmark: Kendal, Penny Post, 16 SE 1820*

## 69

*Mrs Swaine at Mons$^{r}$ Woolmarr's Chantilly, Sep$^{r}$ 25th*
*Mrs Wordsworth, à la poste restante, Paris*

*Tuesday, 19th Sep$^{r}$* [*1820*]

Dearest Friends

I am so delighted to find by your Letter from Milan, rec$^{d}$ yesterday, that you have turned your faces homewards that I must take up my pen to tell you so altho' I do not intend to inflict upon you the plague of another of my long Letters until you are in Paris – Mrs Clarkson will, I trust, write & tell you how well the dear Willy[2] was when she parted with him, and all the other agreeable intelligence respecting his good conduct & manners. She had ascertained, before the receipt of my Letter, that he *had poisoned* himself by eating apples in his journey to Playford – but I hope to hear further news of him before I close my Letter, as I have written to M$^{r}$ Johnson to look after him upon his arrival in Town lest he should have been guilty of similar intemperance during his journey back. Doro[2] too made herself poorly with eating Nuts – or rather she would have been poorly but for Miss Dowling's dose which is always applied as the first symptom appears, viz not eating their dinner. She was with me on Sunday afternoon & was delighted to hear, as I then had heard through Lady Beaumont, that you intended to go no farther than Milan – & great will be her pleasure indeed when she sees this confirmed by your own hand. She is a darling Creature! She wept with joy to hear the praises which dear Mrs. C. so lavishly bestowed upon her Brother – but a little *monkey he* ought to have written to her, according to his promise, for she has most anxiously expected his Letter. – I trust your journey *would* end '*triumphantly*' – for my account of Willy was not doleful – though I wish I had not had anything but good to write about him – for I do not repent having told you though it would occasion you a pang & some anxiety, because I know that it would have made you more uncomfortable when you had found we had concealed it – and it is right that you should know it – that you also may exhort him to *temperance.* John[4] is well & happy.

The Stamp Office Warrant will be down soon. We have had a Letter to say that the Treasury fees must be paid, & a person sent to take the warrant up there, & take it to the Stamp Office – those fees are 4 Guineas – and as we had no one in Town to whom we could apply better than Ri[d] Addison J[ohn] C[arter] wrote to him – so William must remember to call upon him to repay the money. It was very kind in Lady B. to send me news of you – She says that they do not go to Rome this winter in the hope that next summer that, & the neighbourhood of Naples will be more settled. Therefore bade me say they expect that you will visit them at Coleorton in your way home – She wants William's sanction for the sacrifice of some fine Evergreens in the winter Garden. I hope you will go as we are all going on well, & a week or two longer you may easily restrain your impatience to be at home – I expect to have Mary Bill back to receive you – I should be sorry if this smooth-faced, & insincere, creature were here to greet you – I have hired a cook from Keswick, who I hope will do well 'tho I have not seen her. Betty & Johnathan are well pleased to find that you are coming home altho' it will only be half the satisfaction if you leave Dorothy[1] behind which I suppose you will do – We have now delicious weather & I trust the harvest will soon be finished – but it has been a cold summer, indeed we looked for summer in vain – for autumn has succeeded to the Spring.

Mrs Gee was quite gratified to find that you thought the ascent on to Borodale as hard as the Alps – for she was terribly frightened on her ascent from Wasdale – I had changed ponies with her, for her ease on our return (as she said only to the foot of the hill) so when she asked me when I meant to dismount I replied – not at all – supposing it merely politeness that we might again change Poneys, which I did not intend – never dreaming that she was afraid to ride up the hill, or *wished* to walk – so on Mr Gee rode never looking back upon her – she sent forth terrible groans though I did not at first suspect she was afraid – for my part I could not have walked it for the world & when I heard her groans I could not but laugh & repeat '*who comes not hither can he know, how beautiful the vale below*?' for she was forced at last to take my advice & hold by the mane & *shut her eyes* so that till we got to the top she durst not look around her. I wrote to Miss Barker from Borodale to tell her how comfortable we had been in her house – in Doro's Letter, which Doro read to me on Sunday, she says that she could as easily have dined with you at Calais on the day you landed as at the place *she did dine* with a party of Friends – therefore if your route is not through Boulogne you must have her to meet you – else she will be quite in despair. But I hope you will visit her in her home – though you must write as soon as possible to apprize her of your approach as she was meditating a visit into the Country. . . .

Thursday 12st.

John's[4] little Letter which arrived yesterday says that he has got to the 'Ass'es Bridge in Euclid but whether he shall get over it or not does not know' – though he has not found it difficult yet. His Letter is perfectly well spelt & the penmanship is the very same as poor Hartley's – He tells me he has got on one of his white neckcloths but does not think they suit him at all.

Doro is, as you may suppose, overjoyed to hear that you have turned your faces homewards – I went to carry her your Letter on tuesday. . . .

I have this moment recd a Letter from my Brother John[1] in which, after expressing himself most affectionately with regard to his disappointment in not meeting me at home, He speaks of the Children with so much satisfaction that I must transcribe that part for you – 'I was very much pleased with both my nephew and niece – the former is a fine steady young man & I wish any of mine had half his sense & industry. He is most truly desirous to get forward & I have no doubt but he will succeed & become a great man – I think the school, in its present state, the most favorable for him that can be, as the master will, of course, take great pains with his first scholars, & particularly those intended for the University. Dorothy[2] was the very happiest of Housekeepers, while we were with her. She did all in her power, to make us comfortable &, believe me, no people could be more satisfied with their visit, under all the circumstances than we were – the grooming part was the worst, & John C[arter] might have procured us a groom of some kind, but he is I think a mulish short of fellow – & excepting once I never cast eyes upon him during my stay. Dorothy is a very fine Girl. I was mightily taken with her. I believe she & I are great Friends & I hope she will be allowed to visit us. She was much disappointed that G[eorge][2] was not with us: but Chas & she were very kind tho' they soon began to spar & quiz each other &c – I was sure he had been pleased with his visits by the manner in which D. spoke of it – He says George still talks of coming '*but he is uncertain as the wind*' – & will most certainly if I can go back with him – but this is now out of the question as you are about to return – for if I were to go I should not wish to be limited for time & I could not stay comfortably after I knew you were at home – though go I must, as soon as I can – it would be quite unfeeling not to comply with so many pressing entreaties as I have had ever since you went away. Tell me when you expect to reach home. I fear you will not allow John & Doro. to perform their promise at Xmas. I have also had a Letter from Wales with excellent News of dear Mary[2] – she is so much better – indeed so *well* – that she has given up the thought of Aberistyth – Joanna & my Aunt too well – so are all the rest & harvest productive so that Joanna writes in better spirits than usual. Yet she says *you* have *all behaved very shabbily* to them in not writing – From Paris T[om][2] M. might surely find time. Mrs M[onkhouse] could have written to all the nation while at Lucerne or wherever they waited for you, & they would have been mightily gratified I have no doubt by a Letter from her – altho' I do not advise her to take the trouble of writing off her Husbands hands already, else she will have more calls in that way perhaps than she may like. Tell Tom that Penrith races commence on the 3^rd^ oct^r^ – I know not how they are to proceed without him. . . . The Peers have got 3 weeks holiday – what a disgusting business this has been – and the radical & opposition press has in *impudence* & *falsehood* outdone all its former doings – It can only be exceeded by the *Quean*. Some People fear a *row* – but I hope it will pass over quietly – there is nothing to fear if the soldiers are firm – and Gov^t^ will be foolish indeed if it allows her money to squander upon them as she did upon the Mob. – Only think of the D[uke] of W[ellington]s being *insulted* so late their idol – but it is ever so & why wonder? Alas how soon are benefits forgot! Here is Mrs J. Harden canvassing for Smith the Surgeon – Though she knows that Mr Scamblers Friends wish to establish some one who will take to his Stock & Books, being of course well recommeneded. She says it is all party spirit that prevents Smiths being rec^d^ with open arms, because it is party spirit that has moved *her* to espouse his cause & forget all the obligations she used to acknowledge to Mr Scambler. Mr S. was buried on Saturday last – & followed to his grave by his wife & 9 children – for they were all there – all stood round it – the *three* which cannot walk were in the nurses' arms. A most affecting sight! Mr W. Jackson who was there was quite overpowered by it, and ill in consequence all the next day. The whole course of his last illness was most remarkable – for though it ended upon his brain he was *always himself* – & when the violent pain was not upon him perfectly calm – always resigned & praying for his release – being convinced from the moment of his seizure that he had no chance – this was about a month before his death – after which he rallied a little & was out on horseback as far as Clappersgate & at Mr Gees – but death was in his face – He told Mr William on that day that he knew from the turn which his complaint had taken that he could not live above a month – and again at his own home when his Wife had left the room he pointed to his legs which were swoln & said 'I told you how it would be' – When his pulse had nearly ceased to beat & Carr told him so, upon his enquiry, he thanked God – and having desired them all to leave him, except the maid – he asked if no one was at the head of the stairs – then he ba[de] her close the curtains & observing an open place bade her *pin it* 'now I shall die in peace' and he did die instantly. I have not see[n] his poor Widow yet – I called often but did not wish to see her – for she has had so much company that she has been made worse by it – and the fatigue which she underwent during his illness is incalculable. –

Sunday. Being now in possession of the *important document* namely the Bulletin of dear little Willy's health I will finish my Letter lest it should not be ready to greet you upon your arrival in Paris. Mr Johnson writes that he is perfectly well tho' rather thin yet looking clear and healthy – pray God that he may keep off all *excesses* & that you may find him well . . . I had a Letter from Lamb in answer to my communication respecting you and he tells me his Sister is again ill – & that he is trying the experiment of nursing her at home, & they have gone on so far very well – he does not seem himself so much depressed as he has sometimes been – indeed he says so – they are at their 'Suburban Residence' – The Lloyds have been at the Isle of Wight – but are now at home. Mrs C[larkson] tells me that Derwent had been staying a few days with them – and H[artley] *at Montagus* with Jameson I understood – the Ladies of that house were at Blackheath – They are all well at Keswick – have been inundated with visitors – Did I tell you that B[arry] Cornwall left a little note with old Ma[r]y – but it was not sent in until he left the Garden else I should have invited him into the house – He was at Southeys also – Mr de Quinceys Books have literally turned their master & his whole family out of doors – He is *arranging* them – so being strewed about & he meditating a journey to Edin[h] he thought the safest way, as 'his wife did not understand books' (as he expressed himself to Mr W[m]) & they the maids *would be dusting*, was to take another house – and now they are safely lodged at Fox Ghyll which he has taken for 6 months. I predict that there they will remain unless unsettled by an earth-quake or a second accumulation of Books.

I had not finished the foregoing *Topic* when Mr Westall & his Bride dropped in – they stayed tea with me & I sent for Mr Gee – the first time that he has hon[d] me with his company except on the day we came from Borodale – since you went away – The bride is a most homely body – an inferior edition of poor Mary Steele – with an awkwardness of manner which Mary had not & a most coarse expression of countenance & very provincial accent – However I dare say she is very good; and will take good care of her husband a thing very necessary as he is a reckless sort of a Person – Tell T[om][2] M. that his Brother John[2] has applied to me for the 2nd & 3rd N° of the Lakes & I have supplied him – so if he had any intention of providing them he need not. I have also desired W. to send Tom a proof copy of each as he said he had no orders to that effect – & the Prints sell very quickly in London. – Henry[1] came to see me on Saturday – & went off again this morning (Monday) before I was up – so eager is he after his fishing – He brought a fine lot which I potted or rather intended to pot – but Mary Anne, being in love, chose after they were baked to leave them in the way of the dog who dispatched the greater part. Doro[2] says that you Mary promised in the presence of Mr Monkhouse that she should have a pelisse made in London – as she fancies that her ill-made clothes are the, or rather, *cause* the appearance of a '*hump*' as she calls it – However I do believe it is her stays that has pushed out her shoulder blades for they do stick out terribly. I was quite shocked with them yesterday & it really is no fault in her holding herself now but stick out they will – I wish she had had those straps when they were proposed – something might be done by good high backed stays, & if you will try to get her a pair or two I will do my best to send a measure – it is only in a high gown & spencer that this appears at all bad – & having been used to wear a spencer with a cape it was hidden & I supposed it was better – but Mary,[1] her uncle John[1] said it was just like her Mothers back, & Miss Graves of Penrith observed how like her Carriage was to her Mothers at a time when she was holding herself very little to my satisfaction – so now she will think it is inevitable – But I do think they *slander* you – I should be very glad if D. had no more 'hump'. – But to return to the pelisse – I say Miss H can do very well for her – though she would have been glad if you had kept some of the black cloth in Town for this purpose – as she does not care what it is made of if it only be *shapely* – and as I wished also that you had kept as much of it as would make you a habit waist, that you might no longer have an excuse for not riding on horseback, if I have an opportunity must I return you some of it – Miss Charlotte will send a box in a fortnight – Willy[2] also wants new Clothes. Mrs C[larkson] says his old suit was scarcely worth mending – but Mr J[ohnson] thinks it will do till your return if you come quickly – this is a great *bother* you will say and I should not have sent it all the way to Paris but I suppose your stay in Town will not be very long – so answer it in your next. I forgot also to say that there was no black velvet Gown or Pelisse as specified in the list, in the great Trunk but I suppose D. had taken it out for use – If so will she not want some of this black satin to trim it with – Pray dont forget Mrs Ellwood's commission – I hope you got my Letter about Henrys[1] watch – Mr Gee tells me an 8.vo Ed of the *Excursion* is advertized. Mr Westall said last night that he should like much if he had time to make drawings of the scenes described in parts of Williams Poems & bind them up with a copy of the work – sometime they might be engraved but it would be a beautiful book. I wish Doro could ever be able to accomplish such a thing – I sent John his Copy – tho' he poor Fellow finds no time to read – Saint Days & Sundays he says they are hard at work even when they do not attend school – But I am sure he is very happy and does not feel himself upon the whole inferior to the best of his schoolfellows. – Mr Johnson tells me that when he last heard of Dr Wordsworth he was at Cambridge & well – now I think I have got to the end of all that I can say – and you will be glad to be at the end also. If you did not see the Dean of somebody & his Family at Lausanne never face old Mrs Freeman – for she has *dinned* them in my ears eternally – I ought to have reminded you of them before but I forgot. Edith will come to see me when Mr Nash departs. I did not ask her while Keswick was so gay and her Aunt, Miss Southey, only just come – and indeed I have never been lonely – having found plenty of employment either in house or Garden when at home – & whenever I desired society I went down to the Gees – they all [send their] kindest love – The young Ladies were mightily set up by Williams remembrance.

I trust the eyes are entirely recovered, as he does not speak of them – Mr Barber who is at the Lodge made many enquiries after you – He escorted me home on horseback from Church yesterday – for he is *so ill* he cannot walk even to Church & yet I never saw such an old ever green in my life. He is fitting up his Cottage in the *exquisite* Style – I have not seen it but am expected to honor it with my presence. What a creature he is – We have such squabbles about the *Quean* not that he believes her innocent – but is a dreadful radical – Takes the Times & Courier both – the latter he says is full of sedition & Treason. Heaven bless you all. This shall be the last bit – Ever & ever yours – each and all of you. S. H.

D. thanks Miss Barker & is much delig$^{ed}$ with her Letter but really at school she has not time to answer it – evry moment is employed. [*Dora's hand.*]

You ought to have one Letter at Berne, 2 at Geneva – this the 4th.

*Postmark: Kendal, Penny Post, 28 SE 1820*

# 70

*John Monkhouse Esq[re], Stow near Hay, Brecon*

*Rydal Mount, 15th Oct[r] [1820]*

My dear John

Yesterday was forwarded from Kendal *for you* the 2nd & 3rd No of Westall's views in a parcel to M[r] Gethane – also the whole of the Letters which I had at that time of sending received from the Travellers – I have heard twice from Paris where they mean to remain at least a week longer – they are all quite well and seem to continue to enjoy themselves greatly; altho' the party are at present separated as the Hotel, in which Tom[2] & his Ladies took up their abode, was too expensive for the Pockets of their companions who have a private Lodging – the Paris Letters are still more brief than the others – but I am amazed how, in all the hurry of seeing, they have ever found time to write at all – Tom I understand *has* written to you – and Mary[1] W. says that such unsatisfactory Letters, as she was obliged to write, she did not think worth postage which was the sole reason of her not writing to Hindwell – When *you* receive the Pacquet I have no doubt but you will wish that I had come along 'to read it to you' – and guess you will be forced to *save it*, after many attempts, until you go to Hindwell to get it decyphered. They rec[d] all my Letters at Paris – and, to my no small satisfaction, agreed that they were entirely to their's – that I had left nothing untold that they wished to know!!

I wrote a few lines the other day to Mary[2] along with a Letter to little Tom[3] – but as M[r] Gee took it over Kirkstone with him *in the hope only of meeting* a Member (for he was not going to Lowther) perhaps it may not be yet forwarded – and they must think me very idle – but I really have so much to write – so much of the same story – that I am quite weary of the subject – so they must not judge me very hastily. I suppose you expect the Bride & Bridegroom* amongst you, and from them you will hear all their 'Travels Story'.

I went to Kendal on Tuesday last, with W[m] Jackson on his way to Oxford and stayed until Thursday morning – Elizabeth[1] & I sate up till after one o'clock each night talking of Hindwell, the Stowe, &c &c – She was quite as ready to answer my questions as I to put them – and I think I am now in possession of all that has happened *to you all* during her stay among you. It is melancholy to hear the complaints of the

* Thomas Monkhouse and his wife.

Farmers in all Quarters – but this wretched woman occupies the sole attention of the nation – and every thing else seems to be forgotten – one would really suppose that it was expected that her acquittal would remedy all the evils of which they complain! I have seen but little of evidence *in favor* yet but the *Noble witnesses* seem to be of the 'non mi ricordo' class; and *Flynn the very least worthy of credit* of any that have been examined on either side.

I was surprized to find by your Letter to M^r^ C. that Joanna was 'on her way to the North' – She said something of this to me but I thought the scheme was but in nubibus – I hope she does not intend to be off from the Stowe *in great haste*, as certainly I shall not be able to meet her at M^rs^ Hugessen's if she goes thither first – my first visit must be to Stockton – and when I may be at liberty to leave home is very uncertain – she had much better I think have paid her visit here first, as I suppose she will not leave us out among her North Countrie Friends – Dorothy[1] charges *me* not to be off before she returns – but I should not wonder if my visits were paid before we see her face at home again – She goes first to M^rs^ Clarkson's & of course will visit Cambridge on her way home.

I hope you will not be disappointed in the 2 N^os^ now sent; the view of Keswick from Barrow Common, in the 2^nd^, & the Twilight scene in the 3^rd^ are my favorites. Westall tells me that the former has gained him great credit amon[g] the Artists for its *execution* – and I could not have believed than an Engraving could have given the quiet and solemn feeling inspired by such a scene as the latter. The extra 18^d^ upon the 3^rd^ is occasioned by the Letter press; W. would scarcely let me pay it, although he said it really cost him as much, i.e. the paper & printing for Southey furnished the matter gratis – Don't expect from this that it is anything but a mere description – or rather information for it is all about *Becks* & the waters – intended only to be useful – & not like Wm's Preface to Wilkinson's the only part of the Publication worth any thing – *This* publication I think so *cheap* that I should have been quite ashamed had I allowed the 18^d^ to be taken off – Keswick Lake is now finished – Winandermere will be out this Winter we expect – for W. does not go abroad yet – & I hope never will he has foreign views plenty to keep him doing as long as he lives – I have ordered him in future to send one for you to Tom[2] as soon as they are published – so that you must have them down by the first Parcel.

We are all well here 'and about' as Willy[2] expresses it; and have had enchanting weather for some time until today when a watery change has taken place and I greatly fear it will not return to its late course in a hurry – I never saw the Country more beautiful and Rydal in particular in my recollection – The woods are gorgeous beyond example and their beauty has been prolonged by the slow decay occasioned by the mild weather in an unusual degree. But the wind howls and the leaves are driven against the windows today and though the fields are as green as emerald winter seems to be *rushing* upon us – yet the air is not cold – and I could do without a fire were it not for fashions sake – and my tooth ache which has paid me a most unwelcome visit already of four days length and how much longer it may chuse to abide I cannot tell you. Dear Joanna I suppose is with you, else I would say it was very provoking that you are not here what a nice prose we could have had together. But you know I am as well as yourself a good *bider* of solitude – I was invited to spend the day at the Ivy Cot – but it being so rainy & therefore fearing no interruptions I was resolved to have a feast of solitude – I know it is 'bad for one' to be much alone – therefore I do not indulge my *propensity* – else but for the food of my poney, & to visit the old Parson who is sick, I believe I should scarcely have had the virtue to stir from the House. I have ridden a good deal lately – one day a *hunting* – the hounds were at Wytheburne, & I saw them kill the Hare upon the side of Helvellyn!!! Farewell! & may God bless you! Yours most affty S. H. . . .

*Postmark: Kendal, Penny Post*

## 71

*Thos Monkhouse Esq$^{re}$, Gloster Place, 34 Portman Square, London*

*Rydal Mount, 7th Nov$^{r}$* [*1820*]

My dearest Coz.

I have been *perfectly uncomfortable* for the last week in consequence of your nonperformance of the promise to write to me 'at an early opportunity', and above all from my daily expectation of hearing that our Friends were safe in Town once more. I am now not only uneasy, but quite *angry* with them; they seem to have forgotten 'all duties and all cares' – John Carter is in a great dilemma – He ought *to set off* upon his annual journey in 10 days at farthest and he has *yet* not been able to announce the time to his *Subs*, being uncertain whether his Master will be at home, or chuse that the journey should be delayed – I write therefore to you to beg that *the moment* they *arrive in Town* this question may be replied to – If I had had the smallest idea of their remaining so long in Paris I should have written thither for the necessary information. The other Stamp Office business is also undecided; and but for our daily expectation of hearing that Wm[1] was in Town J. C. would have written to Somerset House to *make them* give an *account* of themselves; as he says it will be very irregular if the Stock is not taken into our's before the commencement of next year.

The above cannot be very amusing to you – but you must cast your eye over it & *skip* – it helps, *luckily*, to fill up my paper – for I could scarcely find other matter; it is so long since I have written to you, and such a change has taken place in your circumstances, and consequently a change of *interests* that it will be some time before I know how to suit you* – At all times I am sure you will be glad to hear that I am well – and also my Darling Dorothy[2], who with Mary Calvert, dined with Mr Nash, Edith Southey, & me here on Sunday; & though she looks the picture of health and content she is become very anxious for the return of her Father and Mother – and says 'what *shall* I do when *they do* come?' scarcely being able to contain the pleasure which the anticipation excites – Heaven grant that we may all meet in safety ! – I had a sad fright one night having stumbled upon the account of the loss of one Pacquet boat (in the 'Courier') & of three others being driven ashore – then the thought of their lingering at Paris was a comfort to me –

I hope to hear that Mrs M[onkhouse] is perfectly recovered, and that you are quietly settled in some pleasant residence which is, at least pro tempore, something like a home of your own; and which must be very delightful after all your wandering – I was glad you went upon the Continent altho not a little disappointed, after having had the hope excited, at your not coming hither – especially as I fear you will not in future pay us such frequent visits as heretofore – This has been the most beautiful Autumn I ever remember – though lately the weather has been intolerably wet – I have been *entirely out of patience* with it – indeed the whole of summer was wet also – 6 weeks of fair in the early spring and about 3 in Sepr & Oct are all that we can reckon since our friends left us –

Our Neighbours are all well – Mr Gee had excellent sport upon the moors I cannot venture to tell you how many brace of Game he shot, but Col: Lowther & he together shot 80 brace one day – It was lucky that you were not *along* to frighten the Birds –

* Sara writes under unusual constraint. Thomas Monkhouse's new wife is an unknown, and will probably read the letter. Possibly, too, even at this early date, she has some suspicion that Mrs. Monkhouse's illnesses are more useful than real, a suspicion that grew with the years.

. . . Little M^r^ Nash brought Edith here on Thursday and stayed with us until monday morning – I have therefore no more solitude to *enjoy*, for she will stay until my Friends return – She is quite a delight – one of the very sweetest, & certainly the most lively & entertaining Girl of her age I ever knew – then she is so pretty to look at! This day is almost as bad as a London Fog I cannot see the laurel by the mount – I wonder if you have one of those *beautiful* orange coloured *Suns* today –

Pray now do write whether they are come or not – for I am quite sick with expectation. Tell me how dear little Willy is – He would rejoice in your's and Miss *Jane's* return. God bless you all! My most affectionate regards to your Wife with whom I long to be personally acquainted – Farewell Most truly your's S. H.

(Read this to W. W.)

M^r^ Jackson begs me to tell you (Wm W.) that the Incumbent of Millom is dead & he asks your advice whether his son could with *any propriety* be recommended as a Successor – He has taken it into his head that it would be of the greatest use to his Sons health to be near the Sea (which is I believe true) but I should think that W^m^ would not wish to bury himself there – However I am sorry to say that William Jacksons health is at present in a most precarious state – His Father has written to urge him to give up his College duties in consequence of the alarming accounts we have had of his health – In a Letter which I had from him he *complains more* than ever I knew him before & he had been very unwell for some time before he left us. He says he shall be *most glad* to hear that you mean to take Oxford in your way home. He would *I rather think* wish for a Curacy in the South. Perhaps I did not tell you that he is *now a Fellow*. If you think there is no impropriety M^r^ J. wishes it to be named to *Lord Lowther* from him – but use your own discretion – at any rate old M^r^ J. is the only person concerned in y^e^ application.

Wed: Morning

I have this moment rec^d^ yours for which many thanks altho it has not at all relieved my anxiety with regard to our Friends & increased it as to your good wife – M^rs^ Gees kind regards – the Dog is used by M^r^ Harrison of Kendal at present & does very well – I shall think of your kind invitation – but my first journey must be to Stockton. Adieu

*Postmark: Kendal, Penny Post*

## 72

*Thos Monkhouse Esq$^{re}$, Glo'str Place, 34 Portman Square*

*Stockton, 12th Feb$^{y}$* [*1821*]

My dear Coz.

I have intended for above a week past to write you a long Letter by George[2], who sets off this evening with Anne, but, according to custom, I have procrastinated and now – having been very ill yesterday – I sit down with a head so confused that I cannot but wonder *what it was* that I could possibly have to say to you! – Dorothy[1] tells me that she has received a Letter which was intended for me – for this I must thank you, although I am not the gainer – yet I hope you will not think that your debt is paid or your duty performed, but that you will address a Letter to me here – where it is my intention to sojourn for some time to come – Joanna also is here – very well and very lively; having cast off all her rheumatics, and enjoying herself very much among our old Friends and Neighbours – John's[1] Family is also well – and we do not part with the least of our pleasures when we send Anne to 'your Town' – for she is a sweet Girl as ever lived – Stockton is just the same as ever – bright & clean & dull! but we, the *Hutchinsons* are all so agreeable ourselves, & *to* ourselves, as M$^{rs}$ Clarkson used to say by 'the Bucks' that we are quite independent of all other society –

I am glad to hear that you have got John[2] to Town and that the *bad Times* do not entirely prevent his taking his pleasure – but I must say that he has a great affection for London at a dull time of the year – I suppose he thinks that at a more lively one he should feel the contrast too sensibly on his return home – and therefore one cannot but admire his *philosophy* –

Wed morning

So far I wrote on monday last – in the belief that our youngsters were to set out by the Mail in the afternoon – but, in the delightful uncertainty that attends all the motions of my hopeful nephew, it is impossible for me to guess when this Letter will reach you – though at present it is not intended that *he* shall attend his Sister at all, but that she shall be consigned to the care of the two other Gentlemen who leave this place tomorrow – at all events I must make up my despatch – for I know that unless I send you a Letter, of some kind, that you will not write to me – and I am very anxious to hear how your dear wife is – the state of whose health has given me much concern – Heaven grant that she may do well, & be able to fulfil your intention of travelling northward in the Autumn. It will appear quite strange if two summers should elapse without your visiting the North – at all events, if I am alive and well, I trust that another year will not pass by without your having the pleasure of introducing your wife & me to each other, as I hope to be able to pay you a visit next winter which it would not possibly have been in my power this, even if I had not been under promise to my Brother John; besides, I could not think that though you might at the moment you were writing *just wish* that I was better acquainted with your Rib – yet it was more natural that you should not wish for Intruders until you got a *little tired* of each others Society.

Tell John,[2] if he is still with you, that my Brother John[1] does not approve of emigration for George[1] – He knows that he has no spirit of enterprize in him & without it failure is certain – & he would return upon us in a very short time in a worse condition than before – But what is to be done for him I know not! for to recommend him to any situation in England is impossible, since he has mismanaged both his own and the affairs of all with whom he has been connected – However if he does manifest any eagerness for emigration I do not think we ought to oppose it but do what we can to further the scheme – but I suppose John will have communicated with him through our Friends at Hindwell before this time –

I enclose a few lines for dear Willy[2] who I hope is settled industriously at School again. Our Friends account of his improvement in his Books was not very flattering – I cannot but grieve to think when I look among our youngsters of the present day that if the same advantages had been bestowed upon their *elders* the result would have been more satisfactory. God bless you! My very best love to your wife and John – and believe me, at all times, most affy Your's – S. H.

*Postmark: 7 o'clock 19 Fe*

## 73

*Thos Monkhouse Esq*[re]*, 21 Budge Row, London*

*Rydal Mount, 27th May* [*1821*]

My dear Coz.

The sight of your Letter, which I received at Stockton, whenever I encounter it in my Folio reproaches me with my idleness; but as you are once more in a *single state*, and may sometimes be in want of something to cheer your loneliness I will delay no longer as this circumstance will give value even to a worthless Scrawl which mine may probably turn out to be, as I have a bad head-ache and am not a little stupid – I must first congratulate you upon the recovery of your *Better-half* – and express my most sincere wishes that it may prove permanent – How grievous it is that dear Mary[2] could not join her at Ryde – it would have been a most delightful meeting, and I have no doubt that the sea air would have completely restored Mary's health also – as it has never failed being of service to her whenever she has resorted to it – I cannot but be *vexed* with Tom[1] for continuing in his Farm when there is not the least chance of better Times – much better to retire for a while upon the remnant of their property – how small soever it may be – they would at least be freed from the fears of losing the whole – and having seen so much misery lately from *other causes* than *poverty** I cannot look upon their situation as so pitiable as I used to do – I have often said that *I would rather have Mary's four Children* (with the confidence in their well-doing which her excellent management of them gives rise to) to bring up upon my own slender pittance – than my Brother John's[1] 4 Boys with his own and M^r^ Sutton's property to boot – and this I have told her for her comfort. You can have no idea of the selfish & unfeeling conduct of George[2] Sutton; and the misery he occasions to his whole Family and connexions – His poor Father is almost heart-broken – not only on his own account but from the fear, nay the *certainty*, of the baleful effects of his example upon the other Boys – not an hour passes over his head in which he does not deplore the acquisition of that property which a few years ago seemed so desirable, but which has proved a curse rather than a blessing – this of course is between ourselves – Yet I could not but speak of it to you who have been inclined to judge somewhat harshly of John[1], with regard to George's[1] affairs which I am sure you would not have done had you suspected how unhappy he is, and how much occupied by his own vexations – He might, without doubt, easily give the sum required for George's emigration; but he has already lost much by him, & knows him so thoroughly, that he is entirely without hope concerning him – The plan which he proposes at present is for George to sell his annuity (25 p^r^ ann:) to some Insurance Office – but I should suppose this must be done to a great disadvantage as he is going abroad – perhaps you can give some information on this matter – if you can pray do it, the first time you write to Hindwell, if you have not already been

* She refers to her brother John's worries about his son, George Sutton, who had inherited a fortune.

applied to on this subject – I did not intend when I sate down to have touched upon this – but have slipped unawares into the subject – which it is scarcely possible to avoid for it is always crossing my thoughts.

I left Stockton on Wednesday 15th accompanied by Bessy Hutchinson, who is now at Appleby, and, after staying a few days there & one at Penrith, proceeded hither *via* Keswick on Wednesday last – All the friends whom I saw at Penrith were well, and very particular in their enquiries after you and M^rs^ M. – M^rs^ A. Harrison I did not see, she being in the Straw, and in distress for the loss which her Brother had sustained in a very hopeful young man, his son, who had been in India and was daily expected home when the news of his death arrived – I found all well here, & the country looking most beautifully in spite of the white turbans in which the mountains heads are most unseasonably arrayed – Willy[2], for whose sake I hastened my journey home, is just the same; and I look at him with wonder when I recollect that 20 months have passed over his head working no change in his appearance – I can scarcely believe that he is even an inch & half taller, which his measure upon the wall proves to be the case. He leaves us on Wednesday for Preston and is to be forwarded by his good friends there on the 3^rd^ I believe but they will most probably *announce his approach* to you. He is in good spirits anticipating much pleasure in his visit to them & *fun* upon his Journey with his companions – but his poor Mother I fear will part from him in great anxiety on account of his health, which is certainly far from strong.

The change that has taken place in Miss Wordsworth's *appearance* does not *delight me* much, nor make me very sanguine in my hopes of *improving my own* by a similar operation* – Yet I am resolved to make the trial in the hope of more solid advantages which she certainly has acquired over me – therefore if nothing prevents my visiting you this next winter I hope I shall be enabled to *enjoy* the *good things* which you may place before me. – I am very glad to think that we shall see you here in August, for from the previous report of M^rs^ M's health I had begun to fear that we should not – I am under a promise to return to Penrith for a short visit during the summer – and have been thinking, that as I hope before you go thither (which I guess you intend to do) to be better acquainted with your wife, that it would be more agreeable to her should I be there at the same time and therefore may defer it – You *must* go to Hindwell or Mary will be woefully disappointed – and Joanna say that you care nothing about them. She bade me tell you that had you been married at *Fontainbleau* you would not have forgotten

* Removal of her teeth.

to send them some Bride's Cake – This I told her could not really be the case – that it must have miscarried – else I should have been quite ashamed of my liberal portion.

All our neighbours are well – M^r^ Gee in treaty with Henry Addison for M^r^ Luff's cottage for a residence during the summer months, when his term (next year) is expired in the Ivy Cot – Tillbrook talks of being here for a *day or two* in July – M^r^ de Quincey is still in your favorite Fox Ghyll, with which William came in today in raptures – when Mary took occasion to observe, that she hoped he would no longer oppose your purchasing it, if you should continue inclined so to do – I have not walked that way since my return but the whole neighbourhood appears to me more beautiful than ever and it, I doubt not, will be the same – Even with the country round Appleby I was *enchanted* after the *dearth* I had experienced near Stockton; for during my four months residence there except one day upon the beach at Seaton I derived not the smallest pleasure from any natural object – I was however greatly pleased with my sojourn at Harrowgate and the neighbourhood of Ripon – and above all with York Minster which I saw upon our return for the first time – Perhaps you have not heard of my sad fright and the narrow escape of my Poney at Harrowgate, which was struck by lightening in company with M^r^ Hutchinson's – mine is recovering but his died by the stroke – most providentially the *boy*, who was riding his & leading mine, was uninjured – but I fear that I shall be obliged to forgo the use of mine during the summer – it was not able to leave Harrowgate when I left Stockton – & I have not heard of it since – I had flattered myself that it would have been very useful to M^rs^ M. if you do not bring horses, to enable her to see this Country more thoroughly than she can do in a Carriage – God bless you! Our kindest remembrances to M^rs^ M. when you see her or write, and best wishes for the entire reestablishment of her health – Farewell & believe me most affty Yours S. H.

Mary[1] will thank you to write as soon as you have seen Willy – If another cheap Copy of Percy should fall in your way do not fail to buy it for me & give it to Anne Hutchinson who will send it by the first opportunity to her Father. Love to her when you see her.

*Postmark: Kendal, Penny Post, 31 My 1821*

# 74

## *Mrs Hutchinson*

*Rydal Mount, 27th Sept* [*1821*]

My dearest Mary

I know not whether we are in your debt or not – neither do I seem to have much to write about – yet as William is going to Lowther tomorrow I will prepare a few lines for the sake of a frank – for in these bad times I grudge every Letter that one is obliged to put you to the expense of. – This dreadful weather makes us all melancholy – what will become of the Farmers and you my dearest Friends among the rest! for it seems that the weather *is no worse* here among the mountains than in the open parts of the island – and the reduction in the price of Stock is still more deplorable! Lambs are here sold at 3 shillings a head – even some as low as 2/6 – the best price at Patterdale fair for wethers was 12/.– I cannot express to you how anxious I am concerning your affairs, and how great my fears are that they are not at the worst – surely M^r Lewis will follow the example of all other Landlords and make some return. – I have had no patience with him since he made that *pretending* speech in the house, when he proves so unwilling to act accordingly – Pray write to us – for while you are silent one is apt to imagine the worst; & the accounts which the newspapers give are more doleful than we could conceive, even from the state of the weather in our wet climate – We are all well thank God! except that William's eyes are a constant source of apprehension – and he is the worst manager of himself in the world – & will I fear harm them eventually by too much *care*, & too little *doctoring* – Mary's[1] sprain is nearly well she walked as far as Grasmere today – Willy[2] left us on Saturday, & we hope was safely lodged at the Charterhouse last night – Bessy Hutchinson also left us on Monday – & Henry[1] who came over on Saturday to see her before her departure this morning – so we are now left to ourselves for the first time since the summer began – We were sadly vexed that Bessy made so short a stay – as she really enjoyed herself very much, & was far more lively than ever I saw her – but Miss Weir who had kept her at Appleby all the summer *most reasonably* made her promise to return as soon as Eliza should arrive there – who was expected on Sunday – and I do not believe she would have come hither when she did but that her Father sent her an order for that purpose – I had promised to go to Appleby with her, but I was so vexed at Miss Weir, and thinking that my company would be of little value when Eliza was freshly arrived, I scrupled not to break my promise.

I spent a week very pleasantly with the Gees, in Lodgings, at Keswick – & after they had left it a few days at Southey's which visit I should have lengthened but for Bessy's being here – She came very unexpectedly at last – I had rode over the stake with M[r] Quillinan, called at Miss Barkers house to see William & Dorothy (who were there for a few days for the purpose of climbing the mountains) but not finding them in the house we proceeded to Keswick & overtook them at the Town end – &, proceeding with them to Southeys to our great surprize found Bessy sitting there – She came on in the Coach & M[r] Q. & myself returned on the western side of Wytherburn which was somewhat of a feat of *horsewoman*ship for me, who am not in such practice as formerly – We were i.e. Dorothy (the elder) myself, Bessy, & the two girls from Keswick, to have gone again to Borodale for a few days – but the weather has never been sufficiently favorable – and now she is gone without having accomplished many a scheme of pleasure which we had planned for her – we had one gay Ball at Ambleside whither she went – there were 85 persons there; & she said it was one of the pleasantest she was ever at – but her *party* was very agreeable – Col. & M[rs] Holmes (M[rs] Q's sister) & M[r] Quillinan – & the old Col as Joanna would call him was quite a doating piece of Bessys. – Joanna's Friend Mrs Edmond's & her daughter were the *spectacles* of the room – you would have been amazed with Bessys account of them – by the by I must tell you one piece of news, or rather perhaps a *report* – that old Curwen is *on the point* with a Coz of this very M[rs] E. – the daughter of a M[r] Willan who keeps a Livery Stable in London – an only child – handsome – agreeable – accomplished – 30 years of age, & will have 10,000£ to her fortune!! So much for the attractions of the old Farmer! – And yet if he does get this prize it appears that he does not mean to spend it in bringing himself into Parliament again; for they have already been addressing the Freeholders, & exhorting the *Agriculturists* – to enter into a subscription for this purpose – *now when their hearts shall be opened by the reaping of a plentiful harvest* – but alas! they have reckoned without their host! – The Gees have taken a house at Keswick which they will enter upon next Whitsuntide – *Till* gave them the choice of another year in his; but M[r] Gee is so fidgety, & was so much afraid of being without a house when the time came, that he did not like to let the one he has taken slip; but I have no doubt he will repent long before the time comes, if he has not done it already – Miss Charlotte Lockier is gone, to our very great regret; for she is a most excellent creature – All our

Party are at Mr Gees but myself – and I have a solitary room which is a great rarity, and reminds me of last year when our friends were wandering upon the Continent – I trust that Mrs Monkhouse is well – in her case no news is good news; but until she is safely at her own home it is impossible not to have some fears about her – what an anxious journey it will be! – I can scarcely summon courage to ask after George[1] – for I always try to drive him from my mind whenever, which is not seldom, he comes into it – so hopeless seems his case poor creature! and so powerless are we to amend it. . . .

I called at Capt Southey's in Newlands and found Mrs S. looking very handsome & matronly with 7 Children & in a fair way for the 8th!! *They must* be rich!! You will be sorry to hear that Eliz. Cookson has been very poorly and though recovering is not yet strong enough to leave home else they would have sent her last week hither with Mrs Gee who was at Kendal – they feared our *hill* was too much for her to walk up as she would have been obliged to sleep at Mr Gees we not having at that time a bed. – And for this same reason we have seen little of Henry[1] – we sent for him as soon as Willy had given up his – Dorothy[1] is well but we very seldom see her – Miss Dowlings health is very precarious – she is much afflicted by a tendency to inflammation at her chest & has been obliged to have frequent recourse to blisters and she is so little disposed to give herself ease that I fear it will be long before her disease is subdued – however a fourth sister is about to join them for they have now as many scholars as ever they mean to take 30 boarders 10 day scholars & they hope the day scholars will decrease – Doro[2] will leave school at Xmas with great regret although she will be glad enough to find herself at home. – God bless you all! Our kindest love to all – I hope my aunt is better than when you last wrote. Our poor old parson still suffers greatly – Mr William has taken possession of his church in Whitehaven but returns to Oxford where he stays till March to close up his duties and engagements – A thousand kisses to the Darling. – little Jemima Quillinan reminds us daily of Mary[1] – & no wonder when her papa is like me. They have got another little Girl born by the *Rotha* side & Rotha is the name she is to bear – farewell again God bless you!

Friday. D. has just heard from Miss M. Horrocks that Mrs M. is well thank God!

Mrs Hugesson from whom I have had a Letter tells me that the Doctor says her Sister's complaint is not cancerous – what a blessing! – Tell Julli that we expect Mr Robinson every day – The Kenyons are gone, John to Leamington & Edward to seek, as he said, his register in Carmaerthensh: in case he should want to be married abroad – He will see them in Town probably before they go abroad which was to be in 6 weeks after they left us. – Of course J[ohn] M[onkhouse][2] and his Harvest are included among our anxieties and good wishes tho' I have not spoken of him by name.

I have been employed lately in transcribing *Journals* & *Sonnet* which may account for this legibly written Letter, at which I am myself not a little astonished, my hand is in good *que* so I think I must favor all my correspondents to whom I am in arrears. –

## 75

*Thos Monkhouse Esq^re^, Glo'ster Place, 34 Portman Square*

*Friday Night, 23^rd^ Nov^r^* [*1821*]

My dear Coz.

I have been transcribing Poems for you the whole day – not that it was such a very long job, but William kept altering and improving as I went along to the no small *disfigurement* of my *M.S.*, and the delay of the Work – However, late as it is, I must write you a few hasty lines to thank you for your kind Letter – and to say that the Poems you asked for being a long series of Sonnets (or rather intended to be for they are not complete) which are intended for publication soon, we thought those which I have sent* would be more interesting to you as relating to your *Travels*; and also because you are not likely to see them in print – having been written for the purpose of *ornamenting* 'the *Journals*' – I have just finished a fair Copy of Mary's[1] *Notes*†, which I assure you make a very respectable figure in a Book, and is very *pretty* reading. She was so very shy of exposing it that I was resolved to have a copy of my own that I might lend to whom I liked – I hope Willy[2] will take due care of my pacquet – for we send it to him by one of his old schoolfellows who is going to Town – previous to his embarkation in the India Service –

We were all rejoiced to hear such a good account of your Spouse, and trust that all will go well with her – I had given up all thought of visiting you this winter from the time that I heard of her situation, as

* *Memorials of a Tour on the Continent*: the early manuscript sent by Sara Hutchinson to Thomas Monkhouse is still extant.

† Mary's 'Notes' made up a less extensive journal of the tour than *Dorothy Wordsworth's Journals*.

I think, *that* considered, you are much better without any supernumeraries in the house – To be useful, at such a time, I should have come with the greatest pleasure – but she will be much better supplied and therefore I shall defer my visit until some more seasonable opportunity – I hope nothing will prevent our meeting in Westmorland next summer – It seemed quite strange to me to hear of *Penrith Races* &c and you not amongst the *throng*! – I was at Penrith for a few days a short time ago, where I was delighted to meet M^rs^ Addison looking as well and happy as she used to do many years ago, much better than when I was with her in Wales.

We are all well here except that William's eyes still trouble him – and I am tortured from time to time with my Teeth – Mary has been laid up too with her sprained toe, which she injured upon the Alps; but I hope it will give her no more trouble, and the ease she has given herself has had a good effect upon her looks at least, for she at other times uses far too much exercise for her strength – We are to have John[4] & Doro[2] at home in less than a month – Doro to remain, which will be a great pleasure to us – They (Father & Mother) would not have brought their minds to part with her so soon again even if I had come to Town this winter, though she so much wished it – She is greatly improved in all things, and is a mighty favorite with every Body.

Mary will thank you to take a look at Willy's *best suit*, and if you do not think it fit for Cambridge to get him a new one – and at any rate after his return to keep it for him until Easter when he is to go to Hendon – as if it goes to the C[harter] H[ouse] the old one will be *disposed of*, and the new one not fit for a second visit. If *any* Boys wear *round* Jackets she had much rather his was made in that form, as he looks such a little old man in one with flaps –

I have been long as much out of patience with Frankland Lewis as you can be – He, of all people, to be so loth to lower his rents, who opposed all aid to the farmers in the house, & pointed out this as the only proper method of relief & which he should be willing to resort to! – I cannot bear to think of the Property of our Friends melting away in this manner and they powerless to help it – Your having been with them this summer must have been a great comfort, and could not but have turned aside many a gloomy anticipation – Poor Joe! my heart ached at the account you gave of him – We have had a terrible storm of wind this week I trust he has weathered it! – I should have been very glad to have met my Brother Tom[1] in London – I wonder how you contrived to make him consent to visit it!

Did you ever meet with another cheap copy of Percy for me? If you have not do try to procure one before Anne Hutchinson leaves town & send it from me to her Father – Bye the bye we heard yesterday from Stockton of the Death of the last of the Miss Scarfields who has left behind her no less a sum than 200,000£ – bequeathing 300£ per ann only to her Niece Mrs Gray to whose Children the residue is left – thus rendering them independent of their natural guides & support – and ten to one ruining them in the end – She had far better have given *us*, her next heirs, a share as *we were sure* to have *done credit* to it – She might also have had a sister feeling for some of her *Maiden Cousins*!

I must not forget to say that you are not to give any copy of the Poems to any one. If Mr Robinson should wish it you may let him read them but he even must have no copy. –

We were much grieved to hear of the poor Lambs loss – It is well that Charles had written that nice Article about his Brother, in the *London Mag*:,* as he would not after his death have had the heart to do it – We do not think the Letters in *Blackwood* signed S. T. C.† genuine – But they were too stupid to induce us to read, except a sentence here and there – They seem to think they *are C's* at Keswick, but complain of their being unintelligible – William has never seen them, for he will not allow either of the Mags: to come into the house, he despises their want of principle so much –

God bless you! I must conclude for it is bed time – All here join in kindest love to you and your Better half – And with all good wishes I am ever your's most affty S. H.

Excuse, in consideration of the Poems, this stupid Letter.

Sat. Morng

William has desired Mr R[obinson] to send the Poem upon Goddart‡ to the poor young Man's Mother if he has an opportunity – Therefore *Mrs* M. will be kind enough to transcribe it – for your *hand* he says would be *deadly* for verse, it is bad enough for prose – He has been at work again, & before my M.S. leaves the House, I shall have to scratch & interline till you will not be able to blunder through – He says I am to tell you that it is all his fault & not my inaccurate transcription. Don't supply yourself with any *large* Stock of Socks, as I can soon

* Lamb's essay called 'My Relations'.

† The leading article in *Blackwood's* for Oct. 1821 was entitled 'Selection from Mr. Coleridge's Literary Correspondence' and signed by him. It is undoubtedly his and so evidently that it is difficult to see how anyone could have had any doubts.

‡ *Memorials of a Tour on the Continent*, xxiii.

knit you a few pairs which I will do as soon as I meet with any yarn *soft* enough for your *delicate* skin – this is the only difficulty – the knitting is soon accomplished.

If these Poems do not bring me a Letter 'speedy & soon' I have no hope of ever deserving one – besides we shall be glad to hear of their safe arrival –

## 76

*Thos Monkhouse Esqre, Glo'ster Place, Portman Square*

*Monday* [*26 Nov. 1821*]

My dear Coz.

I forwarded you a *parcel* of Poems with a Letter by an old Schoolfellow of Willy's[2] which I suppose will reach the Charter house before the end of the week – but though we told him to take great care & forward it by the Post you had best enquire after it – as I told you in my Letter we altered, improved, & added all the while the transcription was going forward – and now two new poems are sent which have been written since the other went off – And though Wm says he has finished probably there will be another batch for you in a day or two – You must put them in your Book as neatly as you can & press them to make them look *tidy*.

Tuesday. – As I augured here is another Poem for you besides alterations in the two former – I find that Mr Edmunds & the Parcel did not leave Ambleside as soon as was expected – therefore it will be quite the end of the week before you receive it – I wish I had had my Letter to send instead of this – We are all well – & hope you & Mrs M. are the same to whom & yourself our best love – Your's most truly – S. H.

Thursday. Another & another, have been added – and now it will be impossible for you to put them in order so that you must number them & *read* them in succession – There are more on the Stocks – but here are as many as the Frank will carry –

## 77

*Thos Monkhouse Esq*[re], *Glos'ter Place, 34 Portman Square*

*Jan*[y] *11th* [*1822*]

My dearest Coz.

*Herewith* I send you 2 new Sonnets & one *altered* – there is another Poem, I believe, in progress *about that procession in Chammouny** – but it will not be finished I fear before I must deliver my parcel to M[r] W. Jackson who leaves us by the Coach this Evening for Oxford; but he meditates a speedy journey to Town when he will deliver this with 3 pairs of Socks, which are all that I have been able to accomplish being very busy – You must tell me how they fit for they look to me rather small though I was, as I thought, very careful to make them long enough. – I send also a Necklace & bracelets belonging to your Sister which she gave to Miss Cookson to get cleaned for her at Liverpool, – but as they could not be done there I put them into your hands for that purpose – or to send them back to their owner if they cannot be cleaned in Town which I suppose she would wish to be tried.

As we have heard nothing of you – we trust all is going on well both with your dear Wife & her Nursery. We are all well here – Mary[1] has been at Lancaster carrying M[r] Quillinan's children to their poor mother, who has been there some time under medical care – but she is happily so far recovered that we look forward to the return of the whole family in April, when they will occupy John Flemings house for six months next summer – They have been most agreeable neighbours to us – and but for the prospect of their return our neighbourhood would seem very forlorn – as we shall lose the Gees in May. Tillbrook talks of coming but his plans are very unsettled – I trust you will not desert us next summer – M[r] Kenyon, whom you will have heard is about to be married, tells us that he is to settle in Essex – so the prospect of his becoming our Neighbour is at an end – yet I hope we shall get all the houses occupied by *respectable Folk* – As the White-hosed Knight has suffered so much by his last Tenants that I think he will be wary, & take our advice in future.

I suppose Mary told you that we had lost our old Friend the Rector – William [Jackson] came to his funeral – for though he set out before, the poor old Man was dead when he arrived – We are likely to have

* 'Processions suggested on a Sabbath morning in the Vale of Chamouny'. *Memorials of a Tour on the Continent*, xxxi.

the Church very ill served; as the Living falls to S^r Richard [Fleming] who is it is said, tho' a Reverend, is even more of a Graceless than his Brother Sir Daniel.

William[1] is writing to D^r Russell concerning Willy[2] – who from all accounts does no good at the Charter house; and therefore they have resolved to remove him at the end of the next ½ year – D^r W[ordsworth] who has examined him seems to think that he knows very little more of his Grammar, & that little not accurately, than he did when with him at Sundridge two years ago – therefore if such is to be the result of the enormous expence of the School it would be folly to continue him – and if he will be idle he must be idle at less cost! Poor John[4] what a pity it is, & he himself laments it greatly, that he was not sent thither at the time it was first talked of – It is now too late – and he is so earnest & industrious that we have not the shadow of a doubt but that he will be an admirable Scholar – though it cannot be expected that he will be so well prepared for academical exercises as he might have been – It was a sad error to despair of him, as his father did at one time. He is now *right* proud of him – and for diligence, steadiness, good judgment – and amiable disposition & manners I never saw his equal – and I hope he is not so shy anywhere as at home – and now even he has thrown off much of the fear that he had of his father – and does talk with him freely at times. – He has pursued his studies from duty till his Books are become his delight – and he never leaves them for recreation without reluctance – I hope Willy may come to this in time – for as John says those *little Fellows*, what can you expect from them? – He is very anxious that Willy should not be brought to a North Country School; though he, as well as all of us, think he ought not to remain where he is.

I am loth to talk about Wales – for there is so little comfort in thinking of them, their affairs being so bad – As to M^r Lewis' conduct it is no better than *Swindling* or highway robbery – He demands what he has no claim to – I fear that Tom[1] is not urgent enough, & does not put the case in its strongest light – There is scarcely a Landowner in the Island who has not voluntarily, if not by force, reduced their rents – Just because Tom is not quite ruined he can have no redress! This really is the state of the matter – God bless you & yours! I send you many happy years! – This is a worthless Letter – but when it is to lie so long in the parcel there is no great encouragement to take pains to write *agreeably* – Most affty your's S. H.

# 78

*Thos Monkhouse Esq*[re]*, Glos'ter Place, 34 Portman Square*

[*5 Feb. 1822*]

My dear Coz

I believe, at any rate I *hope*, that this will be sent to you along with the *Ecclesiastical Sketches** (which are going to the Press) through M[r] Beckett – The '*Memorials*' are already in the press – and before I pass to any other subject let me tell you that you are to *buy* them both; as W[m] does not mean to give one copy except to Southey – for his last years acc[t] with Longman was such a *black* one – he had not given away less than 60£ worth, far more than any one year's profits – But I will thank you to buy a copy of each *for me* & send to Mary[2] Hutchinson –

I hope you have received the Stockings, & the rem[dr] of the '*Memorials*', which I sent in a parcel to Hendon – We have got our Cast of the Bust, & like it very much – yet it does not entirely satisfy me or Mary – & I think W[m] & D. are coming into our opinion – It is certainly beautifully executed – the features of course, are exact, but the expression is not William's; & for this cause when you stand a little behind it, on the left side, & dont see the whole length of the nose it is far more like the Doctor – It has the same placid expression of his face. When W[m] looks grave his is more *weighty* & profound, & when cheerful more lively & spirited – I never saw this *medium* in *his* countenance – as far as *likeness* goes nothing has ever satisfied me so well as your portrait† of him – but I dare say people are never satisfied with the busts or portraits of those whom they know so well. If you have not got your's it is waiting your commands at Chantry's.

We are all rejoiced to hear such a good account of your *Nursery*, for I dare say M[rs] M. is chief nurse – I could not but admire the feeling which had prompted the two names, though I was very sorry that my favorite name‡ was robbed of its simplicity – I hope we shall see both Mother & Babe here in the summer – if not I shall rue sadly that I did not come to them this winter – I [have] not been quite well lately – & if not better soon I intend going to Harrowgate & am to take my

* *Ecclesiastical Sketches*, and *Memorials of a Tour on the Continent*, both 1822.

† The Carruthers portrait, owned and possibly commissioned by Thomas Monkhouse.

‡ The child was christened 'Mary Elizabeth'.

darling Edith Southey under my wing – we shall join M^r & M^rs Hutchinson there with whom I spent a fortnight there last year when in that short time the 'virtuable waters' had such a good effect, that I begin to think, with M^r H. that they are the natural remedies for the *Hutchinson* Constitution—

O have you seen our John's[1] *Book**, as he calls it? Never Book surely afforded more fun that it has done! Mary W. alone here was vexed, & somewhat ashamed of it – but we have laughed her out of this – for why should She care at his being laughed at who so evidently laughs at himself with you? Southey was delighted with it – & wrote us such a funny Letter – which I wish I might transcribe for you – For my part, besides the pleasure I had in the spirit & feeling with which the matter is handled, I was delighted to find that Joe could take so much interest in it, & divert his mind in any way, harassed as it is by the misconduct of that unworthy Lad who is constantly before his eyes – An old Lady of our acquaintance, who lived 90 years in this world, used to say that she had *invariably* observed, that when any one obtained the object which they had most set their hearts upon it brought along with it something which either prevented their enjoyment of it or made them wish that it had never been granted – This my poor Brother feels hourly – I dare say he wishes M^r Sutton's Cash were at the bottom of the Sea, as much of it at least as concerns George[2].

You will perhaps have heard from M^r Chapman that William intends taking Willy from the C[harter] H[ouse] in March – at least that is his present intention, unless he has some encouragement from D^r Russel for trying him a little longer – Willy knows nothing of this – from us at least. We were somewhat surprized at your report of D^r W[ordsworth]'s opinion, that he was not so very backward in his scholarship – For the D^r had examined him & said that he knew very little, & *that* not accurately – that he could not have gained less at any school – indeed he seemed to think him very little better, as to his latin, than when 2 years ago he examined him at Sundridge – & certainly with regard to English & penmanship he is much gone off since he left the Central – therefore if, idle as he is, he *can* be idle at the C. H. (which we supposed could not be where the Madras system was practised) it is no better than any other school – & W^m & M. do not think it right to be at such a great expence with him – Yet they are quite at a loss what to do with him – Poor John![4] What would he not give now for the advantages that this little *Monkey* has thrown away! He laments daily that he was not sent to the C. H., or some other great

* John Hutchinson wrote verses, of which some examples, but not this 'book', survive.

School when he was 14 – and is very anxious that Willy should have that advantage – But indeed it is nothing but a waste of money to keep him where he is – He should be where he would be hard worked – where there were fewer Boys, so that the Master could himself see whether Willy did the work himself or not.

I think you will like the *Eccl Sketches* – I delight in them. Nothing that William has ever written has interested me so much at the first – & I think they will even rival my favorite 4th Book of the *Excursion* to which, of all his writings, I the most often turn. – I as well as you like the first *batch* of '*Memorials*' best – and my prime favorite is the 'Eclipse', which you do not notice – tho' this must have been a *forget*, as you could not help being pleased with it – We were much amused at Mr Robinsons *choice* 'the Fish Women' –

Our neighbours are all well – We shall soon lose the Gees – & know not yet who shall occupy the Ivy Cot after them, for Tillbrook seems undecided what to do – If he does not come himself we hope to have Mr & Mrs Quillinan in it for three years – they will be very agreeable neighbours – but we wish we could have the Gees also as they would make an agreeable variety – tho' Mr Q. has much variety of character – & tho a fit companion for William is not the less agreeable & *suitable* to Doro[2] & Willy[2] – He flirts with Doro & plays with Willy & we call him Mary W.'s *Lover* – Doro & he have had a *poetical* correspondence since he went to Lancaster – And Sara[3] Coleridge who is here is quite as fond of him as Doro – So you may guess what a nice good-humoured creature he is – He is very like me, & has been taken for Mary's[1] Nephew. One of his little girls is the image of Mary[2] H. & a great favorite of mine. Mrs Q. is a sweet creature – Wm used to call her Sterne's Maria – and alas! she proved too like her – for since her confinement she has been deranged – though now quite well again, & we believe that it was accidental & not constitutional but this misfortune has, as you may guess, given us a great interest in them.

I hope you intend to buy Sara Coleridges Translation the '*Account of the* [*Abip*]*ones*' published by Murray though not with her name as she does not wish to be ranked among Authoresses.* Derwent began to

* *An Account of the Abipones, an Equestrian People of Paraguay*, translated from the Latin of M. Dobrizhoffer (3 vols. 1822). In a letter to Derwent, 12 Oct. 1821, Sara wrote: 'My blue-stockingism is gone abroad. I hope my dear brother you don't countenance these scandalous reports. I'm really become a perfect bugbear. One gentleman expatiated most pathetically on the *fright* he was in when he first approached our house, the den of the monster! How would Hartley be amused if he could hear that the 'snimpet' [?] 'the dust of a butterfly's wing' could inspire such feelings as these.' (*Unpublished*? In the Fitzwilliam Museum, Cambridge.)

translate it & she to help him – but he could not go on (while he was Tutor at Mr Hopwoods) so she finished it – Southey thinks it very well done, & the matter *interesting* but he is not a fair judge of this, being so much interested himself in all that relates to So. America – But I hope it will sell & she have some reward for her industry – I am glad to see that Southeys Letter* has attracted so much attention – he has far the best of it – What an *ass* that who wrote in the *M. Chron*? He shirked the true cause of hostility & talked as if S. did not allow a man his own thoughts & that nothing were objected to in Ld B. but his political & religious opinions – God bless you & your's and believe me ever most truly your's S. H.

Write soon I very seldom hear from Wales!

5th Feby – 22

Tell Mr Robinson that his Bust† is ready – Mr Kenyon's also but he has no house yet to put it in –

Don't say a word to W[illy] about his removal.

*Postmark: 10 o'Clock, Fe 9 1822*

## 79

*Mr Monkhouse, Stow, nr Hay, Brecon*

*Rydal Mount, Feby 22nd – 1822*

My dear John

If you were not yourself one of the laziest correspondents in the world I should be greatly ashamed at my own tardiness at replying to the many kind messages which I have received from you, throug[h] Joanna – but, considering how difficult it is to *extract* a Letter from you, I think you cannot in conscience think very hardly of me, especially as so many more *years* have passed over my head, which invariably allays the *itch* of Letterwriting – though ones anxiety & interest in the absent suffers, from that cause, no abatement – Indeed I am much more anxious about you all than ever I was in my Life, though I write seldomer & say little about it; for in the present state of affairs it is

* Presumably she refers to the controversy with Byron in 1822 over the *Vision of Judgment*, in the *Courier*. See p. 237 *.

† Chantrey's, of Wordsworth.

much better that you should not be reminded from *abroad* of what presses so hard upon you at home, seeing that sympathy can do no good – How provoked have I been with the *foolish* speeches in Par[t] respecting the agricultural interest! – Nobody has spoken a word of sense except M[r] Ricardo when he said that the *Taxes* could not possibly be the cause of *low prices* – As to the scheme of lending money to Persons & Parishes, who cannot have possibly any chance of repaying the loan, it is only adding another stone to the weight of a drowning Cat! and if all the Taxes of every kind were taken off, & Rents & Poor Rates remaining the same, what better would it be? And as to their *deductions* – these would not mend the matter – the Army would come to the Poors rates after all* – reduced placemen would only have less to spend – the Capitalist alone might be relieved – for all must be made up by the *Land at last* – Not a word have any one of them said about the Poor's Laws, in which a reform would stand the Farmer in much greater stead than a reform in Parliament – which would do nothing but *increase* the *wind* in the House (which is needless) and not '*raise the wind*' in the most desirable sense of the phrase! – 'Patience' is the remedy in every Bodys mouth – but it is only the Farmers who know that Patience & Ruin is their present Lot – I am not patient however – The folly of the Newspapers provoke & irritate me daily – – the *Morning Chronicle*, for instance, had the impudence – or rather *ignorance* to say that 'the most oppressive Tax on Agricul[sts] was that imposed by their own stupidity' which he exemplifies by noticing 'the practice in Surrey of plowing light land with 4 horses, which in *Norfolk* is done by 2' – &, in his wisdom, adds that except in '*one or two*' Counties in England, the same awkwardness, & want of œconomy, are to be found in almost every farming operation. Hence the enormous bills of Labour produced before the Agricul[l] Committee!!!' He notices also the expensive Teams – but these as you know are as *little general* as the other – & I should guess one half of England at least is free from the folly of both practices – & Scotland entirely from both – And yet this as from the best-informed & the most respectable Journal of the *Whigs* – the People who pretend to advocate the cause of the oppressed! – but whose own individual interest is much dearer to them – I wish very much to see these People in place for a while – It was a sad miss that they were not let in to do the Queen's business, & we should have been quiet – and if they were but in we should soon be quiet at least – and soon would the Country be glad to have their own Servants back again – for instead of *relieving*, the load would be *encreased* to satisfy all

* The soldiers, like the poor, would have their pay supplemented out of the parish poor rates.

S.H.—S

the hungry that they must feed! If Statesmen & foreign Ministers are to be reduced to nominal Salaries these employs must fall entirely upon the Aristocracy – others could not support the expence – *they* would do it for honor's sake; & this would be like the wild schemes of stripping the Clergy, & thereby giving up the only property which really does belong to the public, & which every Man of merit & talent has a chance of obtaining – and where will it go! To be locked up, as W^m^ says, 'in everlasting mortmain in the hands of the great Landed proprietors, who are after all the *greatest Sinecurists*' if you push the matter to its natural conclusion.

But what is the use of my wasting my paper with my *wisdom* – but as I said I was *vexed* & you must excuse me for venting my spleen before I pass to other subjects –

We are all well here except that W^ms^ Eyes still continue in an irritable state & I am a little *granky* – but when I get the Miracle of a Poney which I hope will be provided for me from Hindwell, I have no doubt but I shall rally – Your good offers were I assure you, if I had no other feelings to draw me towards you, very tempting – but we expect M^r^ & M^rs^ Clarkson in the Summer – your Brother and his Family (I may say now) & the Doctor & his Boys – all of whom I should like to see at Rydal – besides I have undertaken to furnish Tillbrooks House – & have promised to take Edith Southey to Harrowgate – if My health requires, which I fear it will, a draught of the virtuable waters there – And, as you know, when I *do move* I must make my visit also in London. I wished to have sufficient time upon my hands – else I should greatly have enjoyed the notion of spending this winter among you – and you shall have no reason, when I do come, to complain that You have not a due proportion of my sweet society – for I love the Stow dearly – & often think of your quiet Parlour, & the pleasant view from the end window. – I hope they will send us M^rs^ Walsham's Poney – & then I can leave it behind me for Mary[1], & purchase another if she needs *it* when I am in Wales. My Friend M^r^ Barber has a mind also for a welsh Poney – & thus by sending 3 the expence will be trifling for each – therefore I will thank you to tell Thomas[1] that his must be a *complete one* 13 hands high with a *long Tail* & *Mane* – the height is not an object with him on acc^t^ of the Tax – but he does not like to ride a *higher* horse – & a *dandy* Poney is his fancey – but though a little man he is not very light, & wears heavy *wraps* – so that a Lady's poney would not suit – Now the sooner, for my sake, you can provide for us the better – & I should think that in these times people would not be indisposed to sell though I would not have the Gentlemen suffer on my account – therefore let sufficient time be taken to enable you to meet with what will be worth sending so far. – Thomas must make the entire bargain with the Person who brings them & let nothing be left to *our Generosity* – It will be a nice job for some poor man – & we are all good Chaps – the money will be paid on demand for the whole – M^r^ Barber is not so exact as to *age* as M^r^ Gee though *above* 7 years old he would not like – & neither of them (especially M^r^ B. *who is rich*) would be stingy as to price, if the *article* is completely to their minds – & I think I have been more than sufficiently explicit.

W^m^ has just received the last proofs of his two little works which are in the Press – You will I am sure be delighted with them, especially with the '*Ecclesiastical* [*Ske*]*tches*'. – But I dare say they will fall as flat upon the public as all his other works have done – And no wonder when such stuff as Lord Byron's is read with so much avidity – and when History is only interesting when dressed up in a barbarous Scotch Novel!

I hope you have seen Southeys tickling Letter to Lord Byron* – We long to hear of an answer from his lordship, as S. will then let loose upon him a full sail & if he does not bear him down I shall wonder! – These precious 'Whigs' too make common cause with him – and talk as if Southey were not at war with his Indecencies, Licentiousness, Blasphemy & Infidelity, but simply with his *religious* & *political* creeds – and as if any Man had a right to shock the faith & morals of the community with impunity – Southey has a work in the Press on the same subject as W^ms^ – entitled a concise 'Hist: of the Church *in* Eng^d^'† – His Hist: of the War‡ is also in the Press, & will be out I suppose this Spring – We expect him here in a day or two – Have you read the article on Cromwell§ in the last No (or last but one I forget which) of the *Quarterly* – I hope your poverty has not obliged you to give that up – The *Acc^t^ of the 'Abipones'* which is reviewed in the next is translated by Sara Coleridge|| – & I believe very well done – She is a wonderful little Creature – So laborious at her Books! – She is still with us and enjoys herself greatly, for she has no let or hindrance to her reading all the day through except when she romps with Doro or plays a duet on the Piano forte – Doro is very industrious also – but if [it] were

* 5 Jan. 1822, in the *Courier*, Southey wrote an answer to Byron's personal attacks in *Don Juan III* and *The Two Foscari*. Byron's answer was a parody of *A Vision of Judgment*.

† Southey's *Book of the Church* (2 vols. 1824).

‡ See p. 194 *.

§ The article on Cromwell in the *Quarterly Review* for July 1821 (vol. XXV, 278–347).

|| See p. 233 *. The review was in the *Quarterly Review* for January, 1822 (vol. XXVI, 277–323).

desirable which I do not think it is, she will never be a Book-worm like Sara – John[4] is our miracle now in the way of plodding – if he does not make out something, poor Fellow it will be no fault of his own – John[1] H. has sent Henry[2] to Sedburgh School – those Boys will all be ruined by the example of their Brothers idleness & levity – John says that H. is a fine quick Lad very idle & very entertaining so that all the Boys crowd round him to hear his stories – but he copies his exercises – & says it is of no use his trying to get up – He has by these practices lost so much time – John intended sending Chas. also but Mr Wilkinson declined taking any that had been so long at great Schools – Our John[4] laments sadly that he was not sent to a public school – he thinks now that he would not have thrown away the advantages which our little idle Willy[2] does – but Mr Johnson says that it is the Schools fault & not Willy's – & that he has lost more than he has gained since he left him – I wish I had the old Doctor's ear that I might sound him to it the necessity of his ascertaining whether for the credit of his System it is properly carried into effect at the Charter House – It is some time since I heard from T[om][2] M. and I have often wondered whether he has had any account of poor Joe – beg you will mention the first of you that write. We have had a charming winter – If the Spring is favorable *fodder* in these parts will be most abundant – Mrs Clarkson says they have made 70£ last year by their Farm 'besides the House' what she means by this I suppose only the Corn, Pork, Poultry &c consumed in the House – & even that is more I dare say than any other farmer in the Island has made – they had had the Queen of Hayti & her two Daughters with them all the winter, & Mr C. you may suppose has been in all his glory at the head of his Sable Family* – Wm & I parodied Jonsons 'Hymn to the Moon'† as applicable to them & sent it to Mrs C. & very *funny* she thought it – but I dare say did not let her Husband see it lest he might not have enjoyed even our good-natured quizz. – Mr C. tho' a reform man in part thinks all

* The widow of Henry Christophe, the native king of Hayti, whom Thomas Clarkson made zealous efforts to help towards independence from France. When Henry Christophe ended his life, in Oct. 1820, his wife and daughters fled to England and their friend, Thomas Clarkson. The story of the lengths to which patronage, principles and friendship were tested is told in *Thomas Clarkson, the Friend of the Slaves*, by E. L. Griggs, 1936. Professor Griggs gives an amusing letter from Clarkson on the domestic difficulties involved. *Op. cit.*, 144–6.

† The text of their parody of Jonson's 'Queen and Huntress chaste and fair' is given in a letter of Dorothy Wordsworth to Mrs. Clarkson, 24 Oct. 1821 (*Wordsworth Letters, The Middle Years*, III, 55). Dorothy Wordsworth says the first stanza was Wordsworth's, 'and together they finished it with much loving fun'.

burdens *flea bites* compared to Poors Rates, upon Agriculture! – Kindest love from all to all at Hindwell & yourself – God bless you & believe me most truly yours S. H.

My compts to *Harriet.* –

*Postmark: Kendal, Penny Post*

## 80

*Thos Monkhouse Esq^re^, Glo'ster Place, 34 Portman Square*

*Sunday, 24th Feb^y^* [*1822*]

My dear Coz

. . . We received a Parcel from Longman on Friday & were somewhat disappointed that it contained not a despatch from you as they had previously announced your intention to send one – We long to hear from you & wonder what you are about – D^r^ Satterthwaite is in Cha^s^ St attending upon Lord L. during his confinement under the Oculist – And W^m^ has commissioned him to confer with D^r^ Russel concerning Willy – as the latter is so slow in replying to W^ms^ queries – We hope that he is himself trying to judge of the probability of Willy's doing good where he is – as if there were any chance his Parents would be loth to remove him – but M^r^ Johnson gives a lamentable account of his scholarship – & says that there must be great neglect, as he cannot think the fault is entirely Willys – Mary is very anxious to know upon what grounds you reported D^r^ Wordsworth's favorable report. – I do not think I have a morsel of News for you – W^m^ is as busy as a bee with the new Publication – which will be finished, *for the present*, when it is bound up *tight in boards* but not till then. – I want sadly to know whether you still intend to visit us this summer, & what time your travels are to begin – We hope the Clarksons will also visit us this year. – M^r^ C. talks of it & therefore there is some hope – His Wife has done so year after year for the seven years past.

Chantry has sent Mary a present of a Cast of her Husbands Bust – I think we like them better the longer we look upon them – Have you got yours yet? – Did you see W^m^ Jackson when he was in Town? We have very discouraging reports of his health & fear that he is not long for this world –

We are all pretty well – Williams eyes better than when I last wrote

– Kindest love to Mrs M. & yourself from all & believe me ever most affty Yours S. H.

*Postmark: 7 o'Clock, 4 Mr 1822*

# 81

*Edward Quillinan Esqre, Lee Priory, nr Ickham, Kent*

*Rydal Mount, 28th June* [*1822*]

My dear Friend

As I know you are not, like Mr W. *fidgetty* about the expence of postage I inclose Mr Tillbrook's Letter which I received yesterday, to save myself the trouble of transcribing it – and which I leave you to reply to prevent delay – tho' you need not say that I sent the *Letter*, which perhaps I ought not to have done –

I have had repeated applications from Miss Prichard, & Mrs Elliot, concerning the Terms &c upon which you would part with the Ivy Cottage should Mr T. allow of its being underlet – In consequence I, with the approbation of your other Friends here, proposed that from the time of Dr Wordsworth's quitting it till the 12th of May 1824, the rent should be at the rate of 100£ per Ann: exclusive of the Taxes – reckoning the time from Sepr 12th to May 1823 only as one half year (rent & taxes) which Mr W. though[t] was reasonable, so much of the summer being gone by – The new Tenant to keep all in neat order &c according to Mr T's agreement with you – also to have the liberty of remaining to the end of your lease should neither yourself or Mr T. wish to occupy the House. All this they have agreed to, tho' they added, *of course*, that they thought the terms high 'as there was no Land' – for I reserved the hay for you to return to, or to sell, for the purpose of remunerating you for the expence of the road &c, which unhappily may never be of any use to you – therefore *on this score* you ought not to be a loser – [*10½ lines crossed out*]. I wish you were here for your own sake as well as to spare me all this *bother* in reconciling your separate interests – but I take it for granted that it would not accord with your notions to make up your loss by the increase of rent which has not been obtained by the money laid out by you – the road being no more desirable to the Elliots than Mr T. – Don't suppose that I care for the *bother* any further than that I doubt of my ability to judge properly between you all

I have not much to say respecting your other concerns, except that the Carriers Bill is settled & paid after deducting Mr T's & Mrs M's part of it – the disputed Item proved to be the harp – £1. 1. having been paid by Robinson for Freight & the same sum for the Duty at the Customs House (18[d] only being his charge for carriage from Cockermouth where he received it) as his receipts testify –

So much for business! And I have little else to add – as I doubt not my Sister told you we were rejoiced to hear of your, and the Darlings, safe arrival at Lee – We think, & talk, of you hourly, and look at the print, which is placed upon the dining-room chimney piece, & *wonder* if dear little M'ma is trotting about under those fine Trees – Mr W's eyes are still somewhat inflamed – all else well, except for Willy who returned from School yesterday morning looking wretchedly. He has been very unwell for the last week or 10 days, & I grieve to say that Mr Carr thinks him dropsical – However we trust that his youth may enable him to throw off the disease, tho' Mr C. laments that it has not been discovered sooner, as it has made considerable progress – He is God be thanked! somewhat better this morning. Poor Thing! he has made a thousand enquiries after you & the Children – and all that concerns you – God bless you all! Give that sweetest Mima a hearty kiss for me, & do not let her forget Miss Mutton – The Travellers returned from Borodale greatly pleased with their excursion – and Doro much amended in health & spirits – all join me in kindest remembrances – & best wishes for you & your dear Children – & I am very affty & sincerely

Your Friend S. Hutchinson

Kind regard to Cap[t] Barret & Mr Edgerton – the latter I hope did not think me *rude* in not having bidden him good bye –

Pray write as soon as possible – the Elliots being very anxious for your decision – I have not written to Mr T. nor shall I mention any particulars as to Terms in either case – therefore you are quite at liberty to propose whatever you may think proper – Your expences upon the road garden &c amount to £5 1s. 10½d. – Mr T's to £8. 6 – Miss W. bids me say that she has made a rough calculation of the Bills & with what are yet to come in that not less than 100£ more will be req[d].

After my Letter was finished I erased great part of my *botheration* as it was not approved of by some of our Party therefore I leave it all to yourself – only beg that you will remember that *I* shall be subject to a charge from Tillbrook, if the encreased rent is not allowed him of having made a better bargain for *You* than *him*.

*Postmark: Kendal, Penny Post, 1822*

# 82

*Mr Monkhouse, Stow, nr Hay, Brecon*

*Stockton, Sep$^{tr}$ 12* – [*1822*]

My dear Coz.

You may thank accident for this Letter – therefore I tell you so at the first that you may not feel any undue *gratitude* towards me – John[1] sent George[1] his Dividends some time ago according to Joannas direction – & the Letter never having been called for it has been ret$^{d}$ to the dead Letter office – & this morn$^{g}$ a notice of its being there has arrived – but as the Bill is specially indorsed George must put his name to it & therefore John has ordered the Letter to be sent to you & will thank you to get it forwarded to George & begs you will excuse the liberty – but it was the best way he could contrive – The Bill is past due no doubt & it is provoking that there should have been such a bother – but Geo: should have enquired about it –

You cannot be more surprized to hear that I am here; than I to find myself here – But our John[1] was resolved to have me back with him & Doro[2] put in her claim for a visit to S., which her mother had promised her, & which her Father would only consent to on condition that I should accompany her – We left no one at home but my Aunt, Mary[1], & Willy[2]. W$^{m}$ in his way to Lowther, & Joanna & Miss W. on their way to Edinburgh accompanied us over Kirkstone – & a most pleasant journey we had – *we* spent one night at Penrith & 3 at Appleby – Jane came in the Gig with her Father. & Doro & I rode on horse back & in the Gig also alternately – The weather was delicious & continued so – Bessy – & little Willy[3] H. (who had been his Fathers companion to Rydal) returned to Stockton by Coach from Appleby on the Monday – & now we are a pretty good houseful – Charles H. whom his Father had sent to Sedburgh to wait until he could find him a situation in an Att$^{ys}$ Office – has resolved to remain there – having been inspired by the Sedburgh Lads with a love of Scholarship – & now intends to go to the University which was the wish of his Uncle Hugh & his Father – Our Willy[2] is a very good Boy – & quite attentive to his Books under J. Carter – & I hope his health will soon be reestablished – Now when it is in my head I must tell you that my Poney is a very nice one – It *starts* no more than is agreeable – I have nearly completed its education & it will very soon be quite perfect – My old one has a fine foal but it will be too gay for me in my old age,

Doro[2] – is as you may suppose all alive with her journey & the many strange sights she has seen – Her Uncle quite doats upon her – Poor Thing! She has been very unwell – but I have no doubt change of air will do her good – indeed she already looks much better – John[1] is one of the happiest men alive, notwithstanding all his cares – His verses, & his Short horns make him forget them all – He only stayed 3 days with us at Rydal – but he enjoyed himself greatly notwithstanding we had such a large family, which he is so much afraid of, but in this case they were all friends & he was not annoyed – but we have had *such* a summer for Company as I never remember! – My Aunt I think was the only person who did not complain – but she is, you know, formed for Society – Mary[1] tells me that Willy[2] & they 2 play at Whist with dummy – for their friend M[r] Barber is engaged with company whom they expected to be a never-failing *hand* during their solitude – Joanna who is such a good scribe must have told you all the Rydal News long ago – & news from this place there is none to interest you – John[1] had a Letter from the North on Thursday – The Ladies were full of spirits & enjoyment – altho' Joanna, who was *purse keeper*, found herself already £4 wrong in her reckoning –

We were surprized to find that you had made such a short stay at Preston – the second week, being *musical*, would I thought have had more charms for you –

Pray write & tell me if you enjoyed yourself? &c &c altho' I do not suppose you will think this shabby Letter worth a return – Tell Mary[2] that a Box was sent off from Rydal long ago & I hope she has rec[d] it safe – Kindest love to them all – & beg she will also write when she feels inclined – for I am always far more greedy about Letters when from home – I rode over to Whitten one day & saw our intended new relative – M[r] Fernandez – a very canny young Man – handsome enough for anything – & has an excellent character – but I do not think he will ever set the Thames on fire – tho' I ought not to judge so hastily – God bless you – Ever truly yours S. H.

## 83

*Thos Monkhouse Esq[re], Budge Row, London*

*Stockton, Saturday, 19th Oct[r]* [*1822*]

My dear Coz.

George[2] Sutton, who is about to set out for Italy, has written to beg that his Sister Anne may be allowed to accompany him; & as he is become *quite steady*, & they have a perfect reliance upon Cap^t^ & M^rs^ Bush who are his *Guardians*, his Friends here have consented, & she is to set off immediately to meet Cap^t^ Bush in Town who will conduct her to St. Omer's where George & the Family now are – & they will cross the Simplon & proceed into Italy immediately – where they are to Winter – My Brother would have accompanied her to London himself – but an acquaintance of his, who resides in London, has undertaken the charge of her – & he begs that you & M^rs^ M. will allow him to take the liberty of consigning her to your care upon her arrival – We do not know when Cap^t^ B. will be in Town but certainly not many days after Anne & he is directed to call upon you for her – and we hope it will not be inconvenient to you to give her a few days lodgings – M^r^ Richmond & She are to leave York on Monday morning in some post Coach, & therefore *I guess* that they cannot reach Town before Tuesday *Evening* – probably too late for you to meet or send for her to his House – and as we do not know your exact address (tho' Mary W. tells me you have taken a house in Cumb^d^ St) M^r^ R. cannot bring her to you – therefore be so good as write a note for her (with your address) at M^r^ R's 56 Doughty Street – so that if she is in Town in reasonable time M^r^ R. can send or bring her to your House – but if not she must stay all night at *his*, which will be no great evil (as his wife is a nice Stockton Lady & will be very glad to see her) indeed for the whole time if you had not been in Town. But M^rs^ H[utchinson] is very *fidgetty* about this matter – & vexed that John[1] did not go with her himself, that he is only pacified by the idea of your taking care of her – He is so averse to leaving home & above all to Coach travelling that really when she has such an unexceptionable escort it would have been a folly for him to have harassed himself. If I had not already had *a charge* in Dorothy[2], & had been sure that my visit either to you or Hendon would not have been mistimed I should have set them all at ease & brought her up myself – You will be sure to find her at M^r^ Rs on Wednesday morning if not Tuesday Evening – & if you should be in their neighbourhood before by calling and enquiring for *M^rs^* Richmond you will learn the exact time as she will probably know in what Coach her Husband comes from York – M^rs^ R's Brother John Wilson, was an old lover of your Mary's[3] – now you will say I have told you a long story – but I am so afraid of any blunder or mistake that I fancy I cannot be too explicit – & I beg that you will *by return of post* send me *one line* just to say that you are in Town and that we have not taxed you beyond your convenience – a thing which M^rs^ H. is very solicitous about – & will never be easy until she has better assurances of your good will than either mine or her Husband's – I should not say this exactly –

but she thinks it is a mighty liberty to take – tho' she herself, I am sure, would be as ready to do any good turn she could to her Friends as any body alive –

We are all well here – & my Brother especially quite young and lively – being relieved of so much anxiety by the removal and well-doing of George[2] – & certainly, if Cap[t] B. is to be relied upon, there is good reason for satisfaction in the reports made of him – You will see Cap[t] B. & may learn more than we do from the Letters – & tell us what you think of *him* – He bears an excellent character as does his wife, & they are well known to some people here tho' my Brother does not know him personally – He was in the same Reg[t] with M[r] Quillinan – ask M[r] Q. if you see him what sort of Man he is – for my part notwithstanding all the good which we hear of them *I* would not have trusted a daughter so far away with them – unless her Brother had been older & wiser – But every body else thinks it a most advantageous thing for Anne – & I trust it will not prove otherwise –

Poor Joanna! what a melancholy *finale* to her Scotch Tour – However she is so charmed with the Climate & all that she has seen in Scotland, that I dare say she would not give back the pleasure to be free of the Lumbago – I suppose we shall see her here when she is fit to travel; for she seems to have a perfect horror of Cumb[d] Street. – I am glad to find that you are to be Steward next year – M[rs] M. will be obliged to appear at the Races then – so she must do her best to be strong, for it will be almost as harassing a campaign as Preston Guild – I hope she was benefitted by her residence at Blackpool & that little Ma Ma continues to thrive as well as she did at Rydal – you have doubtless had as much news from Rydal as I have – & none have I had from Wales – & Stockton news neither can interest you or me – I wish very much to hear how you all are, & beg you may not think yourself quite absolved, now that you are a family Man, from the duty of Letter-writing – My kind love to M[rs] M. & a kiss to little Ma who will be much more *to my taste* when I see her again than she was before she could prattle & walk – both of which I hope soon to hear of her attempting – God bless you all Father, Mother & Babe – & believe me ever most affy yours S. Hutchinson.

Doro's love (she is quite well) and all the rest desire their kindest remembrances –

I shall direct this also to M[rs] M. in case you should be out of the way – & she will I am sure *do the needful.*

*Postmark: 19 Oc 1822*

# 84

*Thos Monkhouse Esqre, Budge Row, London*

*Stockton, 9th Novr* [*1822*]

My dear Cousin

I need not say that I was greatly shocked by the account of poor Joe's Death, & I have thought of little else than dear Mary[2], since I received your Letter yesterday, to whom I fear the event was quite unexpected – I have written to my Aunt as you desired – Poor woman it will cast a sad gloom over her visit at Penrith, where I hear she is enjoying herself among her old haunts, & the few old Friends remaining to her – Joanna too will be very much hurt, for she had a most lively regard for your Brother & he was associated with all her youthful recollections – I am sorry to hear such a sad account of his pecuniary affairs – & can only add that I trust you will never feel the loss *on that score* –

I hope Anne Hutchinson has written to Mrs M. – before this time – If she has not it can only be from her modesty in thinking that her Letter was not worth the postage; for she is fully sensible of both your kindness to her – & I hope she is of an affectionate nature – They arrived at St Omer on the Wednesday Evening – found George[2] quite well, & looking so – She is delighted with Capt & Mrs Bush – & says that it is impossible not to be happy with them – They are to proceed in about a week for Italy –

Doro[2] & I have not fixed the time of our departure from this place . . . I think a visit at Miss Lockiers might do her good – but she is too young for a long one in London which would quite unsettle her from her Books – She does not like *this sort of Town* life at all & is very industrious – but London where there is so much novelty would make her quite wild – If it were not for the kindness of our Friends & the flattering attentions which she has recd from every body she would have longed for home in a very short time – for this is the most stupid place in the world – *out of our own agreeable Family of Hutchinson*, which I am happy to say is very numerous, there is no *society* – & for the Country it is detestable. Yet we have exceedingly enjoyed ourselves – My Brothers cheerfulness is a constant delight & Mrs H. is a most amusing person – Doro has seen a play for the first time in her life since she came hither. – . . .

I should have been much better pleased to hear that Mr Lewis had given Tom[1] up his Lease – The Man can have no conscience – When he finds that Farms in the Neighbourhood will now not fetch more than ½ the rent they did – My Brother John[1] is very anxious that I should be in Town to see his fat Heifer shewn at Smithfield at Christmas – You must go to see it at least [once] or never hope to be forgiven – He & Mrs H. send their best thanks to you & Mrs M. for your remembrances & kindnesses to Anne – Your Friend Jenny Nettle is as lively as a Lark – She can find amusement even in this dull Town for her spirits never flag. – Bessy is very chearful too but she is a much more sedate person that Jane. I wish she had gone to the Continent – She would have profitted by it far more than Anne – But perhaps she would not have preferred *the party* –

Mrs Luff told me that the Gov: meant to return in Spring 'She hoped they would not land sooner than April' – Mrs Clarkson said his return was uncertain – If you can learn anything on this head tell me – for tho' we have a daily paper I see it irregularly – I am about to execute a power of Atty to sell out of the Funds – but I do not mean to order them to be sold at present – tho' I should like to lodge it in some ones hands who could depend upon to act without my orders.

God bless you all Husband Wife & Child – I hope Mrs M. has not suffered from this late unseasonable weather – Now we have a nice frost – before it was unnaturally hot – tho' thank God we are all well here – Yours very truly – S. H.

*Postmark: 11 No 1822*

## 85

*Edward Quillinan Esqre, Lee Priory, Wingham, Kent*

*67 Gloucester Place, Saturday* [*March 8 or 15, 1823*]

My dear Friend

Luckily I had a Letter from Coleorton yesterday & can therefore, *in part*, satisfy your enquiries – On the 19th *they* leave Coleorton for Birmingham where *they* are to meet John[4] & proceed with him to Oxford (for Matriculation) & hope to reach Town on the 22nd '& for *a short time* accept of the offered hospitality of your host & hostess'. I give you the very words that you may know as much as I do about the length of *their* stay – but as Mr & Mrs M[onkhouse] talk of going to *Brighton* (for all that I can do I cannot bring Ramsgate into favor) early in April *they* will not be tempted to stay here beyond *their* own time & I dare say *they* will be in haste home. . . .

My cold has left me but I am not quite well, tho' last night Mr M. took me to the Oratorio where we both of us had a comfortable nap in spite of Braham, Mrs Salmon & Miss Stephens – tho' I think if Mad: Camperose had sung all the Time I could have listened – but 2 hours of the best music in the world is quite enough for a feast – & 3½ cannot fail to produce exhaustion in those who enjoy it, & weariness in those who do not. I shall not go to the Theatre again until John comes, & then I shall be sure of amusement in watching its effect upon him should I find no other – but I have outlived my taste for Plays & would not take the trouble to go & see the best of the actors, except to be able *to say that I had seen them.* I never liked Kean entirely in any Character, that I have seen him in, except Sir Giles Overreach* – a bull! is it not?

Mary[1] sent me a long Letter from Rydal the joint production of the Dorothys & Willy – they were all well – Doro[2] reading Horace most industriously – Willy full of Village gossip, & Aunty of Business – so I trust they will keep themselves so – as W^ms^ favorite maxim is that 'when the mind is employed the body takes no harm' tho' he himself proves its falsehood every day of his life –

Mrs M. is quite well – but she is very *naughty* – I could manage Mima, when she was at the very worst, far better than I can her – Baby improves in all things –

Mr M. is in the City – but Mrs M. desires her kind remembrances – and with kisses to Mima & Rotha & I remain very truly yours S. H.

*Postmark: MR 15, 1823*

## 86

*Thos Monkhouse Esq^re^, 24 Budge Row, London*

*Bologne Saturday* – [*28 June 1823*]

My dear Coz

Positively Mons: le C— is playing chess with my hostess & you may thank for this circumstance for my Letter – as it is impossible for me to find a moments leisure except when she is so engaged, even to write to my Friends – altho' the thousand & one stories *have been told*, I have

* In Massinger's *A New Way to Pay Old Debts.*

little doubt but that another will succeed – Your Letter & packet was most acceptable – we had had the day before a note from Miss W. by the Misses Dowling – who, not knowing that I was here, did not call – but whipped off with all *possible* speed by the first Diligence else I should have been tempted to go with them – for even of Boulogne I shall know little for Miss B[arker] is not to be moved – I cannot *tear* her out of the house except for an airing in this charming Country – & Mr Derrington, who is a very agreeable John Bull, has driven us every day – not for want of a Coachman tho' Jean Marie is gone – and his Brother Louis Marie has taken his place – I hope you will come as soon as possible – you, *or all*, as you give me some hopes – and I long to hear how the *voyage* to Dover was performed & what were the consequences – good I hope – & such as will not deter you from making a second trip – As I have said I shall see Nothing by remaining here – &, tho' I spend my time most happily & agreeably, yet when I have stayed a fortnight I shall think I have done my duty considering the other claims I have upon me, which I feel ought not to be set aside for no better purpose than dreaming my time away here – Therefore I hope as soon as you conveniently can you will join me, either for the purpose of making a little Tour, or to give your Ladies an *outing* – for tho' I might meet with companions or even cross by myself (which I had rather do than bring you merely to fetch me) yet the difficulty of getting off would be immense unless you were to *invent* some over-powering reasons for my return –

This is Sunday & we are going to dine at Sir Jere's where I will endeavour to gain some information respecting the means of convey-ance to Ostend &c. Mons: le — told me that it was 30 Leagues to O. but I think it must be farther – & I did not like to engross his conversa-tion upon his first visit to his Love after his confinement – especially as it was a shorter one than usual – He is a very *fine* Man – More like an English than a French man & I liked his looks & manners very much – We have tried this morning to get into the French Church – but it was so full that we were obliged to return – & indeed the *stench* at the door was quite appalling &, much as I wished to witness the ceremonies I had not the *hardihood* to go further – The Churches here are either new or *make-shifts* – the fine old Cathedral was destroyed in the revolu-tion – Some of the views of the Town are very interesting indeed – as a Town I like B— very much – but nothing could make emends to me for the frightful scenery round about – There are some very respectable Chateaux in the neighbourhood with beautiful Gardens – such as I delight in – but except one I have not seen their interior – This I should greatly like to see – the interior & the oeconomics of a french Gentlemans house in the Country – The People in this house Maids included are excellent – The old Gentlemans daughter & her two pretty children are here – & M^r^ *Cass*, as you call him, was at one of Miss B's parties a little Fright of a Man – We have had two other French Gentlemen to Tea with a party – & they seemed very agreeable – & I always can have a *guess* what they are talking about – but their English when they have any, is as funny as my french could well be.

The Play tonight is the *40 Thieves* which I should have liked much to see – but of course could not go – however I hope we may go to Capieure (Tivoli* is another place of the same kind) this evening to see the Matelots dance – & as it is not a night for the English I shall like it much better. M[rs] M. may have a Gros: de Naples Gown at 7 f. pr. ell *of the color she likes* – but she must send or bring a patt[n] old *waist* to make it by – & I think she would like one of the silk Bonnets made with whale bone in the way of *Babys* but far more *tasty* (and which are very fashionable at Paris) & beautiful of whatever color she chuses Gros depap: for 22 fr. but she or Miss H[orrocks] must come to help to *smuggle* them – & if we go to Ostend or else where such things cannot be dragged along with us so I can purchase nothing till this is decided – by the way when you come bring Sovereigns instead of Notes – as we get more by the ex – & you must provide a little for me: but I shall not spend much notwithstanding the temptations – I am writing now on Tuesday morning 1st July. Poor Miss B. has been very unwell since sunday ev[g] but is better today – on Sunday we went to Capieure, a public Garden, where all the lower orders & the Matelots assemble to dance &c on that Evening – & Yesterday Evening I was to have gone, with the Homfrays, to the same place to see all the higher orders who meet there on Mondays for the same purpose – but rain came on & we were prevented. On Sunday I was delighted with our entertainment – they danced so prettily & were so courteous & well-behaved! – in such an assemblage (nay hundreds) of the lower classes in England we should have been insulted or quizzed at least – but here no notice was taken of us and we stood & looked, & made our remarks, at pleasure – Le C— is here again playing at Chess as is his custom twice a week regularly. He is a very fine looking man in spite of his wounds – of very mild manners & not the least like a frenchman – I like very much what I have seen of him but this cannot be much whilst he is playing at Chess – This I find I have told you in the former part of my Letter –

Thursday – I will send off my Letter today tho' it grieves me to think you will have 2/– to pay for it – & for this cause I have written

* Could she mean *Capécure* and *Les Tintelleries*? See also p. 257.

to no one but Edith Southey to whom I could no longer delay without giving more pain than the thing was worth – I learn that there is a regular diligence from this place to Ostend & therefore if you are set upon Antwerp there will be no difficulty on that score – but I fear we should make a poor hand of it with our Stock of French – & to wait for Q[uillinan] is out of the question – nobody can guess when he will be back – If you are inclined to go I shall be most happy to accompany you – but it will not be the least mortification to me to return to Eng[d] direct – I still live in hopes of seeing all these famous sights – & am so anxious to see my Welsh friends that *unless we could go very soon* I had *rather* it was deferred – Miss B. is much better & we have enjoyed ourselves very much in the Carriage at sunset in the Evening – I cannot but regret that we did not come hither all together in April – for this really is a very pleasant place & there is much very good society & plenty of amusement – & in spite of its dearness in comparison with other parts of france one may live for 2/3rds of the expence (including modes of conveyance among housekeeping expences) of Ramsgate – This morning we are going to a *Dej[e]une[r] a la fo[u]rchette* at the hon[ble] M[rs] Mullins *marine Villa* – where we expect much fun – We went yesterday to make a call upon M[rs] Lloyds sister who [with] her Husband & only daughter are arrived from Glocestershire – His name is Ryland, was high Sheriff or is – worth 300,000 & precious vulgar pair I suppose they are – but they are come for seabathing & the advantage of a little french teaching for their daughter & this is one cause why so many *respectable* people are here – so that there would have been no fear of *character* – Gen[l] Hawker & his Family are also newcomers. He called upon Miss B. & she returned the call to his wife yesterday – He made the drawings which are engraved for Southeys *War in the Peninsula* – & seems a very agreeable Man . . .

Now I think you have all the *News* – Let me hear from you – I trust you are all well – & I hope to see some of you soon – If you do not resolve to go to Antwerp could not M[rs] M. & Miss H. accompany you for a few days – I do not think it would be wise for Miss Anne[2] as she *is sick* on the water – *that* would be sure to bring on her hemorrhage – & as you seem doubtful of the prudence of M[rs] M's coming I mean in case you can get to Dover by water – of which I hope there will be no difficulty – God bless you all I long to hear what you decided upon – Most affty Your's S. H. Kiss Ma Ma when you see her –

I direct this to Town as it must go thither

*Postmark: JY 5, 1823*

S.H.—T

# 87

*Miss Joanna Hutchinson, Hindwell, Radnor*

*Boulogne, Rue du Puits d'Amour (The bottomless Pit, I say, it will prove) July 12th the Street opposite 'Rue d'Inferne'*!!! [*1823*]

My dearest Dorothy

You cannot conceive the delight with which I received your Letter & one from M[r] M[onkhouse] yesterday – I had feared that my friends in the North, calculating upon my intention of making a short stay here, would not write to me. – I am truly glad to hear so good an account of you all – for tho' you do not say that your Fathers Eyes are well I feel assured that they will soon be so as he is disposed to try the virtuable waters – but more than all am I surprized to find that he can tolerate H[arrowgate] much less like it. I should have been glad to find that your spots were all gone – but now when I think of it let me tell you that the best thing you can do is to wash *not only your face* but generally, with *sand* (as well as soap) which quickens the circulation & has I know not what other good properties which improve the skin – & *I know* it makes ones feet delightfully warm after they have been cold as stones – now do not fail to profit by this –

How long I shall continue here I know not – I daily regret that the Monkhouses had not come hither when we first talked of it – for as a sea-bathing place I think it is most delightful – &, in spite of all Miss B[arker]s objections to a house near the sea here are many charmingly situated – & the beach is very fine & extensive – Miss B. (who has a small *Phaeton & pair of Ponies*) & I drive out there every evening – this is the most rational way in which we spend our time – but as to seeing anything, either French or English, I have little other opportunity – for she will not walk out herself *& if she would part with* me I cannot even go a shopping alone – which is lucky enough – as I shall keep my money in my pocket – With the Monkhouses I should really have enjoyed the place & Miss B's company – & above all been free to do as I liked – & certainly between this place & Ramsgate there can be no comparison – The Town is beautiful seen from many points – & there is abundance of very good society – & abundance of *scamps* also no doubt – &, dear as the place has become comparatively, one may live for one half of the expence of Ramsgate – I have no chance whatever of going to Paris. Had the Dowlings called I should have been tempted

– but Miss B. cannot afford the expence – besides to go with her would require six months at least to see or do anything – she lives in such a complete dream – planning & scheming, & never executing! Yet believing as firmly as M[r] Coleridge that she never fails! – This being the case I feel uncomfortable at the idea of my stay being prolonged beyond what is necessary & that I ought to be in Wales – yet I do not like to bring M[r] M. over again *just to fetch me* when he cannot be spared from London to take any pleasure to himself – & *I shall never* get off by myself – However I shall wait quietly till I hear that M[r] Q[uillinan] is returned – & then I shall claim his promise to come for me – which I hope will be in a fortnight at farthest – Therefore if you see M[r] Q., or your Mother writes to him, tell him to come as soon as he can after his return – I am glad to hear that dear little Mima is at Ramsgate it will do her good I hope – now as the hot weather is come at last a little bathing will be good for her – as to Rotha she is such a little knotty thing, that she requires no strengthening – M[rs] Irving (Coz: Di) with her Husband & Baby, 3 months old, are just arrived at the Hotel de la Prefecture – she is a charming creature – & the Babe is the largest I ever saw (except perhaps M[rs] Cooksons) at that age – & she, certainly, the most interesting Mama – beautiful as she is she seems not to think of herself – & tho' there is a sad reverse in her prospects, from the failure of profits from their west india property, she seems as if she thought her child was sufficient for all things in this world.

Mons: le C— is really & truly a lover of the Signoras – but I suspect that the Gent: is of the same opinion that I and my (now your) Lover are with respect to matrimony – tho' it appears to me that such an attachment as theirs must end in matrimony else it is great folly – He is a very agreeable & interesting Person – much more like an English than a french man in manners & appearance – Yet he dislikes the English I should say hates them if I thought it possible that a man so good, as I believe him to be, could hate anything but wickedness – He is a royalist – but here they say that the Bonepartists are more liberal, in general, & less prejudiced against the English than the other party. Miss B. & I have many a battle – she defends the French thro' *thick & thin* – tho' she is of the Spanish side in the war – as I *suppose* most in this Town are – In this she is opposed to her lover –

I like the people of this house very much – & wish I could talk with them – the maids especially who appear gracious creatures – but I am grieved to find that in general these fine smooth & obliging manners, which take one so much among the lower orders, are all pretence – Agnes says that they always *mock* you behind your back – I do not mean the Girls of this house whom I like so much that I hope they are an exception – but I have seen it often in others – & another detestable trait is that invariably there is one price for everything to the English & a lower to the French – And then when not one of their friends will deny that the belief is universal among them all, good & bad, that we had no other than self interest as motive for the abolition of the Slave Trade because they have not the virtue to conceive it possible – Yet their politeness their honesty & I know not what virtues are to be thrown in the teeth of the English without fear of contradiction –

I rec^d the french newspaper 'the *Constitutionnel*' every day & can get on with it very well – but I can understand little that is spoken – only just to know *what* they are talking about – Agnes speaks the Patois so well that all the Market people take her for french – & Edward is quite *perfect* & can make himself understood anywhere – Miss B. talks also very well I dare say – she reads & speaks with the C— who visits regularly 2 mornings a week – & she has many french acquaintances – Mad: Fremasoire the daughter of M. Martin an old Gentleman of 85 to whom this house belongs (& from whom I received a beautiful nosegay on the morning after my arrival in great form) is here from Blois with 2 children, Gustave & Elise, pretty creatures as ever you saw – & their Father & mother are clever sensible people – stout republicans they were – according to their account living at B. is very cheap – & it is one of Miss B's schemes to go thither – but she is not very easily moved – & therefore I believe she will end her days in Bologne unless some accident were to determine otherwise for her.

If Miss Dowling should have occasion to write to her sisters beg that she may desire them to call here on their return – as if I should not be in England at that time I should certainly take the opportunity of crossing the channel with them – but I hope to see either M^r M. or M^r Q. before – as I suppose they will stay at least a month longer which I should not wish to do – I shall not be sorry to see the *Fair* which commences on the 25th – I was one night at the Play – & one evening in coming thro one of the Gates we spied a puppet shew into which we went – which proved to be a representation by Puppets of the birth, life, death & resurection of our Saviour!! The exhibition was really very pretty – & the awfulness of the subject prevented the least inclination to laugh – & I was very glad that we had gone – notwithstanding the nasty candles dropped upon my bonnet & spoilt all my ribbons.

I, like your Mother, delight in the profusion of flowers which I see every where – the Gardens are beautiful & we have abundance in the rooms – fine double larkspurs seem to grow wild in the Gardens among the onions & lettuces &c – I long to have them transplanted to England – & would bring seed for ourselves & M^r B but that I know they would not flower in such variety & beauty in our soil – We have taken some rides into the Country – seen one Garden & passed several others which I longed toenter – & I hope to gain admittance before I leave B. to one real old French Garden which surrounds the Chateau of one of Boneys aid du Camp – We went one day to a dejeune[r] a la fourchette at 5 oClock P m in the marine villa or rather *wig wam* of the honble Mrs Mallen – [&] returned home at ½ before 9 – notwithstanding these extraordinary hours the visit was as stupid as ordinary – one of our tea drinkings on Rydal worth 50 such meetings in spite of the champagne, hock, hermitage &c &c which were abundant. – Sir Jere's House is the perfection of french & English – & my Lady is very amusing – She always enquires after your Mother – & bids me ask my Sister what is her opinion of the French & French oeconomics – for it appears they agreed in all things – Yet I like some of the french cookery very much – tho' in some things its want of simplicity [is] detestable – The *kitchen* in this house is as clean as needs be – & [*torn*] in many respects very elegant – but it has a general air of dirt & decay – [*torn*] there is no less than 2000£ worth of plate not a salt spoon – & the plates look as if they had had *biddies* cracked upon them for a century!! – 200 pillow slips all frilled round with scallopped muslin – & other linen in proportion – I believe I must be forced to close my Letter – for Miss B— is up & ready to go with me to the public library to see Denons Work – She bids me say that she wishes you were here to keep us in order – She snuffs as usual in the house but never in the carriage, or a visiting, or when Mons: le C— is playing at Chess &c with her – I am also to say that he is as brave as a Lion, as gentle as a Lamb, as regular in his habits as Mr Southey, & as *philosophical* as Mr Wordsworth – and is a mixture of Amadis de Gaul & uncle Toby. – God bless you all! I shall be glad to hear that you are all well & at Rydal Mount – My best regards to all there & thereabouts – I am vexed to hear of Julia's deceitfulness – but Miss D[owling] always said it was so – & I hope your Mother will tell her that she has done herself more harm in the opinion of her Friends than she has injured Miss D – Ever & ever yours S.H.

Tuesday Morng

My Letter was forgotten last post day – so I have opened it to add a few words – & must redirect it – to Rydal. Last night we went to Capieure – where there is a sort of ball every monday evening for the Gentry french & English – on Sundays the lower orders dance there I had been to see them before & was much delighted especially with the matelots & the general good behaviour of all – Last night we wished for you & some other of our young friends – It is a very nice custom to go out in this way without the trouble of dressing – & tho it is not exactly like dancing in the open air, for there are seats & a screen on each side of the dancing place, yet trees are the only roof & the lamps hang among them & it is much less artificial than Vaux hall – some of the french Girls danced admirably – but we did not stay long & I saw none of the English that were remarkably good dancers tho the Masters say *they* learn much better than the french as they take more pains –

Mrs Lloyds sister Mrs Ryland is here with her Husband & Daughter – come for sea bathing – I have not seen one person that I know in all the multitude that are here – Perhaps if one was always to see the pacquet come in one might meet with friends – The Hugessens I dare say will be returning about this time – if I could meet with them I should go back with them – but indeed I should find little difficulty in meeting with a companion – but as sure as fate we should have a quarrel if I were to take myself off in that manner. Tell your Aunt that I should like to have a little chat with her – & if I were with you I could make you all laugh about the megrims of the Signora – talking of megrims reminds me of the state of medicine here – Miss B. says talk not of the lightness of the french character for to this day they stick to *Galen & Hippocrates*!! You would marvel indeed to hear of their remedies – teasans as they are called, infusions of herbs, for everything – or orange flower water which is a sovereign remedy – for the most violent pains – The old Gent: in this house is afflicted with a very painful complaint – a birch *teasan* is the remedy – & which Victoire, the housekeeper, made one day of a bit of the old besom which had swept the house for months & Mr Martin swallowed it with as good faith as the old women who sit upon the steps of the cross praying to the figures above them – at this cross upon the beach I often see gentlemen even with their hats off at their devotions – but never Ladies. – The road to Paris lies at the head of this street – & we hear daily the cracking of the Postillons whips taking the English either to or from Paris – for very seldom are the carriages filled with any other people – The Duke of Brunswicks Brother is here for the bathing season – a vulgar looking lad as ever you saw. . . .

I suppose they will be ready to receive me at Hendon by the end of the month – again God bless you all – I am vexed to think that any Letter of mine should cost you 2/– & me 10d besides I forget to tell you that I was at one Rout but I hope & trust I shall be at no other it was more stupid if possible than the breakfast

*Postmark: Jy 17, 1823*

# 88

*Thos Monkhouse Esq$^{re}$, 12 Paragon, Ramsgate*

*Boulogne, Wednesday Night, 22nd July* [*1823*]

My dear Cousins

I have wished day after day since I received your Letter to thank you for it and to speak of the time when I should meet you & my other kind Friends at Ramsgate – but Miss B[arker] will not hear of my departure, & I must make my arrangements in spite of her; for were I to remain until this day twelvemonth she would then turn the same deaf ear to them – Next week is the Fair – it commences on Sunday – & as I should wish to see a little of the humours I shall not think of moving till the end of the week or the beginning of the following – If you & Miss H[orrocks] could come to make a pleasure of it you may be sure I should be delighted – or if M$^{r}$ Q[uillinan] is come home & could make it convenient to fetch me I should be greatly obliged to him – but *your* coming alone hither, or to Dover, when your time is so little your own at present would weigh heavy on my conscience – as I may probably be lucky enough to hear of a companion – for I confess that to be left the last in the vessel, sick to death as I was, with no one to assist me ashore is not a very agreeable prospect – especially as the passage is often 4 or 5 hours from the place. If I were but comfortably at the Union at Dover I should do very well – & there is not the least necessity for you coming thither. I every day more & more wish that you had all been here – It is a most delightful sea-bathing place – The Sands are so firm & extensive – we take an airing upon them every evening when the tide does not prevent us & the sunsets are magnificent – besides there are houses near the sea which would be very pleasant – & all the world are upon the pier & the beach – they are the favorite walks both of the French & the English. Then there is that pleasant custom of going to the Gardens of Tivoli* & Capieure where all the Gentry of both nations dance together two Evenings in the week, without the ceremony of dress or the annoyance of heated rooms; & tho' they are shabby places in themselves compared to Vauxhall they are less artificial & you dance under a roof of *natural looking* Trees – Here all the real advantages of the best seabathing place in England with novelty in the amusements – & all is to be had at half the expence. Then if one wished for Balls & routs to shew off fine clothes one might have a *surfeit* if one

* See p. 250 *.

chose – Miss B. is gone to one tonight – but I was obstinate in my refusal – tho' the Lady who she is gone to visit is one of the most agreeable whom I have seen – & there is no lack of either the beautiful or the agreeable in this Town – but the *real parties* are sufficiently stupid – as they always must be to those who do not play cards or dance – & to those I should never wish to go.

We made one very entertaining visit in the Country to an old Col: of Buonapartes – & tomorrow we are to dine with one of his aid de Camps who lives near *Ponbrick* [Pont de Briques?] (well spelt I doubt not) Boneys Country house where there are some beautiful Gardens in the old French style – Mons: le Comt said to us on hearing where we were going 'you will den be forced to make de eloge of Bonaparte!' He is a good-natured creature – & his bad English gives additional simplicity to his character – He always speaks English when I am here – He told us that he had answered an English Gentleman (who spoke to him in bad french) in English – 'because as he had shocked me with his bad french I said to myself that I would shock him with my bad English.'

We dine every Sunday as usual at Sir Jere's – Their daughter with Her Baby have been here a fortnight & she is the most interesting Mother I ever saw – & the baby one of the largest and healthiest looking of its age – they are worth going many miles to see – I am sorry for her poor Thing! for tho' her Husband is all I daresay that she can wish him to be it is very early in life for her to have her fair prospects cut off. Mr Irvings property being in the West Indies they are at present reduced to a very scanty income – with little hope of its being better.

I long to hear how they all are in Wales – tho' I was happy to find by a Letter from Doro[2] that my aunt was something better – I shall make all possible haste to them – & cut my visit near Town as short as possible – You might with reason accuse Wm & Mary of fickleness when you heard, after all! that they had made a visit to Harrowgate. I trust that the *virtuable* waters have had the desired effect upon Williams eyes, & that Doro is quite well – You must tell me all you know when you write – as I do not expect to hear from them again – they will suppose that I have left B. before this time – The Misses Dowling did not even know that I was here – so that there was no unkindness in their not calling – they were not acquainted with Miss B. & probably the Diligences set off to Paris immediately upon the arrival of the Pacquet. – I have said nothing of the journey to Paris – because it is quite out of the question going either there or to Antwerp circumstanced as you are – I wish that I knew when the Misses D. return – or that they might call here before I go which would remove all anxiety on my part as to *fellow travellers* – but I fear they will stay longer than I should wish to do. That dolorous bell is striking twelve – and the wind is blowing a november blast – The day has been altogether boisterous & wet – We have had very few hot days – & the summer will pass over without favoring us with any seasonable weather – Miss B. is so chilly that we have always a fire in the bed room at night; & very seldom has the heat been more than I like tho' I prefer cold to heat at all times – but these winds I detest – & very often when we are in the phaeton I hold the umbrella to shelter myself; by the bye those little Poneys are quite '*miracles*' – they drag us up these hills as if we were kittens only – yesterday we mounted the height towards *Amblet*[*e*]*use* (well spelt also) where Julius Caesar embarked for the conquest of Britain & some of the steeps were little better than parts of Kirkstone – yet if we would have suffered them they would have trotted – & trot they always do at one steady swift pace up & downhill in all our ordinary rides – The Paris road is very pleasant – & upon it are many very handsome & picturesque gentlemans houses – & there is a very pretty little valley on the right of the Calais road which I wish you had seen – that road which we took the day you were here is the least interesting or rather [the] only uninteresting one which I have seen – By this you will [con]clude that I am more disposed to think well of this neighborhood than at first – but I am always the more reconciled to everything about me the longer I am acquainted with them – I like the people of this house *in toto* – Old M^r^ M. tho I scarcely ever see him is as polite as ever – sends a rose now & then – & ordered his cheese to be sent in to me when he heard I liked it, as long as it lasted, & I verily believe that they did not taste it themselves that it might serve me the longer – *M. Siss* as you call him is a *very tidy* man, & speaks very funny English but I have only seen him three times – The drollest English I ever heard of was Mons le C—s when he wished to say that a Lady was in the family way he said '*she was offspring*'! – If this does not make you laugh I despair – God bless you all! I trust you are all well – Kiss the little one for me – & believe me ever & ever most affty yours S. H.

Excuse this horrid scrawl I beseech I am half asleep – and shall not wait for my hostess for the Parties do not separate till 2 or 3 oClock.

I have this moment learnt that Col: Wests 2 Sons whom I know very well leave B. on Monday & I would go with them in spite of the *fair* much as I wish to see it – but having consented to stay till the *end* of the week (what I said about being ready any day after Monday or tuesday was between you & me) unluckily I find that we should have a *downright quarrel* – so you see how difficult it will be to get off alone –

but I will be resolute when I am not shackled by any agreement or promise – Tell your People to *honor* my dft if you should not in Town. I want to buy a few books at the fair. I wish one could buy some Prints. Miss B. has a whole folio which she bought very fine ones for 2^d^ a piece

Thursday. I have rec^d^ your Letter luckily in time to add to this – that I am truly grieved to hear of poor Miss Anne's[2] illness – & the anxieties consequent upon it to you all – I long more than ever to be back to you – as I might be of some use in cheering them – there is such great uncertainty about the boats from Calais to Ramsgate at this distance else I should greatly prefer landing at R. to Dover – but I might arrive at C perhaps 5 minutes too late & have to wait or go to Dover after all. I shall certainly come at the time I have mentioned at the latest – but if Quillinan could fetch me I would be off at any time *after* monday or *tuesday first* – but by myself or with any chance companion I shall not be able to get off before the time *first specified* therefore there will be time for another Letter from you & if Q. comes you must send me a little Cash 5 or 10£ will be plenty – if not I suppose I may draw upon you for that sum – I shall be *rich* again in Sep^r^. I long to see you all again, you will find that I had anticipated the impossibility of *extended* travels at this time. I hope I have made my meaning clear – But pray dont *bother* yourself – Why has Q. been flying about at Bath – he might just as well fly here – My very best love to him and all at Lee. adieu!

This is the way in which Jean Marie folds his Love Letters – I do not think the war will go on as swimmingly as they expected & if I can sell at 82 & have my Sep^r^ Div^d^ also – *Sell*

*Postmark: JY 26, 1823*

## 89

*T. Monkhouse Esq^re^*

*Sat. Night* [*Sept.–Oct. 1823*]

My dear Coz.

M^rs^ M. has been writing a long Letter to her Sister Whitaker, & announced her intention of writing another to you against which imprudent proceeding I put in my protest & upon condition that I should give you a few lines she has submitted, for the first time to my authority – We are all as well as possible in spite of your absence & the Storm which has raged with very little abatement during the day & all last night – the Calais Mail pacquet has been driven in here today – & last night we were rocked, but not to sleep, in our beds – Tonight we shall migrate not from the 'blue to the brown' but from the white bed in the front to the white Bed in the back room to be out of the noise of the wind –

Egerton Brydges has spent the day with us, & was very agreeable, as well as a '*pretty break in*' he did not leave us till 7 oClock & will have a Stormy ride upon Gibb's Horse home – Mrs M. & I have engaged to procure a Wife for him against the time when he is ready to take orders – as he says it is impossible for him to retire to a Parsonage without someone *to talk to* – & adds he promises not to turn up his Nose either upon Manufactures or commerce Mrs M. hopes to succeed among the monied Ladies of Lancashire – We think him much improved – & certainly he is uncommonly handsome – Quill has inlisted the youngest of the Brothers now at Lee into the Corps of Sportsmen – but could not prevail upon Egerton who thinks Q—'s eagerness after the game, as he does *all things*, truly ridiculous –

We know nothing of Ramsgate News – The Ladies walk as usual – & the Town seems as full as ever – therefore I have nothing to add – Baby I believe has not learnt any new words since *Mrs M. wrote last*, but she has the old ones very perfect – 'Gone' – 'Ta ta' – 'By bye' 'Papa Mama' &c – but I have no doubt she will add to the list before your return – God bless you! . . .

## 90

*Edward Quillinan Esqre, Lee Priory*

*Ramsgate, Monday* [*Oct. 1823*]

My dear Friend

Mr Monkhouse & I intended to have given you a pop visit yesterday – the Gig did come to the Church door to take us up but the rain deterred us – & he has left us this morning – we hope to see him again on Saturday to make a little longer stay & then I purpose going to Town with him – In the mean time I hope we shall see you here – & I shall be loth to leave the neighbourhood without seeing your Darlings again – but I can easily accomplish this when Mr. M. returns – Mrs M. bids me say that she has not asked you to come hither because she thought it would be so disagreeable to you to speak in a whisper & walk on tip toe – & not because we should not be most happy to see you –

I have sent every day in vain to the Libraries for Benvenuto Cellini – John[1] is gone to make another attempt but I fear the Box must go without the Book – I enclose Lady Winchelseas Poems, which Mr M. brought from Town with him – You will find one to the Nightingale – & some others which I doubt not will please you – but she has been in general most unfortunate in her subjects.

I had a most amusing adventure with your friend Hoofsletter – at least Mr M— thinks it so amusing that he forbids me to relate it to you except in his presence – it was not however very *amusing* to me tho' I did my best to keep myself in good humour – & I hope he thought I was grateful for what he considered as kindness – . . .

God bless you! Kiss the Trots for me & believe me very sincerely Yours – S. H.

I am afraid Rothas Bonnet will be too small for her – if so send it back again.

## 91

*Edward Quillinan Esq$^{re}$, Lee Priory, nr Wingham*

*Monday* [*13. Oct. 1823*]

My dear Friend

We have this morning been surprized by a visit from Coleridge & lose no time in informing you of it – as we hope it may induce you to give a little rest to the poor Birds which we do not flatter ourselves you would do for our sakes alone – Mrs M[onkhouse] bids me say that we have a Bed at your service for as long a time as you please, but that whilst we stay here you shall not take Mr C[oleridge] to Lee – we have fixed our departure for thursday the 23rd – but we fear that your engagements will not allow you to be our escort as, if I recollect right, you are to be in Essex by the 21st – I expect my hopeful nephew & his Sister will be in Town when we arrive – & also that you will join our party in Gloster Place on your return from Essex if you cannot go with us.

Mr E. Brydges was very kind in coming to see us & we hope he had a pleasant ride home – Mrs M. is quite weary of the winds & complains constantly of a head ache – I am very well –

I hope you gave that vile Man with his vile horses a good 'blowing up' (to use an elegant phrase) I am glad we knew nothing of their evil propensity before you left – indeed I had noticed their wretched appearance and could not have dreamt of their being frisky or obstinate. Dearest little Mima I long, & yet I do not, to see her again! – I should really have enjoyed your disappointment in the non arrival of the Gentlemen, as a proper punishment for your taking her away from us had I known of it.

I shall execute Eliza's commissions the first time I go out, & have them all ready for you when you favor us with a visit – Mima's frocks are all finished – but if I had had leisure I could not have shewn my skill upon Rothas – not having her measure – so she must rely on Mrs Rose for improving her shapes –

Our kind remembrances to all your Party – & as many kisses as you please to the Darlings. Mr C. almost smothered Mary with kisses – he had been, he said, wishing for a baby to kiss which was the next best thing to Bathing in the Sea –

God bless you! & believe me

very truly your Friend S. H.

There is an admirable Letter in the *London Mag*: by Elia to the Poet Laureate* – we have not seen it but from C's report are very anxious, *especially* as there is honorable mention in it of Mr M – & some other Friends –

We shall look out for you tomorrow

*Postmark: Ramsgate, 75*

## 92

*Thos Monkhouse Esq^re^*

*Ramsgate, 14th Oct^r^* [*1823*]

My dear Coz.

I know not why your good Wife presses me to write to you, for, without undervaluing my own performances in the epistolary way, a

* This is the *Letter of Elia to Robert Southey*, 1823 (*Works*, ed. Lucas, 1912, I, 265–77), in which Lamb, stung by Southey's charging him, in the *Quarterly Review* for July 1823, in an article on 'Theo-philanthropism or the spread of Infidelity', with unsound religious feelings, rebukes Southey for intolerance and rigidity. In the *Letter*, Thomas Monkhouse was described by Lamb as 'the noble-minded kinsman by wedlock of Wordsworth'.

Letter from her must be much more acceptable than mine can be to you – However I suppose she hopes that I will confirm the reports, which she has given of herself, as to being very *well-behaved* & *tractable* in your absence – but what will you say when I tell you that our departure from this place is fixed for Thursday the 23[rd]? Indeed during the Stormy weather we were quite out of conceit with our situation – & the more so as M[rs] M. attributed her bad head aches, & other uncomfortable feelings to it – She has now a bad cold I am sorry to say but this day is so delightful that I begin to hope the winds are over & we shall have no more annoyance from them – The sea is as smooth as possible & looks as if it never could be otherwise than delightful – Baby is as well as possible – She comes at Breakfast & holds up her little mouth for 'Tea Tea' – & will I doubt not have many new words to greet you with on your return – she is very ready with her '*How does*' which she pronounces in a most droll way – Coleridge who arrived on Saturday & called upon us yesterday* – almost smothered her with kisses which, tho' she endured them with patience, did not, her Mother observed, give her as much satisfaction as those of a younger Beau – her reception of Egerton Brydges on Saturday was much more flattering. M[rs] M's Beau Gilman is not arrived & she bears the disappointment very well – I think she was rather glad, as she found C. did not require us to exert ourselves for conversation – He gave us an account of Elia's *Letter* (in the *London Mag*:) to the Poet Laureate† – & we are very anxious to see it especially as there is honorable mention of *you* among the list of his Friends – I have written to invite Quill – the attractions of C. may perhaps procure a reprieve for the condemned Birds – but he gives a very bad account of his performances.

Your Letter & *Joanna's double one* received this morning gave us a most agreeable account of you all – How delightful it is to find that dear John[2] can be so cheerful in spite of his misfortune‡ – He is an example for some other of our Friends. I must not scold you about the Tippet because your Wife says you had so very much to think of – but you might have remembered that all in *that drawer* was for Hindwell & Rydal & did you not already see one Tippet in Anne's[1] Box? – We shall now see the Travellers in London – for the 23[rd] happened to be the very day on which they had planned to be there – If they land

* He arrived on Saturday and called on Monday. This visit and later references are evidence that friendly relations did not end with the separation in 1810, and the Wordsworth quarrel.

† See p. 263 *.

‡ His loss of sight. Is there a drop of acid in this remark, with reference to Mrs. Monkhouse's tendency to invalidism?

at Ramsgate (which may be the case without their intending it if the winds return) we shall probably have their company with us to Town – & be a jovial Party – had we been going on Monday Quill & Egerton would have gone with us – but the former is obliged to attend in Essex on the 21st & Egerton to be at Cambridge –

If you have time to call at M^r^ Cooksons on your way do not fail to say all that is kind for me to them all – & that I should be glad to hear from M^rs^ C. herself concerning dear Elizabeth[3] – You will not I think forget the *yarn* if you have not succeeded in Wales. M^rs^ M. wishes you could procure some Mutton Hams in Westmoreland.

It is quite a shame to send you such a shabby Letter but really I cannot spin it out any longer so that you must be contented – I should have cared less about it if I could have given you a better account of your Wifes health – but don't fret about it. I hope this fine weather will enable her to shake off the cold – for it is nothing worse, & will not I trust be of long continuance – My kind remembrances to Mrs H. & all the young Ladies – I need not say I am glad to hear such good accounts of Miss Anne – God bless you! We shall expect a most particular account of the Sports & amusements – a Letter containing the detail will be worth much more in your absence than the relation when you are present – From Joanna I find that our Rydal Friends intend to give you the meeting – I have not heard from them myself – Farewell most affty your's S. H.

Put the enclosed in to the post at Kendal

# 93

*Thos Monkhouse Esq^re^, care of A. Harrison Esq^re^, Penrith*

*Saturday Morn^g^ [18 Oct. 1823]*

My dear Coz.

Your Letter has just arrived & we are glad to find that you are enjoying yourselves so much & hope that you will do the same till the end of your *term* – I wish I could give you a better account of your dear Wife than in my last – but her cold is very obstinate &, tho I hope it will continue in her head & not attack her chest, the weather is now very much against her speedily getting rid of it – this morning is almost as stormy as any we have had – & she complains greatly of the cold – Some days have been so beautiful that we do not despair of having good weather for our voyage & she seems to be confident that her cold will be gone before Thursday – the pain in her head she thinks is rheumatism – All else well – Baby improves hourly – Quill, who is here, is quite astonished at the change in her since his last visit – so I doubt not you will think it almost *miraculous* – Ferdinand Brydges & Q. came yesterday & they stayed to dine with us & Coleridge today, & intend to honor Sachetts concert in the Evening – I have promised to go with them – & we donot despair of enlisting C. to be of the Party...

This is a vile pen & viler Ink – but as we are upon the *saving* plan shall not replenish our Stock – tho' I know not how Quill will get his *Letters of business* written with it, after I have done, which he proposes to write – In spite of the weather he is gone to look after the Ladies having seen some of the indefatigable Walkers out enjoying the Storm –

We shall expect a Letter to greet us on our arrival in G[loucester] P[lace] with a notice of your being safe on the field of action – The Sports I suppose begin on Tuesday – God bless you & send you home safe & well – Don't be anxious about us – We have no Hackney Coachman to deal with – & if M[rs] M. is not quite well again, & the weather good, we will not venture so soon as Thursday –

Kindest remembrances 'to all enquiring Friends' & believe me most affty Your's S. H.

I need not say your Wife sends her love –

Sunday –

M[rs] M. is so much better to day & the weather again calm & promising that she has resolved to take it in good humour & set off in the morning rather than wait for another change for the worse – Q. would have arranged to go with us – but he was obliged to be off to Lee this morning before this was decided – but agreed to enquire for us & escort us from the water side if we did resolve to go which M[rs] M. would have done last night even had M[r] Kirfoot sent the money before this morning – He goes by the Tally Ho & will have got his *urgent* business over before we arrive so that we shall have more of his company but he cannot stay with us till your return – for besides his engagement at home – he takes a farewell dinner at Woolwich [Stodwick?] on Tuesday – We had a most agreeable dinner yesterday – Q. was quite astonished with C. – He had not room to squeeze in a word – tho' he was a little uncomfortable under the feeling that C. was obliged to have the talk all to himself – because he could not presume to talk to him – There was nobody at the Concert – so we did not think it worth while to go – the Gentlemen peeped in & ascertained this – C. will be in despair at our sudden determination – & I am a little sorry to leave R. before the time but I hope it will be for the best – as most certainly the cold weather does not agree with M[rs] M. & she is thoroughly persuaded that she shall be better in Town – God bless you. We shall write on Tuesday –

*Postmark: Ramsgate 20 Oc 1823*

## 94

*Edward Quillinan Esq[re], Lee Priory, nr Wingham, Kent*

*Glos'ter Place, Nov[r] 1st* [*30 Oct. ? 1823*]

My dear Friend

We expect Mr M[onkhouse] home on Saturday & Mrs M. has desired me to write to ask you to give him a meeting & join him at a Cigar in the evening – we shall have a Bed for you & hope you will in future cut your old lodgings at the *Spread Eagle* – I rec[d] your Letter – we had anticipated some blunder but were certain that you would not fail in your visit to Woolwich, as by promise bound.

I had a long Letter from Do yesterday, with a particular & circumstantial account of all the amusements which she had enjoyed, with her Father & Mother, the preceding week at Penrith. – 'Father' was the gayest of the gay in spite of his eyes – made the agreeables to every Lady in the Ball room, & notwithstanding the *lights* was all the better for his exertions. –

My sister says 'No Letter from Q. yet' – I had written & spoke of the probability of your return to the Ivy Cot – which I should not have done but in the confidence that a Letter from you would have preceeded mine – which would give your ultimatum – Tomorrow is the day on which the Elliots ought to know their fate – But I am not sure whether they wish to continue – if they do not, & Till: has no intention of occupying the Ivy Cot himself next year, of course you cannot give it up. I mention this only that if you have not written to T. that you do not leave this to be understood by *inference* – for he is so little of a Man of business that he would immediately fancy you wanted to be rid of your bargain – Mr Gee & he used constantly to have misunderstandings of this kind – & I have had Letters from him more like a *scold* than anything else – In our reckoning we forgot that besides the 19£ you have the 2 years Hay to cover your expences, & T. has no remuneration for his & the extra furniture with which I accommodated *your* Tenant – Now don't *misunderstand* me. I am more anxious that you should not, from forgetfulness, appear less liberal than he is – than in this case, for his interest (for you are to the full a greater *pet* of mine than ever he) [*torn*] knowing from my representations *that* you *would be an excellent* Tenant, *in the way of improving the place*, he lowered his demand of rent – I have ventured to *take the liberty* of reminding you – you say I am plain spoken – but I assure you it is only with *Friends.*

My Sister tells me a good story of Barber – but you shall not have another word till you come – The Party from St Omer arrived on Thursday – & left Town yesterday. – They are the most *entertaining* Travellers I have met with – kept us laughing the whole time – their notices have run in quite a new channel – they have sought *fun* & seen the ludicrous in all things – Mrs M. has had a bad cold since our return but is now nearly well again. We had a prosperous *voyage* until we ran against the boom of a vessel, in the river, & were ordered below in fear of the chimneys falling – but all ended well and we arrived safe before 4 oClock – Mary[5] is as lively as a lark – & quite in Love with the Poets Bull – cries '*pooh pooh*' to it all day long – A thousand Loves & kisses to your Darlings – dear little Trots I wish I could see them! – Never let Mima forget me –

God bless you! and believe me, in great haste,

very truly your Friend S. H.

Mrs M's love to you & our kind remembrances to the Gentlemen – I hope we shall see Cap[t] B[arrett] when *our Master* is at home –

I had nearly forgotten to say that the Man who went with the *Ponee saise* to Lee is unpaid. Five shillings he said was only suf: to pay his expences (turnpikes & Coach hire) this I know was a fib – but bade John[2] give him 2/6 for himself – that was 'not enough for his days work' (which by the bye began at 12 & ended at 7) This was beyond my patience so I said Mr Q. shall pay you himself – 'Then I am to keep this 5/– for my expences & turnpikes' – no, Mr Q. shall pay you the whole I replied, & took the money out of his hand & left him *staring* upon the pier whither he had followed us. – Mrs M. left unpaid at Mrs Bears 8/. for a bot: of Brandy – she would be glad if you could send it to her by a Coachman – & you can at the same time pay the man what you think proper – the 5/– I will return to you – Mr M[onkhouse] says he will be here Sat: A.M. but we think he has forgotten his latin & means P.M.

*Postmark: OC 30, 1823*

# 95

*Mrs Monkhouse, Gloucester Place, 67 Portman Square*

*Hindwell, 23rd Feby* [*1824*]

My dear Friend

I was intending to write to your Husband this morng when your Letter arrived – therefore I have changed my purpose in order to thank you for it, & all the entertainment it contained, which was *no little* – & also to say that I am not *guilty* of the charge of '*shyness*' respecting George's[2] wedding – for a rumour was all that reached us till last Saturday when it was formally announced by Bessy – tho no time specified for the marriage – the *rumour* I *did* communicate either to you or your husband, which was the same thing, & added that Joanna had written G. a droll Letter upon the subject of his taste for *antiquities* – which Letter however, as the offer had been made and accepted, his Father suppressed – The Lady is the third, or youngest, Sister of the Miss Stapylton you know – but she, even this *young one*, is 31 years of age – & therefore I cannot have a very high opinion of her – It is impossible that a woman of her *years* could marry *a young man like G.* for anything but a settlement – His Friends I suppose (tho' my Brother was decidedly averse *on this* score) fancy that an experienced woman will keep him in order – but as Joanna says they will look *much like a pair* 'linking arms' in ten years time –

Mary[2] H. is still at the Stow – but we expect her home today. I ought to have been there also but I have not been quite well & was indisposed to move – I rejoice to hear that you are so well, & have had proof that you are in a *lively mood* – very glad should I be to assist in arranging your new piece of furniture – & contribute, with Thos[2], to your amusement by our deliberations – for you have had proof enough that I am not easily quizzed out of my odd ways – The Case must stand in the little drawing room, must it not? – If you have too many shells – when the Capt has made you the present – (I hope he has not to go to India for them) *Duplicates you know my box is not full & can easily slip them in.* If the *Suttons* are to be married immediately I suppose the House is for this winter's campaign – I dare say George would like it near you – now that he is introduced for he does not like strange people – and your Sister will probably meet her Friend who will most likely be Brides maid – By the bye, talking of *Brides*, Did Dora[2] tell you Miss Dowling was married? – I *was guilty* of keeping *that* secret, but it was because I neither liked to talk or think of the match – However our Rydal Friends are disposed to think better of it – therefore, ill-assorted as it seems, I have no doubt it will prove a happy one –

I am sorry to find that your departure from London is likely to be protracted by the perplexities of Budge Row – for Thos' face will be longer & thinner than ever if he has to stay so many months there – I have no patience with him for complaining of indigestion & yet not refraining from the *pleasures* of the Table – only to think of Sally! but I fear she will be the most refractory patient in the House – & nobody *can watch her* – Here I have not one subject upon which to practise – for all except my Aunt who is too old to mend are true disciples of Abernethy – I must say that I am sorry to hear that little dear Good-Good has been *breeched* – for some of the Faculty *opine* that it is much better that females should not – & Mary H. gave up the practice of putting her Girls into Trowsers, from *her own experience* that it was injurious – and I am sure our little Ebba is as '*decent*' as any young Lady of 15 – & so would Ma Ma be –

Dora I find is most laborious at her employments – but all this will be over if her Aunt & Father come to Town – which I shall be very sorry for on more accounts than one. However it is rather fortunate for her that your stay in Town will be prolonged; for if her Aunt whisks her off to Cambridge & probably to Playford, she would have had no opportunity of visiting you in Gloster Place – Tell Thos[s] that it is not necessary to 'court' *my Tart* for my sake – nor for her own, as perhaps she is already *too much courted* – but I know that if you were once to be thoroughly acquainted with her you would delight in her – as I do – I know not what you mean by *paying me* off in kind for my supposed concealment of the Stockton wedding – My first conjectures turned of course towards York Place – but your *subsequent opinions* & *reflections* put me upon another *tack*, & I am lost – I entirely agree with you in your opinion & wonderment respecting the Att[y] at Law –

I have been called from my chat with you to transcribe on Parchment *the Petition of the Borough to the Ho: of Com:* concerning the Slave Trade, while my Brother was doing the same for the Lords – & now I have neither time to finish my Gossip with you, or write to M[rs] Luff as I intended by this days post – Tell her that Mary[1] Wordsworth desired Dora to write to her & say that Miss D – was married & that she hoped we would both write to congratulate her which I shall do* –

* *SH's* Do[ra] was either too shy or too busy to do it & made a poor excuse that she knew not M[rs] L's address.

also say that *I was not idle* about the Shells, but feared I should spoil them by bad packing – I will write to her when I am settled at the Stow whither I go tomorrow – The Dress is arrived – many thanks to Thos for his trouble – but alas! it ought to have had long sleeves & been made high to the throat – I believe I gave the length of the arm in my directions – but one *never is half particular enough* – & perhaps I relied too much on your memory, thinking you would remember those pretty dresses we used to admire at Ramsgate – this is the same kind as he has been accustomed to wear – It is very very pretty of its kind & I think it very cheap, with all its smart Embroidery – The Saddle Thos need not trouble himself about, as the horse cannot bring it – & we have ascertained that a harness for my Aunt may be had here new for £4: 10 – which, if not so gay as a London one, will do very well – now for my most important business with your Husband – the French Rentes – I *entreat* him to act for me upon his own judgment – for how can I give advice here – Miss Dowling transferred her money to the American upon the supposition that the French Int: was to be reduced – & as the American pays 6 per C^t^ why should not I do the same – now that French Rates are 100 – Of course I expect the Divd: *is paid already* this ½ year & which I hope you will speedily receive – as soon as the Bankers have time to think of anything but their loss – Thos has my power of Att^y^ & I give him full power to *buy or sell & do as he likes* with my money – I shall be satisfied – If you do not see M^rs^ L. very soon pray send her a two-penny – for I ought to have sent her the intelligence before – I have 50 more things to say to you but you must wait until I am at the Stow when I shall not spare my pen whenever my Host is out I shall seek the society of the absent – In the meantime write to me as often as ever you are inclined & never recollect that there is such a thing as postage – I shall not stay less than a fortnight at the Stow – Tell M^r^ Q. that he has used me ill in not sending the Verses* if they were fit for the female eye – which I should not have doubted (coming from his pen) but for an unlucky epithet ('*wanton*') which your Husband bestowed upon the adventure which occasioned them – My kindest love to Q. – kisses to Mary[5] & I pray you & your good Man to write. My best love & good wishes ever most affty yours S. H.

Mary[2] has not come home – the day is so wet & comfortless – we had 2 or three frosty days & the hills put on their white Night Caps but now it is as mild as ever & in spite of the rain the Birds have sung all

* Quillinan had published privately *Carmina Brugesiana, Domestic Poems,* in Geneva, in 1822. But perhaps she refers to something more recent.

day – Have the Ansteys got into their House? I ought to write to them.

*I have hit it now!* Miss Horrocks is going to be married & she is coming up to make arrangements.

# 96

*Thos Monkhouse Esq^re*

*Stow, March 4th* [*1824*]

My dear Coz.

You may guess what an enigma your last night Letter was to us, when I tell you that the last account which we have had, either here or at Hindwell, was the chearful Letter of your wife in which she told me that she was quite well – some Letter must have been lost or missent – From what I can gather from your last she is again, I fear, confined to her couch – How I do pity you both! yet, sad as this news is, and mortifying as the consequences are to us all, I cannot say that I am surprized for I never had any confidence that the half measures which have been pursued would produce any thing more than temporary *alleviation* – & that *unremitting* recumbancy alone could perform a cure – Never listen to any Doctors who would persuade you otherwise – London Doctors are, in general, too *polite* to say disagreeable things – all except Abernethy, & I wish you would consult him – M^r Knight, who was so much interested for poor M^rs Q. as if she had been his sister – & loved her little less – never flattered her that anything but the most rigorous confinement to the couch would be of the least use – and to me (supposing it true that the spine is to be relieved *entirely* from weight of the head) it appears as plain that this is the *only* remedy – as that 2 & 2 make 4 – M^rs Q. had tried the half measures – Sara Coleridge[3] has done so for years – & Miss Fleming received no benefit while she pursued them – M^r Hastler was *cured* in 10 months – M^r Henry Coleridge in about the same time – but they lay *constantly* – and we have good reason to believe that your dear wifes case is not a bad one – When old Jarvy told her that six weeks would complete her cure – he meant six weeks of constant recumbancy – he saw her lying flat upon a hard board &c – & believed that she lay there constantly – he did not suspect that she *trotted*, or would *trot*, upstairs so many times in the day – sate up (tho' not at Table) to all her meals – started up upon any excitement– & spent ½ the 24 hours upon a comparatively soft bed – Dear Mrs M! you know, as well as I, that (unless all which we have heard of the *manner* in which cures *have been* accomplished be a joke) nothing more than an alleviation of pain, or a check to the progress of the disease can have been effected – therefore take heart! and by the blessing of God, I trust, your patience will be rewarded with perfect cure – if not – at least you will have the satisfaction of knowing, that no human means have been neglected which experience, in other cases, has taught us to believe efficacious – I have said nothing *new* in all this *prosing* – but I feel its truth so strongly, and am so deeply interested in the matter, that you must, on this account, excuse me if I press it too much upon you – God bless you! and give you patience for it all – You have plenty of good Friends willing to cheer you in your solitude & privations – I for one will come with pleasure and spend the dullest & *foggiest* months of the year with you – if, which I trust will not be the case, your confinement should be extended over many such – I say nothing of our disappointments here – for they are trifling compared with the cause of them. I am glad that you will so soon have Miss H[orrocks] and our other Friends with you – but Do[a]: I believe is not to come to you until after her visit to Cambridge – and this I should think would be more convenient to you all – and she is very happy where she is – I hope your not coming hither will not induce her Father to take her home without paying her visit here – John[a], who is quite in love with her, says he will fetch her himself rather than this should be – therefore I depend upon you to combat her Fathers '*fraudulent*' inclinations towards us should he have any – besides at Midsummer (about the 20th of June) which is as soon as you expected to leave Town, the Miss Lockiers are coming to Bristol – & would, I doubt not, take charge of her – from when I could fetch her & pay my promised visit to Mrs Gee at the same time.

I am glad to tell you that John[a] is better – not that he believes either the leeches or blisters have done much – but a sort of boil which he has upon his neck, & which is now supperating, he thinks relieves his head & gives him hopes that a seaton which the Hay Doctor recommends might be of permanent service – but he has not yet resolved upon it. He came home yesterday from Brecon with one eye sadly inflamed and in great pain occasioned by the fierce wind which blew almost a hurricane – Our mild weather has departed we have had but 'one mild day of march' – When each minute was sweeter than before '&c' & tho' I was not called upon to put on my 'woodland dress'* I was summoned to array myself in Stultz & mount my Poney & have

* Both quotations are from Wordsworth's 'To my Sister', 'It is the first mild day of March.'

a fine scamper through the mud to Brewerdine to look after some rails in the woods there – and O what roads! no beauty of country can recompence for such annoyance! I really expected my poneys hoofs to be pulled off.

John likes his Mare very much – and will write to J. Addison in a day or two, when he has got a Bill from Kington to enclose for payment. We suspect that you may have sent us a Letter by the Man which he has lost – as the saddle came he must have had communication with you. I did not know that Quill had left Town – but am glad of it – I hope you sent him Johns message that he may be prepared to give us a call when he is again tired of himself – What a disappointment to the Darlings at Hindwell not to see 'little Coz. Mary'[5] – We used to hear stories half an hour long about her arrival &c &c –

God bless you all three! Excuse this wretched scrawl for I never have patience to write *well* when I am eager to express myself upon anything that unusually interests me as in the former part of my letter – Your's ever most truly S. H.

John & I are reading with more delight than with any Book we ever before rec^d the '*Pensées de Pascal*' M^rs M. I am sure would like them.

We had found out the cause of the detention of the Papers – 2 arrived as old as the hills & too dirty for the fingers of *gentle folk* to touch with the Sevenoaks post mark upon them – John thanks you for setting them right – it is a great pleasure to him to have it to expect every evening in this '*uneventful place*' –

Pray write soon for we are very anxious to hear the true state of M^rs Ms present complaint – will thank you to forward the enclosed by 2^d.

Tell M^rs Luff if you see her not to trouble herself about the wheel – I thought she might chance to see one among her wanderings to Gimcrack Shops not that I wished her to *seek* after it –

## 97

*Edward Quillinan Esq^re, Lee Priory, nr Wingham, Kent*

*Hindwell, Ap^l 15th* [*1824*]

My dear Friend

I sent you a message by Mrs M[onkhouse] signifying my intention to defer answering your Letter until I heard that you were again at Lee, & should have leisure to read mine so that if it should prove stupid it would at least be what we here call a 'break-in' – & therefore be welcome. However there was nothing in your's to '*answer*' – to thank you for it, I ought to have said, & for all the agreeable accounts it contained of the Darlings & their attendants – and glad was I also to hear better news of yourself – I hope your last trip to Town has not unsettled you again, & made the solitude of Lee distasteful – I never hear a word of the Pearl now – from any one – Her name even has not occurred in anybody's Letters for weeks except in Mr M's yesterday who said that *she* had been *charmed* by Mr Irving's preaching – Pray were you of the Party to the Caledonian Chap[el]? I only heard that '*all*' were there – but I should like to know if you also were charmed, or not –

I sent you a message in the above mentioned Letter to Mrs M from Mr M concerning *fishing* – which, he promises you, you will find in his neighbourhood very good – & the Parson of the Parish to boot to serve you as guide & Instructor in the art of angling – but I should fear that neither he, or any one, can infuse the necessary stock of patience into your composition to make an angler of you – Here in our Pool there are fish in abundance – & on a calm evening they are leaping as if they wished to be caught – & you will at least have the pleasure of *seeing* them – My Sister (Mrs. H.) says she does not care a fig whether you come or not now, as you do not intend to bring the Children whom she has a great desire to see – and our little ones have their names as *pat* as possible – & are sadly disappointed that all our pleasant stories are at an end of what was to be done when they and Coz. Mary[5] came – Poor T. M.!! – I am most heartily grieved that he will not be able to come amongst us, even for a short visit – since *Ramsgate* is talked of there will be no *necessity* for his leaving Town for Country air elsewhere – & he must be contented to *hum-drum* it up & down in that Steam boat all the summer, instead of the delightful freedom which he might have enjoy'd on the back of a poney upon our airy, green, & unincumbered hills – Mr M begged me also to say that he expected to see you *first* at the Stowe – & has engaged me to meet you there; afterwards you may have a lodging at *The Harp*, if you prefer it; tho' I can insure you a kind welcome *here* notwithstanding Mrs H's indifference! – Of course you could not take the Children from Mrs Lucas – but I fancied you would come all together – bag & baggage – as you talked of leaving Lee should the family return – but I must own it is more *prudent* to let them remain where they are; tho' it is very much more *disagreeable to me* – I hope when you do come you will *try to bring T. M.* with you. If Miss H[orrocks] is with his wife she may spare him very well – & the disappointment of not seeing him this summer will be very great to his sister.

I have been staying six weeks at the Stowe with Mr M[onkhouse] – a nice quiet visit I had which I enjoyed exceedingly – and the more so as I feel myself of so much use, & consequence, to my Host who is unable to read or amuse himself, except by his own thoughts, within doors – And I fear this will very long be the case; for the disease of his eyes advances so slowly that it may be many years before they are ready for an operation – but he is as chearful as the day, & never a murmur escapes him –

I do not suppose you have any weather even at Lee that can give you a hint of the Nightingales – Yet I send you a poem, on the other side, which I transcribed for you some weeks ago – by way of making my Letter worth the postage – as you are always so careful as to procure a frank for me I would gladly do the same, but all our members are upon Duty – & I don't chuse to await their return home – for I never wish any body to defer writing to me for the want of a frank – I hear that our Friends the W[ordsworth]s are to be with you on this Day week – Pray do not tempt them to stay too long – for we all want Miss W. at home again that my Sister may be able to join us here – a visit which has been *due many many* years.

The Nightingale

(From the *Dutch* of *Maria Tesselschade Vischesser*)

Prize thou the Nightingale
Who soothes thee with his tales
And wakes the woods around;
A singing feather he – a wing'd and wandering sound;

Whose tender carolling
Sets all ears listening
Unto that living lyre
Whence flows the airy notes his ecstacies inspire;

Whose shrill capacious song
Breathes like a flute along,
With many a careless tone,
Music of thousand tongues form'd by one tongue alone.

A charming creature rare,
Can aught with thee compare?
Thou art all song; thy breast
Thrills for one month of the year – is tranquil all the rest.

Thee wondrous we may call –
Most wondrous this of all
That such a tiny throat
Should make so wide a sound, & pour so loud a note!

So much for the Dutch Nightingale! but there seems to me something of the *Irish* in the expression of the 4th Stanza – I met with these verses today, in the *Carlisle Patriot*, & think them well worth transcribing – tho' perhaps not of power to reanimate the flame of your passion for your *last year's* favorite – This would be hopeless at present with these March winds howling about our ears – so I shall preserve them till a more genial season when instead of the roaring chimneys of London you shall be among the 'ringing woods' of Lee –

March 3rd – Stowe

Tell Do[2] if she has leisure to write to me from Lee – We shall see her sooner I hope in consequence of the Ramsgate scheme – as I should not think her Father would consent to her going thither – I envy her the pleasure of a good hug of that dear little Mims – for in spite of her *duty* I know she will continue the favourite – God bless them both – and do you give them a good lot of kisses for me – and excuse this worthless Letter – My kind remembrances to Cap$^{t}$ B. & Mr E. B. – who is I suppose with you – I hope he has an agreeable novel to enjoy upon the Sofa in the Drawing room – We read novels sometimes at the Stowe – so tell me if you know of any new ones that are worth *reading aloud* – for I find those that are tolerable when skimmed over silently – become unendurable when you give sound to every world.

Farewell! and believe me every most sincerely Your Friend S. H. –

*Postmark: Radnor, 17 AP 1824*

# 98

*Thos Monkhouse Esq$^{re}$*

*Hindwell, A$^{pl}$ 29th* [*1824*]

My dear Coz

I received yours last Night & take up my pen that I may send you my benediction before you embark again upon the ocean – but I hope it will not be with such a wind as is blowing about us today – or there will be cold comfort both on board the steamboat & in the *Paragon* – Well, I have a sort of an affection for Ramsgate after all, & had I been nearer to you would, with the greatest pleasure in the world, have taken Miss Horrocks place until she was satisfied with the gaieties of London – but in return for what she leaves behind she will be received by the dear Sachett with open arms, besides all the *Tawters* [?] how they will crowd round you with their welcomes!

You may be assured that the *Trouble* of setting off to you, with even *all her* Bairns, would not prevent dear Marys[2] acceding to your wishes – for most happy would she be to gratify you, & herself, if it were convenient or possible from other considerations – but she is doomed to remain at home – & happy is it for her that her home is such a happy one – I am sure that a little sea air would be very useful to her, & little Mary[6] especially & I wish that I could *conscientiously* persuade her to join you – but her objections are too reasonable to be overturned, & it only puts her to pain to be forced to refuse – therefore we must say no more about it; & I trust that in another year you may be at liberty to come to her – for she loves her Friends too well not to consider disappointments like these the worst to bear of all her many privations – To talk of my coming 'along' (as we express ourselves, *elegantly*, in these parts) at this time must have been a mere joke, as I *must* in her absence have remained to take care of those left behind – so I shall make no reply – except by repeating my offer to come to you whenever you wish for my company & my *duties* do not *imperiously* call for me in a contrary way – at present I know you cannot want me so I may say that I really *have some duties to perform* – *Harriet* is about to be married & I am going to make a long sojourn at the Stow in order to *educate* John's[2] new Servants – but after three months have passed over our heads, & if Miss H[orrocks] does not remain with her Sister, I will come & finish out the time at R. with all possible pleasure – but as I know that M^rs^ M. has many other friends who would be glad to do the same she is not to suppose that I should feel offended if she does not accept my offer – only let me beg you will use me with the same sincerity as you would your Sister – for no body can have more desire than I to be as you kindly say 'a *comfort*' to you both – & strange it would be were it not so when we have had so many comfortable & happy days together –

In spite of the winds the Country looks beautiful – nothing can exceed the greenness of the meadows beyond the Pool & those hanging on the side of old Radnor Hill – Fishermen are upon the Pool – & they have had good Sport lately – I have often wished for you &

Quillinan for I think if any where you might have perfected yourselves in the art of angling here – Q— will I hope pop down to see us – we shall not excuse him at the Stow – & he ought to come before the angling season is over – else we shall have no amusements to offer him –

Geo Sutton was married on Easter Wednesday – we have had a long account of the festivities after, & the gaiety of the ceremony from Bessy – they were married at Norton by Mr Anstey – *His* 4 Sisters the Brides 2 & three other Young ladies, *9 in all*, were brides maids. Chas & Geo[1] Hutchinson & Geo Swaine with her Brothers (I know not how many) the Grooms men these all went to Church – the relations & friends, young & old, above 40 in No. breakfasted with them at Mr Stapyltons (where there was a most sumptuous breakfast) the Bride & Bridegroom went off afterwards to Hardwicke – & all the rest of the Party after having departed to their own houses returned to Mr S-s in the Evg where the day was concluded by a Ball which my brother John[1] opened with Miss Stapylton with a contredance to the tune of the Honeymoon!! It was quite a Sir Chas Grandison wedding – such a train of Carriages, favors, & colours. Guns firing & bells ringing as never was seen, or heard, in Norton before – I have been writing the *congratulatory epistle* for the whole family – for I say if there is 'a hard job' in this line I am sure to have it imposed upon me – By the by Bessy said in her letter 'Geo[1] has sent a box off to you, but how he has directed it I know not – I believe to Mr T. M – ' Of course it contains Cake &c – & no doubt a portion for Mrs M: As it is directed to you I am afraid it will [be] sent after you to R[amsgate] so beg it may be opened if it comes to Budge Row, in your absence, & let your part be taken out & the rest forwarded by the Coach – but I suppose it would be directed to G[loucester] P[lace] & ween you had not recd it before you wrote – you have never once taken the least notice of what I said with respect to the F. Rentes – neither Miss W. – but I suppose that you & William think it best to let the money remain where it is – *Remember* you have my power of Atty – I am half affronted at Miss W. (you may tell her so) that she did not execute my commission for Mrs Dew – as it was the only one I troubled her with – & so scrupulous was I on this head that for myself I would not have given her one now as you are all off. I must apply to Quill I think when he comes to town – for Mrs D— sent me a message the other day 'hoping I could get her some more satisfactory information' –

We are all pretty well except little Thos[3] who has been from School for two or three days in a *feverish* complaint. Aunt continues wonderfully well – Joanna is not in her very best way – but She is going to Winandernant & will soon be well – She bids me ask what is to be done with the said Dogs – for they are & will be worse than useless – & have eaten their heads off many times over – I am glad you have let your house – *pretty well* is it not? – God bless you both! Remember me to Miss H— I hope to hear, from her or you, all *the news* of R— But joking apart I shall be anxious to hear how the journey *voyage* is performed – Tell me how long Mr H— will be in Town? because so long as he is there I shall have no scruple in packing off a scrawl like this for him to frank forward – but not for you to have 10d to pay for it.

My love to Q— when you see him & kisses to the three Darlings who will I hope often meet during the Summer – I wish I could drop Ebba amongst them – We have not seen John[2] since my last but in the notes we have had from him he does not mention his health so we hope the best –

I had a Letter from Mrs Gee the other day: She tells me that Mr W. Jacksons match with Miss Crump is off – I think this must be a mistake I have had *no Gin* today – Joanna brought me an excellent bason of broth which may have had the same effect – for she is no disciple of Abernethy but a true Herefordshire woman – 'something to take' shd be her Motto –

Joanna begs Miss W. will not forget to ask Mrs Johnson if she is in want of an *apprentice*.

## 99

*Thos Monkhouse Esqre*

*Stow, June 12th* [*1824*]

My dear Coz.

I doubt not but your late Letters have met with due notice and *return* from Hindwell – and all has been said that *can* be said, from these *uneventful places*. Yet I feel as if I ought to write; having been (*for me, to you*) so long silent – especially as I have to congratulate you upon the good news which we hear, from all quarters, of your wife's *miraculous* recovery – for it appears nothing less, if it does not prove that the complaint (according to my Oracle Abernethy) has proceeded entirely from the Stomach*, & that it is not an affection of the Spine. Well if it be so (which God grant) though she ought to give herself as much ease as possible yet *land travelling* need not be prohibitive – tho' I can-

* In his diagnoses Abernethy emphasized the general health of the patient, especially the digestive system.

not, as I was going to add '*hope*' you will be able to execute your plan in the Autumn for I shall in future for ever despair of the accomplishment of any long-talked-of schemes – for truly when there are not real obstacles, the having so much time beforehand to think & talk about them makes us become *satisfied with thinking* & *talking*; & any new scheme that starts up in ones path appears more easy of accomplishment & often more agreeable – because it is new – Here we (by way of illustrating *part* of the above) have been expecting I know not whom (I need not enumerate to you) to spend the summer with us – & most probably the event will be that no one will visit us except (perhaps) Mrs Blaxland, & Miss Sandford, whom were never expected – To *me* this will be no pleasure – for I never saw the latter & the first only once – & I am not fond of *new folks* – In the Autumn the Rydal Party still talk of coming – but, as I have said, my faith is so shaken that I shall not even *talk* about them.

Joanna, as you will have heard, went off to Kendal yesterday – She had a most beautiful & affecting Letter from Eliz Cookson (*affecting* mainly from its cheerfulness) accepting Joanna's offer & begging her to come immediately – which you may be sure was complied with most freely – notwithstanding she was by this prevented from accepting your kind invitation – for she is always (to use her favorite phrase) desirous of making herself 'useful as well as ornamental' – but your *talking* of visiting us in the autumn prevented any regrets as to Ramsgate – for with half a hope of meeting you, & our other friends all together here, she would not have stirred from home upon any but a humane errand such as the present one. I am very glad she is gone, for I have no doubt that the interest, & occupation which her companion will afford her (melancholy as they will be) will prove salutary to herself – inasmuch as her thoughts will be less occupied by her own *ailments* which, tho bad enough poor thing! are much encreased by her propensity to brood over them – Your good Brother is the Pattern in this respect – He really is the most truly *satisfied* & *chearful* Person I ever met with – He is a daily source of wonder and admiration to me – I never hear any allusion to his affliction except in thankfulness for what he *can enjoy*. I believe the Seaton has been of great service – certainly he suffers much less – indeed scarcely anything from pain in his head – & he can read, a certain quantity at a time, without pain to his eyes which was not the case heretofore – tho' of course the sight is no better – At present he reads *Shakespeare* at every moment when he is able – and he chooses wisely – because being stinted in his quantity of reading he takes that which has most *pith* in it – and never did I see any body more hearilty & deeply enjoy his Book – He never doses over it as you used to do over your Friend Jeremy [? Taylor] – Today he is 'tivying off' to Hereford – or rather yesterday he went intending to go & see little George[3] – of whom we hear very good accounts – I also was off yesterday at Hindwell – tho' only for a few hours to see Joanna before her departure – but neither have I finished my residence or my duties here – nor do I know when they will terminate – for I have so much pleasure in this place – and am so much gratified to find myself both *useful & ornamental*, and above all *greatly prized* in my present situation (a rare thing for an old maid) that if the Blaxland Party come to Hindwell I shall probably remain where I am, as they will be in no want of me – & you know I always like my *company*, & even my *Letters* to *tell* far more than they are worth by being *well-timed* – Mary[2] will have told you that Thos[1] is at last on the alert about a new farm – & certainly will leave Hindwell if there is any prospect of bettering himself – and, if not immediately, will I hope ultimately come over to *this better side of the country* – Indeed it is quite provoking to think they should have lived so long *near to a climate* so much better than theirs – I am sure there is almost 2 *months more summer* here – & never so cold a winter – It would do you good to see John's[2] *grass* – I never saw anything to compare with it – indeed all his crops are admirable – John & Thos are to meet Mr Wakefield about Brinsop Court on Tuesday – Thos has also written to Mr Lewis for his *ultimatum* as to rent at Hindwell for the future – . . . By the bye I think Quill like all the rest is *fickle* as the winds – John often twits me with this – but without joking I am very sorry that he did not come when he proposed, at the end of last month, as the country was so beautiful & John would really have enjoyed his company so much having had so much leisure – We still hope to see him, as he has said nothing to the contrary since I sent him all the particulars which he reqd about the Coaches – I long to hear that dear little GoodGood & the Sweet ones at Lee have had a meeting – the first will have less loss from the change of plans, if she has such good substitutes for her little Cousins – Little Tom[3] & I intend having a long journey together in his holidays – perhaps as far as Bristol – If it suits me to pay my visit to the Gees at that time I intend taking him for my companion – what do you think of my setting off with such a one – *He* I am sure and his *Poney* will be the admiration of all beholders – for they are more like two fairies than anything else – I often think of our *duty* rides at Ramsgate – & have the Gigs &c before the door in my eye – You must have been half roasted during the late hot weather – now it is more temperate – but really it has been unendurable – I have lost my little companion Ebba – She was very good but she pined for her companions & I could not be so selfish as keep her – I hope this will reach you when you are in Town that it may '*tell*' – We are glad to hear you talk more cheerfully about your Budge Row concerns. It must be a wonderful relief to be rid of that ungracious Man & I trust that in the end you will find no more occupation or labour than what is necessary to sweeten enjoyment & ease – for nothing can be more true than as Burns says in his homely words 'Gentleman & Ladies warst &c' – God bless you, & that you may never have heavier sorrow than Budge Row brings in yourself or to those dearest to you, is my most affte wish – kindest remembrances to Mrs M. & Miss H[orrocks] – & kisses to GoodGood who I think must in *the course of nature* have forgotten me by this time – I should like a batch of Ramsgate & Lee News, if anyone would be charitable enough. Again God bless you all! & with most earnest wishes till I may hear good news of you soon. I am very truly yours. S. H.

Pray do answer *this question* – Have you ever recd my Feby Dividends? this I could never learn either from you or Stockton – . . . Remember me to the Lambs if you see them – and also to the Farquhars – I hope you go to see that nice little creature Lady F. sometimes. Poor dear Mrs Luff she has been very poorly – I should have been quite vexed if Dorothy[1] had left her to come hither, glad as we should have been to see D.

If you do send Abernethys Book &c to John enclose for me 2 or 3 quires of the very thickest quarto writing Paper that is made – it is for a book in lieu of the original of all the '*keepsakes*'* which was lost – I have [trans]scribed one since I came hither but the paper was so bad & [*torn*] that I cannot *give it* as a *substitute*. London folk – (Mr Lewis for instance) often write Letters upon the kind I mean – it is not the *blue* sort – and must be large on account of its being to be bound afterwards – but if the paper were uncut at the edges so much the better – it is for Mrs Cookson – the old one was lost in my Trunk – after I had transcribed yours & Henrys[1] from it – I hope you are clever at a puzzle.

I had almost forgotten to congratulate the Ladies upon their prospect of a new Brother in one whom I have heard Mrs M. speak of with so much pleasure. – Her character of her Sister Alice makes one wonder that she should have chosen a *Parson* especially not a rich one – I fear she has not well considered the fate of a Parsons Wife as expressed in the burthen of the old song 'What brats to rear What Stockings to be mended!'

* See Letter 51, p. 148 †.

# 100

*Monday Evg [June–July, 1824]*

My dear Coz.

Your last came, as you expected, the day after it was written – but the one to John[2] rec[d] yesterday had been written on friday – The Man will be sent off without delay either to C— or Gloster, but it is not yet determined which; in the mean time I write to send by him in case he can be off in time to meet you – John is very glad to have the horse; for one of his own has met with an accident which for a short while renders him useless – besides if this was not the case neither his keep or the trouble of him is of any moment here – If you bring a Carriage we think a boy will be indispensable else you will not have a *'genteel turn-out'* – nobody here can clean it – *Your 'friend'* Bill is no better Friend than mine (John[1]) he is gone – & is not remembered with any satisfaction – John has got a nice good-natured *Cimon* in his stead, but quite a novice in Gentleman's work – as for the Maids we shall do very well with them if they are disposed to make themselves useful – but sometimes this is not the case in a strange house & then they are more a 'hindrance than a help' – but all this you will arrange when you come – & right gladly will you be received *bag & baggage – I was thinking to myself,* this afternoon, that if you found a second dose of Cheltenham necessary, & Mary[2] was disposed to join you (but I have had no communication with her on the subject) that Thos[1] might have driven her to Ross & you met her there with Sally[4] & the GoodGood whom he might bring back – but I hope you will both be quite well before that time comes & have no need either to be delayed there, or to visit it from hence – What you say about the operation of the waters convinces me that Harrowgate is the place for you – This is glorious hay weather. John is the complete *bustle* – I never see his face but at meals & half an hour before bed time – except when I walk with him among the Cattle in an Evn[g] – His Crops are quite marvellous – & he has far more Grass than ever can be eaten – so that I *scold* every time we go into the meadows that he has not more stock – but this abundance could not be foreseen – it is unprecedented. He will I hope procure some more stock at Worcester on the 17 of next month – We had thought about the Sofa and will have one if Hereford can furnish it – but it is the most *barren* place in the Island, & I believe it would take a twelvemonth to furnish a Cottage to ones mind from that City.

I cannot tell you any more news about the Farm – as soon as decided you shall hear – Have you heard from Rydal M$^{t}$. Fox Ghyll is to be sold by private Contract? – M$^{rs}$ Luff is trying to buy the house *separately* but it is not likely that she will succeed – She is very happy & enjoys herself very much & they seem to think she will most certainly settle there – All the Robinsons from York are at Rydal – & they have gay *musical parties* & *what* not – Miss R— who is a very superior person has a fine voice – & the pretty Miss Carleton is also in the neighbourhood again – They have also had some very agreeable people at M$^{rs}$ Flemings who have been a great acquisition especially to Do[a]: – 2 Misses Ayling & their Brother – the Ladies were pupils of Miss Lockier & were introduced by them to the Mount – Good hopes that they are to continue at the Mount – but all this you have probably heard, & will be impatient at having the trouble of decyphering old News in this scrawl –

I can marvel at nothing which our Friend Q— does that is queer – & he might say 'I love my love because he is *queer* & hate him because he is a Quiz &c &c' – But I *should have wondered* if M$^{rs}$ M. had 'chaperoned the *young* Ladies' I suppose *he* would say Lee is a *show place* – & why were they not to go to see it? All the *youths* at home too no doubt!! it makes me laugh to myself to think of the oddity of our little Friend. I hope M$^{rs}$ M— will give me another of her lively Letters before we meet – She is very provoking to be so idle – & now when Miss H[orrocks] is with her, she can have no excuse for her Pen as all the writing to Preston will be taken off her hands. Tell Q— we shall be very glad to see him at any time – but we shall be the less *obliged* to him for his company than if he had come for our own Sakes – I wish I could see the three trots all together again – How the wind will blow their little bonnets today! – it has been tremendous – but all in favor of our operations – I rejoice to think this part of the bustle will be over before you come – the Corn harvest is nothing compared to it – & we hope that all the *broken* weather will be mended before that time –

M$^{rs}$ M. must go to Tintern & Chepstow – but I fear she cannot go the most beautiful way (by the towing path from Monmouth) as riding cannot be prudent for her – I was *about to have had* a new poney – a great beauty – but it has put out a Curb & is blistered & lame – so unlucky am I in *Horse flesh* – there is quite a Stud of poneys at Hindwell but only one useful for *adults* – Tom's[1] – which he is kind enough to give up to me –

Tuesday – The Man will be sent off & be at Glo'ster by tomorrow at 2 oClock – therefore as you will not see him I send this by the Coach – We are going to take a ride to Hindwell after Tea to enquire the particulars of the Interview with Mr Lewis – John will endeavour to get a Boy to drive & take care of the Carriage &c – which he thinks may be done & spare you the trouble & expence of bringing him down – as he will not be the kind of Servant you would want to replace John[7] – Say if you approve of this – John was very much grieved that he could not accede to your proposal of a meeting at Ross – but the Sat. & Monday were two most important days with him. You say the Letter *ought* to have been answered – I was of that opinion at first but John said that could not be necessary as he had made a proposal to you to come hither which had you & Mr H[orrocks] agreed to your plans would have been again upset by his acceding to yours – besides he thought you would conclude from his Letter that it was impossible for him to leave home – else he would not have waited for an invitation to a meeting but have come to C[heltenham] – This Paragraph has been written to John's dictation so the sin of it is not upon my head if you find it a *muddle* which we think it is – It is likely that there will be wine enough left for your consumption while here so don't send any more.

My kindest remembrances to all at Ramsgate not omitting the Pearl – altho' her beauty in which I have had so much delight is rivalled in my eyes by Miss Lewins – whose beauty is *celestial* – If she had been in happier circumstances (or rather *more favorable*) she would have been in all respects *angelic* – As it is the expression of her eyes gives ones heart 'a *turn over*' as dear Edith says – Farewell ever most affty yours – S. H.

## 101

*Mr Monkhouse*

*Stowe, Friday Night – [June–July, 1824]*

My dear Coz.

We fully expected a Letter from you this Evg in reply to John's[2] *proposal* for you & your 'Chums' coming over to see us – as you would conclude that it was impossible for John to agree to *your's* for a meeting at Ross – as he is so very busy with his hay & the weather so *ticklish* that he cannot leave home – unless it shld be a *downright wet* morning tomorrow & then he must go to Leominster fair – where business calls him – tho' inclination would carry him to Ross – We are happy to hear that you are already better & trust you will continue so – The

Horse will be most welcome – nay very useful also at present – for we are ill off both here and at H[indwell] so that you could scarcely be accommodated with a *Numbles* – but if you bring a Barouchette the grey Mare will be able to do a little for you in that way – You may either send the Horse – or John will send for him which you think proper – but observe that a Letter posted at Cheltenham on *Monday* does not reach us till Wed. Ev$^{g}$. John could hire a man perhaps cheaper than you but if the Horse is to remain at C— after you have done with him it will make the expence equal – John will take the first opportunity of consulting M$^{r}$ Price respecting the Dogs – We are very sorry that John cannot come – as we trusted to him to keep the Maids in order – for ours are but young ones – As to another Man J. says you must do as you think proper & necessary for your own Comfort – but I think you will find the house *too full* if you bring 2 Maids & a Man –

We are delighted to hear such good accounts of M$^{rs}$ M— God God grant that nothing may prevent a happy meeting among us – Tom & his two eldest Bairns left us this M$^{ng}$ – they came with him in his way to Brinsop Court whither John accompanied him yesterday to view the farm – He expects to see M$^{r}$ Lewis this week – when a final determination must be made respecting Hindwell at least – All seem agreed that Brinsop will be cheaper – a better climate & perhaps as pretty a place – but not so comfortable or so *tidy* a farm – Tom[1] seems inclined to take it – Mary[2] was *scared* by the *rubbish* about the House – M$^{r}$ Ricardo has given the deputation of the Manor to M$^{r}$ Price* of Foxley – but perhaps T. may be able to get the shooting over his own farm – He will try for it – indeed it would be most unreasonable if he were not allowed it – If a Landlord chuses to refuse his Tenant for his own Sport he cannot wish to do it for another's –

You must excuse this scrawl – it is very late I am only just come in from Kington – & finding no Letter from you we thought it necessary to write about the Horse in time – as the post is so *cross* – John says he expects you tomorrow by the Coach – On Sunday I mean –

God bless you – Ever most affty Yours S. H.

Since you request it I will write about the Shooting but I can't see how your delicacy can be spared by it – as it must be your request at last –

* Uvedale Price. See *Wordsworth Letters, Middle Years,* I, 466.

## 102

*Edward Quillinan Esq., Lee Priory*

*Stow, Friday Night, 11 o'Clock* [*10 Sept. 1824*]

My dear Friend

T[om] M[onkhouse] promised to assist in filling the Trunk for you – but he has left me in the lurch & gone off to bed – therefore you can expect only a sleepy epistle from me at this late hour – and tomorrow morning we are to start early for Hindwell where we hope to meet with our Rydal Friends who have been on the wing for above a fortnight – wandering in North Wales – having landed at Bangor from a Liverpool steam Boat on Saturday 29th *ult*: – next day they spent with *the Crumps* & W[m] Jackson at Caernarvon & then went to meet William's old travelling companion Jones at Llanrwst, & with him were to make the tour of North Wales. Whether this is yet accomplished or not I cannot say – but tomorrow we go, at a venture, in the expectation of their arrival, if the day is fine – but the weather is greatly *dis*improved – &, unreasonable Creatures as we are, we are already become impatient for the departure of the clouds tho' they are *novelties* –

I am very sorry to tell you that our good Coz.* mends slowly – for three weeks after he came hither he did not improve the least – and a more ghastly figure I never beheld than he was – since that time he seemed to gain strength & spirits till within the last week – & he has been thrown back I know not how – and we are now more anxious than ever about him, & fear he is in a very precarious state – You never said a *truer* thing in your life than that he was killing himself with *anxiety* – which I firmly believe to have been the cause of all his illness – and that when the Doctors took him in hand he had no other disease – they have handled him too roughly & it will be long (if ever) before their work is repaired. Had he come hither in the spring, instead of going to that cold sea side, and had never consulted a Doctor I am confident he would have escaped all this – now perhaps he will be obliged to seek a still warmer climate – & if not will scarcely be *permitted* to stay quietly – for it is evident that either upon the plea of his own or his wife's health he will never have any rest in this world – but since they have been here Mrs M[onkhouse] has generally [been] very well – yet, tho' she knows that her Husband is happier here than he

* Thomas Monkhouse who had tuberculosis.

would be any where else, she is full of schemes for another removal – *this* is not to be breathed to any body out of *our* own *family* – so take care to *burn it* –

Now I must try to recollect all the messages left for you – The first that T. longs to be among the Lee Partridges – but he does not expect to be strong enough to carry a gun this year – He deserves to have some account of the performances of your Dogs – Mr Whitehead has not been able to procure any ale for you – there is none to be had in Preston. – You will be *obliged* to come into Wales to seek *Civry*. Mr M. bid me say that you were in the condition of the Fox without a Tail (according to the Fable) undervaluing *his constancy* because you were destitute yourself. . . .

You are quite wrong in supposing that any little *Welsh Creatures* can make me forget your Darlings – tho' I am sorry to say I have seen very little of the Hindwell Children lately – they have had the hooping Cough & we have been obliged to keep them apart from Mary[5] M— & as their Mother would not leave them I have been here almost constantly since the M's came – and consequently my visit at Hindwell is unpaid – & I shall most likely winter there – which was not my intention – for I long to have a sight [of] the Westmorland mountains again. – Miss W. tells me that she thinks the Elliots do not intend to take the Ivy Cot for another term – but Tillbrook speaks confidently of becoming Tenant himself next year – So that neither You or T. M. will have a chance for it – T. M. would like it well – but there are others to please in his case besides himself – & he will never occupy it '*I guess*' –

Barber has been at Scarboro', & is now in London. So I suppose he is *about to tire of* solitude – or perhaps he fears that if he remains longer he will cover his *estate* with masonry – for I hear that he has set up numberless edifices.

Well, but it is really late & I must bid you good night – & continue by sending all our *loves to* Cap$^{t}$ B[arrett] and yourself – and our best regards to the youths – we did indeed marvel to hear that you had all *come out* – By the bye we were at Hereford Races – went to stay the three days – but were as eager to leave on the second day, as we were to go on the first. – It was to be sure mighty stupid – for we knew not one person there – & as we could not go to the balls & had no chance of amusement – for the races were very bad – & the ground neither so beautiful or so well attended as at Canterbury – few People go to Race – all meet in the Ball room – But we expectd nothing better & therefore were not disappointed – only I wonder why *we* went! Again good Night! & God bless you! & the Trotts to whom I send the usual quantum of kisses – & I am very truly yours S. H. –

I have 6 pairs of shooting Stockings for you but you ought to have come to fetch them –

## 103

*Edward Quillinan Esq$^{re}$, Lee Priory, nr Wingham, Kent*

*7 Strand, Torquay – Nov$^{r}$ 3rd* [1824]

My dear Friend

I am persuaded that my dislike of Letter-writing is a much greater annoyance to myself than my correspondents – for instance during the last three weeks I have been admonished, entreated, & reproached, on your account – altho' I am not a Letter *in your debt*, & I find that other People are quite as idle as I am – However all this is not intended to excuse myself for knowing that you would be anxious to hear of our Friend.* I ought to have written before this – & have been as angry with myself as any body need wish to be with me – I hope some of our *Rydal Folk* have written to tell you that the Ivy Cot was about to be let *for the winter* – lest when you heard that it *was let* you might have *fancied* that you would have been its Tenant had you known the circumstance – I felt certain that Miss W. would tell you this else I should have written –

My Sister wrote to you from Wales – therefore you will not be surprized to receive this from Devonshire – as at the time she wrote a milder climate than Herefordshire had been recommended to our poor sick Friend – We left the Stow on the 18th of last month, & arrived here on the 22nd after a very prosperous journey – & as pleasant as could be expected in such circumstances – We find the climate delicious – much more mild than we expected; & in all respects the place is very agreeable & the country beautiful – but so weak both in body & spirits is our Friend that he can only 'see not feel how beautiful they are'† – I do not see any change in him since we came hither – he has not much bodily suffering – but when you look at him you wonder how he can have been reduced to his present state without any apparent adequate cause! Heaven grant that our fears may not be realized – I do not think that he *habitually* apprehends any danger – nor does Mrs M at any time – therefore do not write anything that he may not read – I think his spirits have been better for the last few days – till then ever

* Thomas Monkhouse.

† She quotes Coleridge's *Dejection: An Ode*, addressed to her in 1802.

since our parting from our Friends in Herefordshire they have been very low indeed – but we are in expectation of seeing Sartorius soon who will I hope enliven him a little. Also Mr & *Mrs* Birkett (Mary Horrocks) who were to be married yesterday – &, as Mr B. has just had a Living presented to him in this county, they are coming to take possession upon their marriage – so that tho' at first we felt as if we were at the very end of the world I hope our Friends will find us out in time – Mrs M is quite well – & never, or rather scarcely ever, is seen upon a Sofa – this is a blessing indeed for had she been ill also her husband's spirits would have been worse than ever – anxiety of one kind or other has *I am sure* been the cause of his present melancholy state of body – tho' the Drs say that the depression of spirits is the effect & not the cause of his disease – in this *I* am sceptical –

Wm[1], Mary[1] & Doro[2], departed from Hindwell on the same day which we left Stow – They were to have gone via Coleorton but the Beaumonts were called to Worcester on account of the illness of Ly B.'s Sister – there however a meeting would be effected & if Mrs Fermor was better they were to go to C. together – but I have not heard from them – so know not what has been their destination – The Poet was quite well while with us – nobody ever saw him in better plight – & he was the life of our party – doing always his utmost to amuse & keep up our spirits – which he always does God bless him! when there is a real necessity for his exertions – He had enjoyed his tour in Wales very much – & Do had been busy with her Pencil & is most surprizingly improved in Sketching –

So far and not a word of your Trotts – dear little Things! I trust they are both well – Mary[5] improves very much – she talks a great deal tho it is not very intelligible – but I do not quarrel with her for being so long a Baby tho' she is surprizingly backward – not to be wanting in intellect, which she certainly is not – Are your Friends returnd or returning? – We see Sir E[gerton] often advertized – but that is all – have not met with his Books yet – T[om] & Mrs M[onkhouse] desire their kindest remembrances along with mine to you & the Gentlemen who are with you – Your sporting Letter was very amusing to T. tho' he has not had much sport himself – being out only twice in Mr Dews Preserve where he killed a brace of pheasants – If you have a *supera-bundan* of Game a little would be very acceptable to him – as by the Van to Exeter goods come quickly and cheap from London – but across the Country the carriage is very '*promiscuous*' as they say in Wales – I sent you your *shooting* Stockings to the care of Mr Winter Budge row some time ago. I did not bid him forward them as I knew not whether *you* might think them worth car[*riage*] as *I* did not – but

Cap^t B[arrett] can perhaps send for, & bring, them to you if you are not in Town & call for them yourself – This is a *gay* little place in spite of the Invalids which are comparatively numerous – & the People very genteel *looking*. There was a Masquerade last Night at Lord Kilcourcy's (that is the way his name is pronounced if not spelt) whose wife came hither to die 9 months ago! –

I will not cross any more – for the last Paragraph proves Do's[2] saying good, which lately she got from (& would not therefore cross a Letter for the world) somebody, that 'crossed Letters always contain *scandal*' –

God bless you! & kiss the Dears as usual – most truly your Friend S. H.

*Postmark: Newton Abbot, P^y Post, 5 NO 1824*

## 104

*Edward Quillinan Esq^re.*

*Torquay* [*8 Dec. 1824*]

My dear Friend

You are all in the wrong! I never once thought you ungrateful either for not writing, sending Game, or thanking me for the Stockings, because I was sure you were a rambling from home – but *now* I think you very – what shall I say? – unkind for not going to see Mr Monkhouse when you were so near the Stow as Bristol (& probably Malvern) when such a visitor would have been so acceptable in his solitude; & where you would have had such a hearty welcome, & perhaps a little shooting into the bargain. I am not sorry that you did not come hither – glad as I should have been to see you – & much as T[om] M[onkhouse] often says he longs for the day when he can enjoy your society again – but he is prohibited from speaking at all except in a whisper – & in that manner as little as possible & therefore any company which tempts him to break through this rule is injurious to him – He exerted himself more than usual on the evening of the arrival of Cap^t Sartorius & Mr & Mrs Birkett, & the consequence was a spitting of blood – this however was of short duration, and he is now apparently as well as he has been since we came hither – yet still one scarcely *dare* believe that he remains stationary, when there is certainly no change for the better – nor decrease in the unfavorable symptoms – However we have great reason to be thankful that he suffers so little bodily pain – tho' his spirits are in no wise improved – but this cannot be expected whilst the disease remains unabated – and the weather continues so bad that he is unable to take either air or exercise without doors – for the last month we have had only four fine days, & these were not entirely without rain – I have taken the Westmorland climate into high favor again – for here we have as much, or more, *down*right wet – added to high (tho *mild*) winds with roads almost impassable! Yet in spite of the storms the myrtles look as fresh and gay as if they had only been visited by the gales of summer.

We were much pleased, as you may suppose, by both the Sonnets – Little Mary[5] is very much *come out* since the arrival of Capt Sartorius, who is an *untiring* playfellow to her – She talks incessantly, and in sentences – but they are still nearly unintelligible – at least the sounds bear small resemblance to the words she intends to express – She continues as good as needs be, tho' not quite so passive as heretofore – and therefore you would think her greatly improved. *Well*! I wonder whether you will carry back that little red Ro to her native stream! – You must do your best with Tillbrook – I shall not interfere with him – but I tell *you* that when I see how houses, and *hovels*, are let here, I must think . . .

[*Page missing. No address, postmark, &c*]

. . . a Letter from a Friend is to us in this 'uneventful place' – similar circumstances will I hope make even this acceptable. Ever very truly your Friend S. Hutchinson.

## 105

*Thos Monkhouse Esqre, Condon's Hotel, Exeter*

*Wednesday Afternoon* [*2 Feb. 1825*]

My dearest Coz.

I wept many tears of thankfulness over your Letter this morning which I sent for before I was out of bed – Heaven grant that this may find you as comfortable as you must have been when you wrote to me so cheerfully – Believe me I am never hurt at anything you can say or do to me except on your own account well knowing that it is not *you* but your *disease* which chides, & which causes you more suffering than it can do your friends – But no more of this – may God bless you – And now for business –

But first the Darling is as well & happy as possible – She had Tea with me at Mr Wan's yesterday. I wish you could have seen her – she is to go again today with her new Tea things which I sent for some time ago & which are just arrived – Mr F. & Purvis have called Mr F. will do all he can to let the House, if it is not done before we go* – but I find Miss Godfrey expects to have the 60 Guineas paid before we quit – but if the House is let Mr Fenton will remit the money to you as he will remain till our time is out. Dr S. called this Morng & desired his best wishes to you both, & was glad to hear such good news of you, The Lady he said would call to look at the House – (but he was afraid the Bed rooms would not be airy enough) till she has done so I cannot put up a notice in the window.

Such arrivals to day!! 2 brace of Partridges 1 Do Woodcocks – & 3 Snipes from Preston – also a *Tongue cheek* – & a cake of Damson cheese – & from the Major a small box of 'Imperial Plumbs'. My first thought was to distribute the game to Mrs Blisset & Mrs *Wans* but finding that Mrs Monkhouse expected the package from Preston I wait till tomorrow when you may send me some orders about it – or if we should proceed immediately in our Journey it would be no bad thing to make a *pye* of the partridges & boil the Tongue – & send the Woodcocks & snipes to Mrs B. The Plumbs are *beautiful* – If *all* are to be left here perhaps you would give them to Purvis – but this you can tell me when the Carriage comes – We shall be all quite ready to start on Friday at 12 oClock – We could have done it tomorrow had the linen been ready – but the washerwoman cannot let us have it before tomorrow night. I have had 2 enquiries about the Cook – so Mrs Birkett must determine – She will not be able to leave the House before Monday Evening – as, having been employed thus far in washing &c, she cannot till then have it cleaned – I have sent to beg the washerwoman will if possible send home the Linen in time to pack with the Sherry, Books &c in a box to be sent by Marland tomorrow – for tho' I have no doubt but we could bring all the things in the Carriage *to Exeter* yet we shall want a box to send them forward in & I shall pack nothing in it that will be wanted till we are at the end of our Journey, whatever may be our destination, therefore if it arrives before us you need not open it – There will be a hamper & another box full of stores for Mrs Birkett or yourselves as you may determine but of this matter I expect to hear by tomorrows post –

A very short but kind Letter from Mr Bowman enclosed 50£ & a Letter from Mr Winter – the latter I opened, as it looked as if there was

* When Thomas Monkhouse left Torquay for Clifton, Sara was left behind to pack up.

paper enough for me to write upon being, *Mrs Gilpin like*, of a 'frugal mind'. I wished to spare postage – but I saw it would not do – so I send it as it is – but I read M$^{r}$ Bowman's – & also one from the Major which came in the box & which I will send with M$^{r}$ B's by Marland tomorrow – The Major urges you to go to Clifton where he will meet you, or go before, & prepare a Lodging & see the Beds aired himself – M$^{rs}$ Robison he says writes to him that St. Vincents Parade would be the fittest place for you – He begs an answer by return – This is all & the rec$^{t}$ of the Plumbs which he requires answering – the rest of the Letter, as well as this, is all kindness – Capper D. will speak for himself – my frugality does not allow me to withhold his Letter – but we shall not send M$^{rs}$ M's bonnet, as she ordered, tomorrow because we can bring it very well – and the linen will not be ready –

I shall take care to give you *beautiful* accounts – such as will satisfy any old Batchelor – below you will find what I have expended the bills being all paid &, if you do not send money tomorrow, at a venture, I must have the balance by Post on Friday Morn$^{g}$ – that I may settle with old Skin flint – M$^{r}$ Stab will take the Port – there are only 3 bottles – & 7 of Sherry –

| Dr | | |
|---|---|---|
| Last weeks Bills & Prestige's Book | £5. 2 | |
| Mr Wyat | 2.10.0 | He would not allow the 2/6 |
| Do. | 4.6 | |
| Draper's Bill | 16.6 | |
| Poulton's | 2. 8.6 | |
| Cleaning Car 7/6 greasing 1/– loading 1/– | 9.6 | |
| Carriage of Game &c | 3.7 | |
| Poney & Gig | 1. 4.6 | |
| Mrs Cole | 6.5 | |
| Mrs Hearder (Chair) | 5.– | |
| Butchers (this week) | 2.7½ | |
| Bakers Do. | 1.8 | |
| Porter | 15.0 | |
| | £14. 6½ | Errors excepted for I am in haste |

M$^{r}$ Pollard has not sent his Bill
Nor the Milk Bill this week

| Cr £50 | Miss Godfrey |
|---|---|
| 50 | £63 |
| 14 | 14 6 7½ |
| 3 6 | 77 6 7½ |

Poor M^r^ Wans is quite wretched at the thought of losing Ma[ry][5] – when he saw you get into the Carriage yesterday he exclaimed I hope to God the Child is not going – adding when he told me that he is sure he should have wept bitterly if he had not seen her again.

I scarcely dare say I hope dear John[2] is still with you much as I wish it – but I trust we shall not be very long in seeing him again if we are to leave Devonshire – . . . – and now I think I have not forgotten anything & it is nearly post time – for I have waited long for *Pa* who has had many a *tramp* & worry with the People about their Bills before she could get them settled – There will yet be a little more to pay for the washing – & the Cook's wages & food till monday night tho' this last will be a trifle – God bless you all most truly Yours S. H.

*Postmark: Newton Abbot, Penny Post*

## 106

*Mr Monkhouse, Stow, Hereford*

*Taunton, Feb^y^ 7th, Monday Ev^g^* [1825]

My dear John

Here we arrived at 4 o'Clock having left Ex[ete]r at 11 – none of us got out of the carriage & dear Thos[2] complained less of fatigue than any of us – I found him at E^r^ on Saturday very much better *in spirits at least* than when he left Torquay – indeed the change seemed to me miraculous – & as he sleeps so much better, & feels in all other respects more comfortable, we have great reason to be thankful & perfectly satisfied than nothing is to be apprehended from the removal – tho' I dare not flatter myself or you that we have any just grounds to hope that it will work a cure so long as I see the spitting unabated – He complains too a little of his throat tonight – & he tells me that his evil spirit is come back i.e. his fancy about the spitting 'being all for my benefit' – Mrs M. complains *occasionally* of a head-ache – & I have had a little Tooth ache & Sickness today – but I keep '*never heeding*' & have been spending a nice chatty hour with old Miss Southey (the Poets Aunt)*. Last evening I was in Herefordshire – this in Cumberland – Miss Mapleton came to see me yesterday at 3 o'Clock when we had a long gossip together in a room by ourselves till tea Time – ½ past 5 – at ½ past 6 Mr Nash came & escorted us to St Sidwells where he preached – I was at Service in the Cathedral in the morning – walked to the Bridge after dinner, & intended to have been out at 7 this Morng to see the view from the Tiverton road but alas! it rained, & has rained all day – I was sorry not to see more of Ex[ete]r – but right glad to get T. off in in such good heart – tho' he was a little worried with paying bills &c this Morng which made me more than ever thankful that he had had none of the troubles at Torquay which we got over pretty well – tho' the House is unlet & I fear there is much chance for getting it off our hands – Mr Fenton has kindly undertaken it – He was most helpful to me – packed the Carriage out & inside with his own hands & lent me a portmanteau – for Mr M. only sent me one box – & we were in a sad dilemma because we *dared* not fix on a Trunk – for fear of spoiling his Car: – however Mr F. *would do it* – so, as it would have been ungracious to have forbid him, I submitted – but stopped the Carriage when we had got off a Mile & made the driver take it off & put it inside – all the bottom of which it filled & I had a charming easy ride – but this entré nous – There is a Letter from Mrs Lewis tonight – She has not met with a Lodging *to her Mind* – but T. has desired her to take one which is at liberty pro tempore – and we hope to be at Clifton on Wednesday at 2 or 3 oClock – we shall go to Wells tomorrow night & from Wells direct to Bristol not by Bath which we find is only one mile *about* & much more convenient for dividing the journey as there is no decent place to stop at all night by the other road except Bridgewater which would have been a short days journey tomorrow – I am very glad of this arrangement as I shall by this means see Wells Cathedral – most luckily I had a Letter from Hendon the day before I left Torquay telling me that the Gees were returned to West Town – so I shall get my visit paid there which will be convenient enough as these lodgings will scarcely accommodate us all comfortably – therefore I shall probably go to West Town as soon as they are comfortably settled – tho' as yet we have talked nothing about it –

Thos bids me tell you he is enjoying his glass of ale which continues

* Miss Mary Southey who lived at Taunton.

to be palatable to him – His appetite is much improved – indeed I fear he eats too much – when nice things are put before him he cannot risist – He looks forward he says with great pleasure to the Stow – God grant that he may arrive there with health & strength sufficient to enjoy it – I shall be perfectly satisfied to have him at C[lifton] – Unless there is really & truly a change upon which to build hope I shall certainly not encourage to proceed till Ap[l] – tho' I believe he will be inclined to move sooner (if he does not find every *thing to his wish* at C.) now that he has proved to himself that he is able to bear the fatigue of Travilling. Excuse this incoherent Epistle – which in spite of my impatience I must not close without telling you that Sally's *Swain* followed her to Ex[r] within an hour after she had left Torquay & stayed till the Car[riage] came for us – He is a most respectable young man – Nephew to the principal builder & house Proprietor there whose foreman he is (as Carpenter) – I suppose they will now putt off the marriage till the time of our leaving C. – It was to have taken place before we left Torquay – but She was whipped off without even bidding him goodbye – She behaved very well about it – with great feeling & consideration towards her Master & Mistress – so the Stowe will not be graced by Sally. *Pa* tells me that she also is engaged – Her Lover living at Myrthyr – I suppose she was afraid I should think T. the more favoured Person – Good Night! God bless you & all at Hindwell – write to us at the Post Office C. and Mary[2] must think of all she wants me to do for her at Bristol – Little M.[5] is as good as ever – & a more entertaining traveller than she was – she reading the letters on the signs as we pass through the towns & notice all the 'Button Tops' in the Butchers windows again good night – all are gone to bed but myself – & I have had no sleep for 3 nights – little Mary has got a sad cough – but it proceeds from her stomach – remember me to M[rs] D. W. – I hope you got well home – & found your Housekeepers well.

*John Bull*★ tomorrow I want to read the song [to] T. in it – Wilberforces Opium accounts for his *Saintship*.

*Postmark: Taunton, Fe 8, 1825*

★ The *John Bull Magazine* ran only from July 1824 to Dec. 1824, six issues, edited by Theodore Hook. Maginn wrote for it. Possibly she was expecting the Jan. 1825 number which did not materialize, periodicals appearing usually at the *end* of the month. Or she may refer to the newspaper *John Bull*. See Letter 152, p. 402 ★.

# 107

*Mr. Monkhouse, Stow, Hereford*

*30 York Crescent, Clifton, Feb^y 15th* [*1825*]

My dear John

I know not why we have deferred writing to you from day to day – – for to *write* has invariably been our intention – Your's has just arrived for which many thanks – but I am sorry to find that you are not well – pray take care of *feasting* – and dear Mary[2], I fear she will not take [care] of herself – Do not fail to *make* her have some advice – for tho' the '*warmth*' of Brinsop will I trust, with God's blessing do much for her yet she wants something more than warmth to cure her.

Our journey hither from Taunton was prosperous as from Exeter to Taunton with the advantage of better weather – for tho' Monday was not a bad day it was dull & rainy until Ev^g. – but Tuesday was warm & mild & sunny as a day in June – we were all of us sometimes too hot in the Carriage – I almost all the time – we got to Wells at 2 oClock saw the Cathedral &c before dinner – i.e. M^rs M[onkhouse] & I – Thos[2] durst not venture farther than a peep at the palace, & a turn or two upon a sunny walk in its neighbourhood – we had a comfortable Inn & good cheer – & dear little Mary[5] found a host of *e Geas* (little Girls) with whom she was delighted – Thomas went into the Cathedral next Morn^g just for a peep – It is a magnificent building – The Chapter Room uncommonly grand – I am very glad we came that road tho' it was a very hilly stage hither – The morn^g also was dull the whole Vale, or bottom, filled with mist – but when we arrived here all was bright & sunny – Kind M^rs Lewis had prepared every thing for our reception – & her Maid awaited us at the entrance of the Town to direct us to our Lodgings – and in an hour afterwards we were seated at dinner like old settlers. Your dear Brother was certainly fatigued with his journey at last – but I have no hesitation in saying that through the whole of it he seemed to suffer less from languor & lassitude than he used to do at Torquay. But he intends to write a few lines & will speak for himself – M^rs M. is tolerably – but unluckily fell on Sunday off the step at the door and has sprained her leg – which must confine her a little more to the Sofa – . . . M^rs Lewis has introduced a Doctor, a friend of hers & M^rs Robinsons, who has declined practicing – but who will visit T. as a friend – Thos & M^rs M. are much pleased with him – He advises all medicine to be left off except aperients & of those the least possible – to eat anything he *fancies* in moderation – & above all change of air & scene – & not to leave this place till the end of march – he also approves of Thos trying his native air –

Our Lodgings are delightful – and we have seen or felt nothing like cold – I have never seen any snow except that on the heights in Devonshire – We have an excellent airy dining room a large bed room thro' communicating by folding doors – so that dear Thos has not to go upstairs to bed – & by throwing open the door at night he can have plenty of air – 2 other bedrooms a little sitting room for the maids & Mary[5] – kitchen fire, Cooking & Cleaning for 2 Guineas a week – & the situation is the very best in Clifton – full to the sun with a fine paved parade before the door the length of 70 or 80 houses – in short it is the favourite walk of the whole place for those who seek warmth & Health – Yet it is on the 4th tier above the hot well – the hot well situation is always, except on very sunny morn$^{gs}$, cold & damp, *looking* at least – Here are nine nice little close carriages to be had at a reasonable rate which T. intends to avail himself of & will I hope be out in the air as much as possible – for that as well as the exercise does him more good than anything – I know not how long I shall remain at West Town – I shall be content enough there if I only hear daily how he is – because I know there is no want of me here – but I shall be very uneasy if I do not hear regularly.

Dont fail to stir up the workmen that all may be ready before the beginning of April for I am sure T. will not lose his desire, even in this pleasant place, of returning to the Stow as soon as it can be done with safety – He is every day grateful for your exertion in bringing him hither – for his *abduction* as he calls it – He hopes also to see you here – yesterday he said he would give a good deal for a sight of your honest face – He seems very *so so* this morning & will not I fear be able to give much acc$^{t}$ of himself – therefore I must say that I do not think he is quite so well as he was at Ex$^{r}$. He has much uncomfortable feeling in a morn$^{g}$ & does not relish his breakfast always – His cough is certainly better & the phlegm comes up easily – God bless you. My kindest love to all at Hindwell. I hope the *Elderlies* will keep themselves comfortable – Dearest Mary[2], my *heart turned* over when I read of her beginning a new Career at Brinsop – Heaven grant it may be as prosperous and happy a one as she deserves – Ever most truly yours S. H.* . . .

*Postmark: Bristol, Py P*

* Thomas Monkhouse added a few lines.

# 108

*Edward Quillinan Esq$^{r}$, 14 Fludyer Street, Westminster*
Redirected: *Lee Priory, Wingham, Kent*

*Clifton, Feb$^{y}$ 28th [1825]*

My dear Friend

I have no doubt that through Mr Gee you have already heard of the death of my beloved & excellent Cousin – Little hope as I had of his ultimate recovery his death was a dreadful & sudden shock – he had for two days only, previously, been a little worse – still he suffered no pain – & thanks be to God his end was peaceful – He breathed his last without a struggle – scarcely a sign.

It is a great consolation to us that he was removed hither – for he has had one week at least of comparative comfort – never has he been so cheerful & satisfied since we left the Stow – & every day he gave utterance to his thankfulness in being permitted to accomplish the Journey.

Mrs M[onkhouse] is better than we could have expected – I may truly say she has borne her loss thus far with wonderful fortitude – but I fear she has not yet recovered from the astounding blow – & yet she has been even more collected than you can conceive – She desired me to write to inform Cap$^{t}$ Barret of the event – 'because her dear Husband revered him so much' – but feeling that I must write to you I thought he would kindly excuse me – & you will convey to him this wish & the mournful intelligence – Our united regards to him yourself & Mr Gee & believe me most affy Yours S. H.

Mr Monkhouse is here & begs his kind remembrances.

I suppose you to be in Town – Mr Gee having said that he sh$^{d}$ desire you to meet him there.

*Postmark: Bristol, P$^{y}$P. Postage not Paid to London. MR 4, 1825*

[On black-edged notepaper.]

# 109

*Edward Quillinan Esq., Lee Priory, nr Wingham, Kent*

*Hindwell, 29th March* [*1825*]

My dear Friend

It is more than probable that you have already begun your peregrinations, & that my Letter may await your return to Lee for some weeks – but I fancy I *ought* to write, though I have little to say except that I am alive – not in very good health, & in worse spirits, which has been the cause of my neglecting all my Friends – nor would you blame me if you knew how much my sorrow, for the loss of my dearest Cousin, has been encreased by the insensible demeanor of one from whom ( I will not say I *expected*, but) I *might* have expected the most perfect sympathy – However I will not touch upon the subject further than to assure you that your character of her is more than ever true – I have *Tried*, & done my utmost, to disbelieve it – but it has been most painfully confirmed – God forgive us both if we have judged uncharitably! Nothing, I am sure, would give me greater pleasure than to find this was the case – most readily would I acknowledge my error – & my own forgiveness would be less easily obtained than that of the injured party, were she such as I have always wished to find her for the sake of her dear Husband – He is at rest – care & anxiety have done their work! For the first week nothing could exceed my thankfulness for his release – & until I had left Clifton, & parted from his Wife & Child, I thought not of my own loss – and that of Friends here who were so truly & tenderly attached to him, it had been forgotten almost in contemplating his gain. – But now I feel it most bitterly – & the truth cannot be doubted that his life has been destroyed by anxiety of one kind or other – But he was well fitted for a better world – & God knows best what is good for us –

Mrs Monkhouse, [&] Miss Horrocks, with the child returned to Clifton about a week ago – They were all well – but fearing the cold climate of Lancashire at this early season they prefered Clifton to any other Place 'because they had acquaintances there' – We had hoped Mrs M. would have been disposed to remain with us rather than throw herself upon the charities of acquaintances at such a time – but they determined otherwise – Miss H. seemed resolved upon a residence at C. she did not join us there till the night before we left it for the Stow

– having travelled very leisurely from Preston for fear of *night airs* & having also waited for a companion!!

You are under a mistake with regard to my return to Rydal which is not to be until the end of next Term – John[4] has not been at Oxford since Xmas – I almost wish that your journey may be delayed that we may meet in the north – tho' you have behaved so shabbily to me, in breaking all your promises, that I ought to say you are not worth meeting any where – Yet I should not be sorry to see you at this moment upon the Pool where the 'finny fry' are leaping as if they wished to be caught. – We shall leave this place in the course of a month – My Brother & Sister are already gone to their new residence* – but being in the midst of workmen & mortar there is yet no accommodation for the rest of the family – nor will there be any *comfort* there during the whole summer – but at the Stow we have always a quiet harbour – and there I shall often be found whilst I continue in the neighbourhood, & where I hope you will bend your steps in order to make your peace with its master – He is now in London – but we hope to see him home again soon. He has a most painful, & I fear troublesome, duty to perform† – and we wish as much as he does himself that he were in his quiet fields again – Should you be in Town before he leaves it, you will hear of him in Budge Row – or at R. Addison's Esq. 3 Verulam Buildings – or (at *meal times* & nights) 8 Mecklenburg Sq.

So far & not a word about the Darlings – I cannot say bring them hither this summer – because we shall be too far from *The Harp* – and have not accommodations to offer for such a party – else nothing would please Mrs. H. better than to see them – and these Children are already very *intimate* with your's – Little Mary[5] Monkhouse & they have at last been introduced to each other – and they were delighted with her – indeed she is a sweet little creature! greatly improved in all respects, especially in beauty – but she is still very backward in speech & understanding – I believe your Rotha was *wiser* at half Mary's age – I am sure our *little Ebba* must have been so – We have got a north Country Tutor here whose pronunciation & dialect would *charm* you – but he is a respectable youth & of the *genuine upright* north Country character – & competent I have no doubt to accomplish all that he has un[derta]-ken here – Don't be *idle now*, and repay me in kind but write soon & say what are your plans for the summer. I do not in the least expect the *Family*, their return has been so often deferred, & therefore you will continue at Lee – My kind regards to Cap[t] B. & Mr Egerton who

* Brinsop Court in Herefordshire, 10 miles from Stow and John Monkhouse.

† The settlement of Thomas Monkhouse's estate, relations with Mrs. Monkhouse being already strained?

will I suppose be at home by this time – And the full compliment of kisses to the Darlings – & believe me, at all times, very truly your Friend S. H.

Mr Monkhouse writes me that he called last week upon Lamb at the India H[ouse] & found it was His last day – he was about to retire from Office with a *good* Pension I hope –

I have had a very kind Letter from the Daisy since my dear Friend's death – She seems always very *friendly* towards me – tho' I might have been led to think otherwise if I had been disposed to rely on the reports of others.

*Postmark: Radnor, 1 AP 1825*

## 110

*Edward Quillinan Esq[re], Pall Mall, London*

*Brinsop Court, June 2nd* [*1825*]

My dear Friend

As you have given me your address in Town '*I guess*' you expect me to write to you – a little unreasonable if you recollect how long you neglected us after leaving the Stow – sending us nothing but that bit of a Letter from Bronshill [?]. But to tell you the truth I write only to reply to your P.S. by informing you that I shall not leave Herefordshire till the *end* of this month – Mrs H. is still at the Stow where I hope to keep her for a week or two yet – this place being very unfit for her at present – therefore my time cannot possibly suit John Wordsworths & we have given up that scheme – So, if the arrival of your Friends at Lee gives you liberty to go Northward at the end of the Month, I shall be *greatly obliged* by your calling at the Stow – & at the same time both there & here you may gratify your ears with the sound of the crowing Pheasants.

We are vexed at that foolish Davies not letting you have his 'grand' place* – I cannot conceive why he should keep it empty – for I suppose there is no chance of his being able to return to it – I know of nothing else in this neighbourhood to suit you – but indeed I have been so fixed to the House, & the Workmen, since I came hither that I know little of the neighbourhood – The Game *I know* would suit you well – The Family at Whitney Court are very sorry not to have

* Cabaloa of Letter 120, p. 331.

you for a Neighbour – the Dew* would have fallen very gently upon you – as you are in great favour – The Gazelle too (who caught no cold) expressed her best wishes for your success – By the Bye there has been an importation of (a little) *May Dew* at 'the Court' since you left us – all doing well –

Mr Monkhouse is at present from home – gone into Leicestershire upon some farming business – but we hope to see him here on his return on Sunday – I have been here almost ever since you left us – my Brother & I alone. – The young ones are all with their Mother & Mr Milner at Stow – the *old* Ladies, i.e. my Aunt & Joanna, at *Gwayndovenant*† – all snugly out of the way of the bustle and dirt; of which you can have no idea – from the *smooth* & *comfortable* state in which you saw this place – for in sober earnest it has been in ten times more confusion ever since – The House is full of Workmen Masons – Carpenters – Painters – Glaziers – Paperers – Upholsterers &c but we should soon finish, within doors, if they would but be constant to us – but they run off & leave me in the lurch when I least expect it – I advise you, if you wish to preserve your sweetness of temper, never to build or alter a House.

The smell of paint almost killed poor Mrs H – we were seriously alarmed for the state into which she was brought by it – and thankful am I that I was able to relieve her – but she is sadly annoyed by the idea of my troubles & vexations – which do not hurt me at all – & I shall think it one of the *pleasantest visits* I ever spent in my life if her health is restored by means of the little service I am able to render her – for She is one that we *could not spare*.‡

I know not what they *think* of you at Rydal except that they marvel at not hearing from, or seeing you; as a Letter or Letters have already arrived there addressed to you – &, of course, they *had* been looking for you daily. They have had a very interesting visitor, a Miss Jewsbury, with whom they all seem enchanted – The weather has been fine there, as well as else where – & they seem to be enjoying themselves – & executing some scheme of 'particular pleasure' (as Mr Kenyon used to term it) every day. – It is not for *this* – but I *do long to be* with them once again – I trust nothing will detain me beyond the time I mentioned. – Your *Rival* wishes to escort me as far as Chester – but notwithstanding my '*imbecility*' (as Mrs Wordsworth calls it) I should be

* Mary[5] Monkhouse married Rev. Henry Dew, for 58 years Rector of Whitney.

† Gwerndyffnant.

‡ One of the bonds between Quillinan and Sara Hutchinson was that they could let themselves go with regard to Mrs. Thomas Monkhouse, indirectly referred to here.

ashamed to take such a busy Man from his home – but have no scruples in bringing an idle Flibbertygibbet a few miles out of his way – God bless you! Kisses to the Darlings when you return to them – I hope you will soon be wearied of London. – If you want employment perhaps we may favour you with some commissions – Continue to direct to Stow – Kind remembrances to Cap$^{t}$ B—

Your's very truly S. H.

My Brothers best regards –

I hope you have succeeded (with as *little trouble* as usual) in *fitting out* the Children with *becoming* Bonnets &c for the summer, & the arrival of Grandpapa* &c.

*Postmark: Hereford, JU 4, 1825*

## III

*Edward Quillinan Esq., Lee Priory, nr Wingham, Kent*

*Rydal Mount, 5th Oct$^{r}$* [*1825*]

I would not write '*dear Friend*' *good for nothing Creature* D. W.
My dear Friend

If I were not very busy I should *scold* you, as long as there were an inch of blank paper upon this sheet, for your neglecting to write to us – – especially as you left us under the apprehension of being laid up by a bad cold – And, as I infer from your silence you are not very anxious about us, I shall not tell you a word about the good effects of Harrowgate upon Mrs H— or of Dora's[2] perfect restoration to health – nor that we are all well & William[1] & myself set out to Coleorton tomorrow – John[4] to Ox$^{d}$ & Mrs Luff to London – and that we shall leave the House to the Dorothys & Willy[2] for a month – If you wish to hear further particulars, application must be made *to Coleorton Hall Ashby de la Zouch* & Rydal Mount immediately –

Your's, according to your deserts, truly S. H. I cannot leave out the Darlings tho' I send my kisses in the P.S.

*Endorsed:* wrote to Dora Wardour St October 12 – 1825 the day I rec$^{d}$ this at 11 Upper Spring Street, Portman Square. [E.Q.]

*Postmark: Kendal Penny Post, 7 OC 1825*

* Sir Egerton Brydges.

# 112

*(For Edward Quillinan Esq$^{r}$), Capt Barrett, 14 Fludyer Street, Westminster*

*Coleorton Hall, Oct$^{r}$* [*24, 1825*]

My dear Friend

William *commanded* me to write to you immediately upon the receipt of your Letter to Mary[1] – but whether I was prevented by the command, or the want of matter likely to amuse you I know not – at any rate I have been very idle, or stupid, or something that I ought not [to] have been – for we are really very anxious about you; & I know that if we do not *force* you to it you will not send us another word about yourself – Pray be careful – and do not depend too much upon the Doctors – Living *quietly* and *steadily* in the Country is much better for you, in my opinion, than being in a lodging alone in Town, if you are not able to stir out – in which case I cannot imagine how you are to avoid cigars & Porter – which I guess the Doctors will not prescribe – and the Trotts I am sure will do you more good than Physic – so my advice is (unless you can go & take a quiet sojourn, and a little sober sport, among our Herefordshire friends) that you should take a lodging in the country & send for the Children & Mrs Lucas to nurse you –

I have been very poorly myself – or rather uncomfortable from pain – rheumatics I suppose – so that I have wished myself at dear Rydal Mount again many times – But I am somewhat better again & feel that I shall enjoy myself if the weather is tolerable – but for the last four or five days it has been cold beyond all endurance – in spite of hot air & plenty of coal fires it has been impossible to keep oneself warm – We had a covering of snow on Thursday Morning which had an odd effect among the Trees, in their green garments, & the China Roses, Dahlias, & other flowers in full blow [? bloom] upon the Lawn – This is a very beautiful place – I mean the grounds – for the Country is very uninteresting – but there has been so much done by good taste that one can scarcely wish for any residence (*of the kind*) being more delightful – But the Master & Mistress are the charm of the whole – never was there such a well assorted pair – or one so full of enjoyment at such an advanced period of life –

I am forgetting one of the principal motives for writing which was to convey Mr W's thanks to you for the transcript of Sir Egerton's amicable notice of him* with which he was much gratified – & which is written, he says, with the same favor which characterizes all his effusions – it was some such pretty speech as this – but no doubt it has lost much in the reporting – but to tell it in my own way we were all as well as himself mightily pleased both with the manner & matter –

I have nothing to tell you from Rydal because I know that you have had a Letter – and probably in it you may have heard of Mrs Hutchinson's safe arrival at home to the great joy of all her family. . . . She has ordered some good *Beer* to be brewed for you at Brinsop – so I hope you intend to go and drink it –

Mr W & I spent a day at Matlock on our way & were very much pleased with the neighbourhood – the river is indeed charming – we were recommended to go up the Via Gallia &, smitten by the romantic name, took a poney chaise for the purpose (it being too far for me to walk) – we were *disappointed* in what we went to seek viz. '*extraordinary picturesque beauty*' but we were so delighted with our drive that it ended in our purchasing the *poney* – and which after it had been brought hither would have been very useful to us had we not contrived, Mary[1] & I, to overturn the Garden Chair, which we found here, & bruised her Leg & I sprained my ancle so that in addition to my rheumatics I have been a cripple –

Mr W.'s Eyes are very bad I am sorry to say: & he is not in consequence the most lively of the Party – We expect Doctor W. & one of his Boys (for a few days) next Tuesday – and on Thursday 2 Ladies – one a sort of a Russian *Princess* – a Young Lady whose father is a Russian Prince & mother was a sister or daughter or something of L[d] Sherbourne – I had much rather they would stay at their own homes – (these last) for they can neither add to our comfort or cheerfulness let them be as agreeable as they may – & I am sure the Princess, who is very young (I forget her —ousky [orisky?] name) only just presented, will want some young ones to make the visit agreeable to her.

If you can forgive this horrid scrawl it is more than I can do – But tho' I vowed I would write as soon as breakfast was over & not let slip another day I have delayed till the last moment before dinner – having been deep in a *novel* all the morn[g] except when I was forced out into the Garden – By the bye you *must* read the account of the

* The reference appears to be to Brydges's *Gnomica*, 1824, chaps. cxxx–cxxxii, in which he discussed Wordsworth's Preface of 1820.

Vaudois a 'Narrative of an excursion to the mountains of Piedmont with some account of the Vaudois or Waldenses' by a Mr Gilly* – now do read it – not for *spite* do I recommend it – though you will find some truths not very agreeable to the professors of the true Religion – God bless you! W. & M desire their kindest remembrances – I know not how to direct this, you gave not the N°. of your Lodgings – Let us hear from you very soon, & I hope a *very good account* it will be – we are grieved at what you hint concerning Mr Gee – I must say I am not very much surprized – Kind regards to Capt B— from all – Ever most truly Yours S. H. I had forgotten that you have a Brother with you & therefore may not be so *forlorn* as I suppose – I hope you are not *tired* of the Trotts – if you are you may give them to me.

*Postmark: 24 OC 1825*

## 113

*Edward Quillinan Esqr, Lee Priory, nr Wingham, Kent*

*Rydal Mount, Novr 21st* [*1825*]

My dear Friend

I wrote to you from Coleorton, some weeks ago, directing at random to Capt Barret as you had failed to give us your address – Since our return I find that Capt B. is in Ireland and perhaps my Letter has not reached you – I hope that this is the case, and had rather believe that you are nursing your anger against us, for neglecting your request that we would write & help to enliven your 'sick room', than that you are still confined to it & have been prevented by illness from writing to us – We are exceedingly anxious about your health – and if we find that nothing worse than laziness is the cause of your silence we shall be very very angry with you – therefore I beg that this Letter may be answered speedily by a true account of yourself, and good news of the Darlings –

We reached home last week – having left Coleorton on the 9th – William in a '*Pone shase*' (which I bought at Ashby) with our Matlock Poney – and Mary[1] & I by Coach – He arrived at Manchester a day after us, and we remained there, together, on a visit to Miss Jewsbury

* Gilly, William Stephen, *Narrative of an excursion to the mountains of Piedmont and researches among the Vaudois, or Waldenses with maps, plates and an appendix containing copies of ancient manuscripts, etc.*, London, 1824.

until Monday when we proceeded, by our several conveyances, homewards and all arrived here safe & sound – Mr W's eyes much amended by his journey, & the *smoke* of Manchester – they had been very bad during our stay at Coleorton – which, as you may guess, did not enliven our visit – but for this cause it would have been a most agreeable one – our *Princess* was a delightful creature – a sweet unaffected *lass* – such a one as you rarely meet with in these days – and her Friend, Miss Master, a very accomplished and excellent woman. After their departure came a daughter of Lord Beverley – an *elderly young* woman – very good natured but full of affectation. (I was about to say *airs* but I feared you would take the word in its bad sense which she does not deserve) – Such a Person as I never before saw (*among 'quality'* at least) but have often read described in a novel – She amused us greatly & we were not, luckily, long enough with her to be tired of her absurdity & fineness – She was something of a *noisy 'exquisite'*.

We have been exceedingly entertained by your account of the blunder respecting the opium-eater – The real one* is now here *in great force*, his Mother having given him 300£ to pay his debts. He tells Miss W. that he had entirely left off opium before he came hither, but has been obliged to have recourse to it again; 'as he has *no Shoes* to walk in & without exercise he is obliged to take it' – I suppose it is *easier* to send to the Druggists than to the Shoe Makers – We want him to review M. J. J's Book† – & to give her '*a lift*' poor thing! but if he is really *disposed* I fear we must not look for his production before doom's day – therefore we turn our hopes upon you – and wish you would, in your *ingenious* way, try to find out some way or other to help her – as write she *will* & fancies she *must* – so that a little profit is very necessary for her. She is a most meritorious creature – as a Daughter & Sister her conduct is exemplary – and her Friends at Man[r] tell us that her situation is a most arduous & trying one – By the bye we saw some very interesting *females* at M—. One especially which I wished you, who are the slave of beauty, to have seen – She *was* a vision of delight – a lovely apparition sent to be a moment's ornament – But I shall never forget her – Her manners were as fascinating as her

* i.e. de Quincey himself. His *Confessions of an Opium-Eater* had appeared in 1821. Sara's attitude is interesting corroboration of his evident transference there of his own habits to Coleridge in exculpation of himself. In view of the fact that Sara Hutchinson must have suffered considerably from Coleridge's opium addiction, her indirectly defensive attitude towards him *vis à vis* de Quincey is significant. De Quincey's article probably did more to distort the public impression of Coleridge than any other single account of him.

† *Phantasmagoria*, by Maria Jane Jewsbury, 2 vols., 1835, dedicated to William Wordsworth.

face, figure, & countenance; and above all her fortitude under affliction and privation was quite heroic and romantic –

Since I wrote to you I have had two reports from Herefordshire of my dear Sister's health – the first most excellent – but the last I grieve to say not so – but she was better again before she wrote. They sent their love to you – and were unwilling to give up the hope of seeing you before the shooting season is over. Mrs H[utchinson] is in want of a Governess a *steady useful* Person who would undertake the education & charge of the two Girls & younger Boy – perhaps *you* (*who are in that line*) might hear of one – for they are so difficult to meet with that I must try in all quarters – & having succeeded so well for you I think I have some claim on your exertions.

I have another application to make which is for your interest or Cap^t^ B's (if either of you have any) with a Mr Brydges who is a fellow of Merton Col. Oxon. as it has been recommended to John to try for a fellowship there which is obtained by interest, *cheifly*, with the Warden & fellows – I send a list of them – and also the friends through whom they are assailable which has been sent to W^m^ & if you know any of the others he will thank you to make interest for John.

At Preston we saw Mrs. M[onkhouse] and truly she *is*, as report says, 'a *brisk* Widow' – She had written to Mrs H— upon leaving Clifton that the Doctors advised her return to her own family as her ill health was occasioned 'by anxiety of mind' – Another version of the cause of this sudden movement came hither from Preston – Miss Horrocks being upon the point of marriage with a Dr St Clare an old Friend of 15 years standing who according to Mrs M— had not ventured to declare himself till encouraged by her – So Mrs M— is returned to take her Sisters station at P. as long as the novelty charms her* – and probably the *consequence* attached to it may keep her in health till she meets with another husband – We wrote to desire her to meet us, with little Mary[5], at the Inn – but she came alone – 'Mary was not in the way' tho' it came out that she was only *in the Garden* – However she proposed (& I will not doubt her sincerity) to send the Child with Miss H. who is coming to pay Mrs Astley a visit before her marriage – W^m^ saw the Child who is much grown – & very pretty but as he did not hear her talk we fear she is still backward in her speech – He stayed all night at Lark hill – & confirmed our observation that the Lady was well & happy as she could be.

Keep the list – and burn this Letter – Kisses from Dora[2] & me to

* [*SH's note*]: Miss *H's report of the Dr's opinion was that her 'lungs were sound & she* might live any where'.

the Darlings & everybodys love to you all – & believe me ever most sincerely your Friend S. H.

I cannot help sending you an Epigram of Lamb's – Tho' I must preface it in Mr H. [Crabb] Robinsons words who communicated it to us – 'Have you seen L's epigram on L[d] B[yron]'s body being brought to Eng[d]?* There is something unfeeling in it – but as a corrective to the sentimental slang & cant which that event occasioned you may tolerate it'.

'Manners, they say, by climate alter not – Who goes a drunkard will return a Sot.
And lordly Juan, damned to lasting fame, – Went out a *Pickle* & came back the same.'

Warden *Dr. Vaughan*
* Fellows names
* *Capel* Honble Brother to L[d] Essex –
* *Griffith.* Resident at Merton – his friend the B[p] of Oxford –
* *Oglander.* S[r] Wm Oglander & L[d] de Dunstanville –
* *Marsham* – Lord Romney –
* *Addington* L[d] Sidmouth –
* *Whisk.* In the War Off. a friend of Lord Folkstone –
* *Compton* – a Hampshire Family –
* *Herbert* – L[d] Caernarvon his Brother his Friend L. Pembroke – uncle L[d] Egremont –
* *Mills.* * *Mildmay* Friend L Folkstone
* *Cockerell* – S[r] John Leach – Dr Goodenough
* *Hammond* his connections in the diplomatic line
* *Bouverie* L[d] Folkstone
* *Grey*
* *Rooke* S[r] H Burrard Rev[d] G. Burrow
* *Seymour* Serg[t] at Arms to Ho: of Com:
* *Bigon* & * *Tyndall* both Barristers
* *Buckley* L[d] de la Warre
* *Bridges* a Kentish family
* *Tierney*

*Postmark: Kendal, Penny Post, 23 NO 1825*

* Lamb's epigram 'On the Arrival in England of Lord Byron's Remains' appeared first in the *New Times* (ed. Stoddart), 24 Oct. 1825. *Works, ed. cit.*, IV, 121.

# 114

*Edward Quillinan Esq., Lee Priory, nr Wingham, Kent*

*Rydal Mount, 25th Jan$^{y}$* [*1826*]

My dear Friend

You must have thought us all very negligent or forgetful of you for not having written after your communicating to us so important a resolution as that of braving the stormy Bay of Biscay and leaving your Treasures behind you – Yet in the midst of sickness and sorrow both you & yours have been remembered & my prayers for a safe voyage & happy return to you have not been wanting – But after some weeks of great and fearful anxiety, concerning the temporal affairs of our Relatives at Stockton, I have been laid upon my bed by sickness for three weeks – & there I am now writing to you – and not yet able to leave my room – However my strength is recovering daily – & I have considered my 'sickness as a messenger of God sent (in mercy) with purposes of abstraction & separation, with a secret power & a proper efficacy to draw us from unprofitable & useless sorrows' –

You may not perhaps have noticed in the Papers the failure of the 'Tees Bank' – occasioned by their having a very large sum of money locked up in Pole's House at a time when other heavy losses came upon them. After having stood all shocks, & enjoyed, most deservedly, the confidence of the public for 45 years they are become Bankrupt – but heaven be praised no dishonourable conduct has brought them to this; & if they can pay every one their own all the partners *bearing our name* will retire to comparative poverty without a blush – I wish I could say the same of the other Partner in whom they have been deceived, & by whom their late losses have been frightfully increased – My Brother's & my Cousins wives & families are amply provided for – and it is a satisfaction to think that should they not be able (which we trust will not be the case) to answer all demands upon them that upon *this property* the credit of the house was not established – but upon that of our Grandfather & Uncles – great part of which is gone – land which has decended to the family since the time of Henry 8th to pay the creditors of a Man without a shilling – who was admitted into the Concern upon the strength of property which proves to have been borrowed! But why should I trouble you with this – especially as what I say is in confidence – & ought not to be exposed in the present state of affairs – So pray burn this –

Mr W. has been, & kept every one else when they were not employed nursing me, busy in preparing his Poems for republication – Hurst & Robinson were to have been the Publishers – but luckily the bargain was so made that until the delivery of the copy & the cash paid upon it, they had no claim upon it – else he would now have perhaps lost his Edition as they are become Bankrupts – Poor Mr Watts will be a great sufferer in his pecuniary affairs in them – their want of money prevented the timely publication of his '*Souvenir*' & tho' 9000 have been sold, in spite of the delay, he has not rec^d a farthing! –

Had they not been, as I have said, all over head & ears in business, & sick at heart by anxiety some one would have written to you – but it has been reserved for me to write you this worthless Epistle.

Mr Monkhouse was in Town lately. I fear he did not know where to enquire for you or perchance you might have met there. – Dear Mrs Hutchinson is quite well at present, & if she continues so is in the way of adding to her stock of Treasures – she is not very much charmed with this remedy for her other diseases – but trusts that it will prove a blessing.

You must write to us before you leave England – I hope you are not already gone – tell us all about the Darlings whom we most arden[tly] long to see – 'The Family' I suppose are not returned – and you must have ceased to expect them. I have no news from this neighbourhood to amuse you. I know not whether you were told that upon understanding that Mrs Huddlestone was positively to occupy Rydal Mount after May 1827 William bought the little field* behind Tillbrooks Cottage belonging to Backhouse, being resolved to build himself a House rather than quit Rydal – but we have still hopes that Mrs H[uddlestone] will not come hither; & that we may be permitted to stay to prevent the erection of another 'genteel Cottage' a thing very obnoxious to the dignity of the Lady of the Manor – but this is entre nous – If you should meet with the Daisy say not a word that we have any *hopes*, but that Wm is resolved to build if Mrs H. comes – & we are turned out. Mr B[arber] is in great force – he dined here yesterday – more in love with his place than ever – & has been spending his Xmas with the Syren Widow at Fall-foot – Miss Horrocks is married – & he Mr B. spent a day there with the bride & bridegroom – 'a tidy farmer looking Man about 50 not very *refined*' which used to be a desideratum with the Ladies of that family – Miss W. goes to Herefordshire in about a fortnight where she purposes paying a 3 months visit – Dora[2] and I are meditating a journey to Edinburgh on a visit to the *Dentist* – Mr Barber offers to escort us – I said to him 'what can we do with

* 'Dora's Field.'

you' – but I thought to myself if another *little* male Friend of ours had made the proposal I should not have given this same answer – for I think he would not have bothered us so much – I hope however that B. will not press his civilities upon us – Do. is charmed with the idea of the journey & has amused herself, & tried to amuse me, greatly by talking of it – Kiss the Trotts for us all. Every Bodys love to you – My comp^{ts} to Mrs Lucas & Liza ever Yours most truly S. H.

We suppose Cap^{t} B[arrett] is still in Ireland – if not our united regards to him.

*Postmark: Kendal Penny Post 27 JA 1826*

## 115

### *Mr Monkhouse, Stow, Hereford*

*Rydal Mount, 28th Jan^{y} 1826*

My dear John

It is a long time since I have seen your hand-writing – yet I do not take up my pen in order to *extract* a Letter from you, knowing how costly the exertion is to you, but for my own pleasure – And to you I know it will be no small satisfaction to hear that I am now mending rapidly – I was down stairs today while my room was being put in order; & tho' walking ½ a doz times the length of the dining room heated me as much as one of your reapers would have been under a July sun, yet I am no worse for it & am able to sit up great part of the day. I hope I shall be strong enough before the time intended for Miss W's departure that her Journey may be no longer delayed – All else are well and have begun to look upon our other causes of anxiety with less horror since we know the worst – & trust with Gods blessing that the whole will not be purely evil – For our dear Brother himself little will suffice & the effect of his misfortunes* may have a salutary influence upon those of his children who have been a source of anxiety to him hitherto, & consequently produce in the future more happiness than riches could give – Those who have been dutiful have shewn, as might be expected, that their care is only for him – and their reward is sure. Poor Cousin Henry's case is the most lamentable of all – to be reduced at his time of Life, *helpless as he is* to beggary! But his concern now, as

* She refers to John Hutchinson and the failure of the Tees Bank, described in the previous letter.

well as that of all the concern who bear the name of Hutchinson, is that they may be able to pay all – and W$^{m}$ had a Letter from John[1] yesterday – he states that their losses (including M$^{r}$ Perce's debt I suppose) amount to 100,000£ – a frightful sum which I fear all their available property will not be equal to. Could but this be accomplished Time & the consciousness of their own integrity would soften every privation – Great calamities are more easily borne than lesser evils – & are doutless intended as blessings by turning our thoughts to the source from whence, as our Friend Pascal says, flows all the good or evil that happens to us – 'to Him whose counsels are in the deep, & whose footsteps are in the water, and we know not what he shall determine for us' – Of yours & my Aunt's probable losses I say nothing because I feel that had the case been my own it would not have added one regret to what I have endured – & tho' I do not comprehend the messages he has sent me concerning the safety of my property I would not trouble my poor Brother for an explanation for the whole of its value. But enough of this melancholy subject – let me turn to one more grateful to us both – the amended state of your dear sisters health & the satisfaction with which we hear from Joanna that both you & Henry[1] (in spite of his gout) are both in cheerful Spirits – I suspect that you have been too free with your *wine* – & that Coniston fare suits him better than the hospitalities of the Stow – I shall perhaps become his partner in this affliction for I began my 8th bottle of old Sherry today – yet it did not screw up my courage sufficiently to enable me to have my Teeth drawn which M$^{r}$ Carr came to operate upon – having by his advice for the sake of my health consented to be rid of these tormentors – while I was *very ill* my courage would not have failed – but they thought me too weak & when I was in the humour he would only draw two which I endured most heroically – but whether the work will ever be completed or not I cannot say – for as my body becomes stronger my courage seems to be weaker – Joanna will laugh at me I know – Dora[2] & Julia are quite *ashamed* – & Mary[1] W. says 'poor Dora will not get her journey to Edinburgh' with the thoughts of which she has [*torn*] herself & tried 'to amuse me' during my illness. Poor M$^{r}$ Carr! he talked, reasoned, joked, laughed [at] me – did every thing but scold to no effect – the [*torn*] I took upon myself – & did not spare myself [*torn*] easily we can bear pain when we have no choice – but to determine upon it, especially for an uncert[ain and] remote good, I must confess is beyond my philosophy – tho' I do not think I am utterly void of moral courage – my physical would encrease nobodys stock as you all well know.

I think I have written enough about myself & am tired whatever you may be so God bless you all! remember me to your neighbours at the Court – & believe me ever at all times, & in all moods, most truly & affty yours S. H.

I must tell you of William's good luck in having escaped a loss by Hurst & Robinsons failure. They were to have been his publishers – but the bargain was not quite complete & by the greatest chance in the world – Constable also & Ballantyne have failed – S^r^ Walter will be greatly involved there – another *great house* in the Trade in London is expected to follow soon – & not one they say is safe! I wish I could get you a frank for this worthless Epistle – . . .

## 116

*Edward Quillinan Esq., Lee Priory, nr Wingham, Kent*

*Rydal Mount, May 22nd* [*1826*]

My dear Friend

Although the 'middle of may' is past (the time you fixed for my writing to you at Lee) I do not much fear being too late to greet you on your arrival – but before I bid you welcome to old England again I must vent my *illhumour* upon you – or rather the ill humour of the whole house – for leaving England without writing to us – and especially as my Letter had reached you so long before you sailed – Shall I tell you what Mr W. said after having a day by day *for a month* wondered at your silence? 'Well, it seems to me that we have *wasted* a deal of interest & affection upon one who can treat us thus lightly' – word for word – for I was spiteful enough at the time to wish you had heard him – & now that your peace was *partly* made by writing from Oporto I tell it you – I hope you will not be so *naughty* (as Mrs Gee would say) again – but write immediately upon your return – for we are very anxious to hear of the Darlings as well as yourself.

We are all well at present – tho' poor Dora[2] has had a sucession of bad colds during the winter – The weather is now dreafully hot – and we are threatened with a contested election which will not tend to cool the air – It will however bring our Friends among us which will be some satisfaction – Miss Wordsworth has been in Herefordshire since the middle of Feb^y^ & does not intend to return till July – She is very much charmed with her quarters there – the Stow, & Brinsop – & is no hurry to leave them – All Friends there are well – and as little disposed to grumbling as any of his Majesty's subjects, notwithstanding the unprosperous state of the Country – La Gazelle is engaged to be married – but not to Mr M.

Mrs. T. Monkhouse is about to sail with little Mary[5] for the Continent – I had a moist *hoity toity* Letter from her last week – from London – where she had been staying a short time – She seemed in the height of enjoyment – said she had spent an evening with the Atherleys very pleasantly; & had also been staying with Mrs Alderman Thompson in Gloster Place. – Miss Stanley added a few lines to the letter telling me that Mrs M looked uncommonly well – but that she herself was far from strong – and hoped Mrs A. & the family would go to Hastings for the summer – She (the Daisy) enquired after you in a former Letter which I had from her when at Bath – Mrs M— intends to spend the summer, & probably the winter also, at Nantes.

We have little or no hope of spending another summer at dear Rydal Mount. I know not whether I told you of Mr W—'s plan of building – the timber is bought – the plan & elevation all upon Paper &c – and he is eager to begin in good earnest – He – Dora – & Willy are the B*uilders* – Miss W. & J. anti Builders – Mary W. I think is neuter – only she will be satisfied when the determination is made which ever way it may be. – I cannot bear to think of leaving this place – and Mrs Huddlestone who is to succeed us as little relishes leaving her present situation – but My Lady has set her heart upon it – and I suppose, for the sake of her Son, Mrs H. will not refuse – tho' she is wise enough to know that even for his interest they had better have Kirkstone between them. It *vexes* me so I will write no more about it –

I have no more news for you – no changes have taken place yet – tho' we expect new neighbours in plenty – & some old ones are about to take their departure – The Carletons & Whites – from Ambleside – so all our beauty is departing – The Crumps (very plain patterns) are come back to Allan Bank. The Aylings are expected – Dr Wordsworth & his Boys – Mr Tillbrook & some old College Crone – and a shoal of 'Cathedrals' (Cantabs) – John[4] Wordsworth I suppose will be here also to his great joy – but not much I fear for his benefit in the way of *learning* – as Miss B[arker] is returned I guess heart whole from the '*moderate Athens*' – so he will fancy he has still a chance. – Thus you see we shall not be in danger of spending a dull summer if plenty of company can secure us from it – & I hope you do not intend to let the winter come hither again before you make your appearance.

Our Keswick neighbours are all well tho' Mrs C[oleridge] & Sara are in great sorrow and vexation at Hartley's bad conduct – Southey is in Town – Edith paid us a visit lately & talks much of repeating it – She is more delightful than ever – all the house here now delight in her as much as I do – She *affects* to dislike the lakes & mountains & long for her London life again – but she is happier notwithstanding apparently as ever she was before she knew any other life than that she now spends – Her Sister Bertha is a fine young woman – and of a delightful disposition. . . .

All here join me in very best regards to you & your dear little Trotts – and send their best wishes for your safe & speedy return – notwithstanding your delinquencies –

God bless you! And believe me truly your Friend

S Hutchinson.

Barber is in statu quo but raving at the Drought 'quite a calamity'. He has pulled up all his Cabbage &c and strawberry plants in revenge – '*they* shall not grow again' *others* may – Ah you would have been amused with his ravings! Our regards to Cap[t] B[arrett] & Mr Egerton – I don't enquire after '*The Family*'!

*Endorsed:* Miss Hutchinson, Rydal Mount, 22 May. Rec[d] at Lee 18 June. Answered from London 20th D[o] to Mr Wordsworth. Mr Lyddeker, No 3 Wellington Place, Commercial Road. [*E.Q.*]

*Postmark: Kendal Penny Post, 25 MY 1826*

## 117

*Ambleside August twenty three 1826,*
*Edw[d] Quillinan Esq[r], Lee Priory, Wingham, Kent*
*R. T. Farquhar*

*Rydal Mount 23[d] Aug[t]* [*1826*]

My dear Friend

Mrs Wordsworth is too *idle* to take up the pen (which I have urged her to do for the sake of giving you a little variety) so you must be contented with your *more constant* correspondent. Mr *W.* has been from home above a week and I have not had an opportunity of becoming advocate in your cause nor will it be necessary – for he is of a very forgiving disposition & your *misdemeanour* is quite forgotten as well as forgiven – You are right in supposing that we would not even have listened to any 'balderdash' respecting you – It is true that a whole history and statement of the affair was laid before Mr W. – &, *according* to *that*, appearance & facts were in favor of the *Plaintiff* – but not one syllable of blame was attached to *you* – 'it was natural that you should think your father had acted right' – & it was discussed merely as an affair between him & Mr Gee – & not that you were responsible for his conduct – *We* have no doubt but that the case *might* have been *differently* stated – & till both sides were heard it is not likely that Mr. W. would give any judgement, or form an opinion in his own mind – therefore the Gentleman gained & you lost nothing – & it is not worth writing about.

I rejoice to hear such a good account of the Darlings – what a treasure they must be to Grandmama & Aunts! who will I hope bring them up good *protestants* – You have spoiled Mrs Lucas yourself I have no doubt – & have injured her by turning her away in a hurry – don't *bristle-up* at this, for it is true – & all you say of her gossipping &c true enough I doubt not – but if you had not been too *good-natured* & *chatty* with her she would not have taken the liberty to gossip about her betters – I do not presume to blame you for parting with her – only I meant that your doing it in *such a hurry* might hinder the poor woman of another situation – Do you think she would suit Mrs [T.] Hutchinson? Her *vanities* would not be called into action there – she would have no one to set her cap at – unless she took a fancy to Mr M[onkhouse] & thought him *old* enough for her. Answer me this – but don't fancy that I do not think you *quite right* in parting with her – you know the merits of the case better than I do – yet she might do her duty in another situation – but at Mrs Hutchinson's her capability as a *Teacher* would be of more consequence than as nurse.

Mrs H., you will be glad to hear, is much improved in health – Her Brother's eyes are in the same state & he is as cheerful and patient as ever – Miss Wordsworth is so charmed with everything, & ever[y] body, in Herefordshire that I know not when we shall have her at home again – She is also engaged to pay a visit at Coleorton on her return. My Brother & all the Family are well – Joanna & Henry[1] have been with us six weeks – and are now gone to finish out the summer at the Isle of Man – which they visited 3 years ago & were so much charmed that resolved upon a longer sojourn at some future time – We have had a house-ful all the summer – and what a summer it has been! No climate on earth more delightful or more steady – we have scarcely had 3 days *rain* since Feb^y^ and the showers which have fallen have only made the weather more agreeable & kept up the freshness of the verdure – which is really at this time like spring – The *Lakers** have

* *The Lakers.* See p. 63 *.

not been numerous – but all the Lodgings are full – not a house empty – Tillbrook has been at Ivy Cot since June – & stays till Oct[r] – Spring Cottage full of Ladies from NCastle – Mrs Luff has her Friends the Farquhars – & Millar Brig a family from Preston – the Crumps at Grasmere – Hustlers at Tail End – & Barber I know not where – for he has cut us – but no doubt he will *come again* in the winter – & we are not sorry for a reprieve. Elizabeth[3] Cookson has been with us six weeks – she improved greatly during the first three – but beyond a certain point it seems that she cannot advance – She is a perfect Angel & it does one good to look upon her & witness her patient & cheerful endurance.

Mr W's eyes have been very bad since *the election* during which time luckily they were uncommonly well & he was at Appleby & enjoyed the *Sport* – He is now at Lowther whither he went to meet the Atty Gen[l] & Ab[p] of Rork – We hear today that W. Wakefield has forfeited his recognizances & gone off – so there is some *grace* among them. Such a scene of iniquity would have been revealed had the plot been exposed which succeeded in taking off that poor innocent Child! – for an innocent & simple-hearted creature she is – though very quick & clever to boot – *We all* wish that every *Wakefield*, Man & Woman, among them may be hung for they *richly* deserve it – But after all their vaunting they dare not stand a trial –

I have wandered from Mr Wordsworth to these worthless people – else I was going to say that we will deliver to him Sir Egerton's kind messages on his return & you must account for their not being acknowledged sooner. – I can give you no certain information as to our future residence (all that I am anxious about is that we may *not* build) – we have a faint hope that Mrs Huddlestone will directly refuse the offer, & that the Lady will be *ashamed* to *turn us out* – Mrs H. is expected at the Hall tomorrow with Mr & Mrs Hughes – and perhaps something may be determined during this visit – If we do *not* quit – or do *not* build – Mr. W. talks of a journey to Italy next year – but if we do build Cash will be wanting – and we must stay at home – & while houseless those who are not wanted to superintend the building must visit their friends – Apropos of Italy – *The Diary of an Ennunyèe** was written by a Lady when Governess in some Noblemans family *in perfect health* and instead of being dead is now the Wife of a Scotch writer!! I hope you have read the book & have been *taken in* – I am *proud* &

* By Mrs. Anna B. Jameson (1794–1860). It was written when she was Anna Murphy, governess in the family of Lord Hatherton with whom she travelled to Italy. Wordsworth's poems are much quoted in it. See his letter about it to M. J. Jewsbury, *Wordsworth Letters, The Later Years*, I, 249–50.

*conceited* enough to tell you *I was not* but what fools she & her Friends were to let the secret out as they did immediately – for it is a most discreditable hoax at best – & I cannot laugh at it as some do.

Mr Jackson is leaving Whitehaven so I fear your *Trade* will not be encouraged in that part. He has been very ill – and is about to return to Oxford as Bursar of his College (Queens) in the hope of restoring his health by the comparative leisure he will enjoy in that office – at Whitehaven he has had most laborious duties to perform – He is expected here – & I will not forget to canvas for you.

I hear very bad accounts of the Daisy's health – but as Mrs Monkhouse is my informant I hope she has as usual made an extreme case – when she says that she is most certainly consumptive – I know not where she is at present – but in the last Letter I had from her she said they were to spend the summer at Brighton – a bad situation for a consumptive patient. Mrs. M. was on the wing for the Continent – but *in Town* her flight was arrested (I suspect by Papa) tho' the indisposition of a Sister was the ostensible reason for giving up a scheme which 'had been recommended by the Doctors for her own health' but from all other accounts I learn that her health is as good as possible – Mr. M. saw her at Preston on his return from the election – She was as gay as a Lark & met him in her usual frank manner & as if they had never met but in the sunshine – Little Mary[5] he says is a most delightful child – greatly improve in all respects –

A sad sad loss indeed the Southeys have had by the death of that sweet Isabel – It is impossible ever to look or think upon Kate without being reminded of it – They had never been separated – and scarcely did one speak of one without the other – Mr & Mrs S. are better than can be expected – but it has cost them much to bear up – Mrs S. I fear will fall back into her former despondency* when the Summer is over & she is not called upon to appear cheerful among their numerous visitors – but she has borne her sorrow hitherto with more fortitude than on the death of Herbert. Sara[8] Coleridge set off for Town with Mr Gee about a month ago – but unluckily her mother accompanied her to Kendal & there persuaded her she was not fit for the journey, dosed her with Laudanum to make her sleep at a time when she could not have been expected to sleep if she had had the feeling of a stone – viz upon leaving her friends & home under affliction (for it was not more than a week after the poor Child's burial) and brought her back – leaving poor Gee to go alone – after having waited 17 days for her convenience & procured a Carriage in which she could travel at ease –

* Mrs. Southey's despondency amounted to a serious illness which in 1834 made it necessary for her to be confined, at York. See Letter 162.

& have the advantage of staying on the road at Night. Now S[ara] is in despair – Her Father disappointed – Her Lover too (but why does he not fetch her?) and Mama is to accompany her to Derby – So if you want to succor a distressed Damsel you may go thither & escort her up by *slow stages* which is the only mode by which she can travel. – O how I do pity her! & hope that if she gets rid of her Mother that she may turn out something useful before she ceases to be ornamental. I am sorry to tell you (but it is a secret) that she is engaged to one of her Cousins – he who has written the conceited work about West India* and who is very delicate in constitution – having had an affection of the spine – without fortune but what he can make by his wits & the Law – Now I am quite tired of gossip – I hope there is no scandal – tho' I know you will call me *cross* with regard to Sara[3] – but I am vexed at her weakness – & I am more *illnatured to you* because you do not like my favorite Edith so well – Mr W., I must tell you, is as much in love with E. as I am since he has seen more of her – I have not mentioned Dora[2] – she is sadly plagued with the tooth ache & looks like a Ghost – will not take care of herself – nor do anything to cure herself – so she is out of my good graces at present. Seriously Her Looks are sufficient to make one anxious – but do not notice this when you write – Our kindest regards to Col B[arrett] & Mr Egerton – with 50 kisses a piece to the trotts. God bless you all three – & believe me very truly your Friend S. H.

*Postmark: Kendal, Penny Post, TO PAY 1ᵈ ONLY 25 AU 1826*

## 118

*John Monkhouse Esqʳᵉ, Stow, nʳ Hereford*

*Rydal Mount, 19th Sepʳ.* [*1826*]

My dearest Cousin

You are indebted to a wet & a stormy day for this Letter for in spite of my desire to enliven your solitary fire side by a little of my *agreeable chat* (which was my intention as soon as I knew you had lost dear Dorothy's[1]) I have not till this morning found it possible. We

* *Six Weeks in the West Indies*, in 1825, by H. N. Coleridge *q.v.* The first edition was withdrawn on orders from the author's father, objection having been taken to what was considered a disrespectful reference to an aunt in the early pages. The second edition, 1826, appeared anonymously with the obnoxious reference deleted.

have been in such a bustle of *pleasure* it would have been could we have taken it by ease – but having so many friends to attend to unless it had been possible to make each limb do the duty of the whole body or the body could have been in two three places at a time, instead of enjoying the pleasure we have had severe *labour* – Last week began with a large Party at home Sir George [Beaumont] & Mr Rogers & some smaller folk dined with us – & all the rest of our neighbours came in the Evg when Dora's *Syren* Friend, Miss Ayling, charmed all hearts with Handel's music – Monday a wedding at the Crumps – some went to Breakfast – some to dinner – & all the neighbourhood joined the party in the Evg – then came another Day at home with Sir G. &c – then Wm M. & D. set off to Llagstone to a Christening – & I was left at home to entertain all comers, which were no few, & to escort Lady Farquhar & shew her the Lions, attend to Miss Cookson & poor Miss Honeyman who always comes unluckily when we are in a scramble – which is very mortifying – as there is no one in the world we are more disposed to shew attention to, or who better deserves it – so went on last week – & yesterday, Monday, we had a huge picnic party into Easedale – & came home to tea – Wm was not with us and poor Dora laid up with a cold – Wm in the midst of all this bustle busy among his verses – and only *agreeable by fits* – but he is gone off this morning to Keswick to visit Southey – & at the end of the week will join Dora at Halsteads if her cold is well enough for her to leave home – Sir G. & R. are at Keswick – we expect them back after their visit to Lowther is paid – and we are *threatened* with a *visitation* from *Mrs Coleridge* – & have had a Letter proposing a visit from Wms Welsh Friend Mr Jones – so when our *season* is to end I know not. This Evg I forgot to say we are to have a *route* at Mrs Luff's – to which Mary[1], Willy[2], and I *must* go let the equinoxial gale blow as it lists – and but for its fury I should have mounted Nab Scar this morning with Lady F. – I wish you were here to go with us this Evening – I think *Till*, who is *smitten* by Miss A., would have no chance with you – She is certainly a charming person – & it will be a shame if she does not become a wife & enliven some solitary batchelors fire side – such delightful spirits I never before saw – nor any one who was so *instantaneously* attractive – the dear little Lady F. is even more so to me – but she requires to be *known*, being more retired – but her countenance is so benign & so expressive of enjoyment that it is evident in a moment that you must love her *sometime* or *other* – She has won all hearts by her simple manners, & accommodating disposition – Always ready to enjoy whatever was proposed – never making any difficulties, & contented with all things – just like dear Dorothy[1]! She has seen every thing in the

Country on horse back or in a Cart, & never once complained of the jolting – she will, we fear, leave us on Thursday as her sons holidays are over – and she will go with great regret. Her Husband was soon tired of our country, & was not sorry when business called him to Town – tho' he still holds out a hope of returning – and if he does her stay will be prolonged – Walter is a fine spirited good natured youth – & never spent a happier holiday in his life – The Aylings have also a fine young fellow with them – a Nephew of Charlotte Smiths who is very clever & full of fun – Mr Ayling is also a very agreeable Person – of mild manners with a spice of humour – *Till* has had a succession of College Birds – but none of them so agreeable as himself. Poor Mr Jackson, tho' he has been in the Country, has been little among us – for his intended keeps close hold of him – I have often wished for poor *Quill* as well as you – for he would have been both 'useful & ornamental'* – He is however I dare say very happy amongst his sisters-in-law – some of whom he describes as being both pretty & agreeable. Elizabeth[3] Cookson is still with us – and I am glad to say that she has improved very much within the last fortnight – tho' I fear she will fall back again when she returns home – She has been so long accustomed to her own room there without anything to tempt her to leave it that I am convinced the excitement here has been useful – She always sits down to dinner with us – and enjoys company till 10 oC at night – & has frequently been up 9 hours at a time – Now I have given one half of my paper to ourselves & our doings it is time you will think that I should express some interest in your's – & I suspect that unless I am very *urgent* that we shall hear little of you *now* that our *chief scribe* has left you – dear Mary[2] must renew the correspondence – for we cannot tax your eyes very rigidly – and it is in vain to expect John[4] W. to write about others who never tells us half as much about himself as we wish to know – His Mother is very anxious to hear from you *how* he goes on – & she begs me to *entreat you* to discourage in him the habit, which his Aunt said he was inclined to, of sitting over the fire with his books. Tell him that Owen is going to Cambridge to attend Divinity Lectures – & is to be ordained as Mr Dawes' Curate – Derwent is also to be ordained to the curacy of his Cousin James D. Coleridge living in Cornwall –

We are somewhat in a fright respecting Agnes M [?] affairs – these are less important to you than to our dear Friends at Brinsop who have, I find, had their Lease signed – The head Owners will never be able to withstand the clamour of the manufactures – & in the end the latter will be the only part of the people who can *afford* to possess land – &

* Quoting Joanna.

we shall be a nation of white slaves at last. We have not heard from the Isle of *Manners** since Joanna's lively epistle which I believe was forwarded – nor indeed have [we] written to them – as postage is very expensive – and we have not ha[d] any Members near us lately – I am quite provoked that Southey will not make use of his privilege – it is being far too conscientious – especially as he cannot help his own Letters coming free. You will smile when I tell you that Joanna desired some hams might be sent to them from Liverpool! after all her reports of the Land of plenty they were going to – I hope this one winter will satisfy them – but till summer I should not wish them to return – who would cross such a dangerous passage for an uncertain object? – Three Vessels have been wrecked – 14 lives lost in one near Neverstone a week or two ago – it makes one tremble to think of it –

We rec[d] a Durham Paper from Bessy the other day – advertising a Div[d] of 5/– this I hope will not be the whole – sad indeed if it be – John[1] H's private debts also to be paid in full – How does this happen if those if the other partners are not also – of which there was no notification – I had a very kind and *creditable* Letter from M[rs] H. who with her poor Husband & Henry[2] are at Lodgings in Edinburgh – She says the fear of arrest first sent them thither – & they returned to be out of the way of all reports & comments – M[r] H. has suffered much in his health – but is something better – and she hopes that time will do something to restore his serenity of mind – what a strange affair it is† – I mean the *disunion* of the parties – I long to know the whole cause – but I fear we shall never come at the truth – both parties of course will make their own case the best – but in justice to the G.[1] Hutchinsons I must say they have spoken only with kindness & charity of all – M[rs] S[utton] alone with indignation concerning M[r] Place – What an odd thing that young G[2] should have missed Miss Mercer after all – *He* will eventually be as good a match for *her* as ever – but she has only 4000£!! Anne[1] H. is to be married to a M[r] Gide – a young attourney – I believe he is son to M[r] B. near Ledgefields – & I find that Jane's '*strackling*' Lover is constant – which shows some good in him – and if he does but follow his friend Geo Suttons example all may yet be well with her – otherwise she has a poor prospect – even her present poverty would be preferable – I wish we could know that they were all settled again in a home of their own – however humble – and what were their means of retaining that home – but no particulars come from them – & we are painfully in the dark. Do you ever hear from M[rs] M[onkhouse]? She is I suppose at Preston – She is a Letter in my debt so my conscience is at ease – for at her request I wrote her a long account of us all here

* Joanna and Henry Hutchinson. † The episode still eludes explanation.

some time ago – I expect to hear of some movement soon – perhaps she may favor you – as that will be the only excuse now for getting off – her health being so good – & her father unwilling to part with little Mary[5] – You will think we have been very unmindful about the School for little George[3] – but it occurred to me that if Mr Holmes' School was a *cheap* one and they keep the boys over the holidays it might suit – but I have yet had no opportunity of enquiring – Mr H. lives near Great Bridge – was Curate to Dr Saitherthwaite & is an excellent Man & Scholar – he married Mrs Richardsons sister Miss Sidebotham.

I have been talking with Miss Honeyman about the Yorkshire Schools – & she has given me so many instances of neglect towards the health & comfort of the Boys that has come under her own knowledge that they must not be thought of she says they are chiefly kept up by importation of *natural* Children from London. She says there is a good School at Ousely, a cheap one – & where there cannot be too much laxity – but the distance is great Mr Buchannan would make enquiry for you about Mr Holmes – But I fear it is too much of a classical school by Miss H's report.

Excuse the trial that this Letter will be to your eyes – & with kindest love to all at Brinsop & hopes of hearing that my Aunt & dear Mary[2] are in their best health – Thos[1] & you in good heart & the Bairns as happy as they deserve to be. I am & ever will be yours most affty S. H.

*Postmark: Kendal, Penny Post*

## 119

*Edward Quillinan Esq., Lee Priory, nr. Wingham, Kent*

*Rydal Mount,*
[*28*] *Sepr* [*1826*]

My dear Friend

Many thanks to the *Pearl* and the wet morning for your lively Letter – to the latter you are obliged for this my reply – for tho' we have no partridges to shoot here we have almost killed ourselves during the late fine weather with what *might* have been *pleasure* could it have been taken in moderation; but so numerous have been our visitors, and the '*claims upon our attentions*', that for the last two months it would have been desirable that each limb of us all could have performed the duty of the whole body. Never was there known here so delightful a season – we are become so confident *now*, that, if it should chance to rain in the evening or morning, we never fear a wet day – but rejoice in the sight of a cloud which *may* bring a freshening shower. The Country is most beautiful – and it is quite a *shame* that you have not visited it this year – for by all it has been agreed that fine weather is *finer* here than in any other climate in the world – for it is quite free from all annoyances – and most truly have we enjoyed it – but of ourselves hereafter – for I know the Pearl *was*, at least, uppermost in your thoughts when you wrote to me *for the purpose* of gaining some information – which I am sorry to say I cannot give for nobody here knew a word of the matter until her marriage was announced in the Papers – Mr & Mrs Hughes are at the Hall – they & Mr Stanley were as little in the secret as any body – and whether Mrs Atherley was her confidant or not we cannot learn – but I suspect *Mr A.* was not; & I guess she was too wise to consult him lest he, as heretofore, should have marred the plot. Miss Hughes has seen the Bridegroom in Town – &, according to her report, he is handsome & agreeable (but whether rich or not I could not learn) & a Lawyer. The Pearl spent the winter with the Hughes in Bath – & if she had a secret then kept it very close – and greatly do I admire her discretion – If I knew where to address her, & could previously learn that the *match* was *promising*, I would write to congratulate her – and most sincerely do I wish she may be happy. You *of course* will call upon her when you go to Town – so from you I shall expect a just & true account – Your Friend Mrs A will give you all necessary information – My dear Friend *I pity* your *forlorn situation* and should advise you to come hither & fall in love with Miss Ayling (who has bewitched 'old Till') if it were not that the '*Old Sir William*' always comes to mind when I am thinking what a nice lively Wife she would make – and, tho she is the delight of her Brother, what a pity it is that she is not married – for with all her accomplishments* she is a truly useful female of the old-fashioned kind. Every body male & female is delighted with her – so that I needed not to have singled out *Till* – for unlikely as he is to be charmed with anything but his own comforts – he is not more so than Mr Rogers who was smitten at Church with her beauty which is the least of her perfections – indeed she has not much pretentions to mere beauty – and she has passed the meridian – Our Dora is more bewitched than any one – she has neither eyes or ears for anything else – and her Mother sometimes says, in spite of her own love, 'I wish this Miss Ayling had never come hither'. How long they intend to stay I know not – I think they have been here

* Sara Hutchinson appears to share the sceptical views of Jane Austen's Elizabeth Bennet as to 'accomplishments'.

(at Spring Cottage) 3 weeks, Mr & Miss A. & a youth of the name of Fraser – a grand nephew of Charlotte Smith – very clever, handsome, & an excellent *sketcher*. Mrs Luff has had her house full – the Farquhars – Lady F. & her Son were with her 6 weeks – Lady F. was *my pet* – she suits my taste better than even Miss A. – then we have had Sir George Beaumont & Rogers who are now at Patterdale – tomorrow William will join them & go to Lowther where with Southey they are to spend a few days – at present we have Mrs Coleridge & Eliz^h[3] Cookson in the house all the *comers* & *goers* I must beg leave to omit – or I should fill my paper with their names – but they have crammed our rooms & occasioned parties by Land & water innumerable – besides there was a wedding at Allan Bank (not Mr Jackson & Miss C[rump] but a younger sister) and a christening at Cousin Dorothys[3] – where all and a part of this family were called upon to attend – numerous routes at Rydal – some dances &c at Ambleside which we declined – so after this catalogue you cannot suppose we live in retirement & *ease*. But enough of ourselves – only I must tell you that Mr Wordsworth's eyes have been cured by one of our visitors Mr F. Reynolds (son of the Dramatist) who prescribed the touching them with the blue stone* – which acted like magic upon them – & I never saw him look so well & *bonny* as he did yesterday, upon his return from Keswick, for many many years. – Mr Hughes has been making a call here – & says that even Mrs Atherley did not know a word of her sisters intentions till the marriage took place – that the Gent: is unexceptionable – & as he is the only Son of his father Mr H. believes that his pecuniary circumstances are such also – I have been interrupted by a long Letter from Miss W[ordsworth] who is at last on her way home – at present at Leamington with our sick friend Miss Jewsbury who is happily convalescent – from Leamington she goes to Coleorton – thence to Liverpool – & will I suppose end her visits at Preston tho' I suspect she will make a very brief one there. I wonder if Mrs M[onkhouse] was in the Pearls confidence – & had I *owed* her a Letter I should have written to ask the question – but I am not ambitious of a very frequent correspondence from that quarter – of which I have lately been rather apprehensive. All our Herefordshire Friends are well – & will at any time be most happy to see you & give you free range among the Pheasants – – Walter Farquhar had excellent sport at Shap – & *here* in snipe shooting – a capital shot considering his youth. I wish you would come & bring your Trotts for the winter – far better than sauntering away your

* Bluestone or copper sulphate effected a temporary relief to Wordsworth's eye condition which had distressed him as early as 1804. See *The Later Wordsworth*, by Edith C. Batho, 1933, for a full treatment of this subject.

time in Town – for I do not believe you will do much good in the wine Trade which I suppose is the excuse for going thither – You do not answer my question respecting Mrs L[ucas] – but do not suppose that I *blamed* you in either that or the other affair – I should not have *presumed* to do so – even had I doubted your *honor* or *discretion* which in these cases I did not.

Mr W. has no intention at present of visiting London – & I think it is more than probable we shall all content ourselves at home during the winter – whether we are to spend another summer here or not is still a mystery – but it must speedily be explained. – If we leave Rydal Mount we shall be thrown upon the wide world for the building is not begun.

Mr W. begs you will thank Sir Egerton Brydges for his kind message – & has desired me to give you a list of the works which he possesses & feels himself greatly honored by Sir E's intention of completing the set* – Our kindest regards to all – especially Col. B[arrett] and kisses to the Darlings – and I am very truly yours S. H.

*Anti critic* for Aug$^{t}$ 1821 – Mar. 1822.
*Res Lit:* Oct$^{r}$ 1820. May 1821– to Feb: 1822.
*Polyanthea*
*Cimelia*
*Gnomica* imperfect reaching to the 208 page.
*Odo, Count of Lingen* imperfect – 64 pages.
*Carmina Brugesiana*
*Joannis Pierii Valeriani de Litteratorum infeliccitati.*
*Epistola Francisci*
*Petrarchæ Posteritati*

*Postmark: Kendal Penny Post, 28 SE 1826*

# 120

*Edward Quillinan Esq., Lee Priory, nr Wingham, Kent*

*Rydal Mount, Oct$^{r}$ 5th [1826]*

My dear Friend

This is the very first moment in which I could sit down *in comfort* to reply to your Letter – for poor Dora has been ill – very ill – since

* The sale catalogue of Wordsworth's library does not show any additions to this list.

sunday last and not till this morning could we say she was convalescent – I *hope* she *is* so – & then the state of weakness to which she is reduced will not cause the same apprehension which it does at this moment – and by good nursing she will soon be restored to strength – but I am not yet *quite sure* that the disease, tho' abated, is removed. She herself says she is almost well –

You will guess after the above report that I have not had time or opportunity to make *particular* enquiries – & you must excuse a very brief Letter at present – only if you really are in earnest about a northern Journey no time must be lost – two of your questions I can answer – 1st the Carriage *you are most welcome to use* for this or any other journey (Mr W. not doubting that you will be very grateful for the permission) and for Houses you may have great choice – Ivy Cottage and Spring Cottage will *both* be empty – but I do not suppose you *could* occupy either of these – I am sure it would not be *good* for you tho' you used to *talk* of inhabiting Ivy Cot again I advise you not to think of it – but should you feel otherwise Tillbrook is gone to Cambridge & with him you must treat – Allan Bank is ready for a Tenant – and Mr Kings House is to be let – but without furniture – at Ambleside Mrs Whites House to be let furnished – not the old one – but a larger & more comfortable one near it – & I believe very tidily furnished – Mrs Hardens Cottage, at Rotha Bridge, to be let furnished – it is a beautiful situation & the house tho small well *managed* & airy – but no grounds & it literally *hangs over the* River – I like it the best of any of the Lodging Houses in the Country save Tills – & the rent is reasonable (no coach-house or Stable) – Last of all Mrs Luff would let you have her House for *2 years* – but the rent would be high – & I say it would be only a '*misery Trap*' (for your Trotts) with all her *knick nacks* – she could not let house field &c for less than 120£ including Taxes – & I think she would be very foolish to let it at all – it is far too expensively *set out* for any such purpose – Neither should *I* chuse to take it – one does not care whether the furniture is handsome or not in Lodgings. But it is an excellent House & not wanting in any accommodation – far too nice for a batchelor – & even I, an old Maid, would not hire it for *myself*.

Now perhaps after I have written all this I shall hear that you have some new scheme in your head & have forgotten your application – I dare not give you any advice – were I to say it was good for you to come I should bring Lee Priory upon my head – for they cannot bear to part with the Darlings I am sure – Cabaloa would not have appeared such a *frightful* distance – I wish you had got it – especially as I shall not *perhaps* be a *gainer* by your residence here this winter having some thoughts of going to Herefordshire before Xmas – but there will be plenty left behind to *pet* the Trotts – One thing I must not forget to say (lest you should make up your mind to a permanent residence here) that the Children cannot be rec$^{d}$ at Miss Dowlings School except as boarders day & night – you used to *talk* of that school with reference to them – so I mention this that you may know that a Governess will be requisite.

Mr Carr has been here and speaks very hopefully of Dora – who seems *in spirits* so much like herself today that I trust, with God's blessing, she will soon be so in body. Miss W[ordsworth] is at Coleorton – we expect her home in the course of a fortnight – Henry Crabbe Robinson *her Lover* is here – Celestial Blue is safely arrived at Highgate where she is on a visit – but is soon to go to her Cousins (Mrs Pattison) – Excuse this scrawl – I have many other Letters that must be written today – The Mail Coach passed thro to Whitehaven this morn$^{g}$ for the first time – Farewell I hope I have said all that is necessary – Every body's best remembrances – ever very truly your's S. H.

*Postmark: Kendal Penny Post 6 OC*

## 121

*Edward Quillinan Esq$^{re}$., Lee Priory, nr Wingham, Kent*

[*11 Nov. 1826*]

My dear Friend

We have heard, from many quarters, that Trade & Commerce are reviving, & our expectations have been highly raised by an account of the flourishing state of the *Fustain* [Fustian] Manufactory in the venerable City of Canterbury –

*Rydal Mount Nov$^{r}$ 9th 1826* –

The above *wise* paragraph was dictated to me by William some weeks ago (when he was great-coated & setting off over Kirkstone to Lowther) after I had read him the speeches contained in the Paper you sent us – I must not omit telling you he was greatly pleased with this attention – 'Now' he often repeated 'I like this – it looks as if our amusement were not indifferent when absent friends think of us in these trifles' &c – –

I took up my pen at that time intending to write more fully about your talk of flight hither – for it seemed that, in the anxious state of mind in which I had answered your Letter, I had not half replied to your questions – or given you any encouragement to put your plan in execution – but since that time our *anxieties* respecting poor Dora have been so much encreased, that I shrank from the task of writing to any one lest I might communicate *them* – I hope now I may say she is convalescent – but till within the last few days I could not – her debility was so great, & her progress towards amendment so slow, that we were afraid she would ultimately sink under it – Nothing but the advanced state of the year would have prevented us from removing her to a warmer climate – and even now, if it were prudent, we wish much to try change of air – Her nerves are very weak – and she now suffers much from Tooth ache – tho' she has had a Dentist who has done all he can for her – All else well – Mr W's eyes perfectly so –

I take it for granted that you have been induced by the advice & inclinations of your Friends, or perhaps *overruled*, to give up your scheme of returning to Westmorland for the present – though I hope not altogether – poor Dora was never told of your intention & therefore has been spared the disappointment – for weak as she was she would have been wild for joy with half a hope of having the Trotts so near her – however I shall not be quite at ease until I hear that they are well & that in this sickly time their health has not prevented the further thoughts of your scheme – when I wrote I did not know that Tillbrooks Cottage was to be occupied during the winter by Mr Ayling & his young Friend – who returned hither & took possession, last week, after having attended Miss Ayling to her sister's house in Leicestershire.

Miss Wordsworth returned home on Monday last after nine months absence – She is charmed with Herefordshire and I find there is an excellent house at liberty near Brinsop in the midst of *all the abundance of* game which you have heard so much about – and at B. they have no sportsman so you cannot do better but go and look after it and they would be delighted to have you for a neighbour – for I despair of your ever having resolution to set up your rest here –

Our poor dear Pearl – how shall I tell you that she is very ill – that the Drs give no hope of her recovery – alas! I have had many a sad shock lately – two of my eldest Brother's daughters have been at the brink of the grave – one of them is I hope recovering – but the other like poor Miss Stanley is in a confirmed consumption – this last sad news reached me through a Letter from Mrs M[onkhouse]. . . . I can scarcely believe it – so soon cut down that beauteous flower! Mrs M— begged me to write to Mrs A. as she knew it would gratify her – & I have done so also a few lines as cheerful as I could to the poor Bride to enquire after her health – & send my tardy & untimely congratulations. . . . Mrs M. is gone to Clifton – taken a House for a year there. She writes to me upon the spur of an occasion like this – but does not draw towards me habitually – My kindest love & kisses to the Darlings from me & *the rest* – & our united regards to the Family – & believe me ever very truly yours S. H.

Pray write soon – but do not notice our late fears respecting Dora – as she always reads your Letters.

*Postmark: Kendal Py Post, 11 NO 1826*

## 122

*Mr Monkhouse, Stow, near Hereford*

*Tuesday, Feb[y] 6th* [*1827*]

My dear John

I hope my sad habit of procrastinating will not prevent your receiving this before you leave home – as it is necessary you should be able to give a reply to the Bill which André has troubled you with – I have frequently had Hats from his Shop bought & paid for by other People – the *last* by myself in March or Ap[l] 1823 just before we went to Ramsgate which I paid for at the time £1.13 as my old Pocket Book of that year testifies – the date of his Bill is Jan[y] 1st 1824 else I should have supposed that the Shop Woman, of whom I bought it, had forgotten to account for it & it had been booked in the Ev[g] when sent to Glos: Place – Dora had a new hat about that time – but it was bought at your Brother's Hatter – I intended it should have been bought at Andrés but they thought his too expensive. I hope you will succeed in *insensing* them with the truth that we are honest & honorable people – for I should be sorry to find *them* otherwise – & certainly they would lose my *excellent* custom & all that of my friends whom I have recommended if they do not believe my statement. So desirous was I to account for the mistake that I fancied I recollected one had been sent for D.'s approbation by Andrés & returned – she is positive that no such thing was the case – The sum of all however is that no hat is owing for by me – & I hope I shall not be obliged to pay for one. –

I shall be most happy to hear that you have no trouble about this foolish affair – and that you will get all your own comfortably settled – tho' it grieves me sadly to think that so much loss is to be borne exclusively by you – however knowing your contented spirit I trust you will never feel it as such – and for whatever you take upon yourself voluntarily the feeling that you are acting according to your own sense of right will be your recompense – tho' I must add that I think your notions are a little too *refined* – but perhaps you will say I know not what I am writing about so a truce to the subject.

We are all well at present save poor Dora who is still confined to her room in consequence of cold caught when we thought her almost quite well – When spring comes I hope she will revive – but while she is obliged to keep such close quarters we cannot expect that either strength or appetite can return – thankful we are that her cough is nearly gone – It is so long before we can hope for weather fit for a removal that nothing can be decided upon – else I think no place could be better for her than your cheerful home – & bright climate – we have till now wretched weather rain & fog for days & weeks together now it is bright & frosty – pleasant for the strong but too sharp for Invalids – I hope all is going on well at Brinsop – tho' they do not *trouble* us with so many Letters as we could wish – Nor of Joanna have we heard lately – What a fine flourish there has been in the Papers about her *Friend Bolivar*. By the bye I wish you could get her Bonds into your hands while you are in Town – it is very uncomfortable to her not to know where they are – and when she has written to those Nicholsons her Letters are not noticed – Perhaps E. Addison would hold them for her and apply for her dividends if they are ever paid – or your Bankers – now she has to apply always to my Brother John[1] & he poor Man (between ourselves) seems so much overwhelmed by his own distresses as to be unable to think of any body else – Henry[1] has not heard a word about his annuity the value of which would be paid in full at the time the private debts are paid – I have advised him to write to Mr Dickson as John makes no reply. In a Letter which I had from Mrs Sutton a week ago she tells me that both *Bessy* & Jane are in a very precarious state – I had hoped that poor Bessy's disease being removed she would recover but for Jane I fear there is no hope at all – her complaint has been of too long standing to shake off – Poor Things no doubt the troubles of their father have had a baneful effect on their constitutions – What a kind Friend they have had in Mr Sleigh at whose house both have been nursed! –

John[4] Wordsworth is returned to Oxford to attend the Divinity Lectures – which commenced on the 3rd – I suppose he will remain there about 3 weeks or a month – thence he is to go on a visit to Cambridge – & I think his father wished him also to perform his promise of going to Mr Gees – but I dare say he will not – tho' he is less fond of coming home or rather *talks* more of 'seeing the world' than he used to do – of course you will find him out & pay him a visit either as you go or return – he will be heard of at New Col: or at W. Jackson at Queen's – but he is now in Lodgings & will be most happy to see you & you can never have a better opportunity of seeing Ox$^{d}$ thoroughly as now by his & M$^{r}$ J. help – Pray write – or desire Mary[2] to write, to tell me how long you will be in Town – for I have not got my little Box of presents for the Girls yet sent – but perhaps I may have an opportunity while you are in Town – for it is too small to trust by the Carrier & not worth the expence of coach fare – & as I know it will give *such* delight that I am anxious it should be in their hands.

I shall send also some Autographs for M$^{rs}$ Dew – If she wants any others than M$^{r}$ W's I could perhaps furnish her with some of the celebrated – Edith Southey is still with us – she has been here a month & we should be glad to keep her another – & she happy to stay for Dora & she enjoy themselves much together indeed D will be *lost* without her – I am to go home with her to make a longish visit – but direct to me here – as I hope for the sake of others that she will not depart soon – Southey is to come for us – God bless you – & with all our very best love & kind wishes to you & every one at Brinsop ever most truly yours S. H.

Does Mary[2] remember my commission about the *Feathers*? & if [so] can she execute it without much trouble?

*Postmark: Kendal Penny Post*

# 123

*Mrs Hutchinson, Brinsop Court, Hereford*

*Feby 11th* [*1827*]

My dearest Mary[2] –

I hope John[2] has not set out – if so transcribe my little note to him which you will find at the end of this sheet – I find I must not complain of not hearing oftener from you nevertheless I cannot help feeling longings – tho' I refrain from expressing them – we are all well except Dora who still continues an Invalid – indeed she has been very unwell – & is as weak as possible to conceive of one having assertedly no violent disease upon her – since her cold she has not been allowed to take her strengthening medicines till within the last few days – & yesterday returned for the first time to the use of the warm bath – which will I hope have the same good effect as heretofore – tho' she fainted at coming out of it – you know what an anxious creature her poor mother is – & may guess that all this anxiety is not very cheering to an Invalid – but she poor thing keeps up wonderfully – and she has happily a most delightful companion in Edith – but as the Spring advances I hope she will be able to take the air – & that I am sure will restore her appetite & strength sooner than any other thing – she has not been out of her room for 5 weeks except for an hour or two in the Evening during the two last.

From Joanna we had a cheerful Letter on friday – the injury to her hip is exactly what we had anticipated – she cannot lift her leg up stairs but drags it – yet she says that on level ground she can walk better & hopes for very great relief from the warm bath which she had once used – Their expences – every thing included are 30/– per week – and she is in good heart about their income – From my Brother John[1] they had a satisfactory ac[t] respecting H[enry]'s[1] annuity which would all be p[d] with interest in due time – and as Columbians are *looking up* she will be in still better heart – Her Letter was written upon one from poor M[rs] Swaine – who still holds to the intention of visiting the *Island* in summer. Her account of the poor Girls at Stockton is deplorable – Janes case seems hopeless – & Bessy's very precarious – the latter does not know the nature of her complaint which is Dropsy – & John begs that we may not allude to the hopelessness of Janes in our Letters – Poor Man! what a year has this last been to him – but Gods will be done!

I grieve to tell you that we have lost our dear good Friend Sir G. Beaumont – He died last Wednesday of Erysepilas – caused by checked perspiration – We had a Letter from Lady B. after his seizure in which though she expressed her resignation still it was not without apparently a hope of his recovery – 2 days after a Letter from M[r] Mereweather announced the fatal termination – & the day following came a long letter from Lady B. herself written the day after his death with perfect calmness – & in the sweetest possible spirit of resignation. She begs to be left quite alone – no one of her connection to come near her for a time except Miss Wells who is always at C[oleorton] and we trust with Gods blessing she will continue in that same state of mind which it seems her wish & endeavour to preserve – But its a sad separation – for ½ a Century at Shirleys she has been his constant companion – but she draws comfort from the idea of his not having outlived his faculties & enjoyments – & certainly had she gone first he would have been most forlorn. She clings like a true christian as she is to all that part of her lot which exemplifies the goodness and mercy of providence – & this will uphold her. We know nothing further – but are assured that she will not be disturbed at Coleorton – & I hope she will not in her great generosity think of giving it up to the heir as she must know that Sir G had much rather she enjoyed it – if she can –

We have had a cheerful Letter from dear M^rs^ Clarkson. Mr C. is out of all danger & recovering rapidly – & Tom[5] is gaining great reputation in his profession – Perhaps John[2] may see him in Town – I sent my little parcel by M^r^ Ladyman to Budge Row last week – I hope they will take care to keep it dry as there are needles in it which will rust & greatly spoil the beauty of one of the articles contained in it. You will smile when you see how *wisely* we have been employed – but will not wonder when I tell you that those trifles have been wished to amuse a sick room.

I long to hear how the dear Boys take to School & like their Prig of a Master – I am vexed at M^r^ Cooksons decision – as made for Hannahs sake or yours – because I think you would have been a natural advantage to each other. From what M^rs^ Carr says of Miss Scambler I do not think she would do amiss for a year or two if nothing but scholarship were in question but then she must be so wanting in *manners* & *notions* from having associated out of school with vulgar people & in her mothers untidy hands – that she could not be expected to keep the children to tidy ways – & therefore she would not do; if she had been a year or two entirely from home I should not have hesitated to recommend her – for tho' not bright she is very steady to her Books – I have good news to tell you of M^r^ W. Jackson – he is appointed tutor of his Col. & also (upon Wms recommendation by the B^p^ of London) one of the Whitehall Preachers – an office this last of little or no compliment but a great feather in his Cap – especially as the B^p^ was referred to and satisfied by the B^p^ of Cheshire as to his qualifications for the discharge of the duty – it is only to preach 4 sermons a year – I hope *John*[2] will stay a day or two with John[4] at Oxford as he goes up to Town – probably John's time will be out before he returns – Pray write soon – I hope dear old Aunty is well & your nursery thriving – We shall be most anxious about the decision of Parliament respecting the Corn Laws – surely the Land owners will be true to themselves. May God bless you all – & that we may hear good news it is & soon – every bodys best love – ever most truly yours S. H.

My d^r^ John[2] *Maffy* you would call me upon observing that I had not inserted the date of André's Bill – not having it by me at the time I wrote. It is Jany 1st 1824 whereas my last hat bought there was in

March or Apr 1823 – I will thank you to purchase for the Boys '*the broad stone of Honor or Rules for the Gentlemen of England*' published by Rivington Waterloo Place & St. Pauls Ch Yd. There is a spurious *broadstone* – but the true one is written by Kenelm Digby Eq. – who by the bye has become a Catholic since the book was published. it is too *wise* a Book for the Boys at present tho' there are parts in it even entertaining to them – but I wish them to have a present along with the ones for the Girls – the book will be a valuable acquisition to the library of the Adults – God bless you – S. H. Ours is 2nd ed pubd in 23* – but there may be a later – *this* has additions since the first Ed.

Excuse this scrawl written in a great hurry. I gave 2/– to a brief (the first time in my life) today at Church because it was for a *Herefordshire farmer* who had suffered by fire.

*Longman* is printing Wms Poems.†

## 124

*M^r^ Monkhouse, Stow, n^r^ Hereford*

*Keswick, 18th March* [1827]

My dear John

You need not thank Mary Wordsworth for *setting me on* to write to you – for I shall '*afflict*' you with a dull Epistle having lost all wish for Letter-writing & am come into my Brother Johns[1] opinion that it is a very foolish thing – & yet no body in the World (Mary W. excepted) likes to *receive* Letters better than I. –

My business however must be disposed of. 'M^r^ Prince' (I give you W.W.'s words) will not admit that he ever rec^d^ the £18.15 which was paid to him on M^r^ Gees account (as stated in M^r^ T. M. acc^t^ with us settled Oct^r^ 23rd 1823 & also as appears in his book) '*Sep^r^ 18th 1823* paid M^r^ Prince' . . .

I am vexed to have to plague you with this – but there is no hurry till you go to Town – John[4] Wordsworth is in Town at present. He met M^r^ Johnson at Cambridge who invited him to take his house in his very home – and if you are not very long in paying your visit to Town you may probably meet – it would be a great pleasure to him. . .

* *The Broad Stone of Honour; or Rules for the Gentlemen of England . . . with the alterations from the first Edition*, K. H. Digby, 1823. Wordsworth and Coleridge are quoted with approval in the Prologue.

† The five volume edition of 1827.

I had a Letter or rather a note from the Ephesian Matron* (as W^m^ calls her) signifying that early next month she hoped to be happy with D^r^ *Parr's* Dick – supposed I must have heard of her intentions from you – & with remembrances to M^r^ W. & the family concluded without even naming dear little Mary[5] – but memory served before she closed the Letter to send a kiss for her – M^r^ Horrocks told James Cookson that she had had the scarlet fever – & this made her neglect more inexcusable when 'Tunt' wrote her (a long Letter) poor Dora was at death's door – and I scarcely had cheerful news to tell of any body – but no matter! – I only wish I had not the Letter to answer.

I shall certainly be as brief as she – & still take care to tell her that the news did not come from you – but that I had heard it in our own neighbourhood – but that I looked upon it as Preston Gossip which had travelled to Ambleside – turn we to worthier Subjects –

I have been here a fortnight – dear Edith was a kind companion & Nurse to poor Dora for two months – and I am glad to say we left her convalescent – & since we hear that she has been out as far as the *Nab* & has not caught cold – but the weather is sadly against her – & there is no prospect of her being able to change the air yet, even if she were strong enough to move – but her weakness is extreme – with that short ride, Miss W[ordsworth] says, she was more tired than if she *her self* had mounted Helvellyn – & so exhausted that she went to bed & slept for some hours – if she does but keep clear of more colds I hope she will do well – but her state is still very precarious – Poor M^rs^ Southey has not recovered the loss of her Daughter – Southey is very cheerful – & busy – & the kindest creature in the world – and Cuthbert is a Sweet boy – I wish he was not so nice for I seem to like him far too well –

I am rejoiced to hear such good accounts of our Nephews & hope they will continue to like School – The Doctors 2 Boys (I know you like University News) eldest & youngest – stood among upwards of 40 for a Craven Scholarship – After long & weary examinations they (examiners) decided upon reducing the No to 4 – & among the 4 picked out as the best were John[6] & Chris – the others a Son of Capel Lof[f]t & a Leigh or Lee of Trinity – the D^r^ declined being an Ex-

* *The Ephesian Matron*, 1796, by Isaac Bickerstaffe, the Irish dramatist, was a successful 'Comic Serenata, after the manner of the Italian', for which Dibdin wrote the music and in which he played the centurion. The reference may be to this well known popular version of Petronius's story or to the original. The mourning widow in her husband's tomb, hastily re-marrying, is the same character in both, her twentieth-century counterpart being found in Christopher Fry's *Phoenix Too Frequent*. It is interesting to note that Coleridge, referring to *Ephesian Matron* in a notebook, suggests that 'an excellent Farce might be made'.

aminer but he said he thought the L's would beat the W's – but as it is the triumph is not small – besides John[6] has got one or 2 Scholarships before – Our John[4] I ought to tell you is at the Central School Baldwin's Gardens Grays Inn Lane – & if you go there you will see Johnnys* *very very* nice wife –

I have not heard from *Mona* for some time – Joanna I fear does not get so '*well away*' as she expected – and does not like to confirm our fears that she will be *limpsby* (as she would say) for Life –

Mr Southey had a Letter from Joh.[1] H. last week with a parcel of his *vaccine* Verses† – which for the first time I was glad to see as indicative of an improvement in his spirits – He wrote to me about three weeks ago just before the fall of snow to ask me to go to see him at Grassy Nook – & I with my own will should have complied but luckily I was overruled by prudent council – & afterwards he wrote approving of my determination as poor Bessy had had a relapse & Mrs H. being about to join Lucy at Grassy Nook he should not be so solitary but hoped to see me when the weather was warmer – A melancholy visit it will be! but I will not shrink from it – Pray write soon tho' I must trust you are well – My Kindest & best love to every one at Brinsop – & to your neighbours my regards – and may God bless you all – Ever most truly yours S. H.

. . . I have not said any thing of Edith for words are wanting – she is beyond all praise – Sara[3] C. (celestial *blue* as Q. calls her) is at Highgate with her Father.

*Postmark: Keswick*

## 125

*Edward Quillinan Esqr., 12 Bryanstone Street,*
*Bryanstone Square, London*

*Rydal Mount, Apl 10th* [*1827*]

My dear Friend

The sight of your handwriting gave a lively sensation of pleasure throughout the whole house, & the arrival of your Letter was announced at my room door on Sunday Morning before I was out of it – I need not say we were happy to find that you had escaped the late

* i.e. the wife of Mr. Johnson the Master of the Central School.

† On John Hutchinson's verses, cf. Letter 78, p. 232 and note.

storms & were safeley in old England again – and that you had heard good news of the Darlings.

We had a busy Day yesterday among your '*Effects*', which are by this time at Kendal – all packed together in the military chest. Mr Cookson will forward them by the best conveyance – & I desired him to pay the carriage to Town, which will save you at least one third – the difference between the charges to Tradesmen & Gentry – when I know exactly on what day they will arrive, & where you are to enquire after them, I will write again – and also send the keys in a frank.

I hope you will be comfortable & happy in your new home – & not be too much *fashed* with your business – we think your scheme of sending the Children to a day School a very nice one, both for them & yourself – but *think* you will want somebody to look after them & Eliza, & your *roguish* London Servants, & take care of your *property* – & it has just come into my head that I could recommend a person, as housekeeper, who would be entirely trust-worthy – a widow upwards of 50 – of respectable connections, who has had much sorrow, & has been robbed of her little independence by an unprincipled Brother in Law – Her Children are all in the way of providing for themselves – Mrs Hutchinson has known her for 15 years – & she has been with her during her late confinement & for many months last winter, & speaks of her in the highest terms – I too know her well – & a more kind-hearted & honorable person does not breathe – She would require little but a comfortable home, & would make herself thoroughly useful – & in your absence you might leave your children to her care with perfect confidence – She has had, since the death of her husband, the care of a widower & his family – but he is now dead & the Children dispersed among their relatives. I do not know *for certain* whether she is disposed to take another situation – but I believe she is at present without a home of her own – & her Daughter, who has been educated in London for a Governess, is to go to Mrs Hutchinson, in that capacity, at Mid-summer – If you have any inclination or *need* to profit by my (*perhaps* officious) interference in your domestic arrangements, Mrs Hutchinson ('Brinsop Court Hereford') will give you further information – & Mr Monkhouse who will be in Town soon will also tell you that Mrs Urwick, the person in question, is one of the 'best creatures in the world' – She would not do for a *govern*ess – but your children would not but profit under the superintendence of a woman whose manners are gentle & her heart tender & benevolent – & who would not, I would venture my life, give you any *plague* in any way – If I were not sure of this I should not have ventured to suggest the plan – my last attempt to serve you in this way having failed. (She would live in the Nursery & not need a housekeeper's establishment).

We were highly amused with your report of 'Mrs *Marries Nick*'* & glad she had the *grace* to shrink from the sight of you – Pray was little Mary[5] with her – or where has she left the Child? Tell me all that you learn of her from Mrs A[therley]. . . . Poor Thomas[2] Monkhouse! – but *entré nous* – . . .

Now for ourselves – Dora is much better – is able to take an airing every day, when the weather serves – and will, I hope, be strong enough to join a *choice* & *agreeable* party which, Deo volente, will set out for Harrowgate about the end of May – consisting of the Poet Laureate, his Wife, 3 daughters & little Son† – & your friend whom they *impertinently* call 'Hutton'. Dora has set her heart upon the scheme – & says that à la Horrocks it will make her quite well – or rather she *will be well* as such are the conditions upon which she is to be allowed to go – Edith & she are such tender friends that they have set their hearts upon it – and as we are to have private Lodgings & no dissipation – the change of air will we hope quite restore her, & enable her to spend the rest of the summer at home – but she is not to *winter here* again but to go to Herefordshire, & the neighbourhood of Bristol in the Autumn – She desires her kindest regards to you & the Darlings – and we have lamented greatly that we could not procure anything here to send them, as a remembrance of us, when the chest was packed off. – Mr Wordsworth's eyes continue *quite well*. The last corrections of the volumes were sent off yesterday – and they will soon be out – A copy is ordered to be sent to Lee for Col. Barrett – It was ordered to be directed to Sir E. also as we supposed he was in Ireland – but you can order it to be sent from Longmans to him wherever he is –

Can you recollect *if* on Newyears day (*1824* I think it was – the new-years day when Dora, you & I were out shopping) we called at Andrés the Hatter in Bond St & chose a Hat – He has sent me a bill for one dated on that Day – the last I had from him was got in the preceeding March or Ap[l], just before we went to Ramsgate – & paid for at the time as my book shews – but I have an indistinct recollection that I chose one for Dora, & it being too small (& no larger were to be had there) Mr M advised her to have one at his Hatters & it was sent back – but she says, *no such thing*, that it was only *talked of* – at any rate *I owe him* nothing & if you do [not] recollect this circumstance I will not notice

* Mrs. Paris Dick, i.e. formerly Mrs. Thomas Monkhouse. I have deleted a passage on the insincerity of the Horrockses; it is repeated in the next letter, No. 126.

† i.e. Southey, Mrs. S., Edith, Kate, Bertha and Cuthbert.

it – but not being satisfied [my]self, without your assurance, I should think it disingennuous not to try to explain the mistake – Do not forget to answer this – Mr M[onkhouse], to whom the bill was sent, has promised to call & rectify it if he can.

I saw in the Papers that Egerton had taken orders – I hope he will do honor to his cloth – His handsome face in the pulpit will be likely to do execution among the female part of his Audience – *Our* John[4] I suppose intends to follow his example – but is not likely to be successful in the same way. He is not yet at home. He spent a month in Town – from thence went to York – & is now visiting his Uncle & George Sutton and other Durham friends –

With regard to the Bust Mr W[ordsworth] *can* get another at the same *price* – but he will not ask Till to *buy* it (It would not be *becoming* he says) – therefore you must write to T. & say that you [are] about to take it away unless he wishes for a copy – in which case the expence of carriage & packing will be spared to both of you. He will most likely to be in Town at Easter & you will hear of him at the University Club House. – I hope you do not mean to involve yourself so deeply in Business as never to find time to come to see us again – or taking a shooting at the Stow or Brinsop where I am sure you will always give pleasure by your company. Pray do not *miss* Mr Monkhouse when he is in Town – & go with him to see our friends the Lambs – & remind him to look at the Angerstien Gallery where our dear Friends Sir George Beaumonts Pictures also hang. I forgot to tell him this when I wrote last.

Mr W. bids me thank you for your attention about the Carriage – but, as it is very uncertain when if ever he can avail himself of your kindness, begs that you may use it & dispose of it yourself – as it is folly to keep it to spoil – Miss Wordsworth is at Kendal – I sent her your Letter which would give her as much pleasure as the rest of us – My Sister is quite well gone off with her Husband this fine morn[g] (but we have no heat here to make woolen Stockings useless & have had a sad stormy & wet winter) to *swear* & make calls at Calgarth, Rayrigg, &c – but all would send their love if they were here with mine & Doras – God bless you & your's! ever truly S. H.

*Postmark: Kendal Py Post, 12 AP 1827*

# 126

*Mr Monkhouse, Stow, nr Hereford*

[*8 April, 1827*]

My dear John

My best thanks for your kind letter – & all the *good news* it contained – & the next I hope will bring us better of poor old Aunty – & that the Spring will revive & invigorate her – & that with Gods blessing she will be able to enjoy Marys[1] & Doras[2] company when they visit you but which will not be till the autumn or early in the winter—as it is fixed if nothing unforeseen prevents that they are to winter among their southern Friends – Dora is much better, & is in hopes that she may accompany the Southeys to Harrowgate at the end of may – whither they are all going, & I along with them – & the Girls will not be happy if she is not to be of the Party – & as it is a health scheme & not a pleasure one – if Dora is able to go it is hoped it will be of great use to her – & she also has set her heart upon it –

You have been so much interested about dear Lady B[eaumont] that I have been moved to write to you today to communicate the substance of her two last Letters to us – but I will transcribe them at the end of this that you may have her own words – She is in London & will be there till may – being sole executrix she has been obliged to attend to business.

I have had a letter this Morning from Quillinan who is arrived in Town & before you arrive there will be quite settled at 12 Bryanstone St Bryanstone Sq. where I am sure you will be most welcome – & you must give his little Girls many kisses for me – I will give you an extract from his Letter too which will amuse you – 'I called last Evg at Mrs Atherleys (Miss Stanley's Sister) intending to get some tea there; for she is a charming person & a particular favorite with me. Lo & behold! when the door was opened the footman said that Mrs A. was at home & at tea with a Lady. very well said I boldly (for tea was just what I wanted) go & mention my name to her. He did so & came down with a message that "Mrs A. was particularly engaged & would be glad to see me another time." – Away I went muttering wise saws of the caprice & instability of womans mind. – Three short months ago, said I, I seemed welcome here, & now this pretty woman turns me out of doors without the least ceremony. Oh fie Mrs A.! – This morning while I was dressing Mr Atherly called & solved the riddle. Your

Ephesian Matron, your brisk Widow, Miss Jane Horrocks that *was* – M^rs^ M[onkhouse] that *has* been, M^rs^ Morris Nick, no, M^rs^ Paris Dick that *is*, was there & threw herself into such an agitation at the idea of my coming up that M^rs^ A. perforce denied me admittance. What could M^rs^ Dick be afraid of? Poor little Dear I wouldn't have hurt her.' Well, Dora & I say we are glad to find that she had the *grace* to shrink from the sight of him. I wonder if she will like to face the *Major* I think he must have changed his opinion of her – since the talk of this marriage all Ambleside have let loose their tongues – for here are several families connected with Preston – and all the stories of the Ladies feigned illnesses &c are well known – even little Annes are all put on, they say, & not one of the sisters are free from the charge of using these means, of gaining their ends & working upon the feelings of father & husbands – alas! alas! one had need be ashamed of ones sex – & tell yours to beware – for there is a beautiful lady in this, or rather *was*, neighbourhood who can to serve her turn hold herself stiff & motionless as in a trance for 24 hours!! – One had need had a Lady B. to comfort one –

The Poems* will be out in a week – 2 copies are ordered to be sent to Budge Row – one for you, & the other for little Tom[3] from his Godmother – It is not worth while for me to write to André because you will be in Town so soon – & if I am right in my recollection about the Hat sent for Dora it will not be ingenuous to take no notice of it & this I can ascertain from Q. who was out with us on Newyears day (the date of A's bill) & will recollect probably if we were at that Shop – D. is positive we were not & that it was only *talked* of – that your Brother recommended his hatter as cheaper.

I came home from Keswick last Saturday week – after having spent a month very pleasantly to myself, & had the assurance from my good friends there that my company had been of great service to poor M^rs^ Southey & on this account I was induced to consent to accompany them to Harrowgate – I wish you had nothing better to do than join us there – for as Edith says we must press another man or two into our service or poor Papa will have hard work to attend to so many Ladies – She tries her best to induce W^m^ to go – but even her influence, which is very *great with him*, will not prevail – so she says she must be contented if she can wheedle Dora from him. . . .

But I must quit my gossip or I shall not leave room for more worthy matter – so God bless you all! & love to all ever your's S. H.†

Ask M[ary][2] if she rec^d^ a p^r^ of Shoes in a frank for my name sake?

* The five-volume edition of 1827.

† There follows Lady Beaumont's Letter.

Silhouette of Sara Hutchinson at about fifty-two years of age

Let us hear from you – & when in Town remember me to all friends in Mecklen$^{g}$ Sq. mind go to see the Lambs – you will find Cha$^{s}$ every day in the Library of the B$^{h}$ Museum. Colebrook Cottage Colebrook Row is their home. Islington. . . .

John[4] Wordsworth left Town a week ago in company with Tom Robinson via York home – His father wrote to tell him to come from Y. (where he purposed staying a day or two) by way of Stockton to see his Uncle so we do not expect him at home for a week. He would have been glad to meet you – but you will have a much more useful companion in Q.

*Postmark: Kendal, Py post*

## 127

*Edward Quillinan Esq., 12 Bryanstone Street, Bryanstone Square, London*

*Rydal Mount – 21st Ap$^{l}$* [*1827*]

My dear Friend

Your Military chest was forwarded from Kendal on the 11th by John Dowker's, Leeds, Waggon – & will be in Town at the Bull & Mouth Inn B. & M. Street this day – so before you receive this Letter it is probable that it may have reached Bryanstone St – I could not gain the necessary information soon – as often as I have written to Kendal to ask for it – as often have they forgotten to answer my enquiries until yesterday – The keys I sent in a Gov$^{t}$ Frank to Sara[3] Coleridge, & begged she would forward them to you by the 2$^{d}$ post – but her Mama seemed to think this a difficult business *for her* to manage – so that if it has not been accomplished you must be *forced* to call upon her at Mr Rickman's in Palace Y$^{d}$ – I believe she is there at present.

Pray write as soon as you have rec$^{d}$ your goods – for after they were placed in the Cart for Kendal we discovered that the Chest had given way – but begged Mr Cookson would have it properly secured – but if that could not be done – desired Miss W[ordsworth], who was at Kendal, to unpack it & place the contents in other cases. – I forgot to say that your Snuffers are missing – & no one remembers having seen them for a long time – but we have no doubt they will '*cast up*' having been laid *too carefully* away – & a vinegar cruet belonging to the Stand is left behind – so you must come yourself & gather up the remnants –

Poor Dora has had a sad attack of Tooth ache which has weakened &

made her very nervous – but if she would only take care of herself I think she will do well – but you would be shocked to see how changed she is –

My Eldest Brother, whose fortune has been wrecked in the last year, followed one Daughter to the Grave on the 21st of last month – & today his eldest Daughter, Bessy whom you have seen, is to be buried – They have both been confined by sickness during the whole of the Autumn & winter – Bessys complaint was Water in the Chest – & Jane's Consumption – My poor Brothers cup of Affliction is, as you may suppose, full – and we have not yet recovered from the shock which his intelligence has given us – So you must excuse this brief scrawl – for I have no wish to task you with reading what I in my present mood should perforce write – therefore with best wishes to you & your Darlings

I am, very truly, your Friend S. H.

*Postmark: Kendal, Py Post, 23 AP 1827*

## 128

*Edward Quillinan Esq, 12 Bryanston Street, Portman Square, London*

*Grassy Nook, 15th July* [*1827*]

My dear Friend

I had often accused myself of neglect in not acknowledging the receipt of a very kind Letter of yours which I had long before I left home. . . . When we parted I expected to be at home in three weeks – but this being an out-of-the-way place (tho' but 2 miles from Stockton) for Coaches I am dependent upon my brother for forwarding me to the Coach in his Gig & he is very ingenious in making excuses to delay my departure – yet I hope I shall not miss you – if you really visit Rydal – for the chances of our meeting are now so much deminished, by your mercantile engagements, that I should be sadly vexed to lose one of them.

My visit here has been upon the whole a most satisfactory one – for I feel that my presence has cheered my dear Brother*. . . .

I rejoice to hear of the well-doing of your Darlings – and am not disposed to quarrel with you even for spoiling Jemima – Dear little

* She repeats her account of the deaths of Jane and Elizabeth.

Creature! I long to see her before she is really spoilt by becoming a young Lady – which she soon will be – and her rosy cheeks & soft round arms have lost all the beauty of infancy – & instead of being amused by her one will have the trouble of making the agreeable to a young Miss – one of the most irksome tasks that can fall to the lot of an old one – Certainly whenever I do travel southward I shall not forget your invitation to become *Jemimas* guest – or if she was at School should have no scruple, as you know, of becoming yours –

I cannot give you any information respecting Sara[3] Coleridge – but *about* this time I *believe* she was to go upon a visit to Eton to one of her Cousins, a Master in the Col:* – & also she had a visit to pay at Wandsworth to Mary Calvert (*that was*) her visits in Town were nearly finished when I last heard of her – but she may *be heard of* at Highgate – The time of her marriage with her Cousin is *in nubibus* – He is only just called to the Bar – & till he can maintain a Wife his Father will not consent – then, tho' he does not approve, he will not oppose the match – He is a clever young Man but very conceited from all the reports I have had – & his Book confirms them ('*six weeks in the West Indies*') but the most material objection is the state of his health – & the delicacy of his constitution – She I am glad to find has enjoyed good health ever since she left her Mother who *made her fancy* she was ill & unhappy –

As I hope they have written to you from Rydal from them you will learn the fate of your copy of the *Excur*[n] as I am quite ignorant of it – probably my Sister had it among her valuables – laid by out of sight, & therefore out of her mind at the general packing, for if it was left at R. you may depend upon its being safe – as it was never left out among our books – & therefore could neither be stolen or mislaid – there *is* an odd volume or two of your Classics *we know* among our books, which must remain till they *cast up* by accident as Mr. W. searched in vain all the while we were packing for it –

Our residence at Harrowgate was very agreeable – & I think we were all benefitted by the waters – The Poets Party was I assure you quite the fashion – but the place was not full of company – yet as Southey said it was a place where 'acquaintances might be had upon the smallest notice' – & the trade in Autographs was very flourishing – By the bye in your absence last year S[outhey] had application from your mutual friend Sam[l] Simpson for a Frank while he was a M.P. – which he refused as he did every body – but Sim's refusal was heretofore in rhyme – & the rhymes I was desired to send you – which I forgot – but will take care to send them when I return – or if you come

* Edward Coleridge, a brother of H. N. Coleridge, *q.v.*

you will see the whole – your Letters are added to the Simpson correspondence – S. was greatly amused by them – & therefore bade me send you his –

Remember me to your kind neighbour Mrs Atherley – she will be sorry to hear of Bessy's death – they were Schoolfellows – and correspondents –

Best love & kisses to the Darlings – and with my best wishes for your prosperity in all your undertakings I am most truly & aff[t] your's S. H.

*Postmark: Stockton, 15 JU 1827: Stockton, 16 JU 1827: 18 JU 1827*

# 129

*Edward Quillinan Esq., 12 Bryanston Street, Portman Square, London*

*Rydal Mount, Sep[r] 12th [1827]*

My dear Friend

We were all truly grieved to receive such a doleful account of your sufferings mental & bodily . . . But that Preston is according to my definition, given long ago, '*The Town where People lose their Luggage*' – for not one Person of my acquaintance ever passed thro' it, by Coach, that have not been in the same predicament with yourself – While *Guns* are in my head let me say that if you have not bought one for Willy do not – upon second thoughts it must not be – but *if you have* I can dispose of it else where –

My Sister & Dora are gone – & safely arrived at the end of their journey – Brinsop Court – Their departure was hastened by the encreasing weakness of our poor old Aunt, who was diseasedly anxious lest she should die before their arrival – But the old Lady has been cheered by the sight of them – & our accounts of Doras performance of her journey &c. are very good – Mr Monkhouse on the day after they left us arrived – or rather we met him at Threlkeld whither *we all* (except Miss Cookson) the Bishop*, the Poet Laureate's family* & an American Lady* & her Brother had repaired in order to ascend Saddleback – and which we accomplished most *triumphantly* – Our Party consisted of 17 – we dined by the side of the Tarn & all returned delighted & without fatigue – Not one of the Party who knew you

* The Bishop of Chester, their old friend Blomfield, *q.v.* Southey's family, and Harriet Douglas, *q.v.*, with her brother[?s].

failed to express their regret that you were not with us – & more especially did we wish for you while those Americans were with us – A droller person you never met with than the young Lady – Perhaps you may see her at Doncaster Races, whither she is bound – & will be in company with a Yorkshire family of the name of Walker of *Blythe Hall* – She is also an intimate friend of the American Scotts family, now residing at Canterbury – She came over with Gallatin the Minister & spent some time with the Scotts – Her object in Travelling seems to be *Lions* – as Southey says she [is] never happy but in a Lions Dens – She is a most ingenuous & enthusiastic creature – but the oddest manners, & such a speech!! Southey calls them *Hic Haec* & *hoc* Cœlebs – for the elder Brother & she do not scruple to avow their wish to be mated – but *he* says he cannot *fall in love* tho' she would gladly that they could have run off with S. & his Daughter – Dr William & his Wife & Daughter – to Rome, where they are to spend the Winter – In fact poor Things! we were much interested for them – as they seem not only oppressed by the weight of too much liberty, but by the weight of their Purses – If you are acquainted with the Scotts (Sir W[alter's] Brothers Widow & Daughters who live at Canterbury) make some enquiry about the said oddities – Douglas by name from New York – but of course you will (in prudence) not *know them to be oddities* only as they are very – the Lady I mean – *interesting* – the Hoc Cœlebs is neither one thing or other – silent & innofensive – both are inferior to their Sister – She was so bewitched with all she saw at the Mount, that she wished to domesticate with us – It is truly a funny story – & Southey began to parody the Chevy *Chase* – all this is entré nous – when we meet you shall have the whole – such a droll adventure never befel us before – Southey & his 2 Daughters were with us last week – Wm went home with them & is now consoling the Americans at Keswick – but they depart for Doncaster on Friday – If you should meet with them there – you may easily introduce yourself – by using our names discreetly – She was introduced first to Barber & us thro' Mrs Opie – by Mrs Grant to Southey & Mrs Smith of Coniston to whom she was described as a 'Pilgrim to the Shrine of Worth & *departed* Genius' (meaning Elizabeth Smith). She was dressed in high fashion – has red hair white eyebrows & lashes & a fair skin – very Scotch looking – & a little wild –

I must not forget to tell you that Dora says the little Sarah[4] Hutchinson at Brinsop is a fac simile of Rotha at the same age –

You could not but be greatly flattered if you knew how often we have wished for you – we were all, old & young, at a Ball at Coz Dorothys[3] last friday – no less than 65 persons assembled – John[4] &

Willy[2] are not yet returned from Ambleside whither they went to a public Ball last Night – but the dissipation of our family since the departure of Mary[1] & her Daughter has exceeded all former dissipations of the kind – The House was so full that we were obliged to have three beds of our Neighbours – Since Monday Evening, when the Keswick party & Mr M[onkhouse] left us, we have had breathing time – Miss W[ordsworth] Eliz.[3], myself, & the three boys being all that is left – We have had *a* Mr Hare – the most learned Man in Europe & the most entertaining – when you are learned enough for his conversation – but whose appearance & manners are truly remarkable – Sir E. must know him – he lives much abroad – indeed was born at Rome as well as his three Brothers, who are all remarkable men – Augustus – is the Tutor to New Col – Julius at Trinity Camb – & Marcus I know not what – they are the Grandsons of Barber's Friend the late Dean Shipley – or Nephews *I guess* – Perhaps you saw the '*Guesses at Truth*' here – a book by the two Tutor Brothers – with a contribution or two signed R. by the eldest Francis – the one who is in this neighbourhood – He is coming again to stay a few days with us – If you are still confined to the house – this gossip may amuse you – had you been able to take the field I should not have detained you so long – Miss W. did not return till the day before my Sister & Dora set off i.e. on Monday the 3rd – at the same moment (Tuesday 5 o'c—) Edith & I went to Keswick in the poney chair – stayed all night & met along with the rest from K. the Rydal Party, & *Bowness John*[5], & I.M. at Threlkeld – Bertha & Mr. M returned with them & the B[p] with us to K. – next day E. & I came back – to the Ball then followed Southey & Mr Hare – & on Sunday all the Boys from Bowness!* A wet day prevented the B[p] from Preaching at Hawkshead whither all were going to hear him – but he preached for *our* edification at Rydal – We have had much wet & some beautiful weather – but we are thankful that Dora is out of the way – for it is very evident that a dry climate suits her best – I am knitting for you when I am at any work – & hope to be able to send you a supply of Socks by S. Cookson – You have had companions in misery – Southey was obliged to have a Tooth drawn & Dora had had threatenings of a return but she had resolved to part with the offender also – Kind love from every body – & best wishes for you & the darlings – and believe me very truly yours S. H. Barber enq[d] your address yesterday – so perhaps you may have a 'favor' from him –

*Postmark: Kendal, Py Post, 15 SE 1827*

* A Cambridge reading party of which Dr. Christopher Wordsworth's three sons were members.

# 130

*Mrs Hutchinson, Brinsop Court, Hereford*

*Rydal Mount, Wednesday, Dec^r 13th* [*1827*]

My dearest Mary

I was glad of a letter from you though half afraid that something was wrong which made you so unusually communicative, & in consequence, let the letter lay on my knee unopened, to the great surprize of all present, till I had finished *reeling my hank* in which I was engaged when it arrived – I lose no time in replying upon M^rs Urwick's account – tho' I hope you have not said any thing to her on the matter – as M^r Harrison is supplied with a housekeeper – a widow Lady of the name of *Jackson* – the name of his late wife. The Governess which Miss Dowling is in want of is a *musical* one – capable also to teach singing – so that it is not likely that Anne Urwick would be competent for this – they have applied to Cramer, wishing for a superexcellent one – So dear Mary all your schemes, I am sorry to say, for our good friends are overthrown – Poor M^rs U. I pity her greatly – and if I hear of any thing likely to suit will not forget her. Miss W[ordsworth] had a beautiful Letter yesterday from M^rs John Fisher – who, from the delicate state of her health, is obliged to remain at their Living near Weymouth – consequently is at times separated from her Husband he being in residence at Salisbury – & as she says is 'an old fashioned' wife & has not a separate Purse from her Husband till his return she could not determine upon Dorothy's application in behalf of her cousin which she preferred communicating to him personally rather than by letter – She expressed herself as much interested in the case – and said that her thoughts a few days before had dwelt upon her cousin – so I hope they will send her some thing – and not neglect her in future – a more *creditable* Letter to the writer could not have been penned—she thanked D. for the communication – and we are of course glad, for both their sakes that it was made –

Today John[4] Wordsworth's Luggage is arrived – so I suppose some thing or other has made him resolve to return home & he has not received his Fathers advice to pay you a visit – His Love cannot be the cause, as the Lady set off yesterday (& he knew it) for Scotland, where she is to spend the winter – Mary[2] says you wish to know all the *particulars* – but I have none to give – nothing has been cleared up – only we believe that the family is respectable enough – at least they have very respectable friends and acquaintances. But as we have had no communication with the Ullswater Ladies from whom we hoped to have a full account – tho' we do not know it, we believe that most of what we have heard is misrepresentation. How *he stands* we know not – but think that if they suspected his *penchant* they merely smiled at it – & that there is no tenderness on the Lady's side – She is as light hearted as ever – *never* enquiring after him (which they say is hopeful) but her Mother never forgets to do so – I have no doubt he will be very assiduous in his attentions to *her* while she remains at the Wood – which she & Miss Poole intend until January – Miss W. bids me say that John's arrival will determine her journey – as they may travel together part of the way – so about the 20 or 21 of Jan[y] you may expect to see her. – Unluckily Mary wrote to Lady B[eaumont] yesterday – I hope you may have to give her the report of the cyder soon – else she, who is such a methodical piece, will think you remiss in not replying – & Mary W. says if we were to write on purpose, such a round about way, she might suppose you could not write a Letter – this is Mary's *wit*. N.B. Since this was written she has had occasion to write to L[y] B. – & ment[d] the cyder.

We are indeed rejoiced at the good account you give of yourself – but I must still urge you to take care of yourself – all your business will I hope be over before Miss W. arrives – and if the weather be fine you will be able to *take the air* with her in the Gig – you will see by the Letter I wrote John[2] a few days ago, that she intends to be *in residence* with *him* first – wishing her visit to *tell* – and it will do so most during the dreary season – This has been a beautiful morning – but the compliments of the season are returning – in a *skid*ness – *you* have been favoured in the weather beyond any other part of Eng[d] that we have heard of – rain, & snow, seem to have been very plentiful elsewhere – I quarrel most with the scanty favours which the sun sheds on our region. – We are busy reading a novel 'Walladmoor'* translated from the German by De Quincey – freely as he says – for much of it is his own – & much has been left out. It is well worth reading – as the style & descriptions are far very far beyond anything in merit that you meet with in such publications – seldom indeed any where – for every thing that he does must be clever. William writing a sonnet last night upon my spinning wheel – but I have not yet heard it – if it really is finished to his own satisfaction you shall have it by way of paying the postage of this Letter –

I was sure those dear little Creatures would love their uncle Henry[1] – he is always a great favourite with Children – there are few persons

* De Quincey's *Walladmor* appeared in 1825.

been left out. It is well worth reading—as the style & descriptions are far very far beyond any thing in trash that you meet with in such publications. Indeed any where—for every thing that he does must be clever. William writing a Sonnet last night upon my Spinning wheel. but I have not yet read it—If it really is finished to his own satisfaction you shall have it by way of paying the postage of this letter— I was sure those dear little Creatures would love their Uncle Henry—he is always a great favourite with Children—there are few persons whom the young ones love better—Dorothy especially never forgets him he has ceased to give the old scream of pleasure when she hears he is in the house—you do not say whether he intends to pay his visit to Waterloo Bridge.

Sonnet

To a Lady apologizing for her Spinning Wheel." (the noise rather)

Excuse is needless when with love sincere
Of occupation, by caprice not led,
Thou mov'st the Wheel erewhile with dust bespread,
My nerves from no such murmur shrink—tho' near
Soft as the Dor-hawk's to a distant ear
When twilight shades bedim the mountain's head.
She who was feigned to spin the vital thread
Might smile, O Lady, on a task so dear
To household virtues. Venerable Art,
Torn from the Poor! yet will kind Heaven protect
Its own, not left without a guiding chart,
If States, relying with undue respect
On proud discoveries of the Intellect,
Sanction the pillage of man's ancient heart.

Thursday Morng. John & James Cookson arrived last Night—the former had not recd. his fathers letter. it had been sent thro' Mr Becket who has not been in Town—so he was not in possession of the leave to visit you—he seems very sorry—as he does not expect much fun here—& with you, besides the pleasure of seeing you all, he fancies he might have got a hunt or two. He has missed his time just one day! They brought us the sad news of the stoppage of Poles House—and a sleepless & anxious night I have had on account of our Friends at Stockton—for should it be only a temporary suspension there will be a world of anxiety & labour for them, and especially for the elder Brother—I fear also that

Letter to her cousin and sister-in-law Mrs Thomas Hutchinson, 13 December, 1827

Letter to her cousin and sister-in-law Mrs Thomas Hutchinson, 13 December, 182 which the young ones here like better – Dorothy[2], especially, never forgets him – or has ceased to give her old scream of pleasure when she hears he is in the house – you do not say whether he intends to pay his visit to *Waterloo Bridge*.

*Sonnet**

To A Lady Apologizing for her Spinning Wheel (the noise rather)

Excuse is needless when with love sincere
Of occupation, by caprice not led,
Thou turn'st the Wheel erewhile with dust o'erspread;
My nerves from no such murmur shrink – tho' near
Soft as the Dor-hawk's to a distant ear
When twilight shades bedim the mountain's head.
She who was feignèd to spin the vital thread
Might smile, O Lady, on a task so dear
To household Virtues. Venerable art,
Torn from the Poor! Yet will kind Heaven protect
It's own, not left without a guiding chart,
If States, reposing with undue respect
On proud discoveries of the Intellect,
Sanction the pillage of Man's ancient hearth.

Thursday morn[g].

John[4] & James Cookson arrived last night – the former had not rec[d] his father's letter – it had been sent thro' M[rs] Beckett – who has not been in Town – so he was not in possession of the leave to visit you – he seems very sorry – as he does not expect much *fun* here – & with you, besides the pleasure of seeing you all, he fancies he might have got a *hunt* or two. He has missed his love just one day!

They brought us the sad news of the stoppage of Pole's house – and a sleepless & anxious night I have had on account of our Friends at Stockton – for should it be only a temporary suspension there will be a world of anxiety & labour for them and especially for our dear Brother – I fear also that John[2] will not be at ease as he had money in their hands – my aunt's also – But we must hope for the best – and as the Papers say the House has plenty of *security* tho' not *cash*, the alarm I trust will prove a false one. It is most lucky that they have two Houses in London, & that all is not in the hands of Pole's – I have written to Bessy to know the worst.

* The text of the poem given here was considerably altered before it reached the final version. 'Feignèd' for 'feigned' looks like a slip of the pen.

Write soon – I hope to hear that poor old Aunty is better than when *you* last wrote – John's[2] Letter told me she was a wonder. Eliz.[3] Cookson is improving – She comes downstairs every eve[g]. sits & works or plays cards – so she must be better even than when we saw her.

I can give you some *good* news of our sober Friend James Cookson – who will be in your neighbourhood in Feb[y]. but you must not betray me – He will himself probably tell you Joanna, that he is the *accepted* Lover of Miss Thompson, the Sister of the Alderman, she has 15000£ in hand –* is very amiable & he has long been truly attached to her the only drawback that she is 5 years elder – All her Family are in his interest & always have been so – and the Family are so *powerful* in money (which is *power*) that the advantages to the *whole concern* are in prospect most flattering – But as many things may happen between the cup & the lip – do not name it even to Eliz. – tho' of course she knows – Ja[s] is, as you may suppose, in high glee – not the less so for having distanced so many suitors – D[r] Proudfoot, the *wily* Scot, among the rest. – We joke him upon the *effect* of his *shooting* her Brother – which accident brought her from Liverpool where she was upon a visit & surrounded by fortune-hunters – & thus was he furnished with opportunity to shew his natural disposition & prefer his suit – God bless you all! most truly yours S. H.

* her father's property also is immense – & she is the favourite and has always lived with him – the scamp Moreland married one sister greatly against the consent of her friends – M[r] Crawshaw another who gave M[rs] Moreland *1000* & a present of Plate on her marriage! so what think you of our James' prospect.

They are all very bad at Keswick in the hooping cough – a return – Southey himself laid on the Sofa with a bad cold & cough. Our neighbourhood is rather more healthy at present – but the Robinsons are not yet sufficiently purified for our society – . . . This is I think the last word. *Adieu!*

Sometimes they charge your Letters *1/2*. I hope mine do not cost as much.

Sir Robert T. Farquhar Bart: M.P. London – is all that is necessary for M[rs] Luff's address – under cover of course.

*Postmark: Kendal, Penny Post*

# 131

*Edward Quillinan Esq, 12 Bryanston Street, Portman Sq, London*

*Rydal Mount, 27th Jan^y^* [*1828*]

My dear Friend

A 'Kent Herald' which arrived this morning reminded me of my debt to you – & the necessity of giving you the *proper* directions for sending the Hamper – concerning which, or rather your *impertinence* I have had a communication from Brinsop – Your Letter to Dora was sent to us in a parcel – but let that pass – and *observe* that the said Hamper must be directed to Mr Cookson & sent by Jno. Dowker's Waggon ('Leeds & Kendal') from the Bull & Mouth. I have not yet been able to learn the exact sum you are indebted to Mr Cookson for your Chest – the Carriage was upwards of 3£ – but the iron hoops &c had not been paid for, which were put on at Kendal, & till this was settled Mr C. would not make out his account – Mr Wordsworth says he thinks he told you to order a Bust yourself – therefore did not write to Chantrey lest two might come to you – but perhaps Dora has explained this – if not be so good as order one by Mr. W.'s desire to be sent to your house.

So much for business; & now let me thank you for your pleasant Letter from Brinsop which ought, if I were not at all times incorrigibly idle, to have been acknowledged long ago – I am glad you were so much pleased with the Children there – and wish that your little Darlings were nearer to them that they might grow up together – especially as they are so much of the same *cut* – for I am told that my namesake is the image of Rotha – & Mary[6] was once exactly what Mima was when she first came to Rydal – I do wish I could see them all together! Mima has I am afraid quite forgotten me, else I should ask for a Letter from her – as I find she corresponds with you in your absence – but I should not care a fig for it if it were not entirely her own – & this could scarcely be for I can be nothing more than a name to her now.

Mr Wordsworth is not yet returned – He left Brinsop last Tuesday – stayed all night at Chester & part of the next day with the Bp – & is now with the Boltons at Liverpool – and was at a *Ball* in that Town on Thursday Evening – but we hope he will find his way home on Tuesday Morning by the Mail – Miss W. & her Nephews have been alone the greater part of the winter – for I have been rambling to

Appleby, Penrith, & Kendal. We are all well – but Miss W. & I not a little anxious about the Youths – John's[4] Ordination is drawing near – & Willy[2] has got the *Army* so strongly into his head that I am sure there will be no turning him from it, & his poor Mother will be wretched when she finds this to be the case – for she has no idea that he will persist in opposition to his Father's & her wishes –

We had a Letter the other day from the 'hæc Cœlebs' (Miss Douglas) concerning whom you maken enquiries in your Letter to Do. – She & her Brothers (hic & hoc) are still in Dublin – but will in their way to the Continent probably visit Canterbury where their friends *Mrs & Miss Scott* live, i.e. the Widow & Daughter of S^r^ Walters Brother *Cap^t^ Scott* who lived & died in America – & who you may recollect was sometimes reported to be the Author of the Waverly Novels – I wish you might *fall in* (*love* I do not mean) with Miss D[ouglas] for she is really worth knowing – quite an oddity – but overflowing with kindness & generosity. I expect a Letter from her soon – & if I find that they are to be in Town in the Spring it is not impossible that you may meet (if you like it) – *certainly* if '*our folk*' should be there – & if [*she*] had half a hope of meeting them I have little doubt that she would try to effect it – for she is smitten with the whole family – & especially with Mr W. – Southey says she is never happy except in a 'Lions Den' – and she must have had her hearts' content in Ireland – & as I told her I wonder how she has escaped destruction.

I have not seen Barber since my return from Appleby – but hear that after a little cutting at the Wig he likes it very well – at my first return he was ill – & now he has so much amusement at home that he does not take the trouble of coming to see us – and I am not so good natured & Miss W. & therefore do not go to see him – He is building himself a new bed room in anticipation of the time when he may be confined to it – It is to be 30 feet long with a fire place at each end! What a pity that he should be single – when he takes such good care of himself what would he have done for his *better* half?

We suppose the Paper was sent for the *Verses* – nothing else can we find interesting to us in it – The first & last are very pretty especially the last – sweet & tender – but the Moonlight is somewhat too *Moorish* for my taste – Is the Clergyman who lives near you really the Subaltern? & the Author of *Cyril Thornton*?* For some folk say there is another Person whose name I forget who is the Subaltern. Mr W. has written a Sonnet (*Occasion*) upon seeing a Tombstone in Worcester Cathedral without any inscription except the word *Miserrimus* – & one

* *Cyril Thornton*, a novel by Capt. Hamilton, (brother of William Hamilton), Blackwood, 1823.

upon the same arrived here today from the Bp of Chester written by a Gent to whom Mr W. had mentioned the inscription at Chester – They both have the same view of the subject & both are very good – I will send them with Mr Ws permission when he comes home tho perhaps Do. may have sent her father's to you – for he has been very busy sonnetizing.

John & Mrs. Ellwood (who is with us at present) have brought me in a primrose a snowdrop & hypatica – therefore you may guess how mild the season is here – but we have had torrents of rain – such a wet winter was never before known even in this wet climate – Dora complains of Herefordshire but had she been here she could not have stirred out above once a month – I suppose you will see them all in Town as they are to be in Cambridge in April – What a nice Westmorland Party you will be – but when I think of you I shall also feel the party incomplete for poor Thomas[2] Monkhouse used always to be one – God bless you & and with Kisses to the Darlings I am very truly your friend S. H.

I ought to have wished you & the Darlings a happy new year.
Have you seen J. Cookson's Bride? And what is she like unto? I hope when Eliz$^{\text{th}}$[3] goes to visit them you will take the Trotts to see her. Miss Wordsworths love to you & the Children.

*Postmark: Kendal, Py Post, 29 JA 1828*

## 132

*Edward Quillinan Esq$^{\text{re}}$, 12 Bryanstone Street, Portman Square, London*

*Rydal Mount, March 4th* [*1828*]

My dear Friend

I suppose the Valentine which I received on the 15th *ult* is one of the Letters for which I am in your debt but this is not the season to pay you in kind if I were disposed, so for it I must still remain your debtor –

You say you write for news – the first, & best, is that which we have received this morning – viz. Johns[4] ordination, which took place at Cambridge on Sunday last by the Bp of Lincoln & he seems to have gone through his examination to his own satisfaction at least – He returns to the North till May – as his services are not required till then at his Curacy – The old Clerk of Grasmere asked Willy the other day when John was to have 'his commission? as he hoped he would let them hear him at Grasmere'.

Mr Wordsworth is at Keswick – but *I guess** he will be in Town about the 10 of May – They all go to Cambridge in April – but as Dr W. is to be in town on the above mentioned day – they cannot remain longer at C— than that time – We are all well here – and glad to have good accounts of you & your Trotts.

Now for a little business, & a *commission for you* – You have heard of Willy's[2] *Army mania fever* (as our neighbour Mr Robinson would say) & as it was so much against the wishes of his friends you will be glad to hear that it is subsided, & he has turned his thoughts to merchandize – Mr W. has consulted with our neighbour Mr Jaffray, a very intelligent London Mercht & he advises that Willy should be sent into some foreign Country house i.e. 'merely to have the run of the house' & there to have masters to perfect him in the French, & especially in the Spanish Languages – & said he would himself make enquiries – at Havre or else where – (Willy you must know is bent upon being a *foreign* Merch!). Mr W. would prefer his going to Lisbon for this purpose, & we turned our thoughts to Mr Carruthers who would probably take him for this object – not as a *clerk* at a salary – for *that* he is not competent but for education – and as you said you had seen Mr C— in Lisbon, & know of course how to direct to him, Mr W. would thank you most truly if you would write to him immediately, & ask this favor for Mr W— who will write himself if there appears to you and Mr C— any thing possible in the plan – Mr C— had a brother in the City & one also at Lisbon – but one of these is dead – which I know not – therefore except through you we have no clue to guide us to him – Willy has set himself very industriously to work with his accounts & Grammars – which he never could be brought to while he had the Army in his head – I dare say I have expressed myself very muddily – but you must make the best of it – I think my meaning may be guessed at at least.

Our neighbours are all well. Barber dined here last week & I believe wore his Parisian Wig – but as he had, upon its arrival, clipt its wings I did not see anything remarkable – & forgot to admire it.

From Brinsop we have very good news – Dora improves in spite of several colds – but you have probably heard from them – Poor Old Aunty died three weeks ago. It was a blessed release for her – & tho'

* Making fun of Miss Douglas? or Quillinan, if he had picked up this Americanism?

she enjoyed life to the last, she was prepared – & happy in the prospect of death. God grant that the same may be said of us all! –

Mary W. & Dora go to Mrs Gees about the middle of this month – I fear poor Mrs Gee is left in straitened circumstances for we hear that Janetta is going to Hendon where she is to be fitted to take a situation as Governess in a family when an eligible one can be met with – Mrs Gee will probably live with her Sisters – but her plans do not seem fixed – Poor Woman it is a hard case to be in such circumstances at her time of life after having had for so many years a comfortable home of her own!

I have written till I am almost *breathless with haste* – Miss W. is waiting to take my Letter to the post – & has scarcely time to return before dinner – so you must excuse all blunders & God bless you! S. H.

*Postmark: 6 MR 1828*

*Miss Hutchinson, Rydal, Westmoreland, Kendal*

*Sarah my dear, my love; my life,
And soon I hope to be my Wife!
Remember all the pleasant rides
We've had – and all the walks besides
You'll make my tea – I like it strong;
You'll mend my stockings short or long;
You'll scold me when I'm not in fault,
You'll quar̃el with Segars and Malt;
You'll get up scenes like Dog & Cat,
You'll love me dearly for all that,
And I'll love you so help me Jove
And Venus and the God of Love!
So thou art mine and I am thine
My Sarah thou – and *I* thy Valentine

*Postmark: 14 FE 1828*

* Quillinan's valentine to her, returned with her letter on the back.

# 133

*April 28, John Monkhouse Esq., Stow, n^r Hereford*

*Monday Night, Ap^l 28th* [*1828*]

My dear John

Your acceptable, & kind, present arrived safe this morning; & Willy & James immediately obeyed your orders – & in addition tied the corks – but no sooner was this done than the spirit of the liquor scorning further restraint burst 2 bottles – so the strings were cut, & the corks raised; & in a day or two we shall fasten them again – as we suppose it was the warm hands, or the warm air of the house that did the mischief – Now it is safe in a cool Cellar. We drank of the broken bottles – & it is most capital Beverage – I suppose M^r Southey's would be at Keswick on Saturday – I had previously warned them – & I hope their's will fare no worse than our's – but I have not heard from them since I wrote – we have no Coach but the Mail – & have lost the amusement derived from poor M^rs Coleridges *Sybellines**, as we used to call her flying letters written on scraps of Paper.

I have not one word of News for you – Miss W. & I are in the agonies of cleaning – at least we *hear it* in all quarters of the house – but in a day or two we intend to run away from it to Keswick – & tomorrow we go to Kendal to buy a New Carpet. I cannot send you any Drugget *immediately* even if I approved of it – for M^r Cookson will not have any for 6 weeks to come – We once thought of it ourselves to cover our old Study Carpet, as far as the border till we should new paper the room *& make all of a piece* – but, upon calculation, find it would cost ½ as much as a Carpet – so have resolved to do the thing properly at once. And therefore I advise you to do the same, *if you cannot put on* till I come to help you to plan, & execute your alterations. But that cannot be till the *Autumn* (which is the *best time* for Painting) as summer will be far advanced before 'our Folk' come home – & I shall probably be sole housekeeper here till their return – But our Absentees have used us very ill. *John*[4] & *William*[1] went away last thursday week – &, hard as we have been working for them both, have not bestowed a single *line* upon us – neither the Ladies since they got William to Cambridge – therefore we are yet quite uncertain whether Miss W. goes to Whitwick or not – She will regret not seeing you I am sure – but, if she is not there, Mary[1] & Dora[2] will help John[4]

* Coleridge's volume of poems, *Sibylline Leaves*, had appeared in 1817.

to do the honors – We are very anxious to hear what sort of accommodation he has – M^r^ Knight Lady B's Steward who negociated for his furniture says it is very respectable – but altogether fixtures & all it only cost *84£* – & he has a *Spare bed* – a sitting room, & a Study, besides 'kitchen furniture of all sorts' fitting for a batchelor – & we have been *setting him up* with household Linen – and 3 Tea Chests full of Books, Classical & Ecclesiastical, will set off his Bookshelves, & furnish him with matter to work his brains upon.

We have had such horrid rainy weather as never was known at this season which is usually one of our dryest – The poor seeds in the Garden cannot penetrate the beaten soil – & the flowers (of which we have many) are battered & forlorn. – Poor M^rs^ Luff, & Barber, who spare no expence are still more out of humour than I – and *it is* really provoking! – M^rs^ Luff has been amusing herself with making a Grotto – *outside* like a *Hoghouse* but within a palace for the Sea Nymphs – all over coral & shells – & roofed with fir cones – She often *threatens* coming to see you – & says it was dangerous to give her an invitation into your Land of plenty – of which the Misses *Skew* [? Askew] gave her such flaming reports.

Will, or will not, dearest little Ma Ma be allowed to come to see you? But if she is I suppose she will be at Brinsop by this time – O how I wish you could keep her till I come! – else I shall have no chance of seeing her while she is the sweet thing Mary & Dora represent her – and she cannot be so well off as at B. – with such nice companions –

M^r^ Southey is upon the eve of a journey to Town – to Publish his Essays – which I hope I shall have the pleasure of reading to you – & also Bp. Hebers charming Book* which I have not had *time* to get through here – *Our B^p^.* has I see had a bit of a *Squabble* with the old Chancellor – The Bps. are all becoming Liberals I think – Let them beware!

Miss W's best love with mine to you & all at B—. & Remembrances to your Neighbours – Willy is well & sends his Love & bids me say your Cyder nearly *blew* him out of the Cellar – *Comp^ts^* to Ann – Ever truly yours S. H.

Tuesday – I was too late for the Post yesterday – A Letter from our Culprits today tells us they are in the midst of grand Dinners at T[rinity] Lodge. John[4] read Prayers at Coleorton the day after his arrival – very well his Father says & very much to his Rectors satisfaction – He likes his House & Church at Whitwick very much.

If his House is ready before they have finished their visit at C— &

* Probably *Journey through India*, by Bishop Reginald Heber, 1828.

stay a fortnight in Town Miss W. will go – but if not Mary will leave Doro & go herself alone – They go to Town with D^r W. on Saturday week –

*Postmark: Kendal, Penny Post*

# 134

*Edward Quillinan Esq, 12 Bryanstone Street, Portman Square*

*Brinsop Court, 20th Ap^l [1829]*

My dear Friend

I learn, by a Letter from Rydal, that I am accused of having 'forgotten, neglected, given you up' or some thing of the kind – however I hope my accompanying '*annual donation*' will oblige you to confess yourself in the wrong for once . . . All the Children here have been suffering from the '*going about*' complaints – we have had quite an hospital for some time – I have luckily escaped – the only one, among young or old, that has been so favored – The weather is still as cold as Christmas – & till we have a change I fear the sick list will not decrease – Poor Miss Wordsworth, you will have heard, has been dangerously ill at Whitwick & my Sister gone thither to nurse her – I have not heard from them for some days, but Willys last gave a good account of her – so I trust she continues doing well – we expect her to visit us early in the summer – The Children were sorely disappointed that you did not come – the Girls I mean – for I understand you do not patronize Boys – We have 6 in the House at present – four of them visitors during the holidays – with our own two – and if you were here to kick up a riot with the Girls the confusion would be complete – I am only just returned from the Stow, so that the change from Mr. M[onkhouse]'s quiet fire side is as great as can well be imagined –

I send with this a parcel for Mr Stultz – and will venture to give you a commission – viz to order me a riding habit, chuse the cloth, *good*, *stout* & (*dark* blue) pay for it send me the amount of the *damage* & I will return the money by post – He used to charge 10 Gs for a *full sized* habit (2 y^ds long) deducting 10/6 for each ¼ y^d shorter than this – So that as I shall not require a full sized one, I tell you this lest they should charge you the *full price* – If you will be so kind as call & order Stultz to send for the Parcel to your house he will in it find the measure & directions – so that you will have no trouble but in chusing the cloth –

& ordering him to send it by the Mail to Hereford 'to be left at the Greyhound for Mr H. Brinsop Court' – & desire it to be sent as soon as possible – I wish to pay for it immediately that I may have discount –

I understand that you are not much delighted by the Concessions – i.e. you think they will do no good – Is it because they do not go far enough? – Or do you think, as all other *wise people* do, that there are sorer evils to be remedied in Ireland than those occasioned by the restrictions – We are all *antis* here, as you may suspect – and our good neighbour Sir John one of the faithful – our other Member (wise Bobby of Foxley) would have a hard struggle were there a new election –

My Brother will thank you to send us one Number of a Newspaper, lately published, called the '*Record*' – He wishes to have a *Specimen* as he thinks it would suit him better than a weekly paper, & he cannot afford a daily one – It is published twice in the week – & contains the state of the Markets which is important to him – but the Farmers journal which we now have is very stupid for any thing else – I suppose it would be impossible to have the St Ja$^{s}$ Chronicle at second hand else that would cost as little – but at full price would not suit us – as we have 2$^{d}$ postage to pay upon every paper from Hereford which is a *serious* concern to poor farmers – We are all groaning about bad prices, bad crops, & bad seasons – & consequently the poor are poor indeed – nothing can be more wretched than the agricultural population in this neighbourhood – but they are patient & quiet – & those who do not see it fancy all is well – but I am sure there are many families in this neighbourhood little less to be pitied than the Irish about whom we hear so much –

Have your Lee Friends left England again – I hope you will write me a long Letter – & tell me all the news & especially give me a particular account of both the Darlings – I should like well to see them – I do think you ought at least to bring them into the North – where I hope to be again before winter – Mr W. when I last heard was suffering from his Eyes – He has been busy writing & has sent me several sweet Poems – How did you like those in the *Keepsake*?* Would you believe it. I have never seen the Book – so much are we, at least have I been, out of the world for I believe all the rest have seen it – I hope you will condescend to appear in it next year – What a scrawl have I written – but my fingers are literally frozen & it is the more provoking as the fields are as green as emerald in spite of the hail stones which have fallen upon them this morning – Every bodys love to you along

* *The Keepsake*, an annual anthology edited by F. M. Reynolds, *q.v.*

with mine – & to the *Trotts* also – & believe me very truly yours S Hutchinson –

Pray desire Stultz will not make the Sleeves outrageously large – remember I am an old & *little* Body & do not like extremes – Dora's was very neat – but some which I have seen are frightful –

# 135

*Edward Quillinan Esq, 12 Bryanstone St, Portman Square*

*Rydal Mount, 30th Jan$^{y}$* [*1830*]

My dear Friend

Do not suppose that Dora is not very grateful to you for the pains you have taken respecting her Watch because she had deputed me to express her thanks to you, & to say that it is entirely to her satisfaction – & that no Boy of 10 years old was ever *prouder* of one than she is of it – John[4] brought her a pretty seal also from Miss Kinnaird – a remembrance from Mont Blanc – the chain & seal was instantly affixed, & it was hung round her neck in a minute –

The Rector* returned to his Duties this morning – & the consequent bustle of preparations for him prevented her writing other Letters which must be forwarded in this days frank to *the Gorrdon*†. John did not leave Town until monday evening – before which time, *I guess*, you were there – at least I *hope* so – as you said nothing but dear little Mimas illness was likely to detain you – but this he was not aware of – having been told, in Bryanston St, that you were not expected for a fortnight – we shall be most anxious to hear that the Darling has escaped – or rather that she has got well thro' that frightful disease – so pray do not wait for a frank but write to us immediately –

We are all here in our '*better fashion*' – Miss W[ordsworth] & Dora quite well – tho' the former needs great care to keep her so – but I hope she & the leaves will come out together in great force – Poor Willy[2] has been suffering from the severe weather at Bremen – but in other respects Mr Pappendiek gives a most satisfactory account of him –

We have *some* of [us] been in a flame upon *hearing* that those im-

* John Wordsworth, Jr., who had just taken up his duties at Moresby.

† Mr. Gordon of p. 372.

pudent Articles in *Blackwood* were written by *Chancey Hare Townsend** a person professing friendship for Mr Wordsworth, & who was most kindly received in this house at the very time when the most obnoxious of them were about to be published. All the witticisms which are not mere scoffing have been suggested by the Author himself – for T. could not possibly have any feeling or understanding of the beauty of Mr Ws Poetry – to which you will agree when I tell you that he could not go upon Hellvellyn without lugging his Lapdog along with him in a basket – a rather heavier burden, I should guess, than the '*Excursion*' would have been which he deems an impossibility – We have every reason to believe that *he is* the Author, as I have asserted, of the *Articles* except his own acknowledgement – W. has begged Southey to ask him the question – (which as he has known Mr T. for so many years he thought he had a right to do) 'for his general & particular guidance as to those with whom he may in future converse, & under what limitations' – This of course is entré nous – I have not seen all these precious performances. The last was the only one I had looked at till I heard *who* was the Author – for tho' Hartley positively said it was not *Wilson* I did not believe him – because I was sure the person, who ever it might be must either have conversed with Wm or had his conversation reported to him – but some of the others were even *too vulgar* for Mr Wilson – yet Mr C. T. is reckoned one of the most refined, gentle, delicate-minded men in the world – so sensitive & modest that he cannot exhibit himself in the pulpit – so he, I suppose, chuses rather to propagate *christianity* through the medium of *Blackwoods* magazine. There's a little spite for you! written I assure you more for your amusement than from any angry feeling – for he is, I believe, a poor nervous effeminate creature & to be pitied after all – *something of poor Lloyds* kind –

O we had *such* an entertaining Letter from Charles Lamb the other day! I wish you had been here to enjoy it with us – and you might have been in *worse* quarters, even at this season – for the weather has been delightful here – while you southerns have all been annoyed by deep snows we have had nothing beyond a sprinkling – the Poney Chair has been in use daily – & now I am writing in my own room without fire – the laurels on the terrace glittering in the sunshine – & scarcely can I persuade myself that it is only the 30th of January –

Poor Barber has been so bothered with bad, or unsuitable, servants

* Townsend, Chauncey Hare, 1798–1862, wrote four anonymous articles in *Blackwood's Magazine*, Sept.–Dec. 1829. Wordworth later received an apology and renewed acquaintance with him. See the *Wordsworth Letters, Later Years*, I, 448 and note.

since he parted with Mary Kirkby that he is quite out of humour with everything – & *threatens* (as if he thought anybody cared) to shut up his house & take lodgings in Ambleside – *just* as he pulled up his Cabbages & Strawberry plants because the rain did not come to make them grow *at the time* he wished – Of course, poor Man, he has been poorly in consequence of his domestic *distresses*.

. . . Pray write soon, &, with everybodys Love to you & your Darlings, believe me to be very truly your Friend S. Hutchinson.

Mr M[onkhouse] has been suffering from Rheumatism – & I grieve to say his sight grows worse – so his Sister tells me – but he does not seem to be much aware of it as others are –

*Postmark: 1 FE*

## 136

*Miss M. Hutchinson, Brinsop Court*

[*26 March, 1830*]

My dear Mary[6]

Thanks for your nice Letter – & I hope you will often write to me when your Mother is too busy or too idle – I am glad that Coz. Dora[2] sent the Pencils for you from Keswick the other day as M^r^ Newton has sent us a note to say that he has a paper parcel going by the Mail & will enclose us a pacquet or Letter – so I send the stones for Miss Whalley also – but I cannot venture your Mother's Caps – as she says they must be trimmed – so she will be forced to wait till the Ponies are sent for, else they are washed & quite ready. I am going to stay at Keswick very soon – so that I shall not want my Poney else I should have been sorry to wait for it so long as till June – & I suppose it will be better that Maley should stay where she is till her new Mistress comes home – perhaps the Servants might not take such good care of her. Poor Lion, I am sorry he is dead – because I know Mother wished that Sarah[4] might learn to ride upon him as you all had done – I hope she & all of you are better – All the young Ladies at Keswick have had the Influenza except Coz. Dora who has been chief nurse to them all – M^r^ Southey calls her the '*Beguine*' – Beguines are an order of Nuns who go about to visit & attend the sick in some parts of the Continent

– Cousin John[4] was to come to Keswick today to take her to Moresby to spend a month with him there – He has got nice new Lodgings where he has a spare room for a Friend – & she takes her Poney along with her – so that they can ride about together which I hope will do her good – & the sea air also make her quite strong before she comes back again. – Aunt Joanna & Uncle Henry[1] are both here – I believe they will go to Whitehaven next Monday, & stay a week there for the purpose of seeing John & Dora – as she was obliged to go to Keswick before Uncle came, which was a great mortification to her. Uncle Henry is quite well & Aunt Joanna much better than when she came here – indeed she seems very comfortable &, if she has an agreeable voyage will, I dare say, be quite well when she gets to her dear Island again – but I am very sorry for your disappointment in not seeing them at Brinsop this Summer. I hope nothing will prevent dear Father & Thomas[3] from coming hither – poor Totts! we were sorry to hear of his sort-on-a-pleurisy – And the poor Maids too! you must have had a sad house – Mother I suppose was the *Beguine* at Brinsop – We are all delighted to hear of dear M^rs^ Loughs improvement, & do not fear that the Summer will produce still further – & she will become as active as *a Cat* after all her suffering poor Body – I have no Penrith news for her – not having heard from M^rs^ Ellwood lately – or remember to have seen anything in the papers which might interest her. Miss Wordsworth is rather busy writing Letters today which must be finished, else she would have written to her God-daughter – so this Letter of mine must serve for both you & Elizabeth[2] – for I have not news here for you to make two Letters – When you have been at Rydal Mount then I shall have less difficulty in finding something to say to you – I am glad to find that Mrs Wheelwright was so kind as to give you Instructions in Drawing – Cousin Willy[2] too is learning from M^r^ Pappendiek (the Gentleman he lives with in Germany who is a very good Artist) – Willy has been very poorly this Winter – the weather has been so severe – that all the Family he is with were very ill in colds – but they were mending when he last wrote – He sent us one of his Drawings which was very good indeed – but M^r^ P. had *touched* the Trees which he says he cannot yet do well.

Coz. Dora's Doves – Fishes – & Neptune are all well – as I hope your Doves & Prinny* are to whom I send my *compliments*. Tho' before them I ought to have sent all our *loves* to you & the Boys – & to Miss Urwick & M^rs^ Lough – & our remembrances to poor old Wm & Nancy & to Christy & Sally – & mine to the Maids – God bless

* 'Prinny is the dog we have a painting of and Quillinan wrote the epitaph of.' Note by Emma, granddaughter of Thomas and Mary Hutchinson,

you all! And believe me ever dearest Mary & Ebba your affectionate Aunt S. Hutchinson

Rydal Mount, 26th March

## 137

*Edward Quillinan Esq$^{re}$, 12 Bryanston Street, Portman Square*

*Rydal Mount, July 31st* [*1830*]

My dear Friend

Old Lady Diana le Fleming used to say that it was the most *vulgar* thing in Life to be offended, and therefore, knowing you are not one of the vulgar I presume all your messages & taunts were sent in perfect good humour else I should not have dared to take pen in hand to write to you any more after my long & obstinate silence; for which I crave your pardon. Hitherto I have had little but dolefuls to communicate to any of my friends – for poor Dora's state of health has caused us so much anxiety that I had no pleasure in writing to any one – but now I am happy to say she is really convalescent – & for the last ten days has improved so rapidly that had she but a little more flesh upon her bones it would be difficult to believe she had been ill so very lately – Her spirits have always been good – and she & I are about to set out on a tour of the Cumberland coast from which I hope I shall bring her home quite well & strong. We have as usual, a throng of summer visitors & the house has been more like an Inn, for the last six weeks, than a private one – so that quiet which was quite necessary for her could not be had here – & the weather till within the last week so very wet that we could not seek quiet elsewhere as we wished – Now we have got summer weather, &, if it does not prove to[o] hot, on monday we intend to take our departure & leave the pleasure of making the agreeables to those that remain behind – For one *long* fortnight we had Mrs Hemans & one of her boys – he was a sweet interesting creature – but she tho' a good-natured person is so spoilt by the adulation of '*the world*' that her affectation is perfectly unendurable – Don't say this to Miss Jewsbury who idolizes her – Mr W. *pretends* to like her very much – but I believe it is only because we do not – for she is the very opposite, her good-nature excepted, of anything he ever admired before either in *theory or practice* – I wish you had been here – I am sure you would have been amused at least – & with our present visitors, Professor &

Miss Hamilton, delighted – He is a great *genius* in the mathematical & *astronomy* line – & his sister (very plain – Mrs Hemans they say has been a beauty) is a simple modest Girl with ten times the feeling & writes ten times better poetry than Mrs H. tho' *she* would be shocked if she thought *the world* should ever know that she had written a line – We have also had dear little Tom[8] Hutchinson *all the way from Brinsop,* spending his midsummer vacation with us, & Bertha & Cuthbert Southey – and last of all, for nearly three weeks, our Rector & his *intended** – We are glad that you like *her* – for she has won all our hearts – Do you not think his Reverence a bold man to think of entering upon the marriage state with his poor Rectory – In truth we should all have been much better satisfied if this step had not been taken till he had something better in the shape of worldly goods to offer her – but her father has most liberally & disinterestedly made all easy to the young couple that they may not be left to 'pine on from day to day' – & she is so moderate in her desires that I am sure she will be contented even if she were to live her whole life as the Rector of Moresbys Wife – Her Father and Mother are very happy in the choice she has made – & as Wm says '*he is very much gratified that his son has so comported himself as to win the affections of so amiable a young Lady*'. You *do* think her so, but if you had not I would have won you also by telling you that she was charmed with dear Mima – and pleased too with funny little Rotha – You are a provoking creature never to have brought them to see us – I can't forgive that journey to Derbyshire – & now, when I think of it, *that* is the very reason why I have not written to you – & this I confess in spite of Lady Di's opinion given in the beginning of this epistle.

Now for gossip if I can invent any – First Barber has deserted us & *Mr Carr* also, to whom during the Spring he took a violent Fancy & seldom let him take his dinner in peace *until* he was invited to partake of it. But Mrs Hemans; Mrs Fox; & a party of Tyrconnels & Wynyards (who are lodging at Bowness & who go about the country more fantastically dressed than even B. himself) are more engaging than *we* at present – so we are *relieved* – but when winter comes he will return to us – so that we have the satisfaction of knowing that he cannot call us mere *summer friends* – . . . Mrs Hemans is now with her 3 boys at Doves nest – & did talk of coming to Spring Cottage, but I hope she will change her mind & go to Edinburgh whither she has been invited to take a second draught of the flattery which was so agreeable to her there last summer – & of which she has found a scanty supply here – 'Ill natured Creature *you* are' I think I hear you say – but

* John[4], and Isabella Curwen were married 11 Oct. 1830.

I don't care – I am used to such compliments from you – Elizabeth[3] Cookson & her Sister are now settled in a pretty Cottage near Mr Harrison's where they teach a day school & are very comfortable & happy – but perhaps you have not heard that their Father's affairs in consequence of the *bad times* have been somewhat deranged, & they thought it incumbent upon them to do something in order to relieve him from a part of the burthen of his large family – & a *day school* being much wanted for the *Gentry's* Children in Ambleside they have established one which I hope will answer their expectations – Every body is very kind to them & they have by this step raised themselves in the estimation of everyone – Now I think this is all the news I have – You may perhaps have heard from Mr Gordon that Willy has removed from Bremen to *Neweid* (or some such place) on the Rhine – He writes in excellent spirits & says his health is daily improving – so that I hope he will be able to remain long enough to accomplish the end for which he left home – *Every body* in this house send their love to you & the Dears. Dora will be greatly obliged to you to buy for her a *beautiful* & *very small* seal on which the crest must be engraven which I send on the enclosed wax – It is for her Sister *Isabella* – Mr Gordon will frank it when it is ready – Keep the Impression because I shall, *perhaps*, favor you with another commission on which the same crest will require to be engraven. God bless you & yours – & believe me very truly your Friend S. H.

Tell me *how long* you can *put on* without a supply of socks – that I may regulate my fingers according to your need.

It is *tea time*. Mrs Hemans & the Cooksons are come in to tea – What bad taste in me to have been writing to you rather than attending to Mrs. H's '*brilliant*' conversation – for she is always, or would be, brilliant but never natural –

I must not forget to tell you that Barber is in a perfect fury occasioned by the marriage of Mrs Heber – He had been as furious some time ago when the possibility of such an event was named, & he wrote to her Sister that he might have the power of contradicting the Slander by authority – the Widow herself sent a reply that it was neither 'in esse nor posse' – but the Greek Count had not then appeared – Mrs Hemanns says she feels as if she had done something wrong herself – & is quite ashamed of the verses she wrote to Mrs Heber which are in her *Songs of the Affections* – Mr Hamilton made us laugh by his apology for her – that in the intensity of her sorrow she forgot herself & married a greek Count – Mr W. reiterates his opinion that there is no folly a woman will not be guilty of *in this line* – We have never seen the marriage in the papers. Her friends did not know of it for a week after it took place – so she has some grace left – Her Sister Mrs Dashwood has taken [to] her Bed upon it & has written a most heart rending Letter to B—. B. fairly wept in Anguish – *You know* he hates marriages of all kinds – but this is beyond his endurance –

*No postmark. Pencil: 1830*

## 138

*Penrith Sep: eleven 1830,*
*Edward Quillinan Esq, 12 Bryanston Sqe, London*
*W. Marsham*

[*13 Sept. 1830*]

My dear Friend, Hallsteads Sat. Morning – This letter* was brought over the Hill for two reasons – first that I might find leisure here to finish it & secondly that a Frank could be met with at Patterdale – Wm, the Dr, Dora & I came to Patterdale Hall yesterday & after stopping a few hours proceeded here to a dinner Party at which we had all been much rather excused – We return to Patterdale, after breakfast where we remain till Monday – Amongst the luxuries of this House *good* pens are not of the number. I have tried 3 & can scarcely make a stroke – tho' they are all new & tempting looking Pens as you would wish to see – I hope this will find you in Town for we have an important commission for you to execute (if you will be so kind as undertake it) & there is no one else in Town upon whose *taste* we can rely – We have 70 or 75£ to spend in Plate for John & it has been suggested that second hand Plate may be had in London as good as new and at the difference of 7/– old & 10/6 new – Therefore if you just take the trouble of going to Rundles where you are sure to find *good old* if it is to be had – & purchase a Tea & Coffee Pot, Sugar & Cream Jug *to match* – what is called a set – as observe they are not however cheap & handsome to be *odds & ends* – & we should prefer what is called the melon pattern – which is without any chasing or frosting – Also a Toast Rack – A Soup Ladle – Sugar Tongs & Spoon & 4 *old fashioned* salt cellars round ones with little feet which are very common & plentiful in all shops – Dora ought to have made a sketch of this article – for if you do not hit upon the right Pattern She will be

* i.e. Wordsworth's, to which hers was added.

quite unhappy as our little Salt sellars are her *pets* & she wishes these to be the same – If you meet with the Tea set second hand to suit – & the Salts the proper kind second hand also – the smaller articles you will buy new – as they are not likely to be found good – But if second-hand is not to be had I think we can please ourselves with *new* here – & beg you may not trouble yourself any further than going to Rundles – I feared I had made too many words but I have read my production to Dora who lazy thing is yet in bed, & she says it is quite clear & intelligible – but I greatly fear you will not be in Town & we are in wedding haste – Mr W. has given you such a *Newsy* Letter that I have nothing left to say – only love to the dears – & believe me truly yours S. H.

*Postmark: Penrith, FREE, 13 Se 1830*

## 139

*Edward Quillinan Esq*[re] *12 Bryanston Street, Portman Square London*

*Rydal Mount, Nov*[r] *14th* [*1830*]

My dear Friend

Your information is *nearly* correct – My Sister & Dora will be at Cambridge on Tuesday – but as Mr W. travels on *Horseback* perhaps he may be a day or two later. They are all to leave Coleorton (where they have been for the last week) together tomorrow Evening – You will marvel at my saying Mr W. travels on horseback – but it is even so – all the way from Westmorland, or rather from Lancaster, has he ridden his Daughters Poney that she might have the benefit of it during her stay at Cambridge – & he has performed his journey to a miracle – – proud is he of his performance! – I believe they intend to make rather a long stay at Trinity Lodge – & Mr W. talks of 'running up' to Town for a short time – but the *when* was not determined before they left home – but I am sure he would be sorely annoyed if he thought you declined a Tenant for your House on his account – as he will be a Batchelor, while in Town, & may easily be accommodated – My Sister & Dora are not to be with him but remain quietly at Trinity – For my part I can assure you that I should have greatly enjoyed a Christmas Holiday with you & the Dears – but I cannot leave home at present – We could not be easy to leave Miss Wordsworth alone tho' she is well she is not strong, & her health is precarious & uncertain – If we could have left her I should probably have been of the Party to Trinity Lodge – Well, but another Christmas, 'if we live, flourish, & keep *un*married' this pleasant scheme of yours may be put in execution – but the Stockings must be knit here this year – what will you do with the Dears if you let the House? I wish we were not so far off – Miss W. & I would have been glad of their company to make a Stir in our quiet habitation – for doubly quiet does it seem from the usual bustle of company & botheration which we have had all the summer previous to the Wedding – The Pair are returned from their Tour, & are now at Workington Hall, their own house not yet being ready for their reception – When it is I am going to them for a few days to help, as we say here, to '*set up*' the house – then they will be left to Darby & Joan it throughout the winter.

Our Herefordshire Friends were all well when I last heard from them – Tom[3] spent his Midsummer holidays with us, & a happy creature was he – Mary[5] is to come next summer & stay a year with us – so that she *will* be quite a young Lady before she returns – tho' I dare say you would now find her & Ebba as eager for a good romp as heretofore, for they are very childish for their years – and as to the little Sarah[4] she is such an oddity, & so droll, that it would be worth your while, who are so fond of little Girls, to go to see her if you had no other errand – Mr Monkhouse I am afraid is almost blind, tho' he will not allow it – His Sister is very anxious that he should give up his farm – which she thinks leads him at times into great danger –

Barber has left the Country for a while – He was hipped nearly to death before he went – & after his arrival in Wales he wrote to Mrs Carter saying he was miserable and should return – but not having made his appearance I suppose he is more reconciled to his present situation – He went to an old Friend, a Mrs Young – the Aunt of the Ephesian Matron (Mrs Heber) – Mrs Luff also is aweary of her residence & wants to let or even sell – There is no one constant to the Country, thro' fair & foul weather, but ourselves – & even our patience has been sufficiently tried this summer – when the rains will cease I know not – we have had but one fair day for the last fortnight –

You say why do I ask you after the Red Indian? Why did you not give me an entertaining account of her & Egerton in your former Letter & could I help noticing it? – But she is not an *unworthy* tho' a disagreeable body – & not so disagreeable in the Country as when she is among Lions – & vain as she is she is not half as vain as Mrs Hemans that 'the world', as she calls it, runs so much after –

Mr Southey is in London at Mr Rickman's Palace Yard. & Bertha will join him there tomorrow – she called upon us on her way on Tuesday last – I hope you will go to see her for she is a dear Creature – Sara[3] Coleridge perhaps you may have heard has a Son – & is very happy & well – Hartley is going on in the usual way at Grasmere – De Quincey is still at Edinburgh – his Family here – The Ivy Cot has been empty all the Summer – Till. & his Lady never having appeared tho' they talked much about coming –

Willy[4] is at Heidelberg – where he intends to spend the Winter & has entered himself at the University for 3 months as 'Student in Philosophy' – Mother is horrified at the notion of his being enrolled among those *Bears* – but he seems to have very good intentions of making the most of his time, & I dare say she will be quite satisfied with his improvements – Poor Fellow! I know not what he can do with himself when he returns – He is well & happy now but if there is no employment for him at home he will be quite the contrary – Now I have no more news or gossip for you so good bye & with dear love from Miss W. to yourself & the *Bairns* believe me ever most truly your Friend S. H.

. . . We never hear of Mrs Dick – She made a demand of nearly 400 a year for Marys[5] education – & the Chancellor awarded her 150!! . . .

I wish I had had your Letter yesterday then I could have sent this under cover to Mr Gordon for I am sure it is not worth postage – & this I shall conclude is your opinion also unless you write soon to say the contrary.

*Postmark: Kendal, Penny Post, 16 NO 1830*

## 140

*Mrs Hutchinson, Brinsop Court, nr Hereford*

*Jan[y] 6th, Rydal Mount [1831]*

My dearest Mary

Isabella[2], who tells me she has had a kind Letter from you, says that you expect to hear from me – so I *must* write tho' unwillingly as I have neither a frank or much to say that you do not know already – viz. that I love you all dearly & think of you constantly – & thankful am I that you have been hitherto escaped these wicked burnings that have been so frequent in other parts of the country, & even near to you

– John[2] too, Mary[1] tells us, has had a threatening letter – but I trust nothing worse & that the culprit will in due time meet with his reward. Mary desired us to say that she had rec^d your Letter & was thankful that Thos had kept it in his pocket so long as you were enabled to give her a better account of the state of the Sheep – for your previous losses we grieved indeed – but of what use is it – I hope you are all well & enjoying the company of the dear children this Christmas – they, dear things! have no forbodings – & are happy – while all but the *very* children seem in fear & dread of the future – One comfort is that the thing dreaded seldom comes to pass – & mine is that the Whigs & Radicals are *in* power – & the friends of good order out* – from whom we have nothing to fear – & it is but fair that those who have caused the agitation sh^d have the trouble of allaying it – & depend upon it they will not find it either convenient or prudent to make all those sweeping & dangerous reforms which they deemed so necessary when they had no concern in governing the Country. And if the revolutionary spirit subsides on the continent, of which there is at present some sign, *we* shall, I hope, settle into soberness – If each state is wise enough to leave its neighbour to settle its own quarrels they will soon tire of fighting among themselves where nothing is to be gained & much lost – at any rate all is as bad as it can be at present & therefore we may comfort ourselves with the hope that a change may bring some good. Mary would have written to you but their *frankers* being all departed she did not like to put you to the expence of postage. . . .

We have had very pleasant Letters from Willy[2] *the Student at Heidelberg* – He has not any fears of being driven home by disturbances – so I hope he will remain his full time – for, poor Fellow! I know not what is to become of him when he does return – he will not be happy to be an Idler in his fathers house. The poor Cooksons are at their wits end, I have no doubt, about some of their Lads of which the poor mother used to be so proud!! Tom works journeywork *in a mill not their own* – John is at Liverpool getting a job as he may & this of the very humblest kind – Edwin was sent to Manchester in the hopes of a situation – & none can be procured but where he must be engaged for 7 years at a salary of 5£ for the first year, & not more than 30 for the last – in the mean time his board would cost 50 per an. besides washing & clothes – & in these counting houses they are obliged to be dressed smart – so poor M^r C. must have him home again – M^rs C. is with Eliz.[3] who has been very poorly & is mending slowly – Miss W. is gone over to her this morning to persuade her to think of putting the Boy to a handycraft trade or to a druggist in some town where his

* Since the recent election, Nov. 1830.

board will not be so expensive – & I do not see why anyones pride in these times sh[d] prevent their sending a son to be a Cabinet Maker, *with Gillow* at least, or even a house painter which last trade is very profitable and needs little capital – & then what an advantage to send them out to Vandiemens or other lands with a trade in their fingers – & poor M[r] C. himself would have done well if he had followed his own inclinations & gone out with them all some years ago – he knew well enough then that all was going on wrong at home. M[rs] C. is going to London in a fortnight to stay over the confinement of Stricklands wife in April – by the bye *if game* is plentiful could you send a present to them for me – if not a goose or Turkey for which I shall expect to be allowed to pay for in these bad times *farmers* must not make presents. Friday, I was interrupted yesterday by the arrival of M[r] Harrison to escort me to their house where D. had consented to remain to dine & we returned home to tea – for I assure you we take good care of ourselves – wea[ther] is now beautiful – clear & frosty – nice Xmas weather for the young but it pinches us old ones – yet we do not complain as much of it as our absentees – neither do I think it has been so severe in the north. In the neigh[d] of Whitehaven the ploughing has never been stopped by frost – & of snow we have had no more than a sprinkling – I had a very cheerful Letter from Joanna a few days ago she now talks confidently of visiting you in the Summer. . . .

I stayed a few days at Keswick on my way home – all well there – but S[outhey] & Bertha absent. S. I suppose is on his way home – but B. remains in London – Sara[3] Coleridges Baby is quite a wonder – very large & handsome – but Bertha says it does not look *natural* in her arms – Mary[1] & Dora[2] have seen them all – Sara they say is herself more beautiful than ever – & she is very happy – They have also seen M[rs] Gee – & are delighted to find her so comfortable so useful & happy as she seems to be in her situation – & the school is prosperous beyond their utmost hopes – M[rs] Clarkson is very anxious that *our folk* should visit Playford – but I know not whether it will be accomplished. They are so fearful of incurring any additional expence – John's[4] marriage has made a long pull upon W[m] purse for furniture – & the interest of money being so low – that we are all very poor – You will be glad to hear that Brougham has made Tom[5] Clarkson a Comm[r] of Bankruptcy, which in ordinary time will be 400 a year to him—in *good* times (i.e. bad ones for all but Lawyers) it has been 8 or 9 – B. had gratitude in him however – he has made Leo: Edmunds his private sec: the judgment may be doubted that placed a young untried attorney in such a situation – but the kindness cannot – poor M[r] Edmunds lost his life by his exertions previous to the last contest in

West$^{r}$ – they say we are to have a fiercer contest than ever – but I think nobody will care how it goes now – we were sadly alarmed yesterday by a report that Halsteads was burnt to the ground – this is not true but a hunting box at Melmsby belonging to the young Marshalls has been burnt – by Poachers it is supposed to whom they were obnoxious for their strict preservation of the manor which I suppose they hire – All is quiet in this neighbourhood & the people go on feasting as usual in this season. We decline all invitations to these parties—it does not suit D[orothy][1] tho' she likes them which I do not – so we keep snug by our own fire side – and now I think you will be much satisfied with the length of my epistle I have not written so much for months except business – my eyes have been bad – & I fear to use them much – so do nothing but knit or net. Our best love & good wishes to you all dearest Friends both at Brinsop & Stow – I have not room to particularize each of the darlings. . . .

I have almost forgotten, to my shame be it spoken, to enquire after dearest Thomas'[1] *nose*. Pray tell me if he feels the same annoyance from it or what I had rather hear that it is better – W$^{m}$ has bought his money into Louisiana Stock – which is well thought of & pays nearly 5 per C$^{t}$ – but *we* are all too low now to sell – I suppose Thos is in the same predicament with me in the shabby 3½ – God bless you all, for ever, ever your most affly S. H. Write soon.

I have said nothing about the new married pair as I find Isa wrote to you – they are well & as happy as possible & if they have no bairns I hope they will be well enough not to be unhappy on that score for from such Stock there is small hope of a healthy progeny.*

*Postmark: Kendal, Penny Post*

## 141

*Edward Quillinan Esq$^{r}$, 12 Bryanston Street, Portman Square, London*

[*29 April, 1831*]

My dear Friend

Your bright-faced Darling† made her appearance here yesterday Evening along with her Godfather to our no small surprize – as from a

* Sara was unduly pessimistic. The marriage brought six children, some of whom lived well into the twentieth century.

† Rotha Quillinan. Wordsworth was her godfather.

Letter received from Dora the day before we had no hope of seeing any of the Party so soon – my poor Sister having left Cambridge suffering from the Lumbago which she hoped the exercise would cure became so much worse during the journey that on Tuesday morning she could not leave her Bed & a physician was called in who said that it would be impossible for her to travel for some days even if the pain left her as suddenly as it had come on – so Dora & she were left behind & are in comfortable lodgings under the care of *Mary Howitt*, her Husband, & his Brother the physician – Mr W. being *obliged* to leave them brought Rotha with him & a more delightful fellow Traveller he says he never had – we are all charmed with her – She seems as happy & as much at home as if she had known us all her life – was glad to come, she tells me, but adds 'I should have liked it better if Papa & Mima had come also' – She asked Mr W. to shew her the Brook she is named after as soon as she supposed they were drawing near the end of their journey – They came from Kendal in a Car – & during their drive Mr W. said too her 'Now R. you know I am your Godfather & ought to know whether you can say your prayers &c – so let us repeat the Lords Prayer together' with which she instantly complied & having finished she looked up to him with an arch smile (as if conscious there was something ridiculous in their so doing in such a situation) saying 'I hope the Driver did not hear us' – I wish we may not spoil her which will be rather difficult for us to avoid – if we do not the merit will be all her's – Mrs J. Wordsworth who is here was the favorite last night – but this morning I think I have gained ground – having been the only one permitted to peruse her Letter on the other side – which she sate down to write of her own accord – and with as much ease as if Letter writing was her customary occupation – I am sure she is a very clever child – & in her face she is as like yourself as it is possible – Miss W. says she is like me also.* – We shall be glad to hear from you soon – The trip to Paris is very opportune for dear Mima – else she must have felt Rotha's absence very much – God bless you both! & with my best wishes for a pleasant journey believe me very truly your Friend S. H.

*April 29 1831*

My dear Mima

I got to rydal on thur about 7 o'clock. it is such a pretty place. I am sorry to say mrs wordsworth has got the lumbago very bad. there is a picture of you in my room with little flora and I think it is like you.

* Edward Quillinan and Sara Hutchinson were said to look alike.

there is a picture of papa too but I do not think it is much like him. tell Eliza I have bought the doll. it has light hair and blue eyes and also give my love to her. The students at cambridge have such funy caps and gowns. I went one sunday Trinity college chapel and all of the students wear surplises I dont know wether I have spelt it right. Believe me to be your affectionate sister Rotha Quillinan. there is such a larg dog called neptune almost as large as a calf so if he jumped upon me he would most likely turn me over.

*Postmark: Kendal, Penny Post, 2 MY 1831*

## 142

*Edward Quillinan Esq*[r]*, 12 Bryanston Street, Portman Square, London*

*May 10th* [*1831*]

My dear Friend

I know you will be glad to hear that my Sister & Dora are at last safe at home again – tho' detained until last Saturday at Nottingham – My Sister is much better than we could have hoped after such a severe attack, & bore her journey very well – indeed she says she improved during her progress – Dora quite well – & much the better for her wintering in the South – Your Darling well also – & very happy – & in as great favor with all the House as ever – a better & sweeter Child cannot be – My Sister & Dora & myself are all decided in our *opinion* that you *ought* not to take Jemima to Portugal, which we take the liberty of giving as you ask it – My Sister bids me say that you had best leave her at School – if you are not satisfied to leave her in Town – or at Hendon bring her to Miss Dowlings – This is all that I have to say – Rotha, who is now taking her music Lesson, is to fill up the paper which I guess she will do in a more entertaining strain than I can – for we are all in the Dolefuls – I have not had a drop of comfort, except the Camb. Election, in our cups since the return of Mr W. – Miss W. & I dolorus enough before – but he has made us ten times worse. We are very sorry for your friends, the Wakes, & for your disappointment in consequence – *that* trip for Mima would have been both pleasant & useful to her – but, poor Thing! why toss her about on the Seas *for nothing* – No such duty, I trust, will devolve upon us – but, should it, most faithfull will it be performed to this dear little creature.

All send their best love to you & Mima – & believe me ever most truly. Your friend S. H.*

My dear papa
I am very much obliged to you for the nice letter you sent me. it arrived in proper time, mima has not written yet tell her it is a great shame, I have seen the cottage where I was born but It was locked so I could not get in. I went to ivy cottage. I have seen the Rotha but it is no puddle as the young ladyes at school said but a very nice cleair stream, I am so fond of neptune the great dog he doesnt bite any body but beggars but when they come he has his muzzal on. I hope Eliza will not scold for not having written to her but give my love to her and say I will next time, I hope jessy is well believe me to be your affectionate little girl Rotha, excuse the bad writing I am learning to ride; it is very cheap. joseph, mrs john wordsworths man is quite a poet. I will tell you some of his verses. I met your dog at my door step, I understood they called him nep; I put clog shoes to his muzzle and charged him not to get them in his guzzle. mr robinson desires his remembrances to you. his little girl came to spend the day on saturday.

Here is a Blank space (left for Dora I suppose) but I cannot help saying one word – that your little Daughter is writing beside me – copying a poem for her own pleasure – that I *delight* in having her beside me; for she is the best & pleasantest & happiest Child I ever knew – In this judgment of her we all agree – adieu my dear Friend – Yours ever D. W. Sen^r^.

*Postmark: Kendal, Penny Post, 12 MY 1831*

## 143

*Edward Quillinan Esq^r^, 12 Bryanston Street, Portman Square*

*Rydal Mount, May 16th*

My dear Friend
You will be surprized to hear that my Sister in spite of her recent attack of Lumbago has again taken flight & before you receive this will be, I hope, safe at Cheltenham – A Letter reached us yesterday morn^g^

* Following De Selincourt's principle I have not usually included additions by others to Sara's letters, but the preceding one and the two short notes that follow seemed irresistible. The last one is not published in the *Wordsworth Letters*.

from poor old Dr Bell (who has long been in a declining state) containing an earnest request that Miss W[ordsworth] would go to him immediately 'to take care of him & his Sister' – &, as she could not take such a journey (& it would have been quite inhuman to have refused the poor old man under such circumstances) it was resolved that my sister should set off forthwith – which she did by the Mail from Kendal last Night – she was quite well & in hopes that the journey might not be unserviceable to her – as she can have the benefit of warm baths – She will not stay longer than she can possibly avoid – & will return by Brinsop & bring Mary Hutchinson[6] home with her – the prospect of a companion is a great joy to Rotha – By the bye Mrs H. bade me say to you, when I next wrote, that Mr Ricardo had given them full power over the Game at Brinsop & that they hoped you would go & deal destruction amongst it this autumn – Your Darling is quite well – & the Darling of the whole house here – Parlour & kitchen – there is not a dissentient voice – I fancy she is grown a little already – but unluckily I did not think of measuring her height until she had been 3 weeks with us – Barber is returned looking quite blooming, & as young as ever notwithstanding the dolorous account he gives of his sufferings during his absence, & the terrible cough which always comes on when first you meet him – just such an one as is acted by old Gentlemen on the Stage – O had you but seen him when Dora & I called 2 days after his return, you could never have forgotten his figure! – We were standing at his Door – he, coming up from below, announced his approach by this unhappy cough & we discovered him leaning on his staff, as if in extremity, – dressed in a very dirty white frock coat, with black velvet collar & cuffs – *queer* pantaloons of some sort – a black cloth cap like a night cap, or Jelly bag, with a huge tassel reaching to his shoulder – & a Shepherd's *grey plaid* flowing to his feet – He is charmed as you may suppose with the Reform Bill – Mr W. bids me say he is glad you gave your vote in favor of moderation & he thanks you for it – & that he shall be proud as long as he lives of having contributed to the victory at Cambridge – Do you know any thing of a Cap$^{t}$ Beaufoy formerly in the Guards – who is now residing at Bowness & who is, it is said, the author of some inflamatory handbills circulated in this neighbourhood threatening 'war to the knife' if the Reform is not carried – Ro cries out '*my* best love too to Papa' in which we all join – not forgetting dear Mima – we still hope you will not take her to Portugal – God bless you both – & believe me ever most truly your's S Hutchinson.

*Postmark: 25 MY 1831*

# 144

*Miss Elizabeth Hutchinson, Brinsop Court, Hereford*

[*11 Oct. 1831*]

Dearest Friends

You will not call this* a superior performance of dear Polly's, as far as the penwomanship is concerned – this I guess is to be accounted for by the flibberty-gibbet which she had at her side during the writing & Governante not there to keep her in order. They are both rejoiced however in the prospect of her return tho' she threatens in her Letters to keep them very hard at work – Mary[6] has gone 2 days in the week to Ambleside to Dance with Miss Cooksons Children – James generally goes with her on horseback in the morning & she walks back at noon. She likes it very much – She is quite well & looks so – & is very merry & happy. We are all well – but our poor Travellers have had a trieing time with their horse which was far too young for such a journey as I & the wise ones told Wm before he set out – & if they, that is the two Williams, had bought the horse which Dora & I had set our affections upon they would have done well – as it is they are obliged to leave it behind at Bunaw upon Loch Etive at Mr Harrisons Iron Works Farm & come home with a post horse – which is a good thing for they will not be tempted to linger in this broken weather – They have however enjoyed the sights – & Wms Eyes are quite well – They had a pleasant visit at Abbotsford – & also a very short one at Col Campbells in the Isle of Mull – they have never travelled above 15 miles a day with all theyr stoppings to boot – but the horse was far too young for constant work – We expect John[4] & Isabella[2] on their way home tomorrow – their Tour was very prosperous – 'Beau Jones' as Joanna calls him & Quillinan will soon be here & then we shall shut up for the Winter – I do not think Dora will be disposed to leave home again so soon as they wish her to go to Moresby – for I know she will not leave her Bairns & the season is too far advanced for them – so their visit will probably be put off till spring – We expect Ro to winter here as Mima is to continue in Paris for the 6 months that she was entered at School – We have heard once only from Joanna – Mary W. has given up the thoughts of joining her – Wm has promised to take her in the Spring – the weather now would not suit for our open Carriage – even when

* A letter from little Mary[6] Hutchinson to her sister, to which Sara Hutchinson's was added. From M.H.'s we learn it was written on John's[4] wedding day.

we have another horse & she dreads a shaking Coach – yet upon the whole I think her rheumatism is much better – & her general health certainly for I have not seen her look so well for many years past.

I hope you were all rejoiced that The Lords Spiritual & Temp[l] have done their duty – & I do not fear half the bad consequences that would have resulted from the passing of '*The Bill*'* – A Bill I suppose we must have – but a less wise or just one we cannot – & must hope for the best. God grant that the *burnings* may not commence again I do not believe that they ever *originated* among the Peasantry – & there have been the most of them & other atrocities in the *enlightened* Districts Your Country not being of this kind has been one of the *best behaved*. We had a fire at Ambleside on Sunday Night in a new empty house – but it is supposed that the lightening set fire to the shavings – I hope you will write to us soon – as I want to hear how poor old M[rs] Lough is? No better I fear but I trust she will not suffer long. I am vexed to think that J[ohn][2] M. has so much *plague* with his Maidens. Give our best love to him & ask him when he intends to come & see us. Henry Addisons says he always *intends* to come to see you – but when he once gets to London he cannot help staying all the time he [can] spare – Mary[3] is become apparently very strong – certainly she is [very] stout – & not so elegant-looking as before she was married – She is very lively & happy – Richards younger Daughter is a fine stout Girl but not handsome – the elder very very little but young not dwarf-like & has a very sensible countenance – I met them by accident at Patterdale & came over the Hill with them – I had been a day or two with M[rs] W. Marshall – & had my poney along. . . . We will take care that Mary is supplied with all she wants – so you need not concern yourself on this score – She is very tidy & takes care of her clothes – which would never be worse if Coz Willy were not here to romp with her & Ro – what they like well tho they pretend not – poor fellow he goes next week – God bless you all. ever yours S. H.

send the size of your round Table in dining room.

*Postmark: Kendal, Penny Post*

* The reference is to the second version of the Reform Bill which passed the House of Commons on 21 Sept. 1831, but was rejected by the House of Lords on 3 Oct.

# 145

*Edward Quillinin Esq$^{re}$, 7 Rue des Bucherons, St Germain-en-Saye, via Paris*

*Rydal Mount, Jan$^{y}$ 6th 1832*

My dear Friend

First let me express my wishes for a happy new year to you & dear Mima – Your other Darling is as well & happy as you can desire her to be yet she will be over the moon with joy when she sees you & her sister again – Sorry as we shall be to lose her I hope nothing will prevent your fulfilling your intention of being here at the end of the month, for the disappointment would be sore indeed – we have now fine w*inte*r weather, & I hope the snow may not come to stop your journey – if we had you here *we* should not care if you were kept by it & the *trotts* would be less anxious for a sight of Mima were you here – She is not much grown – but looks & is as healthy as possible & as good as needs me [be].

We have been for the last fortnight in great anxiety about dear Miss W[ordsworth] who has had a very bad attack – but I am happy to say that all present danger is over – & for four days her recovery has been very rapid – so that I hope before you come we shall have her down Stairs among us again – I know not whether you expected another Despatch while you were in France – but I now write for the sake of sending you Willy's[2] answers to your questions respecting Heiddelberg which you will find on the other side – He still relies on you for a *coat* tho' he tells us he is obliged to wear his Great Coat to cover his shabbiness – He is very happy & very gay at Carlisle in spite of the little space between C. & the Cholera which I grieve to say is raging at Newcastle & Gateshead – at Sunderland it seems almost to have disappeared – but there is small chance that it will not spread over the Island, which might have been prevented had all communication been cut off with Sunderland by land – & if it was necessary (as has been) to do this by sea one cannot but wonder where the wits of our Gov$^{t}$ have been wandering that Coaches should be allowed to travel 'at their own sweet will' all over the Country.

Dora bids me thank you for your Letter – poor Thing she has been suffering dreadfully from tooth ache for some weeks – but the last two days she has been entirely free – so that I trust the fit is over for this time – all else quite well – Cambridge J[ohn][5] W. is still with us – &

we have Dr Arnold of Rugby at the foot of the Hill & Mr Hamilton (*Cyril Thornton*)* in the Ivy Cot but tho' Mr W. & these two Gentlemen are not in sympathy (especially the Dr) on political matters, they are excellent companions for him – & we look upon their residence here at this time as most fortunate as a diversion of his anxieties respecting his poor Sister during her late attack –

Barber we never see except by chance upon the road – he is furious in favor of Reform – & poor Man has had some vexations which have not contributed to sweeten his temper – & I hardly know whether there is any one of his neighbours with whom he is in any better humor than with himself – perhaps you may pull the black dog off his back & make him more comfortable –

Mr W. will be greatly obliged if you could call at Boxalls† while you are in Town as he asked for an opportunity of sending down *the Picture* which if it be ready perhaps you could bring – & also the Gentleman (Mr W. forgets his name) with whom you dined & met Croly promised him a picture which probably Mr Boxall may have heard something about & if you could be the Carrier or bringer rather of these, without inconvenience, would be a great favour – for we should like to see *the Picture* – & he will never consent to its being sent except by a private hand – All desire their best & kindest love to you & Mima – God bless you! & believe me very sincerely Yours S. Hutchinson.

Pickersgill has not appeared, nor have we heard any thing of him. If you sh[d] chance to meet Mr Gardiner at Boxalls – give Wms *love* to him as he has been most kind in interesting himself about young J.[6] W. who is to be placed with a Surgeon in Town –

*Postmark: 18 JANY 1832*

## 146

*Edward Quillinan Esq[re], Mr George Benson's, Fern Hill, Malvern, Worcestershire*

*[July 10, 1832]*

My dear Friend

So far for Mr W.‡ in whose opinion I entirely coincide with regard to Dora – and for myself I should be utterly worthless under such a

* *Cf.* p. 358 *.

† Sir William Boxall painted a portrait of Wordsworth in 1830.

‡ i.e. Wordsworth's letter declining on Dora's behalf Quillinan's request that Dora and Sara Hutchinson become the guardians of his children in case of his death. Quillinan was about to leave England to travel abroad.

charge – for many years to come our Darlings will be at School – and when they most required the protection of a Guardian I should either be in my grave or become, probably, a helpless old woman & require somebody to take care of me – Some years ago, had I been associated with an efficient person like Henry Coleridge I should not have declined such a flattering testimony of your confidence i[n] me & would have done the utmost in my power – & nothing that Lo[ve] could do would have been wanting towards them – but now it would be injustice both to you & to them, as well as folly in myself to accept of such a Trust – But tho' we are not their lawful Guardians you know we never can lose sight of the Darlings or be other than deeply interested for them at all times & under all circumstances & ever ready to stand forward as their friends – & trust they will ever look to us as such – What I have most at heart is that they should be at a school where the Mistress of it should have a motherly interest in them – & if such is the case with Miss B it is well, as you are satisfied in other respects – but you know *whither* my *judgment* points – God bless you all! & never fear but, sweet Creatures as they are, they will find friends to protect them – should you, unfortunately be taken away from them but I trust that God in his mercy will spare you to them for many years to come.

I have written this in quick time – so excuse any faults you may find in the expression which has been, in truth, dictated by the kindest [*words missing – signature on other side cut away*] & yours – but I have had fifty things to do [*words missing*] Farquhar who is arrived at Fox Ghyll – to go to dine with the Arnolds – & to prepare the Children for their journey to Moresby whither James drives them tomorrow & brings Dora back – I am glad to say that dear Miss W. improves gradually tho' slowly – She joins with us all in love to you & the Darlings – Tell them to write to us – & I want to know if Ro. & George *suited* – as she was very well disposed towards him upon report – Again God bless you and believe me most truly your Friend S. H.

Endorsed: 1832 July

*Postmark: Kendal, Penny Post: Malvern Penny Post*

## 147

*Edward Quillinan Esq$^{re}$, 12 Waterloo Place*

*Rydal Mount, August 7th* [*1832*]

My dear Friend

I did not know when the last despatch was sent off to you else I should have added a few lines in order to remove an impression made on your mind in consequence of having taken the word 'circumstances' (in Mr W's & my joint Letter) in a wrong sense – We used it *properly* – as *scholars* would do – & never dreamt of its being understood by *you* as mere *£.S.D.* Our meaning was that were we, unfortunately, called upon to take charge of and protect your dear Children we could not do our duty to them unless they were under our own eyes – & would they think it just to bring them into this remote spot far from their own natural connections whose mode of life would appear to them much more delightful & suitable to their birth & education. So much did I feel this objection at the time that I quoted the beautiful passage in *Cymbelline* 'Haply this Life is best &c &c'. Dear creatures, we shall all be laid low before they will look upon our circumstances as anything but the walls of a Prison – & therefore I thought that under Mrs Wakes care they would find all the good that they could have with us – besides youthful companions – & all the pleasures which it is natural & right for their years to desire – But I hope, & trust, in God's mercy that you will live to resign them only into the hands of good Husbands whose circumstances in every sense of the word will be unexceptionable – & that they may be as happy as I wish them – Dear *Honeys* there is nothing that I *could* do that I would not for them – I love them both so dearly – & there is not a child in the world that I have so *tender* a love for as Ro – & I can say the same for Dora – tho' she fancies you will not believe it now when we have shrunk from the possibility of being called upon to shew our love in deed as well as word – But I am sure you cannot & do not think anything of the kind – so we will say no more about it – but may God bless you all –

Dora has some commissions for you – but leaves the news to me – the best is that dear Miss W. has been much better for the last few days, which she attributes entirely to exercise in Mrs Harrisons easy carriage, in which she has been 3 times as far as Grasmere – & we hope that she will soon be able to bear the motion of our own – which she can have more under her own command & regulation as to time – All else quite well – & *rather* quiet this week, tho' never alone for an hour –

Before I had finished the last sentence I was called away (nobody else being in the way) to make the agreeables to a party – & now Dora warns me that it is time to finish for we are engaged to pay the dear little Arnolds* a visit at Brathay – their Father & Mother having been called away to attend the sick bed of a Sister – the Children were obliged to be left behind with their Governess – But I was about to tell you that we never had so much company as this summer – the House has been full to overflowing it having been sufficiently so with our regular family – so that even one stranger was more than enough & as to callers & visitors to dinner, tea, &c there has been no end to them!! – The children, i.e. Tom[3] & Mary[6], are now gone – & dear Joanna goes on friday – We sent Mary to Miss Dowlings – for we found it quite impossible to attend to her properly – & thought it a pity to send her home until Christmas when Tom & she will go together – Mr W. is at Lowther – his eyes were better when he set off – & while Mr Hare was with us – & Dr Arnold at Brathay – he took long walks upon the mountains & said he clomb Helvellyn with more ease than he did 15 years ago – Mr Sharp & the Nightingale are in the country – Mr W. & Dora spent 3 days with them at Storrs – they are now at Keswick but will return hither.

This is Regatta Day at Low Wood – there has been one Ball already & another to be to morrow Ev[g] at Ambleside – a Bowness Regatta on the 22nd – So in spite of Cholera you see the folk are determined to enjoy life while they are in it – God bless & preserve you & your Darlings to whom my best love – & believe me ever yours sincerely S. H.

*Postmark: T.P., Charing Cross, 6 SP 1832*

## 148

To Mrs. S. T. Coleridge, c/o Mrs. H. N. Coleridge
Downshire Terrace, Hampstead [9] Feb. [1833]

| | £ | s. | d. |
|---|---|---|---|
| Due to Miss W. after the last settlement - - - - | 1. | 9. | 5 |
| Paid Washerwoman- - - - - - - - - - - - - - | | 16. | 7½ |
| Mrs. Fleming- - - - - - - - - - - - - - - - - | 10. | 13. | 4 |

* One wonders if 'the dear little Arnolds' included Matthew; he was then ten years old.

| | | | |
|---|---|---|---|
| Car[riage] of Books Packing Cases &c. S. T. C. | 1. | 1. | 4 |
| D° Box of Cloathes - - - - - - - - - - - - - - | | 7. | 6 |
| Mrs. Fleming - - - - - - - - - - - - - - - - - - | 8. | 18. | 9 |
| D° - - - - - - - - - - - - - - - - - - - - - - - - | 5. | 5. | |
| D° - - - - - - - - - - - - - - - - - - - - - - - - | 11. | 12. | 2 |
| D° - - - - - - - - - - - - - - - - - - - - - - - - | 11. | 15. | 9 |
| Washerwoman - - - - - - - - - - - - - - - - - | 1. | 1. | 11 |
| Mrs. Fleming - - - - - - - - - - - - - - - - - - | 12. | –. | 6 |
| D° - - - - - - - - - - - - - - - - - - - - - - - - | 5. | – | |
| D° - - - - - - - - - - - - - - - - - - - - - - - - | 9. | 14. | |
| A small debt at Keswick - - - - - - - - - - - - | | 5. | |
| | 80. | 3. | 3½ |
| Rec[d]. from Mrs. C. - - - - - - - - - - - - - - - | 65. | | |
| due to Miss W. | 15. | 3. | 3 |

My dear Friend

The above is a statement of Hartleys account which is now finally settled – I believe it is accurate – but you must excuse dates which I have not given as they would only have puzzled you – as the whole Q[uarte]r was not always paid up when due, in the hope that H. might have paid a part himself (which he did 5£ in one instance) which Mrs F. would not have liked to do unless it had been owing to her – We have heard nothing of him lately – & as he has not come as was reported to be his intention I hope he is still at work & doing well – Poor Mrs. Green you will perhaps have heard is dead, & her Daughter going to settle at Keswick where she is at present so that we shall not have means of hearing of him through that quarter in future.

Many thanks for your kind Letter which should have had a more speedy reply but that I wished to sent you the account at the same time & dearest Dorothy[1] I grieve to say has seldom been in a state fit to be asked any questions about it, & without her aid I could not understand her memorandum book – I wish I could say she was better even now when we have accomplished the matter, but alas! my dear Friend, I fear she will not be long with us – for the last three weeks she has become much worse – tho' gradually – & her weakness & languor are truly deplorable – indeed without the help of stimulants you could scarcely believe her alive – but with these she is kept at times tolerably easy – & even comfortable & *cheer*ful – which is always the case when free from pain & languor – Her patience never forsakes her – & tho' entirely confined to her bed – she never complains of being weary of it – Mr. Carr gives us no hope of her recovery – Her poor Brother strives to hope against hope – & to him we dare not breathe the fears which oppress us – yet he knows but too well that we must soon lose her – Gods will be done! & I trust he will enable us to bear our sad loss, happen when it may, as we ought to do – & be grateful for the time she has been spared to us – it would indeed be selfish to wish her stay among us suffering as she does, & feeling that our loss must be her gain – I ought not to have given *you* these melancholy details who have so much sorrow at home – but as out of the fulness of the heart the mouth speaketh – so will my pen.

We were truly grieved to hear that your dear Child is still a sufferer – but her's is not a hopeless case – & ere this I trust she is something better – pray write soon – & as dear Dorothy is always anxious for news of you, & wishes to see your Letters do not write in the strain which I have done respecting her – We are all else well – Dora's cold gone – tho' it has told its tale upon her strength & looks – & her anxiety on her dear Aunts account has no salutary effect upon her as you may conceive – They are all well at Keswick, & the Isle of Man – Every one here send their kindest remembrances & love to you – dear S. T. C. & Henry & Sara – & may God bless you all! ever prays your aff^te^ Friend

S. H.

Isabella[2] is pretty well – John[4] not quite recovered from his sprain, Willy[2] quite well – tho' he had an accident upon the ice which confin'd him for a few days.

Our Housekeeper, Dora, will thank you to pay £5.11.4 for her (discount to be allowed) to Cotterell & Son Tallow Chandlers Kensington. By writing a note to them they will call at Henrys Chambers for the money – at any time you may appoint – perhaps I had best enclose the Bill –

*Postmark: Fe. 1833*

## 149

*Edward Quillinan Esq^re^, 12 Waterloo Place, London*

*Rydal Mount, 27th of May* [*1833*]

My dear Friend

... I shall be unlucky in not seeing you – but there will be plenty left to give you & yours a hearty welcome – but still I say bring the

Darlings to holidays at Brinsop – especially as Mr W. pronounces it folly to *fag* such little ones into Scotland – however this will be decided by your *ultimate* decision with respect to the school – But first for the Epitaph* with which we are very much pleased – Miss W. is *provoked* that you do not write more – she says "he has more wit (using the word in its oldfashioned sense) than ½ of them" & it is a shame that you should be so *idle*. W^m thought there was an ambiguity in the 3rd line '*& but Few*' when I read it to him – but this is removed when you read & see it yourself – He finds no fault with the fourth – or 7th & 8th on the score you point out – In the last but one he thinks 'And *to* lone anguish' (which makes the construction clearer) better than 'And the lone anguish' – & so ends our criticisms & corrections – except that there ought to be a comma after '*merits*, rest'.

Now I must thank for us for the reading of your Letter – which is a very entertaining one, spite of your perplexities – & a proof that your whirling head does not affect your spirits – tho' I should be glad to know that it *is* merely a nervous affection – & which I trust change of scene will rid you of – yet I do not like to hear of your Italian scheme – tho' Mr W., as you know, thinks travel the sovereign remedy for all things, as well as the highest enjoyment – & approves *therefore* – It depends upon your *object* he says, what shall be your previous study in case you have any *particular* object – I say you might write a most agreeable journal (for you see I want to stimulate you to be industrious) if you could give us any notion of the People & their condition &c – for all who have travelled in Italy are so intent upon the antiquities, works of art, & scenery that of that People & their condition we know as little as of the chinese – as you have read Sismondi's Hist.† It would be as well to read Darus (a frenchman) hist of Venice‡ which bears a high character tho' W^m has not read it – Machiavelli's Hist. of Florence – & refresh your memory with Benvenuto Cellini – Look at Polybius & Livy for the account of Hanibal – but perhaps Forsyth§ will give you the substance of what is necessary for you in this head – We think that if you do resolve to go to Italy you would do well to pay your long promised visit to Cambridge John after Chris returns – and he is expected soon – he has been a most careful observer & will be *fresh* & ready to tell you the all & how about it – Dora would tell you she had a Letter from him begun on the top of Parnassus – & since

* Possibly the epitaph for Prinny? See p. 369 and note.

† Sismondi, J. C. L. de, *History of the Italian Republics*, 1807.

‡ Daru, P. A. N. B., *Histoire de la république de Vénise*, 7 vols., Paris, 1819.

§ Forsyth, Joseph, *Remarks on Antiquities Arts and Letters during an Excursion in Italy in the years 1802 and 1803* (1813).

she has had one from the neighbourhood of Florence on his way home – But Miss Wordsworth's Lover* will do this also if you are not too proud to seek him out – & depend upon it he has not cut you – good-natured creature he cuts nobody – so why should you suspect him – he said he did not know your address. He will be in Town till the middle of June – then comes hither – on the wings of love I suppose – & talks of taking off Mr W. to the Hebrides with him who if his Sister continues tolerably will be nothing loth –

As to the dear Children which after all (excuse me) is the most important matter – *You know* it was always my opinion that they would have done very well at Miss D[owling]'s *from the* first – & I have never ceased to regret that you did not send them there & stay by them tho' according to the regulations of that school you would not have seen as much of them during school times as you have done while they have been with Miss B— & you might have perhaps been spared other perplexities – but this is ungracious – I did not mean to be so – but to counsel & help you to the utmost of my skill – but (as I was going to say) *now*, for Jemima at least, Miss Ds would be a sort of *descent* & she having been used to a school & society of *higher tone* might feel *this* in associating with scotch north country Girls & above all *Kendalians* – You know our opinion of the solid advantages of the school – but Children do not find these out – & even 'little 'cute Ro', W$^{m}$ says, would be ready enough to quizz her companions – & perhaps compare her Teachers with those she has been accustomed to (for there are no Masters) & of course would not profit as she ought – You know the advantages of the *situation* which I need not point out – & I must add that you are quite mistaken with regard to Mr Carrs habit of '*physicing*' – I send you the particulars of the expence – & you must decide for yourself as you say you *will* do, even were I to issue my *orders* – But another plan I will suggest – Can you not find out some Town where there *is* a good school (as at Worcester or Bath or Shrewsbury) where you might send them as day-scholars & keep them at home with you as well as going to Boulogne to finish their Education – & leave your journey to Rome till they were old enough to be your companions on the journey – If they had not wanted *schooling* I am sure we would have *rid* you of them for the next twelvemonth & taken them to Brinsop & given you your liberty to ramble – but they are far beyond my hands in the *eddication* line – we none of us like the notion of Girls being educated in France – unless they had a female English Lady at home with them what would become of them? you could not always have them under your own eye when they were not

* H. Crabb Robinson (?)

at school – & if they had masters at home you could not always be present during their Lessons which it is quite necessary that some one should be. So keep them in old England I pray! unless your good Friend Mrs Wake would take care of them with her own in Scotland – Wms decided opinion is that Jemima is too far advanced for Miss Dowlings – He says if you had had them there till this time you would thought it right to have removed her now to better Masters.

I shall be very anxious to hear from you again for I truly feel for your perplexity & wish for their sakes I had been an accomplished Lady some 10 or 15 years younger. I should have liked no better *fun* than to have taken care of them at Boulogne or some more respectable place English or french for 2 or 3 years – But now even were I an accomplished Lady I have almost a dread not to say horror of the thought of leaving Rydal Mount even to go into Herefordshire lest I should not return & end my Days here – Yet I am well & strong & for these blessing[s] I trust thankful – but I cannot forget that I am not far from 3 score years old – tho I do not feel as old as I fancied when young, that I should be at forty.

All well I believe at Moresby – but we have not heard lately which accounts for our not having had an account of the arrival of the green Album which I hope is not lost – All our neighbours are well save for the Influenza which luckily has not visited us yet – All the Lodgings & houses are taken for the summer – but I dare say notwithstanding there will be a corner for three 'sike lill' ones as you & yours & we shall not quarrel on this score & there will be time enough to contrive the corner for you at *Patterdale* before you come.

Keswick John[6] writes in rather low-spirits about his cough which he says has hung upon him the whole winter – & does not give way to the warm weather – ask Mr G[illman?] what he thinks about it as at his age a cough is not to be trifled with. Our Herefordshire Friends were all well when I last heard – but it is a long time ago – & I am anxious about J[ohn][2] M's Eyes – If he has to go to Town about them I wish it might be before you leave as you would be such a comfort to him there – & I know you would be so disposed – Somebody told us that M[ary][5] M. was not gone to School & that Mrs Atherley did not believe it was Mrs D[ick]'s intention to send her – How can this be? Mr W. despises all Byron's slander & lies – & would not have any body trouble their heads about it – What a *poor creature* he must have been!!

Board & Tuition – including History Chronology, Geography, Globes, Needlework, French & English –

Under 10 years old Gs 40

| | |
|---|---|
| Above that age | 50 Gs |
| Pianoforte | 6 |
| Drawing | 6 |
| Writing & Arithmetic | 2 |
| Dancing | 4 |
| Washing | 4 |
| No extras | |
| | £75.11 [*sic*] |

One Guinea per week during the vacation if remaining which is at Xmas 4, Midsummer 6 weeks.

Of course there are Books, stationary & drawing materials beyond – but they are very frugal in these things – but it is not *cheap* for a North Country school – The School at Worster or near it where Miss Taylor was is I believe a very good one – & in Cathedral Towns there are always good Teachers of music – but of course *Masters* are more expensive – My day school plan would be the most *oeconomical* – & many good schools admit day scholars tho' Miss D's does not. Miss Wordsworth says that the Rawsons say they learnt all that was valuable at Miss D's – & were no better for their London finish – but then they *began* here which makes all the difference & nullifies our objections.

Can't you have a Copy of your Portrait made in a Cap & Ladies Gown & spare me the trouble of sitting for my friends?

Every Bodys love to you & the dear Children & believe me ever most truly your Friend S. H.

Green Book arrived.

Write soon – who is Moxons intended?* we did not know he was engaged – My letter is a sad incoherent scrawl I guess. Shame on you not to go to see poor old Jarvy!

Gee's – Boxall's print his Ruth

*Postmark: Kendal, Penny Post, 29 MY 1833*

* Emma Isola, the adopted daughter of Charles Lamb, later the wife of Wordsworth's publisher, Moxon.

# 150

*Edward Quillinan Esq$^{re}$ (Poste restante) Boulogne sur Mer*

*Rydal Mount, 27th June – 33*

My dear Friend

If I had you here you should be treated with a lecture – but I hold it an unsafe thing to lecture one's Friends by Letter – so I will not tell you how grieved we all were that you had run counter to our *good* advice respecting the dear Children, but had taken them to the very place above all others which we hold in abhorrence – Besides on the score of economy I fear you will be disappointed; for some Friends of ours who went to Boulogne lately, found the place so expensive that they resolved to proceed to Paris – with the example of the Lloyds before us we cannot approve of a French Education – your Darlings will never relish England afterwards – like the Lloyds, perhaps chuse french Husbands – & *cut* all their Friends in Eng$^{d}$ who care more for them than you seem to suppose, else you would not have taken them away – I *was* in hopes that my last Letter would have induced you to bring them to Brinsop – & there I think I could have 'made something of you' as the saying is – I little thought you were hatching such a scheme when you declined speaking of your plans – else I should have ventured upon a scolding Letter take it how you might – I trust however you will think better of the matter & bring them back to old England before any harm is done – and I beg that you will not be so *unkind* as not to write to me – & say how you have sped so far. I hope you have taken Eliza with you that the dears may not be under the care of a French woman – for tho' I do not mean to insinuate that french servants are not quite as good in their way as English ones – yet *their way* is not suitable for English People – & it would grieve me to find your Darlings come back so frenchified as not to be in love & sympathy with their old & true English Friends.

Mary[6] & I are to set off for Brinsop on Tuesday next – you know the address – & if you do not write to me I shall pester *you* with Letters & *postage* until you send them back unopened – Dora is writing & will no doubt tell you all the news – so that I confine myself merely to the *one* subject, & to beg that you will take care of yourself – for Janetta says that you look very ill – and pray break that foolish resolution which you expressed some time ago of making no more complaints – for if you believe that the communication of your troubles & vexations are not received with the same affectionate kindness as your pleasures & satisfactions I say you are – must I write it? an Ingrate! Well, you will say, Miss Hutton! this is something like a scold at last – Nevertheless God bless you & yours & believe her to be ever your (or one of them) most affectionate Friend – S. Hutchinson.

Endorsed: Rec[d] this nice letter at Boulogne Sunday July 1833.

*Postmark: 7 JU 1833,* Angleterre par Calais

## 151

*Edward Quillinan Esq[re]*

*Brinsop Court, 24th Aug[t]* [*1833*]

My dear Friend

I have done as you bade me & waited for a frank – tho' you will believe me, I know, when I say that it was not the postage that prevented my writing to you sooner, but this place does not furnish much subject for Letter writing, & I doubt not you have had all the Rydal news long ago & have been gratified by the good accounts of dear Miss W's gradual improvement in health which in our little world is the most interesting concern.

I was very thankful for your Letter & the assurances contained in it that you will not keep the Darlings too long from their native Land – & I still think you you have enough of the '*flibberty*' remaining in your composition to send you home again in good time – When I first heard of your flight I said to Dora 'Well if I go to Town I shall certainly go over to *look* after them', but I hope you will be in Eng[d] again before that time comes – I do not intend to remain so long from Rydal as heretofore when I paid my Herefordshire visits, but if Miss W's health allows me to be absent till next summer I shall, in the interim, visit both Mrs Clarkson & Mrs Gee & some other friends on the way to them – which will if I am spared so long be my last visitation in that quarter – Netta you know is at Rydal – they seem to have a busier season than usual. Wm has been out of the way for one while – even before I left home he threatened to 'cut & run' – but that time was perfect Desertion & solitude compared to the life they have had since – Here we are all as quiet & still as possible – save for the clacking of Hens, the quacking of Ducks & the gabbling of Geese under my window – but these sounds are so familiar & constant that I never hear them but could in spite of them listen to the Nightingales when they were here – & now the dear little Robins note reaches my ear in the midst of all their din & discords – I wish you could have come to us but I will say nothing about it because I should only end in scolding you for putting it out of your power to oblige your friends – I must however observe that in point of œconomy I do not think much good of your scheme – You might live quite as cheap in England – Tho' I know it would be in a much more hum-drum way – & less suited to a lively sprite like my friend –

We have had most charming weather ever since I came hither & the Harvest has been most favorable & the Crops good – Yet our farmers are in no better heart as far as these concerns go – & my brother talks of winding up his affairs – if he can get rid of his Lease – As to Mr M[onkhouse] his *delight* is *in* his occupation, & he *loses* his money with as cheerful a face as if he were *making* it – We were all spending a week with him lately – & another week we spent at Gwyndovenant* & one day at Hereford which is the sum of all our *seeings* & doings since I came hither – but I enjoy the quiet of this place greatly – only I do not relish such very early going to bed – I can be up with the earliest – but a cozy *sit* by the fire (as we have at Rydal when all is still in the house & all by but one fire side in bed) we never enjoy here – Your young Friends are all well – Ebba most happy in having her Sister at home – but poor little Ta does not now feel herself of so much consequence & is thrown upon the elders for companionship – Your friend Geo.[3] is a wonderful favorite at Rydal – He is not a bit better than my Boy Tom[3] – nay he has a spice of the Pickle in him which makes him more taking –

Have you ever in your rambles (or do you ever ramble?) lit upon Miss Barker's Chateau? It is not far from Boulogne but the Post Town is Marquise. I think she called the Place Pavillion du Paon – She I suppose with her hopeful Husband is at Paris – on some *spee* [spree?] or other I have no doubt. I should like you to make some enquiry after her – but an *acquaintanceship* with her Husband I *guess* would be no credit to anybody – & I believe she is seldom out of his sight – nor can she even write to a friend except by stealth or receive a Letter – but this is entré nous – She has paid dearly for her folly – & I cannot but pity her – & wish that she was at liberty again poor Creature – I long hoped that another wife might *turn up* or something else might break the knott – for I suspect that he is expatriated.

Is Col B[arrett] still at Ambleteuse? How well I remember that place, & how little did I suppose any friend of ours sh[d] chuse such a residence

* Gwerndyffnant, *q.v.*

– Pray write often – don't mind Postage – You have leisure enough & no lack of matter for the least trifle regarding yourself & the Children is interesting to every one here – All desire their best love & believe me very truly & affty yours S Hutchinson.

## 152

*Mrs Hutchinson, Brinsop Court, Hereford*

*Tuesday, Rugby [4 March, 1834]*

Dearest Mary

Many thanks for your Letter which was the most agreeable surprize this morning for I had calculated that mine would only reach you on Sunday & that you would not break the Sabbath. I do not mean to whip another 1/– out of your pocket so soon – but I begin to write & will fill up from time to time – else I know that at one sitting I sh[d] not have patience to put down all you wish to hear, of myself & of others. *Here* I do so long for you that I cannot help writing – such dear Children – such a nice place – tho' an ugly country – & then the master & Mrs of all would delight you. He is most like Southey in his manners & habits at home of any one I ever saw – always occupied & yet always at leisure – the house quiet as a private one – of course we see nothing of the Boys (except in the meadow before the house) & tho' their own bairns when not at lessons wander about the house at 'their own sweet will' it is so large & being carpeted all is still, & every thing goes on like clock work – such a change from Leamington where everyone is busy having nothing to do – breakfasting at eleven – here I was up at the 7 o C bell which calls the *Dr* into school – then down at the 8 to prayers & breakfast to the household – a fine range of domestics as you may suppose to be necessary – with 68 boys in this house – the rest of the 300 Lads are with the other Masters of which there are 10 in all – Edward Hill (the 2nd Brother) is Tutor to D[r] A[rnold]'s 3 eldest boys who do not yet go into school – & perhaps are not intended at any time – He enquired very kindly after you & Thos[1] & all the family – & spoke in a most animated manner of your hospitality. He [Thomas[3]] was truly pleased to see me – tho' he is very strong, D[r] A. complains that he will not talk. He saw Edith [Southey] & her Husband at Oxford where they stayed a week – & are now in Town – I came from L[eamington] yesterday – in a fly alone – I had not fixed my day but

I knew it would be all the same in this House – the Children all popped their faces to a window near the door as we drove up, & were soon upon the steps to meet me – They are all grown except *Bacco* (Mary) who is nevertheless as funny as ever – dear Ta & she would be glorious companions – little Lucy talks incessantly but so fast that I cannot catch one word she says – The house & school were rebuilt in 1816 – & a most handsome building it is – like a College – with towers battlements &c – a nice Chapel – quadrangle & cloisters – but I have as yet only seen the view of the whole from the garden. There is an ugly little Town which is increasing amazingly owing to the celebrity of the school. Many persons especially widows have come to educate their sons more cheaply – but they cannot *build* up this house as the Gardens & Boys meadow will always secure open space –

Thursday. Tomorrow I intend to depart for Cam[bridge]. A Coach passes at 3 miles distance at 1 o['clock] in the morning – which (a slow Coach) will take me to Camb. in 9 hours – I have been as much pressed to stay here longer as good & kind manners would allow – & I sh[d] have liked very well to see all the Boys at Chapel – but I cannot curb my impatience *to be on* & get my journies over – & seem as if when I get to Playford I shall feel like the Poet in that line 'then shield me in the woods again' – I found that there was to be a great party here to dine tomorrow – so that determined me – to be off tomorrow – I have been introduced to all parts of the house except the Schools & Library where D[r] A. teaches his class – & wonderful are the arrangements & order. The Dormitories are immense – some have 6. 9. 12. & 14 beds – all little camps with white hangings & quilt – a wash stand to every bed but no other furniture in the room – their Trunks are ranged on each side of the Gallery leading to the Dormitories in which are their coats &c – All their Linen kept in pigeon holes in the matrons room – & dealt out to them 4 times a week i e laid ready for them on their beds then there are sick rooms apart – hot closets in which are all the Sheets – & another for Blankets and mattresses for the sick rooms – & one less hot for great Coats all so beautiful clean & airy – that even where there are 14 beds there can never be any closeness tho' D[r] A. had had the building he would not have made the dormitory in this way – then there is an immense dining hall & a smaller hall for the head boys when they chuse to be in society – but the funniest of all are the *50* studys – little places under the dormitories just holding a *sofa* (which is their own) Book case, & 2 Tables with room to squeeze in – these are their very own of which they keep the key, & there they learn their Lessons without fire of course but they felt very warm – I do not think they are above 6 feet square – . . . another which I peeped into had a fishing net laying on the Table at which the *Student* had been working – I saw their dinner sent up yesterday – it was salt fish which they ought to have had on Ash Wednesday – & which they did not chuse to be cheated of – 2 huge pewter dishes full – three of mashed potatoes – 120 Eggs chopped for Egg sauce – 2 legs of mutton in case any did not like fish – & 3 immense plumb Puddings baked in 3 large tins like dripping Tins – we had some of the pudding to luncheon which was excellent – there are 14 ser[ts] altogether about 100 in family – on Monday they expect more visitors – & at Easter there is a great concourse of people attends the Speeches – 18 are invited to take up their lodgings here & M[rs] A. will have about 300 to do the agreeable to, – but luckily those who chuse dine with the Governors at an ordinary in the Town – so that as the D[r] and M[rs] A. are expected to do so, they have not to give the callers any dinner – But what a Life it is! Yet by regularity you would be astonished to see how all is accomplished – & how much time they both seem to have to attend upon their own Children (not to teach them for they have both Tutor & Governess) & the poor also. Every moment I wish you were here – The weather has been beautiful ever since I came till today when it looks or rather sounds bleak & wild for I am writing with the blinds down in my own room which I enjoy so much after the squeezed up place at L[eamington] where all is sacrificed to *entertaining rooms* – here is space enough all over – my bed room is 20 f by 18 – at L. what with wardrobe drawers & beds I was so closed up that I could not stir & for the first time of my life uncomfortable for want of room – even in the little spot at Gallow Hill I seemed to have more to turn myself – yet it was not a very small room but so crammed that one could not more than *half* open a drawer & that not without knocking against a Table &c which you must allow to be one of the miseries of human life – I had a Letter from dear M[rs] Hook this morning – & she sent me the *John Bull** – knowing as M[rs] A. said that I sh[d] not see *him* here – I think to myself constantly 'what a fine thing to be a good scholar', happy man D[r] A. must be – working as he does so conscientiously for the good of the many – & being remunerated as he is in such a princely way – all of which is the consequence of his scholarship in the first instance (for interest has had nothing to do with his prosperity) & subsequently his high reputation as a man & a master has raised the school to its present flourishing state – You bade me tell you the *fashions*. Rugby fashions which will be as interesting to you as any, are Hats entirely for Boys & all except the very big ones have their necks open – plain shirt collars turned over their jacket collar – the very

* *John Bull*—the conservative newspaper? *Cf.* Letter 106, p. 298, note.

little, spread down & sometimes frilled just as my Brothers used to have – Poplins for Ladies at L. are *becoming* the fashion – so if you want a Gown you must get an *old shop keeper* cheap before the fashion becomes general – Lady Eastnor wore a dark green one – She is the nicest person I saw at L. & her Girls very sweet ones & they have a pretty house turning i[t]s back upon the *quarry* as I call Leamington & looking upon green fields or a serpentine brook – I *half cried* when I went into her drawing room the sight was so unexpected – That old Noddy Lord Lonneren is on the point of marriage – no very agreeable thing for his family – I must put things down as I think of them – I shall tell D[ora] about the mare – but I think she will not want it yet – as they will surely go off somewhere this spring – & as you are so lamely off for horses it will be better for both parties that you should use it – . . . God bless you! this is my last *stane* at Rugby – it is almost time to dress for dinner – The *Tarts* (i.e. the D^r^ & his wife) are just come in – they take a walk every day between school she on a poney & he by her side – Today is ½ holiday so they are later – I was introduced to the Library Museum & all the School by him before they went out – I wonder how many fires there are about the premises for there are one or 2 in every place such *hugos*. The school field has been full of Boys at play this afternoon – & a pretty sight as you can imagine. The field is smooth as a bowling green – a wide gravel walk round it & fine trees scattered over – on one side of it run the buildings – I have put all my things in train for my final packing at night – it is a weary thing to have to open & shut so often & for so short a time – it really is a *compliment* which I am not gracious enough to say I pay my friend very willingly.

Trin: Lodge Sunday morn^g^ – waiting for my breakfast, my companions being at Chapel – i.e. Chris' H. Cookson – the dear Master* is unluckily absent – But I must begin regularly – Left Rugby at ½ past 9 on friday – had to go 3 miles in a Chaise to meet the coach – which proved a very comfortable one & which I had all to myself – arrived here at 8 – & a pleasant sound was the first voice I heard at the coach door 'A Lady for Trinity?' so off I came hither & to my disappointment find the D^r^ gone to Town on business – & his return to a day uncertain – However Chris welcomed me most cordially – & the whole House (Palace I sh^d^ say) were at my service & here I was importuned to remain till the Drs arrival – but as this could not be ascertained – & I was desired to announce my intentions at Playford that they might meet me at Ipswich I *durst* do no other – besides Chris is obliged to go tomorrow to Harrow being Examiner there this season – So tomorrow also I depart – & will finish this at Playford – yesterday was employed

* Dr. Christopher Wordsworth.

in seeing sights – Chris had engaged H[enry] C[ookson] to dine with us & he would gladly have asked others that I might wish '*to patronize*' but I liked to be snug better – he did invite Hamilton M[r] Hooks nephew whom I know – but he was engaged – also Hymers – but he poor fellow is in the Small Pox* we find which has been rife at St Johns several of the fellows have had it – *Well* this *is* a wonderful place! I do wish for *you* every minute. The statue of Newton in Trin Chapel alone is worth coming to see – it did not strike or affect me less than when I first saw it many years ago – & as nothing else of the kind did. Do not you remember it – expressive of the peaceful & quiet thought so deep† [and] as if one dared [not] breathe when looking upon it – I am sure I held my breath & would not have spoken above a whisper for the world – The new buildings of St John are very fine – those of Kings too fine – but Kings chapel seems more wonderful to me now than before‡ – I did long for dear Thos[3] there – We are going again today – & in the Ev[g] to see the white-robed youths in this Chapel – I have peeped thro the Doctors peep hole in his room at the 460 Fellows & Students at dinner in Hall – a busy scene – & an excellent dinner especially at the fellows Table – which they seemed to enjoy very much. We saw Cloth laid also at Corpus but tho a pretty new Hall their appointments on the Table were somewhat shabby – H. C. wanted me to breakfast at Peter House – but he comes hither in stead & will go with me to Church – then again to Sermon with Chris at St Marys – or to hear D[octor] Simeon if he preaches – then to prayers in the Ev[g] so that I shall have enough Church to[day]. This house (as you must have heard from Mary[1] W.) is a truly magnificent place – I feel like a mouse in a Church being the only inhabitant by night of the principal part – Chris. sleeps in his chambers.

10 o'C. I have had a Letter from Rydal – all well. She has rec[d] some more Langdale Rent £2.10.7 each share – she will keep it for me to meet any charge for the Boys – so you must pay J[ohn][2] M. 2.10.7 for Mary[5] Monkhouse – John's[4] share is always given by him for the Boys – Eldreds I shall continue to pay in Town – The Tenant is still 2 years in arrear – but he is honest & having been unfortunate respecting the quarry wages hitherto they are lenient with him not doubting

* A note by Miss Elizabeth Hutchinson says it was typhoid fever, not smallpox.

† *Cf.* Wordworth's famous lines in Book Three of *The Prelude* on the statue

Of Newton with his prism and silent face
The index of a mind forever
Voyaging through strange seas of thought, alone.

‡ Cf. her account of her earlier visit (p. 13). Her nephew, Thomas[3] Hutchinson, was away with typhoid fever.

that he will pay up in time – She gives me small hopes of a meeting with W^m^ & D[ora] as W^m^ seems to think all money *wasted* in Travelling except to Italy – & that *I* hope they will not accomplish. They are going to the Assizes at Carlisle on business of Stamp Off[ice] . . . so now I must leave the rest of my paper for Playford. I pity your poor Eyes – you must put on your husbands Specs. Heaven bless you all.

I had a little Herefordshire talk with Venables whom C[hristopher] invited to dinner – & with H. Cookson & M^r^ Martin, a Trin Tutor & old friend of mine, we were a nice chatty party – I like Gentlemens parties far better than Ladies – C. says that *this* Venables was in the house at the same time with his Brother & equally disposed to put the question to the fascinating widow – but that the elder got the first start!! – so there must be some truth in the fascination of the Lady or else both Brothers were susceptible to the fascination of the jointure – were disappointed at Church M^r^ Simeon did not preside – so I and my youths are going to chapel at 6 where I shall see the whole of the 'white-robed' youths of this College – (Playford) – And a most touching sight it was – if one could have believed their feelings corresponded with their reverent attitude the sight of so many kneeling youths in their white robes would have been almost overwhelming – I reached this place at 6 oClock this evening – their carriage met me at Ipswich – Dear M^r^ C[larkson] is quite an old man – he pokes about with his hands like blind Bartimeus in Raphaels cartoon of which there is a print in one of the penny mags. He is just the same in all other respects his peculiarities strengthened rather than weakened – I am watched as a cat watches a mouse & am obliged to his bidding – Today was given to me to finish my Letters after telling me the work he had for me in writing & reading for him – he is engaged in a very interesting work I have no doubt, on religion – & M^rs^ Clarkson reads the Bible & takes notes at his suggestion to him for an hour every evening – This is also very interestly to me – Tomorrow after our work we are to go to Wood bridge for a drive. M^rs^ Tom[5] & *the Boys* are there – so I am finishing my Letter tonight before I go to bed – for I have had 4 to prepare for post tomorrow – having written to no one but yourself since our party – Mr C. said in one of his musings I wish I could see your Brother Thos[1]. He & M^rs^ C. had been talking a while before about agriculture & their Farm – She is more of an old woman in appearance but as lively & animated in conversation as heretofore – She would be most happy to see you & your dear Bairns of whom & of dear John she talks with great interest. This place is greatly improved by Trees & shrubs grown *mightily* – The country between this place & Bury is very beautiful – all the rest that I have travelled very dull –

flat & bare except for the churches spires not an object to rest ones eyes upon. The meadows about Northampton Green but very uninteresting – this is a new farming country crops look well – & all is so tidy about the farm houses hedges & cottages that one can scarcely fancy there is any agricultural distress – dear Thos[1] would be *provoked* at that Idiot S[r] W. Inglebys treatment of his *motion* but I have had no time to read newspapers – & I think I have taken up enough of your time, & drawn largely upon your eyesight – so good night! God bless you & loves & kisses to you all ever most affy yours. . . .

The Nightingales were singing when I alighted last night at his gate.

There is a new enquiry making about value of Land & amount of wages paid on each parish – M[r] C's rent is 360 no tithes wages 550 M[rs] Bidell next farm double this size pays 1200£ in wages – there is a superabundance of Laborers & they are obliged to employ them hence the neatness of all about the farmsteads &c – No victuals or drink given but some Malt allowed at harvest which they have at home – M[r] C. wants to know what your labor costs – so you must add to it all the Cider & victuals & interest of money for the hogsheads all kinds of labor. I suppose they reckon or ought to do in their statements tho M[rs] C. said they had forgotten the molecatcher & some other trifles.

Tom[5] C. is on the northern circuit & will see *our folk*. . . .

Don't forget my Shawl. . . .

*Postmark: Mr 6, 1834*

# 153

*Edward Quillinan Esq[re], No 9 sur le Rempart, Bologne-sur-Mer*

*Playford Hall, n[r] Ipswich, Mar. 17th* [*1834*]

My dear Friend

Your most welcome Letter was forwarded to me, by Mrs Gee at this place where I am upon a visit to my dear old Friends Mr & Mrs Clarkson. As this visit was the *principal* motive which induced me to travel farther from home than Brinsop I resolved to pay it *before* I went to Hendon, lest anything should prevent me or hurry me home sooner than I intended – I will not say *than I wished*, for I have been home-sick ever since I left Brinsop – and I assure you that your Letter was a great relief to me – as I had much rather see you in England than at Boulogne – so that I hope to have the pleasure of meeting you in London, & I think, when together, we can contrive some means for my seeing the Darlings also – as you know my sole motive for thinking of going to B[oulogne] was to 'look after you' all. Therefore pursue your own plan & come with the Children to Eng[d] at the time you mention – & long before they have finished their visit at Barham I expect, deo volente, to be at Hendon – and if the Children do not come to me I will certainly go to see them – *with your permission.*

I left Brinsop & all my dear Friends there well on the 11th of Feb[y]. My Brother took me to Che[l]tenham & from thence I went to Leamington where I spent a fortnight with Mrs & Miss Hook – thence to Rugby where I paid a 5 Days visit to Dr & Mrs Arnold – then as my way hither led me through Cambridge I could do no less than spend a couple of days at Trinity Lodge – and after a very prosperous, tho' not *pleasant* journey arrived here on this day fortnight – My intentions were to stay here only a month – but dear Mr C[larkson] who is as nearly blind as possible has found me so useful in reading & writing for him, in aid of a work* which he is engaged in, that I shall feel it almost a duty to prolong my stay beyond that time – tho I hope it will not be much longer – so that in the next month we may meet in Town – & when you are really there pray write to me here & give me your address – that I may announce the time of approach so that if you have nothing better to do you may meet & escort me to Hendon when by the way we may have a good *Westmorland Chat.*

At present you know almost as much of West[d] News as I do – for I have not heard from the Rydal Mount for some time – but have no doubt all is going on well. Miss W[ordsworth] daily improves – & Mr W's Eyes well – if he does not ill-use them.

Of poor Sara[3] Coleridge the account, I grieve to say, is most deplorable – I had a Letter from her Mother a few days ago who tells me she is just in the same state as before her Confinement – Dora[2] will have told you that she had Twins, which both died – & for a short time after they had hoped the Mother was recovering her spirits – if not her strength of Body – but she has relapsed into her former state & they seem perfectly hopeless – (as, she is also herself poor Dear) as to her ultimate restoration – But *I* shall never despair until some *proper* means have been resorted to which, I think, has not yet been the case – All but themselves agree that the only chance is from change of scene & objects – & indeed it is strange that, at the very first, this most obvious & easy remedy should not have been applied – It is a piteous case!

* If Thomas Clarkson's work was his *Researches Anti-deluvian, Patriarchal, and Historical, concerning the way in which Men first acquired their knowledge of God . . .*, London and Ipswich, 1836, Sara deserves sympathy.

she has expressed some pleasure at the prospect of seeing me* – & I shall do my utmost to accomplish a removal.

You say nothing of your own health – I shall be most glad to find that the troublesome complaint in your head has quite left you – We often talked of you in Herefordshire – and *as often* wished for you there – On poor Mr M[onkhouse] you would always confer the greatest favor by a visit – Nobody's society, I am sure, seems to give him so much pleasure as yours – & it is a *real charity* to visit him so that I hope, if you have any leisure upon your hands while in Eng[d], you will not forget Herefordshire – & if you took the Darlings also you would be so much the more welcome at Brinsop – I hope you do not mean to return to Boulogne – But all this we will discuss when we meet – & having this hope before me I have no patience to write more – except my best love to the Darlings & yourself & to beg you to account me ever among your true Friends S. Hutchinson. . . .

*Postmark: Ipswich, 18 MA 1834: 19 MR 1834: Boulogne, 20, Mars 1834: Angleterre par Calais*

## 154

*Mrs Hutchinson, Brinsop Court, Hereford*

[*1 April, 1834*]

Dearest Mary

Thanks for your Letter & M[ary][5] M's also, & for dear little Ta's *intentions.* I intended to write, if I had not rec[d] yours, on the subject of Mays *Corns M*[r] C[larkson] having undertaken the cure of mine!! & I believe he will be successful – He has already cured his own & many in the Parish by 'Denmers Brunswick Corn plaster – Barclay & Sons 95 Fleet Market' – any quack medicine vendor will have it or send for it for you – She must not despair at first as it does not give immediate relief like Ivy Leaves – & tho M[r] C. continues *only to wash one foot at a time he* I dare say did not put his feet in hot water every time the plaster was changed I would advise M[ary] to do so & scrape the corn very well each time – He was such a *martyr* that he was obliged to have his shoes made of the thinnest possible Leather – but now he has neither corn or pain. I have not had a word from Rydal since I came hither –

* She apparently did visit Sara Coleridge at Hampstead, an interesting sidelight on her fundamental kindness even when it was coated with some acerbity; at about the same time, she visited Coleridge at Highgate. See Letter 156.

but I suppose their having been on the move is the cause of their silence. Tom[5] C. saw Wm[1] & Dora[2] at Carlisle – He is now here with his wife & child – she is a sweet mild creature – devoted to her Husband & Bairn, who is a noble Bairn indeed & very good. They stay till about the 12 of next month & if I feel that I am not expected to stay longer I shall go with them – but if dear Mrs C. does not like to part with us all at once I cannot refuse to stay a little while after that – tho' it would be a nice opportunity – especially as they intend to go by steam from Ipswich – & the river Orwell down to Harwich is very beautiful – Quillinan also will be in Town by that time – It will be quite a *godsend* – as dear Mr C. calls my visit here. He tells me his work *never could have been done* without me – for poor Misses is worn out by it – '*twenty-pages-only*-for you to copy Sarah, I have saved them for you'. We have only got thro' 8 of his pages but they are swoln to 28 – besides all the readings & references. The whole *Book of Job* with Dr Clarkes notes – then making notes – looking into all *insides* of books, & finding texts – in the Evg Mr C. reads 2 or 3 Chapters with Dr Cs notes in the Old Testament – which is most interesting. Our mornings (i e Mr Cs & mine) are employed in our work till 12 sometimes till one or 2 & then I either have a duty walk in the Garden or a drive with Mrs C. in the Carriage; & so our days are spent & very happily – I am writing very badly it is not my m.s. hand I assure you. . . . The weather has been delightful here – on Monday & Tuesday we had a shower or two – sleet on the latter day – & it has been colder for the last week than before – but this is all the rain we have had since the day I went to Rugby. That reminds me of the [ ?] yarn. If I had had some of it here I could have knit you such a beautiful shawl Miss Julia Smith (the Wm Smiths) was here for a few days last week with a little nun who was knitting the prettiest I ever saw of 2 shades of crimson quite a new stitch – any 2 shades would do – Miss S. is a very nice lively person, the little girl a *lump* but very clever at her Books &c tho not a forward Miss at all – & her industry was far too great for her age – but I suppose she had been drilled into it – it was the same with her Aunts. Miss S. was well acquainted with your neighbourhood having been at Kinsome when it was in the possession of Mr Nightingale whose wife is her sister. I must give over – I am writing in my own room at bed time – but I have a new fire & all very comfortable & tempting to make me sit up – but I must bear in mind that I shall be expected at my post in the morning – By the way Mrs C. has got *The Dr** from Ipswich today – and she is so amused with it that she will kill herself with laughing – *Old Peter*

* Southey's *The Doctor*, 1834. It was written at Sara Hutchinson's urging and largely dictated to her.

– Aballboozbanganooribo Chap – too almost sent her into fits – she is like John[2] she enjoys every bit – but I must say good night & God bless you. I hope I shall write better tomorrow & I wish I had a frank

Friday. Dear M^rs^ Clarkson would be as happy to see you as you would be to see her. She often talks about you all – but I fear they are fixtures – not for Life perhaps *here* but they will never travel far from home – unless M^r^ C. were to recover his sight & she had more strength than at present – She continues however by means of a good Bailiff to manage the farm well if not profitably – and I must tell you of their good luck in the sheep line which she attributes to the good method they have practised for the last few years – They keep 7 score Ewes – last year & this they did not lose 1 Lamb & only 3 sheep (one an old Ewe & the other two I forget what they were but I think *one* was a rickety Lamb) in the course of the whole 2 years. They dip all their sheep in the beginning of Nov^r^ in a mixture of soft soap & arsenic (probably what killed yours) according to a receipt – taking care that it does not get to their mouth head or eyes – & never give their ewes turnips till *after* Xmas, which she thinks is the best of all regulation – they also give salt. The Crops here of wheat are beautiful – so clean & regular – it is all *planted*. Now after the Sheep for Thos[1] I must give the Girls a receipt to make feather fire screens – of the large Downy Turkey *stiff* feathers – they must be dyed – green or crimson, the lower part light & the upper *dark* (*black* or almost black) which may easily be done after the first dying, by dipping in the tops after the other is dry – there are 2 very pretty ways here they are french manufactury – the wood in the middle & the handles is Tulip wood but any thing would do – I will draw a pattern but I have not a pencil so cannot *shade it well*.

The feathers are stuck into the wood in the middle which is thick enough to hold a close stuck row on each side – so that the edges of

the feathers may meet & by putting them on one side *between* those of the other the stiff part of feather on one side supporting the edges of the feathers in the other makes them as firm as possible. At the dark rim round the wood is a piece of chenille thread gummed on to hide the pens of the feathers – & the inner rim the proportion for the dark part of the feather the outside mark only means that the feathers are to be cut to make the edge *straight* & equally thick which it would not be if they were left in their original or natural shape. If you succeed you may send me some feathers. Good night again – for I have come up with a short candle & cannot write more. No Letter yet from Rydal – it was very creditable to the Cheltenham Innkeepers to thank me – when you go I hope you will not pass by their House for a gayer Hotel. I shall take care to send the Bonnets the very first time I go to Town after my arrival at Hendon – Thos[1] must not forget to send me my 10£ but he need not mind till I am there – as I do not want money here – I shall buy myself a 3£ shawl – which will do quite as well as my 5 Gs one. . . .

We have a *rattling* parson here – but he is not exactly of the same principles as H. W. was – but he scolds dreadfully – is very ill-tempered and told us one day that Playford 'was a place of Devils' we were all so wicked. He is one of the Hymn singing extempory preaching – and long preaching, & nonsensual [*sic*] preaching, Parsons – busy in rectifying everybody though not without need of being rectified himself. Then what provoked me, he is *fat &* [?] & does not look as if he practised the selfdenial & mortification which he recommends – neither does he look as if he were a Student – & he is a great lover of baubles & knick nacks in his House & grounds. He has 3 cures & the other parishes follow him to this so that our own *wicked* parishioners have scarcely room to sit in their own Church. He is very fond of being *glorified* in this way – & is no little of a selfglorifier. But he does a deal of good & dear M^r^ & M^rs^ C. wish the people to think well of him, tho' they cannot but see that it is not all *genuine* – the man may be sincere but the meekness & humility of Christianity seem wanting – at least as far as outward appearance goes. Easter Sunday I have just read 2 Sermons of M^r^ Hook upon the Church Esta^t^ which were about to be pub^d^ when I was at L[eamington] & which M^rs^ H. offered to send me but I said I would buy them as the cost would be less than the Carriage. You *must* get them – but the Bookseller told M^r^ Clarkson when he ordered them for me, that they were in such great request that a cheap ed: was to be published – for greater circulation – tho this only costing 2/6. There is also a set of tracts published at Oxford in a cheap form they are only 1/– per 100 which I would have you get also – & will give you the title of both – 'Tracts for the Times'* printed at Ox$^{d}$ – 35 are advertised – Ja$^{s}$ Garbitt would get you them – M$^{r}$ H's is 'The Church & the Establishment 2 plain sermons' by W. F. Hook. We had such a rigmarole of a discourse today that it required great exertion to compose myself into a fit state for remaining to the Sacrament. The Priest was himself in no good humour because the poor curate forgot the Athanasian Creed & read it in the wrong place – & to mend the matter left out the Litany!! . . .

I desire Molly will persevere with her Corn plaster – mine are nearly gone – dont *pinch for size* that the plaster may cover the whole of the *callous* part. I have not the least pain in mine now – but must not give up till all appearance of corn is gone. You must continue to get a frank when the Members are at home now so that dear little Ta must not be disappointed about writing to me – I hope Thos[1] told D[ora][2] plainly of his objection to Willys[2] having the Horse – it is far better where it is – I have told her so – God bless you all my kindest love to dear John[2] – and remember me also kindly to the Garbitts & to the Misses Whalley – to whom recommend M$^{r}$ Hs sermon – and to the Oliphants not forgetting poor old W$^{m}$ & Nancy – and Bertha & Betty Downs & her Mother & all *enquiring* friends. Ever & ever most truly yours S. H.

If you cant get a *cheap* copy of the Sermon I will send mine with the Bonnets.

M$^{rs}$ Hook has another for *me*.

*Postmark: 1 Ap 1834*

# 155

## *Miss Sarah Hutchinson, Brinsop Court*

[*April-May, 1834*]

My dear little Bedfellow

I thank you most kindly for your Letter – and hope you will send me another soon to tell me how you like your new Bonnet – Father was very saucy – & perhaps he may say I am a fond old Body for making you so smart.

I wish you were here – for there are so many nice little companions for you – especially one little squinting Girl who is like Dody. – You

* *Tracts for the Times*, 1833–41, by Newman, Keble, Pusey, and others in the Oxford Movement.

would be charmed to hear them sing their Psalm before prayers – they sing even better than the Scholars at Brinsop – I wished for you too one Day at Ipswich – when I made a call upon old Admiral & Mrs Page – for their beautiful house is crammed full of curiosities & pretty Things from all parts of the world – beautiful live [&] stuffed Birds – many of the first sang sweetly & there were the dear little Love Birds also which always sit on their Perch with their heads close together – Butterflies of all kinds – Moths – Shells – Pictures, so many that all the walls were covered either with them or books handsomely bound – & all the Tables covered with curiosities in Ivory carved – busts – Minerals – Boxes &c made of precious stones – & shelf after shelf, in the passages, full of the finest China I ever saw – & in the Hall stands of beautiful flowers in blow [? bloom] from the Hot house – There was room after room almost without end & all full of things to be admired – & I had Wine & Brides Cake given me – the Cake out of gold Basket. It was not the old Admirals Bride Cake – but had been sent by some young Friend. I had known him at Rydal – and Uncle W. desired me to call to see them – & I was very sorry I had not done it sooner for they asked me to stay & dine with them, which I should have liked to do that I might have had time to examine all the pretty Things – but Mrs Clarkson was with me, & we were expected home to dinner.

The young Ladies here all chatter French like Parrots – They are now making a pretty noise on the gravel walks about the ground bowling their hoops. They have each a pretty Garden – & the lawn in front is quite a large field with several fine Timber Trees on it – & shrubs all round which shut out the Village in part – but the Country is very pretty in front & we see a long way – Thank dear Polly for her Letter – but she must excuse my writing this time – as I have written so much to Mother – who will read it to you all – My love to old William & Nancy – & to Martha – & to *Davy* – & may God bless you and keep you a good Girl. Ever your most affte Aunt Sarah.

## 156

*Edward Quillinan Esqre, Montagu Street, Portman Square*

[*9 May 1834*]

My dear Friend

I had hoped to have seen you or heard from you before this – but till yesterday I was quite in the dark respecting my Playford Friends whose motions about coming to Town were to determine mine – at all events, deo volente, Mrs Gee & I shall be there on Monday – and if you have no better engagement will find us at Mr Landzelles 22 Lower Grosvenor St at 11 o'Clock – & as we shall have a Coach for the Day shall proceed to Somerset House to see *our Friends* there & do a little business elsewhere, & should be most happy to have your Company – Besides I want to know how or where I am to see the Darlings – as the time passes away alas! very quickly – & it is probable that I may not make any stay in London. In a hasty note just rec[d] from my Sister she says 'Perhaps you may come *before* Mr Parry as Mr Q. talks of visiting us before he goes to Portugal' – This would be delightful to me – & I would suit my time to yours – Only the *Bairns* I must see – Mrs Gee says that if you have no objection she would take them with her to Birmingham – Her friends there would be most happy to have them – they have Children of their own & plenty of House room – Of course there would be no obligation on your part – they would go as part of her family – But you will I hope before this have come to some determination for I feel greatly for you in your anxiety in this matter – Pray write by return if you can – This is a horrid pen. Is it not?

Yesterday I was at Highgate & greatly was I shocked with the changed appearance of my dear old Friend* – So little was I prepared for it by the account I had rec[d] at Hampstead† – He will never rise from his bed more I fear tho' this does not seem to be the opinion of his relatives – & (tho' Mr Gilman does not expect him to rally again) I would not spread it –

Dora says that I must call to see Moxon & his wife – & Pickersgill which last I have done – & the former I fear I shall not be able to do if you *desert* me i.e. if you are going off soon – as my other kind Conductor Mr H. C. Robinson has been called away to see a sick Brother – by which I shall also lose my chance of seeing Lamb.

Mrs Gee & Netta join me in kind regards & all good wishes & believe me ever most truly yours S. H.

My comp[ts] to Mr Holmes.

*Postmark: 9 MY 1834*

* Coleridge. † From Mrs. Coleridge.

# 157

*Hendon, May 27th, Tuesday, 1834*

My dearest Mary

I have not been in a hurry, as you will perceive, to send the screens & cards tho' I have had them by me for some time – but I am waiting for a little music which they may play on a sunday & which Father may accompany them *with his voice & skill* in *psalmody* – besides they are my favorite Tunes & I hope also to get 'the Manly Heart' which used to be such a delight of mine when dear Miss Charlotte played it – but nobody *touched* the instrument as she did! I was most glad to find that the Bonnets gave such universal satisfaction hope they are in better keeping than mine, which, with dust, damp, & sun, looks already mighty shabby but it has had hard service – I have been in Town for a week (I *think*) since I last wrote – but really, having no rest to the sole of my foot, I hardly know *where I am* still less where I left off, or where to *take up* my *adventures* – while in Town I spent 2 days with the Clarksons in Linton Street Finsbury sq: (John Bucks) tho' I slept at Toms[5]) & on the others I was busy with the Dentist – Mr. Q., seeing sights – & *poorly* – very poorly indeed for 2 days or rather nights – for except on *one day* – I did not keep house even – it was first an attack of the Bowels – & then of rhumatism or some most intolerable pain in the Legs – occasioned, I have no doubt, with having walked too much which one does insensibly in London. However on my return here, last Thursday, I got well – & am now very well but don't much relish a return to Town lest I sh[d] have another attack – but go I must for a few days or a week. The Clarksons are coming to Toms – & dear Mary* has made an arrangement to accommodate me at the same time – & I shall then I hope finish my visits to the Dentist & take my leave of Town – though Q. intends to bring his Girls up about the 8th & I suppose I must not go without seeing them – yet it is rather provoking for I shall probably lose my travelling companion M[r] Parry if I wait – & Q. might just as well have brought them up sooner – He is as uncertain as ever what to do with them – He talks sometimes of taking them to Oporto with him.

M[r] Clarksons eye goes on as well as possible. It is *Travers* who was said to be the nervous person. Tyrrels charge is 50£ or Gs for the *operation*† – & a compliment is expected for the subsequent attendance.

* Mary—Mrs. Thomas Clarkson, Jr.

† An operation for cataract.

M^r C. means to give 75 Gs. I saw Tyrrel – he is a very sensible & agreeable man – & for *practice* he must have the most of any operation in the Island. I wish John[2] had come up for inspection while the Cs were here. I send you dear M[ary][5] M.'s note. Her handwriting is very childish for her years – the *inditing* is probably M^rs Sergeants – it is not likely to be her own – & I am sure it is not her Mother's.

I have not had more than a *flying* line from Rydal for an age – but I believe they are well & half-expecting that I am upon the road – but they do not know that I am under the Dentists hands – I mean to surprize them.

I forgot to say that Janetta, who bought the skreens, says that the white card *takes out* to be more handy for drawing upon – & also you may change the picture at pleasure – therefore they are dearer I suppose for this *knick-nackery* & I told her that strength & plainness was more req^d than finery – they cost 8/6. Cards 6/– so that I shall send music to straight *at least* the 5/6 remaining due & I think that Carriage will be paid by it – for I expect to get it *very cheap*. I called upon M^r & M^rs Johnson – & most happy they were to see me – she is a nice creature – they live in Regent St. & he is still at the head of the National Schools but with a Master & Mistress under him – the Central Sch. is removed into the parish of St Georges Westminster. They have 2 children & live in a handsome house – & invited me to stay with them – If I stay till the 5th I shall have pew Tickets from them for St Pauls to see the children – a sight which I wish much to promise for Mary Clarkson.

Let me tell you now lest I forget that M^r & M^rs Prince & probably Miss Lockier, talk of going to the Ware this summer – M^r P. said that he sh^d certainly come to see you – but of course if the Ladies are there you will be so kind as give them a call & an invite to come over to see you – M^r P. is a nice *homely* body. He & I are very great friends – a more worthy creature cannot be – & the Ladies are as good & as kind as they can be – they are all *stirling* People – I do love M^rs Gee more & more every day & my admiration of her is unbounded – Indeed they all seem bent upon making duty a pleasure – for they live more for the good of others than themselves – M^rs Prince is ready to assist every body that is in difficulty, or in want of advice, or a home –

Dorset Place Monday June 1st. To use a favorite expression of Tom Clarkson's 'I am fairly crazed' with heat bustle disappointment & travelling between this place & Hendon – and if I had known the trouble & teasing that I was to encounter I would have minced my meat to all eternity if I were obliged to cut masticable food for so long – Here at 1 o'C I am waiting for a fly to take me to Hendon & in the morning again I must return – I am forced to turn out here because the old folk are coming – & the Bed intended for Mrs C's maid has been found swarming with bugs & unuseable – and as poor Mrs C. is but half a body without her maid there is no alternative but my going to sleep at Hendon to-night. Mr C. is quite well. He already sees better then he has done for 10 years – can read all the Names &c upon the Shops which he never could do in his life before – & when his eye is ready for the proper Spectacles he has no doubt but he shall be able to read any book of tolerable size print. He has not had any fever or inconvenience of any kind – one confined to bed one day – in a darkened *not dark* room about 10 – needed no previous preparation – all that Tyrrell requires is that the patient should be in good health – yet Mr Clarkson (who bids me write all this for dear Johns[2] information) says that Tyrrell & the Nurse both say that very few do quite so well as he has done (I daresay because he was so tractable doing all *to the very letter*) & that it is mostly 6 weeks before the patient attains the state in which he is at the end of a month. But I am also to repeat that the pain is nothing either in operation or afterwards – the first not more than in bleeding & the latter a little soreness as if bruised. I am yet uncertain as to the time of my leaving for home but I shall finish at Hendon. The parcel now waits for Hartleys *Poems** which I lent to Julia Myers & for some Blue Pill – all together I hope you will not think you have too little for your 20/– tho' you have carriage to pay.

Hendon Wed: 4 June – Yesterday I went again to Town by Stage & returned in the same way in the Evg with Mr Prince having kept all day in the Quarter of my Dentist who lives in Bedford Row – called upon S. Cookson & luckily met Henry [Addison] there – then spent several hours with dear old Mrs Addison where I met Mrs C. & Mary Clarkson who came to call upon her – a dinner was provided for Henry A. & me at ½ past 3 but the Cook not being punctual I was forced to hurry off & had the mortification to find myself too early when I reached the place where the Stage stops in Tot:m Court Road & had to wait 25 minutes sufft time for me to have eaten my dinner in comfort – I cannot persuade H. A. to spare time to come & see you – the old Lady is recovering from her accident – but perhaps I have not written since she fell into a hole in the kitchen made by the taking up the flags to repair, & sprained her arm – I have visited her 3 times, & have promised to call tomorrow on my way from Mr Heath when I shall have my teeth to show to her. You will be glad to hear that I am in great hopes that the Teeth will answer & I am charmed with my Dentist tho' I am sorry to find that he is so foolish as to be an Irvingite – His *works* are really pretty to look at – & they cannot change

* Hartley Coleridge's *Poems*, 1833.

– so that there is nothing of disgust can attach to them as there does to the human teeth when set in bone – the very sight makes your flesh creep – which was one of the reasons of my reluctance to have anything to do with them until I heard of Heath's discovery – but the price is *awful.* 50 Gs!! But they will last longer than I shall – & can only be injured by being thrown violently upon a hard stone and even then can be put together again & be as strong as before – so that in the end they must be more than oeconomical. Miss W. has already had 3 sets & is very poorly off at present – But I must wait a little before I can say whether they may not annoy me – & if I cannot wear them I am only worse in pocket – the trouble & travelling I have had after them will soon be forgotten – & I shall never be reproached any more for neglecting to have them. Mr H. does not say that there is any reason to suppose that they will not answer because I have delayed them so long as many would have persuaded me. . . . If my Teeth want no alteration I shall be impatient to set off after this week is over – they want me at home sadly – & I shall leave Mr P. in the lurch rather than exceed *my year* – besides I want to be at home before the Boys go – as I suppose they are to be there – & you must tell me what is to be done respecting Toms[3] Clothes – but I have had so few & such flying Epistles from Rydal that I know nothing further than that dear Toms health was better from which I guess they have had correspondence with them – neither have I heard a word *from* Joanna – if you write to her tell her how busy I have been – & so many Letters to write that I hope she has heard of me thro Rydal – I have had no less than 3 pressing Letters to answer from Mrs Hook – that I would return via Leamington – people are very kind & really it is a most ungracious task to put one to – to refuse so often – I had the same kind request from Mrs Arnold.

Pray do dear Thos[1] call upon Mr Prince when he comes . . . for his kindness & helpfulness to me has been unbounded – & he is such a plain homely body that you need be on no ceremony with him. He has promised me he will come to see you if you do not hear of his being at the Ware. Tomorrow I am going again to that weary Town – to get my Teeth – & to St Paul Mrs Gee goes with me – for Mary C[larkson] after all the trouble I had about getting the Tickets mainly on her acct as I had seen the sight declines going – so rather then lose them

[*Rest of letter missing*]

# 158

*Mrs Clarkson, Playford Hall, Ipswich*

*Sat. June 28th* [*1834*], *Rydal Mount*

My very dear Friend

After a prosperous journey with my attentive young escort (John[6] W.) I reached my dearest home last Sat: Ev[g]. I found poor Dorothy[1] suffering from a bilious attack occasioned by the change of weather – but she is now thank God better – & tho' not so well as she has been is certainly stronger than when I left her last year – She has not been out in the Carriage since my return but the Boys have for the 2 last days dragged her in her Garden Chair for an hour – & I trust if the weather would become dry again I shall see a great improvement in her. William's eyes are pretty well – my Sister thank God as well & active as ever – & poor Dora though in good spirits & uncomplaining looks ill & is thinner than almost any one I ever saw – The Country is as beautiful – more beautiful if possible than when I left it – but I am not reconciled to the changes which have been made at the Mount – Most of the fine Trees at the entrance have been cut down for the sake of Light & Air – some shrubs have been planted which will in part repair the damage when they are grown up – but the p[l]easing gloom thro which you passed to the chearful front of the house is gone – but the advantage when you are in the *Hall*, which is now used as a dining room, is very great – & therefore one *ought* not to quarrel with the change. Dear Dorothy asks much about Playford – & when she is well again talks of taking a Tour to see all her Friends – Poor Thing! I fear there is small chance of this ever being realized – for tho' she has recovered so far her present state is still farther from the point which could make such a scheme practicable – but it amuses her to talk of it.

I long to hear from you now that you are again at your own home – I hope dear Mr C. has not made too free with his Eyes but that all goes on as well as we could desire – and that on his return he has not (to use a country expression) 'spied any farlies' to make him fidgetty or uncomfortable – but has settled himself to his books & left the out-door management to you as usual.

. . . . Did I know before I last saw you that Mrs Deck [Dick] (poor T. Monkhouse's widow) was dead? She died of Typhus at Clifton on this day fortnight & was buried at Clifton on Sat: last. J[ohn][2] M.

& Mary[2] H. attended the funeral where they were met by Mr S. Horrocks (her Brother) & poor little Mary[5] now an Orphan. I told you I had seen the Child at School – She is to spend her holidays this Midsummer at Preston & to go to Brinsop at Christmas. J. M. is sole Trustee & Ex[r] to her fathers will – & Mr S. Horrocks Guardian with him – but from Mary Hutchinson's Letter we conclude that she is to have the care of her – which if so is a most fortunate thing for the poor Child – for tho' Mr S. H. & his Wife are unexceptionable I am sorry to say that her Aunts are not exactly what one could wish them to be – tho' from Mrs St Clair (Miss H.) we have had a very proper & kind Letter in answer to our enquiries – so I hope they will not prejudice the Child against her true friends – as I fear has hitherto been the case –

Dear Tom[5] & Mary & '*Tommy*' are I suppose about to *leave* Town for Ramsgate – Fail not to give my best love to them all. – I shall never forget the kind & hospitable accommodation they afforded me – for I am sure they had not much satisfaction in my society – for I was always on the fidget – I wish I could say that I am entirely at ease with my new *furniture* – but I do not despair – for I have not been used to it for quite a month & that I am told is a too short a time for me to expect complete ease – Every body is satisfied with the appearance – even Mary Wordsworth whom I expected would quarrel with it sees no difference – therefore in this respect I have nothing to regret – for though the trial may fail I shall not care about the cost – once paid it is over.

Pray write soon – tho' this worthless scrawl does not deserve an answer – but you cannot conceive how I have been hurried since I came home – what with my own concerns & the interruptions of numerous visitors – so that I have never sate down to write to any one in peace – & for *peace* I would not wait any longer – The Boys from Sedbergh met me at Kendal & after I had been travelling 2 days & a night I had to run all over the Town after Tailors & Shoemakers for they came home ragged as sheep. John[6] W. is gone to see his Mother at Keswick – but will soon return – he seems greatly to prefer the society here – He is a very fine Lad –

No tidings from Workington – as Dora says they must all have been *daft*. Poor Isabella[2] is quite ashamed of her mistake – but we suppose the Babe will come in its own time – tho' it has not at her's.

Thank you for your little note with the returned Letter – Dear Friend you quite overrate my *services* – but however small the good I may have done to 'you & yours' I have been amply repaid by the pleasure I had in attempting to make myself useful – & I wish I had the opportunity of being more so. May God bless you both – & believe me ever most truly yours – S. H.

I saw dear Coleridge on the Monday before I left Hendon – he was not quite so well as the week before.* Hartley had a Letter from his Mother this week – she said he was better – but I have always found her accounts *past date.* Sara[3] continues the same –

# 159

## *Mrs Hutchinson, Brinsop Court, Hereford*

*Tuesday 8th* [*July, 1834*]

My dearest Mary

I have such a piece of agreeable news for you that I cannot help writing – viz. that dear little M[ary][5] M. is to come to us on Monday. I told you in my last of M[ary][1] W.'s correspondence with M[rs] St. Clair – & this morn[gs] post brought us a Letter to say that M. was delighted with the invitation & that if convenient they would send her by the *Water Witch* (the flying packet Boat) to Kendal & if it was convenient we were to meet her – and if not the person who brought her would see her safe at Rydal next day & be ready at K. to take her back on Saturday. So Tom[3] & either M.W. or I will go to fetch her on Monday Ev[g]. It is most lucky that the Boys are here – we shall have less trouble to entertain her – but indeed Dora is a host – for all the young ones are fond of her & I hope this visit will draw her towards her dear Fathers friends – We have several little schemes in view which we are glad she will be able to join in – & the Arnolds come on friday & there she will find nice female companions – I hope the weather will serve – your own dear Boys are as well as possible & as good & pleasant as ever – They have no Tutor – but always have had a turn at their Books every day – the first thing – & the remainder has been spent principally in reading when not out. W[m] says he likes to encourage Boys in desultory reading & he employs them sometimes in reading to him. Tom is also a constant reader to Dora while she is at work in her own room – & Miss W[ordsworth] likes his reading – she says he reads

* Sara evidently visited Coleridge at Highgate at least two or three times during her stay at Hendon, first in early May (Letter 156), and finally on the Monday before she left for the north, i.e. June 7 or 14, and possibly 'the week before', i.e. May 31 or June 7. He died on July 25th.

as if he understood & *like a Gentlemen* which Geo[3] does not – but G. has been reading to himself *Leonidas – Peter Wilkins* – & now is deep in *the Fool of Quality* – so that tho' they have not yet had much *pleasuring* they seem to enjoy their holidays – & they are so fond of Dora & so loving to us all that happier Boys need not be – One day Dora & they went by boat & spent the day on Winander Mere – dined on the Island – & made a visit to poor John Curwen who with his Servants is there – a happy creature – lord of his domain – He is one of Dora's pets – & he is the *wisest* & best-behaved of all the Sons tho' he *is* daft – but daft in a very odd way – for we never heard him say a foolish thing – but many a wise one. Yesterday the Boys & I drank tea with M^rs^ Ellwood & her Nieces at M. Fishers – the Boys & young Ladies went on the water in the Ev^g^ – and today W^m^ is going to take them to Ivy Lane [? Low] to tea – the Boys & I along.

The Box arrived safe at last & I cannot tell you how much we were all pleased with our Letters & presents – which are most creditable to all parties – but some of them shall speak for themselves.

Now for *business*. You must have Shirts & Stockings ready for Tom[3] against his return as he must leave what he can behind him for Geo.[3] as poor Dody's Shirts are in a very sickly condition – but I hope to mend up as many as will serve him till Sep^r^ if not the whole half year – Tom's Kendal coat is well made as to *fitting* but not swallow tail enough for the fashion – but when I see other Boys Jackets here I am provoked beyond measure with their *nipt carcases*. The Boys here when you look at them before seem as if they had a coat on – & indeed except for the flap there is no difference – & I hope you will not let that Tailor disfigure Geo. again at Xmas – & pray let Tom have a *decent* performer to fit him out for Camb: – M^r^ Green's Bill is £49.8.2. The Items I will send hereafter all very moderate –

Willys[2] toe is better, by his intending to go to Langdale as you may guess – tho' he does not mean to walk – we have a nice light Standby for such expeditions – Dear Miss W. is not so well yesterday & today – we had rain again yesterday morning – which did much good to all but her & those who had their hay out – ours was cut last week & in three days – 9 carts on the Hay field which the first year we had it only produced 2 – the effect of Wms irrigation!!

Miss W. is too poorly to write her thanks so she begs me to send her tender love to you all – & to tell Mary[6] that she is much pleased indeed with the drawings – & thinks her greatly improved – she will be much obliged to her to make her a sketch of the Church – & especially to mark the place of poor old Auntys & Lough's graves . . . how provoking to lose your Cap & dear Pollys nice collar – Aunt W. is charmed with hers – a more acceptable present could not have been made – & Ebba will soon rival Mary[6] if mine is her first performance – I set some edging upon mine & have worn it ever since – they *wash* much better with an edging on the hems. I am sorry to hear poor Polly has been unwell – would not Toms[3] medicine do her good? He had a days head ache & parted with his dinner once since he came – but a dose or two set him immediately to rights – *you* ought to try it yourself – It is nothing but a tea spoonful of Epsom Salt in a cup of camomile Tea – I have said my say so I shall leave the rest of my page for Dora who will fill it to Mary – kindest love to all – not forgetting dear John[2] at the Stow – & Geo.[1] when you see him. . . . God bless you all! S. H.*

*Postmark: Kendal, Penny Post*

## 160

*Edward Quillinan Esq$^{re}$, 7 Gloucester Place, New Road*

*July 20th* [*1834*]

My dear Friend

. . . Dora is I am glad to tell you better than when I came home – but till her appetite improves we cannot expect to see her looks improve – If she will but consent to accept some of the many *eligible* invitations which she has for the Winter I think change of air would do much for her – but she is an unmanageable creature, as you know, & will only do her own way – yet she does sometimes allude to her promised visit to Leamington – Little Mary[5] M. (tho I ought not to call her '*little*' for at ½ *past twelve* she is as tall as I am) is a very sweet Child – tho' there is something of reserve about her that does not quite please me & we suspect that *that Miss Gregg* (the Governess who behaved so ill at Brinsop) is now since her poor Mother is gone her dearest friend – Every farthing of her Mother's Property, Books, Plate & money have been secured by Dr D[ick] all sold – Mr Wordsworth's Portrait I suppose among the rest – & Mr Horrocks is left to pay her debts – even the Governess Salary – of course only for the time she was Governess, or Companion, to the Mother – Mary is to spend her Christmas vacation at Brinsop – but I have no doubt that she has been prejudiced against

* There follows a letter from Dora Wordsworth of which the postscript is worth quoting here: George and Aunt Sarah say the picture we have of Mama is as far as face goes as like as possible but that the painter has greatly improved her figure which is shocking bad really.

her Herefordshire friends – but Mr S. Horrocks disposition towards them, as respecting the Child, is what it ought to be – so I hope the impression upon her mind may be done away – unless she, like her Mother, wants the heart to feel the kindness which will be shewn to her by all her Father's friends – She seems very happy here – & fond of Dora & her Cousins, Tom[3] & Geo.[3], who are luckily here at present.

Perhaps Dora has not told Ro. that her Father has consented to publish the Poems *on hand* – But not with Drawings, as was once talkd of, but in a volume which will make a 5th to the last & uniform also with the preceding ones – a neat little Vol. & not costly. I ought to have told you that the *Teapot* gave entire satisfaction to all Parties – & Mr C. expressed himself more gratified by the inscription than the Gift – We have had wretched wet weather of late in spite of it the Country is more beautiful than ever – yet I hope the rain will have departed before you arrive – and that your business will be safe & speedily accomplished lest you should have to encounter equinoxial gales in the Bay of Biscay – William has often asked me what sends you thither? but I cannot give him any satisfactory answer – Dora I think was quite satisfied with your reasons for withholding dear Ro. and indeed she would not, for her own gratification, have wished you to part the Sisters for any length of time – and still less during your absence from them – but as I told you before the request was made under the idea that they *were* to be parted.

Pray do not be so *stingy* of your Letters – making the want of a frank an excuse for not writing – and we shall in addition to our ordinary wish of hearing of you be anxious to know how the Chancery Business goes on – so do not fail to report progress – A kiss for Ro. & believe me most sincerely your Friend S. H.

## 161

*Mrs Hutchinson, Brinsop Court, Hereford*

*Sunday Ev*[g] [*3 or 10 Aug. 1834*]

My dearest Mary

When I fancy I have much to say to you I always feel disposed to prepare a Letter lest I should not have leisure when the Time comes that I ought to write – then comes in Laziness which says wait till to-morrow's post there may be a Letter & you may have no room to answer it – however I think this sheet will suffice for both purposes –

so I will begin, for for the last fortnight I have been anxious that you should know the state of dear Toms[3] mind & I urged him to write to you which he tells me he has done tho' I guess he would not touch upon the matter – They left us, dear Fellows on Thursday week regretted by all the house, with sad hearts tho' with no unwillingness to return to School – tho' dear Tom had been in very bad spirits for some days previous – his head had been *baddish*, & at first we thought this was the cause – but Dora at last got it out of him that the idea of going to College oppressed him – he was sure he *could* not read hard enough – not on account of his health – but of his want of resolution – that he had broken his resolutions to read hard last half year – & this made him miserable which was the cause of his head aches – & he had no confidence in himself – dear fellow! he cried like a Child when he made this confession – & poor Dora was as much distressed as he – she comforted him as well as she could, but he did not get up his heart – so in a day or two I spoke to him – asked him why he desponded? – was he afraid of not getting thro'? *Yes*, was the reply – & then he repeated his confession to me & distressed me greatly – I reasoned with him the best I could – told him it was a pity he had not spoken out before – that it was too late for him to turn to anything else – even if anything else was more suitable – then I asked him if he had any objection to going into the Church? – No – If he got a degree & a Title did he not think he sh[d] be happy, & do his duty as a Clergyman. '*Yes*' he replied without hesitation – Then I told him he had nothing to be unhappy about – there was no fear of his being plucked – at least that it *depended upon himself* – as at Col: he would have no Master to exact a certain quantity of labor from him unless he had a private Tutor – but sooner than he sh[d] be left to himself, as he had no confidence in himself, he sh[d] have a Tutor at my expence – but that I hoped he would be able, with Gods blessing, to keep to his good resolves hereafter &c &c – Nothing could be more amiable than he was – but still he did not get his heart, & mine was not less sad – but he tells me he is in better spirits now tho he gives me so little reason for the change than, that 'among so many boys he cannot help it tho' he knows not how it might be if he were left to himself' – I told him I should write to you – loth as I was to disturb you – but every body said it was right so to do – If he had opened his mind in the beginning of the holidays – I sh[d] instantly have written to you – & I sh[d] also have tried hard to get someone to read with him – but there was no one likely at hand – & both his Uncle & Owen were all for holiday & desu[l]tory reading – besides his Uncle never had the least fear of his not getting his degree – at first we fancied that being with John[6] W. had turned his thought to London

& Surgery for he once said 'They would not let me be a surgeon'. Nay said I, it was too late when you spake of it – But John W. says he never gave a hint of the kind to him – & from Geo.[3] we could not learn that he had ever been in this despair before – I asked if he was ever accused of neglecting his Lessons at School – No – but Geo. said upon being questioned that Mr W. had told Tom at the Examination that he expected he would have done better – We have had many a talk about him as you may suppose – & after all – as nothing better can be done – his Uncle thinks you will see by the Letter which I have copied to Mr Wilkinson he must go on the course intended – and we must hope for the best – there is no other line in which he can serve him – but he does not fear among so many persons in the family that he will have any difficulty in getting a Title & he has no fear of his doing his duty. He does not regret his not having been put to a Surgeon now – for that profession is even more overdone than the Church – in which you may get a maintenance at least – but Mr Thornton who was here last year (Bp Hebers Friend) said that he was Governor of several medical Institutions & it was melancholy to see the number of clever & accomplished Surgeons who were clamouring for any appointment, however small the emolument, which became vacant – & his advice was decidedly against bringing up a boy to it – If you have not already written to me write immediately to tell me if Tom has said anything of the matter to you – & when you write to him do not reproach but encourage him as much as you can – for he is as much aware of his own defects as you can be – no one can take a juster measure of himself than he does – he wants a little more confidence in himself – 'I cannot read I have not read as I ought to have done at School – I always wish to put the book aside – I cannot take pleasure in it as the other Boys do therefore I make not the same progress' – Such were his confessions expressed in the midst of sobs which went to my heart. But he would not say what he thought he was fitter for – Farming if it had been worth following he did not express any wish for – A Soldier he seemed to relish most – but there was nothing *better* to be done than if that could be – for I talked of all things to him by way of diversion – Dear Fellow! I wish he had a little estate of his own – for a little would serve him – & yet, if he is too young to look for a quiet Life before he has earned it – It was not a *wise* wish of mine & I retract it. George[4] tells me he has got into the first Class – the honest Man is quite satisfied with himself – & there is nothing like it – What *stupes* do go to the University – & yet how few are plucked! I have made a long story of this matter – but much as it has occupied my mind I feel that it must even more concern you & dear Thomas[1] – & I would not willingly leave anything unsaid in the fear of being tedious that might help you to a right conclusion. So I will only add that tho' I know you cannot help being grieved – you have abundant cause for thankfulness in having such a good conscientious & affectionate Son as he is – & owe my life for it, will never grieve you by any moral delinquency – scarcely a day passes in which some of us do not express our thankfulness for the good conduct & disposition of your Boys & the youths of this family & I trust in Gods mercy that though they may not thrive in this world or be eminent for worldly wisdom they will be happy and good Men – John[6] W. is still here but leaves us in a day or two. The Rector is also with us – I know not whether any of y[r] newspapers or the Boys have communicated to you the Birth of his 'Son & Heir' as the Papers designated the Child who was born 3 weeks ago (at 5 months old as we tell him) Mother & child both doing well, a very large one as it *ought* to be after such a long expectation – William is at Lowther with M[r] Rogers who spent 3 days with us last week – His Toe is better i.e. the first complaint he had in it which was ocasioned by the nail setting in after a bruise – but there has since appeared a little lump like a high mole filled with blood which the D[rs] cannot account for unless it is the rupture of some small blood vessels occasioned by the first injury which was the heavy shoe & foot of a man whom he was helping to fell a Tree – Some of his Drs (for he has had 3) advised its being cut off – another said let it alone – for he has no pain – & I hope it will disappear for it does not grow larger – but he cannot wear his shoe – or rather it is not advisable to press upon the part. We have had a good deal of company as usual. . . .*

My d[r] Sir

'I sit down to trouble you with a few lines about my Nephew T. H. He is in very low spirits respecting his prospects at Col: finding in himself notwithstanding his best & firmest resolutions an inability to stick to close reading, & consequently he fears that he will scarcely succeed in procuring a degree. Now as no other line of life is open to him, I do anxiously wish that during the short time he remains with you, you would be so kind as to give him all the encouragement you can – I am well aware of the difficulty of the case. He is a youth of a very nice conscience & of good & excellent dispositions, but deplorably wanting in intellectual propensities & appetites. The only knowledge which he seems capable of acquiring from Books is of a kind destitute of *vital* energy: it is kept together mechanically in his mind without any organic

* There follows her quotation from Wordsworth's letter which does not appear to have been published.

connection; it is against the grain, & as far as it is retained, is retained without pleasure & desire for more. This is a melancholy & appears to me a rare case, for he is not a dunce, nor a stupid Boy incapable of comprehending a thing when plainly stated to him, but he seems almost totally without voluntary activity of mind in literature. But to recur to my wish – Such encouragement as you can give him pray do. So good are his principles & so moderate his desires, that I am persuaded that he would be both happy & useful as a Minister of the Gospel in a small country Parish, & as I said before, unfortunately no other line of Life is at present open to him' –

Monday. No Letter of interest to you & none from you which I had hoped for – as I thought you would write after you had seen M[ary][5] M. – Tell dear Henry[1] that Mary[1] Wordsworth would have had no greater pleasure than in writing to him & receiving Letters from him, but she always understood from Joanna that he did not like to be bothered in that way – & as she contented herself with hearing of him thro' Joanna – & she also supposed that thro the same medium he heard regularly from Rydal Mount, but if they are ever again similarly situated he shall not have the like cause of complaint. John[4] has had a Letter from his Wife – who is going on very well – she has been out airing & the Bairn is a monster for size compared to little Jane – as big as she was at 7 weeks – So far & not a word of Miss W[ordsworth] from which you will augur well – she is indeed wonderful tho' she is never a whole day entirely comfortable – the Papers would tell you that poor dear Coleridge is gone! He died a most calm & happy death – tho' he had suffered great pain for some time previous – He was opened – the disease was at his heart. We have not heard *direct* from any of them since the first announcement by Henry[4] – but Sara[3] is better. Her fathers death rouzed her – but before that she had profitted by my advice & plain speech – as I heard both from herself & others – & she now seems determined to be well – & God grant that she may – for it is a deplorable thing to see a young creature who seems to have every wish of her heart gratified given up to fanciful despondency.* Poor Mr & Mrs Gillman will be true mourners – His own relations had more pride in him than Love for him – at least Pride was the foundation of their Love – & even their Pride did not serve to prevent his being dependent upon the Gillmans for his support since the time when his Pension was withdrawn. . . . Miss Eliza is returned & was greatly pleased with Marys[6] Letter & little remembrance of her – she says that

* In his *Dorothy Wordsworth*, p. 392, de Selincourt attributes this sentence to Dorothy Wordsworth.

she must practise from good copies & then she will acquire facility & knowledge of shading – the sketches in Miss W's room were very creditable to her – She will write to M. by Tom[3] – we are to tell her when he goes – I shall send all the old *Duds* by him – & Ebbas green Gown. – Tom thought that he should come home in about 3 weeks before the Camb. term begins – so you will have time enough for his shirts – & also fronts are more expensive in washing tho perhaps he need not have a *Night* Shirt – as he will probably be obliged to have one a day. I will send you the acc[t] of his debts because it is easier to pay a little than a great bill – one of his 2 p[r] of new white Trowsers are missing from the wash – if they have not been missent to some folk who were at the hall the washerwoman must pay for them –

| Drs | Cr | |
|---|---|---|
| 2 p[r] White Trowsers | £1. 2. 6 | |
| Full suit | 5. – – | Rents £5. 1. |
| Hats & Caps | 1. 7 | |
| Pocket Hfrs | 3. 8 | |
| Trowsers G | 15 | |
| 2 Night Shirts T. | 4. 6 | |
| Making D[o] & mending Clothes | 4. 7 | |
| Waistcoat T | 14 – | |
| Coat | 2. ~~1~~2. 6 [*sic*] | |
| Umbrella | 6. | |
| Black neckcloths | 10 | |
| Gloves | 2. 6 | |
| Shoes | 17 | |
| Shoe Bill last year | 11. 5 | |
| | 13. 16. 8 a heavy sum | |
| | 5. 1. – | |
| | 8. 15. 8 due to me | |

but you need not send it – we shall be getting more rent soon I hope – My best love to dear John[2] in which every body joins as well as to yourselves – and may God bless you all'. I dare say I have forgotten many things but no wonder for my mind was so full of the dear Boy – whom I could not love better if he were my own – ever most truly yours S. H. –

*Postmark: Kendal, Penny Post*

# 162

*Mrs. S. T. Coleridge, c/o Mrs. H. N. Coleridge,*
*21 Downshire Hill, Hampstead*

*Sunday* [*28 Sept. 1834*]

My dear Friend

Bertha & Kate readily accepted my offer of writing to you & I was glad to spare them the painful details which I know you must desire to hear – & I trust that before it is necessary for them to write to you again our hopes that better tidings are in store for you will be confirmed. If patient & cheerful resignation to the divine will under affliction deserve a reward, in this world, the Almighty will I trust manifest it in blessing the human means which have been so wisely & promptly applied for the restoration of your dear suffering Sister – It may be truly said that Southey has 'kissed the rod' – If any man ever deserved the Title of *Christian* Philosopher it is he – so much feeling with so much power to overcome I never before saw exemplified – Often since I came into the house have I said to myself. It is good for us to be afflicted – & felt that it *was* better to go to the House of mourning than of feasting. Kate dear little Creature! is her fathers own child – She has behaved like a Heroine – & dear Bertha has done her best – I have had inexpressible satisfaction in feeling myself a comfort to them as well as to dear Mrs. Lovell – who I am happy to say bears this sad stroke better than I could have hoped – She & all of us are satisfied that the best possible has been done – & we look forward with hope & trust to him whose tender mercy is over all his works.

I do not know exactly what dear Kate wrote to you but doubtless the account was brief – You must have heard that your Sisters depression of spirit had increased greatly of late – probably from the thought of parting with Cuthbert – so soon after the loss of Edith – About a fortnight ago Southey wrote to ask me to come over the week before their intended departure – in which request your Sister most earnestly joined – & I replied that I should be with them in a day or two unless she would consent to come to Rydal with them on their way which we thought would divert her mind a little & make the parting less painful – In reply Southey told me that this could not be accomplished – that she was so much worse that he must give up his journey – & Kate go with her Cousins – & that I had better defer my visit, or rather that I need not come till she was gone – After this I heard no more till last

Tuesdy Morng when a note by post from G. Hill told me that it was Mr. S[outhey]'s last request before he [Mr. Hill] left home, (on Monday) with Mr. S for *York* that I would come to the dear Girls – which I did immediately by that morngs Coach. You may conceive what a shock this was to us at Rydal – Miss W. Dora & I – W$^{m}$. & M[ary] were at Workington – & in their way a week before had used every argument in their power to induce your Sister to come to us but in vain – Mary wrote me that she had a wild & bewildered look – & after this she became so much worse that for a few days she was perfectly unmanageable – & no course was left but the one which was speedily adopted – *Force* alas! was required for her removal – but she evidently improved during the journey (i.e. in calmness – but was not rational) until she approached the end of it – when of course understanding perfectly for what purpose it was taken she was with difficulty removed from the Carriage – but the moment she entered the House she was calm & gentle as a Lamb – Betty you will be happy to hear remains with her – this is not against the rules of the establis$^{t}$. which are humane & mild in the highest degree – & tho' I have heard the efficacy [of] treatment at the retreat questioned on *this point* have no doubt that in this case it will be sufficient – S. was well pleased & satisfied with all he saw & heard – & he left her on Thursdy Evg. as composed as possible – & apparently satisfied – (& more like herself than he had seen her for months previously) only despairing that she should never be well – yet she did not breath a wish to return with him, whether she felt it or not – Her apartments surprized her from their comfort &c. & she could not believe Betty that they were to be hers – S. was much pleased with the Physician – tho' he could give no opinion upon the case – He said the natural strength of her constitution was in her favor – & that there was no hereditary insanity – & that she was not possessed by *one* idea – The unfavourable circumstances were her age & her naturally uncheerful disposition – We look as you may suppose anxiously for a Letter from him, & also from Betty from whom we shall hear the very worst – as she will appear better to those who are Strangers & with whom she is under restraint – I have scarcely time to add more – & I need not say anything to you about my sympathy for you all – All has been done for the best & the very best under the circumstances – there has been nothing left undone that can alleviate – but S. & they all feel that with Gods blessing had she been less yielded to before it came to this – this sad result might have been prevented – but ever since dear E.'s departure she has more than ever indulged her melancholy feelings & anticipations – which *might* have been diverted had they insisted upon her leaving home – & thus the chain might for a time at least have been broken – this they will never cease to regret – but the error was blameless – as it originated in tenderness of feeling – Now, if it pleases God that she recovers, they will act more firmly – & will not suffer her to remain so long at home – & as soon as she is fit for removal which I trust will soon be the case, they will all join her & proceed to Sussex to Worthing – & keep her there for some time – & now I must conclude lest I lose this post – Only let me say dearest little Sara try to rouze yourself – believe me 'quiet' & the presence of the same objects will not so speedily work your cure as change of scene & occupation – & may Gods blessing be upon your endeavours which I trust not will be strengthened by this example which has in mercy no doubt been afforded to us all. I have nothing I grieve to say to tell you of comfort respecting Hartley – & nothing worse than my last report – God bless & support you all is the sincere prayer of your affte Friend S. H.

We shall be glad to hear from you – I know not how long I shall be here – I have not the heart to leave them & S[outhey] tells me the longer I stay the better – Excuse this hasty tho' long Letter & all its blunders for I have not time to look it over – Dorothy is in her best way – Dora a little better.

You will take it for granted that they all send their tenderest love & thanks to dear S[ara][3] for her consoling Letter. Mrs Lovel will thank you to tell Robert the sad news if you have not already done so.

*Postmark: 4 Oct 1834*

## 163

*Thos Hutchinson Esqre, St John's College, Cambridge*

*Keswick, 15th Octr. [1834]*

My dearest Tom

I hope by this time you are comfortably settled & all your fears of Camb[ridge] dissipated – I have had a most kind communication from Mr H. Cookson respecting you – & he I dare say was at the Coach to meet you – & give you his assistance & advice of which you would I am sure feel much need, & be most thankful for. I have written to him & desired that he will undertake to Tutor you – so lose no time if you have not already begun, in attending him for this purpose – & in all things *ask*, & *follow*, his advice with which you can take the liberty of troubling him – He will tell you where to buy books best &c – & I hope it will not be beneath the dignity of Mr Hymers to bestow some regard upon you – tho' it cannot be as in other places – the Dons must not notice such Boys as you –

Now my dear Boy pray write to me – I shall not be comfortable till I hear that you are so – your dear Mother I hope knows it already – for her heart was sorely oppressed by your despondency – and if your spirits are now better I trust you have raised them on a more firm foundation than you did when you returned to Sedbergh else they would not have been again so soon depressed – If you only determine to *use* & not *misuse* your time depend upon it that you will accomplish with credit all that your friends wish or expect you to strive for i.e. simply your degree – if you can do more well – but no wish or expectation will be disappointed if you do not – the only & most important concern is that you continue in morals & principle the same amidst the temptations which may assault you – And I pray to God to give you strength to resist temptation – & that he will preserve you from all evil –

That you should be industrious at College is of two fold importance – for if you are idle you will be sure to be *pestered by* the idle – & all opportunity of being industrious will be taken away – keep out of your Chambers then the Idle – never mind *what they* think of you – practise a little firmness & they will soon give you up – better be reading a novel alone, for your *own amusement,* than enter into scenes of riots & intemperance for theirs – *I* should say to *forswear wine* & the battle would be won before you are called upon to fight it – And an easy victory it will be to you *now* – but delay it & it will become *comparatively* impossible – & though you might lose the society & friendship of some pleasant companions & *more unpleasant* ones – yet you will be amply repaid by the regard & consideration of those whose friendship & good opinion are worth having – This is all very true & very trite you will say – yet I do not shrink from writing it – for I do not think *you* will quiz your old Aunt for her advice, however trite & prosy it may be – for I need not tell you that I am most tenderly & deeply interested in your welfare – & to secure your *well doing* there is nothing in my power that should be wanting, if *that would avail* – but it is in your *own* power *& no one's* else – & follow but the good motions of your own affectionate heart – think of your dear Father & Mother & other tender friends when you are tempted to do wrong, or *leave undone* what you ought to do – & pray to God to enable you to keep the path of your duty to *Him,* & to *them* – & I doubt not you will gain the end of your career at Col. rejoicing – God bless you My dear Boy! & believe me your most afft Aunt S. H.

Write to me at Rob$^{t}$ Southey, Esq$^{re}$, Keswick. If you have not already written to Rydal – & mind you never neglect writing home – & keep strict *accounts* – this is of much more importance than you may suppose – So do not neglect it – Did you go to Mr Heaths about your Teeth? Or was my direction too late? I do wish Dora would go to Camb: We *all wish* it – Is your Uncle's Picture yet arrived at C.?

*Postmark: Keswick*

# 164

*Thos Hutchinson Esqre, St John's College, Cambridge*

*Keswick, Novr 3* [*1834*]

My dear Thomas

Your Letter to me, one forwarded by your Mother addressed to her, & an extract from a latter Letter to her, have all been received by me & read with the most *heartfelt* pleasure. That you are well, & *happy*, is the best assurance I can receive that you are satisfied with yourself, & doing your duty; & tho' much gratified by your kind expressions of obligation to me I should be very disingennuous were I not to tell you that the favor *you say* I have done you – is not *so purely disinterested* as you may suppose – for my dear Boy I assure you the *pain* I felt when I saw you in such a state of despondency I should have been glad to be *rid of* at a much greater price than the payment of a little money – which I can well spare & which I trust, with Gods blessing, will be well bestowed upon you – & I wish no better recompence.

My letters to you & Henry Cookson, which I suppose crossed yours upon the road, were doubtless considered a sufficient answer as I have not heard further from you – & I feel so much confidence in him that I am sure he will further my views to the best of his judgement; & in his hands I leave you with my grateful thanks for his present kindness & further good intentions – & for you I must say that you cannot have a better guide. Therefore, dear Tom, always apply to him for advice in all things as well as in your Studies – and avoid at all times idle company – I do not approve of your working so *furiously* as you appear to have done on the first days of your being at C— but you had soon experience that this would defeat your purpose by rendering you incapable of working at all – & do not fail to take proper & sufficient exercise in the open air – Your having a Tutor will secure your application to the College reading required at present – but when your leisure serves do not fail to improve yourself in general reading –

& especially such as is connected with your future profession – & above all do not neglect your Bible – give some time to it each day – and when you are at Chapel do not think that if you attend seriously to the prayers you have done your duty – but attend also to the Lessons – which people are apt to think they *know* already – but consider that, important as it is for us all to study the Scriptures, no Christian Teacher can be *too familiar* with them – & such *high calling* I trust you will prove yourself worthy of.

And now I have done with my advice for the present, & commit you to the care of that gracious God who careth for us, more than we deserve but who also expects that we shall *care for ourselves* & not neglect our part – then come what will, in this world, the satisfaction arising from a good conscience will secure us that peace of mind which the world cannot give.

I have been here more than a month. Cuthbert is still at home. He was prevented from going to Mr Warters (where he was to have pursued his studies until his entrance at Oxford) by the illness of his Mother who has been obliged to leave home for advice & change of scene but he will go in the Spring. He & I went last week to Workington in their poney Chair – & spent 2 very pleasant Days at the Rectory, where we found all well – Coz. John[4] upon our noticing a very *wee* Church in the neighbourhood told us it was in his Gift – & observed if it should fall vacant in *his* & *your* time it would just suit a *little* Fellow as T. H. – So you see your Friends bear you in mind.

I am sorry to tell you that Dora is very unwell – but as she is under Mr Carr's care, & seems disposed to be obedient to him, I trust she will overcome her complaints & be stronger than she has been for some time – but this will prevent her leaving home at present – tho' I do not despair of her still visiting Cambridge while you are a *freshman.* When she writes to her Coz. Chris. she will desire him to call upon you – but your Aunt W. says *you* must call upon the Dr & put on your Card (for I suppose you are prepared with those *man*ly appendages) '*Brinsop Court*' by way of a more particular introduction. Your Aunt wrote to Mr Hymers to introduce you – but you do not say that you have seen him – She sent her Letter by Professor Sedgwick, who perhaps may not be a *good post.* Miss W. has been very *nice*ly since I left home till within the last week when the change of weather, as usual, affected her, – but in general the season has been very fine – & the Woods have not yet lost their leaves . . . and a happy party I trust you will all be together at Xmas – tho' I must warn you that *yours* must not now be all a *play* holiday – but that you must give a part of each day to study – & then you will enjoy your gun and Mr Peel with double

Zest – But I have got to preaching again, you will perhaps say, so I will conclude my Letter, though not till I have given you a favorite stanza of mine from a very old poet which I hope will stick in your memory as it has done in mine –

'Eschew the Idle Life For never was their idle Bain
Flee, flee, from doing nought But bred an idle thought'*

My kind regards to M^r H[enry] C[ookson] & best thanks for his good services to you. Let me remind you to keep an exact account of your expences – nothing makes economy so *easy* – & in like manner if we would account to ourselves each night *how* the day has been spent, we should never *misspend* our *time*.

I must remind you to take care of your *spelling* & not spell *ghost* again without an *h* as you did in your Letter.† This is only carelessness for you must see the word daily in your Prayer Book. God bless you! & believe me most affectionately & anxiously your Aunt S. H.

I scarcely need say that a Letter from you will always be most welcome but writing to me must not prevent your writing home – where they must be even more anxious to hear of you than I.

*Postmark: Keswick*

## 165

*Edward Quillinan Esq^re, Oporto*

*Rydal Mount, 8th Jan^y – 35*

My dear Friend

If I had supposed that you would be in Eng^d again before this time I should not have been so long in thanking you for your last long & entertaining Letter, tho' I rec^d it when I was about to pay a very distressing visit to our dear Friends at Keswick. I now thank you for it – & also acknowledge the receipt of yours from Oporto to Dora, who poor Thing! is not in a condition fit for using her pen as much as she wishes – indeed she never ought to use it at all – You know how long we have been anxious about her health – & will be grieved to hear that she is now suffering from an inflamation of the Spine – & has been

* From *The Lover to Cupid for Mercy*, George Turberville, c. 1540–1610.

† We must hope that young Tom 'disingennuous'-ly comforted himself. See p. 434, above.

for the last 2 months or more subjected to the troublesome & painful remedies of bleeding & blistering – Sad as this is we felt thankful when the cause of her long indisposition was ascertained – & have no doubt that, by the blessing of God, the means used for her cure will be successful – our only fear is that her strength may fail under these weakening remedies – for her appetite is as bad as ever – she persists in living upon *prison fare* – bread & water – i e Tea as weak as water – though the medical men are of opinion that this spare diet is the cause, in her case, of the complaint – & cannot therefore be the remedy also! You may guess my dear Friend how great our anxiety is & has been – her spirits are as good as ever & were she to write to you herself you could not suspect that anything ailed her except from her hand-writing – which of course from her recumbent position cannot be the same as heretofore – If when the inflamation is entirely subdued, she has strength to bear a removal, & *is willing* to be removed, change may do much to restore her – but it will be a long time before this can be thought of – She is not confined entirely to the Sofa – or obliged to be always upon her back – but allowed to rise occasionally – & to be on her side as much as she chuses – so that the confinement is not so irksome as the old practice was –

I cannot give you one of our very best accounts of dear Miss Wordsworth – She had a bilious attack lately – & has not yet regained the point where it found her – & the severe weather which we have at present keeps her close to her bed. Mr W. is well – his eyes much better than they were last year at this season – He is at present at Lowther – keeping batchelors house with Lord Lowther & the Colonel, who are come down for their election for the County – which we hope will be without opposition – My Sister & I are quite well – John[1] is with us, well also – Willy[2] has been here & he is gone to Lowther in his way home – well – & as noisy as ever – Poor John has all the cares of the world upon him – Rector of a large Parish – Vicar of another where he is building a house – his poor Wife only just recovered from the Typhus fever – but his Bairns are well & thriving – & I hope we shall send him home in better case after his fortnights holiday – the first visit but one he has paid us since last Xmas. Now after this sad catalogue I must tell you that our Keswick friends are in good heart respecting dear Mrs Southey – The accounts from York have for the last three weeks been most favorable – & we look forward with confidence to her restoration to her family in a short time – It has been a sad affliction – but they have all borne it with truly christian fortitude & submission – Sara[3] Coleridge too is better – but not so far as to go about like other People – If you have seen the English Papers you will know that poor C. Lamb is dead – He died of Erysipelas – & was only ill 3 or 4 days – This was a great shock to us – especially to me who had seen him looking so well – & in such pleasant & equable spirits last June when we breakfasted with him at Moxon's!

So far have I written & not one word about your ownself or your Darlings – but I can tell you no more, nor as much as you know yourself on both these subjects – The Children are I doubt not very happy as from their Letters they seem to be – tho' they were sadly disappointed at first that you did not come to spend the holidays with them – Your's is a nice scheme for Easter – so do not mar it by a longer stay at Oporto – We expect Ebba here after Christmas – [she] comes when Geo[3] returns to school – They are all well at Brinsop – Mr Monkhouse's eyes have been operated upon 3 times – with what success the last time I do not know – not have heard from B[rinsop] since his return from Town – he took Mary[5] Monkhouse to B[rinsop] for the Holidays so that if your dears had gone they would have had a pretty round party – Poor Tom[3] had the Cambridge fever – a sort of Typhus – & was obliged to leave Col: to recruit before the end of the Term – but he is quite well & fit for another campaign – I do not send you one word of public news – or gossip – I leave that for the papers & Mags. If you see *Taits* you will have seen a series of infamous Articles upon poor Coleridge by his Friend the Opium Eater – & in the *British Mag.* for last month a most able & gentlemanly answer to it by Julius Hare* – *Our* Vol: is not yet Pub$^{d}$ tho' finished – because an Angel's Book would not be read or looked at in this time of public excitement. I have sent your Queries to Keswick – & hope to receive the answers before I close this – & must leave the rest of my paper to write them upon – So for the present adieu & may God bless you & send you many many happy years is the sincere wish of all your friends at Rydal M.

Mr Southey has replied to your questions – & I enclose you his Letter we sent him that part of your Letter in which they were – We shall send this to the Children who will know probably whether you are likely to receive it at Oporto or in Eng$^{d}$ & forward it accordingly – This of mine is a dull production to send so far – but alas! I am in no heart to write a lively epistle – Again God bless you & preserve you & send you home in health to your dear Children & friends – Ever most truly yours S. H.

*Endorsed:* 1835 Miss Hutchinson, 8th Jan$^{y}$. Rec$^{d}$ at Oporto 22nd Feb$^{y}$. Ans$^{d}$. [*E.Q.*].

* De Quincey's articles appeared in *Tait's Magazine*, Vols. I–II, 1834–5, and J. C. Hare's reply in the *British Magazine*, Vol. VII, 1835.

## 166

*Joseph Henry Green Esq[re], Lincoln's Inn*

*Rydal Mount, Jan[y]. 10th – 35*

My dear Sir

At the request of M[r] Wordsworth I forward to you the Copies of all the notes written by M[r] Coleridge in the Books at Rydal Mount – Also some Extracts from a Common place Book. The Letters of our late Friend have all been examined – but M[r] W. does not find any among them which could be interesting to the public – as they mostly relate to domestic matters.

You will observe by one Ex[t] from a Letter to me that Chapman's *Homer* was a gift of our dear Friend to me – & therefore will not wonder that I am desirous of re-possessing it – His Books were sent from Rydal when I was absent – & I do not know whether it was sent to Highgate or to Helston* – Should you meet with it among the books I shall be greatly obliged if you will retain it for me.

I cannot conclude without telling you how much we have been all gratified by the complete & gentlemanly Answer, which has appeared in the *British Magazine*, to the Opium Eaters infamous Articles in *Taits Magazine*.

I received the ring† by your order some time ago.

M[r] Wordsworth begs me to present to you his respectful regards – & I am

d[r] Sir very truly your's

S. Hutchinson

## 167

*London February twenty 1835,*
*Thomas Hutchinson Es[q], St Johns, Cambridge*

*Rydal Mount, Feb[y] 16th [1835]*

My dear Tom

Your Uncle & Aunt Wordsworth set off tomorrow morning for London & I cannot let slip the opportunity of their forwarding this to

* Helston – where Derwent Coleridge was Master of the Grammar School.
† Coleridge's will gave directions for a mourning ring to be made for her.

you, tho' you have not favored us with a line since your arrival at Cambridge – but we have heard of you – & Ebba would have written had she not had so many other correspondents to satisfy – & for which purpose she has not gone to School today as was intended. You will, I know, be glad to hear that she is to go every morn[g] to Miss Dowlings & return in the Evening – We shall be very sorry to lose her company for so many of the 24 hours – but I thought she would run wild when she was left entirely to my care – I having the charge of two Invalids to boot – *They* are much the same – but Miss W. will, I hope, recruit as the spring advances – & also that the means used for Dora's recovery are in a fair way of being successful –

Your Uncle & Aunt hope to see you & their other Friends at Camb: before they return home. Have you yet taken a look at your Uncle's Picture, which I learn is already put up in the Combination Room of your Col. Pray do not forget to tell us how you like it. Uncle M[onkhouse] will think himself fortunate in being in Town when M[r] W. & your Aunt are there – I hope his eyes will allow of his being with them sometimes.

Ebba has been very gay while with us. She has been at three Parties – one at the Ivy Cot – one at S[r] Thos' & another at M[rs] Godwins – at all which they amused themselves with *Tableaux* i.e. a representation of the paintings of celebrated Masters, by living subjects dressed up in character & placed within a frame – M[r] Fletcher the Statuary (who has been making a Bust of Mr Hamilton) & Sir Minto Farquhar (Lady F's Son) introduced this amusement into the Vale to the great delight of the party-going inhabitants. We have been too much engaged with our Invalids to join in any of the Winter festivities – but Ebba has been kindly admitted among them.

Cousin John[4] is here at present – he is very well – & his Baby which has been very ill better – All else well – God bless you my d[r] Tom & preserve your health – Ever very truly yours S. H.

Remember me kindly to H. Cookson – & I hope you have called at Trin. Lodge* before this time.

*Postmark: Free, 20 Fe 1835*

* Where Dr. Christopher Wordsworth was Master.

# 168

*Mrs Hutchinson, Brinsop Court, Hereford*

[*April–May, 1835*]

My dearest Mary

You may suppose how vexed I have been at this *foolish* Sedbergh affair – Geo.[3] has been impudent no doubt but it was perfectly ridiculous to turn him out for the *worst* of the instances which Mr Green gave me of his impertinence – I wonder how they would have treated Boys who threw the *butter* in the Mistress' face? Transportation or hanging must have been according to their scale of punishment, their desert!!

I send you this Letter, to satisfy you that there is no charge of moral delinquency – & Mr Green says the same but it was unfeeling certainly to make a disturbance when Mr G[reen] was in affliction – but Mr G. is inexcusable in turning him out without telling his friends & suffering him to fix himself elsewhere – & this I shall repeat to Mr Green – & also that he might have satisfied me as to the *respectableness* of the house he is gone to – However there he must stay till Midsummer – I suppose – indeed I cannot think the Greens *wise* people at any rate – or at all calculated to keep Boys in order – far *too strict.*

We have just recd a Letter from Cambridge – the first – they arrived there on Friday week – recognized Tom[3] on the road in a knot of 4 looking very blithe but he did not recognize them – called on him next morning – very well & happy & said he found his work easy – but was very silent – breakfasted with them on the next morning at the Lodge – & they would see him again on Monday the day she wrote – for the Letter had travelled for a frank – Mary[1] says that his Tutor ought to have claimed a scholarship for him as a Sedbergh Boy which he had a right to – & if Tom had been *sharp* he should have known this himself that he can have it next year but this is loss of time & some little emolument – & without it he has no chance of a Sedbergh Fellowship – & unluckily he is not on Hymers side of the Col – else he might have been of more use to him – however we are sure he will do what he can. It was H. who told them this – but I have half a hope that Tom is a scholar as [?] was elected about the time – Yet it is strange that Tom did not tell us – more strange than that H. did not know it.

I hope you have heard of us thro' Mary while she was in Town for really I have not had time to write. Poor Miss W. has been very so so for the last fortnight – a bilious attack which tho not bad she does not throw off as we had hoped. Dora's back is very much better – but she is to have another blister tonight – in other respects she is *a shade* better – We were grieved to hear by Ebba's Letter that dear Johns[2] Eye is still dark – but trust that M$^r$ Tyrrel[l]s hopes are well founded – our best love to him. Bertha & Kate with Joanna left us last Wed: but one – to prepare for their Aunt Lovells departure to the Isle of Man – & their poor Mothers return – Joanna stayed at Keswick till the friday & then went to Workington – & on Wednesday last M$^{rs}$ L. joined her at Whitehaven & on Friday I hope they sail – for the day was mild – M$^r$ & M$^{rs}$ Southey are returned – they spent a week at Scarborough where she was much better – S[outhey] ran up the hill to see us at their coming home on Wed: last – she had been very rambling on their journey, & he looked wretchedly poor man – but said he was perfectly satisfied that he had done right in bringing her home – all the good that could be done had been at York – that if she did not recover she was perfectly manageable – & from Bertha I hear that their meeting passed over better than could be expected & though not *herself* they felt they could bear to see her as she is better than to be separated – She told them all about the Retreat the people &c – & spoke of it with no dislike – but with praise. We all thought M$^{rs}$ Lovells state of health & nervousness would do M$^{rs}$ S. harm & she could ill bear to see her sister in that state – so we persuaded her to go to Miss Eliza – & Martha remains at K. for a while & I have no doubt the change will do her good.

Ebba is well – never has made a complaint of any kind since she came – & she is as good as she need be – a very great favourite with her Godmother & every body – She goes to School dutifully – & gets up in her classes – Mary[1] bids me say that 3 copies of the Poems* are ordered for Brinsop. One for yourselves – one for John[2] – & the other for George[1] – We have got Henrys[1] *Retrospect*† – & are sadly disappointed with it – but don't say so – It is so poor in language – & the incidents he has chosen as far as I have read not worth detailing at length – a mere catalogue [*torn*] places to which he went – but certainly I have not read m[uch?] [*torn*] – He cannot surely wish to publish it!

This is a sad scrawl – but the bells are ringing & when I return from Church I must write a long letter to Camb: for we have never written since they got there – so God bless you all! . . . Remember us to Geo:[1] when you see him we are glad to hear such good accounts of him – I hope they may be depended upon – Farewell! Excuse all omissions – Ever truly yours S. H. In a Letter of Doras to her Father she says

* *Yarrow Revisited and Other Poems*, 1835. † See Letter 1, p. 3, note.

'Aunty bids me say that Ebba is a great pleasure & comfort to her.'

[*Mr. Wilkinson's letter which sheds no further light on George's rudeness to Mr. Green is omitted.*]

. . . I recommended M^r^ G. for the sake of quiet not to insist on the attendance at supper in the parlor, provided they were not out of bounds and were disposed to [*torn*] this.

*Postmark: Kendal, Penny Post*

# 169

## *Mrs Hutchinson, Brinsop Court, Hereford*

[*30–31 May, 1835*]

My dearest Friends

You cannot conceive how anxiously your Letter was expected – poor Ebba thought you had quite forgotten her – & as we had no idea of Mary's[2] remaining so long in Town could not account for *her* silence as only one Letter had she written to Rydal – However we are thankful that all is well – & that Tyrrell gives such good hopes of dear John's[2] ultimate recovery. W^m^ desired me to give a particular message of congratulation from him – & also to say that he was much gratified by M^r^ Robinsons report of the pleasure he had had in the new Volume* – & as he looks upon him as one of his most worthy & intelligent admirers wishes to know *which* of the poems most please him.

I ought not to have said that 'all was well' for you say that poor Thomas is suffering from the rheumatism – but bad as that is to bide it seems a small evil compared with the diseases & afflictions of our other friends which have for so many months past weighed upon our spirits – Poor Miss W. does not rally at all – you never saw any one look more like a *picture* of *exhaustion.* & yet there does not appear to be inwardly either in mind or body any great change – her faculties are the same – & I think she complains less of pain – but is greatly affected by a sort of nausea which obliges her to be perfectly still – & when you go into her room she is lying generally as if she were in a state of insensibility or half asleep – always craving air – so that the change in the weather which we had hoped would have a good effect seemed only to overpower her. I have alas! no better report to give of

* *Yarrow Revisited and Other Poems.*

Dora – though till within the last few days we were in better heart as the shower bath & *porter* we were in hopes were going to do much for her – but unluckily she has got a sad cold – a sort of influenza with sore throat & a very bad *cough* which of things we are most afraid of in her weak state. Her back was much better – nearly well except in one part – & M^r^ Carr thought she might with safety have been removed for change of air &c at the end of this month – but this cannot now be – even if she were willing – but her repugnance to leave home is as strong as ever – & whether it will be accomplished or not I know not – though it seems to be the only chance for her life. W^m^ & Mary came home sooner than they intended in the hope of taking her back when Williams' mouth was ready for his new Teeth – because M^r^ Carr said he was sure that if they remained absent for another 6 weeks, which would have been necessary, that she would not be induced to move soon after their return – & then the season would be so far advanced – that it was a question whether she would get off at all – how it will be I know not – but we must be patient & submit to whatever is ordained for us – melancholy as is our prospect – it is nothing to that of our poor friends at Keswick – M^rs^ Southey is still in the same deplorable state* – seldom herself except in the evening – & then so *cross* that there is no peace or comfort – & those dear Girls – not to say anything of their fathers sufferings will be worn out – but they bear it most heroically – yet such constant anxiety, & with such a melancholy object before them daily, they must suffer in health if not in spirits eventually – Edith is in the family way again – poor thing I hope she will be more fortunate this time – she seems very happy as far as her own lot is concerned – & has borne her other affliction as well as the rest.

Miss W. has always intended to write to you in praise of her God-daughter herself – but as she cannot she desires me to say that she is a great comfort to her – & indeed it is delightful to us all to see how very kind & attentive she is to her – never forgets her – morning & night she is first & last in Ebbas thoughts – & her first question on her return from school is always 'How has Miss W. been'. Miss W. does not like the thought of losing her at the holidays – but independent of this we think it was a very foolish proposal of aunt Joannas – & had not she mentioned it to the Children first, we should have told her so – first the expence – then *she* had, as also *Henry*[1], seen Ebba so lately – & Ebba would have been happy enough here – & George[3] might spend his time more *profitably* here than at the Island – However your Letter has, with respect to him, altered our minds – but I must give you the

* After a few months at York Mrs. Southey was brought home again.

result of our cogitations. First have you any expectation that they would take him in at Budge Row, if he were fitted for business, at Manchester or else where? We cannot but regret that he could not have been *the* Scholar, as he is decidedly fond of Books – & so far we have no notion that he will make a good Tradesman, being inclined to be high spirited – Our Friends are *out* – & if they were not Willys[2] wants stand in the way – though what would suit Geo would not suit Willys age – for the lowest step in a public office would be all that Geo could expect – Now we think that Frankland Lewis might help you to this – & Mary[1] Wordsworth says that if she returns to Town again there will be no objection to *her* applying where she can for him – M[rs] Hemans' Son has got a clerkship in a public office the salary is about 80£, at first, & encreases gradually – & tho this would not maintain him at first – it would be better than nothing which he would have in a merchants counting house till he had been there some time. But whether we can succeed in this or not as he cannot go to Col: we think his remaining at Sedburgh of little use – & till something is determined upon he might spend his time profitably and cheaply at the Island in learning French & Arithmetic both of which will be necessary whether he is to be in Trade or in a public office – & in the mean time you can be looking about, for one of the other situation. Accounts in either will be most necessary – But you must judge for yourself I give these only as hints – yet I think if you could apply, & interest M[r] Lewis in your favor something might be done for him – as he has no friends of his own that stand in the way of such an appointment as would satisfy you at present for Geo. & he is in favor with the present party tho' to be sure they are a *hungry* set. As you have written to Joanna probably the Isle of Man jaunt is decided – but if Geo should go to be tutored there it would be folly to send Ebba to return alone – so we should keep him a while that they might enjoy each others company here – & indeed if we are lucky enough to get Dora off with her Father & Mother I cannot well spare her – but there is a month to come before this need be determined upon. . . .

I was interrupted by a summons from Isabella (who with John[4] the little Girl have been with us since Wed: week) to take a drive with her to shew Janey to Eliz[ths] Cookson – & after stooping to fasten my clog I was punished for having spoken so lightly of dear Thomas'[1] rheumatism by a seizure, without the least previous warning of Lumbago as I suppose it is* – tho' I never had a hint of the disease before – & now

* The beginning of the end; she died on June 23rd, of 'rheumatic fever' or 'influenza' which began as 'lumbago'. See *Wordsworth Letters, the Later Years*, II, 742–7.

my back is as stiff as a tree & I could scarcely get in & out of the Carriage – *Doctor* John[6] is also here – he is of age & is come to settle his affairs during the vacation at Kings College where he attends lectures – we talked about Surgery too this morning – but *his* Education in that profession will, I suppose, cost quite as much as Toms[3] – exclusive of the private Tutor – which would not have been necessary for George[3] – so that *that* would not be desirable – it is *scandalous* to think how expensive all education is become – let it be for what it may. Mary[1] observed that our John[1] at 15 was taken into the bank – & very soon conducted the whole business – yet how little pains were taken with him! – I am sure whatever they may say about the improvement of the age – young Men were far more '*uppart*' & helpful *of old* than now-a-days. I hope G[eorge][4] M[onkhouse] may get a good place where he will be well worked which may be the salvation of him poor Fellow. I never can help lamenting that he was not sent to a Yorkshire School, or at any rate one where he had been less noticed. . . . I hope you have rec^d^ 3 copies of the new Volume – & like the Poems – Williams Eyes are quite well – never have been so well for years – Mary too is well – tho' sadly anxious as you may suppose about poor Dora – I was quite well till 11 o'Clock today when this plaguey pain came on – Our neighbours too are all well – tho' the Hamiltons are absent at Edinburgh & alas are not to be our neighbours longer than July – they have taken Elleray – M^rs^ Luff is at home granking as usual – tho' she has no right to grank – if she rightly compares her situation with that of her neighbours – . . . & now I am at the end of my paper & M^r^ & M^rs^ Elliot are below who wish to take [my] Letter to the post – so God bless you all & believe me ever most truly your loving Sister S. H.

Remember us to George[1] when you see him – I hope he does not come into Joannas scheme of sending Marg^t^ to be a dress maker – she will not be a bit nearer for a suitable place for it – for she is ingenious enough without & may be spoilt – The Columbians are down again, I fear not to rise suddenly. Had they gone further up one knows not what folly might have been the consequence!!

Eliz^th^[3] Cookson is in her best way – very thin – but she has had a good winter *for her*.

*Postmark: Kendal, Penny Post*

# Names of Persons, Houses, Places

Names of persons, including nicknames, are given as used by Sara Hutchinson in alphabetical order according to her citation. As certain Christian names are frequently repeated in various generations and branches of the closely related Hutchinson, Wordsworth and Monkhouse families, it has seemed wise to number the Marys, Henry, Johns, Dorothys, Williams, etc., and apply the numbering to references that may be ambiguous. The contemporary habit of not distinguishing between sisters and sisters-in-law, brothers and brothers-in-law, sometimes is confusing. In some cases it has seemed helpful to list all the children of a family in one place, e.g. the Southeys, Wordsworths and Coleridges. This has been done under the name of the father. The particulars given about persons, places, etc. are not necessarily the most important facts about them, but only details which it is hoped will throw light on references to them in these letters.

Abernethy, Sir John, 1764–1831: physician and physiologist, notoriously blunt with patients.

Addisons, the: Isabella, Jane, Henry, Mary and Richard. Isabella married John Monkhouse in 1807 and lived only a year after her marriage. Richard was a partner of Richard Wordsworth, William's brother.

Anne:

(1) Hutchinson, niece, daughter of John Hutchinson.

(2) Horrocks, sister of Mrs. Thomas Monkhouse.

(3) Cookson, *q.v.*,[1] b. 1745, cousin of W. Wordsworth.

(4) Cookson, daughter of Sara's friends Thomas and Elizabeth Cookson of Kendal.

Antelope: Dr. Andrew Bell's nickname for Dorothy Wordsworth.

Appleby: Miss Weir lived there.

Arnolds: the family of Thomas Arnold of Rugby, 1795–1842. There were nine children.

Ashburner: John, Peggy and their five children, neighbours of the Wordsworths, performed various domestic services for them. They lived opposite Town End.

Atherley, Mrs.: school friend of Bessy Hutchinson.

Aunt (Elizabeth): see Monkhouse. This is the aunt most often mentioned, but it is not always clear to which aunt she is referring.

Ayling: Mr. and Miss, lived in Spring Cottage, and Mr. Ayling proposed marriage to Dora Wordsworth but was refused.

Barber, Mr. Samuel: who lived, was connected socially with Mrs. Thomas Monkhouse.

Barker, Miss: friend of Southey, who lived for a time in the half of Greta Hall not occupied by the Southeys and Coleridges. She built herself a house in Borrodale, and then moved to Boulogne where she married. She is the Bhow Begum of Southey's *The Doctor*.

Barrett, Colonel Brydges: Son of Sir Egerton Brydges, and Quillinan's brother-in-law. He lived at Lee Priory and owned a house in Bryanston St.

Beau, the: John Wilson, *q.v.*

Beaumont, Sir George, 1753–1827: artist and patron of art, principal founder of the National Gallery, friend of Wordsworth and Coleridge.

Beddoes, Thomas, M.D., 1760–1808: patron of Humphry Davy, friend of Coleridge, who published various works on preventive medicine and public health, much in advance of their time.

Bedford Square: where Basil Montagu lived.

Bell, Dr. Andrew, 1753–1832: founder of the Madras system of teaching, staunchly supported by the Wordsworths, Coleridge and Southey. From 1801 onwards he was rector at Swanage in Dorset. Southey wrote his *Life*, in 3 vols.

Bessy, Hutchinson: niece, eldest daughter of John[1] by his first wife.

Betsy, at Greatham: Elizabeth Hutchinson, sister, somewhat under-developed.

Binfield: where Dr. and Mrs. William Cookson lived.

Birkett, Capt. and Mrs.: sister and brother-in-law of Mrs. Thomas Monkhouse.

Bishop, the: see Watson, Richard, Bishop of Llandaff.

Bishop, the, of Chester: see Blomfield.

Blomfield, C. J., 1786–1857: later Bishop of Chester and London. A friend of T. Clarkson.

Brathay, Old: the home, after 1800, of the Charles Lloyds.

Brinsop Court: after Hindwell, the home of Thomas Hutchinson and Mary Monkhouse, six miles from Hereford.

Brydges, Sir Egerton, Bart., 1762–1837: who as a scholar-amateur published many editions of rare works and his own writings, chiefly in small limited editions. Father of Edward Quillinan's first wife. His son, Egerton Brydges, took orders. See *The Literary Career of Sir Egerton Brydges*, by M. K. Woodworth, Oxford, 1935, and *The Times Literary Supplement*, 16 Nov. 1935.

Bury: the Clarksons, *q.v.*, lived at Bury St. Edmunds.

Calgarth: residence of the Bishop of Llandaff, Richard Watson.

Carr, Mr.: a Grasmere Medical man, successor to Mr. Scambler, later of Bolton Abbey.

Carruthers, Richard: painted two portraits of Wordsworth, commissioned perhaps by Thomas Monkhouse.

Carter, John: Wordsworth's deputy as Stamp Distributor.

Catherine, or Kate, Wordsworth: see William Wordsworth.

Celestial Blue: Sara Coleridge, Jr., also called Sariola. Wordsworth described her eyes when she was a baby as of a 'celestial blue', but the nickname seems to have come from de Quincey; she was of course teased about her blue-stocking interests.

Charles Hutchinson: nephew, son of John Hutchinson her eldest brother.
Charlotte, Miss: C. Lockier or C. Crump.
Chippendale: Mr. Chippendale was related to the Wordsworths.
Clarkson, Thomas, 1760–1846: the abolitionist who lived at Eusemere, then Bury St. Edmunds and later at Playford Hall near Ipswitch. Mrs. Clarkson was a close friend of Dorothy Wordsworth and Sara Hutchinson.
Cœlebs, Hæc: is Harriet Douglas, *q.v.* 'Hic' and 'Hoc' are her brothers.
Coleorton: home of Sir George Beaumont, *q.v.*
Coleridge, Henry Nelson, 1798–1843: Coleridge's nephew, son of Colonel James Coleridge, a barrister, who in 1829 married Sara Coleridge, Jr., and on Coleridge's death in 1834 became one of his literary executors.
Coleridge, John Taylor, later Sir John, 1790–1876: Coleridge's nephew, son of Colonel James Coleridge; he was for a time editor of the *Quarterly Review* and later became a Judge.
Coleridge, Samuel Taylor, 1772–1834: for his relation to Sara Hutchinson see Introduction, pp. xxv–xxvi, xxx–xxxi. He married in 1795, went to Germany 1798–9, moved to Keswick in 1800, went to Malta and Italy 1804–6, returned and lived in Keswick and with the Wordsworths in Grasmere, to 1810. After six very unsettled years of ill-health, he found a home with Mr. and Mrs. Gillman, in Highgate. His children were:
Hartley, 1796–1849: poet, and briefly, Fellow of Oriel College, Oxford.
Derwent, 1800–83, divine, and Principal of St. Marks's, Chelsea.
Sara, 1802–52: married H. N. Coleridge, her cousin, in Sept. 1829.
Coleridge, Mrs., *née* Sarah Fricker: at Greta Hall, Keswick, till 1830, and then at Hampstead with her daughter.
Cookson:
(1) Wordsworth's mother was Anne Cookson of Penrith. Her brother was William Cookson, later Dr. and Canon of Windsor. His wife was Dorothy and their children were Mary (b. 1790), Christopher (b. 1791), William (b. 1792), Elizabeth (b. 1793), George (b. 1794), and Anne (b. 1795). Dr. and Mrs. Cookson were Dorothy Wordsworth's favourite uncle and aunt by whom, and her grandmother, she was brought up in Penrith.
(2) Thomas and Elizabeth, of Kendal, friends from her childhood, of Sara Hutchinson. They often exchanged visits with the Wordsworth household. There was no relationship.
Crackanthorpes: cousins of the Wordsworths.
Crump, Mr.: Liverpool Attorney who in 1805 built Allan Bank, the home of the Wordsworths from 1808–11.
Curate at Grasmere: For 50 years it was E. Rowlandson, who died in 1811 to be succeeded by Mr. William Johnson. He persuaded Mary and Dorothy Wordsworth (but not Sara Hutchinson), to teach occasionally in the Sunday School.
Curwen, John: M.P. of Workington Hall. His granddaughter, Isabella Curwen, was the first of John Wordsworth's four wives. They married 11 Oct. 1830.
Daisy, the: sister of Mrs. Thomas Monkhouse, *née* Horrocks.

Dawes, Mr.: master of a school at Ambleside attended by the Coleridge and Wordsworth boys.

Dawsons: a Grasmere family referred to in Wordsworth's *Excursion*.

De Quincey, Thomas, 1785–1859: The Opium Eater – who in 1808 rented Dove Castle to be near Wordsworth and Coleridge. He married Margaret Sympson in 1817, and moved in 1821 to London, and later to Edinburgh.

Derwent: see Coleridge, Derwent.

Dew, Mrs.: Mary[6] Hutchinson married Rev. Henry Dew, rector of Whitney. Mrs. Dew was possibly his mother or aunt.

Dora or 'Do': Dorothy[2].

Dorothy:

(1) Wordsworth, sister of William Wordsworth, 1771–1855.

(2) Wordsworth, 1804–47, niece, daughter of William and Mary Wordsworth; in 1841 married Edward Quillinan, his second wife.

(3) Wordsworth, niece of William Wordsworth, three years older than Dorothy[2], daughter of Richard Wordsworth of Whitehaven.

Douglas, Miss Harriet, of New York, 1790–1872: also called 'Hæc Cœlebs' and 'The Red Indian'. A wealthy heiress who went lion-hunting in Britain to escape fortune-hunters at home. A biography by Angus Davidson, published in 1952, gives two letters of Sara Hutchinson to her, in Appendix I.

Dowling, Miss: friend of Sara Hutchinson, governess in Lord Galloway's family, who in 1818 took charge of a school at Ambleside. Dora Wordsworth was pupil and later teacher there.

Ebba: Elizabeth[2].

Edith: Southey, Edith May, 1804–71, daughter of Robert Southey, *q.v.*

Egerton: see Brydges.

Elizabeth:

(1) Hutchinson, died 1827, niece, daughter of John Hutchinson.

(2) Hutchinson (Ebba), niece, daughter of Thomas and Mary Hutchinson, Dorothy Wordsworth's god-daughter.

(3) Cookson, daughter of Thomas and Elizabeth Cookson of Kendal, *q.v.* See also Monkhouse, Miss Elizabeth, 'Aunt'.

Elleray: a house owned and intermittently occupied by John Wilson from 1808 to 1815, on the slope of Orrest Head, Windermere.

Elstob, Mrs.: took care of Sara Hutchinson's sister Betsy, who was not fully developed.

Ephesian Matron: Mrs. Thomas Monkhouse, *née* Horrocks, of Preston, later Mrs. Paris Dick. It was also applied later to the widow of Bishop Heber.

Farquhar, Sir Robert Townsend, 1776–1830: a politician, and governor of the Mauritius from 1812. He tried to abolish slave-trading there. With his son, Walter, he visited the Wordsworths in Sept. 1826.

Fawleigh: Miss Barker's house in Borrodale.

Fermor, Mrs.: Lady Beaumont's sister.

Fleming, Lady: Diana died 1816; and her daughter Anna Elizabeth Fleming, married to a cousin, Sir Michael Fleming.

Fleming, of Rayrigg: Sir Richard le Fleming, Rector of Grasmere, was inhibited.

Fletcher, Miss: the new schoolmistress of Ambleside, 1813.

Fox Ghyll: The Blakeneys, then de Quincey, and later Mrs. Luff, owned it.

Fox How: built by Dr. Thomas Arnold in 1833–4.

Fricker, Miss Eliza: sister of Mrs. Coleridge and Mrs. Southey.

Gallow Hill: where Sara's brothers, Thomas and George bought a farm when they left Sockburn, in 1800.

Gees: Grasmere neighbours who moved to Hendon, with whom Sara Hutchinson stayed there in 1834.

George:

(1) Hutchinson, 1778–1864, brother, farming with Thomas Hutchinson at Sockburn and Gallow Hill, later at Radnor in Wales.

(2) Hutchinson, 1801–53, nephew, son of John Hutchinson, inherited wealth on condition of taking the name and arms of Sutton; he became a family problem.

(3) Hutchinson, 1818–76, nephew, son of Thomas and Mary Hutchinson.

(4) Monkhouse, a cousin ? collateral with (3)?

Gloucester Place: where Thomas Monkhouse lived.

Godson: Mary Monkhouse Hutchinson's godson was Tommy Wordsworth, *q.v.* Joanna Hutchinson's godson was Willy Wordsworth.

'Good Intent': a coach, three times a week each way, running from Kendal to Whitehaven.

Good-good: Mary[6] Hutchinson, *q.v.*

Grahame, Robert: brother of the poet, James Grahame, 1755–1811.

Grant, Mrs.: of Laggan and Edinburgh, prominent in literary society as a poet and translator of Gaelic poems and songs. She was hostess to Harriet Douglas, *q.v.*

Grassy Nook: a small holding, two miles from Stockton, owned by Sara Hutchinson.

Green, Miss: 'the chatterer' of Dorothy Wordsworth's letters, died 1808.

Green: Grasmere family, of Pavement End, referred to by William Wordsworth in *The Excursion.*

Grosvenor Square: the London home of the Beaumonts.

Gwerndyffnant: three miles from Hindwell, a small farm owned by Thomas[1] Hutchinson. Joanna Hutchinson was attached to it, and Dorothy Wordsworth stayed there in May, 1826. Sara Hutchinson mimics a local pronunciation in her spelling of it.

Halsteads or Hallsteads: Mr. Marshall's house built on Skelly Nab, Ullswater, in 1815.

Hamilton, William, 1788–1856: after 1816, Sir Wm. Professor of Moral Philosophy at Edinburgh, friend of de Quincey; in 1828 married his cousin Janet Marshall. Capt. Thomas Hamilton was his brother.

Hampstead: refers to Thomas Monkhouse in the earlier letters, and to Sara and H. N. Coleridge who lived there later, from 1829 to 1837.

Harden, John: His mother lived in Brathay Hall, 1804–34.

Hare, Julius: visited the Wordsworths in 1832, with his brother Augustus, joint author of *Guesses at Truth*, 1827.

Harrison, Anthony: a lawyer in Penrith, a friend of Coleridge and Wordsworth who was not over-enthusiastic about Wordsworth's poems.

Hartley, Coleridge, 1796–1847: poet, son of S. T. Coleridge.

Haydon, Benjamin Robert, 1786–1846: the painter. In his famous picture, *Christ's Entry into Jerusalem*, Wordsworth's head is used for one of the bystanders.

Hemans, Mrs. Felicia Dorothea, 1793–1835: poetess, friend of the Hamiltons and Scott. In justification of Sara Hutchinson's prejudices, see *Wordsworth Letters, The Later Years*, 700–2.

Hendon: means the Gees.

Henry:

(1) Hutchinson, 1769–1839, the sailor brother, see note p. 3.

(2) Hutchinson, died 1850, nephew, son of John Hutchinson by his second marriage.

(3) Addison, *q.v.*

(4) Coleridge, H. N. C., nephew of S. T. Coleridge, who in 1828 m. Sara[3] Coleridge.

Herbert: Southey, son of Robert Southey, *q.v.*

Hindwell: Radnor, Wales, where her brother Thomas Hutchinson had a farm.

Horrocks, Jane: of Preston, married Thomas Monkhouse, and in early April 1827, Mr. Paris Dick. *See also* Index.

Howitt, Mary and William: both Quakers, both poets, lived in Nottingham.

Hugesson, Mrs.: a friend of Joanna Hutchinson.

Hutchinson: see the family tree, opp. p. 460. Sara Hutchinson's brothers and sisters appear in this list under the Christian names by which she refers to them. The branch of the family most frequently referred to in these letters is that of her brother Thomas.

Hutchinson, Thomas: of Gallow Hill, Park House, Hindwell, and Brinsop Court. He married his cousin Mary Monkhouse and their children were:

Thomas, 1815–1903.

Mary, 1817–37.

George, 1818–76.

Elizabeth, 1820–1905.

Sara, 1821–69.

Elizabeth appears to have been the first collector and preserver of these letters.

'Hutton': Sara Hutchinson, also 'Miss Mutton', both names given by nieces and nephews and Edward Quillinan's two little girls.

Hymers, Mr.: a Cambridge don, St. John's, tutor of Thomas[3] Hutchinson.

Irving, Rev. Edward, 1792–1834: the famous preacher of the chapel in Hatton Gardens.

Isabella:

(1) Addison, *q.v.*, 1784–1807.

(2) Curwen, *q.v.*, d. 1848.

Ivy Cot: owned by Tillbrook, re-modelled, and not lived in by him, but by the Gees, the Christopher Wordsworths, and Edward Quillinan. Now Glen Rothay.

Jack: John[1].

Jackson, Rev. Thomas: in 1811 newly appointed rector of Grasmere, but a better farmer than rector, he elected to live in Langdale; the Wordsworths moved then in May 1811 to the rectory. He died in 1822. His son, Rev. William Jackson, an Oxford don and John[4] Wordsworth's tutor, later became Provost of Queen's College, Oxford. He married S. E. Crump.

Jane, Hutchinson: niece, daughter of John Hutchinson, died 1827.

Jemima Quillinan: daughter of Edward Quillinan by his first wife.

Jere, Sir: according to Mrs. Coleridge, 'Sir Jerry Omphrey', who went to France, like Miss Barker, 'to retrench'. *Among Tritons*, p. 77.

Jewsbury, Maria Jane, 1800–33: 'Her book', *Phantasmagoria, or Sketches of Life and Character*, Leeds, 2 vols., 1825, published with the encouragement of Alaric Watts, was dedicated to Wordsworth, who in turn addressed his poem *Liberty* to her in 1829. Like her sister Geraldine, the friend of Mrs. Carlyle, she wrote much for the *Athenæum*.

Joanna, Hutchinson, 1780–1841: younger sister. She finally settled down with her brother Henry on the Isle of Man.

Joe, Monkhouse: 'honest Joe', the sailor brother of John, Thomas, Mary Monkhouse. He went to the West Indies and died there in 1822.

John:

(1) Hutchinson (Jack), eldest brother, farming at Stockton-on-Tees.

(2) Monkhouse, cousin, brother of Thomas and Mary Monkhouse, at first in business in London, then farming at Stow. In 1806 married Isabella Addison who died about a year later.

(3) Wordsworth, brother of William and Dorothy Wordsworth, who went down with his ship, the *Abergavenny*, in 1805.

(4) Wordsworth (Johnny), later 'the Rector', 1803–75, son of William and Mary Wordsworth; 11 Oct. 1830 married Isabella Curwen.

(5) ? Wordsworth, Bowness John, nephew of William Wordsworth, son of Christopher Wordsworth; on a reading party at Bowness with his two brothers, other Cambridge students and a tutor.

(6) Wordsworth: Keswick John, nephew of William Wordsworth, son of Richard Wordsworth. He studied medicine under Mr. Gardner.

(7) John Monkhouse's groom or manservant.

Johnson, Rev. William, 1784–1864: Curate at Grasmere in 1811. In 1812 he went to London under Dr. A. Bell to be headmaster of the Central School, under the Madras system. Willy Wordsworth was later sent to this school. In 1820 Mr. Johnson was Rector of St. Clements, Eastcheap.

Jones, Robert: Wordsworth's companion on his first trip to Europe in 1790.

Julia: There are at least four Julias and it is not possible always to be certain which one is meant.

Julia Curwen, sister of Jane and Isabella, John Wordsworth's first wife. She was shy and half-blind.

Julia Crump, daughter of the Mrs. Crump, *q.v.*, who built Allan Bank and later married Rev. William Jackson.

Julia Marshall, Dorothy Wordsworth's god-daughter, daughter of her great friend from school days, Jane Marshall.

Julia Myers, who married Rev. J. A. Neakin.

*Keepsake, The:* see Reynolds, F. Mansel.

Kenyon, Mr. John, 1784–1836: friend also of Coleridge, Landor, and later, the Brownings; visited Rydal *c.* Nov. 1819.

King, Mrs.: of The Hollens, Grasmere.

Kinnaird, Miss: adopted daughterof Richard (Conversation) Sharp. W. W. greatly admired her singing. Later Mrs. Drummond.

Knott: family in Grasmere, referred to by William Wordsworth in *The Excursion.*

Lamb, Charles, 1775–1834: introduced to the Wordsworth circle by Coleridge. He visited the Lakes in 1802, entertained them when they went to London, bought books for them, and acted as their London post office.

Lamb, Mary, 1764–1847: sister of Charles Lamb. Sara Hutchinson was afraid to stay with her in London because of her mental illness.

Lambeth: means Christopher Wordsworth, *q.v.*

Lancrigg: Wordsworth negotiated purchase of it for his friend, Lady Richardson, daughter of 'the beautiful Mrs. Feltcher'.

Leamington: M. J. Jewsbury, *q.v.*, lived there, where Dorothy Wordsworth visited her; Sara Hutchinson stayed there with the Rev. W. F. Hook and family.

Lee, or Lee Priory: the home of Sir Egerton Brydges, *q.v.*, who had a private press there. Edward Quillinan made it, his first wife's home, a sort of headquarters for his restless life after her death.

Lewis, Mr.: Thomas Hutchinson's landlord.

Llandaff: see Watson.

Lloyd, Charles, 1775–1839: an old friend of Lamb and Coleridge, writer of verses, and an indiscreetly satirical novel *Edmund Oliver.* He married Sophia Pemberton, and from August 1800 lived at Low Brathay, near Ambleside. He suffered a mental breakdown in 1814 and periodic depressions the rest of his life.

Priscilla: sister of Charles, later Mrs. Christopher Wordsworth.

Lonsdale: see Lowther.

Losh, James: Woodside near Carlisle, an old and intimate friend of William Wordsworth.

Lover: used with the free exaggeration of family teasing, of John Wilson, *q.v.*, and H. Crabb Robinson, linked with Mary Monkhouse and Dorothy[1] Wordsworth respectively. Joanna Hutchinson appears to have had several.

Lowther, Sir William, 1758–1814: 2nd Earl of Lonsdale in 1807 when he repaid his father's debts of £5000 to the Wordsworths. His son, William, 1787–1872, the third Earl, opposed Brougham in 1818, 1820, and 1826. It was the Second Earl to whom Wordsworth dedicated *The Excursion* in 1814. They were both friendly with the Wordsworths and not to be confused with James Lowther, the first ('bad') Earl, 1736–1802, who did not pay his debts.

Lucas, Mrs.: governess to Edward Quillinan's two daughters.

Luff, Capt.: Capt. and Mrs. Luff had a house in Patterdale. They later (1814) suffered financial losses and went to Mauritius, where he died. Mrs. Luff returned to England and lived for a time in Rydal and Grasmere.

Ma-Ma: Mary[5].

Mackareth, George: kept the Swan Inn, 1799 in Grasmere and later moved to the Wyke Cottage. He was Parish clerk, father and son, for over 60 years.

Madras system, the: took its name from the educational experiments of Dr. Andrew Bell, *q.v.*, in the Madras Male Orphan Asylum, 1789–96, where he was superintendent under the East India Co. In 1798 he introduced the system at St. Botolph's, Aldgate, and in 1799 in the Kendal industrial schools. It was also known as the 'mutual method' of instruction and along with the rival Lancastrian scheme was the progressive education of its day, the important aspects of it being the co-operation among the pupils themselves, as well as between pupils and teacher, and stress on positive inducements rather than threats and punishments.

Malcolm, Sir John, 1769–1833: of Burnfoot, soldier and diplomatist, where his father had been a humble farmer. His brothers were almost equally distinguished.

Marshall: see Halsteads.

Marshalls, the: old friends of Dorothy Wordsworth from school days, especially Jane *née* Pollard.

Mary:

(1) Hutchinson, 1770–1859, sister, in 1802 married William Wordsworth.

(2) Monkhouse, 1787–1858, cousin and sister-in-law, sister of Thomas and John; 2 Nov. 1812 married Thomas[1] Hutchinson. They lived at Hindwell in Wales and then at Brinsop Court in Herefordshire.

(3) Addison, *q.v.*

(4) Wordsworth, cousin of William and Dorothy Wordsworth.

(5) Monkhouse, 1821–1900, 'Ma-Ma', daughter of Thomas Monkhouse and Jane Horrocks.

(6) Hutchinson, 1817–37, niece, daughter of Thomas and Mary Hutchinson. also called 'Good-Good' and 'Polly'.

(7) Cookson, b. 1790, cousin of W. Wordsworth.

(8) Hutchinson ? daughter of John H? She is not on the family tree, but a MS. note by a great niece of S. H. so identifies her.

Mentor: William Jackson, *q.v.*, tutor to John Wordsworth.

Mima, or Mims: Jemima Quillinan.

Monkhouse, Miss Elizabeth, 1750–1828: She helped in the upbringing of the Hutchinson and Monkhouse orphaned children, as aunt to both families, and later lived with Thomas and Mary Hutchinson at Radnor and Brinsop Court where she died.

Monkhouse: John, Mary, Thomas, (and Joey the sailor), were Sara Hutchinson's favourite cousins. See under their Christian names.

Montagu, Basil, 1770–1851: a barrister, author of miscellaneous works and legal reforms, a friend of Wordsworth, Coleridge, Godwin, Mackintosh, and many literary men. After the death of his first wife Wordsworth and Dorothy Wordsworth took care for a time of his son.

Moresby: John[4] Wordsworth was Rector there.

Nash, Edward: artist, friend of Southey, who died young, in 1820. He painted a portrait of Wordsworth.

Nightingale, the: Miss Kinnaird, *q.v.*

North, Mr. and Mrs.: of Liverpool, bought Rydal Mt. 1807–8, quarrelled with Lady Fleming about timber rights on Nab Scar and stripped it. After they left Rydal Mt. the Wordsworths occupied it in 1813.

Opie, Mrs. Amelia, 1769–1853: poet and novelist, the wife of John Opie the painter, a memoir of whom she wrote in 1809.

Owen, Mr. Robert, 1771–1858: founder of New Lanark, 1800–24, the philanthropic industrialist who tried to introduce educational and economic reforms along co-operative lines.

Park House: Thomas Hutchinson's farm at the foot of Ullswater before he went to Wales. Sara Hutchinson and Joanna kept house for him there.

Patrick, David and Elizabeth: of Kendal, took care of Sara Hutchinson after her mother's death. Sara's ardent account of his character and intellectual interests went into Wordsworth's pedlar in *The Excursion.*

Patterdale: Wordsworth had a small holding there. The Luffs were there, and the Marshalls, *q.v.*

Peake, Mrs.: Capt. Wordsworth's niece, Mary Wordsworth.

'Pearl, the': Mrs. Hervey, *née* Horrocks, sister of Mrs. Thomas Monkhouse.

Peggy: see Ashburner.

Penny, Miss Jane: in May, 1811 married John Wilson, 'Christopher North'.

Penrith: meant the William Cooksons, or Sara Hutchinson's aunt, Mrs. Elizabeth Monkhouse, or the Addisons.

Playford Hall: nr Ipswich, home of the Clarksons after they left Bury St. Edmunds.

Powley, Mr.: schoolmaster at Grasmere who followed Mr. Johnson in 1812.

Preston: where the Horrocks family lived. Jane Horrocks married Thomas[2] Monkhouse.

Priscilla: see Lloyd.

Quillinan, Edward, 1791–1851, (Quill) published several volumes of verse and engaged in literary controversies. In 1841 he married Wordsworth's daughter Dora, his first wife having died in 1822, of severe burns. There were two daughters by his first marriage, Jemima and Rotha.

Ramstars, Mr.: the government stamp distributor at Haworth.

Rector: at Grasmere, 1811– ?, see Jackson, Rev. Thomas.

Red Indian, the: Harriet Douglas, *q.v.*

Reynolds, F. Mansel: son of the dramatist, editor of *The Keepsake*, a Christmas annual.

Richard: Wordsworth, 1768–1816, William's elder brother whose management of the family finances created many difficulties for Wordsworth.

Rickman, John, 1771–1840: the statistician for the House of Commons; friend of Lamb, Coleridge, and the Wordsworths.

Robinson, Mr.: Henry Crabb Robinson, 1775–1867, the journalist and barrister.

Rogers, Mr. Samuel, 1763–1855: poet, uncle of 'Conversation' Sharp. His influence with Lord Lonsdale may have helped make William Wordsworth Distributor of Stamps; best known as author of *The Pleasures of Memory*, 1792, and *Human Life*, 1819, and of some good *Table Talk*.

Rotha: Quillinan, daughter of Edward Quillinan.

Rydal Hall: home of the Flemings.

Rydal Mt.: the Wordsworth home after May 1813.

Sally: Sara[4] Hutchinson, also Sara[5] Green.

Sara:

(1) Hutchinson, the writer of the letters, 1775–1835.

(2) Coleridge, Mrs. S. T. Coleridge, *née* Fricker.

(3) Coleridge, daughter of S. T. Coleridge, *q.v.*

(4) Hutchinson, 1821–69, niece, daughter of Thomas Hutchinson and Mary Monkhouse.

(5) Green, of the Grasmere family whose tragedy Dorothy Wordsworth described in a moving narrative.

Sartorius: Sertorius, Capt., a friend of Thomas Monkhouse; natural son of George Rose.

Scambler, Mr.: medical man at Grasmere until 1820.

Scott, Mr. and Mrs. Walter: at Kelso, 1814, later Sir Walter Scott. The Wordsworths visited him in Scotland.

Scurfield, Mrs. and Miss: related to the Monkhouses.

Sebergham: a house owned by the Monkhouses.

Sedbergh: school attended by John[4] Wordsworth and Thomas[3] Hutchinson.

Sharp, Richard: 'Conversation' Sharp, 1759–1835, nephew of Samuel Rogers.

Sissy: Dorothy[2].

Smith, Charlotte, 1749–1806: the poet, whose *Elegiac Sonnets*, 1784, Wordsworth admired.

Sockbridge: where Richard Wordsworth lived.

Sockburn-on-Tees, Yorks: Thomas and George Hutchinson farmed there before they moved to Gallow Hill.

Somerset, Lord Robert E. H.: one of the heroes of Waterloo, who franked Sara Hutchinson's letters to the Luffs in the Mauritius, was M.P. for Gloucestershire.

Southey, Dr. H. H., 1783–1865: once of Durham and then of Queen Anne St. London, brother of Robert Southey.

Southey, Robert, 1774–1843: in 1795 married Edith Fricker, sister of Mrs. S. T. Coleridge, and Mrs. Robert Lovell. From 1803 onwards the Southeys lived at Greta Hall, Keswick, sharing the house with the Coleridges. The children were:

Margaret, 1802–3.

Edith May, 1804– ?, married Rev. J. W. Warter, 13 Jan. 1834.

Herbert, 1806–16 (April 17).

Emma, 1808–10.

Bertha, 1809– ?.

Katherine, 1810– ?.
Isabel, 1812–26.
Charles Cuthbert, 1819– ?.

Spring Cottage: occupied by Edward Quillinan; now Loughrigg Holme.

Stanley, Miss: sister of Mrs. Atherley.

Stockton: John[1] and several other Hutchinsons lived there.

Stoddart, Dr. John, 1773–1856: later Sir John; journalist, King's Advocate at Malta while Coleridge was there, founder of the *New Times*; known as 'Dr. Sto'. His sister became Mrs. Hazlitt.

Stow: John[2] farmed there.

Stuart, Daniel, 1766–1840: editor of the *Morning Post* and later of the *Courier*, who drew on the talents of Coleridge, Southey and Wordsworth.

Sundridge: Christopher Wordsworth, *q.v.*, was Rector there.

Sympsons: of Broad Raine, Grasmere, referred to by Wordsworth in *The Excursion*, 'the Patriarch of the Dale', in daily touch with the Wordsworths till his death in 1806.

Ta or Ta-Ta: Sarah[4].

Telemachus: John[4].

Thomas:
(1) Hutchinson, b. 1773, brother, of Sockburn, Gallow Hill, and then Hindwell and Brinsop Court; married Mary Monkhouse, his cousin.
(2) Monkhouse, 1783–1825, possibly her favourite cousin, brother of John and Mary, married Jane Horrocks, in business in London.
(3) Hutchinson, 1815–1903, nephew, son of Thomas Hutchinson and Mary Monkhouse.
(4) Wordsworth (Tommy or Tottie) 1806–Dec. 1812, nephew, son of William and Mary Wordsworth, godson of Mary Monkhouse Hutchinson.
(5) Clarkson, son of Thomas and Catherine Clarkson, *q.v.*

'Till' or Tillbrook: Rev. Samuel Tillbrook, friend of the Clarksons, spent the summer of 1812 at Robert Newton's in Grasmere. Dorothy Wordsworth recorded how he cheered them all, that doleful summer, when he 'stationed himself upon a rock and sounded his flute to the great delight of our party, the cows in the field, and a group of rustic children'. He owned the Ivy Cot 1817–31. He married Miss Ayling.

Tottie, or Totts: Thomas[4] and after 1815, Thomas[3].

Trinity Lodge: Cambridge, where Christopher Wordsworth was Master.

Trots, the: the two daughters of Edward Quillinan, Rotha and Jemima.

Tyrrell, Frederick, 1793–1843: surgeon at St. Thomas's Hospital; in 1840 he published a work in 2 vols., *Diseases of the Eyes*. I have corrected Sara Hutchinson's various spellings of his name.

Warter, Rev. J. W.: married Edith May Southey, 1834.

Watermillock: the Marshalls, friends of the Wordsworths, had a house, Hallsteads, at Watermillock, in Patterdale.

Watson, Richard, 1737–1816: Bishop of Llandaff.

Watts, Alaric, 1797–1864: editor and writer. He edited the *Literary Souvenir*, 1825–35.

Weir, Miss: of Appleby, who had a boarding school there, attended by the Wordsworth, Hutchinson and Monkhouse children.

Westall, William, 1781–1850: painter and engraver. Three sonnets suggested by Mr. Westall's *Views of the Caves . . . Yorkshire*, were printed with *Peter Bell*, 1819.

Wheelwright, Mr.: a business partner of Thomas Monkhouse.

Whitwick: John[4] was appointed rector there in 1828.

Wilberforce, William, 1759–1833: the philanthropist and abolitionist.

Wilkinson, Rev. Joseph: *Select Views in Cumberland, Westmoreland and Lancashire*, by the Rev. Joseph Wilkinson, 1810. The *Introduction* was written by Wordsworth. After several revisions Wordsworth's text in 1835 became his *Guide to the Lakes*.

Willes, Miss: Lady Beaumont's cousin.

William:

(1) Wordsworth, 1770–1850.

(2) Wordsworth, (Willy), 1810–83, nephew, son of William Wordsworth and Mary; Mr. Gordon Wordsworth was his son.

(3) Hutchinson, d. 1890, nephew, son by second marriage of John[1].

William, Mr.: is Rev. William Jackson, *q.v.*

Willy: William[2].

Wilson, John: 'Christopher North' of *Blackwood's*. Mary Monkhouse was teased about him as her 'Lover'. At Elleray, *q.v.*, 1808–15.

Wordsworth: see Family Tree, opp. p. 460, which is, however, not adequate for all Wordsworths mentioned.

Wordsworth, Capt.: a cousin of William and Dorothy Wordsworth, son of Richard Wordsworth of Whitehaven.

Wordsworth, Christopher: brother of William, who had sons, John, Charles and Christopher.

Wordsworth, John: a cousin, a brother of Mary Wordsworth, Mrs. Peake, *q.v.*, whose husband was lost with the *Peacock*.

Wordsworth, Joseph: another cousin possibly Joseph Peake.

Wordsworth, Mary: William Wordsworth's cousin, Mrs. Peake.

Wordsworth, Nanny: married Rev. Ireland. William Wordsworth's mother was Ann, 1748–78. I can find no other; Nanny was perhaps a cousin on their father's side.

Wordsworth, William, 1770–1850: married Mary Hutchinson, October, 1802. From 1799 lived at Grasmere in Dove Cottage, Allan Bank, the Rectory, and then Rydal Mount. His brothers and sister were: Richard, Christopher, and Dorothy. See under their Christian names. His children were:

John, 1803–75, married Isabella Curwen, 11 Oct. 1830.

Dora, 1804–47, married Edward Quillinan, 1841.

Thomas, 1806–12.

Catharine, 1808–12.

William, 1810–83.

Workington Hall: home of the Curwens, *q.v.*

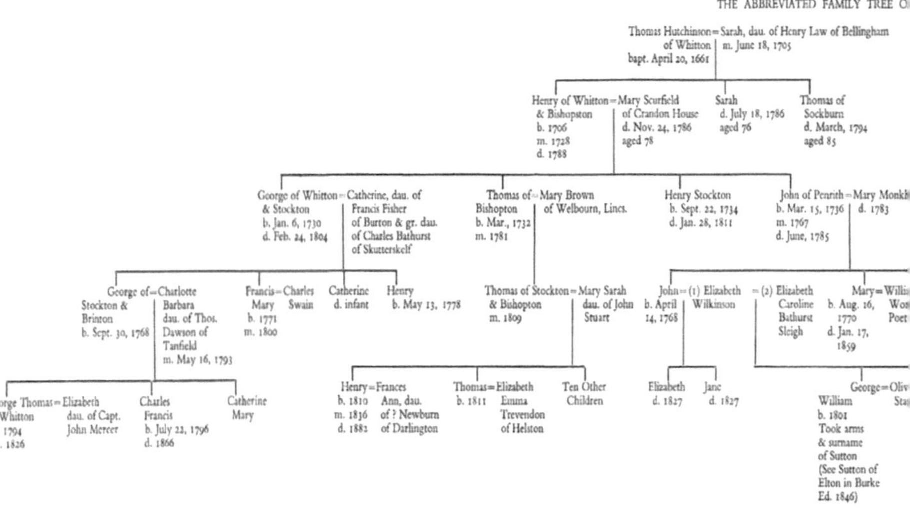
THE ABBREVIATED FAMILY TREE O
Thomas Hutchinson = Sarah, dau. of Henry Law of Bellingham
of Whitton
bapt. April 20, 1661
m. June 18, 1705
Henry of Whitton = Mary Scurfield
& Bishopston
b. 1706
m. 1728
d. 1788
of Crandon House
d. Nov. 24, 1786
aged 78
Sarah
d. July 18, 1786
aged 76
Thomas of
Sockburn
d. March, 1794
aged 85
George of Whitton = Catherine, dau. of
& Stockton
b. Jan. 6, 1730
d. Feb. 24, 1804
Francis Fisher
of Burton & gr. dau.
of Charles Bathurst
of Skutterskelf
Thomas of = Mary Brown
Bishopton
b. Mar., 1732
m. 1781
of Welbourn, Lincs.
Henry Stockton
b. Sept. 22, 1734
d. Jan. 28, 1811
John of Penrith = Mary Monk
b. Mar. 15, 1736
m. 1767
d. June, 1785
d. 1783
George of = Charlotte
Stockton &
Brinton
b. Sept. 30, 1768
Barbara
dau. of Thos.
Dawson of
Tanfield
m. May 16, 1793
Francis = Charles
Mary
b. 1771
m. 1800
Swain
Catherine
d. infant
Henry
b. May 13, 1778
Thomas of Stockton = Mary Sarah
& Bishopton
m. 1809
dau. of John
Stuart
John = (1) Elizabeth
b. April
14, 1768
Wilkinson
= (2) Elizabeth
Caroline
Bathurst
Sleigh
Mary = Willi
b. Aug. 16,
1770
d. Jan. 17,
1859
Wor
Poet
George Thomas = Elizabeth
of Whitton
b. 1794
m. 1826
dau. of Capt.
John Mercer
Charles
Francis
b. July 22, 1796
d. 1866
Catherine
Mary
Henry = Frances
b. 1810
m. 1836
d. 1882
Ann, dau.
of ? Newburn
of Darlington
Thomas = Elizabeth
b. 1811
Emma
Trevendon
of Helston
Ten Other
Children
Elizabeth
d. 1827
Jane
d. 1827
George = Oliv
William
b. 1801
Took arms
& surname
of Sutton
(See Sutton of
Elton in Burke
Ed. 1846)
Sta

NSON FAMILY

9
9

Margaret
b. 1772
d. 1796

Thomas = Mary Monkhouse
b. June 11, 1773 | b. 1783

Sara
b. 1775
d. 1835

Elizabeth
b. 1776
d. 1832

George = Margaret Roberts buried at Brinsop
b. 1778
d. 1864

Joanna
b. 1780
d. 1841

William
b. 1783
d. 1785

Charles Sleigh
b. 1805
m. M. Richmond

Henry William
d. 1850

Lucy

William
d. 1890

Thomas = Emma Sarah dau. of Capt. Gill, R.N.
b. July 14, 1815 | b. Mar. 7, 1820
d. 1903 | d. 1905

George
b. Oct. 10, 1818
d. Oct. 5, 1876

Elizabeth
b. April 3, 1820
d. 1905

Mary Monkhouse
b. Jan. 22, 1817
d. 1837

Sarah
b. 1821
d. 1869

THE ABBREVIATED FAMI

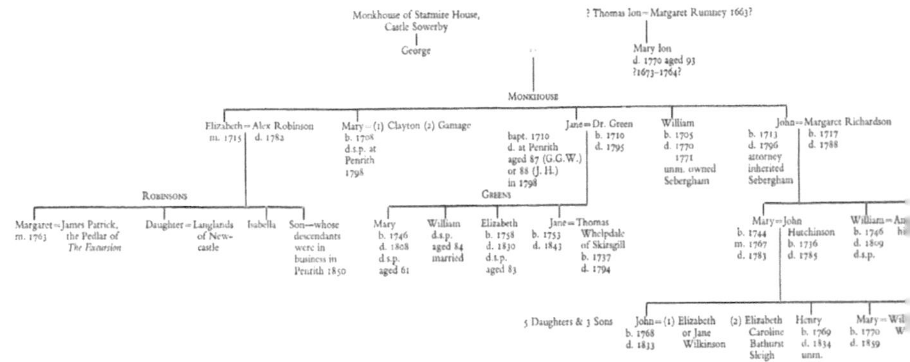

E MONKHOUSE FAMILY

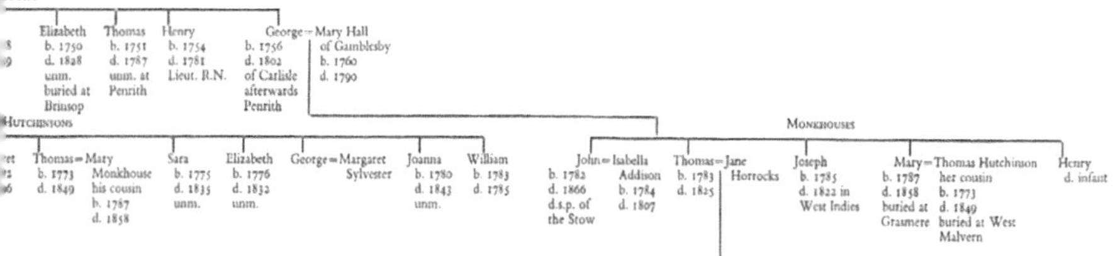

## THE ABBREVIATED FAMILY TREE OF THE WORDSWORTH FAMILY

Richard
1768–1816

William = Mary Hutchinson
b. 1770 | b. 1770
m. 1802 | d. 1859
d. 1850

Dorothy
1771–1855

John
1772–1805

Christopher = Priscilla Lloyd
1774–1846
3 Sons—John, Christopher, Charles

Children of William and Mary:

John = (1) Isabella Christina Curwen = (2) Helen Ross = (3) Mary Ann Dolan = (4) Mary Gamble
John: b. 1803, m. 1830, d. 1875
Isabella Christina Curwen: d. 1848
Helen Ross: m. 1852, d. 1854
Mary Ann Dolan: m. 1856, d. 1866
Mary Gamble: m. 1870, b. 1903

Dora (child of John and Helen Ross)
b. 1858
d. 1934

Dora = Edward Quillinan
Dora: b. 1804, m. 1841, d. 1847
Edward Quillinan: b. 1791, d. 1851

Thomas
b. 1806
d. 1812

Catherine
b. 1808
d. 1812

William = Fanny Eliza Graham
William: b. 1810, m. 1847, d. 1883
Fanny Eliza Graham: b. 1821, d. 1888

Children of John and Isabella Christina Curwen:

Jane Stanley = Bennet Sheward Calcraft Kennedy
Jane Stanley: b. 1833, d. 1912
Bennet Sheward Calcraft Kennedy: b. 1832, d. 1854

Henry Curwen = Adelaide Troutbeck
Henry Curwen: b. 1834, m. 1854, d. 1865
Adelaide Troutbeck: b. 1838, d. 1909

William = (1) Mary Reynolds = (2) Maria Howland Hays (w. of Dr. Bell)
William: b. 1835, d. 1917
Mary Reynolds: b. 1835, d. 1898
Maria Howland Hays: b. 1856, m. 1900, d. 1903

John = Rose Williams
John: b. 1837, m. 1869, d. 1927
Rose Williams: b. 1848

Charles = Elizabeth Flanagen
Charles: b. 1839, d. 1913
John Christian Curwen
b. 1884

Edward
b. 1841
d. 1845

Children of William and Fanny Eliza Graham:

Mary Louisa = William Crosley Siddons Mair
Mary Louisa: b. 1849, m. 1873, d. 1926
William Crosley Siddons Mair: b. 1839, d. 1918

William
b. 1851
d. 1851

Reginald Graham = Annie Frances Dundas
Reginald Graham: b. 1852, m. 1883, d. 1919
Annie Frances Dundas: b. 1857, d. 1887

Gordon
b. 1860
d. 1935

Graham

# INDEX